Contents

First of all, a warm thank you for purchasing this book. The content of this book originally started out as digital letters on the online platform at learnopengl.com. LearnOpenGL quickly evolved from a series of tutorials, to a full online book with years of continuous feedback and improvements that are now finally aggregated into the physical copy you hold in your hands.

The online version at learnopengl.com is free, and will always be free, and for the most up to date content and questions from readers it is still advised to search up articles on the online platform. However, a physical copy makes it easy to read during travel, write notes, and we should never forget that certain charm of printed paper. And not to forget, purchasing a physical copy helps support me as an author for which I again thank you from the bottom of my heart.

The book is structured similarly to the online platform, with a few minor differences to account for the book being offline. Think of a large reduction of hyperlinks, hyperlinks being fully written out, videos now showing static images, and the lack of function hover pop-ups. The content has however been thoroughly revised, and reviewed multiple times, to ensure the book is a first-class citizen that's up to the professional standards you'd expect.

If you'd like to start your journey into graphics programming you've got a great path ahead of you. This book will teach you, step by step, the foundation and skills of becoming a graphics programmer. You'll learn 3D fundamentals, basic and advanced lighting, model loading, blending, post-processing, shadows, debugging, PBR, and so much more; and we'll even walk you through the process of creating a full 2D game. If you're as excited as I amx I will now stop talking and see you in the first chapter.

// Joey

1. Introduction

Since you came here you probably want to learn the inner workings of computer graphics and do all the stuff the cool kids do by yourself. Doing things by yourself is extremely fun and resourceful and gives you a great understanding of graphics programming. However, there are a few items that need to be taken into consideration before starting your journey.

1.1 Prerequisites

Since OpenGL is a graphics API and not a platform of its own, it requires a language to operate in and the language of choice is C++. Therefore a decent knowledge of the C++ programming language is required for these tutorials. However, I will try to explain most of the concepts used, including advanced C++ topics where required so it is not required to be an expert in C++, but you should be able to write more than just a `'Hello World'` program. If you don't have much experience with C++ I can recommend the free tutorials at `www.learncpp.com`.

Also, we will be using some math (linear algebra, geometry, and trigonometry) along the way and I will try to explain all the required concepts of the math required. However, I'm not a mathematician by heart so even though my explanations may be easy to understand, they will most likely be incomplete. So where necessary I will provide pointers to good resources that explain the material in a more complete fashion. Don't be scared about the mathematical knowledge required before starting your journey into OpenGL; almost all the concepts can be understood with a basic mathematical background and I will try to keep the mathematics to a minimum where possible. Most of the functionality doesn't even require you to understand all the math as long as you know how to use it.

1.2 Structure

LearnOpenGL is broken down into a number of general sections. Each section contains several chapters that each explain different concepts in large detail. The subjects are taught in a linear fashion (so it is advised to start from start to finish, unless otherwise instructed) where each chapter explains the background theory and the practical aspects.

To make the concepts easier to follow, and give them some added structure, the book contains *boxes*, *code blocks*, and *color hints*.

1.2.1 Boxes

> **Green** boxes encompasses some notes or useful features/hints about OpenGL or the subject at hand.

> **Red** boxes will contain warnings or other features you have to be extra careful with.

1.2.2 Code

You will find plenty of small pieces of code in the book that are located in dark-gray boxes with syntax-highlighted code as you can see below:

```
// This box contains code
```

Since these provide only snippets of code, wherever necessary you'll find a path to the full source code of the chapter demo(s). The source code paths are relative to the root of the LearnOpenGL repository on GitHub which you can find at: `github.com/JoeyDeVries/learnopengl`. The repository contains full source code samples for every chapter. It's recommended to download the repository and review the full source code samples at the end of each chapter to see how everything fits together as a whole.

1.2.3 Color hints

Some words are displayed with a different color to make it extra clear these words portray a special meaning:

- Definition: green words specify a definition i.e. an important aspect/name of something you're likely to hear more often.
- Program structure: red words specify function names or class names.
- Variables: blue words specify variables including all OpenGL constants.

Now that you got a bit of a feel of the structure of the book, hop over to the Getting Started section to start your journey in OpenGL!

Getting started

2. OpenGL

Before starting our journey we should first define what OpenGL actually is. OpenGL is mainly considered an API (an Application Programming Interface) that provides us with a large set of functions that we can use to manipulate graphics and images. However, OpenGL by itself is not an API, but merely a specification, developed and maintained by the `www.khronos.org/`.

The OpenGL specification specifies exactly what the result/output of each function should be and how it should perform. It is then up to the developers *implementing* this specification to come up with a solution of how this function should operate. Since the OpenGL specification does not give us implementation details, the actual developed versions of OpenGL are allowed to have different implementations, as long as their results comply with the specification (and are thus the same to the user).

The people developing the actual OpenGL libraries are usually the graphics card manufacturers. Each graphics card that you buy supports specific versions of OpenGL which are the versions of OpenGL developed specifically for that card (series). When using an Apple system the OpenGL library is maintained by Apple themselves and under Linux there exists a combination of graphic suppliers' versions and hobbyists' adaptations of these libraries. This also means that whenever OpenGL is showing weird behavior that it shouldn't, this is most likely the fault of the graphics cards manufacturers (or whoever developed/maintained the library).

> Since most implementations are built by graphics card manufacturers. Whenever there is a bug in the implementation this is usually solved by updating your video card drivers; those drivers include the newest versions of OpenGL that your card supports. This is one of the reasons why it's always advised to occasionally update your graphic drivers.

Khronos publicly hosts all specification documents for all the OpenGL versions. The interested reader can find the OpenGL specification[1] of version 3.3 (which is what we'll be using), which is a good read if you want to delve into the details of OpenGL (note how they mostly just describe results and not implementations). The specifications also provide a great reference for finding the **exact** workings of its functions.

2.1 Core-profile vs Immediate mode

In the old days, using OpenGL meant developing in immediate mode (often referred to as the fixed function pipeline) which was an easy-to-use method for drawing graphics. Most of the functionality of OpenGL was hidden inside the library and developers did not have much control over how OpenGL does its calculations. Developers eventually got hungry for more flexibility and over time the specifications became more flexible as a result; developers gained more control over their graphics. The immediate mode is really easy to use and understand, but it is also extremely inefficient. For that reason the specification started to deprecate immediate mode functionality from version 3.2 onwards and started motivating developers to develop in OpenGL's core-profile mode, which is a division of OpenGL's specification that removed all old deprecated functionality.

When using OpenGL's core-profile, OpenGL forces us to use modern practices. Whenever we try to use one of OpenGL's deprecated functions, OpenGL raises an error and stops drawing. The

---

[1] www.opengl.org/registry/doc/glspec33.core.20100311.withchanges.pdf

advantage of learning the modern approach is that it is very flexible and efficient. However, it's also more difficult to learn. The immediate mode abstracted quite a lot from the **actual** operations OpenGL performed and while it was easy to learn, it was hard to grasp how OpenGL actually operates. The modern approach requires the developer to truly understand OpenGL and graphics programming and while it is a bit difficult, it allows for much more flexibility, more efficiency and most importantly: a much better understanding of graphics programming.

This is also the reason why this book is geared at core-profile OpenGL version 3.3. Although it is more difficult, it is greatly worth the effort.

As of today, higher versions of OpenGL are available to choose from (at the time of writing 4.6) at which you may ask: why do I want to learn OpenGL 3.3 when OpenGL 4.6 is out? The answer to that question is relatively simple. All future versions of OpenGL starting from 3.3 add extra useful features to OpenGL without changing OpenGL's core mechanics; the newer versions just introduce slightly more efficient or more useful ways to accomplish the same tasks. The result is that all concepts and techniques remain the same over the modern OpenGL versions so it is perfectly valid to learn OpenGL 3.3. Whenever you're ready and/or more experienced you can easily use specific functionality from more recent OpenGL versions.

> When using functionality from the most recent version of OpenGL, only the most modern graphics cards will be able to run your application. This is often why most developers generally target lower versions of OpenGL and optionally enable higher version functionality.

In some chapters you'll find more modern features which are noted down as such.

2.2 Extensions

A great feature of OpenGL is its support of extensions. Whenever a graphics company comes up with a new technique or a new large optimization for rendering this is often found in an extension implemented in the drivers. If the hardware an application runs on supports such an extension the developer can use the functionality provided by the extension for more advanced or efficient graphics. This way, a graphics developer can still use these new rendering techniques without having to wait for OpenGL to include the functionality in its future versions, simply by checking if the extension is supported by the graphics card. Often, when an extension is popular or very useful it eventually becomes part of future OpenGL versions.

The developer has to query whether any of these extensions are available before using them (or use an OpenGL extension library). This allows the developer to do things better or more efficient, based on whether an extension is available:

```
if(GL_ARB_extension_name)
{
    // Do cool new and modern stuff supported by hardware
}
else
{
    // Extension not supported: do it the old way
}
```

With OpenGL version 3.3 we rarely need an extension for most techniques, but wherever it is necessary proper instructions are provided.

2.3 **State machine**

OpenGL is by itself a large state machine: a collection of variables that define how OpenGL should currently operate. The state of OpenGL is commonly referred to as the OpenGL context. When using OpenGL, we often change its state by setting some options, manipulating some buffers and then render using the current context.

Whenever we tell OpenGL that we now want to draw lines instead of triangles for example, we change the state of OpenGL by changing some context variable that sets how OpenGL should draw. As soon as we change the context by telling OpenGL it should draw lines, the next drawing commands will now draw lines instead of triangles.

When working in OpenGL we will come across several state-changing functions that change the context and several state-using functions that perform some operations based on the current state of OpenGL. As long as you keep in mind that OpenGL is basically one large state machine, most of its functionality will make more sense.

2.4 **Objects**

The OpenGL libraries are written in C and allows for many derivations in other languages, but in its core it remains a C-library. Since many of C's language-constructs do not translate that well to other higher-level languages, OpenGL was developed with several abstractions in mind. One of those abstractions are objects in OpenGL.

An object in OpenGL is a collection of options that represents a subset of OpenGL's state. For example, we could have an object that represents the settings of the drawing window; we could then set its size, how many colors it supports and so on. One could visualize an object as a C-like struct:

```
struct object_name {
    float   option1;
    int     option2;
    char[]  name;
};
```

Whenever we want to use objects it generally looks something like this (with OpenGL's context visualized as a large struct):

```
// The State of OpenGL
struct OpenGL_Context {
    ...
    object_name* object_Window_Target;
    ...
};
```

```
// create object
unsigned int objectId = 0;
glGenObject(1, &objectId);
// bind/assign object to context
glBindObject(GL_WINDOW_TARGET, objectId);
// set options of object currently bound to GL_WINDOW_TARGET
glSetObjectOption(GL_WINDOW_TARGET, GL_OPTION_WINDOW_WIDTH, 800);
glSetObjectOption(GL_WINDOW_TARGET, GL_OPTION_WINDOW_HEIGHT, 600);
// set context target back to default
glBindObject(GL_WINDOW_TARGET, 0);
```

This little piece of code is a workflow you'll frequently see when working with OpenGL. We first create an object and store a reference to it as an id (the real object's data is stored behind the scenes). Then we bind the object (using its id) to the target location of the context (the location of the example window object target is defined as `GL_WINDOW_TARGET`). Next we set the window options and finally we un-bind the object by setting the current object id of the window target to `0`. The options we set are stored in the object referenced by `objectId` and restored as soon as we bind the object back to `GL_WINDOW_TARGET`.

> The code samples provided so far are only approximations of how OpenGL operates; throughout the book you will come across enough actual examples.

The great thing about using these objects is that we can define more than one object in our application, set their options and whenever we start an operation that uses OpenGL's state, we bind the object with our preferred settings. There are objects for example that act as container objects for 3D model data (a house or a character) and whenever we want to draw one of them, we bind the object containing the model data that we want to draw (we first created and set options for these objects). Having several objects allows us to specify many models and whenever we want to draw a specific model, we simply bind the corresponding object before drawing without setting all their options again.

2.5 Let's get started

You now learned a bit about OpenGL as a specification and a library, how OpenGL approximately operates under the hood and a few custom tricks that OpenGL uses. Don't worry if you didn't get all of it; throughout the book we'll walk through each step and you'll see enough examples to really get a grasp of OpenGL.

2.6 Additional resources

- `www.opengl.org/`: official website of OpenGL.
- `www.opengl.org/registry/`: hosts the OpenGL specifications and extensions for all OpenGL versions.

3. Creating a window

The first thing we need to do before we start creating stunning graphics is to create an OpenGL context and an application window to draw in. However, those operations are specific per operating system and OpenGL purposefully tries to abstract itself from these operations. This means we have to create a window, define a context, and handle user input all by ourselves.

Luckily, there are quite a few libraries out there that provide the functionality we seek, some specifically aimed at OpenGL. Those libraries save us all the operation-system specific work and give us a window and an OpenGL context to render in. Some of the more popular libraries are GLUT, SDL, SFML and GLFW. On LearnOpenGL we will be using **GLFW**. Feel free to use any of the other libraries, the setup for most is similar to GLFW's setup.

3.1 GLFW

GLFW is a library, written in C, specifically targeted at OpenGL. GLFW gives us the bare necessities required for rendering goodies to the screen. It allows us to create an OpenGL context, define window parameters, and handle user input, which is plenty enough for our purposes.

The focus of this and the next chapter is to get GLFW up and running, making sure it properly creates an OpenGL context and that it displays a simple window for us to mess around in. This chapter takes a step-by-step approach in retrieving, building and linking the GLFW library. We'll use Microsoft Visual Studio 2019 IDE as of this writing (note that the process is the same on the more recent visual studio versions). If you're not using Visual Studio (or an older version) don't worry, the process will be similar on most other IDEs.

3.2 Building GLFW

GLFW can be obtained from their webpage at `www.glfw.org/download.html`. GLFW already has pre-compiled binaries and header files for Visual Studio 2012 up to 2019, but for completeness' sake we will compile GLFW ourselves from the source code. This is to give you a feel for the process of compiling open-source libraries yourself as not every library will have pre-compiled binaries available. So let's download the *Source package*.

> We'll be building all libraries as 64-bit binaries so make sure to get the 64-bit binaries if you're using their pre-compiled binaries.

Once you've downloaded the source package, extract it and open its content. We are only interested in a few items:

- The resulting library from compilation.
- The **include** folder.

Compiling the library from the source code guarantees that the resulting library is perfectly tailored for your CPU/OS, a luxury pre-compiled binaries don't always provide (sometimes, pre-compiled binaries are not available for your system). The problem with providing source code to the open world however is that not everyone uses the same IDE or build system for developing their application, which means the project/solution files provided may not be compatible with other people's setup. So people then have to setup their own project/solution with the given .c/.cpp and .h/.hpp files, which is cumbersome. Exactly for those reasons there is a tool called CMake.

3.2.1 CMake

CMake is a tool that can generate project/solution files of the user's choice (e.g. Visual Studio, Code::Blocks, Eclipse) from a collection of source code files using pre-defined CMake scripts. This allows us to generate a Visual Studio 2019 project file from GLFW's source package which we can use to compile the library. First we need to download and install CMake which can be downloaded from their download page[1].

Once CMake is installed you can choose to run CMake from the command line or through their GUI. Since we're not trying to overcomplicate things we're going to use the GUI. CMake requires a source code folder and a destination folder for the binaries. For the source code folder we're going to choose the root folder of the downloaded GLFW source package and for the build folder we're creating a new directory *build* and then select that directory.

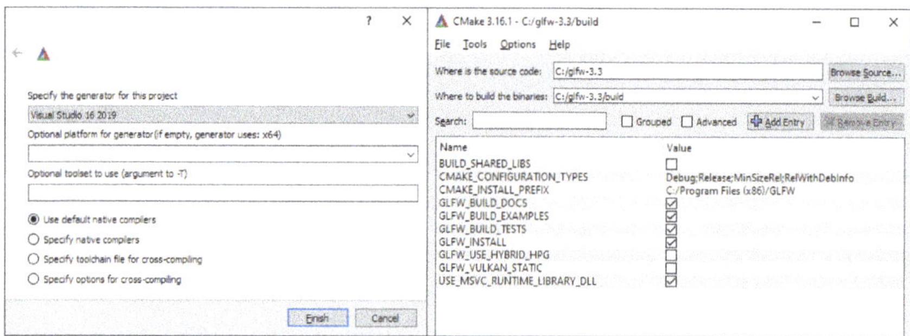

Once the source and destination folders have been set, click the `Configure` button so CMake can read the required settings and the source code. We then have to choose the generator for the project and since we're using Visual Studio 2019 we will choose the `Visual Studio 16` option (Visual Studio 2019 is also known as Visual Studio 16). CMake will then display the possible build options to configure the resulting library. We can leave them to their default values and click `Configure` again to store the settings. Once the settings have been set, we click `Generate` and the resulting project files will be generated in your `build` folder.

3.2.2 Compilation

In the `build` folder a file named `GLFW.sln` can now be found and we open it with Visual Studio 2019. Since CMake generated a project file that already contains the proper configuration settings we only have to build the solution. CMake should've automatically configured the solution so it compiles to a 64-bit library; now hit build solution. This will give us a compiled library file that can be found in `build/src/Debug` named `glfw3.lib`.

Once we generated the library we need to make sure the IDE knows where to find the library and the include files for our OpenGL program. There are two common approaches in doing this:

1. We find the `/lib` and `/include` folders of the IDE/compiler and add the content of GLFW's `include` folder to the IDE's `/include` folder and similarly add `glfw3.lib` to the IDE's `/lib` folder. This works, but it's is not the recommended approach. It's hard to keep track of your library and include files and a new installation of your IDE/compiler results in you having to do this process all over again.
2. Another approach (and recommended) is to create a new set of directories at a location of your choice that contains all the header files/libraries from third party libraries to which you can refer to from your IDE/compiler. You could, for instance, create a single folder that contains a `Libs` and `Include` folder where we store all our library and header files respectively for OpenGL projects. Now all the third party libraries are organized within a single location (that can be shared across multiple computers). The requirement is, however, that each time we create a new project we have to tell the IDE where to find those directories.

---

[1] www.cmake.org/cmake/resources/software.html

Once the required files are stored at a location of your choice, we can start creating our first OpenGL GLFW project.

3.3 Our first project

First, let's open up Visual Studio and create a new project. Choose C++ if multiple options are given and take the `Empty Project` (don't forget to give your project a suitable name). Since we're going to be doing everything in 64-bit and the project defaults to 32-bit, we'll need to change the dropdown at the top next to Debug from x86 to x64:

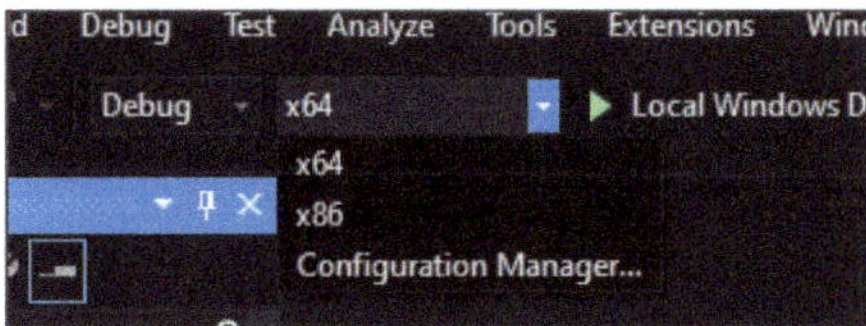

Once that's done, we now have a workspace to create our very first OpenGL application!

3.4 Linking

In order for the project to use GLFW we need to link the library with our project. This can be done by specifying we want to use `glfw3.lib` in the linker settings, but our project does not yet know where to find `glfw3.lib` since we store our third party libraries in a different directory. We thus need to add this directory to the project first.

We can tell the IDE to take this directory into account when it needs to look for library and include files. Right-click the project name in the solution explorer and then go to `VC++ Directories` as seen in the image below:

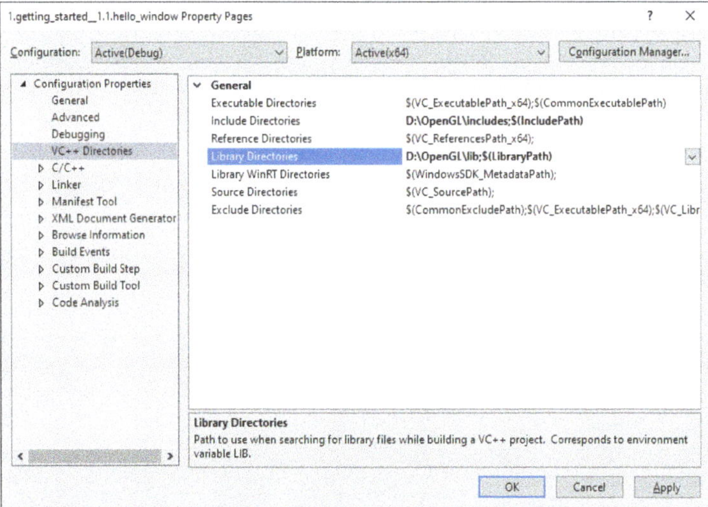

From there on out you can add your own directories to let the project know where to search. This can be done by manually inserting it into the text or clicking the appropriate location string and selecting the `<Edit..>` option. Do this for both the `Library Directories` and `Include Directories`:

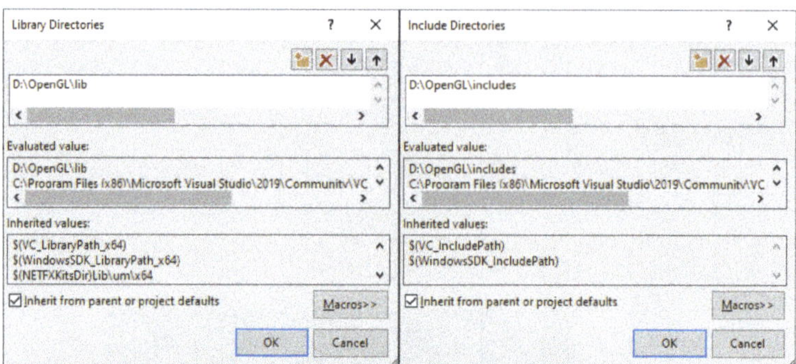

Here you can add as many extra directories as you'd like and from that point on the IDE will also search those directories when searching for library and header files. As soon as your `Include` folder from GLFW is included, you will be able to find all the header files for GLFW by including `<GLFW/..>`. The same applies for the library directories.

Since VS can now find all the required files we can finally link GLFW to the project by going to the `Linker` tab and `Input`:

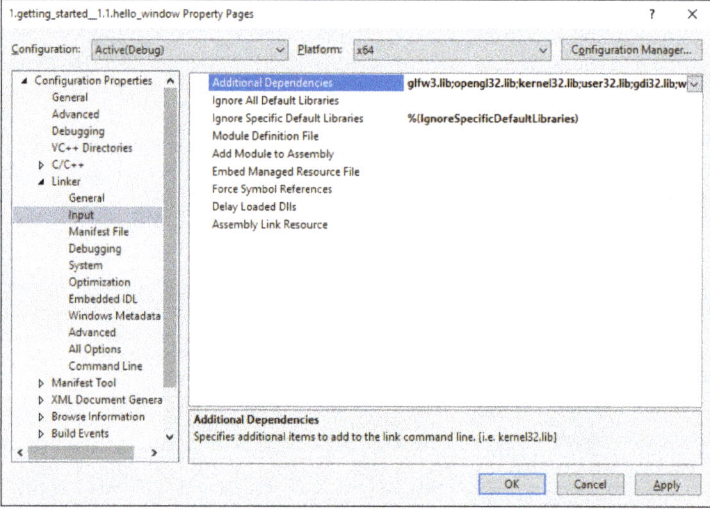

To then link to a library you'd have to specify the name of the library to the linker. Since the library name is `glfw3.lib`, we add that to the `Additional Dependencies` field (either manually or using the `<Edit..>` option) and from that point on GLFW will be linked when we compile. In addition to GLFW we should also add a link entry to the OpenGL library, but this may differ per operating system:

3.4.1 OpenGL library on Windows

If you're on Windows the OpenGL library `opengl32.lib` comes with the Microsoft SDK which is installed by default when you install Visual Studio. Since this chapter uses the VS compiler and is on windows we add `opengl32.lib` to the linker settings. Note that the 64-bit equivalent of the OpenGL library is called `opengl32.lib`, just like the 32-bit equivalent, which is a bit of an unfortunate name.

3.4.2 OpenGL library on Linux

On Linux systems you need to link to the `libGL.so` library by adding `-lGL` to your linker settings. If you can't find the library you probably need to install any of the Mesa, NVidia or AMD dev packages.

Then, once you've added both the GLFW and OpenGL library to the linker settings you can include the header files for GLFW as follows:

```
#include <GLFW\glfw3.h>
```

> For Linux users compiling with GCC, the following command line options may help you compile the project: `-lglfw3 -lGL -lX11 -lpthread -lXrandr -lXi -ldl`. Not correctly linking the corresponding libraries will generate many *undefined reference* errors.

This concludes the setup and configuration of GLFW.

3.5 GLAD

We're still not quite there yet, since there is one other thing we still need to do. Because OpenGL is only really a standard/specification it is up to the driver manufacturer to implement the specification to a driver that the specific graphics card supports. Since there are many different versions of OpenGL drivers, the location of most of its functions is not known at compile-time and needs to be queried at run-time. It is then the task of the developer to retrieve the location of the functions he/she needs and store them in function pointers for later use. Retrieving those locations is OS-specific[1]. In Windows it looks something like this:

```cpp
// define the function's prototype
typedef void (*GL_GENBUFFERS) (GLsizei, GLuint*);
// find the function and assign it to a function pointer
GL_GENBUFFERS glGenBuffers =
    (GL_GENBUFFERS)wglGetProcAddress("glGenBuffers");
// function can now be called as normal
unsigned int buffer;
glGenBuffers(1, &buffer);
```

As you can see the code looks complex and it's a cumbersome process to do this for each function you may need that is not yet declared. Thankfully, there are libraries for this purpose as well where **GLAD** is a popular and up-to-date library.

3.5.1 Setting up GLAD

GLAD is an open source[2] library that manages all that cumbersome work we talked about. GLAD has a slightly different configuration setup than most common open source libraries. GLAD uses a web service[3] where we can tell GLAD for which version of OpenGL we'd like to define and load all relevant OpenGL functions according to that version.

Go to the GLAD web service, make sure the language is set to C++, and in the API section select an OpenGL version of at least 3.3 (which is what we'll be using; higher versions are fine

---

[1] www.khronos.org/opengl/wiki/Load_OpenGL_Functions
[2] github.com/Dav1dde/glad
[3] glad.dav1d.de/

as well). Also make sure the profile is set to *Core* and that the *Generate a loader* option is ticked. Ignore the extensions (for now) and click *Generate* to produce the resulting library files.

GLAD by now should have provided you a zip file containing two include folders, and a single `glad.c` file. Copy both include folders (`glad` and `KHR`) into your include(s) directoy (or add an extra item pointing to these folders), and add the `glad.c` file to your project.

After the previous steps, you should be able to add the following include directive:

```
#include <glad/glad.h>
```

Hitting the compile button shouldn't give you any errors, at which point we're set to go for the next chapter where we'll discuss how we can actually use GLFW and GLAD to configure an OpenGL context and spawn a window. Be sure to check that all your include and library directories are correct and that the library names in the linker settings match the corresponding libraries.

3.6 Additional resources

- `www.glfw.org/docs/latest/window_guide.html`: official GLFW guide on setting up and configuring a GLFW window.
- `www.opengl-tutorial.org/miscellaneous/building-your-own-c-application/`: provides great info about the compilation/linking process of your application and a large list of possible errors (plus solutions) that may come up.
- `wiki.codeblocks.org/index.php?title=Using_GLFW_with_Code::Blocks`: building GLFW in Code::Blocks IDE.
- `www.cmake.org/runningcmake/`: short overview of how to run CMake on both Windows and Linux.
- `learnopengl.com/demo/autotools_tutorial.txt`: an autotools tutorial by Wouter Verholst on how to write a build system in Linux.
- `github.com/Polytonic/Glitter`: a simple boilerplate project that comes pre-configured with all relevant libraries; great for if you want a sample project without the hassle of having to compile all the libraries yourself.

4. Hello Window

Let's see if we can get GLFW up and running. First, create a `.cpp` file and add the following includes to the top of your newly created file.

```cpp
#include <glad/glad.h>
#include <GLFW/glfw3.h>
```

> Be sure to include GLAD before GLFW. The include file for GLAD includes the required OpenGL headers behind the scenes (like `GL/gl.h`) so be sure to include GLAD before other header files that require OpenGL (like GLFW).

Next, we create the `main` function where we will instantiate the GLFW window:

```cpp
int main()
{
    glfwInit();
    glfwWindowHint(GLFW_CONTEXT_VERSION_MAJOR, 3);
    glfwWindowHint(GLFW_CONTEXT_VERSION_MINOR, 3);
    glfwWindowHint(GLFW_OPENGL_PROFILE, GLFW_OPENGL_CORE_PROFILE);
    //glfwWindowHint(GLFW_OPENGL_FORWARD_COMPAT, GL_TRUE);

    return 0;
}
```

In the main function we first initialize GLFW with `glfwInit`, after which we can configure GLFW using `glfwWindowHint`. The first argument of `glfwWindowHint` tells us what option we want to configure, where we can select the option from a large enum of possible options prefixed with `GLFW_`. The second argument is an integer that sets the value of our option. A list of all the possible options and its corresponding values can be found at GLFW's window documentation[1]. If you try to run the application now and it gives a lot of *undefined reference* errors it means you didn't successfully link the GLFW library.

Since the focus of this book is on OpenGL version 3.3 we'd like to tell GLFW that 3.3 is the OpenGL version we want to use. This way GLFW can make the proper arrangements when creating the OpenGL context. This ensures that when a user does not have the proper OpenGL version GLFW fails to run. We set the major and minor version both to 3. We also tell GLFW we want to explicitly use the core-profile. Telling GLFW we want to use the core-profile means we'll get access to a smaller subset of OpenGL features without backwards-compatible features we no longer need. Note that on Mac OS X you need to add `glfwWindowHint(GLFW_OPENGL_FORWARD_COMPAT, GL_TRUE);` to your initialization code for it to work.

> Make sure you have OpenGL versions 3.3 or higher installed on your system/hardware otherwise the application will crash or display undefined behavior. To find the OpenGL version on your machine either call **glxinfo** on Linux machines or use a utility like the OpenGL Extension Viewer[a] for Windows. If your supported version is lower try to check if your video card supports OpenGL 3.3+ (otherwise it's really old) and/or update your drivers.
>
> ---
> [a]download.cnet.com/OpenGL-Extensions-Viewer/3000-18487_4-34442.html

---

[1]www.glfw.org/docs/latest/window.html#window_hints

Next we're required to create a window object. This window object holds all the windowing data and is required by most of GLFW's other functions.

```cpp
GLFWwindow* window = glfwCreateWindow(800, 600, "LearnOpenGL", NULL, NULL);
if (window == NULL)
{
    std::cout << "Failed to create GLFW window" << std::endl;
    glfwTerminate();
    return -1;
}
glfwMakeContextCurrent(window);
```

The `glfwCreateWindow` function requires the window width and height as its first two arguments respectively. The third argument allows us to create a name for the window; for now we call it `"LearnOpenGL"` but you're allowed to name it however you like. We can ignore the last 2 parameters. The function returns a `GLFWwindow` object that we'll later need for other GLFW operations. After that we tell GLFW to make the context of our window the main context on the current thread.

4.1 GLAD

In the previous chapter we mentioned that GLAD manages function pointers for OpenGL so we want to initialize GLAD before we call any OpenGL function:

```cpp
if (!gladLoadGLLoader((GLADloadproc)glfwGetProcAddress))
{
    std::cout << "Failed to initialize GLAD" << std::endl;
    return -1;
}
```

We pass GLAD the function to load the address of the OpenGL function pointers which is OS-specific. GLFW gives us `glfwGetProcAddress` that defines the correct function based on which OS we're compiling for.

4.2 Viewport

Before we can start rendering we have to do one last thing. We have to tell OpenGL the size of the rendering window so OpenGL knows how we want to display the data and coordinates with respect to the window. We can set those *dimensions* via the `glViewport` function:

```cpp
glViewport(0, 0, 800, 600);
```

The first two parameters of `glViewport` set the location of the lower left corner of the window. The third and fourth parameter set the width and height of the rendering window in pixels, which we set equal to GLFW's window size.

We could actually set the viewport dimensions at values smaller than GLFW's dimensions; then all the OpenGL rendering would be displayed in a smaller window and we could for example display other elements outside the OpenGL viewport.

> Behind the scenes OpenGL uses the data specified via `glViewport` to transform the 2D coordinates it processed to coordinates on your screen. For example, a processed point of location $(-0.5, 0.5)$ would (as its final transformation) be mapped to $(200, 450)$ in screen coordinates. Note that processed coordinates in OpenGL are between -1 and 1 so we effectively map from the range (-1 to 1) to (0, 800) and (0, 600).

However, the moment a user resizes the window the viewport should be adjusted as well. We can register a callback function on the window that gets called each time the window is resized. This resize callback function has the following prototype:

```cpp
void framebuffer_size_callback(GLFWwindow* window, int width, int height);
```

The framebuffer size function takes a `GLFWwindow` as its first argument and two integers indicating the new window dimensions. Whenever the window changes in size, GLFW calls this function and fills in the proper arguments for you to process.

```cpp
void framebuffer_size_callback(GLFWwindow* window, int width, int height)
{
    glViewport(0, 0, width, height);
}
```

We do have to tell GLFW we want to call this function on every window resize by registering it:

```cpp
glfwSetFramebufferSizeCallback(window, framebuffer_size_callback);
```

When the window is first displayed `framebuffer_size_callback` gets called as well with the resulting window dimensions. For retina displays `width` and `height` will end up significantly higher than the original input values.

There are many callbacks functions we can set to register our own functions. For example, we can make a callback function to process joystick input changes, process error messages etc. We register the callback functions after we've created the window and before the render loop is initiated.

4.3 Ready your engines

We don't want the application to draw a single image and then immediately quit and close the window. We want the application to keep drawing images and handling user input until the program has been explicitly told to stop. For this reason we have to create a while loop, that we now call the render loop, that keeps on running until we tell GLFW to stop. The following code shows a very simple render loop:

```cpp
while(!glfwWindowShouldClose(window))
{
    glfwSwapBuffers(window);
    glfwPollEvents();
}
```

The `glfwWindowShouldClose` function checks at the start of each loop iteration if GLFW has been instructed to close. If so, the function returns `true` and the render loop stops running, after which we can close the application. The `glfwPollEvents` function checks if any events are triggered (like keyboard input or mouse movement events), updates the window state, and calls the corresponding functions (which we can register via callback methods). The `glfwSwapBuffers` will swap the color buffer (a large 2D buffer that contains color values for each pixel in GLFW's window) that is used to render to during this render iteration and show it as output to the screen.

> **Double buffer** When an application draws in a single buffer the resulting image may display flickering issues. This is because the resulting output image is not drawn in an instant, but drawn pixel by pixel and usually from left to right and top to bottom. Because this image is not displayed at an instant to the user while still being rendered to, the result may contain artifacts. To circumvent these issues, windowing applications apply a double buffer for rendering. The **front** buffer contains the final output image that is shown at the screen, while all the rendering commands draw to the **back** buffer. As soon as all the rendering commands are finished we **swap** the back buffer to the front buffer so the image can be displayed without still being rendered to, removing all the aforementioned artifacts.

4.4 One last thing

As soon as we exit the render loop we would like to properly clean/delete all of GLFW's resources that were allocated. We can do this via the `glfwTerminate` function that we call at the end of the `main` function.

```
glfwTerminate();
return 0;
```

This will clean up all the resources and properly exit the application. Now try to compile your application and if everything went well you should see the following output:

If it's a very dull and boring black image, you did things right! If you didn't get the right image or you're confused as to how everything fits together, check the full source code at `/src/1.getting_started/1.1.hello_window/`. This path is relative to LearnOpenGL's GitHub repository at: `github.com/JoeyDeVries/learnopengl`.

If you have issues compiling the application, first make sure all your linker options are set correctly and that you properly included the right directories in your IDE (as explained in the previous chapter). Also make sure your code is correct; you can verify it by comparing it with the full source code.

4.5 **Input**

We also want to have some form of input control in GLFW and we can achieve this with several of GLFW's input functions. We'll be using GLFW's `glfwGetKey` function that takes the window as input together with a key. The function returns whether this key is currently being pressed. We're creating a `processInput` function to keep all input code organized:

```cpp
void processInput(GLFWwindow *window)
{
    if(glfwGetKey(window, GLFW_KEY_ESCAPE) == GLFW_PRESS)
        glfwSetWindowShouldClose(window, true);
}
```

Here we check whether the user has pressed the escape key (if it's not pressed, `glfwGetKey` returns `GLFW_RELEASE`). If the user did press the escape key, we close GLFW by setting its `WindowShouldClose` property to `true` using `glfwSetwindow ShouldClose`. The next condition check of the main `while` loop will then fail and the application closes.

We then call `processInput` every iteration of the render loop:

```cpp
while (!glfwWindowShouldClose(window))
{
    processInput(window);

    glfwSwapBuffers(window);
    glfwPollEvents();
}
```

This gives us an easy way to check for specific key presses and react accordingly every frame. An iteration of the render loop is more commonly called a frame.

4.6 **Rendering**

We want to place all the rendering commands in the render loop, since we want to execute all the rendering commands each iteration or frame of the loop. This would look a bit like this:

```cpp
// render loop
while(!glfwWindowShouldClose(window))
{
    // input
    processInput(window);

    // rendering commands here
    ...

    // check and call events and swap the buffers
    glfwPollEvents();
    glfwSwapBuffers(window);
}
```

Just to test if things actually work we want to clear the screen with a color of our choice. At the start of frame we want to clear the screen. Otherwise we would still see the results from the previous frame (this could be the effect you're looking for, but usually you don't). We can clear the screen's color buffer using `glClear` where we pass in buffer bits to specify which buffer we would like to clear. The possible bits we can set are `GL_COLOR_BUFFER_BIT`, `GL_DEPTH_BUFFER_BIT` and `GL_STENCIL_BUFFER_BIT`. Right now we only care about the color values so we only clear the color buffer.

```
glClearColor(0.2f, 0.3f, 0.3f, 1.0f);
glClear(GL_COLOR_BUFFER_BIT);
```

Note that we also specify the color to clear the screen with using `glClearColor`. Whenever we call `glClear` and clear the color buffer, the entire color buffer will be filled with the color as configured by `glClearColor`. This will result in a dark green-blueish color.

> As you may recall from the *OpenGL* chapter, the `glClearColor` function is a *state-setting* function and `glClear` is a *state-using* function in that it uses the current state to retrieve the clearing color from.

The full source code of the application can be found at `/src/1.getting_started/1.2.hello_window_clear/`.

So right now we got everything ready to fill the render loop with lots of rendering calls, but that's for the next chapter. I think we've been rambling long enough here.

5. Hello Triangle

In OpenGL everything is in 3D space, but the screen or window is a 2D array of pixels so a large part of OpenGL's work is about transforming all 3D coordinates to 2D pixels that fit on your screen. The process of transforming 3D coordinates to 2D pixels is managed by the graphics pipeline of OpenGL. The graphics pipeline can be divided into two large parts: the first transforms your 3D coordinates into 2D coordinates and the second part transforms the 2D coordinates into actual colored pixels. In this chapter we'll briefly discuss the graphics pipeline and how we can use it to our advantage to create fancy pixels.

The graphics pipeline takes as input a set of 3D coordinates and transforms these to colored 2D pixels on your screen. The graphics pipeline can be divided into several steps where each step requires the output of the previous step as its input. All of these steps are highly specialized (they have one specific function) and can easily be executed in parallel. Because of their parallel nature, graphics cards of today have thousands of small processing cores to quickly process your data within the graphics pipeline. The processing cores run small programs on the GPU for each step of the pipeline. These small programs are called shaders.

Some of these shaders are configurable by the developer which allows us to write our own shaders to replace the existing default shaders. This gives us much more fine-grained control over specific parts of the pipeline and because they run on the GPU, they can also save us valuable CPU time. Shaders are written in the OpenGL Shading Language (GLSL) and we'll delve more into that in the next chapter.

Below you'll find an abstract representation of all the stages of the graphics pipeline. Note that the blue sections represent sections where we can inject our own shaders.

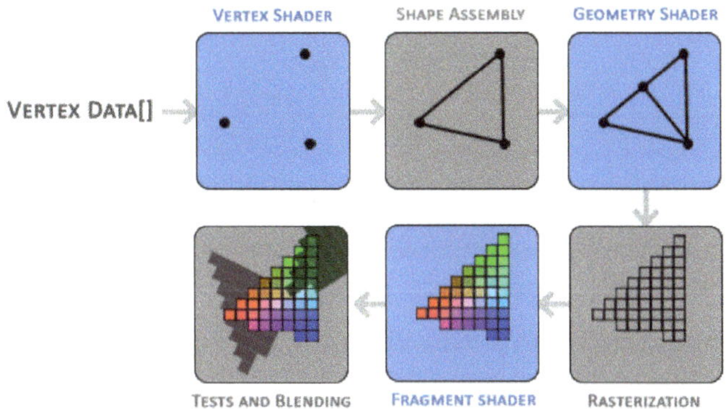

As you can see, the graphics pipeline contains a large number of sections that each handle one specific part of converting your vertex data to a fully rendered pixel. We will briefly explain each part of the pipeline in a simplified way to give you a good overview of how the pipeline operates.

As input to the graphics pipeline we pass in a list of three 3D coordinates that should form a triangle in an array here called `Vertex Data`; this vertex data is a collection of vertices. A vertex is a collection of data per 3D coordinate. This vertex's data is represented using vertex attributes that can contain any data we'd like, but for simplicity's sake let's assume that each vertex consists of just a 3D position and some color value.

> In order for OpenGL to know what to make of your collection of coordinates and color values OpenGL requires you to hint what kind of render types you want to form with the data. Do we want the data rendered as a collection of points, a collection of triangles or perhaps just one long line? Those hints are called primitives and are given to OpenGL while calling any of the drawing commands. Some of these hints are `GL_POINTS`, `GL_TRIANGLES` and `GL_LINE_STRIP`.

The first part of the pipeline is the vertex shader that takes as input a single vertex. The main purpose of the vertex shader is to transform 3D coordinates into different 3D coordinates (more on that later) and the vertex shader allows us to do some basic processing on the vertex attributes.

The primitive assembly stage takes as input all the vertices (or vertex if `GL_POINTS` is chosen) from the vertex shader that form a primitive and assembles all the point(s) in the primitive shape given; in this case a triangle.

The output of the primitive assembly stage is passed to the geometry shader. The geometry shader takes as input a collection of vertices that form a primitive and has the ability to generate other shapes by emitting new vertices to form new (or other) primitive(s). In this example case, it generates a second triangle out of the given shape.

The output of the geometry shader is then passed on to the rasterization stage where it maps the resulting primitive(s) to the corresponding pixels on the final screen, resulting in fragments for the fragment shader to use. Before the fragment shaders run, clipping is performed. Clipping discards all fragments that are outside your view, increasing performance.

> A fragment in OpenGL is all the data required for OpenGL to render a single pixel.

The main purpose of the fragment shader is to calculate the final color of a pixel and this is usually the stage where all the advanced OpenGL effects occur. Usually the fragment shader contains data about the 3D scene that it can use to calculate the final pixel color (like lights, shadows, color of the light and so on).

After all the corresponding color values have been determined, the final object will then pass through one more stage that we call the alpha test and blending stage. This stage checks the corresponding depth (and stencil) value (we'll get to those later) of the fragment and uses those to check if the resulting fragment is in front or behind other objects and should be discarded accordingly. The stage also checks for alpha values (alpha values define the opacity of an object) and blends the objects accordingly. So even if a pixel output color is calculated in the fragment shader, the final pixel color could still be something entirely different when rendering multiple triangles.

As you can see, the graphics pipeline is quite a complex whole and contains many configurable parts. However, for almost all the cases we only have to work with the vertex and fragment shader. The geometry shader is optional and usually left to its default shader. There is also the tessellation stage and transform feedback loop that we haven't depicted here, but that's something for later.

In modern OpenGL we are **required** to define at least a vertex and fragment shader of our own (there are no default vertex/fragment shaders on the GPU). For this reason it is often quite difficult to start learning modern OpenGL since a great deal of knowledge is required before being able to render your first triangle. Once you do get to finally render your triangle at the end of this chapter you will end up knowing a lot more about graphics programming.

5.1 Vertex input

To start drawing something we have to first give OpenGL some input vertex data. OpenGL is a 3D graphics library so all coordinates that we specify in OpenGL are in 3D (x, y and z coordinate). OpenGL doesn't simply transform **all** your 3D coordinates to 2D pixels on your screen; OpenGL only processes 3D coordinates when they're in a specific range between -1.0 and 1.0 on all 3 axes (x, y and z). All coordinates within this so called normalized device coordinates range will end up visible on your screen (and all coordinates outside this region won't).

Because we want to render a single triangle we want to specify a total of three vertices with each vertex having a 3D position. We define them in normalized device coordinates (the visible region of OpenGL) in a `float` array:

```
float vertices[] = {
    -0.5f, -0.5f, 0.0f,
     0.5f, -0.5f, 0.0f,
     0.0f,  0.5f, 0.0f
};
```

Because OpenGL works in 3D space we render a 2D triangle with each vertex having a z coordinate of 0.0. This way the *depth* of the triangle remains the same making it look like it's 2D.

> **Normalized Device Coordinates (NDC)**
> Once your vertex coordinates have been processed in the vertex shader, they should be in normalized device coordinates which is a small space where the x, y and z values vary from -1.0 to 1.0. Any coordinates that fall outside this range will be discarded/clipped and won't be visible on your screen. Below you can see the triangle we specified within normalized device coordinates (ignoring the z axis):
>
> 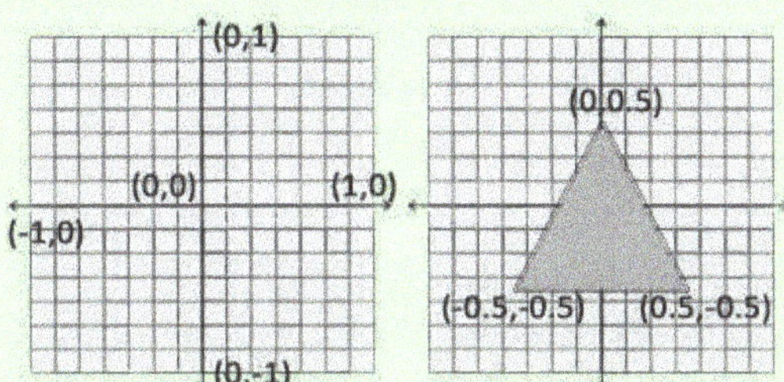
>
>
> Unlike usual screen coordinates the positive y-axis points in the up-direction and the (0,0) coordinates are at the center of the graph, instead of top-left. Eventually you want all the (transformed) coordinates to end up in this coordinate space, otherwise they won't be visible.
>
> Your NDC coordinates will then be transformed to screen-space coordinates via the viewport transform using the data you provided with `glViewport`. The resulting screen-space coordinates are then transformed to fragments as inputs to your fragment shader.

With the vertex data defined we'd like to send it as input to the first process of the graphics pipeline: the vertex shader. This is done by creating memory on the GPU where we store the vertex data, configure how OpenGL should interpret the memory and specify how to send the data to the graphics card. The vertex shader then processes as much vertices as we tell it to from its memory.

We manage this memory via so called vertex buffer objects (VBO) that can store a large number of vertices in the GPU's memory. The advantage of using those buffer objects is that we can send large batches of data all at once to the graphics card, and keep it there if there's enough memory left, without having to send data one vertex at a time. Sending data to the graphics card from the CPU is relatively slow, so wherever we can we try to send as much data as possible at once. Once the data is in the graphics card's memory the vertex shader has almost instant access to the vertices making it extremely fast

A vertex buffer object is our first occurrence of an OpenGL object as we've discussed in the *OpenGL* chapter. Just like any object in OpenGL, this buffer has a unique ID corresponding to that buffer, so we can generate one with a buffer ID using the `glGenBuffers` function:

```
unsigned int VBO;
glGenBuffers(1, &VBO);
```

OpenGL has many types of buffer objects and the buffer type of a vertex buffer object is `GL_ARRAY_BUFFER`. OpenGL allows us to bind to several buffers at once as long as they have a different buffer type. We can bind the newly created buffer to the `GL_ARRAY_BUFFER` target with the `glBindBuffer` function:

```
glBindBuffer(GL_ARRAY_BUFFER, VBO);
```

From that point on any buffer calls we make (on the `GL_ARRAY_BUFFER` target) will be used to configure the currently bound buffer, which is `VBO`. Then we can make a call to the `glBufferData` function that copies the previously defined vertex data into the buffer's memory:

```
glBufferData(GL_ARRAY_BUFFER, sizeof(vertices), vertices, GL_STATIC_DRAW);
```

`glBufferData` is a function specifically targeted to copy user-defined data into the currently bound buffer. Its first argument is the type of the buffer we want to copy data into: the vertex buffer object currently bound to the `GL_ARRAY_BUFFER` target. The second argument specifies the size of the data (in bytes) we want to pass to the buffer; a simple `sizeof` of the vertex data suffices. The third parameter is the actual data we want to send.

The fourth parameter specifies how we want the graphics card to manage the given data. This can take 3 forms:

- `GL_STREAM_DRAW`: the data is set only once and used by the GPU at most a few times.
- `GL_STATIC_DRAW`: the data is set only once and used many times.
- `GL_DYNAMIC_DRAW`: the data is changed a lot and used many times.

The position data of the triangle does not change, is used a lot, and stays the same for every render call so its usage type should best be `GL_STATIC_DRAW`. If, for instance, one would have a buffer with data that is likely to change frequently, a usage type of `GL_DYNAMIC_DRAW` ensures the graphics card will place the data in memory that allows for faster writes.

As of now we stored the vertex data within memory on the graphics card as managed by a vertex buffer object named `VBO`. Next we want to create a vertex and fragment shader that actually processes this data, so let's start building those.

5.2 Vertex shader

The vertex shader is one of the shaders that are programmable by people like us. Modern OpenGL requires that we at least set up a vertex and fragment shader if we want to do some rendering so we will briefly introduce shaders and configure two very simple shaders for drawing our first triangle. In the next chapter we'll discuss shaders in more detail.

The first thing we need to do is write the vertex shader in the shader language GLSL (OpenGL Shading Language) and then compile this shader so we can use it in our application. Below you'll find the source code of a very basic vertex shader in GLSL:

```glsl
#version 330 core
layout (location = 0) in vec3 aPos;

void main()
{
    gl_Position = vec4(aPos.x, aPos.y, aPos.z, 1.0);
}
```

As you can see, GLSL looks similar to C. Each shader begins with a declaration of its version. Since OpenGL 3.3 and higher the version numbers of GLSL match the version of OpenGL (GLSL version 420 corresponds to OpenGL version 4.2 for example). We also explicitly mention we're using core profile functionality.

Next we declare all the input vertex attributes in the vertex shader with the `in` keyword. Right now we only care about position data so we only need a single vertex attribute. GLSL has a vector datatype that contains 1 to 4 floats based on its postfix digit. Since each vertex has a 3D coordinate we create a `vec3` input variable with the name `aPos`. We also specifically set the location of the input variable via `layout (location = 0)` and you'll later see that why we're going to need that location.

> **Vector** In graphics programming we use the mathematical concept of a vector quite often, since it neatly represents positions/directions in any space and has useful mathematical properties. A vector in GLSL has a maximum size of 4 and each of its values can be retrieved via `vec.x`, `vec.y`, `vec.z` and `vec.w` respectively where each of them represents a coordinate in space. Note that the `vec.w` component is not used as a position in space (we're dealing with 3D, not 4D) but is used for something called perspective division. We'll discuss vectors in much greater depth in a later chapter.

To set the output of the vertex shader we have to assign the position data to the predefined `gl_Position` variable which is a `vec4` behind the scenes. At the end of the `main` function, whatever we set `gl_Position` to will be used as the output of the vertex shader. Since our input is a vector of size 3 we have to cast this to a vector of size 4. We can do this by inserting the `vec3` values inside the constructor of `vec4` and set its `w` component to `1.0f` (we will explain why in a later chapter).

The current vertex shader is probably the most simple vertex shader we can imagine because we did no processing whatsoever on the input data and simply forwarded it to the shader's output. In real applications the input data is usually not already in normalized device coordinates so we first have to transform the input data to coordinates that fall within OpenGL's visible region.

5.3 Compiling a shader

We take the source code for the vertex shader and store it in a const C string at the top of the code file for now:

```cpp
const char *vertexShaderSource = "#version 330 core\n"
    "layout (location = 0) in vec3 aPos;\n"
    "void main()\n"
    "{\n"
    " gl_Position = vec4(aPos.x, aPos.y, aPos.z, 1.0);\n"
    "}\0";
```

In order for OpenGL to use the shader it has to dynamically compile it at run-time from its source code. The first thing we need to do is create a shader object, again referenced by an ID. So we store the vertex shader as an `unsigned int` and create the shader with `glCreateShader`:

```cpp
unsigned int vertexShader;
vertexShader = glCreateShader(GL_VERTEX_SHADER);
```

We provide the type of shader we want to create as an argument to `glCreateShader`. Since we're creating a vertex shader we pass in `GL_VERTEX_SHADER`.

Next we attach the shader source code to the shader object and compile the shader:

```cpp
glShaderSource(vertexShader, 1, &vertexShaderSource, NULL);
glCompileShader(vertexShader);
```

The `glShaderSource` function takes the shader object to compile to as its first argument. The second argument specifies how many strings we're passing as source code, which is only one. The third parameter is the actual source code of the vertex shader and we can leave the 4th parameter to `NULL`.

You probably want to check if compilation was successful after the call to `glCompileShader` and if not, what errors were found so you can fix those. Checking for compile-time errors is accomplished as follows:

```cpp
int success;
char infoLog[512];
glGetShaderiv(vertexShader, GL_COMPILE_STATUS, &success);
```

First we define an integer to indicate success and a storage container for the error messages (if any). Then we check if compilation was successful with `glGetShaderiv`. If compilation failed, we should retrieve the error message with `glGetShaderInfoLog` and print the error message.

```cpp
if(!success)
{
    glGetShaderInfoLog(vertexShader, 512, NULL, infoLog);
    std::cout << "ERROR::SHADER::VERTEX::COMPILATION_FAILED\n" <<
            infoLog << std::endl;
}
```

If no errors were detected while compiling the vertex shader it is now compiled.

5.4 **Fragment shader**

The fragment shader is the second and final shader we're going to create for rendering a triangle. The fragment shader is all about calculating the color output of your pixels. To keep things simple the fragment shader will always output an orange-ish color.

> Colors in computer graphics are represented as an array of 4 values: the red, green, blue and alpha (opacity) component, commonly abbreviated to RGBA. When defining a color in OpenGL or GLSL we set the strength of each component to a value between `0.0` and `1.0`. If, for example, we would set red to `1.0` and green to `1.0` we would get a mixture of both colors and get the color yellow. Given those 3 color components we can generate over 16 million different colors!

```glsl
#version 330 core
out vec4 FragColor;

void main()
{
    FragColor = vec4(1.0f, 0.5f, 0.2f, 1.0f);
}
```

The fragment shader only requires one output variable and that is a vector of size 4 that defines the final color output that we should calculate ourselves. We can declare output values with the `out` keyword, that we here promptly named `FragColor`. Next we simply assign a `vec4` to the color output as an orange color with an alpha value of `1.0` (`1.0` being completely opaque).

The process for compiling a fragment shader is similar to the vertex shader, although this time we use the `GL_FRAGMENT_SHADER` constant as the shader type:

```cpp
unsigned int fragmentShader;
fragmentShader = glCreateShader(GL_FRAGMENT_SHADER);
glShaderSource(fragmentShader, 1, &fragmentShaderSource, NULL);
glCompileShader(fragmentShader);
```

Both the shaders are now compiled and the only thing left to do is link both shader objects into a shader program that we can use for rendering. Make sure to check for compile errors here as well!

5.4.1 **Shader program**

A shader program object is the final linked version of multiple shaders combined. To use the recently compiled shaders we have to link them to a shader program object and then activate this shader program when rendering objects. The activated shader program's shaders will be used when we issue render calls.

When linking the shaders into a program it links the outputs of each shader to the inputs of the next shader. This is also where you'll get linking errors if your outputs and inputs do not match.

Creating a program object is easy:

```cpp
unsigned int shaderProgram;
shaderProgram = glCreateProgram();
```

The `glCreateProgram` function creates a program and returns the ID reference to the newly created program object. Now we need to attach the previously compiled shaders to the program object and then link them with `glLinkProgram`:

```
glAttachShader(shaderProgram, vertexShader);
glAttachShader(shaderProgram, fragmentShader);
glLinkProgram(shaderProgram);
```

The code should be pretty self-explanatory, we attach the shaders to the program and link them via `glLinkProgram`.

> Just like shader compilation we can also check if linking a shader program failed and retrieve the corresponding log. However, instead of using `glGetShaderiv` and `glGetShaderInfoLog` we now use:
>
> ```
> glGetProgramiv(shaderProgram, GL_LINK_STATUS, &success);
> if(!success) {
>     glGetProgramInfoLog(shaderProgram, 512, NULL, infoLog);
>     ...
> }
> ```

The result is a program object that we can activate by calling `glUseProgram` with the newly created program object as its argument:

```
glUseProgram(shaderProgram);
```

Every shader and rendering call after `glUseProgram` will now use this program object (and thus the shaders).

Oh yeah, and don't forget to delete the shader objects once we've linked them into the program object; we no longer need them anymore:

```
glDeleteShader(vertexShader);
glDeleteShader(fragmentShader);
```

Right now we sent the input vertex data to the GPU and instructed the GPU how it should process the vertex data within a vertex and fragment shader. We're almost there, but not quite yet. OpenGL does not yet know how it should interpret the vertex data in memory and how it should connect the vertex data to the vertex shader's attributes. We'll be nice and tell OpenGL how to do that.

5.5 Linking Vertex Attributes

The vertex shader allows us to specify any input we want in the form of vertex attributes and while this allows for great flexibility, it does mean we have to manually specify what part of our input data goes to which vertex attribute in the vertex shader. This means we have to specify how OpenGL should interpret the vertex data before rendering.

Our vertex buffer data is formatted as follows:

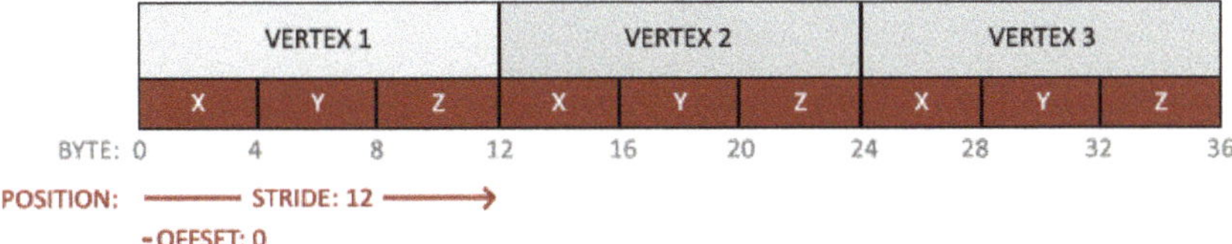

- The position data is stored as 32-bit (4 byte) floating point values.
- Each position is composed of 3 of those values.
- There is no space (or other values) between each set of 3 values. The values are tightly packed in the array.
- The first value in the data is at the beginning of the buffer.

With this knowledge we can tell OpenGL how it should interpret the vertex data (per vertex attribute) using `glVertexAttribPointer`:

```
glVertexAttribPointer(0, 3, GL_FLOAT, GL_FALSE, 3 * sizeof(float),
                      (void*)0);
glEnableVertexAttribArray(0);
```

The function `glVertexAttribPointer` has quite a few parameters so let's carefully walk through them:

- The first parameter specifies which vertex attribute we want to configure. Remember that we specified the location of the `position` vertex attribute in the vertex shader with `layout (location = 0)`. This sets the location of the vertex attribute to 0 and since we want to pass data to this vertex attribute, we pass in 0.
- The next argument specifies the size of the vertex attribute. The vertex attribute is a `vec3` so it is composed of 3 values.
- The third argument specifies the type of the data which is `GL_FLOAT` (a `vec*` in GLSL consists of floating point values).
- The next argument specifies if we want the data to be normalized. If we're inputting integer data types (int, byte) and we've set this to `GL_TRUE`, the integer data is normalized to 0 (or −1 for signed data) and 1 when converted to float. This is not relevant for us so we'll leave this at `GL_FALSE`.
- The fifth argument is known as the stride and tells us the space between consecutive vertex attributes. Since the next set of position data is located exactly 3 times the size of a `float` away we specify that value as the stride. Note that since we know that the array is tightly packed (there is no space between the next vertex attribute value) we could've also specified the stride as 0 to let OpenGL determine the stride (this only works when values are tightly packed). Whenever we have more vertex attributes we have to carefully define the spacing between each vertex attribute but we'll get to see more examples of that later on.
- The last parameter is of type `void*` and thus requires that weird cast. This is the offset of where the position data begins in the buffer. Since the position data is at the start of the data array this value is just 0. We will explore this parameter in more detail later on

> Each vertex attribute takes its data from memory managed by a VBO and which VBO it takes its data from (you can have multiple VBOs) is determined by the VBO currently bound to `GL_ARRAY_BUFFER` when calling `glVertexAttribPointer`. Since the previously defined `VBO` is still bound before calling `glVertexAttribPointer` vertex attribute `0` is now associated with its vertex data.

Now that we specified how OpenGL should interpret the vertex data we should also enable the vertex attribute with `glEnableVertexAttribArray` giving the vertex attribute location as its argument; vertex attributes are disabled by default. From that point on we have everything set up: we initialized the vertex data in a buffer using a vertex buffer object, set up a vertex and fragment shader and told OpenGL how to link the vertex data to the vertex shader's vertex attributes. Drawing an object in OpenGL would now look something like this:

```cpp
// 0. copy our vertices array in a buffer for OpenGL to use
glBindBuffer(GL_ARRAY_BUFFER, VBO);
glBufferData(GL_ARRAY_BUFFER, sizeof(vertices), vertices, GL_STATIC_DRAW);
// 1. then set the vertex attributes pointers
glVertexAttribPointer(0, 3, GL_FLOAT, GL_FALSE, 3 * sizeof(float),
                      (void*)0);
glEnableVertexAttribArray(0);
// 2. use our shader program when we want to render an object
glUseProgram(shaderProgram);
// 3. now draw the object
someOpenGLFunctionThatDrawsOurTriangle();
```

We have to repeat this process every time we want to draw an object. It may not look like that much, but imagine if we have over 5 vertex attributes and perhaps 100s of different objects (which is not uncommon). Binding the appropriate buffer objects and configuring all vertex attributes for each of those objects quickly becomes a cumbersome process. What if there was some way we could store all these state configurations into an object and simply bind this object to restore its state?

5.5.1 Vertex Array Object

A vertex array object (also known as VAO) can be bound just like a vertex buffer object and any subsequent vertex attribute calls from that point on will be stored inside the VAO. This has the advantage that when configuring vertex attribute pointers you only have to make those calls once and whenever we want to draw the object, we can just bind the corresponding VAO. This makes switching between different vertex data and attribute configurations as easy as binding a different VAO. All the state we just set is stored inside the VAO.

> Core OpenGL **requires** that we use a VAO so it knows what to do with our vertex inputs. If we fail to bind a VAO, OpenGL will most likely refuse to draw anything.

A vertex array object stores the following:

- Calls to `glEnableVertexAttribArray` or `glDisableVertexAttrib Array`.
- Vertex attribute configurations via `glVertexAttribPointer`.
- Vertex buffer objects associated with vertex attributes by calls to `glVertexAtt ribPointer`.

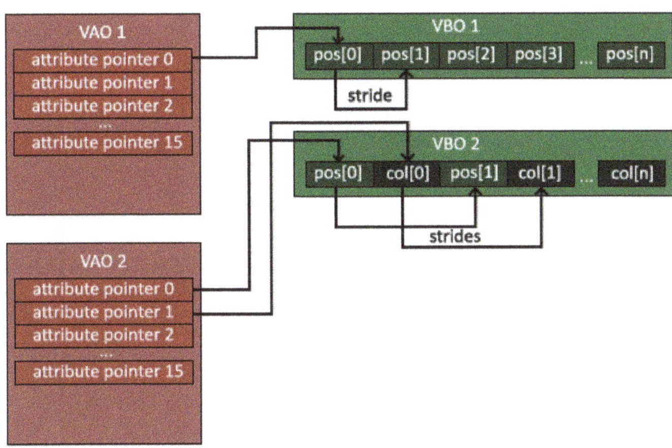

The process to generate a VAO looks similar to that of a VBO:

```cpp
unsigned int VAO;
glGenVertexArrays(1, &VAO);
```

To use a VAO all you have to do is bind the VAO using `glBindVertexArray`. From that point on we should bind/configure the corresponding VBO(s) and attribute pointer(s) and then unbind the VAO for later use. As soon as we want to draw an object, we simply bind the VAO with the preferred settings before drawing the object and that is it. In code this would look a bit like this:

```cpp
// ..:: Initialization code (done once (unless your object frequently
    changes)) :: ..
// 1. bind Vertex Array Object
glBindVertexArray(VAO);
// 2. copy our vertices array in a buffer for OpenGL to use
glBindBuffer(GL_ARRAY_BUFFER, VBO);
glBufferData(GL_ARRAY_BUFFER, sizeof(vertices), vertices, GL_STATIC_DRAW);
// 3. then set our vertex attributes pointers
glVertexAttribPointer(0, 3, GL_FLOAT, GL_FALSE, 3 * sizeof(float),
                      (void*)0);
glEnableVertexAttribArray(0);

[...]

// ..:: Drawing code (in render loop) :: ..
// 4. draw the object
glUseProgram(shaderProgram);
glBindVertexArray(VAO);
someOpenGLFunctionThatDrawsOurTriangle();
```

And that is it! Everything we did the last few million pages led up to this moment, a VAO that stores our vertex attribute configuration and which VBO to use. Usually when you have multiple objects you want to draw, you first generate/configure all the VAOs (and thus the required VBO and attribute pointers) and store those for later use. The moment we want to draw one of our objects, we take the corresponding VAO, bind it, then draw the object and unbind the VAO again.

5.5.2 The triangle we've all been waiting for

To draw our objects of choice, OpenGL provides us with the `glDrawArrays` function that draws primitives using the currently active shader, the previously defined vertex attribute configuration and with the VBO's vertex data (indirectly bound via the VAO).

```
glUseProgram(shaderProgram);
glBindVertexArray(VAO);
glDrawArrays(GL_TRIANGLES, 0, 3);
```

The `glDrawArrays` function takes as its first argument the OpenGL primitive type we would like to draw. Since I said at the start we wanted to draw a triangle, and I don't like lying to you, we pass in `GL_TRIANGLES`. The second argument specifies the starting index of the vertex array we'd like to draw; we just leave this at 0. The last argument specifies how many vertices we want to draw, which is 3 (we only render 1 triangle from our data, which is exactly 3 vertices long).

Now try to compile the code and work your way backwards if any errors popped up. As soon as your application compiles, you should see the following result:

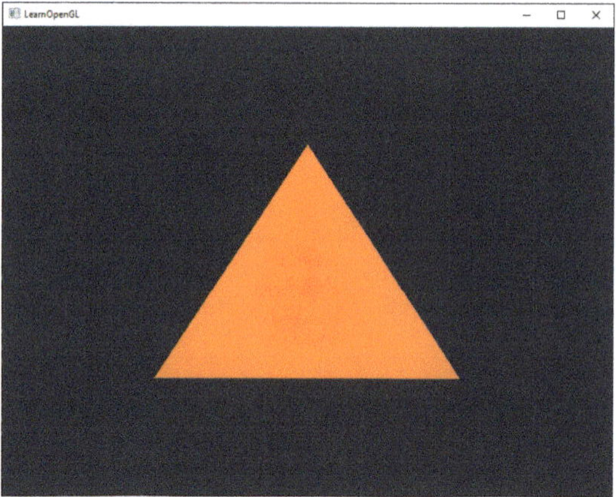

The source code for the complete program can be found at `/src/1.getting_started/2.1.hello_triangle/`.

If your output does not look the same you probably did something wrong along the way so check the complete source code and see if you missed anything.

5.6 Element Buffer Objects

There is one last thing we'd like to discuss when rendering vertices and that is element buffer objects abbreviated to EBO. To explain how element buffer objects work it's best to give an example: suppose we want to draw a rectangle instead of a triangle. We can draw a rectangle using two triangles (OpenGL mainly works with triangles). This will generate the following set of vertices:

```cpp
float vertices[] = {
    // first triangle
     0.5f,  0.5f, 0.0f, // top right
     0.5f, -0.5f, 0.0f, // bottom right
    -0.5f,  0.5f, 0.0f, // top left
    // second triangle
     0.5f, -0.5f, 0.0f, // bottom right
    -0.5f, -0.5f, 0.0f, // bottom left
    -0.5f,  0.5f, 0.0f  // top left
};
```

As you can see, there is some overlap on the vertices specified. We specify `bottom right` and `top left` twice! This is an overhead of 50% since the same rectangle could also be specified with only 4 vertices, instead of 6. This will only get worse as soon as we have more complex models that have over 1000s of triangles where there will be large chunks that overlap. What would be a better solution is to store only the unique vertices and then specify the order at which we want to draw these vertices in. In that case we would only have to store 4 vertices for the rectangle, and then just specify at which order we'd like to draw them. Wouldn't it be great if OpenGL provided us with a feature like that?

Thankfully, element buffer objects work exactly like that. An EBO is a buffer, just like a vertex buffer object, that stores indices that OpenGL uses to decide what vertices to draw. This so called indexed drawing is exactly the solution to our problem. To get started we first have to specify the (unique) vertices and the indices to draw them as a rectangle:

```cpp
float vertices[] = {
     0.5f,  0.5f, 0.0f, // top right
     0.5f, -0.5f, 0.0f, // bottom right
    -0.5f, -0.5f, 0.0f, // bottom left
    -0.5f,  0.5f, 0.0f  // top left
};
unsigned int indices[] = { // note that we start from 0!
    0, 1, 3, // first triangle
    1, 2, 3  // second triangle
};
```

You can see that, when using indices, we only need 4 vertices instead of 6. Next we need to create the element buffer object:

```cpp
unsigned int EBO;
glGenBuffers(1, &EBO);
```

Similar to the VBO we bind the EBO and copy the indices into the buffer with `glBufferData`. Also, just like the VBO we want to place those calls between a bind and an unbind call, although this time we specify `GL_ELEMENT_ARRAY_BUFFER` as the buffer type.

```cpp
glBindBuffer(GL_ELEMENT_ARRAY_BUFFER, EBO);
glBufferData(GL_ELEMENT_ARRAY_BUFFER, sizeof(indices), indices,
    GL_STATIC_DRAW);
```

Note that we're now giving `GL_ELEMENT_ARRAY_BUFFER` as the buffer target. The last thing left to do is replace the `glDrawArrays` call with `glDrawElements` to indicate we want to render the triangles from an index buffer. When using `glDrawElements` we're going to draw using indices provided in the element buffer object currently bound:

```
glBindBuffer(GL_ELEMENT_ARRAY_BUFFER, EBO);
glDrawElements(GL_TRIANGLES, 6, GL_UNSIGNED_INT, 0);
```

The first argument specifies the mode we want to draw in, similar to `glDrawArrays`. The second argument is the count or number of elements we'd like to draw. We specified 6 indices so we want to draw 6 vertices in total. The third argument is the type of the indices which is of type `GL_UNSIGNED_INT`. The last argument allows us to specify an offset in the EBO (or pass in an index array, but that is when you're not using element buffer objects), but we're just going to leave this at 0.

The `glDrawElements` function takes its indices from the EBO currently bound to the `GL_ELEMENT_ARRAY_BUFFER` target. This means we have to bind the corresponding EBO each time we want to render an object with indices which again is a bit cumbersome. It just so happens that a vertex array object also keeps track of element buffer object bindings. The last element buffer object that gets bound while a VAO is bound, is stored as the VAO's element buffer object. Binding to a VAO then also automatically binds that EBO.

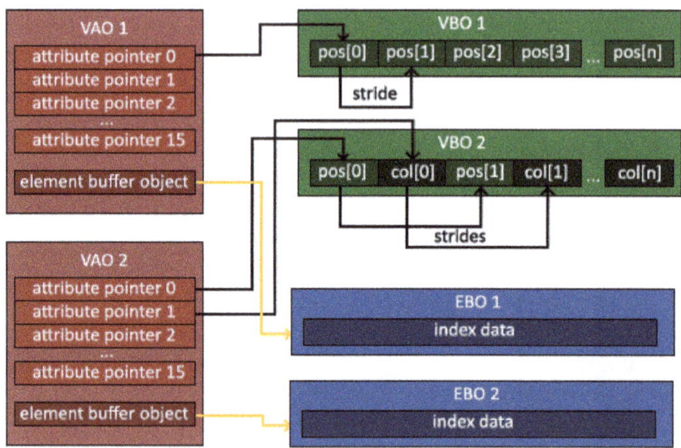

A VAO stores the `glBindBuffer` calls when the target is `GL_ELEMENT_ARRAY_BUFFER`. This also means it stores its unbind calls so make sure you don't unbind the element array buffer before unbinding your VAO, otherwise it doesn't have an EBO configured.

The resulting initialization and drawing code now looks something like this:

```
// ..:: Initialization code :: ..
// 1. bind Vertex Array Object
glBindVertexArray(VAO);
// 2. copy our vertices array in a vertex buffer for OpenGL to use
glBindBuffer(GL_ARRAY_BUFFER, VBO);
glBufferData(GL_ARRAY_BUFFER, sizeof(vertices), vertices, GL_STATIC_DRAW);
// 3. copy our index array in a element buffer for OpenGL to use
glBindBuffer(GL_ELEMENT_ARRAY_BUFFER, EBO);
glBufferData(GL_ELEMENT_ARRAY_BUFFER, sizeof(indices), indices,
             GL_STATIC_DRAW);
// 4. then set the vertex attributes pointers
```

```
glVertexAttribPointer(0, 3, GL_FLOAT, GL_FALSE, 3 * sizeof(float),
                      (void*)0);
glEnableVertexAttribArray(0);

[...]

// ..:: Drawing code (in render loop) :: ..
glUseProgram(shaderProgram);
glBindVertexArray(VAO);
glDrawElements(GL_TRIANGLES, 6, GL_UNSIGNED_INT, 0)
glBindVertexArray(0);
```

Running the program should give an image as depicted below. The left image should look familiar and the right image is the rectangle drawn in wireframe mode. The wireframe rectangle shows that the rectangle indeed consists of two triangles.

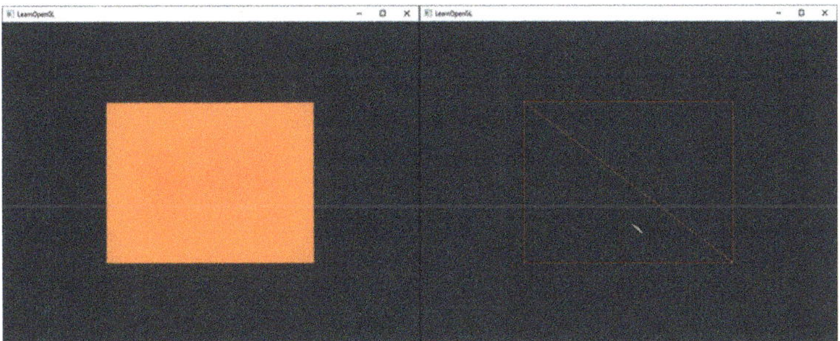

> **Wireframe mode** To draw your triangles in wireframe mode, you can configure how OpenGL draws its primitives via `glPolygonMode(GL_FRONT_AND_BACK, GL_LINE)`. The first argument says we want to apply it to the front and back of all triangles and the second line tells us to draw them as lines. Any subsequent drawing calls will render the triangles in wireframe mode until we set it back to its default using `glPolygonMode(GL_FRONT_AND_BACK, GL_FILL)`.

If you have any errors, work your way backwards and see if you missed anything. You can find the complete source code at `/src/1.getting_started/2.2.hello_triangle_indexed/`.

If you managed to draw a triangle or a rectangle just like we did then congratulations, you managed to make it past one of the hardest parts of modern OpenGL: drawing your first triangle. This is a difficult part since there is a large chunk of knowledge required before being able to draw your first triangle. Thankfully, we now made it past that barrier and the upcoming chapters will hopefully be much easier to understand.

5.7 Additional resources

- `antongerdelan.net/opengl/hellotriangle.html`: Anton Gerdelan's take on rendering the first triangle.
- `open.gl/drawing`: Alexander Overvoorde's take on rendering the first triangle.
- `antongerdelan.net/opengl/vertexbuffers.html`: some extra insights into vertex buffer objects.
- `learnopengl.com/In-Practice/Debugging` (Chapter 47): there are a lot of steps involved in this chapter; if you're stuck it may be worthwhile to read a bit on debugging in

OpenGL (up until the debug output section).

5.8 Exercises

To really get a good grasp of the concepts discussed a few exercises were set up. It is advised to work through them before continuing to the next subject to make sure you get a good grasp of what's going on.

1. Try to draw 2 triangles next to each other using `glDrawArrays` by adding more vertices to your data. Solution: `/src/1.getting_started/2.3.hello_triangle_exercise1/`.
2. Now create the same 2 triangles using two different VAOs and VBOs for their data. Solution: `/src/1.getting_started/2.4.hello_triangle_exercise2/`.
3. Create two shader programs where the second program uses a different fragment shader that outputs the color yellow; draw both triangles again where one outputs the color yellow. Solution: `/src/1.getting_started/2.5.hello_triangle_exercise3/`.

6. Shaders

As mentioned in the previous chapter, shaders are little programs that rest on the GPU. These programs are run for each specific section of the graphics pipeline. In a basic sense, shaders are nothing more than programs transforming inputs to outputs. Shaders are also very isolated programs in that they're not allowed to communicate with each other; the only communication they have is via their inputs and outputs.

In the previous chapter we briefly touched the surface of shaders and how to properly use them. We will now explain shaders, and specifically the OpenGL Shading Language, in a more general fashion.

6.1 GLSL

Shaders are written in the C-like language GLSL. GLSL is tailored for use with graphics and contains useful features specifically targeted at vector and matrix manipulation.

Shaders always begin with a version declaration, followed by a list of input and output variables, uniforms and its `main` function. Each shader's entry point is at its `main` function where we process any input variables and output the results in its output variables. Don't worry if you don't know what uniforms are, we'll get to those shortly.

A shader typically has the following structure:

```glsl
#version version_number
in type in_variable_name;
in type in_variable_name;

out type out_variable_name;

uniform type uniform_name;

void main()
{
// process input(s) and do some weird graphics stuff
...
// output processed stuff to output variable
out_variable_name = weird_stuff_we_processed;
}
```

When we're talking specifically about the vertex shader each input variable is also known as a vertex attribute. There is a maximum number of vertex attributes we're allowed to declare limited by the hardware. OpenGL guarantees there are always at least 16 4-component vertex attributes available, but some hardware may allow for more which you can retrieve by querying `GL_MAX_VERTEX_ATTRIBS`:

```cpp
int nrAttributes;
glGetIntegerv(GL_MAX_VERTEX_ATTRIBS, &nrAttributes);
std::cout << "Maximum nr of vertex attributes supported: " << nrAttributes
    << std::endl;
```

This often returns the minimum of `16` which should be more than enough for most purposes.

6.2 Types

GLSL has, like any other programming language, data types for specifying what kind of variable we want to work with. GLSL has most of the default basic types we know from languages like C: `int`, `float`, `double`, `uint` and `bool`. GLSL also features two container types that we'll be using a lot, namely `vectors` and `matrices`. We'll discuss matrices in a later chapter.

6.2.1 Vectors

A vector in GLSL is a 1,2,3 or 4 component container for any of the basic types just mentioned. They can take the following form (n represents the number of components):

- `vecn`: the default vector of n floats.
- `bvecn`: a vector of n booleans.
- `ivecn`: a vector of n integers.
- `uvecn`: a vector of n unsigned integers.
- `dvecn`: a vector of n double components.

Most of the time we will be using the basic `vecn` since floats are sufficient for most of our purposes.

Components of a vector can be accessed via `vec.x` where x is the first component of the vector. You can use `.x`, `.y`, `.z` and `.w` to access their first, second, third and fourth component respectively. GLSL also allows you to use `rgba` for colors or `stpq` for texture coordinates, accessing the same components.

The vector datatype allows for some interesting and flexible component selection called swizzling. Swizzling allows us to use syntax like this:

```
vec2 someVec;
vec4 differentVec = someVec.xyxx;
vec3 anotherVec   = differentVec.zyw;
vec4 otherVec     = someVec.xxxx + anotherVec.yxzy;
```

You can use any combination of up to 4 letters to create a new vector (of the same type) as long as the original vector has those components; it is not allowed to access the `.z` component of a `vec2` for example. We can also pass vectors as arguments to different vector constructor calls, reducing the number of arguments required:

```
vec2 vect = vec2(0.5, 0.7);
vec4 result = vec4(vect, 0.0, 0.0);
vec4 otherResult = vec4(result.xyz, 1.0);
```

Vectors are thus a flexible datatype that we can use for all kinds of input and output. Throughout the book you'll see plenty of examples of how we can creatively manage vectors.

6.3 Ins and outs

Shaders are nice little programs on their own, but they are part of a whole and for that reason we want to have inputs and outputs on the individual shaders so that we can move stuff around. GLSL defined the `in` and `out` keywords specifically for that purpose. Each shader can specify inputs and outputs using those keywords and wherever an output variable matches with an input variable of the next shader stage they're passed along. The vertex and fragment shader differ a bit though.

The vertex shader **should** receive some form of input otherwise it would be pretty ineffective. The vertex shader differs in its input, in that it receives its input straight from the vertex data. To define how the vertex data is organized we specify the input variables with location metadata so we can configure the vertex attributes on the CPU. We've seen this in the previous chapter as `layout (location = 0)`. The vertex shader thus requires an extra layout specification for its inputs so we can link it with the vertex data.

It is also possible to omit the `layout (location = 0)` specifier and query for the attribute locations in your OpenGL code via `glGetAttribLocation`, but I'd prefer to set them in the vertex shader. It is easier to understand and saves you (and OpenGL) some work.

The other exception is that the fragment shader requires a `vec4` color output variable, since the fragment shaders needs to generate a final output color. If you fail to specify an output color in your fragment shader, the color buffer output for those fragments will be undefined (which usually means OpenGL will render them either black or white).

So if we want to send data from one shader to the other we'd have to declare an output in the sending shader and a similar input in the receiving shader. When the types and the names are equal on both sides OpenGL will link those variables together and then it is possible to send data between shaders (this is done when linking a program object). To show you how this works in practice we're going to alter the shaders from the previous chapter to let the vertex shader decide the color for the fragment shader.

Vertex shader

```glsl
#version 330 core
layout (location = 0) in vec3 aPos; // position has attribute position 0

out vec4 vertexColor; // specify a color output to the fragment shader

void main()
{
    gl_Position = vec4(aPos, 1.0); // we give a vec3 to vec4's constructor
    vertexColor = vec4(0.5, 0.0, 0.0, 1.0); // output variable to dark-red
}
```

Fragment shader

```glsl
#version 330 core
out vec4 FragColor;

in vec4 vertexColor; // input variable from vs (same name and type)

void main()
{
    FragColor = vertexColor;
}
```

You can see we declared a `vertexColor` variable as a `vec4` output that we set in the vertex shader and we declare a similar `vertexColor` input in the fragment shader. Since they both have the same type and name, the `vertexColor` in the fragment shader is linked to the `vertexColor` in the vertex shader. Because we set the color to a dark-red color in the vertex shader, the resulting fragments should be dark-red as well. The following image shows the output:

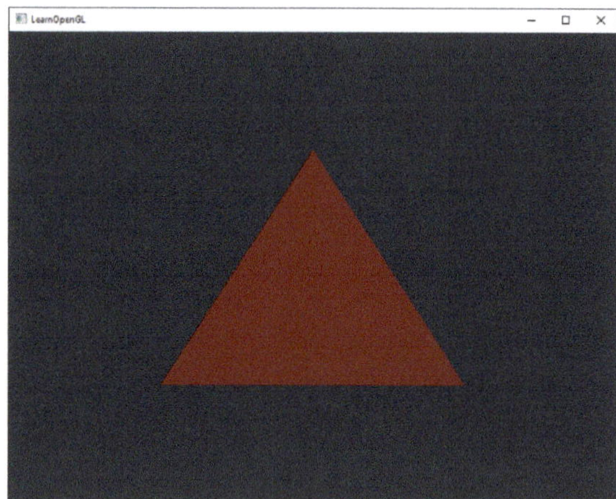

There we go! We just managed to send a value from the vertex shader to the fragment shader. Let's spice it up a bit and see if we can send a color from our application to the fragment shader!

6.4 Uniforms

Uniforms are another way to pass data from our application on the CPU to the shaders on the GPU. Uniforms are however slightly different compared to vertex attributes. First of all, uniforms are global. Global, meaning that a uniform variable is unique per shader program object, and can be accessed from any shader at any stage in the shader program. Second, whatever you set the uniform value to, uniforms will keep their values until they're either reset or updated.

To declare a uniform in GLSL we simply add the `uniform` keyword to a shader with a type and a name. From that point on we can use the newly declared uniform in the shader. Let's see if this time we can set the color of the triangle via a uniform:

```glsl
#version 330 core
out vec4 FragColor;

uniform vec4 ourColor; // we set this variable in the OpenGL code.

void main()
{
    FragColor = ourColor;
}
```

We declared a uniform `vec4 ourColor` in the fragment shader and set the fragment's output color to the content of this uniform value. Since uniforms are global variables, we can define them in any shader stage we'd like so no need to go through the vertex shader again to get something to the fragment shader. We're not using this uniform in the vertex shader so there's no need to define it there.

> If you declare a uniform that isn't used anywhere in your GLSL code the compiler will silently remove the variable from the compiled version which is the cause for several frustrating errors; keep this in mind!

The uniform is currently empty; we haven't added any data to the uniform yet so let's try that. We first need to find the index/location of the uniform attribute in our shader. Once we have the index/location of the uniform, we can update its values. Instead of passing a single color to the fragment shader, let's spice things up by gradually changing color over time:

```cpp
float timeValue = glfwGetTime();
float greenValue = (sin(timeValue) / 2.0f) + 0.5f;
int vertexColorLocation = glGetUniformLocation(shaderProgram, "ourColor");
glUseProgram(shaderProgram);
glUniform4f(vertexColorLocation, 0.0f, greenValue, 0.0f, 1.0f);
```

First, we retrieve the running time in seconds via `glfwGetTime()`. Then we vary the color in the range of `0.0 - 1.0` by using the `sin` function and store the result in `greenValue`.

Then we query for the location of the `ourColor` uniform using `glGetUniformLocation`. We supply the shader program and the name of the uniform (that we want to retrieve the location from) to the query function. If `glGetUniformLocation` returns `-1`, it could not find the location. Lastly we can set the uniform value using the `glUniform4f` function. Note that finding the uniform location does not require you to use the shader program first, but updating a uniform **does** require you to first use the program (by calling `glUseProgram`), because it sets the uniform on the currently active shader program.

Because OpenGL is in its core a C library it does not have native support for function overloading, so wherever a function can be called with different types OpenGL defines new functions for each type required; `glUniform` is a perfect example of this. The function requires a specific postfix for the type of the uniform you want to set. A few of the possible postfixes are:

- `f`: the function expects a `float` as its value.
- `i`: the function expects an `int` as its value.
- `ui`: the function expects an `unsigned int` as its value.
- `3f`: the function expects 3 `float`s as its value.
- `fv`: the function expects a `float` vector/array as its value.

Whenever you want to configure an option of OpenGL simply pick the overloaded function that corresponds with your type. In our case we want to set 4 floats of the uniform individually so we pass our data via `glUniform4f` (note that we also could've used the `fv` version).

Now that we know how to set the values of uniform variables, we can use them for rendering. If we want the color to gradually change, we want to update this uniform every frame, otherwise the triangle would maintain a single solid color if we only set it once. So we calculate the `greenValue` and update the uniform each render iteration:

```cpp
while(!glfwWindowShouldClose(window))
{
    // input
    processInput(window);

    // render
    // clear the colorbuffer
    glClearColor(0.2f, 0.3f, 0.3f, 1.0f);
    glClear(GL_COLOR_BUFFER_BIT);

    // be sure to activate the shader
```

```cpp
glUseProgram(shaderProgram);

// update the uniform color
float timeValue = glfwGetTime();
float greenValue = sin(timeValue) / 2.0f + 0.5f;
int vertexColorLocation = glGetUniformLocation(shaderProgram,
                                               "ourColor");
glUniform4f(vertexColorLocation, 0.0f, greenValue, 0.0f, 1.0f);

// now render the triangle
glBindVertexArray(VAO);
glDrawArrays(GL_TRIANGLES, 0, 3);

// swap buffers and poll IO events
glfwSwapBuffers(window);
glfwPollEvents();
}
```

The code is a relatively straightforward adaptation of the previous code. This time, we update a uniform value each frame before drawing the triangle. If you update the uniform correctly you should see the color of your triangle gradually change from green to black and back to green.

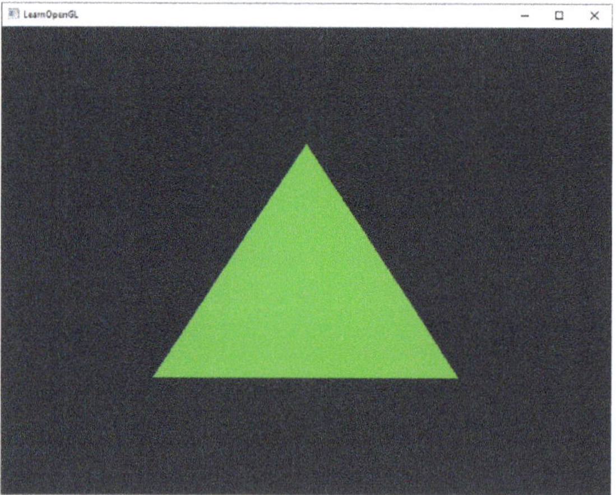

Check out the source code at `/src/1.getting_started/3.1.shaders_uniform/` if you're stuck.

As you can see, uniforms are a useful tool for setting attributes that may change every frame, or for interchanging data between your application and your shaders, but what if we want to set a color for each vertex? In that case we'd have to declare as many uniforms as we have vertices. A better solution would be to include more data in the vertex attributes which is what we're going to do now.

6.5 More attributes!

We saw in the previous chapter how we can fill a VBO, configure vertex attribute pointers and store it all in a VAO. This time, we also want to add color data to the vertex data. We're going to add color data as 3 `floats` to the `vertices` array. We assign a red, green and blue color to each of the corners of our triangle respectively:

```
float vertices[] = {
    // positions         // colors
     0.5f, -0.5f, 0.0f,  1.0f, 0.0f, 0.0f,  // bottom right
    -0.5f, -0.5f, 0.0f,  0.0f, 1.0f, 0.0f,  // bottom left
     0.0f,  0.5f, 0.0f,  0.0f, 0.0f, 1.0f   // top
};
```

Since we now have more data to send to the vertex shader, it is necessary to adjust the vertex shader to also receive our color value as a vertex attribute input. Note that we set the location of the aColor attribute to 1 with the layout specifier:

```
#version 330 core
layout (location = 0) in vec3 aPos;    // position has attribute position 0
layout (location = 1) in vec3 aColor;  // color has attribute position 1

out vec3 ourColor; // output a color to the fragment shader

void main()
{
    gl_Position = vec4(aPos, 1.0);
    ourColor = aColor; // set ourColor to input color from the vertex data
}
```

Since we no longer use a uniform for the fragment's color, but now use the ourColor output variable we'll have to change the fragment shader as well:

```
#version 330 core
out vec4 FragColor;
in vec3 ourColor;

void main()
{
    FragColor = vec4(ourColor, 1.0);
}
```

Because we added another vertex attribute and updated the VBO's memory we have to re-configure the vertex attribute pointers. The updated data in the VBO's memory now looks a bit like:

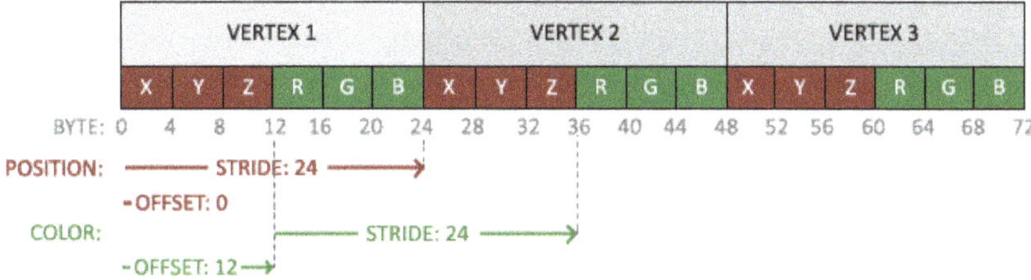

Knowing the current layout we can update the vertex format with glVertexAttrib Pointer:

```cpp
// position attribute
glVertexAttribPointer(0, 3, GL_FLOAT, GL_FALSE, 6 * sizeof(float),
                      (void*)0);
glEnableVertexAttribArray(0);
// color attribute
glVertexAttribPointer(1, 3, GL_FLOAT, GL_FALSE, 6 * sizeof(float),
                      (void*)(3* sizeof(float)));
glEnableVertexAttribArray(1);
```

The first few arguments of `glVertexAttribPointer` are relatively straightforward. This time we are configuring the vertex attribute on attribute location 1. The color values have a size of 3 `floats` and we do not normalize the values.

Since we now have two vertex attributes we have to re-calculate the *stride* value. To get the next attribute value (e.g. the next x component of the position vector) in the data array we have to move 6 `floats` to the right, three for the position values and three for the color values. This gives us a stride value of 6 times the size of a `float` in bytes (= 24 bytes). Also, this time we have to specify an offset. For each vertex, the position vertex attribute is first so we declare an offset of 0. The color attribute starts after the position data so the offset is 3 * `sizeof(float)` in bytes (= 12 bytes).

Running the application should result in the following image:

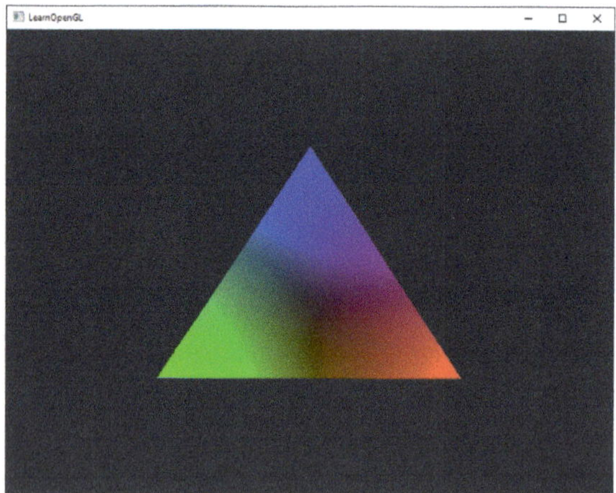

Check out the source code at `/src/1.getting_started/3.2.shaders_interpola tion/` if you're stuck.

The image may not be exactly what you would expect, since we only supplied 3 colors, not the huge color palette we're seeing right now. This is all the result of something called fragment interpolation in the fragment shader. When rendering a triangle the rasterization stage usually results in a lot more fragments than vertices originally specified. The rasterizer then determines the positions of each of those fragments based on where they reside on the triangle shape. Based on these positions, it interpolates all the fragment shader's input variables. Say for example we have a line where the upper point has a green color and the lower point a blue color. If the fragment shader is run at a fragment that resides around a position at `70%` of the line, its resulting color input attribute would then be a linear combination of green and blue; to be more precise: `30%` blue and `70%` green.

This is exactly what happened at the triangle. We have 3 vertices and thus 3 colors, and judging from the triangle's pixels it probably contains around 50000 fragments, where the fragment shader interpolated the colors among those pixels. If you take a good look at the colors you'll see it all makes sense: red to blue first gets to purple and then to blue. Fragment interpolation is applied to all the fragment shader's input attributes.

6.6 Our own shader class

Writing, compiling and managing shaders can be quite cumbersome. As a final touch on the shader subject we're going to make our life a bit easier by building a shader class that reads shaders from disk, compiles and links them, checks for errors and is easy to use. This also gives you a bit of an idea how we can encapsulate some of the knowledge we learned so far into useful abstract objects.

We will create the shader class entirely in a header file, mainly for learning purposes and portability. Let's start by adding the required includes and by defining the class structure:

```cpp
#ifndef SHADER_H
#define SHADER_H

#include <glad/glad.h> // include glad to get the required OpenGL headers

#include <string>
#include <fstream>
#include <sstream>
#include <iostream>


class Shader
{
public:
    // the program ID
    unsigned int ID;

    // constructor reads and builds the shader
    Shader(const char* vertexPath, const char* fragmentPath);
    // use/activate the shader
    void use();
    // utility uniform functions
    void setBool(const std::string &name, bool value) const;
    void setInt(const std::string &name, int value) const;
    void setFloat(const std::string &name, float value) const;
};

#endif
```

> We used several preprocessor directives at the top of the header file. Using these little lines of code informs your compiler to only include and compile this header file if it hasn't been included yet, even if multiple files include the shader header. This prevents linking conflicts.

The shader class holds the ID of the shader program. Its constructor requires the file paths of the source code of the vertex and fragment shader respectively that we can store on disk as simple text files. To add a little extra we also add several utility functions to ease our lives a little: `use` activates the shader program, and all `set...` functions query a uniform location and set its value.

6.7 Reading from file

We're using C++ filestreams to read the content from the file into several `string` objects:

```cpp
Shader(const char* vertexPath, const char* fragmentPath)
{
    // 1. retrieve the vertex/fragment source code from filePath
    std::string vertexCode;
    std::string fragmentCode;
    std::ifstream vShaderFile;
    std::ifstream fShaderFile;
    // ensure ifstream objects can throw exceptions:
    vShaderFile.exceptions (std::ifstream::failbit | std::ifstream::badbit);
    fShaderFile.exceptions (std::ifstream::failbit | std::ifstream::badbit);
    try
    {
        // open files
        vShaderFile.open(vertexPath);
        fShaderFile.open(fragmentPath);
        std::stringstream vShaderStream, fShaderStream;
        // read file's buffer contents into streams
        vShaderStream << vShaderFile.rdbuf();
        fShaderStream << fShaderFile.rdbuf();
        // close file handlers
        vShaderFile.close();
        fShaderFile.close();
        // convert stream into string
        vertexCode = vShaderStream.str();
        fragmentCode = fShaderStream.str();
    }
    catch(std::ifstream::failure e)
    {
        std::cout << "ERROR::SHADER::FILE_NOT_SUCCESFULLY_READ" << std::endl;
    }
    const char* vShaderCode = vertexCode.c_str();
    const char* fShaderCode = fragmentCode.c_str();
    [...]
```

Next we need to compile and link the shaders. Note that we're also reviewing if compilation/linking failed and if so, print the compile-time errors. This is extremely useful when debugging (you are going to need those error logs eventually):

```cpp
// 2. compile shaders
unsigned int vertex, fragment;
int success;
char infoLog[512];

// vertex Shader
vertex = glCreateShader(GL_VERTEX_SHADER);
glShaderSource(vertex, 1, &vShaderCode, NULL);
glCompileShader(vertex);
// print compile errors if any
glGetShaderiv(vertex, GL_COMPILE_STATUS, &success);
if(!success)
{
    glGetShaderInfoLog(vertex, 512, NULL, infoLog);
    std::cout << "ERROR::SHADER::VERTEX::COMPILATION_FAILED\n" <<
            infoLog << std::endl;
};

// similiar for Fragment Shader
[...]

// shader Program
```

```cpp
ID = glCreateProgram();
glAttachShader(ID, vertex);
glAttachShader(ID, fragment);
glLinkProgram(ID);
// print linking errors if any
glGetProgramiv(ID, GL_LINK_STATUS, &success);
if(!success)
{
    glGetProgramInfoLog(ID, 512, NULL, infoLog);
    std::cout << "ERROR::SHADER::PROGRAM::LINKING_FAILED\n" <<
                 infoLog << std::endl;
}

// delete shaders; they're linked into our program and no longer necessary
glDeleteShader(vertex);
glDeleteShader(fragment);
```

The `use` function is straightforward:

```cpp
void use()
{
    glUseProgram(ID);
}
```

Similarly for any of the uniform setter functions:

```cpp
void setBool(const std::string &name, bool value) const
{
    glUniform1i(glGetUniformLocation(ID, name.c_str()), (int)value);
}
void setInt(const std::string &name, int value) const
{
    glUniform1i(glGetUniformLocation(ID, name.c_str()), value);
}
void setFloat(const std::string &name, float value) const
{
    glUniform1f(glGetUniformLocation(ID, name.c_str()), value);
}
```

And there we have it, a completed shader class at `/includes/learnopengl/shader_s.h`. Using the shader class is fairly easy; we create a shader object once and from that point on simply start using it:

```cpp
Shader ourShader("path/to/shaders/shader.vs", "path/to/shaders/shader.fs");
[...]
while(...)
{
    ourShader.use();
    ourShader.setFloat("someUniform", 1.0f);
    DrawStuff();
}
```

Here we stored the vertex and fragment shader source code in two files called `shader.vs` and `shader.fs`. You're free to name your shader files however you like; I personally find the extensions `.vs` and `.fs` quite intuitive.

You can find the source code at `/src/1.getting_started/3.3.shaders_class/`

using our newly created shader class. Note that you can click the shader file paths online to find the shaders' source code.

6.8 Exercises

1. Adjust the vertex shader so that the triangle is upside down. Solution: `/src/1.getting_started/3.4.shaders_exercise1/shaders_exercise1.cpp`.

2. Specify a horizontal offset via a uniform and move the triangle to the right side of the screen in the vertex shader using this offset value. Solution `/src/1.getting_started/3.5.shaders_exercise2/shaders_exercise2.cpp`.

3. Output the vertex position to the fragment shader using the `out` keyword and set the fragment's color equal to this vertex position (see how even the vertex position values are interpolated across the triangle). Once you managed to do this; try to answer the following question: why is the bottom-left side of our triangle black? Solution: `/src/1.getting_started/3.6.shaders_exercise3/shaders_exercise3.cpp`.

7. Textures

We learned that to add more detail to our objects we can use colors for each vertex to create some interesting images. However, to get a fair bit of realism we'd have to have many vertices so we could specify a lot of colors. This takes up a considerable amount of extra overhead, since each model needs a lot more vertices and for each vertex a color attribute as well.

What artists and programmers generally prefer is to use a texture. A texture is a 2D image (even 1D and 3D textures exist) used to add detail to an object; think of a texture as a piece of paper with a nice brick image (for example) on it neatly folded over your 3D house so it looks like your house has a stone exterior. Because we can insert a lot of detail in a single image, we can give the illusion the object is extremely detailed without having to specify extra vertices.

> Next to images, textures can also be used to store a large collection of arbitrary data to send to the shaders, but we'll leave that for a different topic.

Below you'll see a texture image of a brick wall[1] mapped to the triangle from the previous chapter.

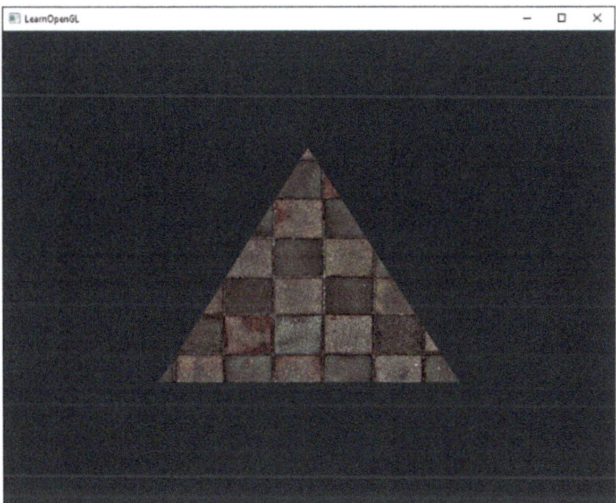

In order to map a texture to the triangle we need to tell each vertex of the triangle which part of the texture it corresponds to. Each vertex should thus have a texture coordinate associated with them that specifies what part of the texture image to sample from. Fragment interpolation then does the rest for the other fragments.

Texture coordinates range from 0 to 1 in the x and y axis (remember that we use 2D texture images). Retrieving the texture color using texture coordinates is called sampling. Texture coordinates start at (0,0) for the lower left corner of a texture image to (1,1) for the upper right corner of a texture image. The following image shows how we map texture coordinates to the triangle:

---

[1]learnopengl.com/img/textures/wall.jpg

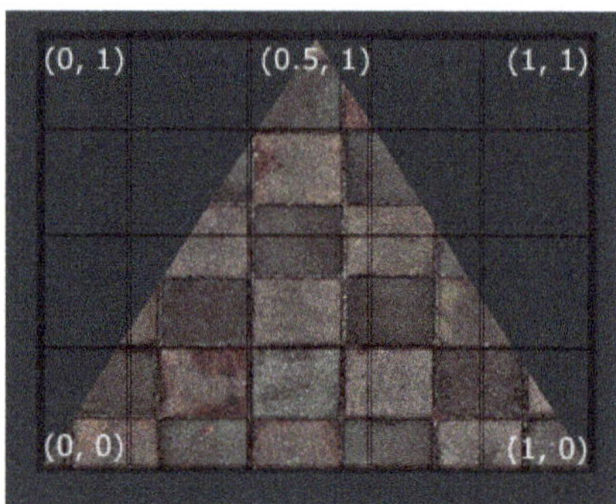

We specify 3 texture coordinate points for the triangle. We want the bottom-left side of the triangle to correspond with the bottom-left side of the texture so we use the `(0,0)` texture coordinate for the triangle's bottom-left vertex. The same applies to the bottom-right side with a `(1,0)` texture coordinate. The top of the triangle should correspond with the top-center of the texture image so we take `(0.5,1.0)` as its texture coordinate. We only have to pass 3 texture coordinates to the vertex shader, which then passes those to the fragment shader that neatly interpolates all the texture coordinates for each fragment.

The resulting texture coordinates would then look like this:

```
float texCoords[] = {
    0.0f, 0.0f,  // lower-left corner
    1.0f, 0.0f,  // lower-right corner
    0.5f, 1.0f   // top-center corner
};
```

Texture sampling has a loose interpretation and can be done in many different ways. It is thus our job to tell OpenGL how it should *sample* its textures.

7.1 Texture Wrapping

Texture coordinates usually range from `(0,0)` to `(1,1)` but what happens if we specify coordinates outside this range? The default behavior of OpenGL is to repeat the texture images (we basically ignore the integer part of the floating point texture coordinate), but there are more options OpenGL offers:

- `GL_REPEAT`: The default behavior for textures. Repeats the texture image.
- `GL_MIRRORED_REPEAT`: Same as `GL_REPEAT` but mirrors the image with each repeat.
- `GL_CLAMP_TO_EDGE`: Clamps the coordinates between 0 and 1. The result is that higher coordinates become clamped to the edge, resulting in a stretched edge pattern.
- `GL_CLAMP_TO_BORDER`: Coordinates outside the range are now given a user-specified border color.

Each of the options have a different visual output when using texture coordinates outside the default range. Let's see what these look like on a sample texture image (original image by Hólger Rezende):

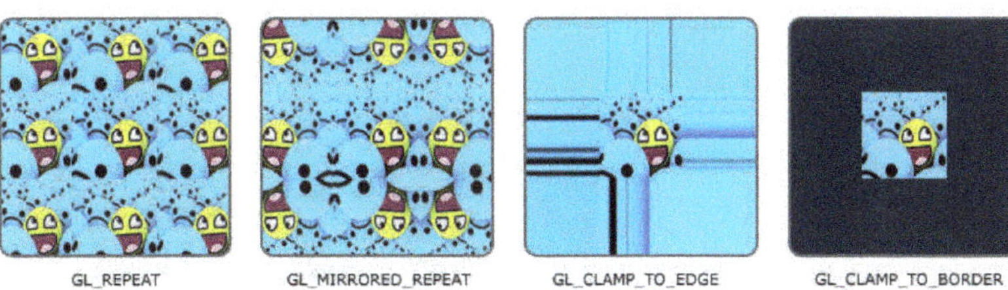

Each of the aforementioned options can be set per coordinate axis (s, t (and r if you're using 3D textures) equivalent to x,y,z) with the `glTexParameter*` function:

```
glTexParameteri(GL_TEXTURE_2D, GL_TEXTURE_WRAP_S, GL_MIRRORED_REPEAT);
glTexParameteri(GL_TEXTURE_2D, GL_TEXTURE_WRAP_T, GL_MIRRORED_REPEAT);
```

The first argument specifies the texture target; we're working with 2D textures so the texture target is `GL_TEXTURE_2D`. The second argument requires us to tell what option we want to set and for which texture axis; we want to configure it for both the S and T axis. The last argument requires us to pass in the texture wrapping mode we'd like and in this case OpenGL will set its texture wrapping option on the currently active texture with `GL_MIRRORED_REPEAT`.

If we choose the `GL_CLAMP_TO_BORDER` option we should also specify a border color. This is done using the `fv` equivalent of the `glTexParameter` function with `GL_TEXTURE_BORDER_COLOR` as its option where we pass in a float array of the border's color value:

```
float borderColor[] = { 1.0f, 1.0f, 0.0f, 1.0f };
glTexParameterfv(GL_TEXTURE_2D, GL_TEXTURE_BORDER_COLOR, borderColor);
```

7.2 Texture Filtering

Texture coordinates do not depend on resolution but can be any floating point value, thus OpenGL has to figure out which texture pixel (also known as a texel) to map the texture coordinate to. This becomes especially important if you have a very large object and a low resolution texture. You probably guessed by now that OpenGL has options for this texture filtering as well. There are several options available but for now we'll discuss the most important options: `GL_NEAREST` and `GL_LINEAR`.

`GL_NEAREST` (also known as nearest neighbor or point filtering) is the default texture filtering method of OpenGL. When set to `GL_NEAREST`, OpenGL selects the texel that center is closest to the texture coordinate. Below you can see 4 pixels where the cross represents the exact texture coordinate. The upper-left texel has its center closest to the texture coordinate and is therefore chosen as the sampled color:

`GL_LINEAR` (also known as (bi)linear filtering) takes an interpolated value from the texture coordinate's neighboring texels, approximating a color between the texels. The smaller the distance from the texture coordinate to a texel's center, the more that texel's color contributes to the sampled color. Below we can see that a mixed color of the neighboring pixels is returned:

But what is the visual effect of such a texture filtering method? Let's see how these methods work when using a texture with a low resolution on a large object (texture is therefore scaled upwards and individual texels are noticeable):

`GL_NEAREST` results in blocked patterns where we can clearly see the pixels that form the texture while `GL_LINEAR` produces a smoother pattern where the individual pixels are less visible. `GL_LINEAR` produces a more realistic output, but some developers prefer a more 8-bit look and as a result pick the `GL_NEAREST` option.

Texture filtering can be set for magnifying and minifying operations (when scaling up or downwards) so you could for example use nearest neighbor filtering when textures are scaled downwards and linear filtering for upscaled textures. We thus have to specify the filtering method for both options via `glTexParameter*`. The code should look similar to setting the wrapping method:

```
glTexParameteri(GL_TEXTURE_2D, GL_TEXTURE_MIN_FILTER, GL_NEAREST);
glTexParameteri(GL_TEXTURE_2D, GL_TEXTURE_MAG_FILTER, GL_LINEAR);
```

7.2.1 Mipmaps

Imagine we had a large room with thousands of objects, each with an attached texture. There will be objects far away that have the same high resolution texture attached as the objects close to the viewer. Since the objects are far away and probably only produce a few fragments, OpenGL has difficulties retrieving the right color value for its fragment from the high resolution texture, since it has to pick a texture color for a fragment that spans a large part of the texture. This will produce visible artifacts on small objects, not to mention the waste of memory bandwidth using high resolution textures on small objects.

To solve this issue OpenGL uses a concept called mipmaps that is basically a collection of texture images where each subsequent texture is twice as small compared to the previous one. The idea behind mipmaps should be easy to understand: after a certain distance threshold from the viewer, OpenGL will use a different mipmap texture that best suits the distance to the object. Because the object is far away, the smaller resolution will not be noticeable to the user. OpenGL is then able to sample the correct texels, and there's less cache memory involved when sampling that part of the mipmaps. Let's take a closer look at what a mipmapped texture looks like:

Creating a collection of mipmapped textures for each texture image is cumbersome to do manually, but luckily OpenGL is able to do all the work for us with a single call to `glGenerateMipmaps` after we've created a texture.

When switching between mipmaps levels during rendering OpenGL may show some artifacts like sharp edges visible between the two mipmap layers. Just like normal texture filtering, it is also possible to filter between mipmap levels using `NEAREST` and `LINEAR` filtering for switching between mipmap levels. To specify the filtering method between mipmap levels we can replace the original filtering methods with one of the following four options:

- `GL_NEAREST_MIPMAP_NEAREST`: takes the nearest mipmap to match the pixel size and uses nearest neighbor interpolation for texture sampling.
- `GL_LINEAR_MIPMAP_NEAREST`: takes the nearest mipmap level and samples that level using linear interpolation.
- `GL_NEAREST_MIPMAP_LINEAR`: linearly interpolates between the two mipmaps that most closely match the size of a pixel and samples the interpolated level via nearest neighbor interpolation.
- `GL_LINEAR_MIPMAP_LINEAR`: linearly interpolates between the two closest mipmaps and samples the interpolated level via linear interpolation.

Just like texture filtering we can set the filtering method to one of the 4 aforementioned methods using `glTexParameteri`:

```cpp
glTexParameteri(GL_TEXTURE_2D, GL_TEXTURE_MIN_FILTER,
                GL_LINEAR_MIPMAP_LINEAR);
glTexParameteri(GL_TEXTURE_2D, GL_TEXTURE_MAG_FILTER, GL_LINEAR);
```

A common mistake is to set one of the mipmap filtering options as the magnification filter. This doesn't have any effect since mipmaps are primarily used for when textures get downscaled: texture magnification doesn't use mipmaps and giving it a mipmap filtering option will generate an OpenGL `GL_INVALID_ENUM` error code.

7.3 Loading and creating textures

The first thing we need to do to actually use textures is to load them into our application. Texture images can be stored in dozens of file formats, each with their own structure and ordering of data, so how do we get those images in our application? One solution would be to choose a file format we'd like to use, say `.PNG` and write our own image loader to convert the image format into a large array of bytes. While it's not very hard to write your own image loader, it's still cumbersome and what if you want to support more file formats? You'd then have to write an image loader for each format you want to support.

Another solution, and probably a good one, is to use an image-loading library that supports several popular formats and does all the hard work for us. A library like `stb_image.h`.

7.4 stb_image.h

`stb_image.h` is a very popular single header image loading library by Sean Barrett that is able to load most popular file formats and is easy to integrate in your project(s). `stb_image.h` can be downloaded from its GitHub page: `github.com/nothings/stb/blob/master/stb_image.h`. Simply download the single header file, add it to your project as `stb_image.h`, and create an additional C++ file with the following code:

```
#define STB_IMAGE_IMPLEMENTATION
#include "stb_image.h"
```

By defining `STB_IMAGE_IMPLEMENTATION` the preprocessor modifies the header file such that it only contains the relevant definition source code, effectively turning the header file into a `.cpp` file, and that's about it. Now simply include `stb_image.h` somewhere in your program and compile.

For the following texture sections we're going to use an image of a wooden container: wooden container[1]. To load an image using `stb_image.h` we use its `stbi_load` function:

```
int width, height, nrChannels;
unsigned char *data = stbi_load("container.jpg", &width, &height,
                                &nrChannels, 0);
```

The function first takes as input the location of an image file. It then expects you to give three `int`s as its second, third and fourth argument that `stb_image.h` will fill with the resulting image's *width*, *height* and *number* of color channels. We need the image's width and height for generating textures later on.

7.5 Generating a texture

Like any of the previous objects in OpenGL, textures are referenced with an ID; let's create one:

```
unsigned int texture;
glGenTextures(1, &texture);
```

The `glGenTextures` function first takes as input how many textures we want to generate and stores them in a `unsigned int` array given as its second argument (in our case just a single `unsigned int`). Just like other objects we need to bind it so any subsequent texture commands will configure the currently bound texture:

```
glBindTexture(GL_TEXTURE_2D, texture);
```

Now that the texture is bound, we can start generating a texture using the previously loaded image data. Textures are generated with `glTexImage2D`:

---

[1]learnopengl.com/img/textures/container.jpg

```cpp
glTexImage2D(GL_TEXTURE_2D, 0, GL_RGB, width, height, 0, GL_RGB,
             GL_UNSIGNED_BYTE, data);
glGenerateMipmap(GL_TEXTURE_2D);
```

This is a large function with quite a few parameters so we'll walk through them step-by-step:

- The first argument specifies the texture target; setting this to `GL_TEXTURE_2D` means this operation will generate a texture on the currently bound texture object at the same target (so any textures bound to targets `GL_TEXTURE_1D` or `GL_TEXTURE_3D` will not be affected).
- The second argument specifies the mipmap level for which we want to create a texture for if you want to set each mipmap level manually, but we'll leave it at the base level which is 0.
- The third argument tells OpenGL in what kind of format we want to store the texture. Our image has only `RGB` values so we'll store the texture with `RGB` values as well.
- The 4th and 5th argument sets the width and height of the resulting texture. We stored those earlier when loading the image so we'll use the corresponding variables.
- The next argument should always be 0 (some legacy stuff).
- The 7th and 8th argument specify the format and datatype of the source image. We loaded the image with `RGB` values and stored them as `chars` (bytes) so we'll pass in the corresponding values.
- The last argument is the actual image data.

Once `glTexImage2D` is called, the currently bound texture object now has the texture image attached to it. However, currently it only has the base-level of the texture image loaded and if we want to use mipmaps we have to specify all the different images manually (by continually incrementing the second argument) or, we could call `glGenerateMipmap` after generating the texture. This will automatically generate all the required mipmaps for the currently bound texture.

After we're done generating the texture and its corresponding mipmaps, it is good practice to free the image memory:

```cpp
stbi_image_free(data);
```

The whole process of generating a texture thus looks something like this:

```cpp
unsigned int texture;
glGenTextures(1, &texture);
glBindTexture(GL_TEXTURE_2D, texture);
// set the texture wrapping/filtering options (on currently bound texture)
glTexParameteri(GL_TEXTURE_2D, GL_TEXTURE_WRAP_S, GL_REPEAT);
glTexParameteri(GL_TEXTURE_2D, GL_TEXTURE_WRAP_T, GL_REPEAT);
glTexParameteri(GL_TEXTURE_2D, GL_TEXTURE_MIN_FILTER, GL_LINEAR);
glTexParameteri(GL_TEXTURE_2D, GL_TEXTURE_MAG_FILTER, GL_LINEAR);
// load and generate the texture
int width, height, nrChannels;
unsigned char *data = stbi_load("container.jpg", &width, &height,
                                &nrChannels, 0);
if (data)
{
    glTexImage2D(GL_TEXTURE_2D, 0, GL_RGB, width, height, 0, GL_RGB,
                 GL_UNSIGNED_BYTE, data);
    glGenerateMipmap(GL_TEXTURE_2D);
}
else
{
    std::cout << "Failed to load texture" << std::endl;
}
```

```
stbi_image_free(data);
```

7.6 Applying textures

For the upcoming sections we will use the rectangle shape drawn with `glDrawElements` from the final part of the *Hello Triangle* chapter. We need to inform OpenGL how to sample the texture so we'll have to update the vertex data with the texture coordinates:

```
float vertices[] = {
    // positions        // colors           // texture coords
     0.5f,  0.5f, 0.0f, 1.0f, 0.0f, 0.0f, 1.0f, 1.0f, // top right
     0.5f, -0.5f, 0.0f, 0.0f, 1.0f, 0.0f, 1.0f, 0.0f, // bottom right
    -0.5f, -0.5f, 0.0f, 0.0f, 0.0f, 1.0f, 0.0f, 0.0f, // bottom left
    -0.5f,  0.5f, 0.0f, 1.0f, 1.0f, 0.0f, 0.0f, 1.0f  // top left
};
```

Since we've added an extra vertex attribute we again have to notify OpenGL of the new vertex format:

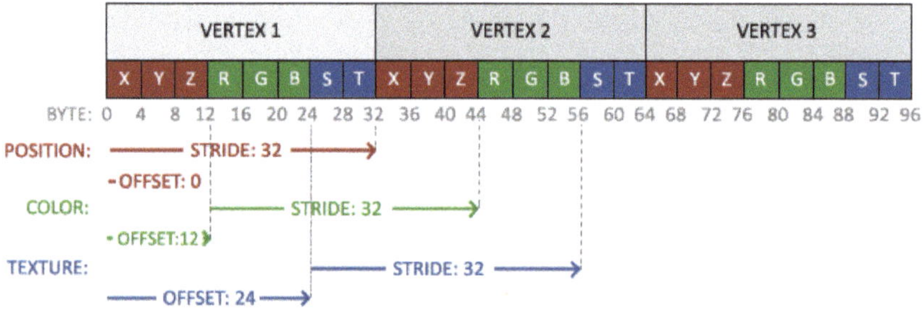

```
glVertexAttribPointer(2, 2, GL_FLOAT, GL_FALSE, 8 * sizeof(float),
                      (void*)(6 * sizeof(float)));
glEnableVertexAttribArray(2);
```

Note that we have to adjust the stride parameter of the previous two vertex attributes to 8 * `sizeof(float)` as well.

Next we need to alter the vertex shader to accept the texture coordinates as a vertex attribute and then forward the coordinates to the fragment shader:

```
#version 330 core
layout (location = 0) in vec3 aPos;
layout (location = 1) in vec3 aColor;
layout (location = 2) in vec2 aTexCoord;

out vec3 ourColor;
out vec2 TexCoord;

void main()
{
    gl_Position = vec4(aPos, 1.0);
    ourColor = aColor;
    TexCoord = aTexCoord;
}
```

The fragment shader should then accept the `TexCoord` output variable as an input variable.

The fragment shader should also have access to the texture object, but how do we pass the texture object to the fragment shader? GLSL has a built-in data-type for texture objects called a sampler that takes as a postfix the texture type we want e.g. `sampler1D`, `sampler3D` or in our case `sampler2D`. We can then add a texture to the fragment shader by simply declaring a `uniform sampler2D` that we later assign our texture to.

```glsl
#version 330 core
out vec4 FragColor;

in vec3 ourColor;
in vec2 TexCoord;

uniform sampler2D ourTexture;

void main()
{
    FragColor = texture(ourTexture, TexCoord);
}
```

To sample the color of a texture we use GLSL's built-in `texture` function that takes as its first argument a texture sampler and as its second argument the corresponding texture coordinates. The `texture` function then samples the corresponding color value using the texture parameters we set earlier. The output of this fragment shader is then the (filtered) color of the texture at the (interpolated) texture coordinate.

All that's left to do now is to bind the texture before calling `glDrawElements` and it will then automatically assign the texture to the fragment shader's sampler:

```cpp
glBindTexture(GL_TEXTURE_2D, texture);
glBindVertexArray(VAO);
glDrawElements(GL_TRIANGLES, 6, GL_UNSIGNED_INT, 0);
```

If you did everything right you should see the following image:

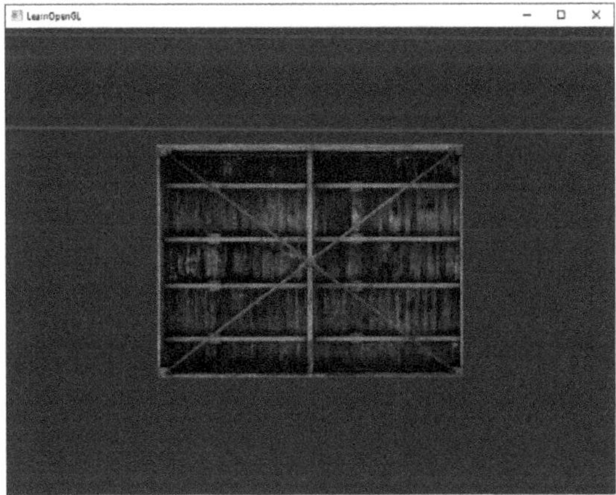

If your rectangle is completely white or black you probably made an error along the way. Check your shader logs and try to compare your code with the application's source code: `/src/1. getting_started/4.1.textures/`.

> If your texture code doesn't work or shows up as completely black, continue reading and
> work your way to the last example that **should** work. On some drivers it is **required** to
> assign a texture unit to each sampler uniform, which is something we'll discuss further in
> this chapter.

To get a little funky we can also mix the resulting texture color with the vertex colors. We simply
multiply the resulting texture color with the vertex color in the fragment shader to mix both colors:

```
FragColor = texture(ourTexture, TexCoord) * vec4(ourColor, 1.0);
```

The result should be a mixture of the vertex's color and the texture's color:

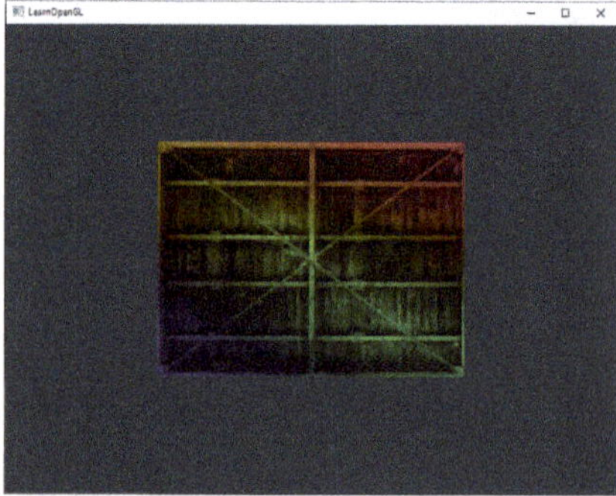

I guess you could say our container likes to disco.

7.7 Texture Units

You probably wondered why the `sampler2D` variable is a uniform if we didn't even assign it
some value with `glUniform`. Using `glUniform1i` we can actually assign a *location* value to
the texture sampler so we can set multiple textures at once in a fragment shader. This location of
a texture is more commonly known as a texture unit. The default texture unit for a texture is 0
which is the default active texture unit so we didn't need to assign a location in the previous section;
note that not all graphics drivers assign a default texture unit so the previous section may not have
rendered for you.

The main purpose of texture units is to allow us to use more than 1 texture in our shaders. By
assigning texture units to the samplers, we can bind to multiple textures at once as long as we
activate the corresponding texture unit first. Just like `glBindTexture` we can activate texture
units using `glActiveTexture` passing in the texture unit we'd like to use:

```
glActiveTexture(GL_TEXTURE0); // activate texture unit first
glBindTexture(GL_TEXTURE_2D, texture);
```

After activating a texture unit, a subsequent `glBindTexture` call will bind that texture to
the currently active texture unit. Texture unit `GL_TEXTURE0` is always by default activated, so we
didn't have to activate any texture units in the previous example when using `glBindTexture`.

OpenGL should have a at least a minimum of 16 texture units for you to use which you can activate using `GL_TEXTURE0` to `GL_TEXTURE15`. They are defined in order so we could also get `GL_TEXTURE8` via `GL_TEXTURE0 + 8` for example, which is useful when we'd have to loop over several texture units.

We still however need to edit the fragment shader to accept another sampler. This should be relatively straightforward now:

```glsl
#version 330 core
...

uniform sampler2D texture1;
uniform sampler2D texture2;

void main()
{
    FragColor = mix(texture(texture1, TexCoord),
                    texture(texture2, TexCoord), 0.2);
}
```

The final output color is now the combination of two texture lookups. GLSL's built-in `mix` function takes two values as input and linearly interpolates between them based on its third argument. If the third value is `0.0` it returns the first input; if it's `1.0` it returns the second input value. A value of `0.2` will return `80%` of the first input color and `20%` of the second input color, resulting in a mixture of both our textures.

We now want to load and create another texture; you should be familiar with the steps now. Make sure to create another texture object, load the image and generate the final texture using `glTexImage2D`. For the second texture we'll use an image of your facial expression[1] while learning OpenGL:

```cpp
unsigned char *data = stbi_load("awesomeface.png", &width, &height,
                               &nrChannels, 0);
if (data)
{
    glTexImage2D(GL_TEXTURE_2D, 0, GL_RGB, width, height, 0, GL_RGBA,
                 GL_UNSIGNED_BYTE, data);
    glGenerateMipmap(GL_TEXTURE_2D);
}
```

Note that we now load a `.png` image that includes an alpha (transparency) channel. This means we now need to specify that the image data contains an alpha channel as well by using `GL_RGBA`; otherwise OpenGL will incorrectly interpret the image data.

To use the second texture (and the first texture) we'd have to change the rendering procedure a bit by binding both textures to the corresponding texture unit:

```cpp
glActiveTexture(GL_TEXTURE0);
glBindTexture(GL_TEXTURE_2D, texture1);
glActiveTexture(GL_TEXTURE1);
glBindTexture(GL_TEXTURE_2D, texture2);

glBindVertexArray(VAO);
```

---

[1]learnopengl.com/img/textures/awesomeface.png

```
glDrawElements(GL_TRIANGLES, 6, GL_UNSIGNED_INT, 0);
```

We also have to tell OpenGL to which texture unit each shader sampler belongs to by setting each sampler using `glUniform1i`. We only have to set this once, so we can do this before we enter the render loop:

```cpp
shader.use(); // don't forget to activate the shader first!
glUniform1i(glGetUniformLocation(shader.ID, "texture1"), 0); // manually
shader.setInt("texture2", 1); // or with shader class

while(...)
{
    [...]
}
```

By setting the samplers via `glUniform1i` we make sure each uniform sampler corresponds to the proper texture unit. You should get the following result:

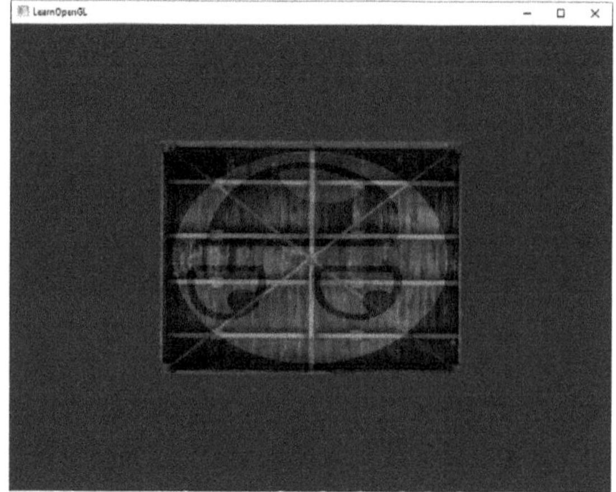

You probably noticed that the texture is flipped upside-down! This happens because OpenGL expects the `0.0` coordinate on the y-axis to be on the bottom side of the image, but images usually have `0.0` at the top of the y-axis. Luckily for us, `stb_image.h` can flip the y-axis during image loading by adding the following statement before loading any image:

```cpp
stbi_set_flip_vertically_on_load(true);
```

After telling `stb_image.h` to flip the y-axis when loading images you should get the following result:

If you see one happy container, you did things right. You can compare it with the source code at `/src/1.getting_started/4.2.textures_combined/`.

7.8 Exercises

To get more comfortable with textures it is advised to work through these exercises before continuing.

- Make sure **only** the happy face looks in the other/reverse direction by changing the fragment shader. Solution: `/src/1.getting_started/4.3.textures_exercise1/textures_exercise1.cpp`.
- Experiment with the different texture wrapping methods by specifying texture coordinates in the range `0.0f` to `2.0f` instead of `0.0f` to `1.0f`. See if you can display 4 smiley faces on a single container image clamped at its edge. Solution: `/src/1.getting_started/4.4.textures_exercise2/`, result: `learnopengl.com/img/getting-started/textures_exercise2.png`. See if you can experiment with other wrapping methods as well.
- Try to display only the center pixels of the texture image on the rectangle in such a way that the individual pixels are getting visible by changing the texture coordinates. Try to set the texture filtering method to `GL_NEAREST` to see the pixels more clearly. Solution: `/src/1.getting_started/4.5.textures_exercise3/`.
- Use a uniform variable as the `mix` function's third parameter to vary the amount the two textures are visible. Use the up and down arrow keys to change how much the container or the smiley face is visible. Solution: `/src/1.getting_started/4.6.textures_exercise4/`.

8. Transformations

We now know how to create objects, color them and/or give them a detailed appearance using textures, but they're still not that interesting since they're all static objects. We could try and make them move by changing their vertices and re-configuring their buffers each frame, but that's cumbersome and costs quite some processing power. There are much better ways to transform an object and that's by using (multiple) matrix objects. This doesn't mean we're going to talk about Kung Fu and a large digital artificial world.

Matrices are very powerful mathematical constructs that seem scary at first, but once you'll grow accustomed to them they'll prove extremely useful. When discussing matrices, we'll have to make a small dive into some mathematics and for the more mathematically inclined readers I'll post additional resources for further reading.

However, to fully understand transformations we first have to delve a bit deeper into vectors before discussing matrices. The focus of this chapter is to give you a basic mathematical background in topics we will require later on. If the subjects are difficult, try to understand them as much as you can and come back to this chapter later to review the concepts whenever you need them.

8.1 Vectors

In its most basic definition, vectors are directions and nothing more. A vector has a direction and a magnitude (also known as its strength or length). You can think of vectors like directions on a treasure map: 'go left 10 steps, now go north 3 steps and go right 5 steps'; here 'left' is the direction and '10 steps' is the magnitude of the vector. The directions for the treasure map thus contains 3 vectors. Vectors can have any dimension, but we usually work with dimensions of 2 to 4. If a vector has 2 dimensions it represents a direction on a plane (think of 2D graphs) and when it has 3 dimensions it can represent any direction in a 3D world.

Below you'll see 3 vectors where each vector is represented with (x, y) as arrows in a 2D graph. Because it is more intuitive to display vectors in 2D (rather than 3D) you can think of the 2D vectors as 3D vectors with a z coordinate of 0. Since vectors represent directions, the origin of the vector does not change its value. In the graph below we can see that the vectors $\bar{v}$ and $\bar{w}$ are equal even though their origin is different:

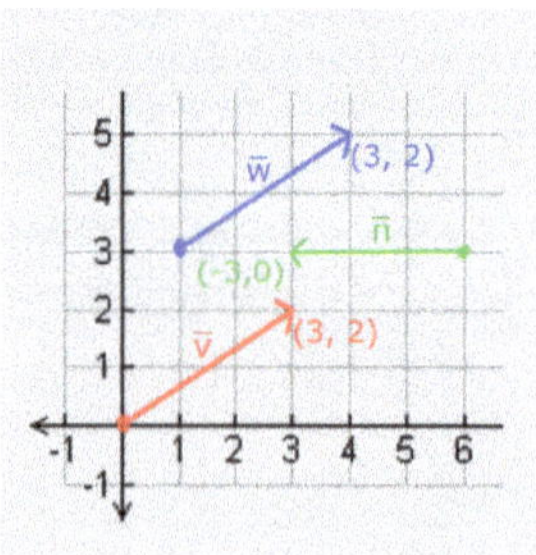

When describing vectors mathematicians generally prefer to describe vectors as character symbols with a little bar over their head like $\bar{v}$. Also, when displaying vectors in formulas they are generally displayed as follows:

$$\bar{v} = \begin{pmatrix} x \\ y \\ z \end{pmatrix}$$

Because vectors are specified as directions it is sometimes hard to visualize them as positions. If we want to visualize vectors as positions we can imagine the origin of the direction vector to be

$(0,0,0)$ and then point towards a certain direction that specifies the point, making it a position vector (we could also specify a different origin and then say: 'this vector points to that point in space from this origin'). The position vector $(3,5)$ would then point to $(3,5)$ on the graph with an origin of $(0,0)$. Using vectors we can thus describe directions **and** positions in 2D and 3D space.

Just like with normal numbers we can also define several operations on vectors (some of which you've already seen).

8.2 Scalar vector operations

A scalar is a single digit. When adding/subtracting/multiplying or dividing a vector with a scalar we simply add/subtract/multiply or divide each element of the vector by the scalar. For addition it would look like this:

$$\begin{pmatrix}1\\2\\3\end{pmatrix}+x \rightarrow \begin{pmatrix}1\\2\\3\end{pmatrix}+\begin{pmatrix}x\\x\\x\end{pmatrix}=\begin{pmatrix}1+x\\2+x\\3+x\end{pmatrix}$$

Where $+$ can be $+,-,\cdot$ or $\div$ where $\cdot$ is the multiplication operator.

8.3 Vector negation

Negating a vector results in a vector in the reversed direction. A vector pointing north-east would point south-west after negation. To negate a vector we add a minus-sign to each component (you can also represent it as a scalar-vector multiplication with a scalar value of -1):

$$-\bar{v}=-\begin{pmatrix}v_x\\v_y\\v_z\end{pmatrix}=\begin{pmatrix}-v_x\\-v_y\\-v_z\end{pmatrix}$$

8.4 Addition and subtraction

Addition of two vectors is defined as component-wise addition, that is each component of one vector is added to the same component of the other vector like so:

$$\bar{v}=\begin{pmatrix}1\\2\\3\end{pmatrix},\bar{k}=\begin{pmatrix}4\\5\\6\end{pmatrix}\rightarrow \bar{v}+\bar{k}=\begin{pmatrix}1+4\\2+5\\3+6\end{pmatrix}=\begin{pmatrix}5\\7\\9\end{pmatrix}$$

Visually, it looks like this on vectors $v=(4,2)$ and $k=(1,2)$, where the second vector is added on top of the first vector's end to find the end point of the resulting vector (head-to-tail method):

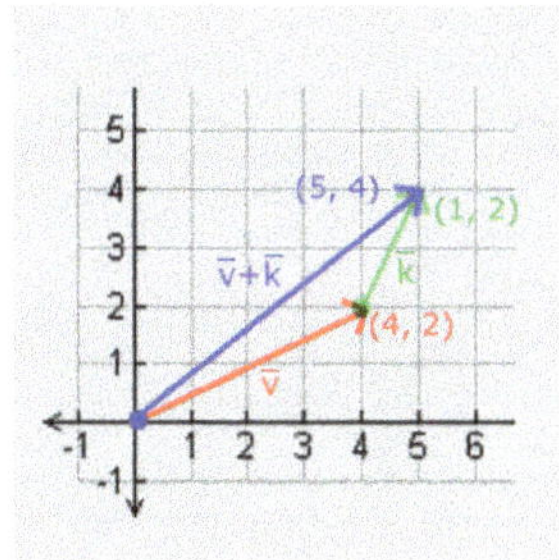

Just like normal addition and subtraction, vector subtraction is the same as addition with a negated second vector:

$$\bar{v} = \begin{pmatrix} 1 \\ 2 \\ 3 \end{pmatrix}, \bar{k} = \begin{pmatrix} 4 \\ 5 \\ 6 \end{pmatrix} \rightarrow \bar{v} + -\bar{k} = \begin{pmatrix} 1+(-4) \\ 2+(-5) \\ 3+(-6) \end{pmatrix} = \begin{pmatrix} -3 \\ -3 \\ -3 \end{pmatrix}$$

Subtracting two vectors from each other results in a vector that's the difference of the positions both vectors are pointing at. This proves useful in certain cases where we need to retrieve a vector that's the difference between two points.

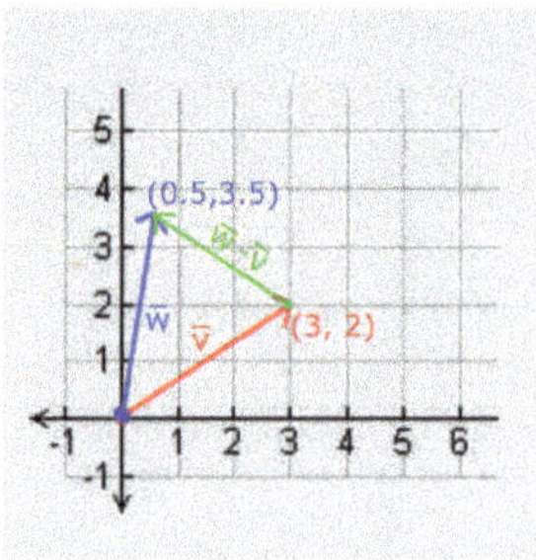

8.5 Length

To retrieve the length/magnitude of a vector we use the Pythagoras theorem that you may remember from your math classes. A vector forms a triangle when you visualize its individual x and y component as two sides of a triangle:

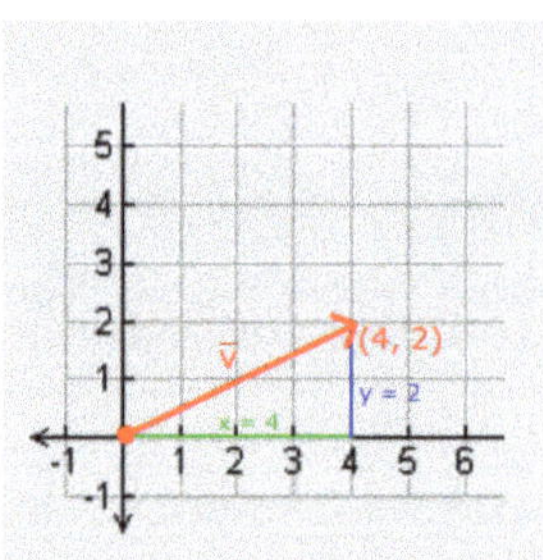

Since the length of the two sides (x, y) are known and we want to know the length of the tilted side $\bar{v}$ we can calculate it using the Pythagoras theorem as:

$$||\bar{v}|| = \sqrt{x^2 + y^2}$$

Where $||\bar{v}||$ is denoted as *the length of vector $\bar{v}$*. This is easily extended to 3D by adding z^2 to the equation.

In this case the length of vector (4, 2) equals:

$$||\bar{v}|| = \sqrt{4^2 + 2^2} = \sqrt{16 + 4} = \sqrt{20} = 4.47$$

Which is 4.47.

The same rules apply for matrix subtraction:

$$\begin{bmatrix} 4 & 2 \\ 1 & 6 \end{bmatrix} - \begin{bmatrix} 2 & 4 \\ 0 & 1 \end{bmatrix} = \begin{bmatrix} 4-2 & 2-4 \\ 1-0 & 6-1 \end{bmatrix} = \begin{bmatrix} 2 & -2 \\ 1 & 5 \end{bmatrix}$$

8.9 Matrix-scalar products

A matrix-scalar product multiples each element of the matrix by a scalar. The following example illustrates the multiplication:

$$2 \cdot \begin{bmatrix} 1 & 2 \\ 3 & 4 \end{bmatrix} = \begin{bmatrix} 2 \cdot 1 & 2 \cdot 2 \\ 2 \cdot 3 & 2 \cdot 4 \end{bmatrix} = \begin{bmatrix} 2 & 4 \\ 6 & 8 \end{bmatrix}$$

Now it also makes sense as to why those single numbers are called scalars. A scalar basically *scales* all the elements of the matrix by its value. In the previous example, all elements were scaled by 2.

So far so good, all of our cases weren't really too complicated. That is, until we start on matrix-matrix multiplication.

8.10 Matrix-matrix multiplication

Multiplying matrices is not necessarily complex, but rather difficult to get comfortable with. Matrix multiplication basically means to follow a set of pre-defined rules when multiplying. There are a few restrictions though:

1. You can only multiply two matrices if the number of columns on the left-hand side matrix is equal to the number of rows on the right-hand side matrix.
2. Matrix multiplication is not commutative that is $A \cdot B \neq B \cdot A$.

Let's get started with an example of a matrix multiplication of 2 2x2 matrices:

$$\begin{bmatrix} 1 & 2 \\ 3 & 4 \end{bmatrix} \cdot \begin{bmatrix} 5 & 6 \\ 7 & 8 \end{bmatrix} = \begin{bmatrix} 1 \cdot 5 + 2 \cdot 7 & 1 \cdot 6 + 2 \cdot 8 \\ 3 \cdot 5 + 4 \cdot 7 & 3 \cdot 6 + 4 \cdot 8 \end{bmatrix} = \begin{bmatrix} 19 & 22 \\ 43 & 50 \end{bmatrix}$$

Right now you're probably trying to figure out what the hell just happened? Matrix multiplication is a combination of normal multiplication and addition using the left-matrix's rows with the right-matrix's columns. Let's try discussing this with the following image:

$$\begin{bmatrix} 1 & 2 \\ 3 & 4 \end{bmatrix} \cdot \begin{bmatrix} 5 & 6 \\ 7 & 8 \end{bmatrix} = \begin{bmatrix} 1 \cdot 5 + 2 \cdot 7 & 1 \cdot 6 + 2 \cdot 8 \\ 3 \cdot 5 + 4 \cdot 7 & 3 \cdot 6 + 4 \cdot 8 \end{bmatrix} = \begin{bmatrix} 19 & 22 \\ 43 & 50 \end{bmatrix}$$

We first take the upper row of the left matrix and then take a column from the right matrix. The row and column that we picked decides which output value of the resulting $2x2$ matrix we're going to calculate. If we take the first row of the left matrix the resulting value will end up in the first row of the result matrix, then we pick a column and if it's the first column the result value will end up in the first column of the result matrix. This is exactly the case of the red pathway. To calculate the bottom-right result we take the bottom row of the first matrix and the rightmost column of the second matrix.

To calculate the resulting value we multiply the first element of the row and column together using normal multiplication, we do the same for the second elements, third, fourth etc. The results of the individual multiplications are then summed up and we have our result. Now it also makes sense that one of the requirements is that the size of the left-matrix's columns and the right-matrix's rows are equal, otherwise we can't finish the operations!

The result is then a matrix that has dimensions of (n, m) where n is equal to the number of rows of the left-hand side matrix and m is equal to the columns of the right-hand side matrix.

Don't worry if you have difficulties imagining the multiplications inside your head. Just keep trying to do the calculations by hand and return to this page whenever you have difficulties. Over time, matrix multiplication becomes second nature to you.

Let's finish the discussion of matrix-matrix multiplication with a larger example. Try to visualize the pattern using the colors. As a useful exercise, see if you can come up with your own answer of the multiplication and then compare them with the resulting matrix (once you try to do a matrix multiplication by hand you'll quickly get the grasp of them).

$$\begin{bmatrix} 4 & 2 & 0 \\ 0 & 8 & 1 \\ 0 & 1 & 0 \end{bmatrix} \cdot \begin{bmatrix} 4 & 2 & 1 \\ 2 & 0 & 4 \\ 9 & 4 & 2 \end{bmatrix} = \begin{bmatrix} 4\cdot4+2\cdot2+0\cdot9 & 4\cdot2+2\cdot0+0\cdot4 & 4\cdot1+2\cdot4+0\cdot2 \\ 0\cdot4+8\cdot2+1\cdot9 & 0\cdot2+8\cdot0+1\cdot4 & 0\cdot1+8\cdot4+1\cdot2 \\ 0\cdot4+1\cdot2+0\cdot9 & 0\cdot2+1\cdot0+0\cdot4 & 0\cdot1+1\cdot4+0\cdot2 \end{bmatrix}$$

$$= \begin{bmatrix} 20 & 8 & 12 \\ 25 & 4 & 34 \\ 2 & 0 & 4 \end{bmatrix}$$

As you can see, matrix-matrix multiplication is quite a cumbersome process and very prone to errors (which is why we usually let computers do this) and this gets problematic real quick when the matrices become larger. If you're still thirsty for more and you're curious about some more of the mathematical properties of matrices I strongly suggest you take a look at the Khan Academy videos[1] about matrices.

Anyways, now that we know how to multiply matrices together, we can start getting to the good stuff.

8.11 Matrix-Vector multiplication

Up until now we've had our fair share of vectors. We used them to represent positions, colors and even texture coordinates. Let's move a bit further down the rabbit hole and tell you that a vector is basically a `Nx1` matrix where `N` is the vector's number of components (also known as an N-dimensional vector). If you think about it, it makes a lot of sense. Vectors are just like matrices an array of numbers, but with only 1 column. So, how does this new piece of information help us? Well, if we have a `MxN` matrix we can multiply this matrix with our `Nx1` vector, since the columns of the matrix are equal to the number of rows of the vector, thus matrix multiplication is defined.

But why do we care if we can multiply matrices with a vector? Well, it just so happens that there are lots of interesting 2D/3D transformations we can place inside a matrix, and multiplying that matrix with a vector then *transforms* that vector. In case you're still a bit confused, let's start with a few examples and you'll soon see what we mean.

8.12 Identity matrix

In OpenGL we usually work with 4×4 transformation matrices for several reasons and one of them is that most of the vectors are of size 4. The most simple transformation matrix that we can think of is the identity matrix. The identity matrix is an `NxN` matrix with only 0s except on its diagonal. As you'll see, this transformation matrix leaves a vector completely unharmed:

---

[1] www.khanacademy.org/math/algebra2/algebra-matrices

$$\begin{bmatrix} 1 & 0 & 0 & 0 \\ 0 & 1 & 0 & 0 \\ 0 & 0 & 1 & 0 \\ 0 & 0 & 0 & 1 \end{bmatrix} \cdot \begin{bmatrix} 1 \\ 2 \\ 3 \\ 4 \end{bmatrix} = \begin{bmatrix} 1 \cdot 1 \\ 1 \cdot 2 \\ 1 \cdot 3 \\ 1 \cdot 4 \end{bmatrix} = \begin{bmatrix} 1 \\ 2 \\ 3 \\ 4 \end{bmatrix}$$

The vector is completely untouched. This becomes obvious from the rules of multiplication: the first result element is each individual element of the first row of the matrix multiplied with each element of the vector. Since each of the row's elements are 0 except the first one, we get: $1 \cdot 1 + 0 \cdot 2 + 0 \cdot 3 + 0 \cdot 4 = 1$ and the same applies for the other 3 elements of the vector.

> You may be wondering what the use is of a transformation matrix that does not transform? The identity matrix is usually a starting point for generating other transformation matrices and if we dig even deeper into linear algebra, a very useful matrix for proving theorems and solving linear equations.

8.13 Scaling

When we're scaling a vector we are increasing the length of the arrow by the amount we'd like to scale, keeping its direction the same. Since we're working in either 2 or 3 dimensions we can define scaling by a vector of 2 or 3 scaling variables, each scaling one axis (x, y or z).

Let's try scaling the vector $\bar{v} = (3,2)$. We will scale the vector along the x-axis by 0.5, thus making it twice as narrow; and we'll scale the vector by 2 along the y-axis, making it twice as high. Let's see what it looks like if we scale the vector by $(0.5,2)$ as $\bar{s}$:

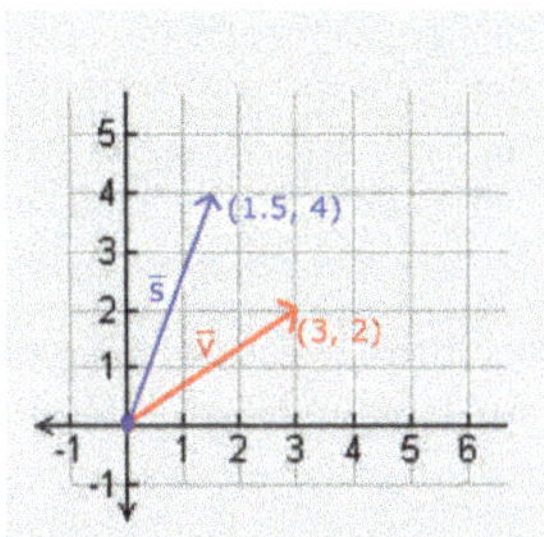

Keep in mind that OpenGL usually operates in 3D space so for this 2D case we could set the z-axis scale to 1, leaving it unharmed. The scaling operation we just performed is a non-uniform scale, because the scaling factor is not the same for each axis. If the scalar would be equal on all axes it would be called a uniform scale.

Let's start building a transformation matrix that does the scaling for us. We saw from the identity matrix that each of the diagonal elements were multiplied with its corresponding vector element. What if we were to change the 1s in the identity matrix to 3s? In that case, we would be multiplying each of the vector elements by a value of 3 and thus effectively uniformly scale the vector by 3. If we represent the scaling variables as (S_1, S_2, S_3) we can define a scaling matrix on any vector (x, y, z) as:

$$\begin{bmatrix} S_1 & 0 & 0 & 0 \\ 0 & S_2 & 0 & 0 \\ 0 & 0 & S_3 & 0 \\ 0 & 0 & 0 & 1 \end{bmatrix} \cdot \begin{pmatrix} x \\ y \\ z \\ 1 \end{pmatrix} = \begin{pmatrix} S_1 \cdot x \\ S_2 \cdot y \\ S_3 \cdot z \\ 1 \end{pmatrix}$$

Note that we keep the 4th scaling value `1`. The `w` component is used for other purposes as we'll see later on.

8.14 Translation

Translation is the process of adding another vector on top of the original vector to return a new vector with a different position, thus *moving* the vector based on a translation vector. We've already discussed vector addition so this shouldn't be too new.

Just like the scaling matrix there are several locations on a 4-by-4 matrix that we can use to perform certain operations and for translation those are the top-3 values of the 4th column. If we represent the translation vector as (T_x, T_y, T_z) we can define the translation matrix by:

$$\begin{bmatrix} 1 & 0 & 0 & T_x \\ 0 & 1 & 0 & T_y \\ 0 & 0 & 1 & T_z \\ 0 & 0 & 0 & 1 \end{bmatrix} \cdot \begin{pmatrix} x \\ y \\ z \\ 1 \end{pmatrix} = \begin{pmatrix} x + T_x \\ y + T_y \\ z + T_z \\ 1 \end{pmatrix}$$

This works because all of the translation values are multiplied by the vector's `w` column and added to the vector's original values (remember the matrix-multiplication rules). This wouldn't have been possible with a 3-by-3 matrix.

> **Homogeneous coordinates** The `w` component of a vector is also known as a homogeneous coordinate. To get the 3D vector from a homogeneous vector we divide the x, y and z coordinate by its w coordinate. We usually do not notice this since the w component is `1.0` most of the time. Using homogeneous coordinates has several advantages: it allows us to do matrix translations on 3D vectors (without a w component we can't translate vectors) and in the next chapter we'll use the w value to create 3D perspective. Also, whenever the homogeneous coordinate is equal to 0, the vector is specifically known as a direction vector since a vector with a w coordinate of 0 cannot be translated.

With a translation matrix we can move objects in any of the 3 axis directions (x, y, z), making it a very useful transformation matrix for our transformation toolkit.

8.15 Rotation

The last few transformations were relatively easy to understand and visualize in 2D or 3D space, but rotations are a bit trickier. If you want to know exactly how these matrices are constructed I'd recommend that you watch the rotation videos of Khan Academy's linear algebra section[1].

First let's define what a rotation of a vector actually is. A rotation in 2D or 3D is represented with an angle. An angle could be in degrees or radians where a whole circle has 360 degrees or 2 PI[2] radians. I prefer explaining rotations using degrees as we're generally more accustomed to them.

> Most rotation functions require an angle in radians, but luckily degrees are easily converted to radians: `angle in degrees = angle in radians * (180 / PI)` `angle in radians = angle in degrees * (PI / 180)` Where `PI` equals (rounded) `3.14159265359`.

[1] www.khanacademy.org/math/linear-algebra/matrix_transformations
[2] en.wikipedia.org/wiki/Pi

Rotating half a circle rotates us 360/2 = 180 degrees and rotating 1/5th to the right means we rotate 360/5 = 72 degrees to the right. This is demonstrated for a basic 2D vector where $\bar{v}$ is rotated 72 degrees to the right, or clockwise, from $\bar{k}$:

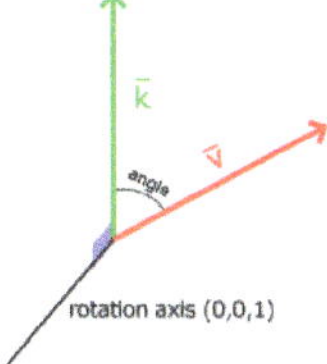

Rotations in 3D are specified with an angle **and** a rotation axis. The angle specified will rotate the object along the rotation axis given. Try to visualize this by spinning your head a certain degree while continually looking down a single rotation axis. When rotating 2D vectors in a 3D world for example, we set the rotation axis to the z-axis (try to visualize this).

Using trigonometry it is possible to transform vectors to newly rotated vectors given an angle. This is usually done via a smart combination of the `sine` and `cosine` functions (commonly abbreviated to `sin` and `cos`). A discussion of how the rotation matrices are generated is out of this chapter's scope.

A rotation matrix is defined for each unit axis in 3D space where the angle is represented as the theta symbol θ.

Rotation around the X-axis:

$$\begin{bmatrix} 1 & 0 & 0 & 0 \\ 0 & \cos\theta & -\sin\theta & 0 \\ 0 & \sin\theta & \cos\theta & 0 \\ 0 & 0 & 0 & 1 \end{bmatrix} \cdot \begin{pmatrix} x \\ y \\ z \\ 1 \end{pmatrix} = \begin{pmatrix} x \\ \cos\theta \cdot y - \sin\theta \cdot z \\ \sin\theta \cdot y + \cos\theta \cdot z \\ 1 \end{pmatrix}$$

Rotation around the Y-axis:

$$\begin{bmatrix} \cos\theta & 0 & \sin\theta & 0 \\ 0 & 1 & 0 & 0 \\ -\sin\theta & 0 & \cos\theta & 0 \\ 0 & 0 & 0 & 1 \end{bmatrix} \cdot \begin{pmatrix} x \\ y \\ z \\ 1 \end{pmatrix} = \begin{pmatrix} \cos\theta \cdot x + \sin\theta \cdot z \\ y \\ -\sin\theta \cdot x + \cos\theta \cdot z \\ 1 \end{pmatrix}$$

Rotation around the Z-axis:

$$\begin{bmatrix} \cos\theta & -\sin\theta & 0 & 0 \\ \sin\theta & \cos\theta & 0 & 0 \\ 0 & 0 & 1 & 0 \\ 0 & 0 & 0 & 1 \end{bmatrix} \cdot \begin{pmatrix} x \\ y \\ z \\ 1 \end{pmatrix} = \begin{pmatrix} \cos\theta \cdot x - \sin\theta \cdot y \\ \sin\theta \cdot x + \cos\theta \cdot y \\ z \\ 1 \end{pmatrix}$$

Using the rotation matrices we can transform our position vectors around one of the three unit axes. To rotate around an arbitrary 3D axis we can combine all 3 them by first rotating around the X-axis, then Y and then Z for example. However, this quickly introduces a problem called Gimbal lock. We won't discuss the details, but a better solution is to rotate around an arbitrary unit axis e.g. `(0.662,0.2,0.722)` (note that this is a unit vector) right away instead of combining the rotation matrices. Such a (verbose) matrix exists and is given below with (R_x, R_y, R_z) as the arbitrary rotation axis:

$$\begin{bmatrix} \cos\theta + R_x^2(1-\cos\theta) & R_xR_y(1-\cos\theta) - R_z\sin\theta & R_xR_z(1-\cos\theta) + R_y\sin\theta & 0 \\ R_yR_x(1-\cos\theta) + R_z\sin\theta & \cos\theta + R_y^2(1-\cos\theta) & R_yR_z(1-\cos\theta) - R_x\sin\theta & 0 \\ R_zR_x(1-\cos\theta) - R_y\sin\theta & R_zR_y(1-\cos\theta) + R_x\sin\theta & \cos\theta + R_z^2(1-\cos\theta) & 0 \\ 0 & 0 & 0 & 1 \end{bmatrix}$$

A mathematical discussion of generating such a matrix is out of the scope of this chapter. Keep in mind that even this matrix does not completely prevent gimbal lock (although it gets a lot harder). To truly prevent Gimbal locks we have to represent rotations using quaternions, that are not only safer, but also more computationally friendly. However, a discussion of quaternions is out of the scope of this chapter.

8.16 Combining matrices

The true power from using matrices for transformations is that we can combine multiple transformations in a single matrix thanks to matrix-matrix multiplication. Let's see if we can generate a transformation matrix that combines several transformations. Say we have a vector (x, y, z) and we want to scale it by 2 and then translate it by $(1, 2, 3)$. We need a translation and a scaling matrix for our required steps. The resulting transformation matrix would then look like:

$$Trans.Scale = \begin{bmatrix} 1 & 0 & 0 & 1 \\ 0 & 1 & 0 & 2 \\ 0 & 0 & 1 & 3 \\ 0 & 0 & 0 & 1 \end{bmatrix} \cdot \begin{bmatrix} 2 & 0 & 0 & 0 \\ 0 & 2 & 0 & 0 \\ 0 & 0 & 2 & 0 \\ 0 & 0 & 0 & 1 \end{bmatrix} = \begin{bmatrix} 2 & 0 & 0 & 1 \\ 0 & 2 & 0 & 2 \\ 0 & 0 & 2 & 3 \\ 0 & 0 & 0 & 1 \end{bmatrix}$$

Note that we first do a translation and then a scale transformation when multiplying matrices. Matrix multiplication is not commutative, which means their order is important. When multiplying matrices the right-most matrix is first multiplied with the vector so you should read the multiplications from right to left. It is advised to first do scaling operations, then rotations and lastly translations when combining matrices otherwise they may (negatively) affect each other. For example, if you would first do a translation and then scale, the translation vector would also scale!

Running the final transformation matrix on our vector results in the following vector:

$$\begin{bmatrix} 2 & 0 & 0 & 1 \\ 0 & 2 & 0 & 2 \\ 0 & 0 & 2 & 3 \\ 0 & 0 & 0 & 1 \end{bmatrix} \cdot \begin{bmatrix} x \\ y \\ z \\ 1 \end{bmatrix} = \begin{bmatrix} 2x+1 \\ 2y+2 \\ 2z+3 \\ 1 \end{bmatrix}$$

Great! The vector is first scaled by two and then translated by $(1, 2, 3)$.

Now that we've explained all the theory behind transformations, it's time to see how we can actually use this knowledge to our advantage. OpenGL does not have any form of matrix or vector knowledge built in, so we have to define our own mathematics classes and functions. In this book we'd rather abstract from all the tiny mathematical details and simply use pre-made mathematics libraries. Luckily, there is an easy-to-use and tailored-for-OpenGL mathematics library called GLM.

8.17 GLM

GLM stands for **OpenGL M**athematics and is a *header-only* library, which means that we only have to include the proper header files and we're done; no linking and compiling necessary. GLM can be downloaded from their website: `glm.g-truc.net/0.9.8/index.html`. Copy the root directory of the header files into your *includes* folder and let's get rolling.

Most of GLM's functionality that we need can be found in 3 headers files that we'll include as follows:

```cpp
#include <glm/glm.hpp>
#include <glm/gtc/matrix_transform.hpp>
#include <glm/gtc/type_ptr.hpp>
```

Let's see if we can put our transformation knowledge to good use by translating a vector of (1,0,0) by (1,1,0) (note that we define it as a `glm::vec4` with its homogeneous coordinate set to 1.0:

```cpp
glm::vec4 vec(1.0f, 0.0f, 0.0f, 1.0f);
glm::mat4 trans = glm::mat4(1.0f);
trans = glm::translate(trans, glm::vec3(1.0f, 1.0f, 0.0f));
vec = trans * vec;
std::cout << vec.x << vec.y << vec.z << std::endl;
```

We first define a vector named `vec` using GLM's built-in vector class. Next we define a `mat4` and explicitly initialize it to the identity matrix by initializing the matrix's diagonals to 1.0; if we do not initialize it to the identity matrix the matrix would be a null matrix (all elements 0) and all subsequent matrix operations would end up a null matrix as well.

The next step is to create a transformation matrix by passing our identity matrix to the `glm::translate` function, together with a translation vector (the given matrix is then multiplied with a translation matrix and the resulting matrix is returned). Then we multiply our vector by the transformation matrix and output the result. If we still remember how matrix translation works then the resulting vector should be (1+1,0+1,0+0) which is (2,1,0). This snippet of code outputs 210 so the translation matrix did its job.

Let's do something more interesting and scale and rotate the container object from the previous chapter:

```cpp
glm::mat4 trans = glm::mat4(1.0f);
trans = glm::rotate(trans, glm::radians(90.0f), glm::vec3(0.0, 0.0, 1.0));
trans = glm::scale(trans, glm::vec3(0.5, 0.5, 0.5));
```

First we scale the container by 0.5 on each axis and then rotate the container 90 degrees around the Z-axis. GLM expects its angles in radians so we convert the degrees to radians using `glm::radians`. Note that the textured rectangle is on the XY plane so we want to rotate around the Z-axis. Keep in mind that the axis that we rotate around should be a unit vector, so be sure to normalize the vector first if you're not rotating around the X, Y, or Z axis. Because we pass the matrix to each of GLM's functions, GLM automatically multiples the matrices together, resulting in a transformation matrix that combines all the transformations.

The next big question is: how do we get the transformation matrix to the shaders? We shortly mentioned before that GLSL also has a `mat4` type. So we'll adapt the vertex shader to accept a `mat4` uniform variable and multiply the position vector by the matrix uniform:

```glsl
#version 330 core
layout (location = 0) in vec3 aPos;
layout (location = 1) in vec2 aTexCoord;

out vec2 TexCoord;
```

```glsl
uniform mat4 transform;

void main()
{
    gl_Position = transform * vec4(aPos, 1.0f);
    TexCoord = vec2(aTexCoord.x, aTexCoord.y);
}
```

> GLSL also has `mat2` and `mat3` types that allow for swizzling-like operations just like
> vectors. All the aforementioned math operations (like scalar-matrix multiplication, matrix-
> vector multiplication and matrix-matrix multiplication) are allowed on the matrix types.
> Wherever special matrix operations are used we'll be sure to explain what's happening.

We added the uniform and multiplied the position vector with the transformation matrix before
passing it to `gl_Position`. Our container should now be twice as small and rotated 90 degrees
(tilted to the left). We still need to pass the transformation matrix to the shader though:

```cpp
unsigned int transformLoc = glGetUniformLocation(ourShader.ID,"transform");
glUniformMatrix4fv(transformLoc, 1, GL_FALSE, glm::value_ptr(trans));
```

We first query the location of the uniform variable and then send the matrix data to the shaders
using `glUniform` with `Matrix4fv` as its postfix. The first argument should be familiar by now
which is the uniform's location. The second argument tells OpenGL how many matrices we'd like
to send, which is `1`. The third argument asks us if we want to transpose our matrix, that is to swap
the columns and rows. OpenGL developers often use an internal matrix layout called column-major
ordering which is the default matrix layout in GLM so there is no need to transpose the matrices;
we can keep it at `GL_FALSE`. The last parameter is the actual matrix data, but GLM stores their
matrices' data in a way that doesn't always match OpenGL's expectations so we first convert the
data with GLM's built-in function `value_ptr`.

We created a transformation matrix, declared a uniform in the vertex shader and sent the matrix
to the shaders where we transform our vertex coordinates. The result should look something like
this:

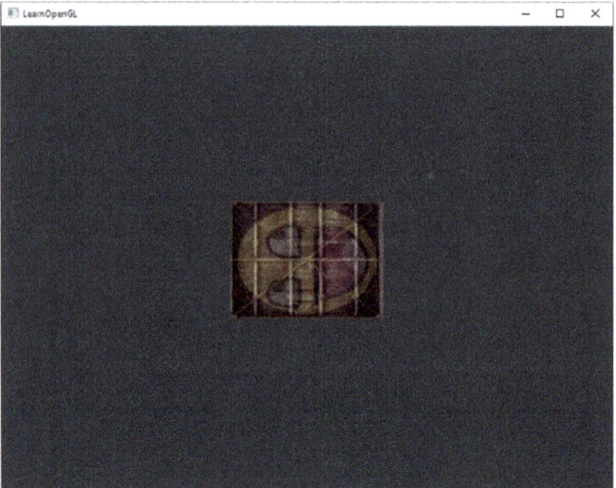

Perfect! Our container is indeed tilted to the left and twice as small so the transformation was
successful. Let's get a little more funky and see if we can rotate the container over time, and for fun

we'll also reposition the container at the bottom-right side of the window. To rotate the container over time we have to update the transformation matrix in the render loop because it needs to update each frame. We use GLFW's time function to get an angle over time:

```cpp
glm::mat4 trans = glm::mat4(1.0f);
trans = glm::translate(trans, glm::vec3(0.5f, -0.5f, 0.0f));
trans = glm::rotate(trans, (float)glfwGetTime(),
                    glm::vec3(0.0f, 0.0f, 1.0f));
```

Keep in mind that in the previous case we could declare the transformation matrix anywhere, but now we have to create it every iteration to continuously update the rotation. This means we have to re-create the transformation matrix in each iteration of the render loop. Usually when rendering scenes we have several transformation matrices that are re-created with new values each frame.

Here we first rotate the container around the origin (0,0,0) and once it's rotated, we translate its rotated version to the bottom-right corner of the screen. Remember that the actual transformation order should be read in reverse: even though in code we first translate and then later rotate, the actual transformations first apply a rotation and then a translation. Understanding all these combinations of transformations and how they apply to objects is difficult to understand. Try and experiment with transformations like these and you'll quickly get a grasp of it.

If you did things right you should get the following result:

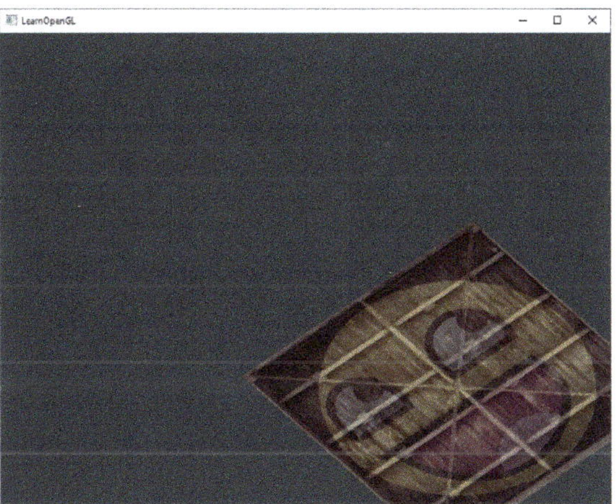

And there you have it. A translated container that's rotated over time, all done by a single transformation matrix! Now you can see why matrices are such a powerful construct in graphics land. We can define an infinite amount of transformations and combine them all in a single matrix that we can re-use as often as we'd like. Using transformations like this in the vertex shader saves us the effort of re-defining the vertex data and saves us some processing time as well, since we don't have to re-send our data all the time (which is quite slow); all we need to do is update the transformation uniform.

If you didn't get the right result or you're stuck somewhere else, take a look at the source code at /src/1.getting_started/5.1.transformations/ and the updated shader class at /includes/learnopengl/shader_m.h.

In the next chapter we'll discuss how we can use matrices to define different coordinate spaces for our vertices. This will be our first step into 3D graphics!

8.18 Further reading

- `www.youtube.com/playlist?list=PLZHQObOWTQDPD3MizzM2xVFit`
  `gF8hE_ab`: great video tutorial series by Grant Sanderson about the underlying mathematics
  of transformations and linear algebra.

8.19 Exercises

- Using the last transformation on the container, try switching the order around by first rotating
  and then translating. See what happens and try to reason why this happens. Solution:
  `/src/1.getting_started/5.2.transformations_exercise1/`.
- Try drawing a second container with another call to `glDrawElements` but place it at a
  different position using transformations **only**. Make sure this second container is placed at the
  top-left of the window and instead of rotating, scale it over time (using the `sin` function is
  useful here; note that using `sin` will cause the object to invert as soon as a negative scale is applied). Solution: `/src/1.getting_started/5.2.transformations_exercis`
  `e2/`.

9. Coordinate Systems

In the last chapter we learned how we can use matrices to our advantage by transforming all vertices with transformation matrices. OpenGL expects all the vertices, that we want to become visible, to be in normalized device coordinates after each vertex shader run. That is, the x, y and z coordinates of each vertex should be between -1.0 and 1.0; coordinates outside this range will not be visible. What we usually do, is specify the coordinates in a range (or space) we determine ourselves and in the vertex shader transform these coordinates to normalized device coordinates (NDC). These NDC are then given to the rasterizer to transform them to 2D coordinates/pixels on your screen.

Transforming coordinates to NDC is usually accomplished in a step-by-step fashion where we transform an object's vertices to several coordinate systems before finally transforming them to NDC. The advantage of transforming them to several *intermediate* coordinate systems is that some operations/calculations are easier in certain coordinate systems as will soon become apparent. There are a total of 5 different coordinate systems that are of importance to us:

- Local space (or Object space)
- World space
- View space (or Eye space)
- Clip space
- Screen space

Those are all a different state at which our vertices will be transformed in before finally ending up as fragments.

You're probably quite confused by now by what a space or coordinate system actually is so we'll explain them in a more high-level fashion first by showing the total picture and what each specific space represents.

9.1 The global picture

To transform the coordinates from one space to the next coordinate space we'll use several transformation matrices of which the most important are the model, view and projection matrix. Our vertex coordinates first start in local space as local coordinates and are then further processed to world coordinates, view coordinates, clip coordinates and eventually end up as screen coordinates. The following image displays the process and shows what each transformation does:

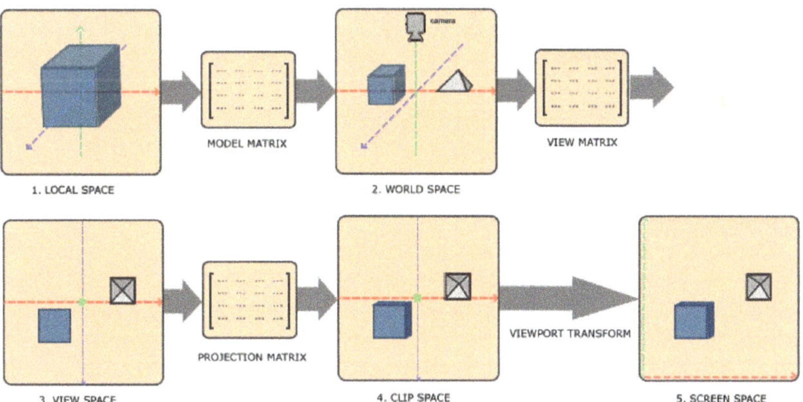

1. Local coordinates are the coordinates of your object relative to its local origin; they're the coordinates your object begins in.
2. The next step is to transform the local coordinates to world-space coordinates which are

    coordinates in respect of a larger world. These coordinates are relative to some global origin of the world, together with many other objects also placed relative to this world's origin.

3. Next we transform the world coordinates to view-space coordinates in such a way that each coordinate is as seen from the camera or viewer's point of view.

4. After the coordinates are in view space we want to project them to clip coordinates. Clip coordinates are processed to the `-1.0` and `1.0` range and determine which vertices will end up on the screen. Projection to clip-space coordinates can add perspective if using perspective projection.

5. And lastly we transform the clip coordinates to screen coordinates in a process we call viewport transform that transforms the coordinates from `-1.0` and `1.0` to the coordinate range defined by `glViewport`. The resulting coordinates are then sent to the rasterizer to turn them into fragments.

You probably got a slight idea what each individual space is used for. The reason we're transforming our vertices into all these different spaces is that some operations make more sense or are easier to use in certain coordinate systems. For example, when modifying your object it makes most sense to do this in local space, while calculating certain operations on the object with respect to the position of other objects makes most sense in world coordinates and so on. If we want, we could define one transformation matrix that goes from local space to clip space all in one go, but that leaves us with less flexibility.

We'll discuss each coordinate system in more detail below.

9.2 Local space

Local space is the coordinate space that is local to your object, i.e. where your object begins in. Imagine that you've created your cube in a modeling software package (like Blender). The origin of your cube is probably at $(0,0,0)$ even though your cube may end up at a different location in your final application. Probably all the models you've created all have $(0,0,0)$ as their initial position. All the vertices of your model are therefore in *local* space: they are all local to your object.

    The vertices of the container we've been using were specified as coordinates between -0.5 and 0.5 with 0.0 as its origin. These are local coordinates.

9.3 World space

If we would import all our objects directly in the application they would probably all be somewhere positioned inside each other at the world's origin of $(0,0,0)$ which is not what we want. We want to define a position for each object to position them inside a larger world. The coordinates in world space are exactly what they sound like: the coordinates of all your vertices relative to a (game) world. This is the coordinate space where you want your objects transformed to in such a way that they're all scattered around the place (preferably in a realistic fashion). The coordinates of your object are transformed from local to world space; this is accomplished with the model matrix.

The model matrix is a transformation matrix that translates, scales and/or rotates your object to place it in the world at a location/orientation they belong to. Think of it as transforming a house by scaling it down (it was a bit too large in local space), translating it to a suburbia town and rotating it a bit to the left on the y-axis so that it neatly fits with the neighboring houses. You could think of the matrix in the previous chapter to position the container all over the scene as a sort of model matrix as well; we transformed the local coordinates of the container to some different place in the scene/world.

9.4 **View space**

The view space is what people usually refer to as the camera of OpenGL (it is sometimes also known as camera space or eye space). The view space is the result of transforming your world-space coordinates to coordinates that are in front of the user's view. The view space is thus the space as seen from the camera's point of view. This is usually accomplished with a combination of translations and rotations to translate/rotate the scene so that certain items are transformed to the front of the camera. These combined transformations are generally stored inside a view matrix that transforms world coordinates to view space. In the next chapter we'll extensively discuss how to create such a view matrix to simulate a camera.

9.5 **Clip space**

At the end of each vertex shader run, OpenGL expects the coordinates to be within a specific range and any coordinate that falls outside this range is clipped. Coordinates that are clipped are discarded, so the remaining coordinates will end up as fragments visible on your screen. This is also where clip space gets its name from.

Because specifying all the visible coordinates to be within the range -1.0 and 1.0 isn't really intuitive, we specify our own coordinate set to work in and convert those back to NDC as OpenGL expects them.

To transform vertex coordinates from view to clip-space we define a so called projection matrix that specifies a range of coordinates e.g. -1000 and 1000 in each dimension. The projection matrix then transforms coordinates within this specified range to normalized device coordinates $(-1.0, 1.0)$. All coordinates outside this range will not be mapped between -1.0 and 1.0 and therefore be clipped. With this range we specified in the projection matrix, a coordinate of $(1250, 500, 750)$ would not be visible, since the x coordinate is out of range and thus gets converted to a coordinate higher than 1.0 in NDC and is therefore clipped.

> Note that if only a part of a primitive e.g. a triangle is outside the clipping volume OpenGL will reconstruct the triangle as one or more triangles to fit inside the clipping range.

This *viewing box* a projection matrix creates is called a frustum and each coordinate that ends up inside this frustum will end up on the user's screen. The total process to convert coordinates within a specified range to NDC that can easily be mapped to 2D view-space coordinates is called projection since the projection matrix projects 3D coordinates to the easy-to-map-to-2D normalized device coordinates.

Once all the vertices are transformed to clip space a final operation called perspective division is performed where we divide the x, y and z components of the position vectors by the vector's homogeneous w component; perspective division is what transforms the 4D clip space coordinates to 3D normalized device coordinates. This step is performed automatically at the end of the vertex shader step.

It is after this stage where the resulting coordinates are mapped to screen coordinates (using the settings of `glViewport`) and turned into fragments.

The projection matrix to transform view coordinates to clip coordinates usually takes two different forms, where each form defines its own unique frustum. We can either create an orthographic projection matrix or a perspective projection matrix.

9.5.1 Orthographic projection

An orthographic projection matrix defines a cube-like frustum box that defines the clipping space where each vertex outside this box is clipped. When creating an orthographic projection matrix we specify the width, height and length of the visible frustum. All the coordinates inside this frustum will end up within the NDC range after transformed by its matrix and thus won't be clipped. The frustum looks a bit like a container:

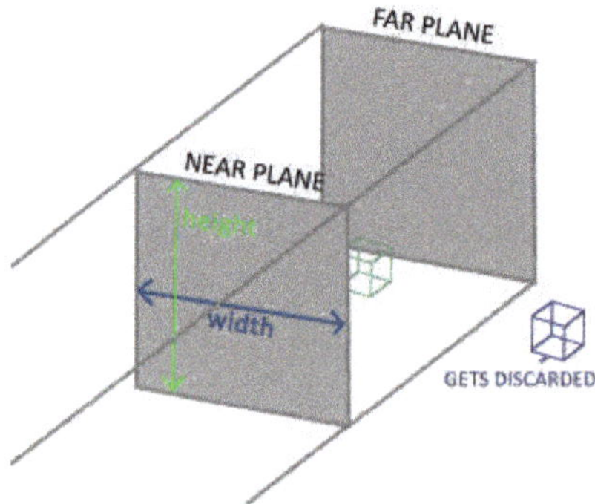

The frustum defines the visible coordinates and is specified by a width, a height and a near and far plane. Any coordinate in front of the near plane is clipped and the same applies to coordinates behind the far plane. The orthographic frustum **directly** maps all coordinates inside the frustum to normalized device coordinates without any special side effects since it won't touch the w component of the transformed vector; if the w component remains equal to 1.0 perspective division won't change the coordinates.

To create an orthographic projection matrix we make use of GLM's built-in function glm::ortho:

```
glm::ortho(0.0f, 800.0f, 0.0f, 600.0f, 0.1f, 100.0f);
```

The first two parameters specify the left and right coordinate of the frustum and the third and fourth parameter specify the bottom and top part of the frustum. With those 4 points we've defined the size of the near and far planes and the 5th and 6th parameter then define the distances between the near and far plane. This specific projection matrix transforms all coordinates between these x, y and z range values to normalized device coordinates.

An orthographic projection matrix directly maps coordinates to the 2D plane that is your screen, but in reality a direct projection produces unrealistic results since the projection doesn't take perspective into account. That is something the perspective projection matrix fixes for us.

9.5.2 Perspective projection

If you ever were to enjoy the graphics the *real life* has to offer you'll notice that objects that are farther away appear much smaller. This weird effect is something we call perspective. Perspective is especially noticeable when looking down the end of an infinite motorway or railway as seen in the following image:

As you can see, due to perspective the lines seem to coincide at a far enough distance. This is exactly the effect perspective projection tries to mimic and it does so using a perspective projection matrix. The projection matrix maps a given frustum range to clip space, but also manipulates the w value of each vertex coordinate in such a way that the further away a vertex coordinate is from the viewer, the higher this w component becomes. Once the coordinates are transformed to clip space they are in the range $-w$ to w (anything outside this range is clipped). OpenGL requires that the visible coordinates fall between the range -1.0 and 1.0 as the final vertex shader output, thus once the coordinates are in clip space, perspective division is applied to the clip space coordinates:

$$out = \begin{pmatrix} x/w \\ y/w \\ z/w \end{pmatrix}$$

Each component of the vertex coordinate is divided by its w component giving smaller vertex coordinates the further away a vertex is from the viewer. This is another reason why the w component is important, since it helps us with perspective projection. The resulting coordinates are then in normalized device space. If you're interested to figure out how the orthographic and perspective projection matrices are actually calculated (and aren't too scared of the mathematics) I can recommend this excellent article by Songho: `www.songho.ca/opengl/gl_projectionmatrix.html`.

A perspective projection matrix can be created in GLM as follows:

```
glm::mat4 proj = glm::perspective(glm::radians(45.0f), (float)width /
                                  (float)height, 0.1f, 100.0f);
```

What `glm::perspective` does is again create a large *frustum* that defines the visible space, anything outside the frustum will not end up in the clip space volume and will thus become clipped. A perspective frustum can be visualized as a non-uniformly shaped box from where each coordinate inside this box will be mapped to a point in clip space. An image of a perspective frustum is seen below:

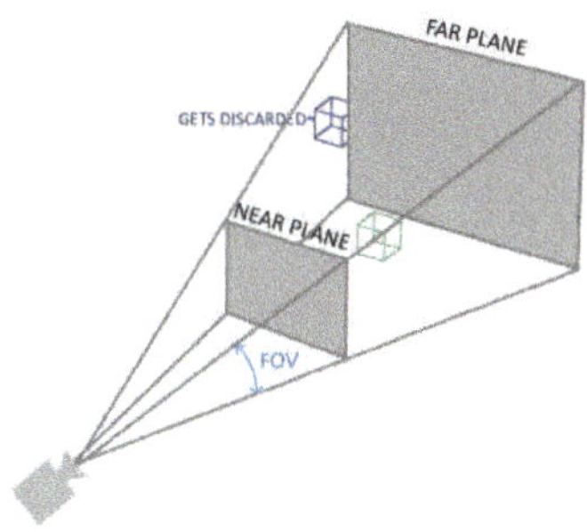

Its first parameter defines the fov value, that stands for field of view and sets how large the viewspace is. For a realistic view it is usually set to 45 degrees, but for more doom-style results you could set it to a higher value. The second parameter sets the aspect ratio which is calculated by dividing the viewport's width by its height. The third and fourth parameter set the *near* and *far* plane of the frustum. We usually set the near distance to 0.1 and the far distance to 100.0. All the vertices between the near and far plane and inside the frustum will be rendered.

> Whenever the *near* value of your perspective matrix is set too high (like 10.0), OpenGL will clip all coordinates close to the camera (between 0.0 and 10.0), which can give a visual result you maybe have seen before in videogames where you could see through certain objects when moving uncomfortably close to them.

When using orthographic projection, each of the vertex coordinates are directly mapped to clip space without any fancy perspective division (it still does perspective division, but the w component is not manipulated (it stays 1) and thus has no effect). Because the orthographic projection doesn't use perspective projection, objects farther away do not seem smaller, which produces a weird visual output. For this reason the orthographic projection is mainly used for 2D renderings and for some architectural or engineering applications where we'd rather not have vertices distorted by perspective. Applications like *Blender* that are used for 3D modeling sometimes use orthographic projection for modeling, because it more accurately depicts each object's dimensions. Below you'll see a comparison of both projection methods in Blender:

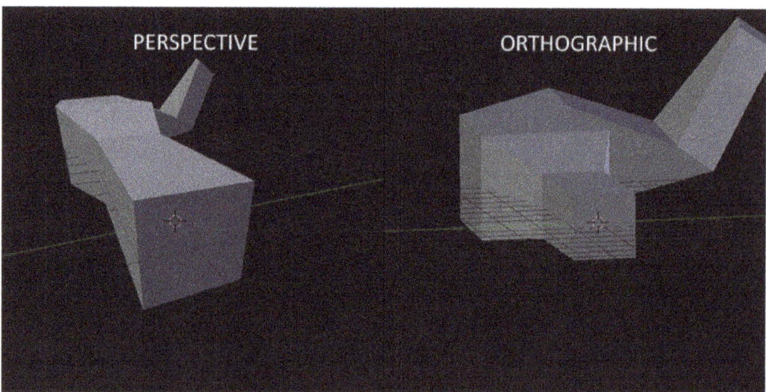

You can see that with perspective projection, the vertices farther away appear much smaller, while in orthographic projection each vertex has the same distance to the user.

9.6 Putting it all together

We create a transformation matrix for each of the aforementioned steps: model, view and projection matrix. A vertex coordinate is then transformed to clip coordinates as follows:

$$V_{clip} = M_{projection} \cdot M_{view} \cdot M_{model} \cdot V_{local}$$

Note that the order of matrix multiplication is reversed (remember that we need to read matrix multiplication from right to left). The resulting vertex should then be assigned to gl_Position in the vertex shader and OpenGL will then automatically perform perspective division and clipping.

And then? The output of the vertex shader requires the coordinates to be in clip-space which is what we just did with the transformation matrices. OpenGL then performs *perspective division* on the *clip-space coordinates* to transform them to *normalized-device coordinates*. OpenGL then uses the parameters from `glViewPort` to map the normalized-device coordinates to *screen coordinates* where each coordinate corresponds to a point on your screen (in our case a 800x600 screen). This process is called the *viewport transform*.

This is a difficult topic to understand so if you're still not exactly sure about what each space is used for you don't have to worry. Below you'll see how we can actually put these coordinate spaces to good use and enough examples will follow in the upcoming chapters.

9.7 Going 3D

Now that we know how to transform 3D coordinates to 2D coordinates we can start rendering real 3D objects instead of the lame 2D plane we've been showing so far.

To start drawing in 3D we'll first create a model matrix. The model matrix consists of translations, scaling and/or rotations we'd like to apply to *transform* all object's vertices to the global world space. Let's transform our plane a bit by rotating it on the x-axis so it looks like it's laying on the floor. The model matrix then looks like this:

```cpp
glm::mat4 model = glm::mat4(1.0f);
model = glm::rotate(model, glm::radians(-55.0f),
                    glm::vec3(1.0f, 0.0f, 0.0f));
```

By multiplying the vertex coordinates with this model matrix we're transforming the vertex coordinates to world coordinates. Our plane that is slightly on the floor thus represents the plane in the global world.

Next we need to create a view matrix. We want to move slightly backwards in the scene so the object becomes visible (when in world space we're located at the origin `(0,0,0)`). To move around the scene, think about the following:

- To move a camera backwards, is the same as moving the entire scene forward.

That is exactly what a view matrix does, we move the entire scene around inversed to where we want the camera to move. Because we want to move backwards and since OpenGL is a right-handed system we have to move in the positive z-axis. We do this by translating the scene towards the negative z-axis. This gives the impression that we are moving backwards.

Right-handed system

By convention, OpenGL is a right-handed system. What this basically says is that the positive x-axis is to your right, the positive y-axis is up and the positive z-axis is backwards. Think of your screen being the center of the 3 axes and the positive z-axis going through your screen towards you. The axes are drawn as follows:

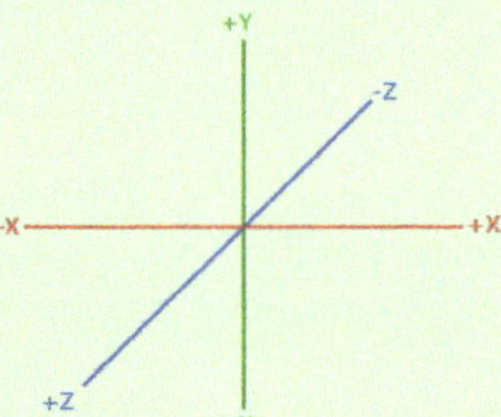

To understand why it's called right-handed do the following:

- Stretch your right-arm along the positive y-axis with your hand up top.
- Let your thumb point to the right.
- Let your pointing finger point up.
- Now bend your middle finger downwards 90 degrees.

If you did things right, your thumb should point towards the positive x-axis, the pointing finger towards the positive y-axis and your middle finger towards the positive z-axis. If you were to do this with your left-arm you would see the z-axis is reversed. This is known as a left-handed system and is commonly used by DirectX. Note that in normalized device coordinates OpenGL actually uses a left-handed system (the projection matrix switches the handedness).

We'll discuss how to move around the scene in more detail in the next chapter. For now the view matrix looks like this:

```cpp
glm::mat4 view = glm::mat4(1.0f);
// note that we're translating the scene in the reverse direction
view = glm::translate(view, glm::vec3(0.0f, 0.0f, -3.0f));
```

The last thing we need to define is the projection matrix. We want to use perspective projection for our scene so we'll declare the projection matrix like this:

```cpp
glm::mat4 projection;
projection = glm::perspective(glm::radians(45.0f), 800.0f / 600.0f, 0.1f,
                              100.0f);
```

Now that we created the transformation matrices we should pass them to our shaders. First let's declare the transformation matrices as uniforms in the vertex shader and multiply them with the vertex coordinates:

```glsl
#version 330 core
layout (location = 0) in vec3 aPos;
...
uniform mat4 model;
uniform mat4 view;
uniform mat4 projection;
```

```
void main()
{
    // note that we read the multiplication from right to left
    gl_Position = projection * view * model * vec4(aPos, 1.0);
    ...
}
```

We should also send the matrices to the shader (this is usually done each frame since transformation matrices tend to change a lot):

```
int modelLoc = glGetUniformLocation(ourShader.ID, "model");
glUniformMatrix4fv(modelLoc, 1, GL_FALSE, glm::value_ptr(model));
... // same for View Matrix and Projection Matrix
```

Now that our vertex coordinates are transformed via the model, view and projection matrix the final object should be:

- Tilted backwards to the floor.
- A bit farther away from us.
- Be displayed with perspective (it should get smaller, the further its vertices are).

Let's check if the result actually does fulfill these requirements:

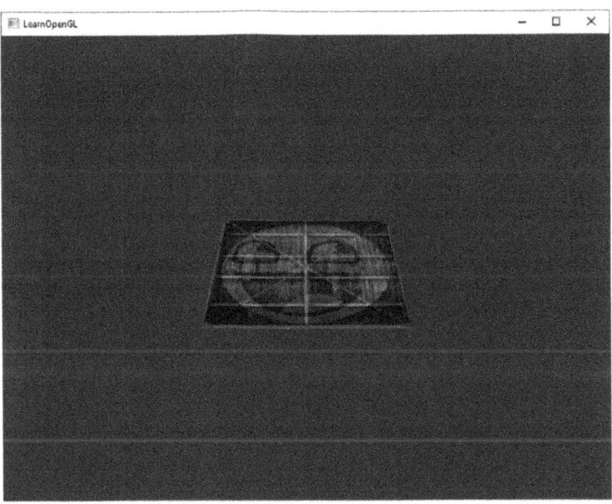

It does indeed look like the plane is a 3D plane that's resting at some imaginary floor. If you're not getting the same result, compare your code with the complete source code at /src/1. getting_started/6.1.coordinate_systems/.

9.8 More 3D

So far we've been working with a 2D plane, even in 3D space, so let's take the adventurous route and extend our 2D plane to a 3D cube. To render a cube we need a total of 36 vertices (6 faces * 2 triangles * 3 vertices each). 36 vertices are a lot to sum up, but let's list them here anyways:

```
float vertices[] = {
    -0.5f, -0.5f, -0.5f,  0.0f, 0.0f,
     0.5f, -0.5f, -0.5f,  1.0f, 0.0f,
     0.5f,  0.5f, -0.5f,  1.0f, 1.0f,
     0.5f,  0.5f, -0.5f,  1.0f, 1.0f,
```

```cpp
    -0.5f,  0.5f, -0.5f,  0.0f, 1.0f,
    -0.5f, -0.5f, -0.5f,  0.0f, 0.0f,

    -0.5f, -0.5f,  0.5f,  0.0f, 0.0f,
     0.5f, -0.5f,  0.5f,  1.0f, 0.0f,
     0.5f,  0.5f,  0.5f,  1.0f, 1.0f,
     0.5f,  0.5f,  0.5f,  1.0f, 1.0f,
    -0.5f,  0.5f,  0.5f,  0.0f, 1.0f,
    -0.5f, -0.5f,  0.5f,  0.0f, 0.0f,

    -0.5f,  0.5f,  0.5f,  1.0f, 0.0f,
    -0.5f,  0.5f, -0.5f,  1.0f, 1.0f,
    -0.5f, -0.5f, -0.5f,  0.0f, 1.0f,
    -0.5f, -0.5f, -0.5f,  0.0f, 1.0f,
    -0.5f, -0.5f,  0.5f,  0.0f, 0.0f,
    -0.5f,  0.5f,  0.5f,  1.0f, 0.0f,

     0.5f,  0.5f,  0.5f,  1.0f, 0.0f,
     0.5f,  0.5f, -0.5f,  1.0f, 1.0f,
     0.5f, -0.5f, -0.5f,  0.0f, 1.0f,
     0.5f, -0.5f, -0.5f,  0.0f, 1.0f,
     0.5f, -0.5f,  0.5f,  0.0f, 0.0f,
     0.5f,  0.5f,  0.5f,  1.0f, 0.0f,

    -0.5f, -0.5f, -0.5f,  0.0f, 1.0f,
     0.5f, -0.5f, -0.5f,  1.0f, 1.0f,
     0.5f, -0.5f,  0.5f,  1.0f, 0.0f,
     0.5f, -0.5f,  0.5f,  1.0f, 0.0f,
    -0.5f, -0.5f,  0.5f,  0.0f, 0.0f,
    -0.5f, -0.5f, -0.5f,  0.0f, 1.0f,

    -0.5f,  0.5f, -0.5f,  0.0f, 1.0f,
     0.5f,  0.5f, -0.5f,  1.0f, 1.0f,
     0.5f,  0.5f,  0.5f,  1.0f, 0.0f,
     0.5f,  0.5f,  0.5f,  1.0f, 0.0f,
    -0.5f,  0.5f,  0.5f,  0.0f, 0.0f,
    -0.5f,  0.5f, -0.5f,  0.0f, 1.0f
};
```

For fun, we'll let the cube rotate over time:

```cpp
model = glm::rotate(model, (float)glfwGetTime() * glm::radians(50.0f),
                    glm::vec3(0.5f, 1.0f, 0.0f));
```

And then we'll draw the cube using `glDrawArrays` (as we didn't specify indices), but this time with a count of 36 vertices.

```cpp
glDrawArrays(GL_TRIANGLES, 0, 36);
```

You should get something similar to the following:

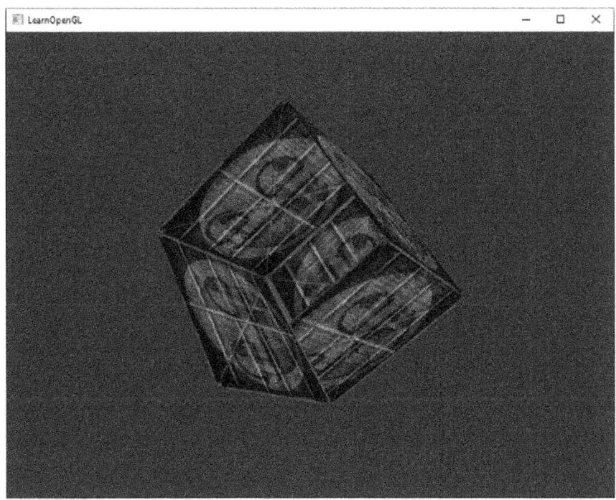

It does resemble a cube slightly but something's off. Some sides of the cubes are being drawn over other sides of the cube. This happens because when OpenGL draws your cube triangle-by-triangle, fragment by fragment, it will overwrite any pixel color that may have already been drawn there before. Since OpenGL gives no guarantee on the order of triangles rendered (within the same draw call), some triangles are drawn on top of each other even though one should clearly be in front of the other.

Luckily, OpenGL stores depth information in a buffer called the z-buffer that allows OpenGL to decide when to draw over a pixel and when not to. Using the z-buffer we can configure OpenGL to do depth-testing.

9.8.1 Z-buffer

OpenGL stores all its depth information in a z-buffer, also known as a depth buffer. GLFW automatically creates such a buffer for you (just like it has a color-buffer that stores the colors of the output image). The depth is stored within each fragment (as the fragment's z value) and whenever the fragment wants to output its color, OpenGL compares its depth values with the z-buffer. If the current fragment is behind the other fragment it is discarded, otherwise overwritten. This process is called depth testing and is done automatically by OpenGL.

However, if we want to make sure OpenGL actually performs the depth testing we first need to tell OpenGL we want to enable depth testing; it is disabled by default. We can enable depth testing using `glEnable`. The `glEnable` and `glDisable` functions allow us to enable/disable certain functionality in OpenGL. That functionality is then enabled/disabled until another call is made to disable/enable it. Right now we want to enable depth testing by enabling `GL_DEPTH_TEST`:

```
glEnable(GL_DEPTH_TEST);
```

Since we're using a depth buffer we also want to clear the depth buffer before each render iteration (otherwise the depth information of the previous frame stays in the buffer). Just like clearing the color buffer, we can clear the depth buffer by specifying the `DEPTH_BUFFER_BIT` bit in the `glClear` function:

```
glClear(GL_COLOR_BUFFER_BIT | GL_DEPTH_BUFFER_BIT);
```

Let's re-run our program and see if OpenGL now performs depth testing:

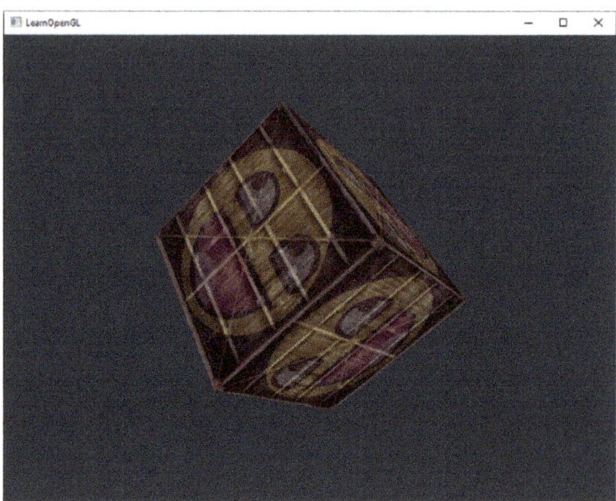

There we go! A fully textured cube with proper depth testing that rotates over time. Check the source code at `/src/1.getting_started/6.2.coordinate_systems_depth/`.

9.8.2 More cubes!

Say we wanted to display 10 of our cubes on screen. Each cube will look the same but will only differ in where it's located in the world with each a different rotation. The graphical layout of the cube is already defined so we don't have to change our buffers or attribute arrays when rendering more objects. The only thing we have to change for each object is its model matrix where we transform the cubes into the world.

First, let's define a translation vector for each cube that specifies its position in world space. We'll define 10 cube positions in a `glm::vec3` array:

```cpp
glm::vec3 cubePositions[] = {
    glm::vec3( 0.0f,  0.0f,   0.0f),
    glm::vec3( 2.0f,  5.0f, -15.0f),
    glm::vec3(-1.5f, -2.2f,  -2.5f),
    glm::vec3(-3.8f, -2.0f, -12.3f),
    glm::vec3( 2.4f, -0.4f,  -3.5f),
    glm::vec3(-1.7f,  3.0f,  -7.5f),
    glm::vec3( 1.3f, -2.0f,  -2.5f),
    glm::vec3( 1.5f,  2.0f,  -2.5f),
    glm::vec3( 1.5f,  0.2f,  -1.5f),
    glm::vec3(-1.3f,  1.0f,  -1.5f)
};
```

Now, within the render loop we want to call `glDrawArrays` 10 times, but this time send a different model matrix to the vertex shader each time before we send out the draw call. We will create a small loop within the render loop that renders our object 10 times with a different model matrix each time. Note that we also add a small unique rotation to each container.

```cpp
glBindVertexArray(VAO);
for(unsigned int i = 0; i < 10; i++)
{
    glm::mat4 model = glm::mat4(1.0f);
    model = glm::translate(model, cubePositions[i]);
    float angle = 20.0f * i;
    model = glm::rotate(model, glm::radians(angle),
                        glm::vec3(1.0f, 0.3f, 0.5f));
```

```
    ourShader.setMat4("model", model);

    glDrawArrays(GL_TRIANGLES, 0, 36);
}
```

This snippet of code will update the model matrix each time a new cube is drawn and do this 10 times in total. Right now we should be looking into a world filled with 10 oddly rotated cubes:

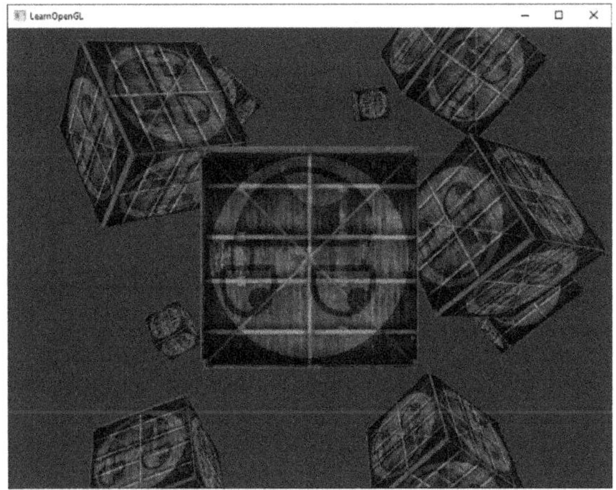

Perfect! It looks like our container found some like-minded friends. If you're stuck see if you can compare your code with the full source code at `/src/1.getting_started/6.3.coordinate_systems_multiple/`.

9.9 Exercises

- Try experimenting with the `FoV` and `aspect-ratio` parameters of GLM's `projection` function. See if you can figure out how those affect the perspective frustum.
- Play with the view matrix by translating in several directions and see how the scene changes. Think of the view matrix as a camera object.
- Try to make every 3rd container (including the 1st) rotate over time, while leaving the other containers static using just the model matrix. Solution: `/src/1.getting_started/6.4.coordinate_systems_exercise3/`.

10. Camera

In the previous chapter we discussed the view matrix and how we can use the view matrix to move around the scene (we moved backwards a little). OpenGL by itself is not familiar with the concept of a *camera*, but we can try to simulate one by moving all objects in the scene in the reverse direction, giving the illusion that **we** are moving.

In this chapter we'll discuss how we can set up a camera in OpenGL. We will discuss a fly style camera that allows you to freely move around in a 3D scene. We'll also discuss keyboard and mouse input and finish with a custom camera class.

10.1 Camera/View space

When we're talking about camera/view space we're talking about all the vertex coordinates as seen from the camera's perspective as the origin of the scene: the view matrix transforms all the world coordinates into view coordinates that are relative to the camera's position and direction. To define a camera we need its position in world space, the direction it's looking at, a vector pointing to the right and a vector pointing upwards from the camera. A careful reader may notice that we're actually going to create a coordinate system with 3 perpendicular unit axes with the camera's position as the origin.

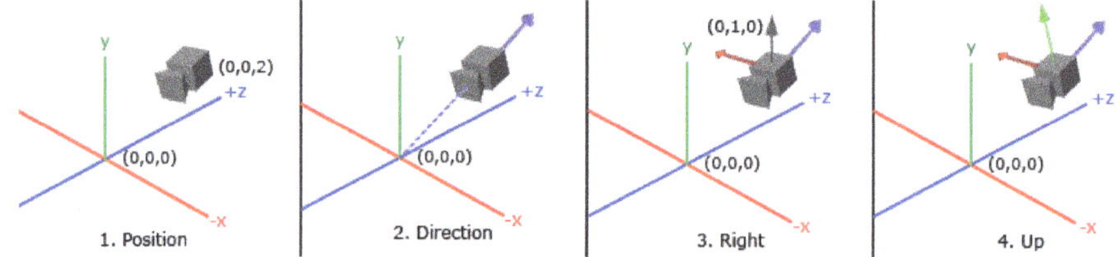

10.1.1 1. Camera position

Getting the camera position is easy. The camera position is a vector in world space that points to the camera's position. We set the camera at the same position we've set the camera in the previous chapter:

```
glm::vec3 cameraPos = glm::vec3(0.0f, 0.0f, 3.0f);
```

> Don't forget that the positive z-axis is going through your screen towards you so if we want the camera to move backwards, we move along the positive z-axis.

10.1.2 2. Camera direction

The next vector required is the camera's direction e.g. at what direction it is pointing at. For now we let the camera point to the origin of our scene: $(0,0,0)$. Remember that if we subtract two vectors from each other we get a vector that's the difference of these two vectors? Subtracting the camera position vector from the scene's origin vector thus results in the direction vector we want. For the view matrix's coordinate system we want its z-axis to be positive and because by convention (in OpenGL) the camera points towards the negative z-axis we want to negate the direction vector. If we switch the subtraction order around we now get a vector pointing towards the camera's positive z-axis:

```
glm::vec3 cameraTarget = glm::vec3(0.0f, 0.0f, 0.0f);
glm::vec3 cameraDirection = glm::normalize(cameraPos - cameraTarget);
```

> The name *direction* vector is not the best chosen name, since it is actually pointing in the reverse direction of what it is targeting.

10.1.3 3. Right axis

The next vector that we need is a *right* vector that represents the positive x-axis of the camera space. To get the *right* vector we use a little trick by first specifying an *up* vector that points upwards (in world space). Then we do a cross product on the up vector and the direction vector from step 2. Since the result of a cross product is a vector perpendicular to both vectors, we will get a vector that points in the positive x-axis's direction (if we would switch the cross product order we'd get a vector that points in the negative x-axis):

```cpp
glm::vec3 up = glm::vec3(0.0f, 1.0f, 0.0f);
glm::vec3 cameraRight = glm::normalize(glm::cross(up, cameraDirection));
```

10.1.4 4. Up axis

Now that we have both the x-axis vector and the z-axis vector, retrieving the vector that points to the camera's positive y-axis is relatively easy: we take the cross product of the right and direction vector:

```cpp
glm::vec3 cameraUp = glm::cross(cameraDirection, cameraRight);
```

With the help of the cross product and a few tricks we were able to create all the vectors that form the view/camera space. For the more mathematically inclined readers, this process is known as the Gram-Schmidt process[1] in linear algebra. Using these camera vectors we can now create a LookAt matrix that proves very useful for creating a camera.

10.2 Look At

A great thing about matrices is that if you define a coordinate space using 3 perpendicular (or non-linear) axes you can create a matrix with those 3 axes plus a translation vector and you can transform any vector to that coordinate space by multiplying it with this matrix. This is exactly what the *LookAt* matrix does and now that we have 3 perpendicular axes and a position vector to define the camera space we can create our own LookAt matrix:

$$LookAt = \begin{bmatrix} R_x & R_y & R_z & 0 \\ U_x & U_y & U_z & 0 \\ D_x & D_y & D_z & 0 \\ 0 & 0 & 0 & 1 \end{bmatrix} * \begin{bmatrix} 1 & 0 & 0 & -P_x \\ 0 & 1 & 0 & -P_y \\ 0 & 0 & 1 & -P_z \\ 0 & 0 & 0 & 1 \end{bmatrix}$$

Where R is the right vector, U is the up vector, D is the direction vector and P is the camera's position vector. Note that the rotation (left matrix) and translation (right matrix) parts are inverted (transposed and negated respectively) since we want to rotate and translate the world in the opposite direction of where we want the camera to move. Using this LookAt matrix as our view matrix effectively transforms all the world coordinates to the view space we just defined. The LookAt matrix then does exactly what it says: it creates a view matrix that *looks* at a given target.

Luckily for us, GLM already does all this work for us. We only have to specify a camera position, a target position and a vector that represents the up vector in world space (the up vector we used for calculating the right vector). GLM then creates the LookAt matrix that we can use as our view matrix:

---

[1] en.wikipedia.org/wiki/Gram-Schmidt_process

```
glm::mat4 view;
view = glm::lookAt(glm::vec3(0.0f, 0.0f, 3.0f),
                   glm::vec3(0.0f, 0.0f, 0.0f),
                   glm::vec3(0.0f, 1.0f, 0.0f));
```

The `glm::LookAt` function requires a position, target and up vector respectively. This example creates a view matrix that is the same as the one we created in the previous chapter.

Before delving into user input, let's get a little funky first by rotating the camera around our scene. We keep the target of the scene at `(0,0,0)`. We use a little bit of trigonometry to create an `x` and `z` coordinate each frame that represents a point on a circle and we'll use these for our camera position. By re-calculating the `x` and `y` coordinate over time we're traversing all the points in a circle and thus the camera rotates around the scene. We enlarge this circle by a pre-defined `radius` and create a new view matrix each frame using GLFW's `glfwGetTime` function:

```
const float radius = 10.0f;
float camX = sin(glfwGetTime()) * radius;
float camZ = cos(glfwGetTime()) * radius;
glm::mat4 view;
view = glm::lookAt(glm::vec3(camX, 0.0, camZ), glm::vec3(0.0, 0.0, 0.0),
                   glm::vec3(0.0, 1.0, 0.0));
```

If you run this code you should get something like this:

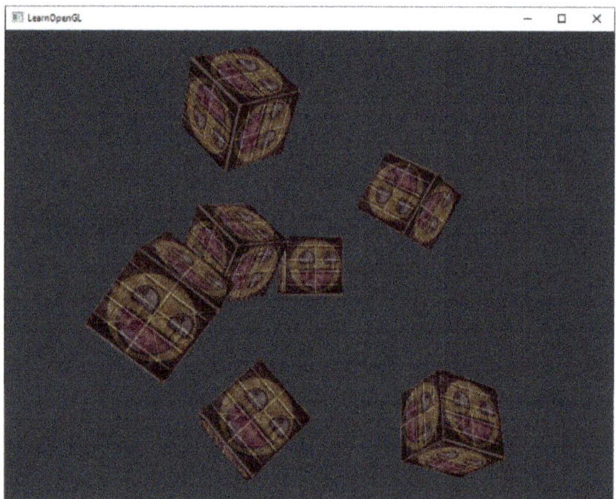

With this little snippet of code the camera now circles around the scene over time. Feel free to experiment with the radius and position/direction parameters to get the feel of how this *LookAt* matrix works. Also, check the source code at `/src/1.getting_started/7.1.camera_circle/` if you're stuck.

10.3 Walk around

Swinging the camera around a scene is fun, but it's more fun to do all the movement ourselves! First we need to set up a camera system, so it is useful to define some camera variables at the top of our program:

```
glm::vec3 cameraPos   = glm::vec3(0.0f, 0.0f, 3.0f);
glm::vec3 cameraFront = glm::vec3(0.0f, 0.0f, -1.0f);
glm::vec3 cameraUp    = glm::vec3(0.0f, 1.0f, 0.0f);
```

The `LookAt` function now becomes:

```cpp
view = glm::lookAt(cameraPos, cameraPos + cameraFront, cameraUp);
```

First we set the camera position to the previously defined `cameraPos`. The direction is the current position + the direction vector we just defined. This ensures that however we move, the camera keeps looking at the target direction. Let's play a bit with these variables by updating the `cameraPos` vector when we press some keys.

We already defined a `processInput` function to manage GLFW's keyboard input so let's add a few extra key commands:

```cpp
void processInput(GLFWwindow *window)
{
    ...
    const float cameraSpeed = 0.05f; // adjust accordingly
    if (glfwGetKey(window, GLFW_KEY_W) == GLFW_PRESS)
        cameraPos += cameraSpeed * cameraFront;
    if (glfwGetKey(window, GLFW_KEY_S) == GLFW_PRESS)
        cameraPos -= cameraSpeed * cameraFront;
    if (glfwGetKey(window, GLFW_KEY_A) == GLFW_PRESS)
        cameraPos -= glm::normalize(glm::cross(cameraFront, cameraUp)) *
    cameraSpeed;
    if (glfwGetKey(window, GLFW_KEY_D) == GLFW_PRESS)
        cameraPos += glm::normalize(glm::cross(cameraFront, cameraUp)) *
    cameraSpeed;
}
```

Whenever we press one of the `WASD` keys, the camera's position is updated accordingly. If we want to move forward or backwards we add or subtract the direction vector from the position vector scaled by some speed value. If we want to move sideways we do a cross product to create a *right* vector and we move along the right vector accordingly. This creates the familiar strafe effect when using the camera.

> Note that we normalize the resulting *right* vector. If we wouldn't normalize this vector, the resulting cross product may return differently sized vectors based on the `cameraFront` variable. If we would not normalize the vector we would move slow or fast based on the camera's orientation instead of at a consistent movement speed.

By now, you should already be able to move the camera somewhat, albeit at a speed that's system-specific so you may need to adjust `cameraSpeed`.

10.4 Movement speed

Currently we used a constant value for movement speed when walking around. In theory this seems fine, but in practice people's machines have different processing powers and the result of that is that some people are able to render much more frames than others each second. Whenever a user renders more frames than another user he also calls `processInput` more often. The result is that some people move really fast and some really slow depending on their setup. When shipping your application you want to make sure it runs the same on all kinds of hardware.

Graphics applications and games usually keep track of a deltatime variable that stores the time it took to render the last frame. We then multiply all velocities with this `deltaTime` value. The result is that when we have a large `deltaTime` in a frame, meaning that the last frame took longer than average, the velocity for that frame will also be a bit higher to balance it all out. When using this approach it does not matter if you have a very fast or slow pc, the velocity of the camera will be balanced out accordingly so each user will have the same experience.

To calculate the `deltaTime` value we keep track of 2 global variables:

```
float deltaTime = 0.0f; // Time between current frame and last frame
float lastFrame = 0.0f; // Time of last frame
```

Within each frame we then calculate the new `deltaTime` value for later use:

```
float currentFrame = glfwGetTime();
deltaTime = currentFrame - lastFrame;
lastFrame = currentFrame;
```

Now that we have `deltaTime` we can take it into account when calculating the velocities:

```
void processInput(GLFWwindow *window)
{
    float cameraSpeed = 2.5f * deltaTime;
    [...]
}
```

Since we're using `deltaTime` the camera will now move at a constant speed of `2.5` units per second. Together with the previous section we should now have a much smoother and more consistent camera system for moving around the scene:

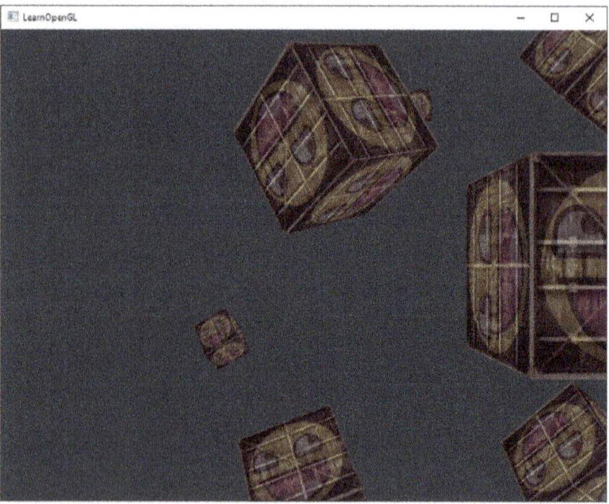

And now we have a camera that walks and looks equally fast on any system. Again, check the source code at `/src/1.getting_started/7.2.camera_keyboard_dt/` if you're stuck. We'll see the `deltaTime` value frequently return with anything movement related.

10.5 Look around

Only using the keyboard keys to move around isn't that interesting. Especially since we can't turn around making the movement rather restricted. That's where the mouse comes in!

To look around the scene we have to change the `cameraFront` vector based on the input of the mouse. However, changing the direction vector based on mouse rotations is a little complicated and requires some trigonometry. If you do not understand the trigonometry, don't worry, you can just skip to the code sections and paste them in your code; you can always come back later if you want to know more.

10.6 **Euler angles**

Euler angles are 3 values that can represent any rotation in 3D, defined by Leonhard Euler somewhere in the 1700s. There are 3 Euler angles: *pitch*, *yaw* and *roll*. The following image gives them a visual meaning:

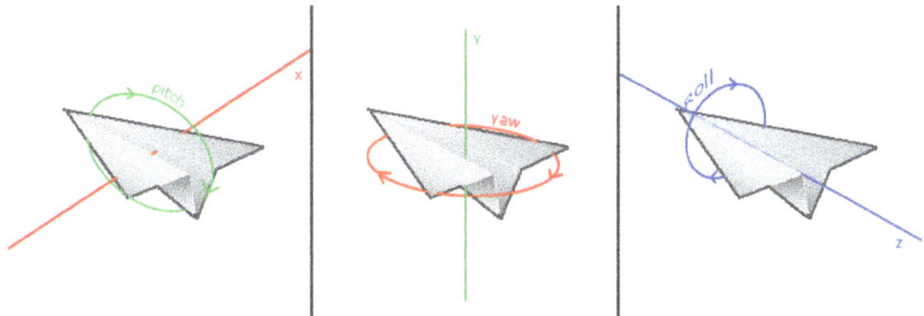

The pitch is the angle that depicts how much we're looking up or down as seen in the first image. The second image shows the yaw value which represents the magnitude we're looking to the left or to the right. The roll represents how much we *roll* as mostly used in space-flight cameras. Each of the Euler angles are represented by a single value and with the combination of all 3 of them we can calculate any rotation vector in 3D.

For our camera system we only care about the yaw and pitch values so we won't discuss the roll value here. Given a pitch and a yaw value we can convert them into a 3D vector that represents a new direction vector. The process of converting yaw and pitch values to a direction vector requires a bit of trigonometry. and we start with a basic case:

Let's start with a bit of a refresher and check the general right triangle case (with one side at a 90 degree angle):

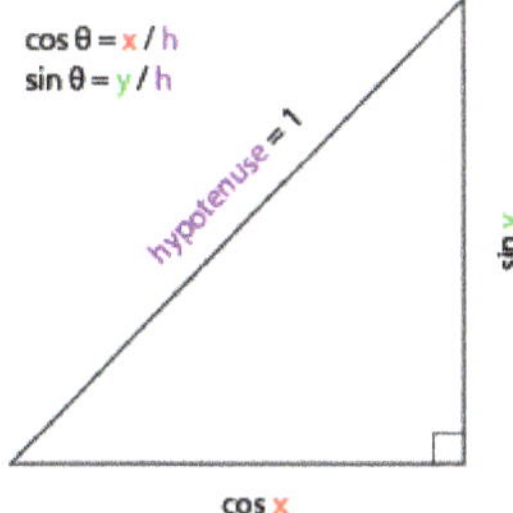

If we define the hypotenuse to be of length 1 we know from trigonometry (soh cah toa) that the adjacent side's length is $\cos x/h = \cos x/1 = \cos x$ and that the opposing side's length is $\sin y/h = \sin y/1 = \sin y$. This gives us some general formulas for retrieving the length in both the x and y sides on right triangles, depending on the given angle. Let's use this to calculate the components of the direction vector.

Let's imagine this same triangle, but now looking at it from a top perspective with the adjacent and opposite sides being parallel to the scene's x and z axis (as if looking down the y-axis).

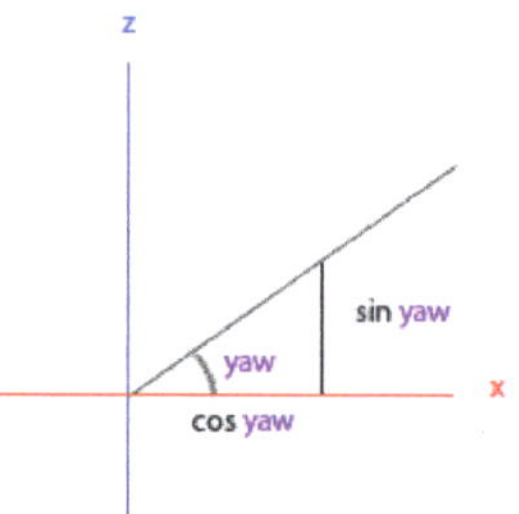

If we visualize the yaw angle to be the counter-clockwise angle starting from the x side we can see that the length of the x side relates to `cos(yaw)`. And similarly how the length of the z side relates to `sin(yaw)`.

If we take this knowledge and a given `yaw` value we can use it to create a camera direction vector:

```cpp
glm::vec3 direction;
direction.x = cos(glm::radians(yaw)); // convert to radians first
direction.z = sin(glm::radians(yaw));
```

This solves how we can get a 3D direction vector from a yaw value, but pitch needs to be included as well. Let's now look at the y axis side as if we're sitting on the xz plane:

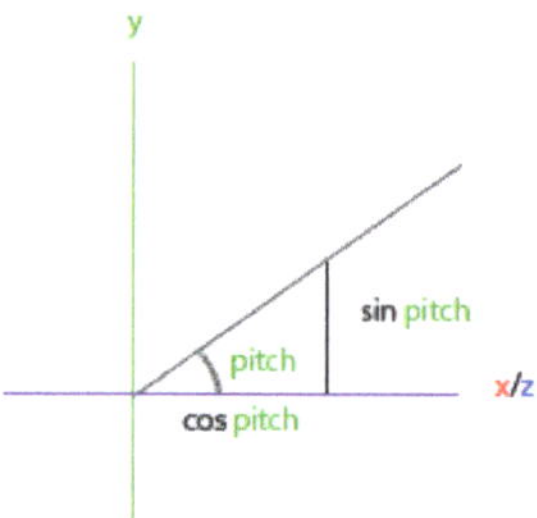

Similarly, from this triangle we can see that the direction's y component equals `sin(pitch)` so let's fill that in:

```cpp
direction.y = sin(glm::radians(pitch));
```

However, from the pitch triangle we can also see the xz sides are influenced by `cos(pitch)` so we need to make sure this is also part of the direction vector. With this included we get the final direction vector as translated from yaw and pitch Euler angles:

```cpp
direction.x = cos(glm::radians(yaw)) * cos(glm::radians(pitch));
direction.y = sin(glm::radians(pitch));
direction.z = sin(glm::radians(yaw)) * cos(glm::radians(pitch));
```

This gives us a formula to convert yaw and pitch values to a 3-dimensional direction vector that we can use for looking around.

We've set up the scene world so everything's positioned in the direction of the negative z-axis. However, if we look at the x and z yaw triangle we see that a θ of 0 results in the camera's `direction` vector to point towards the positive x-axis. To make sure the camera points towards the negative z-axis by default we can give the `yaw` a default value of a 90 degree clockwise rotation. Positive degrees rotate counter-clockwise so we set the default `yaw` value to:

```
yaw = -90.0f;
```

You've probably wondered by now: how do we set and modify these yaw and pitch values?

10.7 Mouse input

The yaw and pitch values are obtained from mouse (or controller/joystick) movement where horizontal mouse-movement affects the yaw and vertical mouse-movement affects the pitch. The idea is to store the last frame's mouse positions and calculate in the current frame how much the mouse values changed. The higher the horizontal or vertical difference, the more we update the pitch or yaw value and thus the more the camera should move.

First we will tell GLFW that it should hide the cursor and capture it. Capturing a cursor means that, once the application has focus, the mouse cursor stays within the center of the window (unless the application loses focus or quits). We can do this with one simple configuration call:

```
glfwSetInputMode(window, GLFW_CURSOR, GLFW_CURSOR_DISABLED);
```

After this call, wherever we move the mouse it won't be visible and it should not leave the window. This is perfect for an FPS camera system.

To calculate the pitch and yaw values we need to tell GLFW to listen to mouse-movement events. We do this by creating a callback function with the following prototype:

```
void mouse_callback(GLFWwindow* window, double xpos, double ypos);
```

Here `xpos` and `ypos` represent the current mouse positions. As soon as we register the callback function with GLFW each time the mouse moves, the `mouse_callback` function is called:

```
glfwSetCursorPosCallback(window, mouse_callback);
```

When handling mouse input for a fly style camera there are several steps we have to take before we're able to fully calculate the camera's direction vector:

1. Calculate the mouse's offset since the last frame.
2. Add the offset values to the camera's yaw and pitch values.
3. Add some constraints to the minimum/maximum pitch values.
4. Calculate the direction vector.

The first step is to calculate the offset of the mouse since last frame. We first have to store the last mouse positions in the application, which we initialize to be in the center of the screen (screen size is 800 by 600) initially:

```
float lastX = 400, lastY = 300;
```

Then in the mouse's callback function we calculate the offset movement between the last and current frame:

```
float xoffset = xpos - lastX;
float yoffset = lastY - ypos; // reversed: y ranges bottom to top
lastX = xpos;
lastY = ypos;

const float sensitivity = 0.1f;
xoffset *= sensitivity;
yoffset *= sensitivity;
```

Note that we multiply the offset values by a `sensitivity` value. If we omit this multiplication the mouse movement would be way too strong; fiddle around with the sensitivity value to your liking.

Next we add the offset values to the globally declared `pitch` and `yaw` values:

```
yaw   += xoffset;
pitch += yoffset;
```

In the third step we'd like to add some constraints to the camera so users won't be able to make weird camera movements (also causes a LookAt flip once direction vector is parallel to the world up direction). The pitch needs to be constrained in such a way that users won't be able to look higher than 89 degrees (at 90 degrees we get the LookAt flip) and also not below -89 degrees. This ensures the user will be able to look up to the sky or below to his feet but not further. The constraints work by replacing the Euler value with its constraint value whenever it breaches the constraint:

```
if(pitch > 89.0f)
    pitch = 89.0f;
if(pitch < -89.0f)
    pitch = -89.0f;
```

Note that we set no constraint on the yaw value since we don't want to constrain the user in horizontal rotation. However, it's just as easy to add a constraint to the yaw as well if you feel like it.

The fourth and last step is to calculate the actual direction vector using the formula from the previous section:

```
glm::vec3 direction;
direction.x = cos(glm::radians(yaw)) * cos(glm::radians(pitch));
direction.y = sin(glm::radians(pitch));
direction.z = sin(glm::radians(yaw)) * cos(glm::radians(pitch));
cameraFront = glm::normalize(direction);
```

This computed direction vector then contains all the rotations calculated from the mouse's movement. Since the `cameraFront` vector is already included in glm's `lookAt` function we're set to go.

If you'd now run the code you'll notice the camera makes a large sudden jump whenever the window first receives focus of your mouse cursor. The cause for this sudden jump is that as soon as your cursor enters the window the mouse callback function is called with an `xpos` and `ypos` position equal to the location your mouse entered the screen from. This is often a position that is significantly far away from the center of the screen, resulting in large offsets and thus a large movement jump. We can circumvent this issue by defining a global `bool` variable to check if this is the first time we receive mouse input. If it is the first time, we update the initial mouse positions to the new `xpos` and `ypos` values. The resulting mouse movements will then use the newly entered mouse's position coordinates to calculate the offsets:

```cpp
if (firstMouse) // initially set to true
{
    lastX = xpos;
    lastY = ypos;
    firstMouse = false;
}
```

The final code then becomes:

```cpp
void mouse_callback(GLFWwindow* window, double xpos, double ypos)
{
    if (firstMouse)
    {
        lastX = xpos;
        lastY = ypos;
        firstMouse = false;
    }

    float xoffset = xpos - lastX;
    float yoffset = lastY - ypos;
    lastX = xpos;
    lastY = ypos;

    float sensitivity = 0.1f;
    xoffset *= sensitivity;
    yoffset *= sensitivity;

    yaw += xoffset;
    pitch += yoffset;

    if(pitch > 89.0f)
        pitch = 89.0f;
    if(pitch < -89.0f)
        pitch = -89.0f;

    glm::vec3 direction;
    direction.x = cos(glm::radians(yaw)) * cos(glm::radians(pitch));
    direction.y = sin(glm::radians(pitch));
    direction.z = sin(glm::radians(yaw)) * cos(glm::radians(pitch));
    cameraFront = glm::normalize(direction);
}
```

There we go! Give it a spin and you'll see that we can now freely move through our 3D scene!

10.8 Zoom

As a little extra to the camera system we'll also implement a zooming interface. In the previous chapter we said the *Field of view* or *fov* largely defines how much we can see of the scene. When the field of view becomes smaller, the scene's projected space gets smaller. This smaller space is projected over the same NDC, giving the illusion of zooming in. To zoom in, we're going to use the mouse's scroll wheel. Similar to mouse movement and keyboard input we have a callback function for mouse scrolling:

```cpp
void scroll_callback(GLFWwindow* window, double xoffset, double yoffset)
{
    Zoom -= (float)yoffset;
    if (Zoom < 1.0f)
        Zoom = 1.0f;
    if (Zoom > 45.0f)
        Zoom = 45.0f;
}
```

When scrolling, the `yoffset` value tells us the amount we scrolled vertically. When the `scroll_callback` function is called we change the content of the globally declared `fov` variable. Since `45.0` is the default fov value we want to constrain the zoom level between `1.0` and `45.0`.

We now have to upload the perspective projection matrix to the GPU each frame, but this time with the `fov` variable as its field of view:

```cpp
projection = glm::perspective(glm::radians(fov), 800.0f / 600.0f, 0.1f,
                              100.0f);
```

And lastly don't forget to register the scroll callback function:

```cpp
glfwSetScrollCallback(window, scroll_callback);
```

And there you have it. We implemented a simple camera system that allows for free movement in a 3D environment.

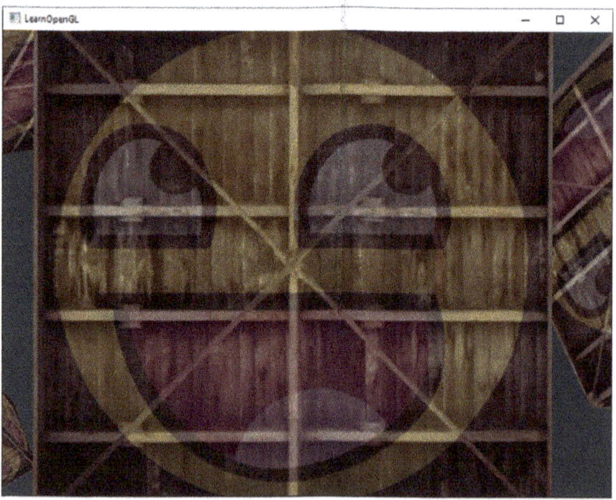

Feel free to experiment a little and if you're stuck compare your code with the full source code at `/src/1.getting_started/7.3.camera_mouse_zoom/`.

10.9 Camera class

In the upcoming chapters we'll always use a camera to easily look around the scenes and see the results from all angles. However, since the camera code can take up a significant amount of space on each chapter we'll abstract its details a little and create our own camera object that does most of the work for us with some neat little extras. Unlike the Shader chapter we won't walk you through creating the camera class, but provide you with the (fully commented) source code if you want to know the inner workings.

Like the `Shader` object, we define the camera class entirely in a single header file. You can find the class object at `/includes/learnopengl/camera.h`; you should be able to understand the code after this chapter. It is advised to at least check the class out once as an example on how you could create your own camera system.

> The camera system we introduced is a fly like camera that suits most purposes and works well with Euler angles, but be careful when creating different camera systems like an FPS camera, or a flight simulation camera. Each camera system has its own tricks and quirks so be sure to read up on them. For example, this fly camera doesn't allow for pitch values higher than or equal to `90` degrees and a static up vector of `(0,1,0)` doesn't work when we take roll values into account.

The updated version of the source code using the new camera object can be found at `/src/1.getting_started/7.4.camera_class/`.

10.10 Exercises

- See if you can transform the camera class in such a way that it becomes a **true** fps camera where you cannot fly; you can only look around while staying on the `xz` plane. Solution: `/src/1.getting_started/7.5.camera_exercise1/`.
- Try to create your own LookAt function where you manually create a view matrix as discussed at the start of this chapter. Replace glm's LookAt function with your own implementation and see if it still acts the same. Solution: `/src/1.getting_started/7.6.camera_exercise2/`.

11. Review

Congratulations on reaching the end of the *Getting started* chapters. By now you should be able to create a window, create and compile shaders, send vertex data to your shaders via buffer objects or uniforms, draw objects, use textures, understand vectors and matrices and combine all that knowledge to create a full 3D scene with a camera to play around with.

Phew, there is a lot that we learned these last few chapters. Try to play around with what you learned, experiment a bit or come up with your own ideas and solutions to some of the problems. As soon as you feel you got the hang of all the materials we've discussed it's time to move on to the Lighting chapters.

11.1 Glossary

- `OpenGL`: a formal specification of a graphics API that defines the layout and output of each function.
- `GLAD`: an extension loading library that loads and sets all OpenGL's function pointers for us so we can use all (modern) OpenGL's functions.
- `Viewport`: the 2D window region where we render to.
- `Graphics Pipeline`: the entire process vertices have to walk through before ending up as one or more pixels on the screen.
- `Shader`: a small program that runs on the graphics card. Several stages of the graphics pipeline can use user-made shaders to replace existing functionality.
- `Vertex`: a collection of data that represent a single point.
- `Normalized Device Coordinates`: the coordinate system your vertices end up in after perspective division is performed on clip coordinates. All vertex positions in NDC between -1.0 and 1.0 will not be discarded or clipped and end up visible.
- `Vertex Buffer Object`: a buffer object that allocates memory on the GPU and stores all the vertex data there for the graphics card to use.
- `Vertex Array Object`: stores buffer and vertex attribute state information.
- `Element Buffer Object`: a buffer object that stores indices on the GPU for indexed drawing.
- `Uniform`: a special type of GLSL variable that is global (each shader in a shader program can access this uniform variable) and only has to be set once.
- `Texture`: a special type of image used in shaders and usually wrapped around objects, giving the illusion an object is extremely detailed.
- `Texture Wrapping`: defines the mode that specifies how OpenGL should sample textures when texture coordinates are outside the range: $(0, 1)$.
- `Texture Filtering`: defines the mode that specifies how OpenGL should sample the texture when there are several texels (texture pixels) to choose from. This usually occurs when a texture is magnified.
- `Mipmaps`: stored smaller versions of a texture where the appropriate sized version is chosen based on the distance to the viewer.
- `stb_image`: image loading library.
- `Texture Units`: allows for multiple textures on a single shader program by binding multiple textures, each to a different texture unit.
- `Vector`: a mathematical entity that defines directions and/or positions in any dimension.
- `Matrix`: a rectangular array of mathematical expressions with useful transformation properties.
- `GLM`: a mathematics library tailored for OpenGL.
- `Local Space`: the space an object begins in. All coordinates relative to an object's origin.
- `World Space`: all coordinates relative to a global origin.
- `View Space`: all coordinates as viewed from a camera's perspective.
- `Clip Space`: all coordinates as viewed from the camera's perspective but with projection applied. This is the space the vertex coordinates should end up in, as output of the vertex

shader. OpenGL does the rest (clipping/perspective division).

- `Screen Space`: all coordinates as viewed from the screen. Coordinates range from 0 to screen width/height.
- `LookAt`: a special type of view matrix that creates a coordinate system where all coordinates are rotated and translated in such a way that the user is looking at a given target from a given position.
- `Euler Angles`: defined as `yaw`, `pitch` and `roll` that allow us to form any 3D direction vector from these 3 values.

II Lighting

12. Colors

We briefly used and manipulated colors in the previous chapters, but never defined them properly. Here we'll discuss what colors are and start building the scene for the upcoming Lighting chapters.

In the real world, colors can take any known color value with each object having its own color(s). In the digital world we need to map the (infinite) real colors to (limited) digital values and therefore not all real-world colors can be represented digitally. Colors are digitally represented using a `red`, `green` and `blue` component commonly abbreviated as RGB. Using different combinations of just those 3 values, within a range of `[0,1]`, we can represent almost any color there is. For example, to get a *coral* color, we define a color vector as:

```cpp
glm::vec3 coral(1.0f, 0.5f, 0.31f);
```

The color of an object we see in real life is not the color it actually has, but is the color reflected from the object. The colors that aren't absorbed (rejected) by the object is the color we perceive of it. As an example, the light of the sun is perceived as a white light that is the combined sum of many different colors (as you can see in the image). If we would shine this white light on a blue toy, it would absorb all the white color's sub-colors except the blue color. Since the toy does not absorb the blue color part, it is reflected. This reflected light enters our eye, making it look like the toy has a blue color. The following image shows this for a coral colored toy where it reflects several colors with varying intensity:

You can see that the white sunlight is a collection of all the visible colors and the object absorbs a large portion of those colors. It only reflects those colors that represent the object's color and the combination of those is what we perceive (in this case a coral color).

Technically it's a bit more complicated, but we'll get to that in the PBR chapters.

These rules of color reflection apply directly in graphics-land. When we define a light source in OpenGL we want to give this light source a color. In the previous paragraph we had a white color so we'll give the light source a white color as well. If we would then multiply the light source's color with an object's color value, the resulting color would be the reflected color of the object (and thus its perceived color). Let's revisit our toy (this time with a coral value) and see how we would calculate its perceived color in graphics-land. We get the resulting color vector by doing a component-wise multiplication between the light and object color vectors:

```cpp
glm::vec3 lightColor(1.0f, 1.0f, 1.0f);
glm::vec3 toyColor(1.0f, 0.5f, 0.31f);
glm::vec3 result = lightColor * toyColor; // = (1.0f, 0.5f, 0.31f);
```

We can see that the toy's color *absorbs* a large portion of the white light, but reflects several red, green and blue values based on its own color value. This is a representation of how colors would work in real life. We can thus define an object's color as *the amount of each color component it reflects from a light source*. Now what would happen if we used a green light?

```cpp
glm::vec3 lightColor(0.0f, 1.0f, 0.0f);
glm::vec3 toyColor(1.0f, 0.5f, 0.31f);
glm::vec3 result = lightColor * toyColor; // = (0.0f, 0.5f, 0.0f);
```

As we can see, the toy has no red and blue light to absorb and/or reflect. The toy also absorbs half of the light's green value, but also reflects half of the light's green value. The toy's color we perceive would then be a dark-greenish color. We can see that if we use a green light, only the green color components can be reflected and thus perceived; no red and blue colors are perceived. As a result the coral object suddenly becomes a dark-greenish object. Let's try one more example with a dark olive-green light:

```cpp
glm::vec3 lightColor(0.33f, 0.42f, 0.18f);
glm::vec3 toyColor(1.0f, 0.5f, 0.31f);
glm::vec3 result = lightColor * toyColor; // = (0.33f, 0.21f, 0.06f);
```

As you can see, we can get interesting colors from objects using different light colors. It's not hard to get creative with colors.

But enough about colors, let's start building a scene where we can experiment in.

12.1 A lighting scene

In the upcoming chapters we'll be creating interesting visuals by simulating real-world lighting making extensive use of colors. Since now we'll be using light sources we want to display them as visual objects in the scene and add at least one object to simulate the lighting from.

The first thing we need is an object to cast the light on and we'll use the infamous container cube from the previous chapters. We'll also be needing a light object to show where the light source is located in the 3D scene. For simplicity's sake we'll represent the light source with a cube as well.

So, filling a vertex buffer object, setting vertex attribute pointers and all that jazz should be familiar for you by now so we won't walk you through those steps. If you still have no idea what's going on with those I suggest you review the previous chapters, and work through the exercises if possible, before continuing.

So, the first thing we'll need is a vertex shader to draw the container. The vertex positions of the container remain the same (although we won't be needing texture coordinates this time) so the code should be nothing new. We'll be using a stripped down version of the vertex shader from the last chapters:

```glsl
#version 330 core
layout (location = 0) in vec3 aPos;

uniform mat4 model;
uniform mat4 view;
uniform mat4 projection;

void main()
{
    gl_Position = projection * view * model * vec4(aPos, 1.0);
}
```

Make sure to update the vertex data and attribute pointers to match the new vertex shader (if you want, you can actually keep the texture data and attribute pointers active; we're just not using them right now).

Because we're also going to render a light source cube, we want to generate a new VAO specifically for the light source. We could render the light source with the same VAO and then do a few light position transformations on the `model` matrix, but in the upcoming chapters we'll be changing the vertex data and attribute pointers of the container object quite often and we don't want these changes to propagate to the light source object (we only care about the light cube's vertex positions), so we'll create a new VAO:

```cpp
unsigned int lightVAO;
glGenVertexArrays(1, &lightVAO);
glBindVertexArray(lightVAO);
// we only need to bind to the VBO, the container's VBO's data
// already contains the data.
glBindBuffer(GL_ARRAY_BUFFER, VBO);
// set the vertex attributes (only position data for our lamp)
glVertexAttribPointer(0, 3, GL_FLOAT, GL_FALSE, 3 * sizeof(float),
                      (void*)0);
glEnableVertexAttribArray(0);
```

The code should be relatively straightforward. Now that we created both the container and the light source cube there is one thing left to define and that is the fragment shader for both the container and the light source:

```glsl
#version 330 core
out vec4 FragColor;

uniform vec3 objectColor;
uniform vec3 lightColor;

void main()
{
    FragColor = vec4(lightColor * objectColor, 1.0);
}
```

The fragment shader accepts both an object color and a light color from a uniform variable. Here we multiply the light's color with the object's (reflected) color like we discussed at the beginning of this chapter. Again, this shader should be easy to understand. Let's set the object's color to the last section's coral color with a white light:

```cpp
// don't forget to use the corresponding shader program first
lightingShader.use();
lightingShader.setVec3("objectColor", 1.0f, 0.5f, 0.31f);
lightingShader.setVec3("lightColor", 1.0f, 1.0f, 1.0f);
```

One thing left to note is that when we start to update these *lighting shaders* in the next chapters, the light source cube would also be affected and this is not what we want. We don't want the light source object's color to be affected the lighting calculations, but rather keep the light source isolated from the rest. We want the light source to have a constant bright color, unaffected by other color changes (this makes it look like the light source cube really is the source of the light).

To accomplish this we need to create a second set of shaders that we'll use to draw the light source cube, thus being safe from any changes to the lighting shaders. The vertex shader is the same as the lighting vertex shader so you can simply copy the source code over. The fragment shader of the light source cube ensures the cube's color remains bright by defining a constant white color on the lamp:

```glsl
#version 330 core
out vec4 FragColor;

void main()
{
    FragColor = vec4(1.0); // set all 4 vector values to 1.0
}
```

When we want to render, we want to render the container object (or possibly many other objects) using the lighting shader we just defined, and when we want to draw the light source we use the light source's shaders. During the Lighting chapters we'll gradually be updating the lighting shaders to slowly achieve more realistic results.

The main purpose of the light source cube is to show where the light comes from. We usually define a light source's position somewhere in the scene, but this is simply a position that has no visual meaning. To show where the light source actually is we render a cube at the same location of the light source. We render this cube with the light source cube shader to make sure the cube always stays white, regardless of the light conditions of the scene.

So let's declare a global `vec3` variable that represents the light source's location in world-space coordinates:

```cpp
glm::vec3 lightPos(1.2f, 1.0f, 2.0f);
```

We then translate the light source cube to the light source's position and scale it down before rendering it:

```cpp
model = glm::mat4(1.0f);
model = glm::translate(model, lightPos);
model = glm::scale(model, glm::vec3(0.2f));
```

The resulting render code for the light source cube should then look something like this:

```cpp
lightCubeShader.use();
// set the model, view and projection matrix uniforms
[...]
// draw the light cube object
glBindVertexArray(lightCubeVAO);
glDrawArrays(GL_TRIANGLES, 0, 36);
```

Injecting all the code fragments at their appropriate locations would then result in a clean OpenGL application properly configured for experimenting with lighting. If everything compiles it should look like this:

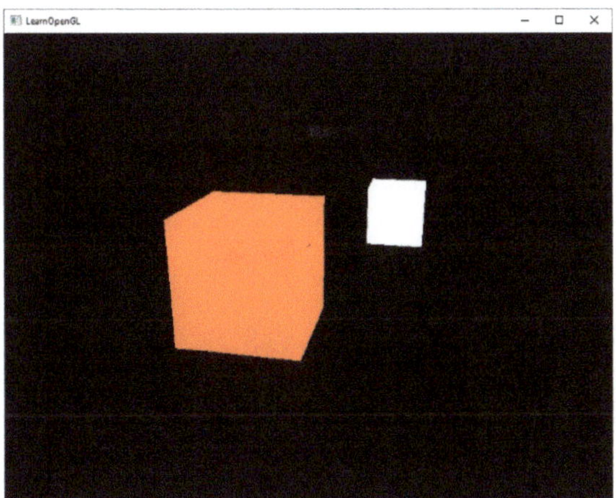

Not really much to look at right now, but I'll promise it'll get more interesting in the upcoming chapters.

If you have difficulties finding out where all the code snippets fit together in the application as a whole, check the source code at `/src/2.lighting/1.colors/` and carefully work your way through the code/comments.

13. Basic Lighting

Lighting in the real world is extremely complicated and depends on way too many factors, something we can't afford to calculate on the limited processing power we have. Lighting in OpenGL is therefore based on approximations of reality using simplified models that are much easier to process and look relatively similar. These lighting models are based on the physics of light as we understand it. One of those models is called the Phong lighting model. The major building blocks of the Phong lighting model consist of 3 components: ambient, diffuse and specular lighting. Below you can see what these lighting components look like on their own and combined:

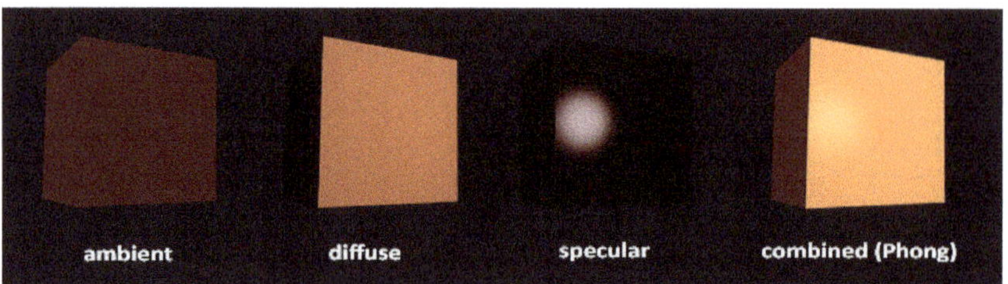

- Ambient lighting: even when it is dark there is usually still some light somewhere in the world (the moon, a distant light) so objects are almost never completely dark. To simulate this we use an ambient lighting constant that always gives the object some color.
- Diffuse lighting: simulates the directional impact a light object has on an object. This is the most visually significant component of the lighting model. The more a part of an object faces the light source, the brighter it becomes.
- Specular lighting: simulates the bright spot of a light that appears on shiny objects. Specular highlights are more inclined to the color of the light than the color of the object.

To create visually interesting scenes we want to at least simulate these 3 lighting components. We'll start with the simplest one: *ambient lighting*.

13.1 Ambient lighting

Light usually does not come from a single light source, but from many light sources scattered all around us, even when they're not immediately visible. One of the properties of light is that it can scatter and bounce in many directions, reaching spots that aren't directly visible; light can thus *reflect* on other surfaces and have an indirect impact on the lighting of an object. Algorithms that take this into consideration are called global illumination algorithms, but these are complicated and expensive to calculate.

Since we're not big fans of complicated and expensive algorithms we'll start by using a very simplistic model of global illumination, namely ambient lighting. As you've seen in the previous section we use a small constant (light) color that we add to the final resulting color of the object's fragments, thus making it look like there is always some scattered light even when there's not a direct light source.

Adding ambient lighting to the scene is really easy. We take the light's color, multiply it with a small constant ambient factor, multiply this with the object's color, and use that as the fragment's color in the cube object's shader:

```
void main()
{
    float ambientStrength = 0.1;
    vec3 ambient = ambientStrength * lightColor;

    vec3 result = ambient * objectColor;
    FragColor = vec4(result, 1.0);
}
```

If you'd now run the program, you'll notice that the first stage of lighting is now successfully applied to the object. The object is quite dark, but not completely since ambient lighting is applied (note that the light cube is unaffected because we use a different shader). It should look something like this:

13.2 Diffuse lighting

Ambient lighting by itself doesn't produce the most interesting results, but diffuse lighting however will start to give a significant visual impact on the object. Diffuse lighting gives the object more brightness the closer its fragments are aligned to the light rays from a light source. To give you a better understanding of diffuse lighting take a look at the following image:

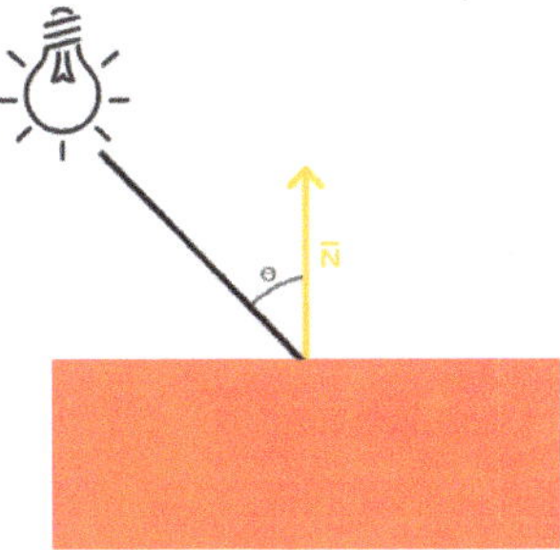

To the left we find a light source with a light ray targeted at a single fragment of our object. We need to measure at what angle the light ray touches the fragment. If the light ray is perpendicular to the object's surface the light has the greatest impact. To measure the angle between the light ray and the fragment we use something called a normal vector, that is a vector perpendicular to the fragment's surface (here depicted as a yellow arrow); we'll get to that later. The angle between the two vectors can then easily be calculated with the dot product.

You may remember from the *Transformations* chapter that, the lower the angle between two unit vectors, the more the dot product is inclined towards a value of 1. When the angle between both vectors is 90 degrees, the dot product becomes 0. The same applies to θ: the larger θ becomes, the less of an impact the light should have on the fragment's color.

> Note that to get (only) the cosine of the angle between both vectors we will work with *unit vectors* (vectors of length 1) so we need to make sure all the vectors are normalized, otherwise the dot product returns more than just the cosine (see the *Transformations* chapters).

The resulting dot product thus returns a scalar that we can use to calculate the light's impact on the fragment's color, resulting in differently lit fragments based on their orientation towards the light.

So, what do we need to calculate diffuse lighting:

- Normal vector: a vector that is perpendicular to the vertex' surface.
- The directed light ray: a direction vector that is the difference vector between the light's position and the fragment's position. To calculate this light ray we need the light's position vector and the fragment's position vector.

13.3 Normal vectors

A normal vector is a (unit) vector that is perpendicular to the surface of a vertex. Since a vertex by itself has no surface (it's just a single point in space) we retrieve a normal vector by using its surrounding vertices to figure out the surface of the vertex. We can use a little trick to calculate the normal vectors for all the cube's vertices by using the cross product, but since a 3D cube is not a complicated shape we can simply manually add them to the vertex data. We'll list the updated vertex data array next. Try to visualize that the normals are indeed vectors perpendicular to each plane's surface (a cube consists of 6 planes).

```
float vertices[] = {
    // positions          // normals           // texture coords
    -0.5f, -0.5f, -0.5f,  0.0f,  0.0f, -1.0f,  0.0f, 0.0f,
     0.5f, -0.5f, -0.5f,  0.0f,  0.0f, -1.0f,  1.0f, 0.0f,
     0.5f,  0.5f, -0.5f,  0.0f,  0.0f, -1.0f,  1.0f, 1.0f,
     0.5f,  0.5f, -0.5f,  0.0f,  0.0f, -1.0f,  1.0f, 1.0f,
    -0.5f,  0.5f, -0.5f,  0.0f,  0.0f, -1.0f,  0.0f, 1.0f,
    -0.5f, -0.5f, -0.5f,  0.0f,  0.0f, -1.0f,  0.0f, 0.0f,

    -0.5f, -0.5f,  0.5f,  0.0f,  0.0f,  1.0f,  0.0f, 0.0f,
     0.5f, -0.5f,  0.5f,  0.0f,  0.0f,  1.0f,  1.0f, 0.0f,
     0.5f,  0.5f,  0.5f,  0.0f,  0.0f,  1.0f,  1.0f, 1.0f,
     0.5f,  0.5f,  0.5f,  0.0f,  0.0f,  1.0f,  1.0f, 1.0f,
    -0.5f,  0.5f,  0.5f,  0.0f,  0.0f,  1.0f,  0.0f, 1.0f,
    -0.5f, -0.5f,  0.5f,  0.0f,  0.0f,  1.0f,  0.0f, 0.0f,

    -0.5f,  0.5f,  0.5f, -1.0f,  0.0f,  0.0f,  1.0f, 0.0f,
    -0.5f,  0.5f, -0.5f, -1.0f,  0.0f,  0.0f,  1.0f, 1.0f,
    -0.5f, -0.5f, -0.5f, -1.0f,  0.0f,  0.0f,  0.0f, 1.0f,
    -0.5f, -0.5f, -0.5f, -1.0f,  0.0f,  0.0f,  0.0f, 1.0f,
    -0.5f, -0.5f,  0.5f, -1.0f,  0.0f,  0.0f,  0.0f, 0.0f,
    -0.5f,  0.5f,  0.5f, -1.0f,  0.0f,  0.0f,  1.0f, 0.0f,
```

```
     0.5f,   0.5f,   0.5f,   1.0f,   0.0f,   0.0f,   1.0f,  0.0f,
     0.5f,   0.5f,  -0.5f,   1.0f,   0.0f,   0.0f,   1.0f,  1.0f,
     0.5f,  -0.5f,  -0.5f,   1.0f,   0.0f,   0.0f,   0.0f,  1.0f,
     0.5f,  -0.5f,  -0.5f,   1.0f,   0.0f,   0.0f,   0.0f,  1.0f,
     0.5f,  -0.5f,   0.5f,   1.0f,   0.0f,   0.0f,   0.0f,  0.0f,
     0.5f,   0.5f,   0.5f,   1.0f,   0.0f,   0.0f,   1.0f,  0.0f,

    -0.5f,  -0.5f,  -0.5f,   0.0f,  -1.0f,   0.0f,   0.0f,  1.0f,
     0.5f,  -0.5f,  -0.5f,   0.0f,  -1.0f,   0.0f,   1.0f,  1.0f,
     0.5f,  -0.5f,   0.5f,   0.0f,  -1.0f,   0.0f,   1.0f,  0.0f,
     0.5f,  -0.5f,   0.5f,   0.0f,  -1.0f,   0.0f,   1.0f,  0.0f,
    -0.5f,  -0.5f,   0.5f,   0.0f,  -1.0f,   0.0f,   0.0f,  0.0f,
    -0.5f,  -0.5f,  -0.5f,   0.0f,  -1.0f,   0.0f,   0.0f,  1.0f,

    -0.5f,   0.5f,  -0.5f,   0.0f,   1.0f,   0.0f,   0.0f,  1.0f,
     0.5f,   0.5f,  -0.5f,   0.0f,   1.0f,   0.0f,   1.0f,  1.0f,
     0.5f,   0.5f,   0.5f,   0.0f,   1.0f,   0.0f,   1.0f,  0.0f,
     0.5f,   0.5f,   0.5f,   0.0f,   1.0f,   0.0f,   1.0f,  0.0f,
    -0.5f,   0.5f,   0.5f,   0.0f,   1.0f,   0.0f,   0.0f,  0.0f,
    -0.5f,   0.5f,  -0.5f,   0.0f,   1.0f,   0.0f,   0.0f,  1.0f
};
```

Since we added extra data to the vertex array we should update the cube's vertex shader:

```glsl
#version 330 core
layout (location = 0) in vec3 aPos;
layout (location = 1) in vec3 aNormal;
...
```

Now that we added a normal vector to each of the vertices and updated the vertex shader we should update the vertex attribute pointers as well. Note that the light source's cube uses the same vertex array for its vertex data, but the lamp shader has no use of the newly added normal vectors. We don't have to update the lamp's shaders or attribute configurations, but we have to at least modify the vertex attribute pointers to reflect the new vertex array's size:

```cpp
glVertexAttribPointer(0, 3, GL_FLOAT, GL_FALSE, 8 * sizeof(float),
                      (void*)0);
glEnableVertexAttribArray(0);
```

We only want to use the first 3 floats of each vertex and ignore the last 5 floats so we only need to update the *stride* parameter to 8 times the size of a `float` and we're done.

> It may look inefficient using vertex data that is not completely used by the lamp shader, but the vertex data is already stored in the GPU's memory from the container object so we don't have to store new data into the GPU's memory. This actually makes it more efficient compared to allocating a new **VBO** specifically for the lamp.

All the lighting calculations are done in the fragment shader so we need to forward the normal vectors from the vertex shader to the fragment shader. Let's do that:

```glsl
out vec3 Normal;

void main()
{
    gl_Position = projection * view * model * vec4(aPos, 1.0);
    Normal = aNormal;
}
```

What's left to do is declare the corresponding input variable in the fragment shader:

```glsl
in vec3 Normal;
```

13.4 Calculating the diffuse color

We now have the normal vector for each vertex, but we still need the light's position vector and the fragment's position vector. Since the light's position is a single static variable we can declare it as a uniform in the fragment shader:

```glsl
uniform vec3 lightPos;
```

And then update the uniform in the render loop (or outside since it doesn't change per frame). We use the `lightPos` vector declared in the previous chapter as the location of the diffuse light source:

```cpp
lightingShader.setVec3("lightPos", lightPos);
```

Then the last thing we need is the actual fragment's position. We're going to do all the lighting calculations in world space so we want a vertex position that is in world space first. We can accomplish this by multiplying the vertex position attribute with the model matrix only (not the view and projection matrix) to transform it to world space coordinates. This can easily be accomplished in the vertex shader so let's declare an output variable and calculate its world space coordinates:

```glsl
out vec3 FragPos;
out vec3 Normal;

void main()
{
    gl_Position = projection * view * model * vec4(aPos, 1.0);
    FragPos = vec3(model * vec4(aPos, 1.0));
    Normal = aNormal;
}
```

And lastly add the corresponding input variable to the fragment shader:

```glsl
in vec3 FragPos;
```

This `in` variable will be interpolated from the 3 world position vectors of the triangle to form the `FragPos` vector that is the per-fragment world position. Now that all the required variables are set we can start the lighting calculations.

The first thing we need to calculate is the direction vector between the light source and the fragment's position. From the previous section we know that the light's direction vector is the difference vector between the light's position vector and the fragment's position vector. As you may remember from the *Transformations* chapter we can easily calculate this difference by subtracting both vectors from each other. We also want to make sure all the relevant vectors end up as unit vectors so we normalize both the normal and the resulting direction vector:

```
vec3 norm = normalize(Normal);
vec3 lightDir = normalize(lightPos - FragPos);
```

> When calculating lighting we usually do not care about the magnitude of a vector or their position; we only care about their direction. Because we only care about their direction almost all the calculations are done with unit vectors since it simplifies most calculations (like the dot product). So when doing lighting calculations, make sure you always normalize the relevant vectors to ensure they're actual unit vectors. Forgetting to normalize a vector is a popular mistake.

Next we need to calculate the diffuse impact of the light on the current fragment by taking the dot product between the `norm` and `lightDir` vectors. The resulting value is then multiplied with the light's color to get the diffuse component, resulting in a darker diffuse component the greater the angle between both vectors:

```
float diff = max(dot(norm, lightDir), 0.0);
vec3 diffuse = diff * lightColor;
```

If the angle between both vectors is greater than 90 degrees then the result of the dot product will actually become negative and we end up with a negative diffuse component. For that reason we use the `max` function that returns the highest of both its parameters to make sure the diffuse component (and thus the colors) never become negative. Lighting for negative colors is not really defined so it's best to stay away from that, unless you're one of those eccentric artists.

Now that we have both an ambient and a diffuse component we add both colors to each other and then multiply the result with the color of the object to get the resulting fragment's output color:

```
vec3 result = (ambient + diffuse) * objectColor;
FragColor = vec4(result, 1.0);
```

If your application (and shaders) compiled successfully you should see something like this:

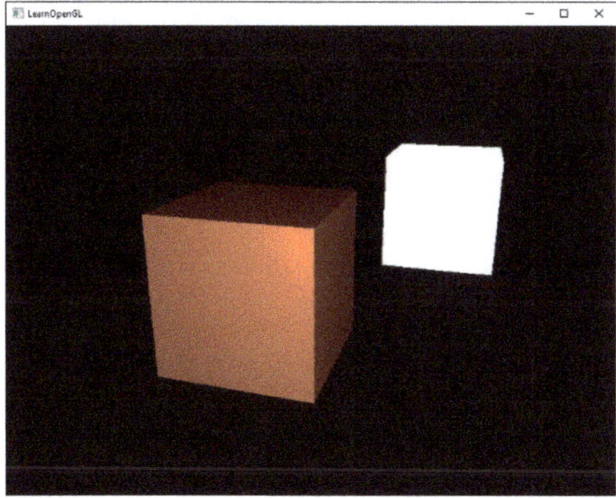

You can see that with diffuse lighting the cube starts to look like an actual cube again. Try visualizing the normal vectors in your head and move the camera around the cube to see that the larger the angle between the normal vector and the light's direction vector, the darker the fragment becomes.

Feel free to compare your source code with the complete source code at `/src/2.lighting/ 2.1.basic_lighting_diffuse/` if you're stuck.

13.5 One last thing

in the previous section we passed the normal vector directly from the vertex shader to the fragment shader. However, the calculations in the fragment shader are all done in world space, so shouldn't we transform the normal vectors to world space coordinates as well? Basically yes, but it's not as simple as simply multiplying it with a model matrix.

First of all, normal vectors are only direction vectors and do not represent a specific position in space. Second, normal vectors do not have a homogeneous coordinate (the w component of a vertex position). This means that translations should not have any effect on the normal vectors. So if we want to multiply the normal vectors with a model matrix we want to remove the translation part of the matrix by taking the upper-left $3x3$ matrix of the model matrix (note that we could also set the w component of a normal vector to 0 and multiply with the 4x4 matrix).

Second, if the model matrix would perform a non-uniform scale, the vertices would be changed in such a way that the normal vector is not perpendicular to the surface anymore. The following image shows the effect such a model matrix (with non-uniform scaling) has on a normal vector:

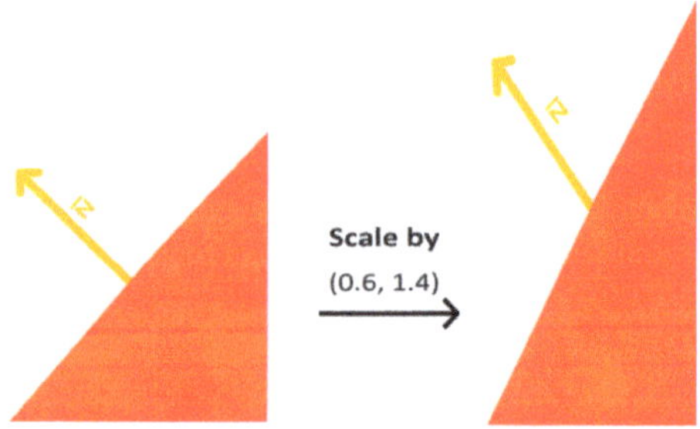

Whenever we apply a non-uniform scale (note: a uniform scale only changes the normal's magnitude, not its direction, which is easily fixed by normalizing it) the normal vectors are not perpendicular to the corresponding surface anymore which distorts the lighting.

The trick of fixing this behavior is to use a different model matrix specifically tailored for normal vectors. This matrix is called the normal matrix and uses a few linear algebraic operations to remove the effect of wrongly scaling the normal vectors. If you want to know how this matrix is calculated, I suggest the normal matrix article[1] from LightHouse3D.

The normal matrix is defined as 'the transpose of the inverse of the upper-left 3x3 part of the model matrix'. Phew, that's a mouthful and if you don't really understand what that means, don't worry; we haven't discussed inverse and transpose matrices yet. Note that most resources define the normal matrix as derived from the model-view matrix, but since we're working in world space (and not in view space) we will derive it from the model matrix.

---

[1] www.lighthouse3d.com/tutorials/glsl-tutorial/the-normal-matrix/

In the vertex shader we can generate the normal matrix by using the `inverse` and `transpose` functions in the vertex shader that work on any matrix type. Note that we cast the matrix to a 3x3 matrix to ensure it loses its translation properties and that it can multiply with the `vec3` normal vector:

```
Normal = mat3(transpose(inverse(model))) * aNormal;
```

> Inversing matrices is a costly operation for shaders, so wherever possible try to avoid doing inverse operations since they have to be done on each vertex of your scene. For learning purposes this is fine, but for an efficient application you'll likely want to calculate the normal matrix on the CPU and send it to the shaders via a uniform before drawing (just like the model matrix).

In the diffuse lighting section the lighting was fine because we didn't do any scaling on the object, so there was not really a need to use a normal matrix and we could've just multiplied the normals with the model matrix. If you are doing a non-uniform scale however, it is essential that you multiply your normal vectors with the normal matrix.

13.6 Specular Lighting

If you're not exhausted already by all the lighting talk we can start finishing the Phong lighting model by adding specular highlights.

Similar to diffuse lighting, specular lighting is based on the light's direction vector and the object's normal vectors, but this time it is also based on the view direction e.g. from what direction the player is looking at the fragment. Specular lighting is based on the reflective properties of surfaces. If we think of the object's surface as a mirror, the specular lighting is the strongest wherever we would see the light reflected on the surface. You can see this effect in the following image:

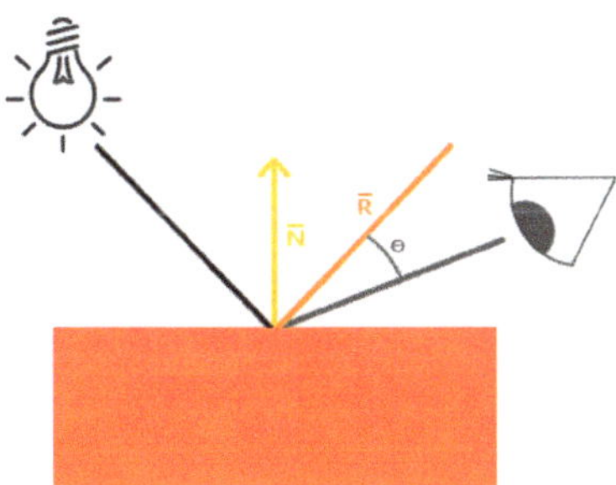

We calculate a reflection vector by reflecting the light direction around the normal vector. Then we calculate the angular distance between this reflection vector and the view direction. The closer the angle between them, the greater the impact of the specular light. The resulting effect is that we see a bit of a highlight when we're looking at the light's direction reflected via the surface.

The view vector is the one extra variable we need for specular lighting which we can calculate using the viewer's world space position and the fragment's position. Then we calculate the specular's intensity, multiply this with the light color and add this to the ambient and diffuse components.

> We chose to do the lighting calculations in world space, but most people tend to prefer doing lighting in view space. An advantage of view space is that the viewer's position is always at $(0, 0, 0)$ so you already got the position of the viewer for free. However, I find calculating lighting in world space more intuitive for learning purposes. If you still want to calculate lighting in view space you want to transform all the relevant vectors with the view matrix as well (don't forget to change the normal matrix too).

To get the world space coordinates of the viewer we simply take the position vector of the camera object (which is the viewer of course). So let's add another uniform to the fragment shader and pass the camera position vector to the shader:

```
uniform vec3 viewPos;
```

```
lightingShader.setVec3("viewPos", camera.Position);
```

Now that we have all the required variables we can calculate the specular intensity. First we define a specular intensity value to give the specular highlight a medium-bright color so that it doesn't have too much of an impact:

```
float specularStrength = 0.5;
```

If we would set this to `1.0f` we'd get a really bright specular component which is a bit too much for a coral cube. In the next chapter we'll talk about properly setting all these lighting intensities and how they affect the objects. Next we calculate the view direction vector and the corresponding reflect vector along the normal axis:

```
vec3 viewDir = normalize(viewPos - FragPos);
vec3 reflectDir = reflect(-lightDir, norm);
```

Note that we negate the `lightDir` vector. The `reflect` function expects the first vector to point **from** the light source towards the fragment's position, but the `lightDir` vector is currently pointing the other way around: from the fragment **towards** the light source (this depends on the order of subtraction earlier on when we calculated the `lightDir` vector). To make sure we get the correct `reflect` vector we reverse its direction by negating the `lightDir` vector first. The second argument expects a normal vector so we supply the normalized `norm` vector.

Then what's left to do is to actually calculate the specular component. This is accomplished with the following formula:

```
float spec = pow(max(dot(viewDir, reflectDir), 0.0), 32);
vec3 specular = specularStrength * spec * lightColor;
```

We first calculate the dot product between the view direction and the reflect direction (and make sure it's not negative) and then raise it to the power of 32. This 32 value is the shininess value of the highlight. The higher the shininess value of an object, the more it properly reflects the light instead of scattering it all around and thus the smaller the highlight becomes. Below you can see an image that shows the visual impact of different shininess values:

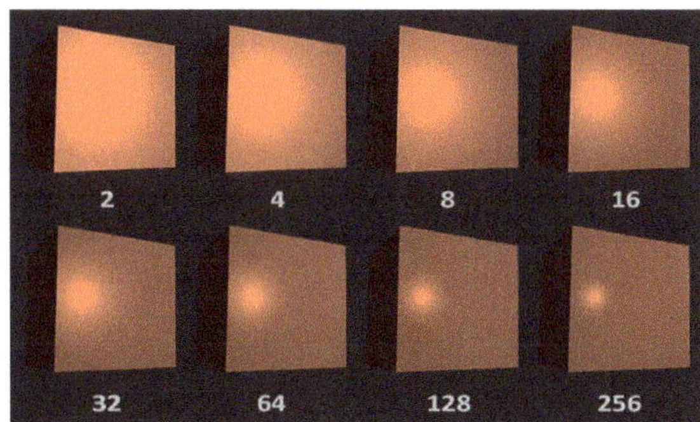

We don't want the specular component to be too distracting so we keep the exponent at 32. The only thing left to do is to add it to the ambient and diffuse components and multiply the combined result with the object's color:

```
vec3 result = (ambient + diffuse + specular) * objectColor;
FragColor = vec4(result, 1.0);
```

We now calculated all the lighting components of the Phong lighting model. Based on your point of view you should see something like this:

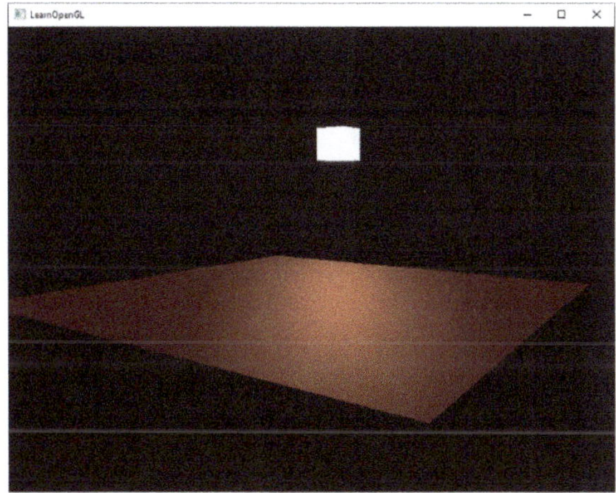

You can find the complete source code of the application at `/src/2.lighting/2.2.basic_lighting_specular/`.

In the earlier days of lighting shaders, developers used to implement the Phong lighting model in the vertex shader. The advantage of doing lighting in the vertex shader is that it is a lot more efficient since there are generally a lot less vertices compared to fragments, so the (expensive) lighting calculations are done less frequently. However, the resulting color value in the vertex shader is the resulting lighting color of that vertex only and the color values of the surrounding fragments are then the result of interpolated lighting colors. The result was that the lighting was not very realistic unless large amounts of vertices were used:

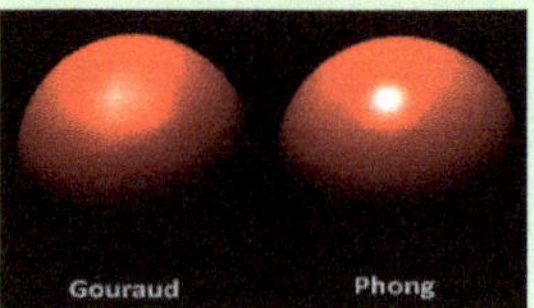

When the Phong lighting model is implemented in the vertex shader it is called Gouraud shading instead of Phong shading. Note that due to the interpolation the lighting looks somewhat off. The Phong shading gives much smoother lighting results.

By now you should be starting to see just how powerful shaders are. With little information shaders are able to calculate how lighting affects the fragment's colors for all our objects. In the next chapters we'll be delving much deeper into what we can do with the lighting model.

13.7 Exercises

- Right now the light source is a boring static light source that doesn't move. Try to move the light source around the scene over time using either `sin` or `cos`. Watching the lighting change over time gives you a good understanding of Phong's lighting model. Solution: `/src/2.lighting/2.3.basic_lighting_exercise1/`.
- Play around with different ambient, diffuse and specular strengths and see how they impact the result. Also experiment with the shininess factor. Try to comprehend why certain values have a certain visual output.
- Do Phong shading in view space instead of world space. Solution: `/src/2.lighting/2.4.basic_lighting_exercise2/`.
- Implement Gouraud shading instead of Phong shading. If you did things right the lighting should look a bit off as you can see at: `learnopengl.com/img/lighting/basic_lighting_exercise3.png` (especially the specular highlights) with the cube object. Try to reason why it looks so weird. Solution: `/src/2.lighting/2.5.basic_lighting_exercise3/`.

14. Materials

In the real world, each object has a different reaction to light. Steel objects are often shinier than a clay vase for example and a wooden container doesn't react the same to light as a steel container. Some objects reflect the light without much scattering resulting in small specular highlights and others scatter a lot giving the highlight a larger radius. If we want to simulate several types of objects in OpenGL we have to define material properties specific to each surface.

In the previous chapter we defined an object and light color to define the visual output of the object, combined with an ambient and specular intensity component. When describing a surface we can define a material color for each of the 3 lighting components: ambient, diffuse and specular lighting. By specifying a color for each of the components we have fine-grained control over the color output of the surface. Now add a shininess component to those 3 colors and we have all the material properties we need:

```glsl
#version 330 core
struct Material {
    vec3  ambient;
    vec3  diffuse;
    vec3  specular;
    float shininess;
};

uniform Material material;
```

In the fragment shader we create a `struct` to store the material properties of the surface. We can also store them as individual uniform values, but storing them as a struct keeps it more organized. We first define the layout of the struct and then simply declare a uniform variable with the newly created struct as its type.

As you can see, we define a color vector for each of the Phong lighting's components. The `ambient` material vector defines what color the surface reflects under ambient lighting; this is usually the same as the surface's color. The `diffuse` material vector defines the color of the surface under diffuse lighting. The diffuse color is (just like ambient lighting) set to the desired surface's color. The `specular` material vector sets the color of the specular highlight on the surface (or possibly even reflect a surface-specific color). Lastly, the `shininess` impacts the scattering/radius of the specular highlight.

With these 4 components that define an object's material we can simulate many real-world materials. A table as found at `devernay.free.fr/cours/opengl/materials.html` shows a list of material properties that simulate real materials found in the outside world. The following image shows the effect several of these real world material values have on our cube:

As you can see, by correctly specifying the material properties of a surface it seems to change the perception we have of the object. The effects are clearly noticeable, but for the more realistic results we'll need to replace the cube with something more complicated. In the later *Model Loading* chapters we'll discuss more complicated shapes.

Figuring out the right material settings for an object is a difficult feat that mostly requires experimentation and a lot of experience. It's not that uncommon to completely destroy the visual quality of an object by a misplaced material.

Let's try implementing such a material system in the shaders.

14.1 Setting materials

We created a uniform material struct in the fragment shader so next we want to change the lighting calculations to comply with the new material properties. Since all the material variables are stored in a struct we can access them from the `material` uniform:

```glsl
void main()
{
    // ambient
    vec3 ambient = lightColor * material.ambient;

    // diffuse
    vec3 norm = normalize(Normal);
    vec3 lightDir = normalize(lightPos - FragPos);
    float diff = max(dot(norm, lightDir), 0.0);
    vec3 diffuse = lightColor * (diff * material.diffuse);

    // specular
    vec3 viewDir = normalize(viewPos - FragPos);
    vec3 reflectDir = reflect(-lightDir, norm);
    float spec = pow(max(dot(viewDir, reflectDir), 0.0),
                     material.shininess);
    vec3 specular = lightColor * (spec * material.specular);

    vec3 result = ambient + diffuse + specular;
    FragColor = vec4(result, 1.0);
}
```

As you can see we now access all of the material struct's properties wherever we need them and this time calculate the resulting output color with the help of the material's colors. Each of the object's material attributes are multiplied with their respective lighting components.

We can set the material of the object in the application by setting the appropriate uniforms. A struct in GLSL however is not special in any regard when setting uniforms; a struct only really acts as a namespace of uniform variables. If we want to fill the struct we will have to set the individual uniforms, but prefixed with the struct's name:

```cpp
lightingShader.setVec3("material.ambient", 1.0f, 0.5f, 0.31f);
lightingShader.setVec3("material.diffuse", 1.0f, 0.5f, 0.31f);
lightingShader.setVec3("material.specular", 0.5f, 0.5f, 0.5f);
lightingShader.setFloat("material.shininess", 32.0f);
```

We set the ambient and diffuse component to the color we'd like the object to have and set the specular component of the object to a medium-bright color; we don't want the specular component to be too strong. We also keep the shininess at 32.

We can now easily influence the object's material from the application. Running the program gives you something like this:

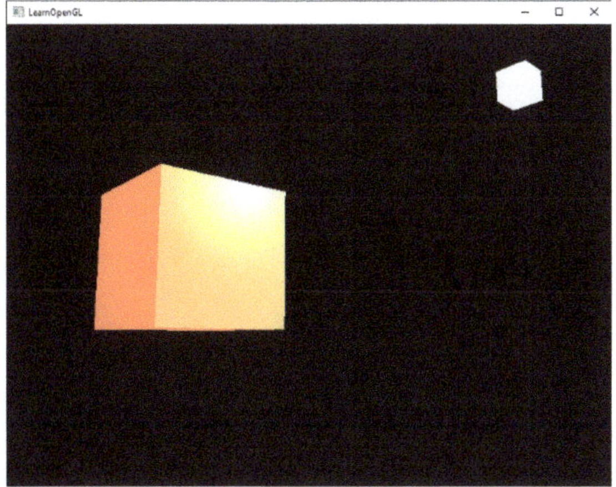

It doesn't really look right though?

14.2 Light properties

The object is way too bright. The reason for the object being too bright is that the ambient, diffuse and specular colors are reflected with full force from any light source. Light sources also have different intensities for their ambient, diffuse and specular components respectively. In the previous chapter we solved this by varying the ambient and specular intensities with a strength value. We want to do something similar, but this time by specifying intensity vectors for each of the lighting components. If we'd visualize `lightColor` as vec3(1.0) the code would look like this:

```
vec3 ambient  = vec3(1.0) * material.ambient;
vec3 diffuse  = vec3(1.0) * (diff * material.diffuse);
vec3 specular = vec3(1.0) * (spec * material.specular);
```

So each material property of the object is returned with full intensity for each of the light's components. These vec3(1.0) values can be influenced individually as well for each light source and this is usually what we want. Right now the ambient component of the object is fully influencing the color of the cube. The ambient component shouldn't really have such a big impact on the final color so we can restrict the ambient color by setting the light's ambient intensity to a lower value:

```
vec3 ambient = vec3(0.1) * material.ambient;
```

We can influence the diffuse and specular intensity of the light source in the same way. This is closely similar to what we did in the previous chapter; you could say we already created some light properties to influence each lighting component individually. We'll want to create something similar to the material struct for the light properties:

```glsl
struct Light {
    vec3 position;

    vec3 ambient;
    vec3 diffuse;
    vec3 specular;
};
uniform Light light;
```

A light source has a different intensity for its `ambient`, `diffuse` and `specular` components. The ambient light is usually set to a low intensity because we don't want the ambient color to
be too dominant. The diffuse component of a light source is usually set to the exact color we'd like a
light to have; often a bright white color. The specular component is usually kept at `vec3(1.0)`
shining at full intensity. Note that we also added the light's position vector to the struct.

Just like with the material uniform we need to update the fragment shader:

```glsl
vec3 ambient = light.ambient * material.ambient;
vec3 diffuse = light.diffuse * (diff * material.diffuse);
vec3 specular = light.specular * (spec * material.specular);
```

We then want to set the light intensities in the application:

```cpp
lightingShader.setVec3("light.ambient", 0.2f, 0.2f, 0.2f);
lightingShader.setVec3("light.diffuse", 0.5f, 0.5f, 0.5f); // darkened
lightingShader.setVec3("light.specular", 1.0f, 1.0f, 1.0f);
```

Now that we modulated how the light influences the object's material we get a visual output that
looks much like the output from the previous chapter. This time however we got full control over
the lighting and the material of the object:

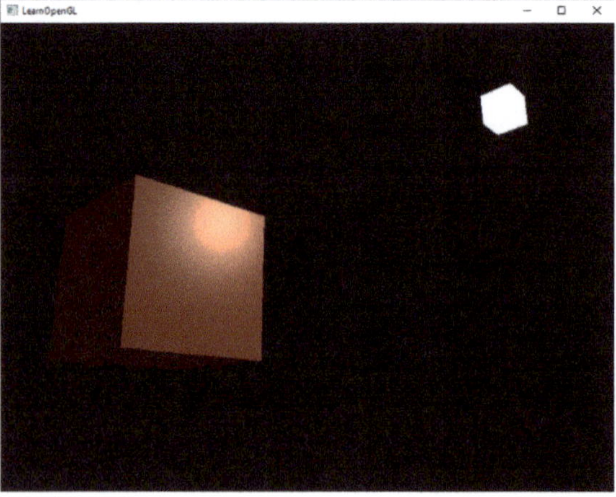

Changing the visual aspects of objects is relatively easy right now. Let's spice things up a bit!

14.3 Different light colors

So far we used light colors to only vary the intensity of their individual components by choosing
colors that range from white to gray to black, not affecting the actual colors of the object (only its
intensity). Since we now have easy access to the light's properties we can change their colors over

time to get some really interesting effects. Since everything is already set up in the fragment shader, changing the light's colors is easy and immediately creates some funky effects:

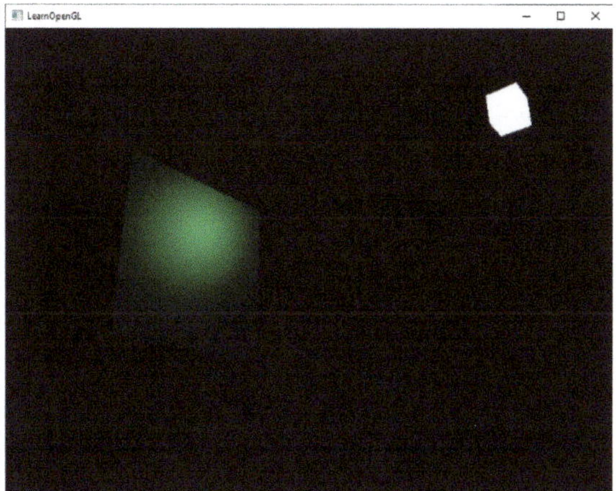

As you can see, a different light color greatly influences the object's color output. Since the light color directly influences what colors the object can reflect (as you may remember from the *Colors* chapter) it has a significant impact on the visual output.

We can easily change the light's colors over time by changing the light's ambient and diffuse colors via `sin` and `glfwGetTime`:

```cpp
glm::vec3 lightColor;
lightColor.x = sin(glfwGetTime() * 2.0f);
lightColor.y = sin(glfwGetTime() * 0.7f);
lightColor.z = sin(glfwGetTime() * 1.3f);

glm::vec3 diffuseColor = lightColor * glm::vec3(0.5f);
glm::vec3 ambientColor = diffuseColor * glm::vec3(0.2f);

lightingShader.setVec3("light.ambient", ambientColor);
lightingShader.setVec3("light.diffuse", diffuseColor);
```

Try and experiment with several lighting and material values and see how they affect the visual output. You can find the source code of the application at `/src/2.lighting/3.1.materials/`.

14.4 Exercises

- Can you make it so that changing the light color changes the color of the light's cube object?
- Can you simulate some of the real-world objects by defining their respective materials like we've seen at the start of this chapter? Note that the linked table's ambient values are not the same as the diffuse values; they didn't take light intensities into account. To correctly set their values you'd have to set all the light intensities to `vec3(1.0)` to get the same output. Solution: `/src/2.lighting/3.2.materials_exercise1/` of cyan plastic container.

15. Lighting Maps

In the previous chapter we discussed the possibility of each object having a unique material of its own that reacts differently to light. This is great for giving each object a unique look in comparison to other objects, but still doesn't offer much flexibility on the visual output of an object.

In the previous chapter we defined a material for an entire object as a whole. Objects in the real world however usually do not consist of a single material, but of several materials. Think of a car: its exterior consists of a shiny fabric, it has windows that partly reflect the surrounding environment, its tires are all but shiny so they don't have specular highlights and it has rims that are super shiny (if you actually washed your car alright). The car also has diffuse and ambient colors that are not the same for the entire object; a car displays many different ambient/diffuse colors. All by all, such an object has different material properties for each of its different parts.

So the material system in the previous chapter isn't sufficient for all but the simplest models so we need to extend the system by introducing *diffuse* and *specular* maps. These allow us to influence the diffuse (and indirectly the ambient component since they should be the same anyways) and the specular component of an object with much more precision.

15.1 Diffuse maps

What we want is some way to set the diffuse colors of an object for each individual fragment. Some sort of system where we can retrieve a color value based on the fragment's position on the object?

This should probably all sound familiar and we've been using such a system for a while now. This sounds just like *textures* we've extensively discussed in the earlier chapters and it basically is just that: a texture. We're just using a different name for the same underlying principle: using an image wrapped around an object that we can index for unique color values per fragment. In lit scenes this is usually called a diffuse map (this is generally how 3D artists call them before PBR) since a texture image represents all of the object's diffuse colors.

To demonstrate diffuse maps we're going to use an image of a wooden container with a steel border[1].

Using a diffuse map in shaders is exactly like we showed in the texture chapter. This time however we store the texture as a `sampler2D` inside the `Material` struct. We replace the earlier defined `vec3` diffuse color vector with the diffuse map.

---

[1] learnopengl.com/img/textures/container2.png

Keep in mind that `sampler2D` is a so called opaque type which means we can't instanti-ate these types, but only define them as uniforms. If the struct would be instantiated other than as a uniform (like a function parameter) GLSL could throw strange errors; the same thus applies to any struct holding such opaque types.

We also remove the ambient material color vector since the ambient color is equal to the diffuse color anyways now that we control ambient with the light. So there's no need to store it separately:

```
struct Material {
    sampler2D diffuse;
    vec3      specular;
    float     shininess;
};
...
in vec2 TexCoords;
```

If you're a bit stubborn and still want to set the ambient colors to a different value (other than the diffuse value) you can keep the ambient `vec3`, but then the ambient colors would still remain the same for the entire object. To get different ambient values for each fragment you'd have to use another texture for ambient values alone.

Note that we are going to need texture coordinates again in the fragment shader, so we declared an extra input variable. Then we simply sample from the texture to retrieve the fragment's diffuse color value:

```
vec3 diffuse = light.diffuse * diff * vec3(texture(material.diffuse,
                                           TexCoords));
```

Also, don't forget to set the ambient material's color equal to the diffuse material's color as well:

```
vec3 ambient = light.ambient * vec3(texture(material.diffuse, TexCoords));
```

And that's all it takes to use a diffuse map. As you can see it is nothing new, but it does provide a dramatic increase in visual quality. To get it working we do need to update the vertex attributes, transfer texture coordinates to the fragment shader, load the texture, and bind the texture to the appropriate texture unit.

Let's update the vertex shader to accept texture coordinates as a vertex attribute and forward them to the fragment shader:

```
#version 330 core
layout (location = 0) in vec3 aPos;
layout (location = 1) in vec3 aNormal;
layout (location = 2) in vec2 aTexCoords;
...
out vec2 TexCoords;

void main()
{
    ...
    TexCoords = aTexCoords;
}
```

Be sure to update the vertex attribute pointers of both VAOs to match the new vertex data and load the container image as a texture. Before rendering the cube we want to assign the right texture unit to the `material.diffuse` uniform sampler and bind the container texture to this texture unit:

```
lightingShader.setInt("material.diffuse", 0);
...
glActiveTexture(GL_TEXTURE0);
glBindTexture(GL_TEXTURE_2D, diffuseMap);
```

Now using a diffuse map we get an enormous boost in detail again and this time the container really starts to shine (quite literally). Your container now probably looks something like this:

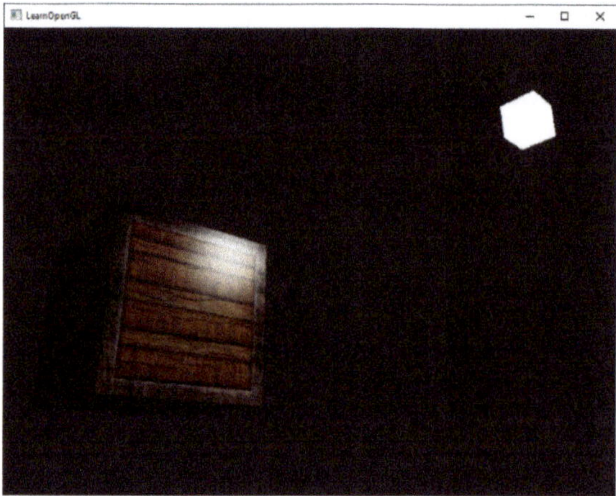

You can find the full source code of the application at `/src/2.lighting/4.1.lighting_maps_diffuse_map/`.

15.2 Specular maps

You probably noticed that the specular highlight looks a bit odd since the object is a container that mostly consists of wood and wood doesn't have specular highlights like that. We can fix this by setting the specular material of the object to `vec3(0.0)` but that would mean that the steel borders of the container would stop showing specular highlights as well and steel **should** show specular highlights. We would like to control what parts of the object should show a specular highlight with varying intensity. This is a problem that sounds familiar. Coincidence? I think not.

We can also use a texture map just for specular highlights. This means we need to generate a black and white (or colors if you feel like it) texture[1] that defines the specular intensities of each part of the object.

---

[1]learnopengl/img/textures/container2_specular.png

The intensity of the specular highlight comes from the brightness of each pixel in the image. Each pixel of the specular map can be displayed as a color vector where black represents the color vector `vec3(0.0)` and gray the color vector `vec3(0.5)` for example. In the fragment shader we then sample the corresponding color value and multiply this value with the light's specular intensity. The more 'white' a pixel is, the higher the result of the multiplication and thus the brighter the specular component of an object becomes.

Because the container mostly consists of wood, and wood as a material should have no specular highlights, the entire wooden section of the diffuse texture was converted to black: black sections do not have any specular highlight. The steel border of the container has varying specular intensities with the steel itself being relatively susceptible to specular highlights while the cracks are not.

> Technically wood also has specular highlights although with a much lower shininess value (more light scattering) and less impact, but for learning purposes we can just pretend wood doesn't have any reaction to specular light.

Using tools like *Photoshop* or *Gimp* it is relatively easy to transform a diffuse texture to a specular image like this by cutting out some parts, transforming it to black and white and increasing the brightness/contrast.

15.3 Sampling specular maps

A specular map is just like any other texture so the code is similar to the diffuse map code. Make sure to properly load the image and generate a texture object. Since we're using another texture sampler in the same fragment shader we have to use a different texture unit (see the *Textures* chapter) for the specular map so let's bind it to the appropriate texture unit before rendering:

```
lightingShader.setInt("material.specular", 1);
...
glActiveTexture(GL_TEXTURE1);
glBindTexture(GL_TEXTURE_2D, specularMap);
```

Then update the material properties of the fragment shader to accept a `sampler2D` as its specular component instead of a `vec3`:

```
struct Material {
    sampler2D diffuse;
    sampler2D specular;
    float     shininess;
};
```

And lastly we want to sample the specular map to retrieve the fragment's corresponding specular intensity:

```
vec3 ambient = light.ambient * vec3(texture(material.diffuse, TexCoords));
vec3 diffuse = light.diffuse * diff * vec3(texture(material.diffuse,
                                           TexCoords));
vec3 specular = light.specular * spec * vec3(texture(material.specular,
                                             TexCoords));
FragColor = vec4(ambient + diffuse + specular, 1.0);
```

By using a specular map we can specify with enormous detail what parts of an object have *shiny* properties and we can even control the corresponding intensity. Specular maps give us an added layer of control over lighting on top of the diffuse map.

> If you don't want to be too mainstream you could also use actual colors in the specular map to not only set the specular intensity of each fragment, but also the color of the specular highlight. Realistically however, the color of the specular highlight is mostly determined by the light source itself so it wouldn't generate realistic visuals (that's why the images are usually black and white: we only care about the intensity).

If you would now run the application you can clearly see that the container's material now closely resembles that of an actual wooden container with steel frames:

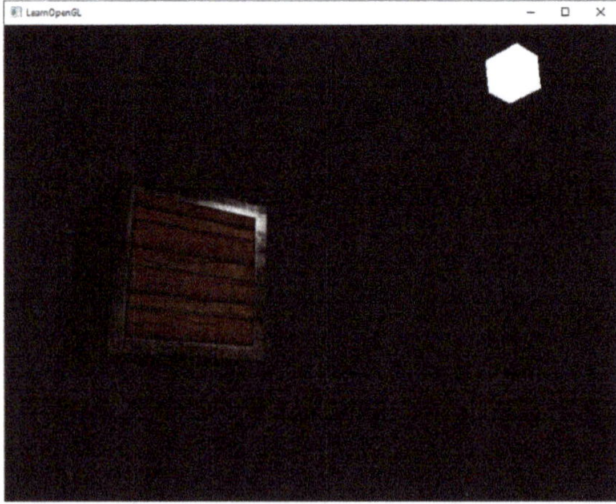

You can find the full source code of the application at /src/2.lighting/4.2.lighting_maps_specular_map/.

Using diffuse and specular maps we can really add an enormous amount of detail into relatively simple objects. We can even add more detail into the objects using other texture maps like normal/bump maps and/or reflection maps, but that is something we'll reserve for later chapters. Show your container to all your friends and family and be content with the fact that our container can one day become even prettier than it already is!

15.4 Exercises

- Fool around with the light source's ambient, diffuse and specular vectors and see how they affect the visual output of the container.

- Try inverting the color values of the specular map in the fragment shader so that the wood shows specular highlights and the steel borders do not (note that due to the cracks in the steel border the borders still show some specular highlight, although with less intensity). Solution: `/src/2.lighting/4.3.lighting_maps_exercise2/`.
- Try creating a specular map from the diffuse texture that uses actual colors instead of black and white and see that the result doesn't look too realistic. You can use the following image if you can't generate one yourself: `learnopengl.com/img/lighting/lighting_maps_specular_color.png`. Result: `learnopengl.com/img/lighting/lighting_maps_exercise3.png`.
- Also add something they call an emission map which is a texture that stores emission values per fragment. Emission values are colors an object may *emit* as if it contains a light source itself; this way an object can glow regardless of the light conditions. Emission maps are often what you see when objects in a game glow (like the eyes of a robot, or light strips on a container). Add the following texture (by creativesam) as an emission map onto the container as if the letters emit light: `learnopengl.com/img/textures/matrix.jpg`. Solution: `/src/2.lighting/4.4.lighting_maps_exercise4/`; result: `learnopengl.com/img/lighting/lighting_maps_exercise4.png`.

16. Light Casters

All the lighting we've used so far came from a single source that is a single point in space. It gives good results, but in the real world we have several types of light that each act different. A light source that *casts* light upon objects is called a light caster. In this chapter we'll discuss several different types of light casters. Learning to simulate different light sources is yet another tool in your toolbox to further enrich your environments.

We'll first discuss a directional light, then a point light which is an extension of what we had before, and lastly we'll discuss spotlights. In the next chapter we'll combine several of these different light types into one scene.

16.1 Directional Light

When a light source is far away the light rays coming from the light source are close to parallel to each other. It looks like all the light rays are coming from the same direction, regardless of where the object and/or the viewer is. When a light source is modeled to be *infinitely* far away it is called a directional light since all its light rays have the same direction; it is independent of the location of the light source.

A fine example of a directional light source is the sun as we know it. The sun is not infinitely far away from us, but it is so far away that we can perceive it as being infinitely far away in the lighting calculations. All the light rays from the sun are then modeled as parallel light rays as we can see in the following image:

Because all the light rays are parallel it does not matter how each object relates to the light source's position since the light direction remains the same for each object in the scene. Because the light's direction vector stays the same, the lighting calculations will be similar for each object in the scene.

We can model such a directional light by defining a light direction vector instead of a position vector. The shader calculations remain mostly the same except this time we directly use the light's `direction` vector instead of calculating the `lightDir` vector using the light's `position` vector:

```glsl
struct Light {
    // vec3 position; // no longer necessary when using directional lights.
    vec3 direction;

    vec3 ambient;
    vec3 diffuse;
    vec3 specular;
};
[...]
void main()
{
    vec3 lightDir = normalize(-light.direction);
    [...]
}
```

Note that we first negate the `light.direction` vector. The lighting calculations we used so far expect the light direction to be a direction from the fragment **towards** the light source, but people generally prefer to specify a directional light as a global direction pointing **from** the light source. Therefore we have to negate the global light direction vector to switch its direction; it's now a direction vector pointing towards the light source. Also, be sure to normalize the vector since it is unwise to assume the input vector to be a unit vector.

The resulting `lightDir` vector is then used as before in the diffuse and specular computations.

To demonstrate that a directional light has the same effect on multiple objects we'll revisit the container party scene from the end of the *Coordinate systems* chapter:

```cpp
for(unsigned int i = 0; i < 10; i++)
{
    glm::mat4 model = glm::mat4(1.0f);
    model = glm::translate(model, cubePositions[i]);
    float angle = 20.0f * i;
    model = glm::rotate(model, glm::radians(angle),
                        glm::vec3(1.0f, 0.3f, 0.5f));
    lightingShader.setMat4("model", model);

    glDrawArrays(GL_TRIANGLES, 0, 36);
}
```

Also, don't forget to actually specify the direction of the light source (note that we define the direction as a direction **from** the light source; you can quickly see the light's direction is pointing downwards):

```cpp
lightingShader.setVec3("light.direction", -0.2f, -1.0f, -0.3f);
```

We've been passing the light's position and direction vectors as `vec3`s for a while now, but some people tend to prefer to keep all the vectors defined as `vec4`. When defining position vectors as a `vec4` it is important to set the w component to `1.0` so translation and projections are properly applied. However, when defining a direction vector as a `vec4` we don't want translations to have an effect (since they just represent directions, nothing more) so then we define the w component to be `0.0`.

Direction vectors can then be represented as: `vec4(-0.2f, -1.0f, -0.3f, 0.0f)`. This can also function as an easy check for light types: you could check if the w component is equal to `1.0` to see that we now have a light's position vector and if w is equal to `0.0` we have a light's direction vector; so adjust the calculations based on that:

```cpp
if (lightVector.w == 0.0) // be careful for floating point errors
    // do directional light calculations
else if (lightVector.w == 1.0)
    // do light calculations using the light's position
```

Fun fact: this is actually how the old OpenGL (fixed-functionality) determined if a light source was a directional light or a positional light source and adjusted its lighting based on that.

If you'd now compile the application and fly through the scene it looks like there is a sun-like light source casting light on all the objects. Can you see that the diffuse and specular components all react as if there was a light source somewhere in the sky? It'll look something like this:

You can find the full source code of the application at `/src/2.lighting/5.1.light_casters_directional/`.

16.2 Point lights

Directional lights are great for global lights that illuminate the entire scene, but we usually also want several point lights scattered throughout the scene. A point light is a light source with a given position somewhere in a world that illuminates in all directions, where the light rays fade out over distance. Think of light bulbs and torches as light casters that act as a point light.

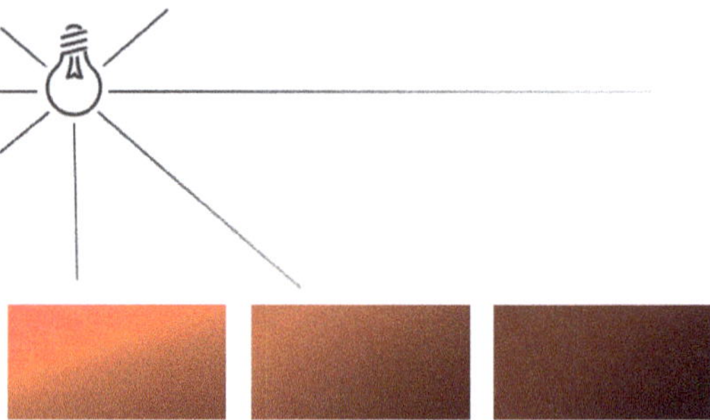

In the earlier chapters we've been working with a simplistic point light. We had a light source at a given position that scatters light in all directions from that given light position. However, the light source we defined simulated light rays that never fade out thus making it look like the light source is extremely strong. In most 3D applications we'd like to simulate a light source that only illuminates an area close to the light source and not the entire scene.

If you'd add the 10 containers to the lighting scene from the previous chapters, you'd notice that the container all the way in the back is lit with the same intensity as the container in front of the light; there is no logic yet that diminishes light over distance. We want the container in the back to only be slightly lit in comparison to the containers close to the light source.

16.3 **Attenuation**

To reduce the intensity of light over the distance a light ray travels is generally called attenuation. One way to reduce the light intensity over distance is to simply use a linear equation. Such an equation would linearly reduce the light intensity over the distance thus making sure that objects at a distance are less bright. However, such a linear function tends to look a bit fake. In the real world, lights are generally quite bright standing close by, but the brightness of a light source diminishes quickly at a distance; the remaining light intensity then slowly diminishes over distance. We are thus in need of a different equation for reducing the light's intensity.

Luckily some smart people already figured this out for us. The following formula calculates an attenuation value based on a fragment's distance to the light source which we later multiply with the light's intensity vector:

$$F_{\text{att}} = \frac{1.0}{K_c + K_l * d + K_q * d^2}$$

Here d represents the distance from the fragment to the light source. Then to calculate the attenuation value we define 3 (configurable) terms: a constant term K_c, a linear term K_l and a quadratic term K_q.

- The constant term is usually kept at `1.0` which is mainly there to make sure the denominator never gets smaller than `1` since it would otherwise boost the intensity with certain distances, which is not the effect we're looking for.
- The linear term is multiplied with the distance value that reduces the intensity in a linear fashion.
- The quadratic term is multiplied with the quadrant of the distance and sets a quadratic decrease of intensity for the light source. The quadratic term will be less significant compared to the linear term when the distance is small, but gets much larger as the distance grows.

Due to the quadratic term the light will diminish mostly at a linear fashion until the distance becomes large enough for the quadratic term to surpass the linear term and then the light intensity will decrease a lot faster. The resulting effect is that the light is quite intense when at a close range, but quickly loses its brightness over distance until it eventually loses its brightness at a more slower pace. The following graph shows the effect such an attenuation has over a distance of `100`:

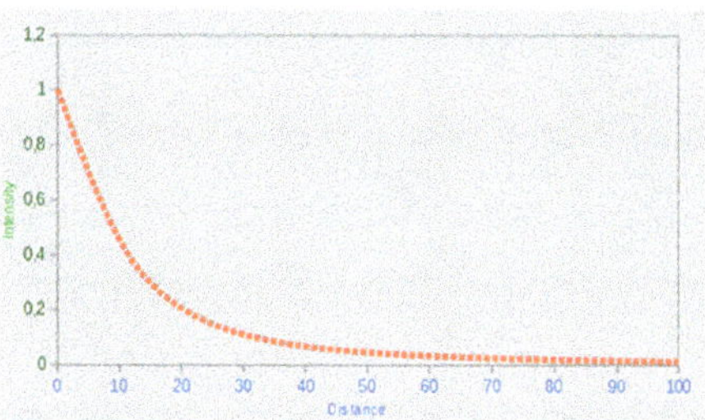

You can see that the light has the highest intensity when the distance is small, but as soon as the distance grows its intensity is significantly reduced and slowly reaches `0` intensity at around a distance of `100`. This is exactly what we want.

16.3.1 **Choosing the right values**

But at what values do we set those 3 terms? Setting the right values depend on many factors: the environment, the distance you want a light to cover, the type of light etc. In most cases, it simply is a question of experience and a moderate amount of tweaking. The following table shows some of the values these terms could take to simulate a realistic (sort of) light source that covers a specific radius (distance). The first column specifies the distance a light will cover with the given terms. These values are good starting points for most lights, with courtesy of Ogre3D's wiki[1]:

Distance	Constant	Linear	Quadratic
7	1.0	0.7	1.8
13	1.0	0.35	0.44
20	1.0	0.22	0.20
32	1.0	0.14	0.07
50	1.0	0.09	0.032
65	1.0	0.07	0.017
100	1.0	0.045	0.0075
160	1.0	0.027	0.0028
200	1.0	0.022	0.0019
325	1.0	0.014	0.0007
600	1.0	0.007	0.0002
3250	1.0	0.0014	0.000007

As you can see, the constant term K_c is kept at 1.0 in all cases. The linear term K_l is usually quite small to cover larger distances and the quadratic term K_q is even smaller. Try to experiment a bit with these values to see their effect in your implementation. In our environment a distance of 32 to 100 is generally enough for most lights.

16.3.2 Implementing attenuation

To implement attenuation we'll be needing 3 extra values in the fragment shader: namely the constant, linear and quadratic terms of the equation. These are best stored in the `Light` struct we defined earlier. Note that we need to calculate `lightDir` again using `position` as this is a point light (as we did in the previous chapter) and not a directional light.

```glsl
struct Light {
    vec3 position;

    vec3 ambient;
    vec3 diffuse;
    vec3 specular;

    float constant;
    float linear;
    float quadratic;
};
```

Then we set the terms in our application: we want the light to cover a distance of 50 so we'll use the appropriate constant, linear and quadratic terms from the table:

```cpp
lightingShader.setFloat("light.constant",  1.0f);
lightingShader.setFloat("light.linear",    0.09f);
lightingShader.setFloat("light.quadratic", 0.032f);
```

Implementing attenuation in the fragment shader is relatively straightforward: we simply calculate an attenuation value based on the equation and multiply this with the ambient, diffuse and specular components.

---

[1] www.ogre3d.org/tikiwiki/tiki-index.php?page=-Point+Light+Attenuation

We do need the distance to the light source for the equation to work though. Remember how we can calculate the length of a vector? We can retrieve the distance term by calculating the difference vector between the fragment and the light source and take that resulting vector's length. We can use GLSL's built-in `length` function for that purpose:

```glsl
float distance    = length(light.position - FragPos);
float attenuation = 1.0 / (light.constant + light.linear * distance +
                    light.quadratic * (distance * distance));
```

Then we include this attenuation value in the lighting calculations by multiplying the attenuation value with the ambient, diffuse and specular colors.

> We could leave the ambient component alone so ambient lighting is not decreased over distance, but if we were to use more than 1 light source all the ambient components will start to stack up. In that case we want to attenuate ambient lighting as well. Simply play around with what's best for your environment.

```glsl
ambient  *= attenuation;
diffuse  *= attenuation;
specular *= attenuation;
```

If you'd run the application you'd get something like this:

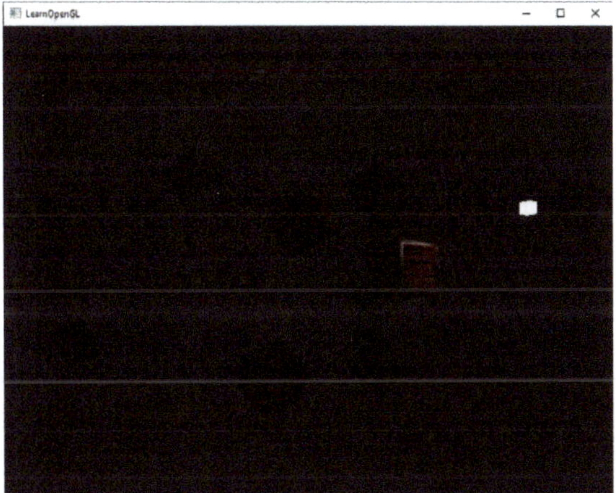

You can see that right now only the front containers are lit with the closest container being the brightest. The containers in the back are not lit at all since they're too far from the light source. You can find the source code of the application at `/src/2.lighting/5.2.light_casters_point/`.

A point light is thus a light source with a configurable location and attenuation applied to its lighting calculations. Yet another type of light for our lighting arsenal.

16.4 Spotlight

The last type of light we're going to discuss is a spotlight. A spotlight is a light source that is located somewhere in the environment that, instead of shooting light rays in all directions, only shoots them in a specific direction. The result is that only the objects within a certain radius of the spotlight's direction are lit and everything else stays dark. A good example of a spotlight would be a street lamp or a flashlight.

A spotlight in OpenGL is represented by a world-space position, a direction and a cutoff angle that specifies the radius of the spotlight. For each fragment we calculate if the fragment is between the spotlight's cutoff directions (thus in its cone) and if so, we lit the fragment accordingly. The following image gives you an idea of how a spotlight works:

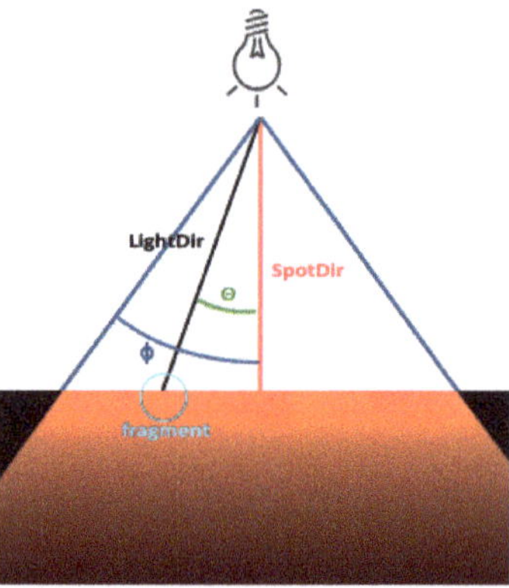

- `LightDir`: the vector pointing from the fragment to the light source.
- `SpotDir`: the direction the spotlight is aiming at.
- `Phi` ϕ: the cutoff angle that specifies the spotlight's radius. Everything outside this angle is not lit by the spotlight.
- `Theta` θ: the angle between the `LightDir` vector and the `SpotDir` vector. The θ value should be smaller than Φ to be inside the spotlight.

So what we basically need to do, is calculate the dot product (returns the cosine of the angle between two unit vectors) between the `LightDir` vector and the `SpotDir` vector and compare this with the cutoff angle ϕ. Now that you (sort of) understand what a spotlight is all about we're going to create one in the form of a flashlight.

16.5 Flashlight

A flashlight is a spotlight located at the viewer's position and usually aimed straight ahead from the player's perspective. A flashlight is basically a normal spotlight, but with its position and direction continually updated based on the player's position and orientation.

So, the values we're going to need for the fragment shader are the spotlight's position vector (to calculate the fragment-to-light's direction vector), the spotlight's direction vector and the cutoff angle. We can store these values in the `Light` struct:

```glsl
struct Light {
    vec3 position;
    vec3 direction;
    float cutOff;
    ...
};
```

Next we pass the appropriate values to the shader:

```cpp
lightingShader.setVec3("light.position", camera.Position);
lightingShader.setVec3("light.direction", camera.Front);
lightingShader.setFloat("light.cutOff", glm::cos(glm::radians(12.5f)));
```

As you can see we're not setting an angle for the cutoff value but calculate the cosine value based on an angle and pass the cosine result to the fragment shader. The reason for this is that in the fragment shader we're calculating the dot product between the `LightDir` and the `SpotDir` vector and the dot product returns a cosine value and not an angle; and we can't directly compare an angle with a cosine value. To get the angle in the shader we then have to calculate the inverse cosine of the dot product's result which is an expensive operation. So to save some performance we calculate the cosine value of a given cutoff angle beforehand and pass this result to the fragment shader. Since both angles are now represented as cosines, we can directly compare between them without expensive operations.

Now what's left to do is calculate the theta θ value and compare this with the cutoff ϕ value to determine if we're in or outside the spotlight:

```cpp
float theta = dot(lightDir, normalize(-light.direction));

if(theta > light.cutOff)
{
    // do lighting calculations
}
else // use ambient light so scene isn't black outside the spotlight.
    color = vec4(light.ambient * vec3(texture(material.diffuse,
                                TexCoords)), 1.0);
```

We first calculate the dot product between the `lightDir` vector and the negated `direction` vector (negated, because we want the vectors to point towards the light source, instead of from). Be sure to normalize all the relevant vectors.

You may be wondering why there is a > sign instead of a < sign in the `if` guard. Shouldn't `theta` be smaller than the light's cutoff value to be inside the spotlight? That is right, but don't forget angle values are represented as cosine values and an angle of 0 degrees is represented as the cosine value of `1.0` while an angle of 90 degrees is represented as the cosine value of `0.0` as you can see here:

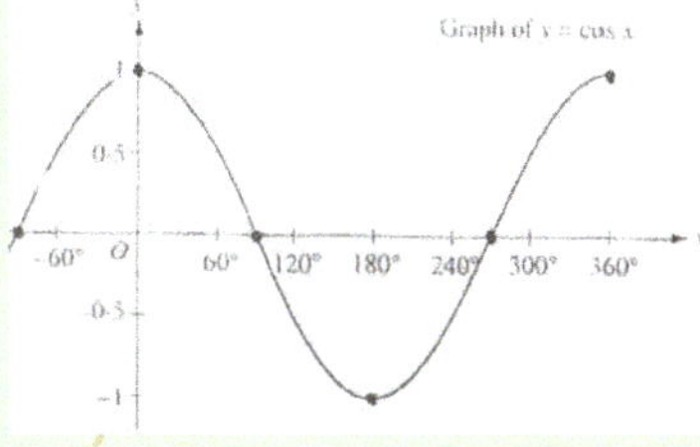

You can now see that the closer the cosine value is to `1.0` the smaller its angle. Now it makes sense why `theta` needs to be larger than the cutoff value. The cutoff value is currently set at the cosine of `12.5` which is equal to `0.976` so a cosine `theta` value between `0.976` and `1.0` would result in the fragment being lit as if inside the spotlight.

Running the application results in a spotlight that only lights the fragments that are directly inside the cone of the spotlight. It'll look something like this:

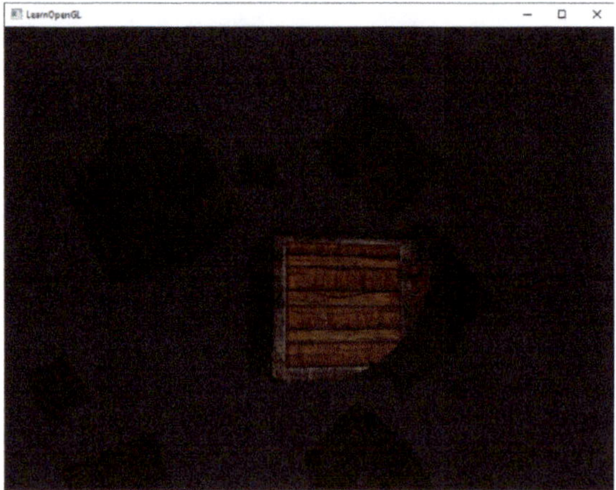

You can find the full source code at `/src/2.lighting/5.3.light_casters_spot/`.

It still looks a bit fake though, mostly because the spotlight has hard edges. Wherever a fragment reaches the edge of the spotlight's cone it is shut down completely instead of with a nice smooth fade. A realistic spotlight would reduce the light gradually around its edges.

16.6 Smooth/Soft edges

To create the effect of a smoothly-edged spotlight we want to simulate a spotlight having an inner and an outer cone. We can set the inner cone as the cone defined in the previous section, but we also want an outer cone that gradually dims the light from the inner to the edges of the outer cone.

To create an outer cone we simply define another cosine value that represents the angle between the spotlight's direction vector and the outer cone's vector (equal to its radius). Then, if a fragment is between the inner and the outer cone it should calculate an intensity value between `0.0` and `1.0`. If the fragment is inside the inner cone its intensity is equal to `1.0` and `0.0` if the fragment is outside the outer cone.

We can calculate such a value using the following equation:

$$I = \frac{\theta - \gamma}{\varepsilon}$$

Here ε (epsilon) is the cosine difference between the inner (ϕ) and the outer cone (γ) ($\varepsilon = \phi - \gamma$). The resulting I value is then the intensity of the spotlight at the current fragment.

It is a bit hard to visualize how this formula actually works so let's try it out with a few sample values:

θ	θ in degrees	ϕ (inner cutoff)	ϕ in degrees	γ (outer cutoff)	γ in degrees	ε	I
0.87	30	0.91	25	0.82	35	0.91 - 0.82 = 0.09	0.87 - 0.82 / 0.09 = 0.56
0.9	26	0.91	25	0.82	35	0.91 - 0.82 = 0.09	0.9 - 0.82 / 0.09 = 0.89
0.97	14	0.91	25	0.82	35	0.91 - 0.82 = 0.09	0.97 - 0.82 / 0.09 = 1.67
0.97	14	0.91	25	0.82	35	0.91 - 0.82 = 0.09	0.97 - 0.82 / 0.09 = 1.67
0.83	34	0.91	25	0.82	35	0.91 - 0.82 = 0.09	0.83 - 0.82 / 0.09 = 0.11
0.64	50	0.91	25	0.82	35	0.91 - 0.82 = 0.09	0.64 - 0.82 / 0.09 = -2.0
0.966	15	0.9978	12.5	0.953	17.5	0.966 - 0.953 = 0.0448	0.966 - 0.953 / 0.0448 = 0.29

As you can see we're basically interpolating between the outer cosine and the inner cosine based on the θ value. If you still don't really see what's going on, don't worry, you can simply take the formula for granted and return here when you're much older and wiser.

We now have an intensity value that is either negative when outside the spotlight, higher than 1.0 when inside the inner cone, and somewhere in between around the edges. If we properly clamp the values we don't need an if-else in the fragment shader anymore and we can simply multiply the light components with the calculated intensity value:

```glsl
float theta     = dot(lightDir, normalize(-light.direction));
float epsilon = light.cutOff - light.outerCutOff;
float intensity = clamp((theta - light.outerCutOff) / epsilon, 0.0, 1.0);
...
// we'll leave ambient unaffected so we always have a little light.
diffuse *= intensity;
specular *= intensity;
...
```

Note that we use the clamp function that clamps its first argument between the values 0.0 and 1.0. This makes sure the intensity values won't end up outside the [0, 1] range.

Make sure you add the outerCutOff value to the Light struct and set its uniform value in the application. For the following image an inner cutoff angle of 12.5 and an outer cutoff angle of 17.5 was used:

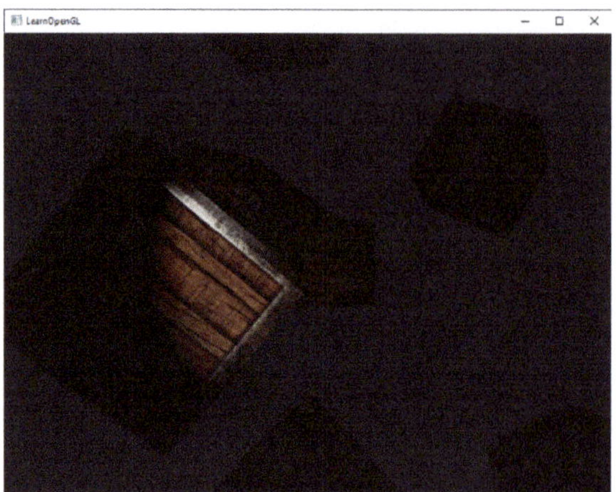

Ahhh, that's much better. Play around with the inner and outer cutoff angles and try to create a spotlight that better suits your needs. You can find the source code of the application at `/src/2.lighting/5.4.light_casters_spot_soft/`.

Such a flashlight/spotlight type of lamp is perfect for horror games and combined with directional and point lights the environment will really start to light up.

16.7 Exercises

- Try experimenting with all the different light types and their fragment shaders. Try inverting some vectors and/or use < instead of >. Try to explain the different visual outcomes.

17. Multiple lights

In the previous chapters we learned a lot about lighting in OpenGL. We learned about Phong shading, materials, lighting maps and different types of light casters. In this chapter we're going to combine all the previously obtained knowledge by creating a fully lit scene with 6 active light sources. We are going to simulate a sun-like light as a directional light source, 4 point lights scattered throughout the scene and we'll be adding a flashlight as well.

To use more than one light source in the scene we want to encapsulate the lighting calculations into GLSL functions. The reason for that is that the code quickly gets nasty when we do lighting computations with multiple light types, each requiring different computations. If we were to do all these calculations in the `main` function only, the code quickly becomes difficult to understand.

Functions in GLSL are just like C-functions. We have a function name, a return type and we need to declare a prototype at the top of the code file if the function hasn't been declared yet before the main function. We'll create a different function for each of the light types: directional lights, point lights and spotlights.

When using multiple lights in a scene the approach is usually as follows: we have a single color vector that represents the fragment's output color. For each light, the light's contribution to the fragment is added to this output color vector. So each light in the scene will calculate its individual impact and contribute that to the final output color. A general structure would look something like this:

```glsl
out vec4 FragColor;

void main()
{
    // define an output color value
    vec3 output = vec3(0.0);
    // add the directional light's contribution to the output
    output += someFunctionToCalculateDirectionalLight();
    // do the same for all point lights
    for(int i = 0; i < nr_of_point_lights; i++)
        output += someFunctionToCalculatePointLight();
    // and add others lights as well (like spotlights)
    output += someFunctionToCalculateSpotLight();

    FragColor = vec4(output, 1.0);
}
```

The actual code will likely differ per implementation, but the general structure remains the same. We define several functions that calculate the impact per light source and add its resulting color to an output color vector. If for example two light sources are close to the fragment, their combined contribution would result in a more brightly lit fragment compared to the fragment being lit by a single light source.

17.1 Directional light

We want to define a function in the fragment shader that calculates the contribution a directional light has on the corresponding fragment: a function that takes a few parameters and returns the calculated directional lighting color.

First we need to set the required variables that we minimally need for a directional light source. We can store the variables in a struct called `DirLight` and define it as a uniform. The struct's variables should be familiar from the previous chapter:

```glsl
struct DirLight {
    vec3 direction;

    vec3 ambient;
    vec3 diffuse;
    vec3 specular;
};
uniform DirLight dirLight;
```

We can then pass the `dirLight` uniform to a function with the following prototype:

```glsl
vec3 CalcDirLight(DirLight light, vec3 normal, vec3 viewDir);
```

> Just like C and C++, when we want to call a function (in this case inside the `main` function) the function should be defined somewhere before the caller's line number. In this case we'd prefer to define the functions below the `main` function so this requirement doesn't hold. Therefore we declare the function's prototypes somewhere above the `main` function, just like we would in C.

You can see that the function requires a `DirLight` struct and two other vectors required for its computation. If you successfully completed the previous chapter then the content of this function should come as no surprise:

```glsl
vec3 CalcDirLight(DirLight light, vec3 normal, vec3 viewDir)
{
    vec3 lightDir = normalize(-light.direction);
    // diffuse shading
    float diff = max(dot(normal, lightDir), 0.0);
    // specular shading
    vec3 reflectDir = reflect(-lightDir, normal);
    float spec = pow(max(dot(viewDir, reflectDir), 0.0),
                     material.shininess);
    // combine results
    vec3 ambient = light.ambient * vec3(texture(material.diffuse,
                                                TexCoords));
    vec3 diffuse = light.diffuse * diff * vec3(texture(material.diffuse,
                                                       TexCoords));
    vec3 specular = light.specular * spec * vec3(texture(material.specular,
                                                         TexCoords));
    return (ambient + diffuse + specular);
}
```

We basically copied the code from the previous chapter and used the vectors given as function arguments to calculate the directional light's contribution vector. The resulting ambient, diffuse and specular contributions are then returned as a single color vector.

17.2 Point light

Similar to directional lights we also want to define a function that calculates the contribution a point light has on the given fragment, including its attenuation. Just like directional lights we want to define a struct that specifies all the variables required for a point light:

```glsl
struct PointLight {
    vec3 position;

    float constant;
    float linear;
    float quadratic;

    vec3 ambient;
    vec3 diffuse;
    vec3 specular;
};
#define NR_POINT_LIGHTS 4
uniform PointLight pointLights[NR_POINT_LIGHTS];
```

As you can see we used a pre-processor directive in GLSL to define the number of point lights we want to have in our scene. We then use this `NR_POINT_LIGHTS` constant to create an array of `PointLight` structs. Arrays in GLSL are just like C arrays and can be created by the use of two square brackets. Right now we have 4 `PointLight` structs to fill with data.

The prototype of the point light's function is as follows:

```glsl
vec3 CalcPointLight(PointLight light, vec3 normal, vec3 fragPos,
                    vec3 viewDir);
```

The function takes all the data it needs as its arguments and returns a `vec3` that represents the color contribution that this specific point light has on the fragment. Again, some intelligent copy-and-pasting results in the following function:

```glsl
vec3 CalcPointLight(PointLight light, vec3 normal, vec3 fragPos, vec3
    viewDir)
{
    vec3 lightDir = normalize(light.position - fragPos);
    // diffuse shading
    float diff = max(dot(normal, lightDir), 0.0);
    // specular shading
    vec3 reflectDir = reflect(-lightDir, normal);
    float spec = pow(max(dot(viewDir, reflectDir), 0.0),
                     material.shininess);
    // attenuation
    float distance    = length(light.position - fragPos);
    float attenuation = 1.0 / (light.constant + light.linear * distance +
                              light.quadratic * (distance * distance));
    // combine results
    vec3 ambient = light.ambient * vec3(texture(material.diffuse,
                                        TexCoords));
    vec3 diffuse = light.diffuse * diff * vec3(texture(material.diffuse,
                                        TexCoords));
    vec3 specular = light.specular * spec * vec3(texture(material.specular,
                                        TexCoords));
    ambient *= attenuation;
    diffuse *= attenuation;
    specular *= attenuation;
    return (ambient + diffuse + specular);
}
```

Abstracting this functionality away in a function like this has the advantage that we can easily calculate the lighting for multiple point lights without the need for duplicated code. In the `main` function we simply create a loop that iterates over the point light array that calls `CalcPointLight` for each point light.

17.3 Putting it all together

Now that we defined both a function for directional lights and a function for point lights we can put it all together in the `main` function.

```glsl
void main()
{
    // properties
    vec3 norm = normalize(Normal);
    vec3 viewDir = normalize(viewPos - FragPos);

    // phase 1: Directional lighting
    vec3 result = CalcDirLight(dirLight, norm, viewDir);
    // phase 2: Point lights
    for(int i = 0; i < NR_POINT_LIGHTS; i++)
        result += CalcPointLight(pointLights[i], norm, FragPos, viewDir);
    // phase 3: Spot light
    //result += CalcSpotLight(spotLight, norm, FragPos, viewDir);

    FragColor = vec4(result, 1.0);
}
```

Each light type adds its contribution to the resulting output color until all light sources are processed. The resulting color contains the color impact of all the light sources in the scene combined. We leave the `CalcSpotLight` function as an exercise for the reader.

> There are lot of duplicated calculations in this approach spread out over the light type functions (e.g. calculating the reflect vector, diffuse and specular terms, and sampling the material textures) so there's room for optimization here.

Setting the uniforms for the directional light struct shouldn't be too unfamiliar, but you may be wondering how to set the uniform values of the point lights since the point light uniform is actually an array of `PointLight` structs. This isn't something we've discussed before.

Luckily for us, it isn't too complicated. Setting the uniform values of an array of structs works just like setting the uniforms of a single struct, although this time we also have to define the appropriate index when querying the uniform's location:

```cpp
lightingShader.setFloat("pointLights[0].constant", 1.0f);
```

Here we index the first `PointLight` struct in the `pointLights` array and internally retrieve the location of its `constant` variable, which we set to `1.0`.

Let's not forget that we also need to define a position vector for each of the 4 point lights so let's spread them up a bit around the scene. We'll define another `glm::vec3` array that contains the pointlights' positions:

```cpp
glm::vec3 pointLightPositions[] = {
    glm::vec3( 0.7f,  0.2f,   2.0f),
    glm::vec3( 2.3f, -3.3f,  -4.0f),
    glm::vec3(-4.0f,  2.0f, -12.0f),
    glm::vec3( 0.0f,  0.0f,  -3.0f)
};
```

Then we index the corresponding `PointLight` struct from the `pointLights` array and set its `position` attribute as one of the positions we just defined. Also be sure to now draw 4 light cubes instead of just 1. Simply create a different model matrix for each of the light objects just like we did with the containers.

If you'd also use a flashlight, the result of all the combined lights looks something like this:

As you can see there appears to be some form of a global light (like a sun) somewhere in the sky, we have 4 lights scattered throughout the scene and a flashlight is visible from the player's perspective. Looks pretty neat doesn't it?

You can find the full source code of the final application at `/src/2.lighting/6.multiple _lights/`.

The image shows all the light sources set with the default light properties we've used in the previous chapters, but if you play around with these values you can get pretty interesting results. Artists and level designers generally tweak all these lighting variables in a large editor to make sure the lighting matches the environment. Using our simple environment you can already create some pretty interesting visuals simply by tweaking the lights' attributes:

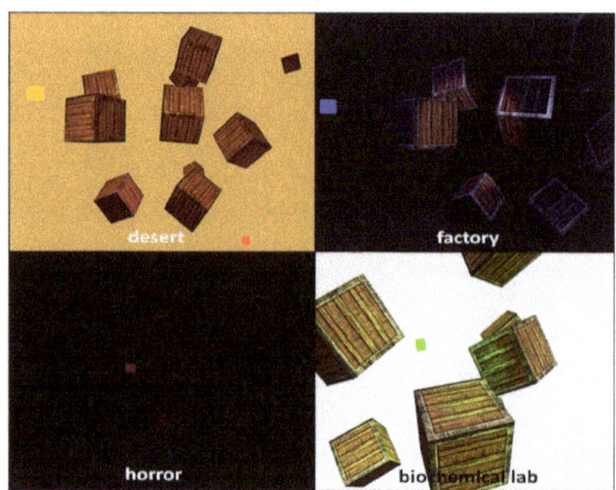

We also changed the clear color to better reflect the lighting. You can see that by simply adjusting some of the lighting parameters you can create completely different atmospheres.

By now you should have a pretty good understanding of lighting in OpenGL. With the knowledge so far we can already create interesting and visually rich environments and atmospheres. Try playing around with all the different values to create your own atmospheres.

17.4 Exercises

- Can you (sort of) re-create the different atmospheres of the last image by tweaking the light's attribute values? Solution: `/src/2.lighting/6.multiple_lights_exercise1/`.

18. Review

Congratulations on making it this far! I'm not sure if you noticed, but over all the lighting chapters we learned nothing new about OpenGL itself aside from a few minor items like accessing uniform arrays. All of the lighting chapters so far were all about manipulating shaders using techniques and equations to achieve realistic lighting results. This again shows you the power of shaders. Shaders are extremely flexible and you witnessed first-hand that with just a few 3D vectors and some configurable variables we were able to create amazing graphics!

The last few chapters you learned about colors, the Phong lighting model (that includes ambient, diffuse and specular lighting), object materials, configurable light properties, diffuse and specular maps, different types of lights, and how to combine all the knowledge into a single fully lit scene. Be sure to experiment with different lights, material colors, light properties, and try to create your own environments with the help of a little bit of creativity.

In the next chapters we'll be adding more advanced geometry shapes to our scene that look really well in the lighting models we've discussed.

18.1 Glossary

- `Color vector`: a vector portraying most of the real world colors via a combination of red, green and blue components (abbreviated to `RGB`). The color of an object is the reflected color components that an object did not absorb.
- `Phong lighting model`: a model for approximating real-world lighting by computing an ambient, diffuse and specular component.
- `Ambient lighting`: approximation of global illumination by giving each object a small brightness so that objects aren't completely dark if not directly lit.
- `Diffuse shading`: lighting that gets stronger the more a vertex/fragment is aligned to a light source. Makes use of normal vectors to calculate the angles.
- `Normal vector`: a unit vector that is perpendicular to a surface.
- `Normal matrix`: a 3x3 matrix that is the model (or model-view) matrix without translation. It is also modified in such a way (inverse-transpose) that it keeps normal vectors facing in the correct direction when applying non-uniform scaling. Otherwise normal vectors get distorted when using non-uniform scaling.
- `Specular lighting`: sets a specular highlight the closer the viewer is looking at the reflection of a light source on a surface. Based on the viewer's direction, the light's direction and a shininess value that sets the amount of scattering of the highlight.
- `Phong shading`: the Phong lighting model applied in the fragment shader.
- `Gouraud shading`: the Phong lighting model applied in the vertex shader. Produces noticeable artifacts when using a small number of vertices. Gains efficiency for loss of visual quality.
- `GLSL struct`: a C-like struct that acts as a container for shader variables. Mostly used for organizing input, output, and uniforms.
- `Material`: the ambient, diffuse and specular color an object reflects. These set the colors an object has.
- `Light (properties)`: the ambient, diffuse and specular intensity of a light. These can take any color value and define at what color/intensity a light source shines for each specific Phong component.
- `Diffuse map`: a texture image that sets the diffuse color per fragment.
- `Specular map`: a texture map that sets the specular intensity/color per fragment. Allows for specular highlights only on certain areas of an object.
- `Directional light`: a light source with only a direction. It is modeled to be at an infinite distance which has the effect that all its light rays seem parallel and its direction vector thus stays the same over the entire scene.
- `Point light`: a light source with a location in a scene with light that fades out over

distance.

- `Attenuation`: the process of light reducing its intensity over distance, used in point lights and spotlights.
- `Spotlight`: a light source that is defined by a cone in one specific direction.
- `Flashlight`: a spotlight positioned from the viewer's perspective.
- `GLSL uniform array`: an array of uniform values. Work just like a C-array, except that they can't be dynamically allocated.

Model Loading

19. Assimp

In all the scenes so far we've been extensively playing with our little container friend, but over time, even our best friends can get a little boring. In bigger graphics applications, there are usually lots of complicated and interesting models that are much prettier to look at than a static container. However, unlike the container object, we can't really manually define all the vertices, normals, and texture coordinates of complicated shapes like houses, vehicles, or human-like characters. What we want instead, is to *import* these models into the application; models that were carefully designed by 3D artists in tools like Blender[1], 3DS Max[2] or Maya[3].

These so called 3D modeling tools allow artists to create complicated shapes and apply textures to them via a process called uv-mapping. The tools then automatically generate all the vertex coordinates, vertex normals, and texture coordinates while exporting them to a model file format we can use. This way, artists have an extensive toolkit to create high quality models without having to care too much about the technical details. All the technical aspects are hidden in the exported model file. We, as graphics programmers, **do** have to care about these technical details though.

It is our job to parse these exported model files and extract all the relevant information so we can store them in a format that OpenGL understands. A common issue is that there are dozens of different file formats where each exports the model data in its own unique way. Model formats like the Wavefront.obj[4] format only contains model data with minor material information like model colors and diffuse/specular maps, while model formats like the XML-based Collada file format[5] are extremely extensive and contain models, lights, many types of materials, animation data, cameras, complete scene information, and much more. The wavefront object format is generally considered to be an easy-to-parse model format. It is recommended to visit the Wavefront's wiki page at least once to see how such a file format's data is structured. This should give you a basic perception of how model file formats are generally structured.

All by all, there are many different file formats where a common general structure between them usually does not exist. So if we want to import a model from these file formats, we'd have to write an importer ourselves for each of the file formats we want to import. Luckily for us, there just happens to be a library for this.

19.1 A model loading library

A very popular model importing library out there is called Assimp that stands for *Open Asset Import Library*. Assimp is able to import dozens of different model file formats (and export to some as well) by loading all the model's data into Assimp's generalized data structures. As soon as Assimp has loaded the model, we can retrieve all the data we need from Assimp's data structures. Because the data structure of Assimp stays the same, regardless of the type of file format we imported, it abstracts us from all the different file formats out there.

When importing a model via Assimp it loads the entire model into a *scene* object that contains all the data of the imported model/scene. Assimp then has a collection of nodes where each node contains indices to data stored in the scene object where each node can have any number of children.

---

[1] www.blender.org

[2] www.autodesk.nl/products/3ds-max/overview

[3] www.autodesk.com/products/autodesk-maya/overview

[4] en.wikipedia.org/wiki/Wavefront_.obj_file

[5] en.wikipedia.org/wiki/COLLADA

A (simplistic) model of Assimp's structure is shown below:

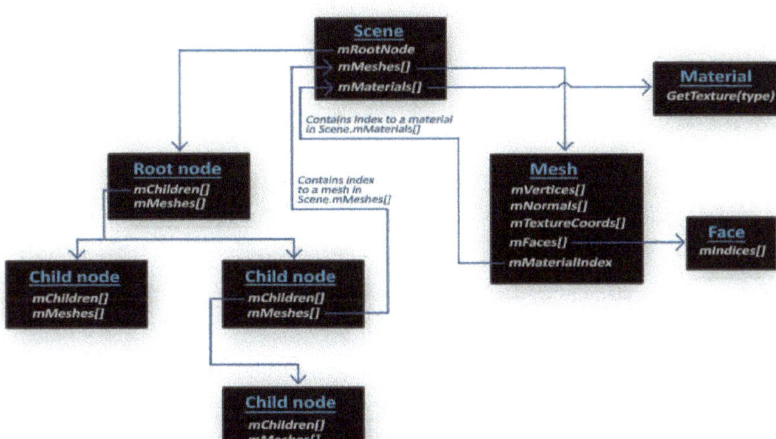

- All the data of the scene/model is contained in the Scene object like all the materials and the meshes. It also contains a reference to the root node of the scene.
- The Root node of the scene may contain children nodes (like all other nodes) and could have a set of indices that point to mesh data in the scene object's `mMeshes` array. The scene's `mMeshes` array contains the actual Mesh objects, the values in the `mMeshes` array of a node are only indices for the scene's meshes array.
- A Mesh object itself contains all the relevant data required for rendering, think of vertex positions, normal vectors, texture coordinates, faces, and the material of the object.
- A mesh contains several faces. A Face represents a render primitive of the object (triangles, squares, points). A face contains the indices of the vertices that form a primitive. Because the vertices and the indices are separated, this makes it easy for us to render via an index buffer (see *Hello Triangle* chapter).
- Finally a mesh also links to a Material object that hosts several functions to retrieve the material properties of an object. Think of colors and/or texture maps (like diffuse and specular maps).

What we want to do is: first load an object into a Scene object, recursively retrieve the corresponding Mesh objects from each of the nodes (we recursively search each node's children), and process each Mesh object to retrieve the vertex data, indices, and its material properties. The result is then a collection of mesh data that we want to contain in a single `Model` object.

> **Mesh** When modeling objects in modeling toolkits, artists generally do not create an entire model out of a single shape. Usually, each model has several sub-models/shapes that it consists of. Each of those single shapes is called a mesh. Think of a human-like character: artists usually model the head, limbs, clothes, and weapons all as separate components, and the combined result of all these meshes represents the final model. A single mesh is the minimal representation of what we need to draw an object in OpenGL (vertex data, indices, and material properties). A model (usually) consists of several meshes.

In the next chapters we'll create our own `Model` and `Mesh` class that load and store imported models using the structure we've just described. If we then want to draw a model, we do not render the model as a whole, but we render all of the individual meshes that the model is composed of. However, before we can start importing models, we first need to actually include Assimp in our project.

19.2 Building Assimp

You can download Assimp from their download page[1] and choose the corresponding version. For this writing, the Assimp version used was version `3.1.1`. It is advised to compile the libraries by yourself, since their pre-compiled libraries don't always work on all systems. Review the *Creating a window* chapter if you forgot how to compile a library by yourself via CMake.

A few issues can come up while building Assimp, so I'll note them down here with their solutions in case any of you get the same errors:

- CMake continually gives errors while retrieving the configuration list about DirectX libraries missing, messages like:

```
Could not locate DirectX
CMake Error at cmake-modules/FindPkgMacros.cmake:110 (message):
Required library DirectX not found! Install the library (including dev
    packages)
and try again. If the library is already installed, set the missing
    variables
manually in cmake.
```

  The solution here is to install the DirectX SDK in case you haven't installed this before. You can download the SDK at: `www.microsoft.com/en-us/download/details.aspx?id=6812`.
- While installing the DirectX SDK, a possible error code of `s1023` could pop up. In that case you first want to de-install the C++ Redistributable package(s) before installing the SDK.

Once the configuration is completed, you can generate a solution file, open it, and compile the libraries (either as a release version or a debug version, whatever floats your boat). Be sure to compile it for 64-bit as all LearnOpenGL code is 64 bit.

The default configuration builds Assimp as a dynamic library so we need to include the resulting DLL named `assimp.dll` (or with some post-fix) alongside the application's binaries. You can simply copy the DLL to the same folder where your application's executable is located.

After compiling the generated solution, the resulting library and DLL file are located in the `code/Debug` or `code/Release` folder. Then simply move the lib and DLL to their appropriate locations, link them from your solution, and be sure to copy Assimp's headers to your `include` directory (the header files are found in the `include` folder in the files downloaded from Assimp).

By now you should have compiled Assimp and linked it to your application. If you still received any unreported error, feel free to ask for help in the comments.

---

[1] assimp.org/index.php/downloads

20. Mesh

With Assimp we can load many different models into the application, but once loaded they're all stored in Assimp's data structures. What we eventually want is to transform that data to a format that OpenGL understands so that we can render the objects. We learned from the previous chapter that a mesh represents a single drawable entity, so let's start by defining a mesh class of our own.

Let's review a bit of what we've learned so far to think about what a mesh should minimally have as its data. A mesh should at least need a set of vertices, where each vertex contains a position vector, a normal vector, and a texture coordinate vector. A mesh should also contain indices for indexed drawing, and material data in the form of textures (diffuse/specular maps).

Now that we set the minimal requirements for a mesh class we can define a vertex in OpenGL:

```cpp
struct Vertex {
    glm::vec3 Position;
    glm::vec3 Normal;
    glm::vec2 TexCoords;
};
```

We store each of the required vertex attributes in a struct called `Vertex`. Next to a `Vertex` struct we also want to organize the texture data in a `Texture` struct:

```cpp
struct Texture {
    unsigned int id;
    string type;
};
```

We store the id of the texture and its type e.g. a diffuse or specular texture.

Knowing the actual representation of a vertex and a texture we can start defining the structure of the mesh class:

```cpp
class Mesh {
    public:
        // mesh data
        vector<Vertex>       vertices;
        vector<unsigned int> indices;
        vector<Texture>      textures;

        Mesh(vector<Vertex> vertices, vector<unsigned int> indices,
            vector<Texture> textures);
        void Draw(Shader &shader);
    private:
        // render data
        unsigned int VAO, VBO, EBO;

        void setupMesh();
};
```

As you can see, the class isn't too complicated. In the constructor we give the mesh all the necessary data, we initialize the buffers in the `setupMesh` function, and finally draw the mesh via the `Draw` function. Note that we give a shader to the `Draw` function; by passing the shader to the mesh we can set several uniforms before drawing (like linking samplers to texture units).

The function content of the constructor is pretty straightforward. We simply set the class's public variables with the constructor's corresponding argument variables. We also call the `setupMesh` function in the constructor:

```cpp
Mesh(vector<Vertex> vertices, vector<unsigned int> indices,
     vector<Texture> textures)
{
    this->vertices = vertices;
    this->indices = indices;
    this->textures = textures;

    setupMesh();
}
```

Nothing special going on here. Let's delve right into the `setupMesh` function now.

20.1 Initialization

Thanks to the constructor we now have large lists of mesh data that we can use for rendering. We do need to setup the appropriate buffers and specify the vertex shader layout via vertex attribute pointers. By now you should have no trouble with these concepts, but we've spiced it up a bit this time with the introduction of vertex data in structs:

```cpp
void setupMesh()
{
    glGenVertexArrays(1, &VAO);
    glGenBuffers(1, &VBO);
    glGenBuffers(1, &EBO);

    glBindVertexArray(VAO);
    glBindBuffer(GL_ARRAY_BUFFER, VBO);

    glBufferData(GL_ARRAY_BUFFER, vertices.size() * sizeof(Vertex),
                 &vertices[0], GL_STATIC_DRAW);

    glBindBuffer(GL_ELEMENT_ARRAY_BUFFER, EBO);
    glBufferData(GL_ELEMENT_ARRAY_BUFFER, indices.size() *
                 sizeof(unsigned int), &indices[0], GL_STATIC_DRAW);

    // vertex positions
    glEnableVertexAttribArray(0);
    glVertexAttribPointer(0, 3, GL_FLOAT, GL_FALSE, sizeof(Vertex),
                          (void*)0);
    // vertex normals
    glEnableVertexAttribArray(1);
    glVertexAttribPointer(1, 3, GL_FLOAT, GL_FALSE, sizeof(Vertex),
                          (void*)offsetof(Vertex, Normal));
    // vertex texture coords
    glEnableVertexAttribArray(2);
    glVertexAttribPointer(2, 2, GL_FLOAT, GL_FALSE, sizeof(Vertex),
                          (void*)offsetof(Vertex, TexCoords));

    glBindVertexArray(0);
}
```

The code is not much different from what you'd expect, but a few little tricks were used with the help of the `Vertex` struct.

Structs have a great property in C++ that their memory layout is sequential. That is, if we were to represent a struct as an array of data, it would only contain the struct's variables in sequential order which directly translates to a float (actually byte) array that we want for an array buffer. For example, if we have a filled `Vertex` struct, its memory layout would be equal to:

```
Vertex vertex;
vertex.Position  = glm::vec3(0.2f, 0.4f, 0.6f);
vertex.Normal    = glm::vec3(0.0f, 1.0f, 0.0f);
vertex.TexCoords = glm::vec2(1.0f, 0.0f);
// = [0.2f, 0.4f, 0.6f, 0.0f, 1.0f, 0.0f, 1.0f, 0.0f];
```

Thanks to this useful property we can directly pass a pointer to a large list of `Vertex` structs as the buffer's data and they translate perfectly to what `glBufferData` expects as its argument:

```
glBufferData(GL_ARRAY_BUFFER, vertices.size() * sizeof(Vertex),
             vertices[0], GL_STATIC_DRAW);
```

Naturally the `sizeof` operator can also be used on the struct for the appropriate size in bytes. This should be `32` bytes (8 floats * 4 bytes each).

Another great use of structs is a preprocessor directive called `offsetof(s,m)` that takes as its first argument a struct and as its second argument a variable name of the struct. The macro returns the byte offset of that variable from the start of the struct. This is perfect for defining the offset parameter of the `glVertexAttribPointer` function:

```
glVertexAttribPointer(1, 3, GL_FLOAT, GL_FALSE, sizeof(Vertex),
                      (void*)offsetof(Vertex, Normal));
```

The offset is now defined using the `offsetof` macro that, in this case, sets the byte offset of the normal vector equal to the byte offset of the normal attribute in the struct which is 3 floats and thus `12` bytes.

Using a struct like this doesn't only get us more readable code, but also allows us to easily extend the structure. If we want another vertex attribute we can simply add it to the struct and due to its flexible nature, the rendering code won't break.

20.2 Rendering

The last function we need to define for the `Mesh` class to be complete is its `Draw` function. Before rendering the mesh, we first want to bind the appropriate textures before calling `glDrawElements`. However, this is somewhat difficult since we don't know from the start how many (if any) textures the mesh has and what type they may have. So how do we set the texture units and samplers in the shaders?

To solve the issue we're going to assume a certain naming convention: each diffuse texture is named `texture_diffuseN`, and each specular texture should be named `texture_specularN` where `N` is any number ranging from `1` to the maximum number of texture samplers allowed. Let's say we have 3 diffuse textures and 2 specular textures for a particular mesh, their texture samplers should then be called:

```
uniform sampler2D texture_diffuse1;
uniform sampler2D texture_diffuse2;
uniform sampler2D texture_diffuse3;
uniform sampler2D texture_specular1;
uniform sampler2D texture_specular2;
```

By this convention we can define as many texture samplers as we want in the shaders (up to OpenGL's maximum) and if a mesh actually does contain (so many) textures, we know what their names are going to be. By this convention we can process any amount of textures on a single mesh and the shader developer is free to use as many of those as he wants by defining the proper samplers.

> There are many solutions to problems like this and if you don't like this particular solution
> it is up to you to get creative and come up with your own approach.

The resulting drawing code then becomes:

```cpp
void Draw(Shader &shader)
{
    unsigned int diffuseNr = 1;
    unsigned int specularNr = 1;
    for(unsigned int i = 0; i < textures.size(); i++)
    {
        glActiveTexture(GL_TEXTURE0 + i); // activate texture unit first
        // retrieve texture number (the N in diffuse_textureN)
        string number;
        string name = textures[i].type;
        if(name == "texture_diffuse")
            number = std::to_string(diffuseNr++);
        else if(name == "texture_specular")
            number = std::to_string(specularNr++);

        shader.setFloat(("material." + name + number).c_str(), i);
        glBindTexture(GL_TEXTURE_2D, textures[i].id);
    }
    glActiveTexture(GL_TEXTURE0);

    // draw mesh
    glBindVertexArray(VAO);
    glDrawElements(GL_TRIANGLES, indices.size(), GL_UNSIGNED_INT, 0);
    glBindVertexArray(0);
}
```

We first calculate the N-component per texture type and concatenate it to the texture's type string to get the appropriate uniform name. We then locate the appropriate sampler, give it the location value to correspond with the currently active texture unit, and bind the texture. This is also the reason we need the shader in the `Draw` function.

We also added `"material."` to the resulting uniform name because we usually store the textures in a material struct (this may differ per implementation).

> Note that we increment the diffuse and specular counters the moment we convert them
> to `string`. In C++ the increment call: `variable++` returns the variable as is and
> **then** increments the variable while `++variable` **first** increments the variable and **then**
> returns it. In our case the value passed to `std::string` is the original counter value.
> After that the value is incremented for the next round.

You can find the full source code of the `Mesh` class at `/includes/learnopengl/mesh.h`.

The `Mesh` class we just defined is an abstraction for many of the topics we've discussed in the early chapters. In the next chapter we'll create a model that acts as a container for several mesh objects and implements Assimp's loading interface.

21. Model

Now it is time to get our hands dirty with Assimp and start creating the actual loading and translation code. The goal of this chapter is to create another class that represents a model in its entirety, that is, a model that contains multiple meshes, possibly with multiple textures. A house, that contains a wooden balcony, a tower, and perhaps a swimming pool, could still be loaded as a single model. We'll load the model via Assimp and translate it to multiple `Mesh` objects we've created in the previous chapter.

Without further ado, I present you the class structure of the `Model` class:

```cpp
class Model
{
    public:
        Model(char *path)
        {
            loadModel(path);
        }
        void Draw(Shader &shader);
    private:
        // model data
        vector<Mesh> meshes;
        string directory;

        void loadModel(string path);
        void processNode(aiNode *node, const aiScene *scene);
        Mesh processMesh(aiMesh *mesh, const aiScene *scene);
        vector<Texture> loadMaterialTextures(aiMaterial *mat,
            aiTextureType type, string typeName);
};
```

The `Model` class contains a vector of `Mesh` objects and requires us to give it a file location in its constructor. It then loads the file right away via the `loadModel` function that is called in the constructor. The private functions are all designed to process a part of Assimp's import routine and we'll cover them shortly. We also store the directory of the file path that we'll later need when loading textures.

The `Draw` function is nothing special and basically loops over each of the meshes to call their respective `Draw` function:

```cpp
void Draw(Shader &shader)
{
    for(unsigned int i = 0; i < meshes.size(); i++)
        meshes[i].Draw(shader);
}
```

21.1 Importing a 3D model into OpenGL

To import a model and translate it to our own structure, we first need to include the appropriate headers of Assimp:

```cpp
#include <assimp/Importer.hpp>
#include <assimp/scene.h>
#include <assimp/postprocess.h>
```

The first function we're calling is `loadModel`, that's directly called from the constructor. Within `loadModel`, we use Assimp to load the model into a data structure of Assimp called a scene object. You may remember from the first chapter of the model loading series that this is the root object of Assimp's data interface. Once we have the scene object, we can access all the data we need from the loaded model.

The great thing about Assimp is that it neatly abstracts from all the technical details of loading all the different file formats and does all this with a single one-liner:

```cpp
Assimp::Importer importer;
const aiScene *scene = importer.ReadFile(path, aiProcess_Triangulate |
                                         aiProcess_FlipUVs);
```

We first declare an `Importer` object from Assimp's namespace and then call its `ReadFile` function. The function expects a file path and several post-processing options as its second argument. Assimp allows us to specify several options that forces Assimp to do extra calculations/operations on the imported data. By setting `aiProcess_Triangulate` we tell Assimp that if the model does not (entirely) consist of triangles, it should transform all the model's primitive shapes to triangles first. The `aiProcess_FlipUVs` flips the texture coordinates on the y-axis where necessary during processing (you may remember from the *Textures* chapter that most images in OpenGL were reversed around the y-axis; this little postprocessing option fixes that for us). A few other useful options are:

- `aiProcess_GenNormals`: creates normal vectors for each vertex if the model doesn't contain normal vectors.
- `aiProcess_SplitLargeMeshes`: splits large meshes into smaller sub-meshes which is useful if your rendering has a maximum number of vertices allowed and can only process smaller meshes.
- `aiProcess_OptimizeMeshes`: does the reverse by trying to join several meshes into one larger mesh, reducing drawing calls for optimization.

Assimp provides a great set of postprocessing options and you can find all of them in their documentation[1]. Loading a model via Assimp is (as you can see) surprisingly easy. The hard work is in using the returned scene object to translate the loaded data to an array of `Mesh` objects.

The complete `loadModel` function is listed here:

```cpp
void loadModel(string path)
{
    Assimp::Importer import;
    const aiScene *scene = import.ReadFile(path, aiProcess_Triangulate |
    aiProcess_FlipUVs);

    if(!scene || scene->mFlags & AI_SCENE_FLAGS_INCOMPLETE ||
        !scene->mRootNode)
    {
        cout << "ERROR::ASSIMP::" << import.GetErrorString() << endl;
        return;
    }
    directory = path.substr(0, path.find_last_of('/'));

    processNode(scene->mRootNode, scene);
}
```

After we load the model, we check if the scene and the root node of the scene are not null and check one of its flags to see if the returned data is incomplete. If any of these error conditions are

---

[1] assimp.sourceforge.net/lib_html/postprocess_8h.html

met, we report the error retrieved from the importer's `GetErrorString` function and return. We also retrieve the directory path of the given file path.

If nothing went wrong, we want to process all of the scene's nodes. We pass the first node (root node) to the recursive `processNode` function. Because each node (possibly) contains a set of children we want to first process the node in question, and then continue processing all the node's children and so on. This fits a recursive structure, so we'll be defining a recursive function. A recursive function is a function that does some processing and recursively calls the same function with different parameters until a certain condition is met. In our case the exit condition is met when all nodes have been processed.

As you may remember from Assimp's structure, each node contains a set of mesh indices where each index points to a specific mesh located in the scene object. We thus want to retrieve these mesh indices, retrieve each mesh, process each mesh, and then do this all again for each of the node's children nodes. The content of the `processNode` function is shown below:

```cpp
void processNode(aiNode *node, const aiScene *scene)
{
    // process all the node's meshes (if any)
    for(unsigned int i = 0; i < node->mNumMeshes; i++)
    {
        aiMesh *mesh = scene->mMeshes[node->mMeshes[i]];
        meshes.push_back(processMesh(mesh, scene));
    }
    // then do the same for each of its children
    for(unsigned int i = 0; i < node->mNumChildren; i++)
    {
        processNode(node->mChildren[i], scene);
    }
}
```

We first check each of the node's mesh indices and retrieve the corresponding mesh by indexing the scene's `mMeshes` array. The returned mesh is then passed to the `processMesh` function that returns a `Mesh` object that we can store in the `meshes` list/vector.

Once all the meshes have been processed, we iterate through all of the node's children and call the same `processNode` function for each its children. Once a node no longer has any children, the recursion stops.

A careful reader may have noticed that we could forget about processing any of the nodes and simply loop through all of the scene's meshes directly, without doing all this complicated stuff with indices. The reason we're doing this is that the initial idea for using nodes like this is that it defines a parent-child relation between meshes. By recursively iterating through these relations, we can define certain meshes to be parents of other meshes. An example use case for such a system is when you want to translate a car mesh and make sure that all its children (like an engine mesh, a steering wheel mesh, and its tire meshes) translate as well; such a system is easily created using parent-child relations. Right now however we're not using such a system, but it is generally recommended to stick with this approach for whenever you want extra control over your mesh data. These node-like relations are after all defined by the artists who created the models.

The next step is to process Assimp's data into the `Mesh` class from the previous chapter.

21.1.1 Assimp to Mesh

Translating an `aiMesh` object to a mesh object of our own is not too difficult. All we need to do, is access each of the mesh's relevant properties and store them in our own object. The general structure of the `processMesh` function then becomes:

```cpp
Mesh processMesh(aiMesh *mesh, const aiScene *scene)
{
    vector<Vertex> vertices;
    vector<unsigned int> indices;
    vector<Texture> textures;

    for(unsigned int i = 0; i < mesh->mNumVertices; i++)
    {
        Vertex vertex;
        // process vertex positions, normals and texture coordinates
        [...]
        vertices.push_back(vertex);
    }
    // process indices
    [...]
    // process material
    if(mesh->mMaterialIndex >= 0)
    {
        [...]
    }

    return Mesh(vertices, indices, textures);
}
```

Processing a mesh is a 3-part process: retrieve all the vertex data, retrieve the mesh's indices, and finally retrieve the relevant material data. The processed data is stored in one of the 3 vectors and from those a `Mesh` is created and returned to the function's caller.

Retrieving the vertex data is pretty simple: we define a `Vertex` struct that we add to the `vertices` array after each loop iteration. We loop for as much vertices there exist within the mesh (retrieved via `mesh->mNumVertices`). Within the iteration we want to fill this struct with all the relevant data. For vertex positions this is done as follows:

```cpp
glm::vec3 vector;
vector.x = mesh->mVertices[i].x;
vector.y = mesh->mVertices[i].y;
vector.z = mesh->mVertices[i].z;
vertex.Position = vector;
```

Note that we define a temporary `vec3` for transferring Assimp's data to. This is necessary as Assimp maintains its own data types for vector, matrices, strings etc. and they don't convert that well to glm's data types.

> Assimp calls their vertex position array `mVertices` which isn't the most intuitive name.

The procedure for normals should come as no surprise now:

```
vector.x = mesh->mNormals[i].x;
vector.y = mesh->mNormals[i].y;
vector.z = mesh->mNormals[i].z;
vertex.Normal = vector;
```

Texture coordinates are roughly the same, but Assimp allows a model to have up to 8 different texture coordinates per vertex. We're not going to use 8, we only care about the first set of texture coordinates. We'll also want to check if the mesh actually contains texture coordinates (which may not be always the case):

```
if(mesh->mTextureCoords[0]) // does the mesh contain texture coordinates?
{
    glm::vec2 vec;
    vec.x = mesh->mTextureCoords[0][i].x;
    vec.y = mesh->mTextureCoords[0][i].y;
    vertex.TexCoords = vec;
}
else
    vertex.TexCoords = glm::vec2(0.0f, 0.0f);
```

The `vertex` struct is now completely filled with the required vertex attributes and we can push it to the back of the `vertices` vector at the end of the iteration. This process is repeated for each of the mesh's vertices.

21.1.2 Indices

Assimp's interface defines each mesh as having an array of faces, where each face represents a single primitive, which in our case (due to the `aiProcess_Triangulate` option) are always triangles. A face contains the indices of the vertices we need to draw in what order for its primitive. So if we iterate over all the faces and store all the face's indices in the `indices` vector we're all set:

```
for(unsigned int i = 0; i < mesh->mNumFaces; i++)
{
    aiFace face = mesh->mFaces[i];
    for(unsigned int j = 0; j < face.mNumIndices; j++)
        indices.push_back(face.mIndices[j]);
}
```

After the outer loop has finished, we now have a complete set of vertices and index data for drawing the mesh via `glDrawElements`. However, to finish the discussion and to add some detail to the mesh, we want to process the mesh's material as well.

21.1.3 Material

Similar to nodes, a mesh only contains an index to a material object. To retrieve the material of a mesh, we need to index the scene's `mMaterials` array. The mesh's material index is set in its `mMaterialIndex` property, which we can also query to check if the mesh contains a material or not:

```
if(mesh->mMaterialIndex >= 0)
{
    aiMaterial *material = scene->mMaterials[mesh->mMaterialIndex];
    vector<Texture> diffuseMaps = loadMaterialTextures(material,
        aiTextureType_DIFFUSE, "texture_diffuse");
    textures.insert(textures.end(), diffuseMaps.begin(), diffuseMaps.end());
    vector<Texture> specularMaps = loadMaterialTextures(material,
```

```
            aiTextureType_SPECULAR, "texture_specular");
    textures.insert(textures.end(), specularMaps.begin(),
                    specularMaps.end());
}
```

We first retrieve the `aiMaterial` object from the scene's `mMaterials` array. Then we want to load the mesh's diffuse and/or specular textures. A material object internally stores an array of texture locations for each texture type. The different texture types are all prefixed with `aiTextureType_`. We use a helper function called `loadMaterialTextures` to retrieve, load, and initialize the textures from the material. The function returns a vector of `Texture` structs that we store at the end of the model's `textures` vector.

The `loadMaterialTextures` function iterates over all the texture locations of the given texture type, retrieves the texture's file location and then loads and generates the texture and stores the information in a `Vertex` struct. It looks like this:

```
vector<Texture> loadMaterialTextures(aiMaterial *mat, aiTextureType type,
                                     string typeName)
{
    vector<Texture> textures;
    for(unsigned int i = 0; i < mat->GetTextureCount(type); i++)
    {
        aiString str;
        mat->GetTexture(type, i, &str);
        Texture texture;
        texture.id = TextureFromFile(str.C_Str(), directory);
        texture.type = typeName;
        texture.path = str;
        textures.push_back(texture);
    }
    return textures;
}
```

We first check the amount of textures stored in the material via its `GetTextureCount` function that expects one of the texture types we've given. We retrieve each of the texture's file locations via the `GetTexture` function that stores the result in an `aiString`. We then use another helper function called `TextureFromFile` that loads a texture (with `stb_image.h`) for us and returns the texture's ID. You can check the complete code listing at the end for its content if you're not sure how such a function is written.

> Note that we make the assumption that texture file paths in model files are local to the actual model object e.g. in the same directory as the location of the model itself. We can then simply concatenate the texture location string and the directory string we retrieved earlier (in the `loadModel` function) to get the complete texture path (that's why the `GetTexture` function also needs the directory string).

And that is all there is to importing a model with Assimp.

21.2 An optimization

We're not completely done yet, since there is still a large (but not completely necessary) optimization we want to make. Most scenes re-use several of their textures onto several meshes; think of a house again that has a granite texture for its walls. This texture could also be applied to the floor, its ceilings, the staircase, perhaps a table, and maybe even a small well close by. Loading textures is not a cheap operation and in our current implementation a new texture is loaded and generated for each mesh, even though the exact same texture could have been loaded several times before. This quickly becomes the bottleneck of your model loading implementation.

So we're going to add one small tweak to the model code by storing all of the loaded textures globally. Wherever we want to load a texture, we first check if it hasn't been loaded already. If so, we take that texture and skip the entire loading routine, saving us a lot of processing power. To be able to compare textures we need to store their path as well:

```cpp
struct Texture {
    unsigned int id;
    string type;
    string path; // store path of texture to compare with other textures
};
```

Then we store all the loaded textures in another vector declared at the top of the model's class file as a private variable:

```cpp
vector<Texture> textures_loaded;
```

In the `loadMaterialTextures` function, we want to compare the texture path with all the textures in the `textures_loaded` vector to see if the current texture path equals any of those. If so, we skip the texture loading/generation part and simply use the located texture struct as the mesh's texture. The (updated) function is shown below:

```cpp
vector<Texture> loadMaterialTextures(aiMaterial *mat, aiTextureType type,
                                     string typeName)
{
    vector<Texture> textures;
    for(unsigned int i = 0; i < mat->GetTextureCount(type); i++)
    {
        aiString str;
        mat->GetTexture(type, i, &str);
        bool skip = false;
        for(unsigned int j = 0; j < textures_loaded.size(); j++)
        {
            if(std::strcmp(textures_loaded[j].path.data(),
                           str.C_Str()) == 0)
            {
                textures.push_back(textures_loaded[j]);
                skip = true;
                break;
            }
        }
        if(!skip)
        { // if texture hasn't been loaded already, load it
            Texture texture;
            texture.id = TextureFromFile(str.C_Str(), directory);
            texture.type = typeName;
            texture.path = str.C_Str();
            textures.push_back(texture);
            textures_loaded.push_back(texture); // add to loaded textures
        }
    }
    return textures;
}
```

> Some versions of Assimp tend to load models quite slow when using the debug version
> and/or the debug mode of your IDE, so be sure to test it out with release versions as well
> if you run into slow loading times.

You can find the complete source code of the `Model` class at `/includes/learnopengl/model.h`.

21.3 No more containers!

So let's give our implementation a spin by actually importing a model created by genuine artists, not something done by the creative genius that I am. Because I don't want to give myself too much credit, I'll occasionally allow some other artists to join the ranks and this time we're going to load this amazing Survival Guitar Backpack[1] by Berk Gedik. I've modified the material and paths a bit so it works directly with the way we've set up the model loading. The model is exported as a `.obj` file together with a `.mtl` file that links to the model's diffuse, specular, and normal maps (we'll get to those later). You can download the adjusted model for this chapter at: `learnopengl.com/data/models/backpack.zip`. Note that there's a few extra texture types we won't be using yet, and that all the textures and the model file(s) should be located in the same directory for the textures to load.

> The modified version of the backpack uses local relative texture paths, and renamed the
> albedo and metallic textures to diffuse and specular respectively.

Now, declare a `Model` object and pass in the model's file location. The model should then automatically load and (if there were no errors) render the object in the render loop using its `Draw` function and that is it. No more buffer allocations, attribute pointers, and render commands, just a simple one-liner. If you create a simple set of shaders where the fragment shader only outputs the object's diffuse texture, the result looks a bit like this:

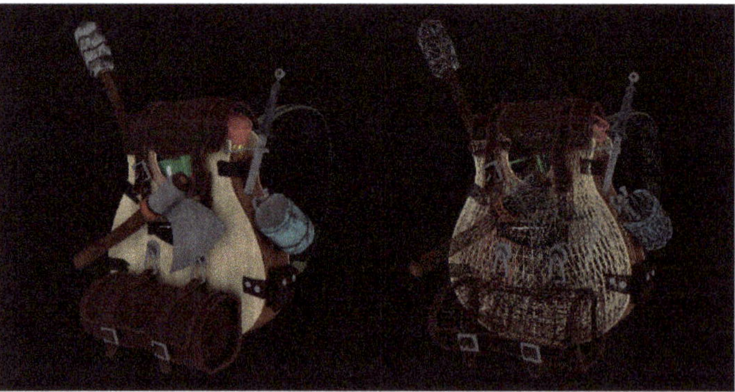

You can find the complete source code at `/src/3.model_loading/1.model_loading/`. Note that we tell `stb_image.h` to flip textures vertically, if you haven't done so already, before we load the model. Otherwise the textures will look all messed up.

---

[1] sketchfab.com/3d-models/survival-guitar-backpack-low-poly-799f8c4511f84fab8c3f12887f7e6b36

We can also get more creative and introduce point lights to the render equation as we learned from the *Lighting* chapters and together with specular maps get amazing results:

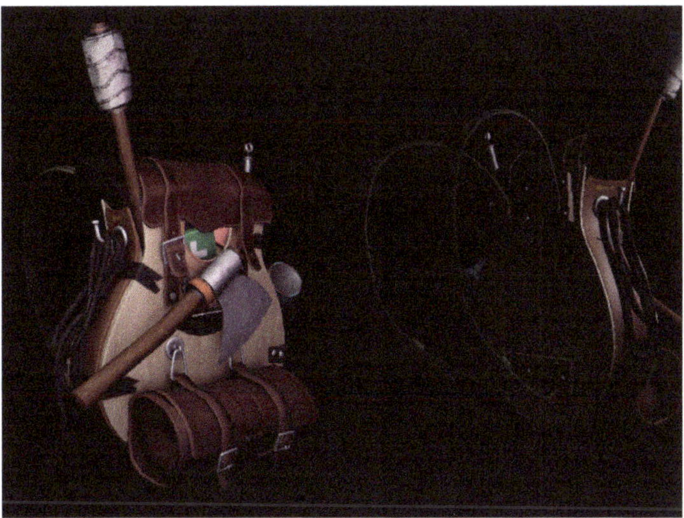

Even I have to admit that this is maybe a bit more fancy than the containers we've used so far. Using Assimp you can load tons of models found over the internet. There are quite a few resource websites that offer free 3D models for you to download in several file formats. Do note that some models still won't load properly, have texture paths that won't work, or are simply exported in a format even Assimp can't read.

21.4 Further reading

- `www.youtube.com/watch?v=4DQquG_o-Ac`: great video guide by Matthew Early on how to set up 3D models in Blender so they directly work with the current model loader (as the texture setup we've chosen doesn't always work out of the box).

IV Advanced OpenGL

22. Depth Testing

In the *coordinate systems* chapter we've rendered a 3D container and made use of a depth buffer to prevent triangles rendering in the front while they're supposed to be behind other triangles. In this chapter we're going to elaborate a bit more on those depth values the depth buffer (or z-buffer) stores and how it actually determines if a fragment is in front.

The depth-buffer is a buffer that, just like the color buffer (that stores all the fragment colors: the visual output), stores information per fragment and has the same width and height as the color buffer. The depth buffer is automatically created by the windowing system and stores its depth values as 16, 24 or 32 bit floats. In most systems you'll see a depth buffer with a precision of 24 bits.

When depth testing is enabled, OpenGL tests the depth value of a fragment against the content of the depth buffer. OpenGL performs a depth test and if this test passes, the fragment is rendered and the depth buffer is updated with the new depth value. If the depth test fails, the fragment is discarded.

Depth testing is done in screen space after the fragment shader has run (and after the stencil test which we'll get to in the next chapter. The screen space coordinates relate directly to the viewport defined by OpenGL's `glViewport` function and can be accessed via GLSL's built-in `gl_FragCoord` variable in the fragment shader. The x and y components of `gl_FragCoord` represent the fragment's screen-space coordinates (with (0,0) being the bottom-left corner). The `gl_FragCoord` variable also contains a z-component which contains the depth value of the fragment. This z value is the value that is compared to the depth buffer's content.

> Today most GPUs support a hardware feature called early depth testing. Early depth testing allows the depth test to run before the fragment shader runs. Whenever it is clear a fragment isn't going to be visible (it is behind other objects) we can prematurely discard the fragment. Fragment shaders are usually quite expensive so wherever we can avoid running them we should. A restriction on the fragment shader for early depth testing is that you shouldn't write to the fragment's depth value. If a fragment shader would write to its depth value, early depth testing is impossible; OpenGL won't be able to figure out the depth value beforehand.

Depth testing is disabled by default so to enable depth testing we need to enable it with the `GL_DEPTH_TEST` option:

```
glEnable(GL_DEPTH_TEST);
```

Once enabled, OpenGL automatically stores fragments their z-values in the depth buffer if they passed the depth test and discards fragments if they failed the depth test accordingly. If you have depth testing enabled you should also clear the depth buffer before each frame using `GL_DEPTH_BUFFER_BIT`; otherwise you're stuck with the depth values from last frame:

```
glClear(GL_COLOR_BUFFER_BIT | GL_DEPTH_BUFFER_BIT);
```

There are certain scenarios imaginable where you want to perform the depth test on all fragments and discard them accordingly, but **not** update the depth buffer. Basically, you're (temporarily) using a read-only depth buffer. OpenGL allows us to disable writing to the depth buffer by setting its depth mask to GL_FALSE:

```
glDepthMask(GL_FALSE);
```

Note that this only has effect if depth testing is enabled.

22.1 Depth test function

OpenGL allows us to modify the comparison operators it uses for the depth test. This allows us to control when OpenGL should pass or discard fragments and when to update the depth buffer. We can set the comparison operator (or depth function) by calling `glDepthFunc`:

```
glDepthFunc(GL_LESS);
```

The function accepts several comparison operators that are listed in the table below:

Function	Description
GL_ALWAYS	The depth test always passes.
GL_NEVER	The depth test never passes.
GL_LESS	Passes if the fragment's depth value is less than the stored depth value.
GL_EQUAL	Passes if the fragment's depth value is equal to the stored depth value.
GL_LEQUAL	Passes if the fragment's depth value is less than or equal to the stored depth value.
GL_GREATER	Passes if the fragment's depth value is greater than the stored depth value.
GL_NOTEQUAL	Passes if the fragment's depth value is not equal to the stored depth value.
GL_GEQUAL	Passes if the fragment's depth value is greater than or equal to the stored depth value.

By default the depth function `GL_LESS` is used that discards all the fragments that have a depth value higher than or equal to the current depth buffer's value.

Let's show the effect that changing the depth function has on the visual output. We'll use a fresh code setup that displays a basic scene with two textured cubes sitting on a textured floor with no lighting. You can find the source code at `/src/4.advanced_opengl/1.1.depth_testing/`.

Within the source code we changed the depth function to `GL_ALWAYS`:

```
glEnable(GL_DEPTH_TEST);
glDepthFunc(GL_ALWAYS);
```

This simulates the same behavior we'd get if we didn't enable depth testing. The depth test always passes so the fragments that are drawn last are rendered in front of the fragments that were drawn before, even though they should've been at the front. Since we've drawn the floor plane last, the plane's fragments overwrite each of the container's previously written fragments:

Setting it all back to `GL_LESS` gives us the type of scene we're used to:

22.2 Depth value precision

The depth buffer contains depth values between `0.0` and `1.0` and it compares its content with the z-values of all the objects in the scene as seen from the viewer. These z-values in view space can be any value between the projection-frustum's `near` and `far` plane. We thus need some way to transform these view-space z-values to the range of `[0,1]` and one way is to linearly transform them. The following (linear) equation transforms the z-value to a depth value between `0.0` and `1.0`:

$$F_{depth} = \frac{z - near}{far - near}$$

Here *near* and *far* are the *near* and *far* values we used to provide to the projection matrix to set the visible frustum (see *Coordinate Systems* chapter). The equation takes a depth value z within the frustum and transforms it to the range `[0,1]`. The relation between the z-value and its corresponding depth value is presented in the following graph:

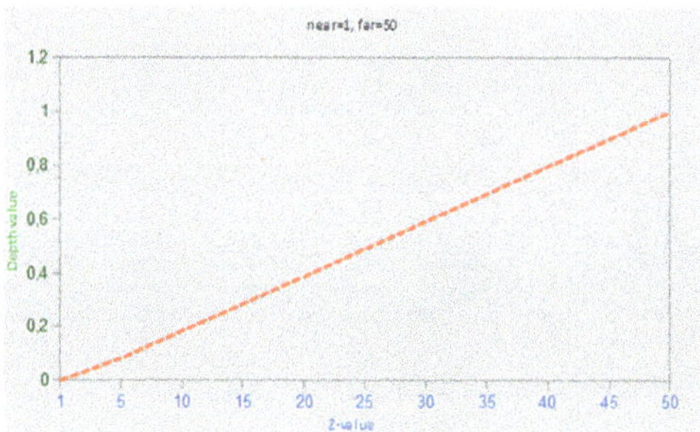

> Note that all equations give a depth value close to `0.0` when the object is close by and a depth value close to `1.0` when the object is close to the far plane.

In practice however, a linear depth buffer like this is almost never used. Because of projection properties a non-linear depth equation is used that is proportional to 1/z. The result is that we get enormous precision when z is small and much less precision when z is far away.

Since the non-linear function is proportional to 1/z, z-values between `1.0` and `2.0` would result in depth values between `1.0` and `0.5` which is half of the [0,1] range, giving us enormous precision at small z-values. Z-values between `50.0` and `100.0` would account for only 2% of the [0,1] range. Such an equation, that also takes near and far distances into account, is given below:

$$F_{\text{depth}} = \frac{1/z - 1/near}{1/far - 1/near}$$

Don't worry if you don't know exactly what is going on with this equation. The important thing to remember is that the values in the depth buffer are not linear in clip-space (they are linear in view-space before the projection matrix is applied). A value of `0.5` in the depth buffer does not mean the pixel's z-value is halfway in the frustum; the z-value of the vertex is actually quite close to the near plane! You can see the non-linear relation between the z-value and the resulting depth buffer's value in the following graph:

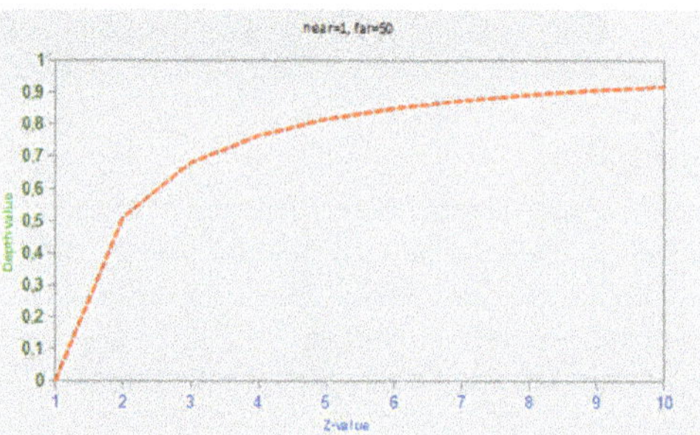

As you can see, the depth values are greatly determined by the small z-values giving us large depth precision to the objects close by. The equation to transform z-values (from the viewer's perspective) is embedded within the projection matrix so when we transform vertex coordinates from view to clip, and then to screen-space the non-linear equation is applied.

The effect of this non-linear equation quickly becomes apparent when we try to visualize the depth buffer.

22.3 Visualizing the depth buffer

We know that the z-value of the built-in `gl_FragCoord` vector in the fragment shader contains the depth value of that particular fragment. If we were to output this depth value of the fragment as a color we could display the depth values of all the fragments in the scene:

```glsl
void main()
{
    FragColor = vec4(vec3(gl_FragCoord.z), 1.0);
}
```

If you'd then run the program you'll probably notice that everything is white, making it look like all of our depth values are the maximum depth value of `1.0`. So why aren't any of the depth values closer to `0.0` and thus darker?

In the previous section we described that depth values in screen space are non-linear e.g. they have a very high precision for small z-values and a low precision for large z-values. The depth value of the fragment increases rapidly over distance so almost all the vertices have values close to `1.0`. If we were to carefully move really close to an object you may eventually see the colors getting darker, their z-values becoming smaller:

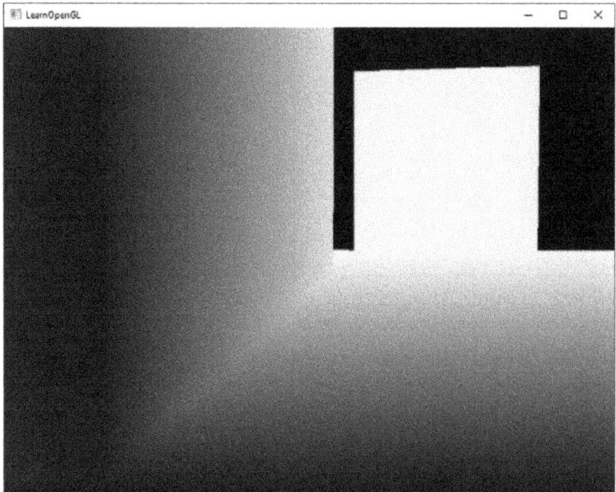

This clearly shows the non-linearity of the depth value. Objects close by have a much larger effect on the depth value than objects far away. Only moving a few inches can result in the colors going from dark to completely white.

We can however, transform the non-linear depth values of the fragment back to its linear sibling. To achieve this we basically need to reverse the process of projection for the depth values alone. This means we have to first re-transform the depth values from the range `[0,1]` to normalized device coordinates in the range `[-1,1]`. Then we want to reverse the non-linear equation (equation 2) as done in the projection matrix and apply this inversed equation to the resulting depth value. The result is then a linear depth value.

First we transform the depth value to NDC which is not too difficult:

```
float ndc = depth * 2.0 - 1.0;
```

We then take the resulting `ndc` value and apply the inverse transformation to retrieve its linear depth value:

```
float linearDepth = (2.0 * near * far) / (far + near - ndc * (far - near));
```

This equation is derived from the projection matrix for non-linearizing the depth values, returning depth values between `near` and `far`. The math-heavy projection matrix article[1] by Song Ho Ahn explains the projection matrix in enormous detail for the interested reader; it also shows where the equations come from.

The complete fragment shader that transforms the non-linear depth in screen-space to a linear depth value is then as follows:

```
#version 330 core
out vec4 FragColor;

float near = 0.1;
float far = 100.0;

float LinearizeDepth(float depth)
{
```

---

[1]www.songho.ca/opengl/gl_projectionmatrix.html

```glsl
    float z = depth * 2.0 - 1.0; // back to NDC
    return (2.0 * near * far) / (far + near - z * (far - near));
}

void main()
{
    float depth = LinearizeDepth(gl_FragCoord.z) / far; // / far for demo
    FragColor = vec4(vec3(depth), 1.0);
}
```

Because the linearized depth values range from `near` to `far` most of its values will be above `1.0` and displayed as completely white. By dividing the linear depth value by `far` in the `main` function we convert the linear depth value to the range [0, 1]. This way we can gradually see the scene become brighter the closer the fragments are to the projection frustum's far plane, which works better for visualization purposes.

If we'd now run the application we get depth values that are linear over distance. Try moving around the scene to see the depth values change in a linear fashion.

The colors are mostly black because the depth values range linearly from the `near` plane (`0.1`) to the `far` plane (`100`) which is still quite far away from us. The result is that we're relatively close to the near plane and therefore get lower (darker) depth values.

22.4 Z-fighting

A common visual artifact may occur when two planes or triangles are so closely aligned to each other that the depth buffer does not have enough precision to figure out which one of the two shapes is in front of the other. The result is that the two shapes continually seem to switch order which causes weird glitchy patterns. This is called z-fighting, because it looks like the shapes are fighting over who gets on top.

In the scene we've been using so far there are a few spots where z-fighting can be noticed. The containers were placed at the exact height of the floor which means the bottom plane of the container is coplanar with the floor plane. The depth values of both planes are then the same so the resulting depth test has no way of figuring out which is the right one.

If you move the camera inside one of the containers the effects are clearly visible, the bottom part of the container is constantly switching between the container's plane and the floor's plane in a zigzag pattern:

Z-fighting is a common problem with depth buffers and it's generally more noticeable when objects are further away (because the depth buffer has less precision at larger z-values). Z-fighting can't be completely prevented, but there are a few tricks that will help to mitigate or completely prevent z-fighting in your scene.

22.4.1 Prevent z-fighting

The first and most important trick is *never place objects too close to each other in a way that some of their triangles closely overlap.* By creating a small offset between two objects you can completely remove z-fighting between the two objects. In the case of the containers and the plane we could've easily moved the containers slightly upwards in the positive y direction. The small change of the container's positions would probably not be noticeable at all and would completely reduce the z-fighting. However, this requires manual intervention of each of the objects and thorough testing to make sure no objects in a scene produce z-fighting.

A second trick is to *set the near plane as far as possible.* In one of the previous sections we've discussed that precision is extremely large when close to the `near` plane so if we move the `near` plane away from the viewer, we'll have significantly greater precision over the entire frustum range. However, setting the `near` plane too far could cause clipping of near objects so it is usually a matter of tweaking and experimentation to figure out the best `near` distance for your scene.

Another great trick at the cost of some performance is to *use a higher precision depth buffer.* Most depth buffers have a precision of 24 bits, but most GPUs nowadays support 32 bit depth buffers, increasing the precision by a significant amount. So at the cost of some performance you'll get much more precision with depth testing, reducing z-fighting.

The 3 techniques we've discussed are the most common and easy-to-implement anti z-fighting techniques. There are some other techniques out there that require a lot more work and still won't completely disable z-fighting. Z-fighting is a common issue, but if you use the proper combination of the listed techniques you probably won't need to deal with z-fighting that much.

23. Stencil testing

Once the fragment shader has processed the fragment a so called stencil test is executed that, just like the depth test, has the option to discard fragments. After that the remaining fragments are passed to the depth test where OpenGL could possibly discard even more fragments. The stencil test is based on the content of yet another buffer called the stencil buffer that we're allowed to update during rendering to achieve interesting effects.

A stencil buffer (usually) contains 8 bits per stencil value that amounts to a total of 256 different stencil values per pixel. We can set these stencil values to values of our liking and we can discard or keep fragments whenever a particular fragment has a certain stencil value.

> Each windowing library needs to set up a stencil buffer for you. GLFW does this automatically so we don't have to tell GLFW to create one, but other windowing libraries may not create a stencil buffer by default so be sure to check your library's documentation.

A simple example of a stencil buffer is shown below (pixels not-to-scale):

Color buffer   Stencil buffer   After stencil test

The stencil buffer is first cleared with zeros and then an open rectangle of 1s is stored in the stencil buffer. The fragments of the scene are then only rendered (the others are discarded) wherever the stencil value of that fragment contains a 1.

Stencil buffer operations allow us to set the stencil buffer at specific values wherever we're rendering fragments. By changing the content of the stencil buffer while we're rendering, we're *writing* to the stencil buffer. In the same (or following) frame(s) we can *read* these values to discard or pass certain fragments. When using stencil buffers you can get as crazy as you like, but the general outline is usually as follows:

- Enable writing to the stencil buffer.
- Render objects, updating the content of the stencil buffer.
- Disable writing to the stencil buffer.
- Render (other) objects, this time discarding certain fragments based on the content of the stencil buffer.

By using the stencil buffer we can thus discard certain fragments based on the fragments of other drawn objects in the scene.

You can enable stencil testing by enabling GL_STENCIL_TEST. From that point on, all rendering calls will influence the stencil buffer in one way or another.

```cpp
glEnable(GL_STENCIL_TEST);
```

Note that you also need to clear the stencil buffer each iteration just like the color and depth buffer:

```
glClear(GL_COLOR_BUFFER_BIT | GL_DEPTH_BUFFER_BIT | GL_STENCIL_BUFFER_BIT);
```

Also, just like the depth testing's `glDepthMask` function, there is an equivalent function for the stencil buffer. The function `glStencilMask` allows us to set a bitmask that is ANDed with the stencil value about to be written to the buffer. By default this is set to a bitmask of all 1s not affecting the output, but if we were to set this to `0x00` all the stencil values written to the buffer end up as 0s. This is equivalent to depth testing's `glDepthMask(GL_FALSE)`:

```
glStencilMask(0xFF); // each bit is written to as is
glStencilMask(0x00); // each bit ends up as 0 (disabling writes)
```

Most of the cases you'll only be using `0x00` or `0xFF` as the stencil mask, but it's good to know there are options to set custom bit-masks.

23.1 Stencil functions

Similar to depth testing, we have a certain amount of control over when a stencil test should pass or fail and how it should affect the stencil buffer. There are a total of two functions we can use to configure stencil testing: `glStencilFunc` and `glStencilOp`.

The `glStencilFunc(GLenum func, GLint ref, GLuint mask)` has three parameters:

- `func`: sets the stencil test function that determines whether a fragment passes or is discarded. This test function is applied to the stored stencil value and the `glStencilFunc`'s ref value. Possible options are: `GL_NEVER`, `GL_LESS`, `GL_LEQUAL`, `GL_GREATER`, `GL_GEQUAL`, `GL_EQUAL`, `GL_NOTEQUAL` and `GL_ALWAYS`. The semantic meaning of these is similar to the depth buffer's functions.
- `ref`: specifies the reference value for the stencil test. The stencil buffer's content is compared to this value.
- `mask`: specifies a mask that is ANDed with both the reference value and the stored stencil value before the test compares them. Initially set to all 1s.

In the case of the simple stencil example we've shown at the start, the function would be set to:

```
glStencilFunc(GL_EQUAL, 1, 0xFF)
```

This tells OpenGL that whenever the stencil value of a fragment is equal (`GL_EQUAL`) to the reference value 1, the fragment passes the test and is drawn, otherwise discarded.

But `glStencilFunc` only describes whether OpenGL should pass or discard fragments based on the stencil buffer's content, not how we can actually update the buffer. That is where `glStencilOp` comes in.

The `glStencilOp(GLenum sfail, GLenum dpfail, GLenum dppass)` contains three options of which we can specify for each option what action to take:

- `sfail`: action to take if the stencil test fails.
- `dpfail`: action to take if the stencil test passes, but the depth test fails.
- `dppass`: action to take if both the stencil and the depth test pass.

Then for each of the options you can take any of the following actions:

Action	Description
GL_KEEP	The currently stored stencil value is kept.
GL_ZERO	The stencil value is set to 0.
GL_REPLACE	The stencil value is replaced with the reference value set with glStencilFunc.
GL_INCR	The stencil value is increased by 1 if it is lower than the maximum value.
GL_INCR_WRAP	Same as GL_INCR, but wraps it back to 0 as soon as the maximum value is exceeded.
GL_DECR	The stencil value is decreased by 1 if it is higher than the minimum value.
GL_DECR_WRAP	Same as GL_DECR, but wraps it to the maximum value if it ends up lower than 0.
GL_INVERT	Bitwise inverts the current stencil buffer value.

By default the glStencilOp function is set to (GL_KEEP, GL_KEEP, GL_KEEP) so whatever the outcome of any of the tests, the stencil buffer keeps its values. The default behavior does not update the stencil buffer, so if you want to write to the stencil buffer you need to specify at least one different action for any of the options.

So using glStencilFunc and glStencilOp we can precisely specify when and how we want to update the stencil buffer and when to pass or discard fragments based on its content.

23.2 Object outlining

It would be unlikely if you completely understood how stencil testing works from the previous sections alone so we're going to demonstrate a particular useful feature that can be implemented with stencil testing alone called object outlining.

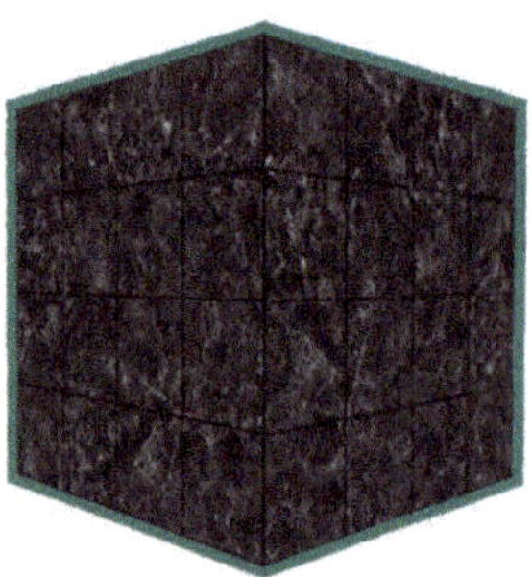

Object outlining does exactly what it says it does. For each object (or only one) we're creating a small colored border around the (combined) objects. This is a particular useful effect when you want to select units in a strategy game for example and need to show the user which of the units were selected. The routine for outlining your objects is as follows:

1. Enable stencil writing.
2. Set the stencil op to GL_ALWAYS before drawing the (to be outlined) objects, updating the stencil buffer with 1s wherever the objects' fragments are rendered.
3. Render the objects.
4. Disable stencil writing and depth testing.
5. Scale each of the objects by a small amount.
6. Use a different fragment shader that outputs a single (border) color.
7. Draw the objects again, but only if their fragments' stencil values are not equal to 1.
8. Enable depth testing again and restore stencil func to GL_KEEP.

This process sets the content of the stencil buffer to 1s for each of the object's fragments and when it's time to draw the borders, we draw scaled-up versions of the objects only where the stencil test passes. We're effectively discarding all the fragments of the scaled-up versions that are part of the original objects' fragments using the stencil buffer.

So we're first going to create a very basic fragment shader that outputs a border color. We simply set a hardcoded color value and call the shader `shaderSingleColor`:

```
void main()
{
    FragColor = vec4(0.04, 0.28, 0.26, 1.0);
}
```

Using the scene from the previous chapter we're going to add object outlining to the two containers, so we'll leave the floor out of it. We want to first draw the floor, then the two containers (while writing to the stencil buffer), and then draw the scaled-up containers (while discarding the fragments that write over the previously drawn container fragments).

We first need to enable stencil testing:

```
glEnable(GL_STENCIL_TEST);
```

And then in each frame we want to specify the action to take whenever any of the stencil tests succeed or fail:

```
glStencilOp(GL_KEEP, GL_KEEP, GL_REPLACE);
```

If any of the tests fail we do nothing; we simply keep the currently stored value that is in the stencil buffer. If both the stencil test and the depth test succeed however, we want to replace the stored stencil value with the reference value set via `glStencilFunc` which we later set to 1.

We clear the stencil buffer to 0s at the start of the frame and for the containers we update the stencil buffer to 1 for each fragment drawn:

```
glStencilOp(GL_KEEP, GL_KEEP, GL_REPLACE);
glStencilFunc(GL_ALWAYS, 1, 0xFF); // all fragments pass the stencil test
glStencilMask(0xFF); // enable writing to the stencil buffer
normalShader.use();
DrawTwoContainers();
```

By using `GL_REPLACE` as the stencil op function we make sure that each of the containers' fragments update the stencil buffer with a stencil value of 1. Because the fragments always pass the stencil test, the stencil buffer is updated with the reference value wherever we've drawn them.

Now that the stencil buffer is updated with 1s where the containers were drawn we're going to draw the upscaled containers, but this time with the appropriate test function and disabling writes to the stencil buffer:

```
glStencilFunc(GL_NOTEQUAL, 1, 0xFF);
glStencilMask(0x00); // disable writing to the stencil buffer
glDisable(GL_DEPTH_TEST);
shaderSingleColor.use();
DrawTwoScaledUpContainers();
```

We set the stencil function to `GL_NOTEQUAL` to make sure that we're only drawing parts of the containers that are not equal to 1. This way we only draw the part of the containers that are outside the previously drawn containers. Note that we also disable depth testing so the scaled up containers (e.g. the borders) do not get overwritten by the floor. Make sure to enable the depth buffer again once you're done.

The total object outlining routine for our scene looks something like this:

```
glEnable(GL_DEPTH_TEST);
glStencilOp(GL_KEEP, GL_KEEP, GL_REPLACE);

glClear(GL_COLOR_BUFFER_BIT | GL_DEPTH_BUFFER_BIT | GL_STENCIL_BUFFER_BIT);

glStencilMask(0x00); // don't update stencil buffer while drawing the floor
normalShader.use();
DrawFloor()

glStencilFunc(GL_ALWAYS, 1, 0xFF);
glStencilMask(0xFF);
DrawTwoContainers();

glStencilFunc(GL_NOTEQUAL, 1, 0xFF);
glStencilMask(0x00);
glDisable(GL_DEPTH_TEST);
shaderSingleColor.use();
DrawTwoScaledUpContainers();
glStencilMask(0xFF);
glStencilFunc(GL_ALWAYS, 1, 0xFF);
glEnable(GL_DEPTH_TEST);
```

As long as you understand the general idea behind stencil testing this shouldn't be too hard
to understand. Otherwise try to carefully read the previous sections again and try to completely
understand what each of the functions does now that you've seen an example of it can be used.

The result of the outlining algorithm then looks like this:

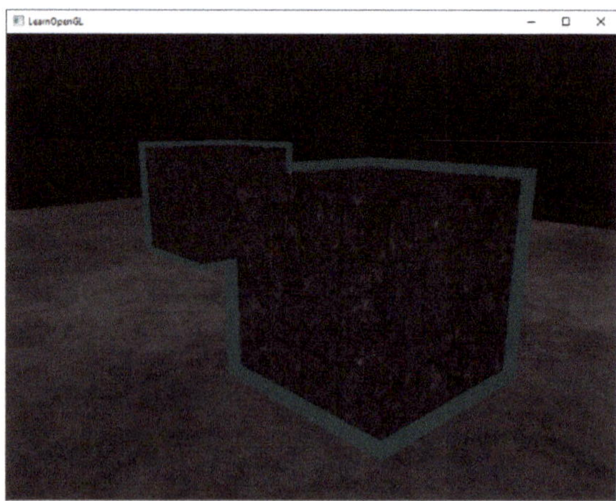

Check the source code at `/src/4.advanced_opengl/2.stencil_testing/` to see
the complete code of the object outlining algorithm.

You can see that the borders overlap between both containers which is usually the effect
that we want (think of strategy games where we want to select 10 units; merging borders
is generally preferred). If you want a complete border per object you'd have to clear the
stencil buffer per object and get a little creative with the depth buffer.

The object outlining algorithm you've seen is commonly used in games to visualize selected objects (think of strategy games) and an algorithm like this can easily be implemented within a model class. You could set a boolean flag within the model class to draw either with borders or without. If you want to be creative you could even give the borders a more natural look with the help of post-processing filters like Gaussian Blur.

Stencil testing has many more purposes (beside outlining objects) like drawing textures inside a rear-view mirror so it neatly fits into the mirror shape, or rendering real-time shadows with a stencil buffer technique called shadow volumes. Stencil buffers give us with yet another nice tool in our already extensive OpenGL toolkit.

24. Blending

Blending in OpenGL is commonly known as the technique to implement transparency within objects. Transparency is all about objects (or parts of them) not having a solid color, but having a combination of colors from the object itself and any other object behind it with varying intensity. A colored glass window is a transparent object; the glass has a color of its own, but the resulting color contains the colors of all the objects behind the glass as well. This is also where the name blending comes from, since we blend several pixel colors (from different objects) to a single color. Transparency thus allows us to see through objects.

Full transparent window   Partially transparent window

Transparent objects can be completely transparent (letting all colors through) or partially transparent (letting colors through, but also some of its own colors). The amount of transparency of an object is defined by its color's alpha value. The alpha color value is the 4th component of a color vector that you've probably seen quite often now. Up until this chapter, we've always kept this 4th component at a value of `1.0` giving the object `0.0` transparency. An alpha value of `0.0` would result in the object having complete transparency. An alpha value of `0.5` tells us the object's color consist of 50% of its own color and 50% of the colors behind the object.

The textures we've used so far all consisted of 3 color components: red, green and blue, but some textures also have an embedded alpha channel that contains an alpha value per texel. This alpha value tells us exactly which parts of the texture have transparency and by how much. For example, the window texture[1] below has an alpha value of `0.25` at its glass part and an alpha value of `0.0` at its corners. The glass part would normally be completely red, but since it has 75% transparency it largely shows the page's background through it, making it seem a lot less red:

We'll soon be adding this windowed texture to the scene from the depth testing chapter, but first we'll discuss an easier technique to implement transparency for pixels that are either fully transparent or fully opaque.

24.1 Discarding fragments

Some effects do not care about partial transparency, but either want to show something or nothing at all based on the color value of a texture. Think of grass; to create something like grass with little effort you generally paste a grass texture onto a 2D quad and place that quad into your scene.

---

[1]learnopengl.com/img/advanced/blending_transparent_window.png

However, grass isn't exactly shaped like a 2D square so you only want to display some parts of the grass texture and ignore the others.

The grass texture[1] below is exactly such a texture where it either is full opaque (an alpha value of 1.0) or it is fully transparent (an alpha value of 0.0) and nothing in between. You can see that wherever there is no grass, the image shows the paper's color instead of its own.

So when adding vegetation to a scene we don't want to see a square image of grass, but rather only show the actual grass and see through the rest of the image. We want to discard the fragments that show the transparent parts of the texture, not storing that fragment into the color buffer.

Before we get into that we first need to learn how to load a transparent texture. To load textures with alpha values there's not much we need to change. stb_image automatically loads an image's alpha channel if it's available, but we do need to tell OpenGL our texture now uses an alpha channel in the texture generation procedure:

```cpp
glTexImage2D(GL_TEXTURE_2D, 0, GL_RGBA, width, height, 0, GL_RGBA,
             GL_UNSIGNED_BYTE, data);
```

Also make sure that you retrieve all 4 color components of the texture in the fragment shader, not just the RGB components:

```glsl
void main()
{
    // FragColor = vec4(vec3(texture(texture1, TexCoords)), 1.0);
    FragColor = texture(texture1, TexCoords);
}
```

Now that we know how to load transparent textures it's time to put it to the test by adding several of these leaves of grass throughout the basic scene introduced in the *Depth Testing* chapter.

We create a small vector array where we add several glm::vec3 vectors to represent the location of the grass leaves:

```cpp
vector<glm::vec3> vegetation;
vegetation.push_back(glm::vec3(-1.5f, 0.0f, -0.48f));
vegetation.push_back(glm::vec3( 1.5f, 0.0f,  0.51f));
vegetation.push_back(glm::vec3( 0.0f, 0.0f,  0.7f));
vegetation.push_back(glm::vec3(-0.3f, 0.0f, -2.3f));
vegetation.push_back(glm::vec3( 0.5f, 0.0f, -0.6f));
```

Each of the grass objects is rendered as a single quad with the grass texture attached to it. It's not a perfect 3D representation of grass, but it's a lot more efficient than loading and rendering a

---

[1] learnopengl.com/img/textures/grass.png

large number of complex models. With a few tricks like adding randomized rotations and scales you can get pretty convincing results with quads.

Because the grass texture is going to be displayed on a quad object we'll need to create another VAO again, fill the VBO, and set the appropriate vertex attribute pointers. Then after we've rendered the floor and the two cubes we're going to render the grass leaves:

```cpp
glBindVertexArray(vegetationVAO);
glBindTexture(GL_TEXTURE_2D, grassTexture);
for(unsigned int i = 0; i < vegetation.size(); i++)
{
    model = glm::mat4(1.0f);
    model = glm::translate(model, vegetation[i]);
    shader.setMat4("model", model);
    glDrawArrays(GL_TRIANGLES, 0, 6);
}
```

Running the application will now look a bit like this:

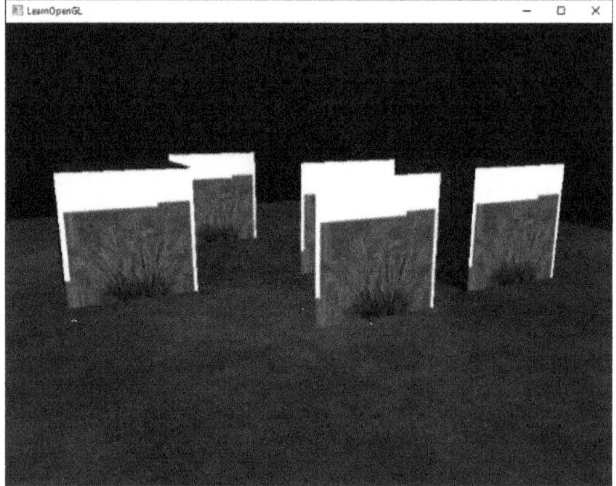

This happens because OpenGL by default does not know what to do with alpha values, nor when to discard them. We have to manually do this ourselves. Luckily this is quite easy thanks to the use of shaders. GLSL gives us the `discard` command that (once called) ensures the fragment will not be further processed and thus not end up into the color buffer. Thanks to this command we can check whether a fragment has an alpha value below a certain threshold and if so, discard the fragment as if it had never been processed:

```glsl
#version 330 core
out vec4 FragColor;

in vec2 TexCoords;

uniform sampler2D texture1;

void main()
{
    vec4 texColor = texture(texture1, TexCoords);
    if(texColor.a < 0.1)
        discard;
    FragColor = texColor;
}
```

Here we check if the sampled texture color contains an alpha value lower than a threshold of `0.1` and if so, discard the fragment. This fragment shader ensures us that it only renders fragments that are not (almost) completely transparent. Now it'll look like it should:

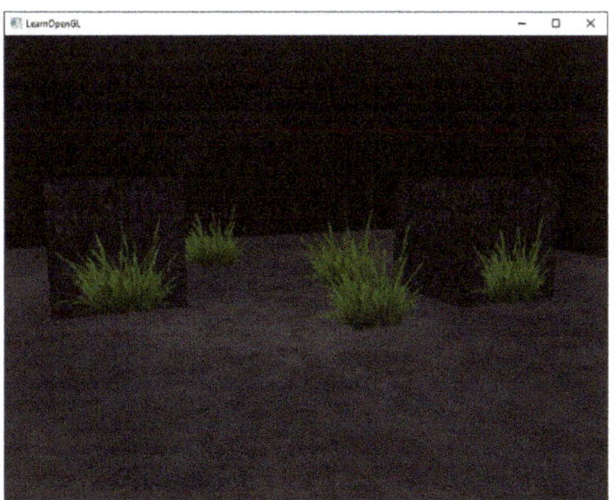

> Note that when sampling textures at their borders, OpenGL interpolates the border values with the next repeated value of the texture (because we set its wrapping parameters to `GL_REPEAT` by default). This is usually okay, but since we're using transparent values, the top of the texture image gets its transparent value interpolated with the bottom border's solid color value. The result is then a slightly semi-transparent colored border you may see wrapped around your textured quad. To prevent this, set the texture wrapping method to `GL_CLAMP_TO_EDGE` whenever you use alpha textures that you don't want to repeat:
>
> ```cpp
> glTexParameteri( GL_TEXTURE_2D, GL_TEXTURE_WRAP_S, GL_CLAMP_TO_EDGE);
> glTexParameteri( GL_TEXTURE_2D, GL_TEXTURE_WRAP_T, GL_CLAMP_TO_EDGE);
> ```

You can find the source code at `/src/4.advanced_opengl/3.1.blending_discard/`.

24.2 Blending

While discarding fragments is great and all, it doesn't give us the flexibility to render semi-transparent images; we either render the fragment or completely discard it. To render images with different levels of transparency we have to enable blending. Like most of OpenGL's functionality we can enable blending by enabling `GL_BLEND`:

```cpp
glEnable(GL_BLEND);
```

Now that we've enabled blending we need to tell OpenGL **how** it should actually blend.

Blending in OpenGL happens with the following equation:

$$\bar{C}_{\text{result}} = \bar{C}_{\text{source}} * F_{\text{source}} + \bar{C}_{\text{destination}} * F_{\text{destination}}$$

- $\bar{C}_{\text{source}}$: the source color vector. This is the color output of the fragment shader.
- $\bar{C}_{\text{destination}}$: the destination color vector. This is the color vector that is currently stored in the color buffer.
- F_{source}: the source factor value. Sets the impact of the alpha value on the source color.
- $F_{\text{destination}}$: the destination factor value. Sets the impact of the alpha value on the destination color.

After the fragment shader has run and all the tests have passed, this blend equation is let loose on the fragment's color output and with whatever is currently in the color buffer. The source and destination colors will automatically be set by OpenGL, but the source and destination factor can be set to a value of our choosing. Let's start with a simple example:

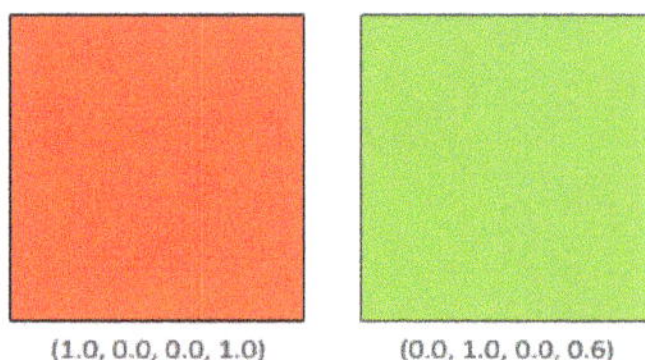

(1.0, 0.0, 0.0, 1.0)   (0.0, 1.0, 0.0, 0.6)

We have two squares where we want to draw the semi-transparent green square on top of the red square. The red square will be the destination color (and thus should be first in the color buffer) and we are now going to draw the green square over the red square.

The question then arises: what do we set the factor values to? Well, we at least want to multiply the green square with its alpha value so we want to set the F_{src} equal to the alpha value of the source color vector which is 0.6. Then it makes sense to let the destination square have a contribution equal to the remainder of the alpha value. If the green square contributes 60% to the final color we want the red square to contribute 40% of the final color e.g. $1.0 - 0.6$. So we set $F_{destination}$ equal to one minus the alpha value of the source color vector. The equation thus becomes:

$$\bar{C}_{result} = \begin{pmatrix} 0.0 \\ 1.0 \\ 0.0 \\ 0.6 \end{pmatrix} * 0.6 + \begin{pmatrix} 1.0 \\ 0.0 \\ 0.0 \\ 1.0 \end{pmatrix} * (1 - 0.6)$$

The result is that the combined square fragments contain a color that is 60% green and 40% red:

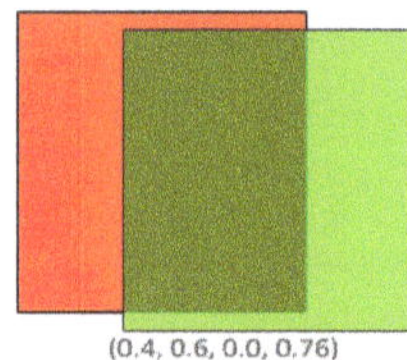

(0.4, 0.6, 0.0, 0.76)

The resulting color is then stored in the color buffer, replacing the previous color.

So this is great and all, but how do we actually tell OpenGL to use factors like that? Well it just so happens that there is a function for this called `glBlendFunc`.

The `glBlendFunc(GLenum sfactor, GLenum dfactor)` function expects two parameters that set the option for the source and destination factor. OpenGL defined quite a few options for us to set of which we'll list the most common options below. Note that the constant color vector $\bar{C}_{constant}$ can be separately set via the `glBlendColor` function.

Option	Value
GL_ZERO	Factor is equal to 0.
GL_ONE	Factor is equal to 1.
GL_SRC_COLOR	Factor is equal to the source color vector $\bar{C}_{\text{source}}$.
GL_ONE_MINUS_SRC_COLOR	Factor is equal to 1 minus the source color vector: $1 - \bar{C}_{\text{source}}$.
GL_DST_COLOR	Factor is equal to the destination color vector $\bar{C}_{\text{destination}}$
GL_ONE_MINUS_DST_COLOR	Factor is equal to 1 minus the destination color vector: $1 - \bar{C}_{\text{destination}}$.
GL_SRC_ALPHA	Factor is equal to the *alpha* component of the source color vector $\bar{C}_{\text{source}}$.
GL_ONE_MINUS_SRC_ALPHA	Factor is equal to $1 - alpha$ of the source color vector $\bar{C}_{\text{source}}$.
GL_DST_ALPHA	Factor is equal to the *alpha* component of the destination color vector $\bar{C}_{\text{destination}}$.
GL_ONE_MINUS_DST_ALPHA	Factor is equal to $1 - alpha$ of the destination color vector $\bar{C}_{\text{destination}}$.
GL_CONSTANT_COLOR	Factor is equal to the constant color vector $\bar{C}_{\text{constant}}$.
GL_ONE_MINUS_CONSTANT_COLOR	Factor is equal to 1 - the constant color vector $\bar{C}_{\text{constant}}$.
GL_CONSTANT_ALPHA	Factor is equal to the *alpha* component of the constant color vector $\bar{C}_{\text{constant}}$.
GL_ONE_MINUS_CONSTANT_ALPHA	Factor is equal to $1 - alpha$ of the constant color vector $\bar{C}_{\text{constant}}$.

To get the blending result of our little two square example, we want to take the *alpha* of the source color vector for the source factor and $1 - alpha$ of the same color vector for the destination factor. This translates to `glBlendFunc` as follows:

```
glBlendFunc(GL_SRC_ALPHA, GL_ONE_MINUS_SRC_ALPHA);
```

It is also possible to set different options for the RGB and alpha channel individually using `glBlendFuncSeparate`:

```
glBlendFuncSeparate(GL_SRC_ALPHA, GL_ONE_MINUS_SRC_ALPHA, GL_ONE, GL_ZERO);
```

This function sets the RGB components as we've set them previously, but only lets the resulting alpha component be influenced by the source's alpha value.

OpenGL gives us even more flexibility by allowing us to change the operator between the source and destination part of the equation. Right now, the source and destination components are added together, but we could also subtract them if we want. `glBlendEquation(GLenum mode)` allows us to set this operation and has 5 possible options:

- `GL_FUNC_ADD`: the default, adds both colors to each other: $\bar{C}_{\text{result}} = Src + Dst$.
- `GL_FUNC_SUBTRACT`: subtracts both colors from each other: $\bar{C}_{\text{result}} = Src - Dst$.
- `GL_FUNC_REVERSE_SUBTRACT`: subtracts both colors, but reverses order: $\bar{C}_{\text{result}} = Dst - Src$.
- `GL_MIN`: takes the component-wise minimum of both colors: $\bar{C}_{\text{result}} = min(Dst, Src)$.
- `GL_MAX`: takes the component-wise maximum of both colors: $\bar{C}_{\text{result}} = max(Dst, Src)$.

Usually we can simply omit a call to `glBlendEquation` because `GL_FUNC_ADD` is the preferred blending equation for most operations, but if you're really trying your best to break the mainstream circuit any of the other equations could suit your needs.

24.3 Rendering semi-transparent textures

Now that we know how OpenGL works with regards to blending it's time to put our knowledge to the test by adding several semi-transparent windows. We'll be using the same scene as in the start of this chapter, but instead of rendering a grass texture we're now going to use the transparent window texture from the start of this chapter.

First, during initialization we enable blending and set the appropriate blending function:

```
glEnable(GL_BLEND);
glBlendFunc(GL_SRC_ALPHA, GL_ONE_MINUS_SRC_ALPHA);
```

Since we enabled blending there is no need to discard fragments so we'll reset the fragment shader to its original version:

```
#version 330 core
out vec4 FragColor;

in vec2 TexCoords;

uniform sampler2D texture1;

void main()
{
    FragColor = texture(texture1, TexCoords);
}
```

This time (whenever OpenGL renders a fragment) it combines the current fragment's color with the fragment color currently in the color buffer based on the alpha value of `FragColor`. Since the glass part of the window texture is semi-transparent we should be able to see the rest of the scene by looking through this window.

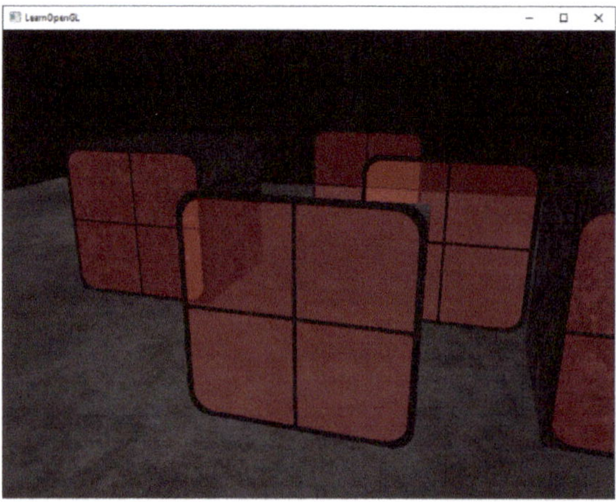

If you take a closer look however, you may notice something is off. The transparent parts of the front window are occluding the windows in the background. Why is this happening?

The reason for this is that depth testing works a bit tricky combined with blending. When writing to the depth buffer, the depth test does not care if the fragment has transparency or not, so the transparent parts are written to the depth buffer as any other value. The result is that the background windows are tested on depth as any other opaque object would be, ignoring transparency. Even though the transparent part should show the windows behind it, the depth test discards them.

So we cannot simply render the windows however we want and expect the depth buffer to solve all our issues for us; this is also where blending gets a little nasty. To make sure the windows show the windows behind them, we have to draw the windows in the background first. This means we have to manually sort the windows from furthest to nearest and draw them accordingly ourselves.

> Note that with fully transparent objects like the grass leaves we have the option to discard the transparent fragments instead of blending them, saving us a few of these headaches (no depth issues).

24.4 Don't break the order

To make blending work for multiple objects we have to draw the most distant object first and the closest object last. The normal non-blended objects can still be drawn as normal using the depth buffer so they don't have to be sorted. We do have to make sure they are drawn first before drawing the (sorted) transparent objects. When drawing a scene with non-transparent and transparent objects the general outline is usually as follows:

1. Draw all opaque objects first.
2. Sort all the transparent objects.
3. Draw all the transparent objects in sorted order.

One way of sorting the transparent objects is to retrieve the distance of an object from the viewer's perspective. This can be achieved by taking the distance between the camera's position vector and the object's position vector. We then store this distance together with the corresponding position vector in a `map` data structure from the STL library. A `map` automatically sorts its values based on its keys, so once we've added all positions with their distance as the key they're automatically sorted on their distance value:

```cpp
std::map<float, glm::vec3> sorted;
for (unsigned int i = 0; i < windows.size(); i++)
{
    float distance = glm::length(camera.Position - windows[i]);
    sorted[distance] = windows[i];
}
```

The result is a sorted container object that stores each of the window positions based on their `distance` key value from lowest to highest distance.

Then, this time when rendering, we take each of the map's values in reverse order (from farthest to nearest) and then draw the corresponding windows in correct order:

```cpp
for(std::map<float,glm::vec3>::reverse_iterator it = sorted.rbegin(); it !=
    sorted.rend(); ++it)
{
    model = glm::mat4(1.0f);
    model = glm::translate(model, it->second);
    shader.setMat4("model", model);
    glDrawArrays(GL_TRIANGLES, 0, 6);
}
```

We take a reverse iterator from the `map` to iterate through each of the items in reverse order and then translate each window quad to the corresponding window position. This relatively simple approach to sorting transparent objects fixes the previous problem and now the scene looks like this:

You can find the complete source code with sorting at `/src/4.advanced_opengl/3.2.blending_sort/`.

While this approach of sorting the objects by their distance works well for this specific scenario, it doesn't take rotations, scaling or any other transformation into account and weirdly shaped objects need a different metric than simply a position vector.

Sorting objects in your scene is a difficult feat that depends greatly on the type of scene you have, let alone the extra processing power it costs. Completely rendering a scene with solid and transparent objects isn't all that easy. There are more advanced techniques like order independent transparency but these are out of the scope of this chapter. For now you'll have to live with normally blending your objects, but if you're careful and know the limitations you can get pretty decent blending implementations.

25. Face culling

Try mentally visualizing a 3D cube and count the maximum number of faces you'll be able to see from any direction. If your imagination is not too creative you probably ended up with a maximum number of 3. You can view a cube from any position and/or direction, but you would never be able to see more than 3 faces. So why would we waste the effort of drawing those other 3 faces that we can't even see. If we could discard those in some way we would save more than 50% of this cube's total fragment shader runs!

> We say *more than 50%* instead of 50%, because from certain angles only 2 or even 1 face could be visible. In that case we'd save **more** than 50%.

This is a really great idea, but there's one problem we need to solve: how do we know if a face of an object is not visible from the viewer's point of view? If we imagine any closed shape, each of its faces has two sides. Each side would either *face* the user or show its back to the user. What if we could only render the faces that are *facing* the viewer?

This is exactly what face culling does. OpenGL checks all the faces that are front facing towards the viewer and renders those while discarding all the faces that are back facing, saving us a lot of fragment shader calls. We do need to tell OpenGL which of the faces we use are actually the front faces and which faces are the back faces. OpenGL uses a clever trick for this by analyzing the winding order of the vertex data.

25.1 Winding order

When we define a set of triangle vertices we're defining them in a certain winding order that is either clockwise or counter-clockwise. Each triangle consists of 3 vertices and we specify those 3 vertices in a winding order as seen from the center of the triangle.

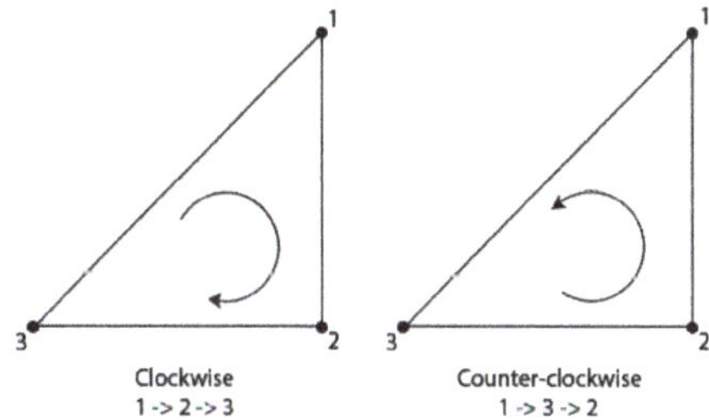

As you can see in the image we first define vertex 1 and from there we can choose whether the next vertex is 2 or 3. This choice defines the winding order of this triangle. The following code illustrates this:

```
float vertices[] = {
    // clockwise
    vertices[0], // vertex 1
    vertices[1], // vertex 2
    vertices[2], // vertex 3
    // counter-clockwise
    vertices[0], // vertex 1
    vertices[2], // vertex 3
    vertices[1]  // vertex 2
};
```

Each set of 3 vertices that form a triangle primitive thus contain a winding order. OpenGL uses this information when rendering your primitives to determine if a triangle is a front-facing or a back-facing triangle. By default, triangles defined with counter-clockwise vertices are processed as front-facing triangles.

When defining your vertex order you visualize the corresponding triangle as if it was facing you, so each triangle that you're specifying should be counter-clockwise as if you're directly facing that triangle. The cool thing about specifying all your vertices like this is that the actual winding order is calculated at the rasterization stage, so when the vertex shader has already run. The vertices are then seen as from the **viewer's point of view**.

All the triangle vertices that the viewer is then facing are indeed in the correct winding order as we specified them, but the vertices of the triangles at the other side of the cube are now rendered in such a way that their winding order becomes reversed. The result is that the triangles we're facing are seen as front-facing triangles and the triangles at the back are seen as back-facing triangles. The following image shows this effect:

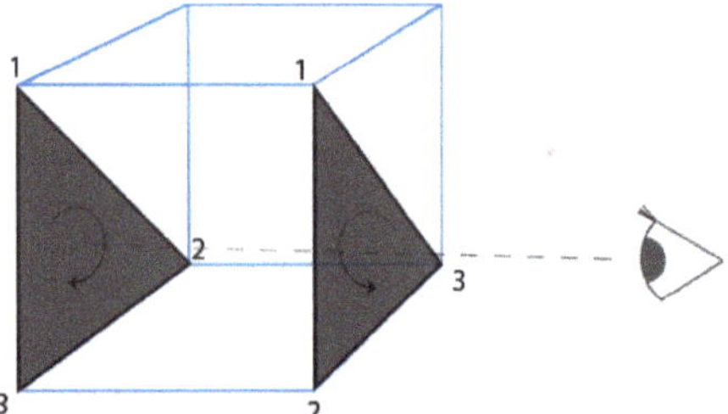

In the vertex data we defined both triangles in counter-clockwise order (the front and back triangle as 1, 2, 3). However, from the viewer's direction the back triangle is rendered clockwise if we draw it in the order of 1, 2 and 3 from the viewer's current point of view. Even though we specified the back triangle in counter-clockwise order, it is now rendered in a clockwise order. This is exactly what we want to cull (discard) non-visible faces!

25.2 Face culling

At the start of the chapter we said that OpenGL is able to discard triangle primitives if they're rendered as back-facing triangles. Now that we know how to set the winding order of the vertices we can start using OpenGL's face culling option which is disabled by default.

The cube vertex data we used in the previous chapters wasn't defined with the counter-clockwise winding order in mind, so an updated set of vertex data to reflect a counter-clockwise winding order can be copied from the following code listing:

```cpp
float vertices[] = {
    // back face
    -0.5f, -0.5f, -0.5f,  0.0f, 0.0f, // bottom-left
     0.5f,  0.5f, -0.5f,  1.0f, 1.0f, // top-right
     0.5f, -0.5f, -0.5f,  1.0f, 0.0f, // bottom-right
     0.5f,  0.5f, -0.5f,  1.0f, 1.0f, // top-right
    -0.5f, -0.5f, -0.5f,  0.0f, 0.0f, // bottom-left
    -0.5f,  0.5f, -0.5f,  0.0f, 1.0f, // top-left
    // front face
    -0.5f, -0.5f,  0.5f,  0.0f, 0.0f, // bottom-left
     0.5f, -0.5f,  0.5f,  1.0f, 0.0f, // bottom-right
     0.5f,  0.5f,  0.5f,  1.0f, 1.0f, // top-right
     0.5f,  0.5f,  0.5f,  1.0f, 1.0f, // top-right
    -0.5f,  0.5f,  0.5f,  0.0f, 1.0f, // top-left
```

```cpp
    -0.5f, -0.5f,  0.5f,  0.0f, 0.0f, // bottom-left
    // left face
    -0.5f,  0.5f,  0.5f,  1.0f, 0.0f, // top-right
    -0.5f,  0.5f, -0.5f,  1.0f, 1.0f, // top-left
    -0.5f, -0.5f, -0.5f,  0.0f, 1.0f, // bottom-left
    -0.5f, -0.5f, -0.5f,  0.0f, 1.0f, // bottom-left
    -0.5f, -0.5f,  0.5f,  0.0f, 0.0f, // bottom-right
    -0.5f,  0.5f,  0.5f,  1.0f, 0.0f, // top-right
    // right face
     0.5f,  0.5f,  0.5f,  1.0f, 0.0f, // top-left
     0.5f, -0.5f, -0.5f,  0.0f, 1.0f, // bottom-right
     0.5f,  0.5f, -0.5f,  1.0f, 1.0f, // top-right
     0.5f, -0.5f, -0.5f,  0.0f, 1.0f, // bottom-right
     0.5f,  0.5f,  0.5f,  1.0f, 0.0f, // top-left
     0.5f, -0.5f,  0.5f,  0.0f, 0.0f, // bottom-left
    // bottom face
    -0.5f, -0.5f, -0.5f,  0.0f, 1.0f, // top-right
     0.5f, -0.5f, -0.5f,  1.0f, 1.0f, // top-left
     0.5f, -0.5f,  0.5f,  1.0f, 0.0f, // bottom-left
     0.5f, -0.5f,  0.5f,  1.0f, 0.0f, // bottom-left
    -0.5f, -0.5f,  0.5f,  0.0f, 0.0f, // bottom-right
    -0.5f, -0.5f, -0.5f,  0.0f, 1.0f, // top-right
    // top face
    -0.5f,  0.5f, -0.5f,  0.0f, 1.0f, // top-left
     0.5f,  0.5f,  0.5f,  1.0f, 0.0f, // bottom-right
     0.5f,  0.5f, -0.5f,  1.0f, 1.0f, // top-right
     0.5f,  0.5f,  0.5f,  1.0f, 0.0f, // bottom-right
    -0.5f,  0.5f, -0.5f,  0.0f, 1.0f, // top-left
    -0.5f,  0.5f,  0.5f,  0.0f, 0.0f  // bottom-left
};
```

It's a good practice to try and visualize that these vertices are indeed all defined in a counter-clockwise order for each triangle.

To enable face culling we only have to enable OpenGL's `GL_CULL_FACE` option:

```cpp
glEnable(GL_CULL_FACE);
```

From this point on, all the faces that are not front-faces are discarded (try flying inside the cube to see that all inner faces are indeed discarded). Currently we save over 50% of performance on rendering fragments if OpenGL decides to render the back faces first (otherwise depth testing would've discarded them already). Do note that this only really works with closed shapes like a cube. We do have to disable face culling again when we draw the grass leaves from the previous chapter, since their front **and** back face should be visible.

OpenGL allows us to change the type of face we want to cull as well. What if we want to cull front faces and not the back faces? We can define this behavior with `glCullFace`:

```cpp
glCullFace(GL_FRONT);
```

The `glCullFace` function has three possible options:

- `GL_BACK`: Culls only the back faces.
- `GL_FRONT`: Culls only the front faces.
- `GL_FRONT_AND_BACK`: Culls both the front and back faces.

The initial value of `glCullFace` is `GL_BACK`. We can also tell OpenGL we'd rather prefer clockwise faces as the front-faces instead of counter-clockwise faces via `glFrontFace`:

```
glFrontFace(GL_CCW);
```

The default value is GL_CCW that stands for counter-clockwise ordering with the other option being GL_CW which (obviously) stands for clockwise ordering.

As a simple test we could reverse the winding order by telling OpenGL that the front-faces are now determined by a clockwise ordering instead of a counter-clockwise ordering:

```
glEnable(GL_CULL_FACE);
glCullFace(GL_BACK);
glFrontFace(GL_CW);
```

The result is that only the back faces are rendered:

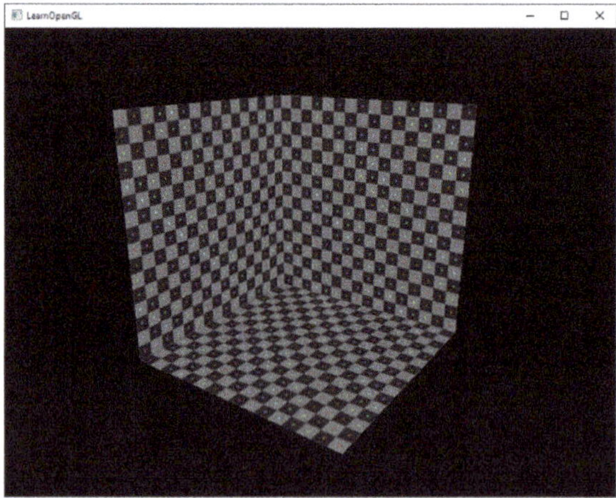

Note that you can create the same effect by culling front faces with the default counter-clockwise winding order:

```
glEnable(GL_CULL_FACE);
glCullFace(GL_FRONT);
```

As you can see, face culling is a great tool for increasing performance of your OpenGL applications with minimal effort; especially as all 3D applications export models with consistent winding orders (CCW by default). You do have to keep track of the objects that will actually benefit from face culling and which objects shouldn't be culled at all.

25.3 Exercises

- Can you re-define the vertex data by specifying each triangle in clockwise order and then render the scene with clockwise triangles set as the front faces. Solution: /src/4.advanced_opengl/4.face_culling_exercise1.

26. Framebuffers

So far we've used several types of screen buffers: a color buffer for writing color values, a depth buffer to write and test depth information, and finally a stencil buffer that allows us to discard certain fragments based on some condition. The combination of these buffers is stored somewhere in GPU memory and is called a framebuffer. OpenGL gives us the flexibility to define our own framebuffers and thus define our own color (and optionally a depth and stencil) buffer.

The rendering operations we've done so far were all done on top of the render buffers attached to the default framebuffer. The default framebuffer is created and configured when you create your window (GLFW does this for us). By creating our own framebuffer we can get an additional target to render to.

The application of framebuffers may not immediately make sense, but rendering your scene to a different framebuffer allows us to use that result to create mirrors in a scene, or do cool post-processing effects for example. First we'll discuss how they actually work and then we'll use them by implementing those cool post-processing effects.

26.1 Creating a framebuffer

Just like any other object in OpenGL we can create a framebuffer object (abbreviated to FBO) by using a function called `glGenFramebuffers`:

```
unsigned int fbo;
glGenFramebuffers(1, &fbo);
```

This pattern of object creation and usage is something we've seen dozens of times now so their usage functions are similar to all the other object's we've seen: first we create a framebuffer object, bind it as the active framebuffer, do some operations, and unbind the framebuffer. To bind the framebuffer we use `glBindFramebuffer`:

```
glBindFramebuffer(GL_FRAMEBUFFER, fbo);
```

By binding to the `GL_FRAMEBUFFER` target all the next *read* and *write* framebuffer operations will affect the currently bound framebuffer. It is also possible to bind a framebuffer to a read or write target specifically by binding to `GL_READ_FRAMEBUFFER` or `GL_DRAW_FRAMEBUFFER` respectively. The framebuffer bound to `GL_READ_FRAMEBUFFER` is then used for all read operations like `glReadPixels` and the framebuffer bound to `GL_DRAW_FRAMEBUFFER` is used as the destination for rendering, clearing and other write operations. Most of the times you won't need to make this distinction though and you generally bind to both with `GL_FRAMEBUFFER`.

Unfortunately, we can't use our framebuffer yet because it is not complete. For a framebuffer to be complete the following requirements have to be satisfied:

- We have to attach at least one buffer (color, depth or stencil buffer).
- There should be at least one color attachment.
- All attachments should be complete as well (reserved memory).
- Each buffer should have the same number of samples.

Don't worry if you don't know what samples are, we'll get to those in a later chapter.

From the requirements it should be clear that we need to create some kind of attachment for the framebuffer and attach this attachment to the framebuffer. After we've completed all requirements we can check if we actually successfully completed the framebuffer by calling `glCheckFramebufferStatus` with `GL_FRAMEBUFFER`. It then checks the currently bound

framebuffer and returns an enum of values[1] found in the specification. If it returns GL_FRAMEBUFFE
R_COMPLETE we're good to go:

```
if(glCheckFramebufferStatus(GL_FRAMEBUFFER) == GL_FRAMEBUFFER_COMPLETE)
    // execute victory dance
```

All subsequent rendering operations will now render to the attachments of the currently bound
framebuffer. Since our framebuffer is not the default framebuffer, the rendering commands will have
no impact on the visual output of your window. For this reason it is called off-screen rendering when
rendering to a different framebuffer. If you want all rendering operations to have a visual impact
again on the main window we need to make the default framebuffer active by binding to 0:

```
glBindFramebuffer(GL_FRAMEBUFFER, 0);
```

When we're done with all framebuffer operations, do not forget to delete the framebuffer object:

```
glDeleteFramebuffers(1, &fbo);
```

Now before the completeness check is executed we need to attach one or more attachments to
the framebuffer. An attachment is a memory location that can act as a buffer for the framebuffer,
think of it as an image. When creating an attachment we have two options to take: textures or
renderbuffer objects.

26.1.1 Texture attachments

When attaching a texture to a framebuffer, all rendering commands will write to the texture as if it
was a normal color/depth or stencil buffer. The advantage of using textures is that the render output
is stored inside the texture image that we can then easily use in our shaders.

Creating a texture for a framebuffer is roughly the same as creating a normal texture:

```
unsigned int texture;
glGenTextures(1, &texture);
glBindTexture(GL_TEXTURE_2D, texture);

glTexImage2D(GL_TEXTURE_2D, 0, GL_RGB, 800, 600, 0, GL_RGB,
    GL_UNSIGNED_BYTE, NULL);

glTexParameteri(GL_TEXTURE_2D, GL_TEXTURE_MIN_FILTER, GL_LINEAR);
glTexParameteri(GL_TEXTURE_2D, GL_TEXTURE_MAG_FILTER, GL_LINEAR);
```

The main differences here is that we set the dimensions equal to the screen size (although this
is not required) and we pass NULL as the texture's data parameter. For this texture, we're only
allocating memory and not actually filling it. Filling the texture will happen as soon as we render to
the framebuffer. Also note that we do not care about any of the wrapping methods or mipmapping
since we won't be needing those in most cases.

> If you want to render your whole screen to a texture of a smaller or larger size you need to
> call glViewport again (before rendering to your framebuffer) with the new dimensions
> of your texture, otherwise render commands will only fill part of the texture.

---

[1] www.khronos.org/registry/OpenGL-Refpages/gl4/html/%67lCheckFramebufferStatus.xhtml

Now that we've created a texture, the last thing we need to do is actually attach it to the framebuffer:

```
glFramebufferTexture2D(GL_FRAMEBUFFER, GL_COLOR_ATTACHMENT0, GL_TEXTURE_2D,
                       texture, 0);
```

The `glFrameBufferTexture2D` function has the following parameters:

- `target`: the framebuffer type we're targeting (draw, read or both).
- `attachment`: the type of attachment we're going to attach. Right now we're attaching a color attachment. Note that the `0` at the end suggests we can attach more than 1 color attachment. We'll get to that in a later chapter.
- `textarget`: the type of the texture you want to attach.
- `texture`: the actual texture to attach.
- `level`: the mipmap level. We keep this at `0`.

Next to the color attachments we can also attach a depth and a stencil texture to the framebuffer object. To attach a depth attachment we specify the attachment type as `GL_DEPTH_ATTACHMENT`. Note that the texture's format and internalformat type should then become `GL_DEPTH_COMPONENT` to reflect the depth buffer's storage format. To attach a stencil buffer you use `GL_STENCIL_ATTAC HMENT` as the second argument and specify the texture's formats as `GL_STENCIL_INDEX`.

It is also possible to attach both a depth buffer and a stencil buffer as a single texture. Each 32 bit value of the texture then contains 24 bits of depth information and 8 bits of stencil information. To attach a depth and stencil buffer as one texture we use the `GL_DEPTH_STENCIL_ATTACHMENT` type and configure the texture's formats to contain combined depth and stencil values. An example of attaching a depth and stencil buffer as one texture to the framebuffer is given below:

```
glTexImage2D(GL_TEXTURE_2D, 0, GL_DEPTH24_STENCIL8, 800, 600, 0,
             GL_DEPTH_STENCIL, GL_UNSIGNED_INT_24_8, NULL);

glFramebufferTexture2D(GL_FRAMEBUFFER, GL_DEPTH_STENCIL_ATTACHMENT,
                       GL_TEXTURE_2D, texture, 0);
```

26.1.2 Renderbuffer object attachments

Renderbuffer objects were introduced to OpenGL after textures as a possible type of framebuffer attachment, Just like a texture image, a renderbuffer object is an actual buffer e.g. an array of bytes, integers, pixels or whatever. However, a renderbuffer object can not be directly read from. This gives it the added advantage that OpenGL can do a few memory optimizations that can give it a performance edge over textures for off-screen rendering to a framebuffer.

Renderbuffer objects store all the render data directly into their buffer without any conversions to texture-specific formats, making them faster as a writeable storage medium. You cannot read from them directly, but it is possible to read from them via the slow `glReadPixels`. This returns a specified area of pixels from the currently bound framebuffer, but not directly from the attachment itself.

Because their data is in a native format they are quite fast when writing data or copying data to other buffers. Operations like switching buffers are therefore quite fast when using renderbuffer objects. The `glfwSwapBuffers` function we've been using at the end of each frame may as well be implemented with renderbuffer objects: we simply write to a renderbuffer image, and swap to the other one at the end. Renderbuffer objects are perfect for these kind of operations.

Creating a renderbuffer object looks similar to the framebuffer's code:

```cpp
unsigned int rbo;
glGenRenderbuffers(1, &rbo);
```

And similarly we want to bind the renderbuffer object so all subsequent renderbuffer operations affect the current `rbo`:

```cpp
glBindRenderbuffer(GL_RENDERBUFFER, rbo);
```

Since renderbuffer objects are write-only they are often used as depth and stencil attachments, since most of the time we don't really need to read values from them, but we do care about depth and stencil testing. We **need** the depth and stencil values for testing, but don't need to *sample* these values so a renderbuffer object suits this perfectly. When we're not sampling from these buffers, a renderbuffer object is generally preferred.

Creating a depth and stencil renderbuffer object is done by calling the `glRenderbufferStorage` function:

```cpp
glRenderbufferStorage(GL_RENDERBUFFER, GL_DEPTH24_STENCIL8, 800, 600);
```

Creating a renderbuffer object is similar to texture objects, the difference being that this object is specifically designed to be used as a framebuffer attachment, instead of a general purpose data buffer like a texture. Here we've chosen `GL_DEPTH24_STENCIL8` as the internal format, which holds both the depth and stencil buffer with 24 and 8 bits respectively.

The last thing left to do is to actually attach the renderbuffer object:

```cpp
glFramebufferRenderbuffer(GL_FRAMEBUFFER, GL_DEPTH_STENCIL_ATTACHMENT,
                          GL_RENDERBUFFER, rbo);
```

Renderbuffer objects can be more efficient for use in your off-screen render projects, but it is important to realize when to use renderbuffer objects and when to use textures. The general rule is that if you never need to sample data from a specific buffer, it is wise to use a renderbuffer object for that specific buffer. If you need to sample data from a specific buffer like colors or depth values, you should use a texture attachment instead.

26.2 Rendering to a texture

Now that we know how framebuffers (sort of) work it's time to put them to good use. We're going to render the scene into a color texture attached to a framebuffer object we created and then draw this texture over a simple quad that spans the whole screen. The visual output is then exactly the same as without a framebuffer, but this time it's all printed on top of a single quad. Now why is this useful? In the next section we'll see why.

First thing to do is to create an actual framebuffer object and bind it, this is all relatively straightforward:

```cpp
unsigned int framebuffer;
glGenFramebuffers(1, &framebuffer);
glBindFramebuffer(GL_FRAMEBUFFER, framebuffer);
```

Next we create a texture image that we attach as a color attachment to the framebuffer. We set the texture's dimensions equal to the width and height of the window and keep its data uninitialized:

```cpp
// generate texture
unsigned int texColorBuffer;
glGenTextures(1, &texColorBuffer);
glBindTexture(GL_TEXTURE_2D, texColorBuffer);
glTexImage2D(GL_TEXTURE_2D, 0, GL_RGB, 800, 600, 0, GL_RGB,
    GL_UNSIGNED_BYTE, NULL);
glTexParameteri(GL_TEXTURE_2D, GL_TEXTURE_MIN_FILTER, GL_LINEAR );
glTexParameteri(GL_TEXTURE_2D, GL_TEXTURE_MAG_FILTER, GL_LINEAR);
glBindTexture(GL_TEXTURE_2D, 0);

// attach it to currently bound framebuffer object
glFramebufferTexture2D(GL_FRAMEBUFFER, GL_COLOR_ATTACHMENT0, GL_TEXTURE_2D,
    texColorBuffer, 0);
```

We also want to make sure OpenGL is able to do depth testing (and optionally stencil testing) so we have to make sure to add a depth (and stencil) attachment to the framebuffer. Since we'll only be sampling the color buffer and not the other buffers we can create a renderbuffer object for this purpose.

Creating a renderbuffer object isn't too hard. The only thing we have to remember is that we're creating it as a depth **and** stencil attachment renderbuffer object. We set its *internal format* to `GL_DEPTH24_STENCIL8` which is enough precision for our purposes:

```cpp
unsigned int rbo;
glGenRenderbuffers(1, &rbo);
glBindRenderbuffer(GL_RENDERBUFFER, rbo);
glRenderbufferStorage(GL_RENDERBUFFER, GL_DEPTH24_STENCIL8, 800, 600);
glBindRenderbuffer(GL_RENDERBUFFER, 0);
```

Once we've allocated enough memory for the renderbuffer object we can unbind the renderbuffer.

Then, as a final step before we complete the framebuffer, we attach the renderbuffer object to the depth **and** stencil attachment of the framebuffer:

```cpp
glFramebufferRenderbuffer(GL_FRAMEBUFFER, GL_DEPTH_STENCIL_ATTACHMENT,
                          GL_RENDERBUFFER, rbo);
```

Then we want to check if the framebuffer is complete and if it's not, we print an error message.

```cpp
if(glCheckFramebufferStatus(GL_FRAMEBUFFER) != GL_FRAMEBUFFER_COMPLETE)
    std::cout << "ERROR::FRAMEBUFFER:: Framebuffer is not complete!" <<
    std::endl;
glBindFramebuffer(GL_FRAMEBUFFER, 0);
```

Be sure to unbind the framebuffer to make sure we're not accidentally rendering to the wrong framebuffer.

Now that the framebuffer is complete, all we need to do to render to the framebuffer's buffers instead of the default framebuffers is to simply bind the framebuffer object. All subsequent render commands will then influence the currently bound framebuffer. All the depth and stencil operations will also read from the currently bound framebuffer's depth and stencil attachments if they're available. If you were to omit a depth buffer for example, all depth testing operations will no longer work.

So, to draw the scene to a single texture we'll have to take the following steps:

1. Render the scene as usual with the new framebuffer bound as the active framebuffer.
2. Bind to the default framebuffer.
3. Draw a quad that spans the entire screen with the new framebuffer's color buffer as its texture.

We'll render the same scene we've used in the *Depth Testing* chapter, but this time with the old-school *container* texture.

To render the quad we're going to create a fresh set of simple shaders. We're not going to include fancy matrix transformations since we'll be supplying the quad's vertex coordinates as normalized device coordinates so we can directly forward them as output of the vertex shader.

```cpp
float quadVertices[] = {
    // positions   // texCoords
    -1.0f,  1.0f,  0.0f, 1.0f,
    -1.0f, -1.0f,  0.0f, 0.0f,
     1.0f, -1.0f,  1.0f, 0.0f,

    -1.0f,  1.0f,  0.0f, 1.0f,
     1.0f, -1.0f,  1.0f, 0.0f,
     1.0f,  1.0f,  1.0f, 1.0f
};
```

The vertex shader looks like this:

```glsl
#version 330 core
layout (location = 0) in vec2 aPos;
layout (location = 1) in vec2 aTexCoords;

out vec2 TexCoords;

void main()
{
    gl_Position = vec4(aPos.x, aPos.y, 0.0, 1.0);
    TexCoords = aTexCoords;
}
```

Nothing too fancy. The fragment shader is even more basic since the only thing we have to do is sample from a texture:

```glsl
#version 330 core
out vec4 FragColor;

in vec2 TexCoords;

uniform sampler2D screenTexture;

void main()
{
    FragColor = texture(screenTexture, TexCoords);
}
```

It is then up to you to create and configure a VAO for the screen quad. A single render iteration of the framebuffer procedure has the following structure:

```
// first pass
glBindFramebuffer(GL_FRAMEBUFFER, framebuffer);
glClearColor(0.1f, 0.1f, 0.1f, 1.0f);
glClear(GL_COLOR_BUFFER_BIT | GL_DEPTH_BUFFER_BIT);
glEnable(GL_DEPTH_TEST);
DrawScene();

// second pass
glBindFramebuffer(GL_FRAMEBUFFER, 0); // back to default
glClearColor(1.0f, 1.0f, 1.0f, 1.0f);
glClear(GL_COLOR_BUFFER_BIT);

screenShader.use();
glBindVertexArray(quadVAO);
glDisable(GL_DEPTH_TEST);
glBindTexture(GL_TEXTURE_2D, textureColorbuffer);
glDrawArrays(GL_TRIANGLES, 0, 6);
```

There are a few things to note. First, since each framebuffer we're using has its own set of buffers, we want to clear each of those buffers with the appropriate bits set by calling `glClear`. Second, when drawing the quad, we're disabling depth testing since we want to make sure the quad always renders in front of everything else; we'll have to enable depth testing again when we draw the normal scene though.

There are quite some steps that could go wrong here, so if you have no output, try to debug where possible and re-read the relevant sections of the chapter. If everything did work out successfully you'll get a visual result that looks like this:

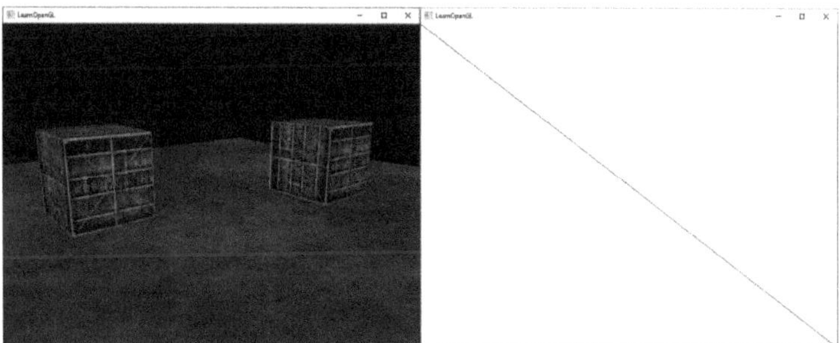

The left shows the visual output, exactly the same as we've seen in the *Depth Testing* chapter, but this time rendered on a simple quad. If we render the scene in wireframe it's obvious we've only drawn a single quad in the default framebuffer.

You can find the source code of the application at `/src/4.advanced_opengl/5.1.framebuffers/`.

So what was the use of this again? Well, because we can now freely access each of the pixels of the completely rendered scene as a single texture image, we can create some interesting effects in the fragment shader.

26.3 Post-processing

Now that the entire scene is rendered to a single texture we can create cool post-processing effects by manipulating the scene texture. In this section we'll show you some of the more popular post-processing effects and how you may create your own with some added creativity.

Let's start with one of the simplest post-processing effects.

26.3.1 Inversion

We have access to each of the colors of the render output so it's not so hard to return the inverse of these colors in the fragment shader. We can take the color of the screen texture and inverse it by subtracting it from `1.0`:

```glsl
void main()
{
    FragColor = vec4(vec3(1.0 - texture(screenTexture, TexCoords)), 1.0);
}
```

While inversion is a relatively simple post-processing effect it already creates funky results:

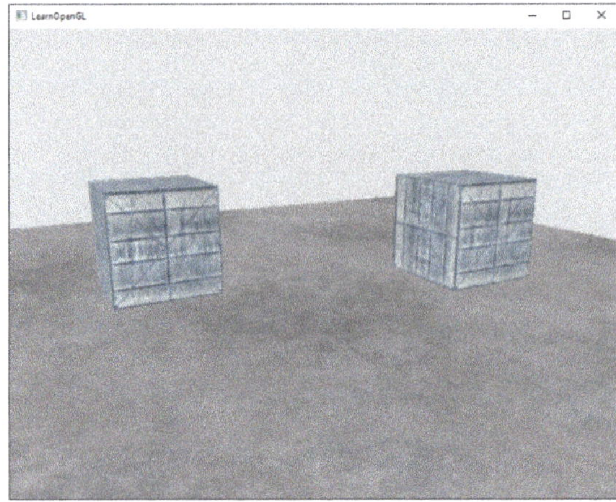

The entire scene now has all its colors inversed with a single line of code in the fragment shader. Pretty cool huh?

26.3.2 Grayscale

Another interesting effect is to remove all colors from the scene except the white, gray and black colors; effectively grayscaling the entire image. An easy way to do this is by taking all the color components and averaging their results:

```glsl
void main()
{
    FragColor = texture(screenTexture, TexCoords);
    float average = (FragColor.r + FragColor.g + FragColor.b) / 3.0;
    FragColor = vec4(average, average, average, 1.0);
}
```

This already creates pretty good results, but the human eye tends to be more sensitive to green colors and the least to blue. So to get the most physically accurate results we'll need to use weighted channels:

```
void main()
{
    FragColor = texture(screenTexture, TexCoords);
    float average = 0.2126 * FragColor.r + 0.7152 * FragColor.g +
                    0.0722 * FragColor.b;
    FragColor = vec4(average, average, average, 1.0);
}
```

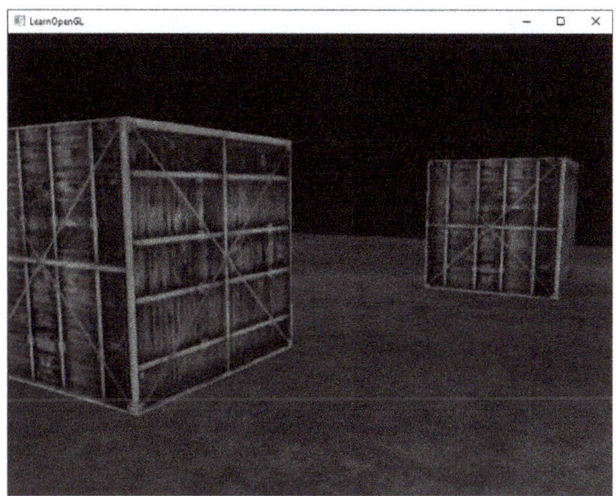

You probably won't notice the difference right away, but with more complicated scenes, such a weighted grayscaling effect tends to be more realistic.

26.4 Kernel effects

Another advantage about doing post-processing on a single texture image is that we can sample color values from other parts of the texture not specific to that fragment. We could for example take a small area around the current texture coordinate and sample multiple texture values around the current texture value. We can then create interesting effects by combining them in creative ways.

A kernel (or convolution matrix) is a small matrix-like array of values centered on the current pixel that multiplies surrounding pixel values by its kernel values and adds them all together to form a single value. We're adding a small offset to the texture coordinates in surrounding directions of the current pixel and combine the results based on the kernel. An example of a kernel is given below:

$$\begin{bmatrix} 2 & 2 & 2 \\ 2 & -15 & 2 \\ 2 & 2 & 2 \end{bmatrix}$$

This kernel takes 8 surrounding pixel values and multiplies them by 2 and the current pixel by -15. This example kernel multiplies the surrounding pixels by several weights determined in the kernel and balances the result by multiplying the current pixel by a large negative weight.

Most kernels you'll find over the internet all sum up to 1 if you add all the weights together. If they don't add up to 1 it means that the resulting texture color ends up brighter or darker than the original texture value.

Kernels are an extremely useful tool for post-processing since they're quite easy to use and experiment with, and a lot of examples can be found online. We do have to slightly adapt the fragment shader a bit to actually support kernels. We make the assumption that each kernel we'll be using is a 3x3 kernel (which most kernels are):

```glsl
const float offset = 1.0 / 300.0;

void main()
{
    vec2 offsets[9] = vec2[](
        vec2(-offset,  offset), // top-left
        vec2( 0.0f,    offset), // top-center
        vec2( offset,  offset), // top-right
        vec2(-offset,  0.0f),   // center-left
        vec2( 0.0f,    0.0f),   // center-center
        vec2( offset,  0.0f),   // center-right
        vec2(-offset, -offset), // bottom-left
        vec2( 0.0f,   -offset), // bottom-center
        vec2( offset, -offset)  // bottom-right
    );

    float kernel[9] = float[](
        -1, -1, -1,
        -1,  9, -1,
        -1, -1, -1
    );

    vec3 sampleTex[9];
    for(int i = 0; i < 9; i++)
    {
        sampleTex[i] = vec3(texture(screenTexture, TexCoords.st +
                                    offsets[i]));
    }
    vec3 col = vec3(0.0);
    for(int i = 0; i < 9; i++)
        col += sampleTex[i] * kernel[i];

    FragColor = vec4(col, 1.0);
}
```

In the fragment shader we first create an array of 9 `vec2` offsets for each surrounding texture coordinate. The offset is a constant value that you could customize to your liking. Then we define the kernel, which in this case is a sharpen kernel that sharpens each color value by sampling all surrounding pixels in an interesting way. Lastly, we add each offset to the current texture coordinate when sampling and multiply these texture values with the weighted kernel values that we add together.

This particular sharpen kernel looks like this:

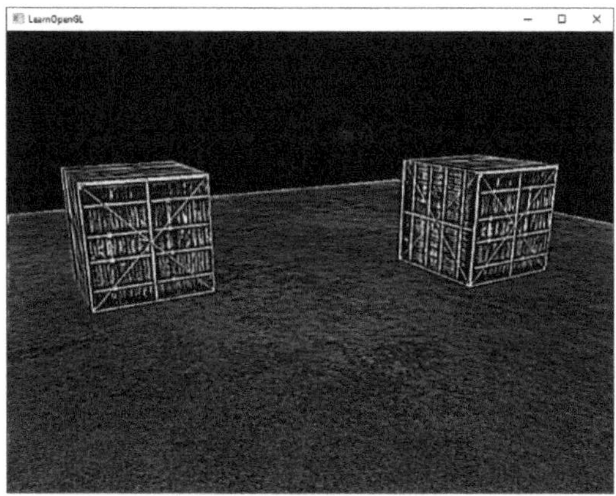

This could be the base of some interesting effects where your player may be on a narcotic adventure.

26.4.1 Blur

A kernel that creates a blur effect is defined as follows:

$$\begin{bmatrix} 1 & 2 & 1 \\ 2 & 4 & 2 \\ 1 & 2 & 1 \end{bmatrix} /16$$

Because all values add up to 16, directly returning the combined sampled colors would result in an extremely bright color so we have to divide each value of the kernel by 16. The resulting kernel array then becomes:

```
float kernel[9] = float[](
    1.0 / 16, 2.0 / 16, 1.0 / 16,
    2.0 / 16, 4.0 / 16, 2.0 / 16,
    1.0 / 16, 2.0 / 16, 1.0 / 16
);
```

By only changing the kernel array in the fragment shader we can completely change the post-processing effect. It now looks something like this:

Such a blur effect creates interesting possibilities. We could vary the blur amount over time to create the effect of someone being drunk, or increase the blur whenever the main character is not wearing glasses. Blurring can also be a useful tool for smoothing color values which we'll see use of in later chapters.

You can see that once we have such a little kernel implementation in place it is quite easy to create cool post-processing effects. Let's show you a last popular effect to finish this discussion.

26.4.2 Edge detection

Below you can find an edge-detection kernel that is similar to the sharpen kernel:

$$\begin{bmatrix} 1 & 1 & 1 \\ 1 & -8 & 1 \\ 1 & 1 & 1 \end{bmatrix}$$

This kernel highlights all edges and darkens the rest, which is pretty useful when we only care about edges in an image.

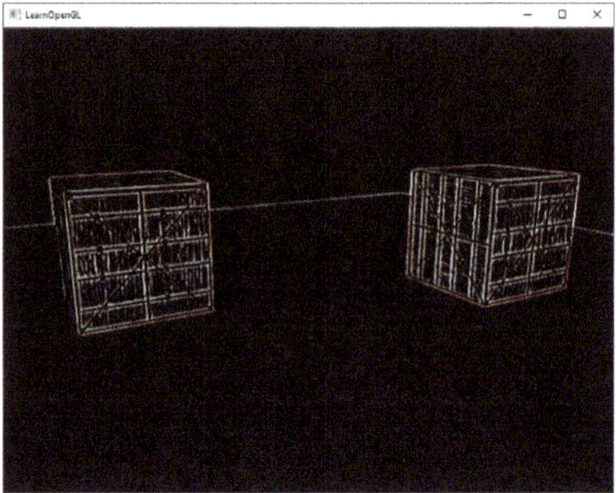

It probably does not come as a surprise that kernels like this are used as image-manipulating tools/filters in tools like Photoshop. Because of a graphic card's ability to process fragments with extreme parallel capabilities, we can manipulate images on a per-pixel basis in real-time with relative ease. Image-editing tools therefore tend to use graphics cards for image-processing.

26.5 Exercises

- Can you use framebuffers to create a rear-view mirror? For this you'll have to draw your scene twice: one with the camera rotated 180 degrees and the other as normal. Try to create a small quad at the top of your screen to apply the mirror texture on. Solution: `/src/4.advanced_opengl/5.2.framebuffers_exercise1/`.
- Play around with the kernel values and create your own interesting post-processing effects. Try searching the internet as well for other interesting kernels.

27. Cubemaps

We've been using 2D textures for a while now, but there are more texture types we haven't explored yet and in this chapter we'll discuss a texture type that is a combination of multiple textures mapped into one: a cube map.

A cubemap is a texture that contains 6 individual 2D textures that each form one side of a cube: a textured cube. You may be wondering what the point is of such a cube? Why bother combining 6 individual textures into a single entity instead of just using 6 individual textures? Well, cube maps have the useful property that they can be indexed/sampled using a direction vector. Imagine we have a 1x1x1 unit cube with the origin of a direction vector residing at its center. Sampling a texture value from the cube map with an orange direction vector looks a bit like this:

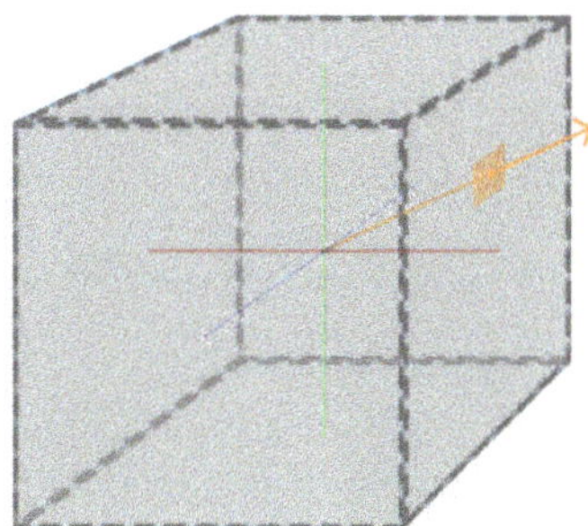

> The magnitude of the direction vector doesn't matter. As long as a direction is supplied, OpenGL retrieves the corresponding texels that the direction hits (eventually) and returns the properly sampled texture value.

If we imagine we have a cube shape that we attach such a cubemap to, this direction vector would be similar to the (interpolated) local vertex position of the cube. This way we can sample the cubemap using the cube's actual position vectors as long as the cube is centered on the origin. We thus consider all vertex positions of the cube to be its texture coordinates when sampling a cubemap. The result is a texture coordinate that accesses the proper individual face texture of the cubemap.

27.1 Creating a cubemap

A cubemap is a texture like any other texture, so to create one we generate a texture and bind it to the proper texture target before we do any further texture operations. This time binding it to `GL_TEXTURE_CUBE_MAP`:

```cpp
unsigned int textureID;
glGenTextures(1, &textureID);
glBindTexture(GL_TEXTURE_CUBE_MAP, textureID);
```

Because a cubemap contains 6 textures, one for each face, we have to call `glTexImage2D` six times with their parameters set similarly to the previous chapters. This time however, we have to set the texture *target* parameter to match a specific face of the cubemap, telling OpenGL which side of the cubemap we're creating a texture for. This means we have to call `glTexImage2D` once for each face of the cubemap.

Since we have 6 faces OpenGL gives us 6 special texture targets for targeting a face of the cubemap:

Texture target	Orientation
`GL_TEXTURE_CUBE_MAP_POSITIVE_X`	Right
`GL_TEXTURE_CUBE_MAP_NEGATIVE_X`	Left
`GL_TEXTURE_CUBE_MAP_POSITIVE_Y`	Top
`GL_TEXTURE_CUBE_MAP_NEGATIVE_Y`	Bottom
`GL_TEXTURE_CUBE_MAP_POSITIVE_Z`	Back
`GL_TEXTURE_CUBE_MAP_NEGATIVE_Z`	Front

Like many of OpenGL's enums, their behind-the-scenes `int` value is linearly incremented, so if we were to have an array or vector of texture locations we could loop over them by starting with `GL_TEXTURE_CUBE_MAP_POSITIVE_X` and incrementing the enum by 1 each iteration, effectively looping through all the texture targets:

```cpp
int width, height, nrChannels;
unsigned char *data;
for(unsigned int i = 0; i < textures_faces.size(); i++)
{
    data = stbi_load(textures_faces[i].c_str(), &width, &height,
                     &nrChannels, 0);
    glTexImage2D(GL_TEXTURE_CUBE_MAP_POSITIVE_X + i, 0, GL_RGB, width,
                 height, 0, GL_RGB, GL_UNSIGNED_BYTE, data);
}
```

Here we have a `vector` called `textures_faces` that contain the locations of all the textures required for the cubemap in the order as given in the table. This generates a texture for each face of the currently bound cubemap.

Because a cubemap is a texture like any other texture, we will also specify its wrapping and filtering methods:

```cpp
glTexParameteri(GL_TEXTURE_CUBE_MAP, GL_TEXTURE_MAG_FILTER, GL_LINEAR);
glTexParameteri(GL_TEXTURE_CUBE_MAP, GL_TEXTURE_MIN_FILTER, GL_LINEAR);
glTexParameteri(GL_TEXTURE_CUBE_MAP, GL_TEXTURE_WRAP_S, GL_CLAMP_TO_EDGE);
glTexParameteri(GL_TEXTURE_CUBE_MAP, GL_TEXTURE_WRAP_T, GL_CLAMP_TO_EDGE);
glTexParameteri(GL_TEXTURE_CUBE_MAP, GL_TEXTURE_WRAP_R, GL_CLAMP_TO_EDGE);
```

Don't be scared by the `GL_TEXTURE_WRAP_R`, this simply sets the wrapping method for the texture's R coordinate which corresponds to the texture's 3rd dimension (like z for positions). We set the wrapping method to `GL_CLAMP_TO_EDGE` since texture coordinates that are exactly between two faces may not hit an exact face (due to some hardware limitations) so by using `GL_CLAMP_TO_EDGE` OpenGL always returns their edge values whenever we sample between faces.

Then before drawing the objects that will use the cubemap, we activate the corresponding texture unit and bind the cubemap before rendering; not much of a difference compared to normal 2D textures.

Within the fragment shader we also have to use a different sampler of the type `samplerCube` that we sample from using the `texture` function, but this time using a `vec3` direction vector instead of a `vec2`. An example of fragment shader using a cubemap looks like this:

```glsl
in vec3 textureDir; // direction vector: a 3D texture coordinate
uniform samplerCube cubemap; // cubemap texture sampler

void main()
{
    FragColor = texture(cubemap, textureDir);
}
```

That is still great and all, but why bother? Well, it just so happens that there are quite a few interesting techniques that are a lot easier to implement with a cubemap. One of those techniques is creating a skybox.

27.2 Skybox

A skybox is a (large) cube that encompasses the entire scene and contains 6 images of a surrounding environment, giving the player the illusion that the environment he's in is actually much larger than it actually is. Some examples of skyboxes used in videogames are images of mountains, of clouds, or of a starry night sky. An example of a skybox, using starry night sky images, can be seen in the following screenshot of the third elder scrolls game:

You probably guessed by now that skyboxes like this suit cubemaps perfectly: we have a cube that has 6 faces and needs to be textured per face. In the previous image they used several images of a night sky to give the illusion the player is in some large universe while he's actually inside a tiny little box.

There are usually enough resources online where you could find skyboxes like that. These skybox images usually have the following pattern:

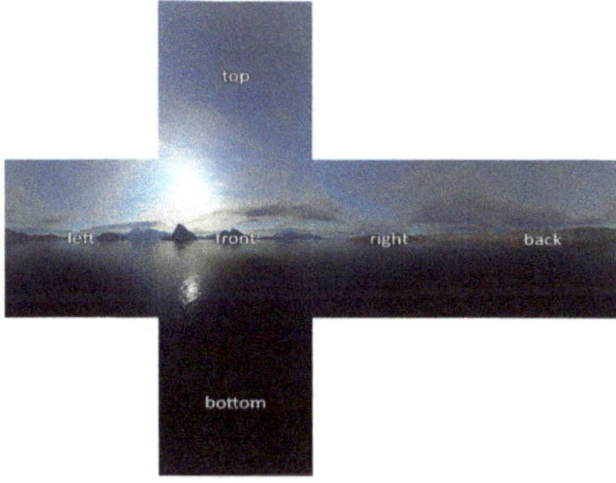

If you would fold those 6 sides into a cube you'd get the completely textured cube that simulates a large landscape. Some resources provide the skybox in a format like that in which case you'd have to manually extract the 6 face images, but in most cases they're provided as 6 single texture images.

This particular (high-quality) skybox is what we'll use for our scene and can be downloaded from `learnopengl.com/img/textures/skybox.zip`.

27.3 Loading a skybox

Since a skybox is by itself just a cubemap, loading a skybox isn't too different from what we've seen at the start of this chapter. To load the skybox we're going to use the following function that accepts a `vector` of 6 texture locations:

```cpp
unsigned int loadCubemap(vector<std::string> faces)
{
    unsigned int textureID;
    glGenTextures(1, &textureID);
    glBindTexture(GL_TEXTURE_CUBE_MAP, textureID);

    int width, height, nrChannels;
    for (unsigned int i = 0; i < faces.size(); i++)
    {
        unsigned char *data = stbi_load(faces[i].c_str(), &width, &height,
                                        &nrChannels, 0);
        if (data)
        {
            glTexImage2D(GL_TEXTURE_CUBE_MAP_POSITIVE_X + i, 0, GL_RGB,
                         width, height, 0, GL_RGB, GL_UNSIGNED_BYTE, data);
            stbi_image_free(data);
        }
        else
        {
            std::cout << "Cubemap failed to load at path: " << faces[i]
                      << std::endl;
            stbi_image_free(data);
        }
    }
    glTexParameteri(GL_TEXTURE_CUBE_MAP, GL_TEXTURE_MIN_FILTER, GL_LINEAR);
    glTexParameteri(GL_TEXTURE_CUBE_MAP, GL_TEXTURE_MAG_FILTER, GL_LINEAR);
    glTexParameteri(GL_TEXTURE_CUBE_MAP, GL_TEXTURE_WRAP_S,
                    GL_CLAMP_TO_EDGE);
    glTexParameteri(GL_TEXTURE_CUBE_MAP, GL_TEXTURE_WRAP_T,
                    GL_CLAMP_TO_EDGE);
    glTexParameteri(GL_TEXTURE_CUBE_MAP, GL_TEXTURE_WRAP_R,
                    GL_CLAMP_TO_EDGE);

    return textureID;
}
```

The function itself shouldn't be too surprising. It is basically all the cubemap code we've seen in the previous section, but combined in a single manageable function.

Now, before we call this function we'll load the appropriate texture paths in a vector in the order as specified by the cubemap enums:

```cpp
vector<std::string> faces;
{
    "right.jpg",
    "left.jpg",
    "top.jpg",
    "bottom.jpg",
    "front.jpg",
    "back.jpg"
};
unsigned int cubemapTexture = loadCubemap(faces);
```

We loaded the skybox as a cubemap with `cubemapTexture` as its id. We can now finally bind it to a cube to replace that lame clear color we've been using all this time.

27.4 Displaying a skybox

Because a skybox is drawn on a cube we'll need another VAO, VBO and a set of (cube) vertices like any other 3D object.

A cubemap used to texture a 3D cube can be sampled using the local positions of the cube as its texture coordinates. When a cube is centered on the origin (0,0,0) each of its position vectors is also a direction vector from the origin. This direction vector is exactly what we need to get the corresponding texture value at that specific cube's position. For this reason we only need to supply position vectors and don't need texture coordinates.

To render the skybox we'll need a new set of shaders which aren't too complicated. Because we only have one vertex attribute the vertex shader is quite simple:

```glsl
#version 330 core
layout (location = 0) in vec3 aPos;

out vec3 TexCoords;

uniform mat4 projection;
uniform mat4 view;

void main()
{
    TexCoords = aPos;
    gl_Position = projection * view * vec4(aPos, 1.0);
}
```

The interesting part of this vertex shader is that we set the incoming local position vector as the outcoming texture coordinate for (interpolated) use in the fragment shader. The fragment shader then takes these as input to sample a `samplerCube`:

```glsl
#version 330 core
out vec4 FragColor;

in vec3 TexCoords;

uniform samplerCube skybox;

void main()
{
    FragColor = texture(skybox, TexCoords);
}
```

The fragment shader is relatively straightforward. We take the vertex attribute's interpolated position vector as the texture's direction vector and use it to sample the texture values from the cubemap.

Rendering the skybox is easy now that we have a cubemap texture, we simply bind the cubemap texture and the `skybox` sampler is automatically filled with the skybox cubemap. To draw the skybox we're going to draw it as the first object in the scene and disable depth writing. This way the skybox will always be drawn at the background of all the other objects since the unit cube is most likely smaller than the rest of the scene.

```cpp
glDepthMask(GL_FALSE);
skyboxShader.use();
// ... set view and projection matrix
glBindVertexArray(skyboxVAO);
glBindTexture(GL_TEXTURE_CUBE_MAP, cubemapTexture);
glDrawArrays(GL_TRIANGLES, 0, 36);
glDepthMask(GL_TRUE);
// ... draw rest of the scene
```

If you run this you will get into difficulties though. We want the skybox to be centered around the player so that no matter how far the player moves, the skybox won't get any closer, giving the impression the surrounding environment is extremely large. The current view matrix however transforms all the skybox's positions by rotating, scaling and translating them, so if the player moves, the cubemap moves as well! We want to remove the translation part of the view matrix so only rotation will affect the skybox's position vectors.

You may remember from the *Basic Lighting* chapter that we can remove the translation section of transformation matrices by taking the upper-left 3x3 matrix of the 4x4 matrix. We can achieve this by converting the view matrix to a 3x3 matrix (removing translation) and converting it back to a 4x4 matrix:

```cpp
glm::mat4 view = glm::mat4(glm::mat3(camera.GetViewMatrix()));
```

This removes any translation, but keeps all rotation transformations so the user can still look around the scene.

The result is a scene that instantly looks enormous due to our skybox. If you'd fly around the basic container you immediately get a sense of scale which dramatically improves the realism of the scene. The result looks something like this:

Try experimenting with different skyboxes and see how they can have an enormous impact on the look and feel of your scene.

27.5 An optimization

Right now we've rendered the skybox first before we rendered all the other objects in the scene. This works great, but isn't too efficient. If we render the skybox first we're running the fragment shader for each pixel on the screen even though only a small part of the skybox will eventually be visible; fragments that could have easily been discarded using early depth testing saving us valuable bandwidth.

So to give us a slight performance boost we're going to render the skybox last. This way, the depth buffer is completely filled with all the scene's depth values so we only have to render the skybox's fragments wherever the early depth test passes, greatly reducing the number of fragment shader calls. The problem is that the skybox will most likely fail to render since it's only a 1x1x1 cube, failing most depth tests. Simply rendering it without depth testing is not a solution since the skybox will then overwrite all the other objects in the scene. We need to trick the depth buffer into believing that the skybox has the maximum depth value of `1.0` so that it fails the depth test wherever there's a different object in front of it.

In the *Coordinate Systems* chapter we said that *perspective division* is performed after the vertex shader has run, dividing the `gl_Position`'s `xyz` coordinates by its `w` component. We also know from the *Depth Testing* chapter that the `z` component of the resulting division is equal to that vertex's depth value. Using this information we can set the `z` component of the output position equal to its `w` component which will result in a `z` component that is always equal to `1.0`, because when the perspective division is applied its `z` component translates to `w / w = 1.0`:

```
void main()
{
    TexCoords = aPos;
    vec4 pos = projection * view * vec4(aPos, 1.0);
    gl_Position = pos.xyww;
}
```

The resulting *normalized device coordinates* will then always have a z value equal to `1.0`: the maximum depth value. The skybox will as a result only be rendered wherever there are no objects visible (only then it will pass the depth test, everything else is in front of the skybox).

We do have to change the depth function a little by setting it to `GL_LEQUAL` instead of the default `GL_LESS`. The depth buffer will be filled with values of `1.0` for the skybox, so we need to make sure the skybox passes the depth tests with values *less than or equal* to the depth buffer instead of *less than*.

You can find the more optimized version of the source code at `/src/4.advanced_opengl/6.1.cubemaps_skybox/`.

27.6 Environment mapping

We now have the entire surrounding environment mapped in a single texture object and we could use that information for more than just a skybox. Using a cubemap with an environment, we could give objects reflective or refractive properties. Techniques that use an environment cubemap like this are called environment mapping techniques and the two most popular ones are reflection and refraction.

27.6.1 Reflection

Reflection is the property that an object (or part of an object) reflects its surrounding environment e.g. the object's colors are more or less equal to its environment based on the angle of the viewer. A mirror for example is a reflective object: it reflects its surroundings based on the viewer's angle.

The basics of reflection are not that difficult. The following image shows how we can calculate a reflection vector and use that vector to sample from a cubemap:

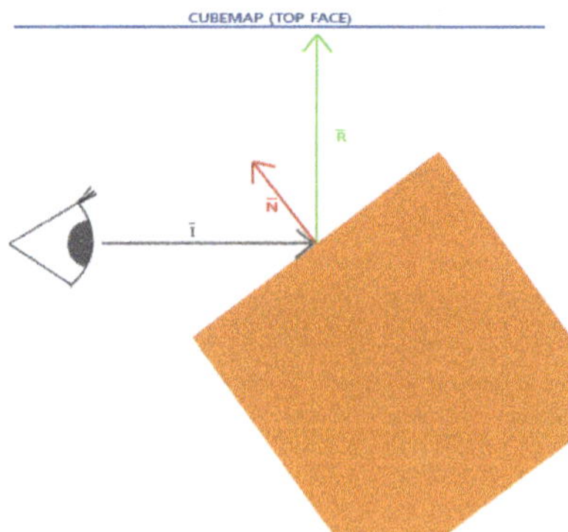

We calculate a reflection vector $\bar{R}$ around the object's normal vector $\bar{N}$ based on the view direction vector $\bar{I}$. We can calculate this reflection vector using GLSL's built-in `reflect` function. The resulting vector $\bar{R}$ is then used as a direction vector to index/sample the cubemap, returning a color value of the environment. The resulting effect is that the object seems to reflect the skybox.

Since we already have a skybox setup in our scene, creating reflections isn't too difficult. We'll change the fragment shader used by the container to give the container reflective properties:

```glsl
#version 330 core
out vec4 FragColor;

in vec3 Normal;
in vec3 Position;

uniform vec3 cameraPos;
uniform samplerCube skybox;

void main()
```

```
{
    vec3 I = normalize(Position - cameraPos);
    vec3 R = reflect(I, normalize(Normal));
    FragColor = vec4(texture(skybox, R).rgb, 1.0);
}
```

We first calculate the view/camera direction vector `I` and use this to calculate the reflect vector `R` which we then use to sample from the skybox cubemap. Note that we have the fragment's interpolated `Normal` and `Position` variable again so we'll need to adjust the vertex shader as well:

```
#version 330 core
layout (location = 0) in vec3 aPos;
layout (location = 1) in vec3 aNormal;

out vec3 Normal;
out vec3 Position;

uniform mat4 model;
uniform mat4 view;
uniform mat4 projection;

void main()
{
    Normal = mat3(transpose(inverse(model))) * aNormal;
    Position = vec3(model * vec4(aPos, 1.0));
    gl_Position = projection * view * vec4(Position, 1.0);
}
```

We're using normal vectors so we'll want to transform them with a normal matrix again. The `Position` output vector is a world-space position vector. This `Position` output of the vertex shader is used to calculate the view direction vector in the fragment shader.

Because we're using normals you'll want to update the vertex data with normals, if you haven't done so already, and update the attribute pointers as well. Also make sure to set the `cameraPos` uniform.

Then we also want to bind the cubemap texture before rendering the container:

```
glBindVertexArray(cubeVAO);
glBindTexture(GL_TEXTURE_CUBE_MAP, skyboxTexture);
glDrawArrays(GL_TRIANGLES, 0, 36);
```

Compiling and running your code gives you a container that acts like a perfect mirror. The surrounding skybox is perfectly reflected on the container:

You can find the full source code at `/src/4.advanced_opengl/6.2.cubemaps_ environment_mapping/`.

When reflection is applied to an entire object (like the container) the object looks as if it has a high reflective material like steel or chrome. If we were to load a more interesting object (like the backpack model from the *Model Loading* chapters) we'd get the effect that the object looks to be entirely made out of chrome:

This looks quite awesome, but in reality most models aren't all completely reflective. We could for instance introduce reflection maps that give the models another extra level of detail. Just like diffuse and specular maps, reflection maps are texture images that we can sample to determine the reflectivity of a fragment. Using these reflection maps we can determine which parts of the model show reflection and by what intensity.

27.6.2 Refraction

Another form of environment mapping is called refraction and is similar to reflection. Refraction is the change in direction of light due to the change of the material the light flows through. Refraction is what we commonly see with water-like surfaces where the light doesn't enter straight through, but bends a little. It's like looking at your arm when it's halfway in the water.

Refraction is described by Snell's law[1] that with environment maps looks a bit like this:

---

[1]en.wikipedia.org/wiki/Snell%27s_law

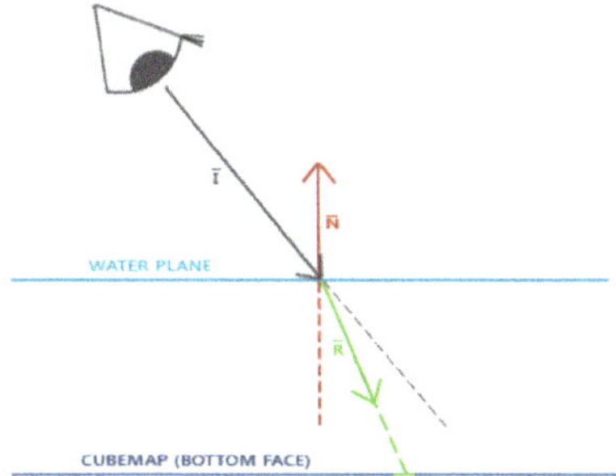

Again, we have a view vector $\bar{I}$, a normal vector $\bar{N}$ and this time a resulting refraction vector $\bar{R}$. As you can see, the direction of the view vector is slightly bend. This resulting bended vector $\bar{R}$ is then used to sample from the cubemap.

Refraction is fairly easy to implement using GLSL's built-in `refract` function that expects a normal vector, a view direction, and a ratio between both materials' refractive indices.

The refractive index determines the amount light distorts/bends in a material where each material has its own refractive index. A list of the most common refractive indices are given in the following table:

Material	Refractive index
Air	1.00
Water	1.33
Ice	1.309
Glass	1.52
Diamond	2.42

We use these refractive indices to calculate the ratio between both materials the light passes through. In our case, the light/view ray goes from *air* to *glass* (if we assume the object is made of glass) so the ratio becomes $\frac{1.00}{1.52} = 0.658$.

We already have the cubemap bound, supplied the vertex data with normals, and set the camera position as a uniform. The only thing we have to change is the fragment shader:

```
void main()
{
    float ratio = 1.00 / 1.52;
    vec3 I = normalize(Position - cameraPos);
    vec3 R = refract(I, normalize(Normal), ratio);
    FragColor = vec4(texture(skybox, R).rgb, 1.0);
}
```

By changing the refractive indices you can create completely different visual results. Compiling the application and running the results on the container object is not so interesting though as it doesn't really show the effect refraction has aside that it acts as a magnifying glass right now. Using the same shaders on the loaded 3D model however does show us the effect we're looking for: a glass-like object.

You can imagine that with the right combination of lighting, reflection, refraction and vertex movement, you can create pretty neat water graphics. Do note that for physically accurate results we should refract the light **again** when it leaves the object; now we simply used single-sided refraction which is fine for most purposes.

27.7 Dynamic environment maps

Right now we've been using a static combination of images as the skybox, which looks great, but it doesn't include the actual 3D scene with possibly moving objects. We didn't really notice this so far, because we only used a single object. If we had a mirror-like objects with multiple surrounding objects, only the skybox would be visible in the mirror as if it was the only object in the scene.

Using framebuffers it is possible to create a texture of the scene for all 6 different angles from the object in question and store those in a cubemap each frame. We can then use this (dynamically generated) cubemap to create realistic reflection and refractive surfaces that include all other objects. This is called dynamic environment mapping, because we dynamically create a cubemap of an object's surroundings and use that as its environment map.

While it looks great, it has one enormous disadvantage: we have to render the scene 6 times per object using an environment map, which is an enormous performance penalty on your application. Modern applications try to use the skybox as much as possible and where possible pre-render cubemaps wherever they can to still sort-of create dynamic environment maps. While dynamic environment mapping is a great technique, it requires a lot of clever tricks and hacks to get it working in an actual rendering application without too many performance drops.

28. Advanced Data

Throughout most chapters we've been extensively using buffers in OpenGL to store data on the GPU. This chapter we'll briefly discuss a few alternative approaches to managing buffers.

A buffer in OpenGL is, at its core, an object that manages a certain piece of GPU memory and nothing more. We give meaning to a buffer when binding it to a specific buffer target. A buffer is only a vertex array buffer when we bind it to `GL_ARRAY_BUFFER`, but we could just as easily bind it to `GL_ELEMENT_ARRAY_BUFFER`. OpenGL internally stores a reference to the buffer per target and, based on the target, processes the buffer differently.

So far we've been filling the buffer's memory by calling `glBufferData`, which allocates a piece of GPU memory and adds data into this memory. If we were to pass `NULL` as its data argument, the function would only allocate memory and not fill it. This is useful if we first want to *reserve* a specific amount of memory and later come back to this buffer.

Instead of filling the entire buffer with one function call we can also fill specific regions of the buffer by calling `glBufferSubData`. This function expects a buffer target, an offset, the size of the data and the actual data as its arguments. What's new with this function is that we can now give an offset that specifies from *where* we want to fill the buffer. This allows us to insert/update only certain parts of the buffer's memory. Do note that the buffer should have enough allocated memory so a call to `glBufferData` is necessary before calling `glBufferSubData` on the buffer.

```cpp
// Range: [24, 24 + sizeof(data)]
glBufferSubData(GL_ARRAY_BUFFER, 24, sizeof(data), &data);
```

Yet another method for getting data into a buffer is to ask for a pointer to the buffer's memory and directly copy the data in memory yourself. By calling `glMapBuffer` OpenGL returns a pointer to the currently bound buffer's memory for us to operate on:

```cpp
float data[] = {
    0.5f, 1.0f, -0.35f
    [...]
};
glBindBuffer(GL_ARRAY_BUFFER, buffer);
// get pointer
void *ptr = glMapBuffer(GL_ARRAY_BUFFER, GL_WRITE_ONLY);
// now copy data into memory
memcpy(ptr, data, sizeof(data));
// make sure to tell OpenGL we're done with the pointer
glUnmapBuffer(GL_ARRAY_BUFFER);
```

By telling OpenGL we're finished with the pointer operations via `glUnmapBuffer`, OpenGL knows you're done. By unmapping, the pointer becomes invalid and the function returns `GL_TRUE` if OpenGL was able to map your data successfully to the buffer.

Using `glMapBuffer` is useful for directly mapping data to a buffer, without first storing it in temporary memory. Think of directly reading data from file and copying it into the buffer's memory.

28.1 Batching vertex attributes

Using `glVertexAttribPointer` we were able to specify the attribute layout of the vertex array buffer's content. Within the vertex array buffer we interleaved the attributes; that is, we placed the position, normal and/or texture coordinates next to each other in memory for each vertex. Now that we know a bit more about buffers we can take a different approach.

What we could also do is batch all the vector data into large chunks per attribute type instead of interleaving them. Instead of an interleaved layout `123123123123` we take a batched approach

```
111122223333.
```

When loading vertex data from file you generally retrieve an array of positions, an array of normals and/or an array of texture coordinates. It may cost some effort to combine these arrays into one large array of interleaved data. Taking the batching approach is then an easier solution that we can easily implement using `glBufferSubData`:

```cpp
float positions[] = { ... };
float normals[] = { ... };
float tex[] = { ... };
// fill buffer
glBufferSubData(GL_ARRAY_BUFFER, 0, sizeof(positions), &positions);
glBufferSubData(GL_ARRAY_BUFFER, sizeof(positions),
                sizeof(normals), &normals);
glBufferSubData(GL_ARRAY_BUFFER, sizeof(positions) + sizeof(normals),
                sizeof(tex), &tex);
```

This way we can directly transfer the attribute arrays as a whole into the buffer without first having to process them. We could have also combined them in one large array and fill the buffer right away using `glBufferData`, but using `glBufferSubData` lends itself perfectly for tasks like these.

We'll also have to update the vertex attribute pointers to reflect these changes:

```cpp
glVertexAttribPointer(0, 3, GL_FLOAT, GL_FALSE, 3 * sizeof(float), 0);
glVertexAttribPointer(1, 3, GL_FLOAT, GL_FALSE, 3 * sizeof(float),
                      (void*)(sizeof(positions)));
glVertexAttribPointer(2, 2, GL_FLOAT, GL_FALSE, 2 * sizeof(float),
                      (void*)(sizeof(positions) + sizeof(normals)));
```

Note that the `stride` parameter is equal to the size of the vertex attribute, since the next vertex attribute vector can be found directly after its 3 (or 2) components.

This gives us yet another approach of setting and specifying vertex attributes. Using either approach is feasible, it is mostly a more organized way to set vertex attributes. However, the interleaved approach is still the recommended approach as the vertex attributes for each vertex shader run are then closely aligned in memory.

28.2 Copying buffers

Once your buffers are filled with data you may want to share that data with other buffers or perhaps copy the buffer's content into another buffer. The function `glCopyBufferSubData` allows us to copy the data from one buffer to another buffer with relative ease. The function's prototype is as follows:

```cpp
void glCopyBufferSubData(GLenum readtarget, GLenum writetarget,
                         GLintptr readoffset, GLintptr writeoffset,
                         GLsizeiptr size);
```

The `readtarget` and `writetarget` parameters expect to give the buffer targets that we want to copy from and to. We could for example copy from a VERTEX_ARRAY_BUFFER buffer to a VERTEX_ELEMENT_ARRAY_BUFFER buffer by specifying those buffer targets as the read and write targets respectively. The buffers currently bound to those buffer targets will then be affected.

But what if we wanted to read and write data into two different buffers that are both vertex array buffers? We can't bind two buffers at the same time to the same buffer target. For this reason, and this reason alone, OpenGL gives us two more buffer targets called `GL_COPY_READ_BUFFER` and `GL_COPY_WRITE_BUFFER`. We then bind the buffers of our choice to these new buffer targets and set those targets as the `readtarget` and `writetarget` argument.

`glCopyBufferSubData` then reads data of a given `size` from a given `readoffset` and writes it into the `writetarget` buffer at `writeoffset`. An example of copying the content of two vertex array buffers is shown below:

```
glBindBuffer(GL_COPY_READ_BUFFER, vbo1);
glBindBuffer(GL_COPY_WRITE_BUFFER, vbo2);
glCopyBufferSubData(GL_COPY_READ_BUFFER, GL_COPY_WRITE_BUFFER, 0, 0,
                    8 * sizeof(float));
```

We could've also done this by only binding the `writetarget` buffer to one of the new buffer target types:

```
float vertexData[] = { ... };
glBindBuffer(GL_ARRAY_BUFFER, vbo1);
glBindBuffer(GL_COPY_WRITE_BUFFER, vbo2);
glCopyBufferSubData(GL_ARRAY_BUFFER, GL_COPY_WRITE_BUFFER, 0, 0,
                    8 * sizeof(float));
```

With some extra knowledge about how to manipulate buffers we can already use them in more interesting ways. The further you get in OpenGL, the more useful these new buffer methods start to become. In the next chapter, where we'll discuss uniform buffer objects, we'll make good use of `glBufferSubData`.

29. Advanced GLSL

This chapter won't really show you super advanced cool new features that give an enormous boost to your scene's visual quality. This chapter goes more or less into some interesting aspects of GLSL and some nice tricks that may help you in your future endeavors. Basically some *good to knows* and *features that may make your life easier* when creating OpenGL applications in combination with GLSL.

We'll discuss some interesting built-in variables, new ways to organize shader input and output, and a very useful tool called uniform buffer objects.

29.1 GLSL's built-in variables

Shaders are extremely pipelined, if we need data from any other source outside of the current shader we'll have to pass data around. We learned to do this via vertex attributes, uniforms, and samplers. There are however a few extra variables defined by GLSL prefixed with `gl_` that give us an extra means to gather and/or write data. We've already seen two of them in the chapters so far: `gl_Position` that is the output vector of the vertex shader, and the fragment shader's `gl_FragCoord`.

We'll discuss a few interesting built-in input and output variables that are built-in in GLSL and explain how they may benefit us. Note that we won't discuss all built-in variables that exist in GLSL so if you want to see all built-in variables you can check OpenGL's wiki[1].

29.2 Vertex shader variables

We've already seen `gl_Position` which is the clip-space output position vector of the vertex shader. Setting `gl_Position` in the vertex shader is a strict requirement if you want to render anything on the screen. Nothing we haven't seen before.

29.2.1 gl_PointSize

One of the render primitives we're able to choose from is `GL_POINTS` in which case each single vertex is a primitive and rendered as a point. It is possible to set the size of the points being rendered via OpenGL's `glPointSize` function, but we can also influence this value in the vertex shader.

One output variable defined by GLSL is called `gl_PointSize` that is a `float` variable where you can set the point's width and height in pixels. By setting the point's size in the vertex shader we get per-vertex control over this point's dimensions.

Influencing the point sizes in the vertex shader is disabled by default, but if you want to enable this you'll have to enable OpenGL's `GL_PROGRAM_POINT_SIZE`:

```
glEnable(GL_PROGRAM_POINT_SIZE);
```

A simple example of influencing point sizes is by setting the point size equal to the clip-space position's z value which is equal to the vertex's distance to the viewer. The point size should then increase the further we are from the vertices as the viewer.

```
void main()
{
    gl_Position = projection * view * model * vec4(aPos, 1.0);
    gl_PointSize = gl_Position.z;
}
```

---

[1]www.khronos.org/opengl/wiki/Built-in_Variable_(GLSL)

The result is that the points we've drawn are rendered larger the more we move away from them:

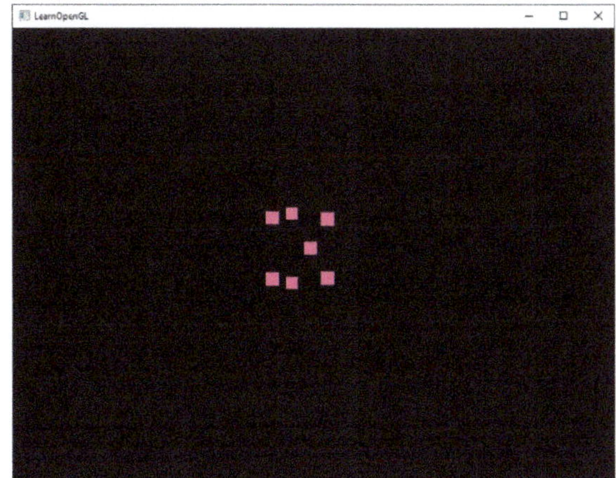

You can imagine that varying the point size per vertex is interesting for techniques like particle generation.

29.2.2 gl_VertexID

The `gl_Position` and `gl_PointSize` are *output variables* since their value is read as output from the vertex shader; we can influence the result by writing to them. The vertex shader also gives us an interesting *input variable*, that we can only read from, called `gl_VertexID`.

The integer variable `gl_VertexID` holds the current ID of the vertex we're drawing. When doing *indexed rendering* (with `glDrawElements`) this variable holds the current index of the vertex we're drawing. When drawing without indices (via `glDrawArrays`) this variable holds the number of the currently processed vertex since the start of the render call.

29.3 Fragment shader variables

Within the fragment shader we also have access to some interesting variables. GLSL gives us two interesting input variables called `gl_FragCoord` and `gl_FrontFacing`.

29.3.1 gl_FragCoord

We've seen the `gl_FragCoord` a couple of times before during the discussion of depth testing, because the z component of the `gl_FragCoord` vector is equal to the depth value of that particular fragment. However, we can also use the x and y component of that vector for some interesting effects.

The `gl_FragCoord`'s x and y component are the window- or screen-space coordinates of the fragment, originating from the bottom-left of the window. We specified a render window of 800x600 with `glViewport` so the screen-space coordinates of the fragment will have x values between 0 and 800, and y values between 0 and 600.

Using the fragment shader we could calculate a different color value based on the screen coordinate of the fragment. A common usage for the `gl_FragCoord` variable is for comparing visual output of different fragment calculations, as usually seen in tech demos. We could for example split the screen in two by rendering one output to the left side of the window and another output to the right side of the window. An example fragment shader that outputs a different color based on the fragment's screen coordinates is given below:

```
void main()
{
    if(gl_FragCoord.x < 400)
        FragColor = vec4(1.0, 0.0, 0.0, 1.0);
    else
        FragColor = vec4(0.0, 1.0, 0.0, 1.0);
}
```

Because the width of the window is equal to 800, whenever a pixel's x-coordinate is less than 400 it must be at the left side of the window and we'll give that fragment a different color.

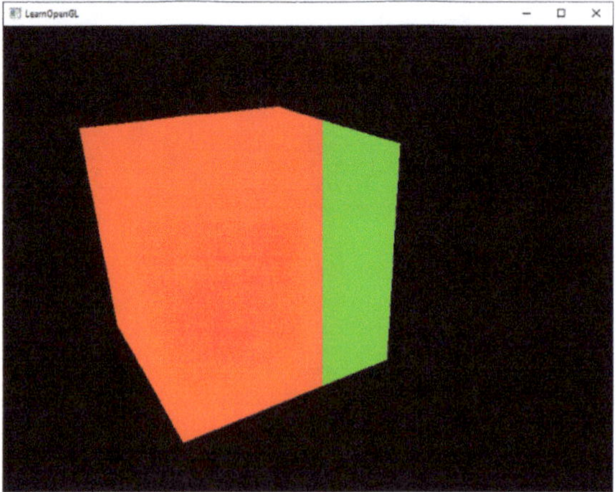

We can now calculate two completely different fragment shader results and display each of them on a different side of the window. This is great for testing out different lighting techniques for example.

29.3.2 gl_FrontFacing

Another interesting input variable in the fragment shader is the `gl_FrontFacing` variable. In the *Face Culling* chapter we mentioned that OpenGL is able to figure out if a face is a front or back face due to the winding order of the vertices. The `gl_FrontFacing` variable tells us if the current fragment is part of a front-facing or a back-facing face. We could, for example, decide to output different colors for all back faces.

The `gl_FrontFacing` variable is a `bool` that is `true` if the fragment is part of a front face and `false` otherwise. We could create a cube this way with a different texture on the inside than on the outside:

```glsl
#version 330 core
out vec4 FragColor;

in vec2 TexCoords;

uniform sampler2D frontTexture;
uniform sampler2D backTexture;

void main()
{
    if(gl_FrontFacing)
        FragColor = texture(frontTexture, TexCoords);
    else
        FragColor = texture(backTexture, TexCoords);
}
```

If we take a peek inside the container we can now see a different texture being used.

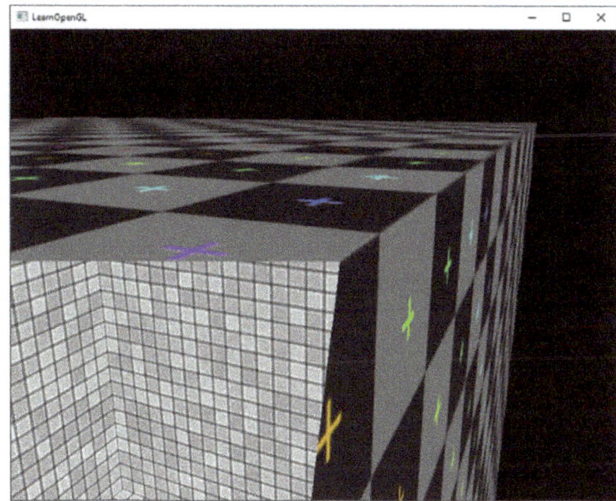

Note that if you enabled face culling you won't be able to see any faces inside the container and using `gl_FrontFacing` would then be pointless.

29.3.3 gl_FragDepth

The input variable `gl_FragCoord` is an input variable that allows us to read screen-space coordinates and get the depth value of the current fragment, but it is a read-only variable. We can't influence the screen-space coordinates of the fragment, but it is possible to set the depth value of the fragment. GLSL gives us an output variable called `gl_FragDepth` that we can use to manually set the depth value of the fragment within the shader.

To set the depth value in the shader we write any value between `0.0` and `1.0` to the output variable:

```glsl
gl_FragDepth = 0.0; // this fragment now has a depth value of 0.0
```

If the shader does not write anything to `gl_FragDepth`, the variable will automatically take its value from `gl_FragCoord.z`.

Setting the depth value manually has a major disadvantage however. That is because OpenGL disables early depth testing (as discussed in the *Depth Testing* chapter) as soon as we write to `gl_FragDepth` in the fragment shader. It is disabled, because OpenGL cannot know what depth value the fragment will have *before* we run the fragment shader, since the fragment shader may actually change this value.

By writing to `gl_FragDepth` you should take this performance penalty into consideration. From OpenGL 4.2 however, we can still sort of mediate between both sides by redeclaring the `gl_FragDepth` variable at the top of the fragment shader with a depth condition:

```
layout (depth_<condition>) out float gl_FragDepth;
```

This `condition` can take the following values:

Condition	Description
any	The default value. Early depth testing is disabled and you lose most performance.
greater	You can only make the depth value larger compared to `gl_FragCoord.z`.
less	You can only make the depth value smaller compared to `gl_FragCoord.z`.
unchanged	If you write to `gl_FragDepth`, you will write exactly `gl_FragCoord.z`.

By specifying `greater` or `less` as the depth condition, OpenGL can make the assumption that you'll only write depth values larger or smaller than the fragment's depth value. This way OpenGL is still able to do early depth testing when the depth buffer value is part of the other direction of `gl_FragCoord.z`.

An example of where we increase the depth value in the fragment shader, but still want to preserve some of the early depth testing is shown in the fragment shader below:

```glsl
#version 420 core // note the GLSL version!
out vec4 FragColor;
layout (depth_greater) out float gl_FragDepth;

void main()
{
    FragColor = vec4(1.0);
    gl_FragDepth = gl_FragCoord.z + 0.1;
}
```

Do note that this feature is only available from OpenGL version 4.2 or higher.

29.4 Interface blocks

So far, every time we sent data from the vertex to the fragment shader we declared several matching input/output variables. Declaring these one at a time is the easiest way to send data from one shader to another, but as applications become larger you probably want to send more than a few variables over.

To help us organize these variables GLSL offers us something called interface blocks that allows us to group variables together. The declaration of such an interface block looks a lot like a `struct` declaration, except that it is now declared using an `in` or `out` keyword based on the block being an input or an output block.

```glsl
#version 330 core
layout (location = 0) in vec3 aPos;
layout (location = 1) in vec2 aTexCoords;

uniform mat4 model;
```

```glsl
uniform mat4 view;
uniform mat4 projection;

out VS_OUT
{
    vec2 TexCoords;
} vs_out;

void main()
{
    gl_Position = projection * view * model * vec4(aPos, 1.0);
    vs_out.TexCoords = aTexCoords;
}
```

This time we declared an interface block called `vs_out` that groups together all the output variables we want to send to the next shader. This is kind of a trivial example, but you can imagine that this helps organize your shaders' inputs/outputs. It is also useful when we want to group shader input/output into arrays as we'll see in the next chapter about geometry shaders.

Then we also need to declare an input interface block in the next shader which is the fragment shader. The block name (`VS_OUT`) should be the same in the fragment shader, but the instance name (`vs_out` as used in the vertex shader) can be anything we like - avoiding confusing names like `vs_out` for a fragment struct containing input values.

```glsl
#version 330 core
out vec4 FragColor;

in VS_OUT
{
    vec2 TexCoords;
} fs_in;

uniform sampler2D texture;

void main()
{
    FragColor = texture(texture, fs_in.TexCoords);
}
```

As long as both interface block names are equal, their corresponding input and output is matched together. This is another useful feature that helps organize your code and proves useful when crossing between certain shader stages like the geometry shader.

29.5 Uniform buffer objects

We've been using OpenGL for quite a while now and learned some pretty cool tricks, but also a few annoyances. For example, when using more than one shader we continuously have to set uniform variables where most of them are exactly the same for each shader.

OpenGL gives us a tool called uniform buffer objects that allow us to declare a set of *global* uniform variables that remain the same over any number of shader programs. When using uniform buffer objects we set the relevant uniforms only **once** in fixed GPU memory. We do still have to manually set the uniforms that are unique per shader. Creating and configuring a uniform buffer object requires a bit of work though.

Because a uniform buffer object is a buffer like any other buffer we can create one via `glGenBuffers`, bind it to the `GL_UNIFORM_BUFFER` buffer target and store all the relevant uniform data into the buffer. There are certain rules as to how the data for uniform buffer objects should be stored and we'll get to that later. First, we'll take a simple vertex shader and store our `projection` and `view` matrix in a so called uniform block:

```glsl
#version 330 core
layout (location = 0) in vec3 aPos;

layout (std140) uniform Matrices
{
    mat4 projection;
    mat4 view;
};

uniform mat4 model;

void main()
{
    gl_Position = projection * view * model * vec4(aPos, 1.0);
}
```

In most of our samples we set a projection and view uniform matrix every frame for each shader we're using. This is a perfect example of where uniform buffer objects become useful since now we only have to store these matrices once.

Here we declared a uniform block called `Matrices` that stores two 4x4 matrices. Variables in a uniform block can be directly accessed without the block name as a prefix. Then we store these matrix values in a buffer somewhere in the OpenGL code and each shader that declares this uniform block has access to the matrices.

You're probably wondering right now what the `layout (std140)` statement means. What this says is that the currently defined uniform block uses a specific memory layout for its content; this statement sets the uniform block layout.

29.6 Uniform block layout

The content of a uniform block is stored in a buffer object, which is effectively nothing more than a reserved piece of global GPU memory. Because this piece of memory holds no information on what kind of data it holds, we need to tell OpenGL what parts of the memory correspond to which uniform variables in the shader.

Imagine the following uniform block in a shader:

```glsl
layout (std140) uniform ExampleBlock
{
    float value;
    vec3 vector;
    mat4 matrix;
    float values[3];
    bool boolean;
    int integer;
};
```

What we want to know is the size (in bytes) and the offset (from the start of the block) of each of these variables so we can place them in the buffer in their respective order. The size of each of the elements is clearly stated in OpenGL and directly corresponds to C++ data types; vectors and matrices being (large) arrays of floats. What OpenGL doesn't clearly state is the spacing between the variables. This allows the hardware to position or pad variables as it sees fit. The hardware is able to place a `vec3` adjacent to a `float` for example. Not all hardware can handle this and pads the `vec3` to an array of 4 floats before appending the `float`. A great feature, but inconvenient for us.

By default, GLSL uses a uniform memory layout called a shared layout - shared because once the offsets are defined by the hardware, they are consistently *shared* between multiple programs. With a shared layout GLSL is allowed to reposition the uniform variables for optimization as long as the variables' order remains intact. Because we don't know at what offset each uniform variable will be we don't know how to precisely fill our uniform buffer. We can query this information with functions like `glGetUniformIndices`, but that's not the approach we're going to take in this chapter.

While a shared layout gives us some space-saving optimizations, we'd need to query the offset for each uniform variable which translates to a lot of work. The general practice however is to not use the shared layout, but to use the std140 layout. The std140 layout **explicitly** states the memory layout for each variable type by standardizing their respective offsets governed by a set of rules. Since this is standardized we can manually figure out the offsets for each variable.

Each variable has a base alignment equal to the space a variable takes (including padding) within a uniform block using the std140 layout rules. For each variable, we calculate its aligned offset: the byte offset of a variable from the start of the block. The aligned byte offset of a variable **must** be equal to a multiple of its base alignment. This is a bit of a mouthful, but we'll get to see some examples soon enough to clear things up.

The exact layout rules can be found at OpenGL's uniform buffer specification[1], but we'll list the most common rules below. Each variable type in GLSL such as `int`, `float` and `bool` are defined to be four-byte quantities with each entity of 4 bytes represented as N.

Type	Layout rule
Scalar e.g. `int` or `bool`	Each scalar has a base alignment of N.
Vector Either 2N or 4N.	This means that a `vec3` has a base alignment of 4N.
Array of scalars or vectors	Each element has a base alignment equal to that of a `vec4`.
Matrices	Stored as a large array of column vectors, where each of those vectors has a base alignment of `vec4`.
Struct	Equal to the computed size of its elements according to the previous rules, but padded to a multiple of the size of a `vec4`.

Like most of OpenGL's specifications it's easier to understand with an example. We're taking the uniform block called `ExampleBlock` we introduced earlier and calculate the aligned offset for each of its members using the std140 layout:

---

[1]www.opengl.org/registry/specs/ARB/uniform_buffer_object.txt

```
layout (std140) uniform ExampleBlock
{
                           // base alignment // aligned offset
    float value;      // 4                 // 0
    vec3 vector;      // 16                // 16 (multiple of 16: 4->16)
    mat4 matrix;      // 16                // 32 (column 0)
                      // 16                // 48 (column 1)
                      // 16                // 64 (column 2)
                      // 16                // 80 (column 3)
    float values[3];  // 16                // 96 (values[0])
                      // 16                // 112 (values[1])
                      // 16                // 128 (values[2])
    bool boolean;     // 4                 // 144
    int integer;      // 4                 // 148
};
```

As an exercise, try to calculate the offset values yourself and compare them to this table. With these calculated offset values, based on the rules of the std140 layout, we can fill the buffer with data at the appropriate offsets using functions like `glBufferSubData`. While not the most efficient, the std140 layout does guarantee us that the memory layout remains the same over each program that declared this uniform block.

By adding the statement `layout (std140)` in the definition of the uniform block we tell OpenGL that this uniform block uses the std140 layout. There are two other layouts to choose from that require us to query each offset before filling the buffers. We've already seen the `shared` layout, with the other remaining layout being `packed`. When using the `packed` layout, there is no guarantee that the layout remains the same between programs (not shared) because it allows the compiler to optimize uniform variables away from the uniform block which may differ per shader.

29.7 Using uniform buffers

We've defined uniform blocks and specified their memory layout, but we haven't discussed how to actually use them yet.

First, we need to create a uniform buffer object which is done via the familiar `glGenBuffers`. Once we have a buffer object we bind it to the GL_UNIFORM_BUFFER target and allocate enough memory by calling `glBufferData`.

```
unsigned int uboExampleBlock;
glGenBuffers(1, &uboExampleBlock);
glBindBuffer(GL_UNIFORM_BUFFER, uboExampleBlock);
glBufferData(GL_UNIFORM_BUFFER, 152, NULL, GL_STATIC_DRAW); // 152 bytes
glBindBuffer(GL_UNIFORM_BUFFER, 0);
```

Now whenever we want to update or insert data into the buffer, we bind to uboExampleBlock and use `glBufferSubData` to update its memory. We only have to update this uniform buffer once, and all shaders that use this buffer now use its updated data. But, how does OpenGL know what uniform buffers correspond to which uniform blocks?

In the OpenGL context there is a number of binding points defined where we can link a uniform buffer to. Once we created a uniform buffer we link it to one of those binding points and we also link the uniform block in the shader to the same binding point, effectively linking them together. The following diagram illustrates this:

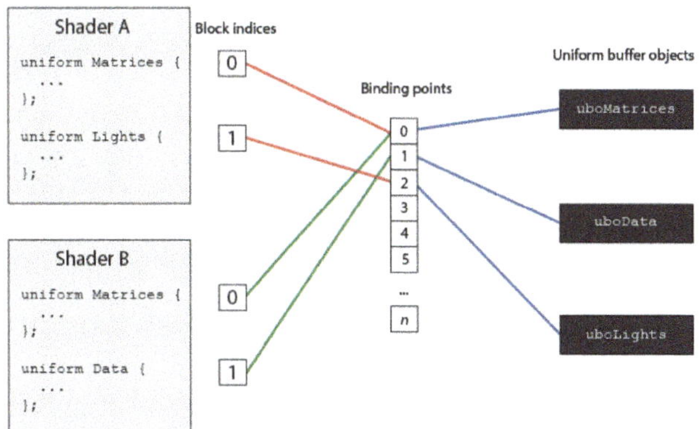

As you can see we can bind multiple uniform buffers to different binding points. Because shader A and shader B both have a uniform block linked to the same binding point 0, their uniform blocks share the same uniform data found in uboMatrices; a requirement being that both shaders defined the same Matrices uniform block.

To set a shader uniform block to a specific binding point we call glUniformBlockBinding that takes a program object, a uniform block index, and the binding point to link to. The uniform block index is a location index of the defined uniform block in the shader. This can be retrieved via a call to glGetUniformBlockIndex that accepts a program object and the name of the uniform block. We can set the Lights uniform block from the diagram to binding point 2 as follows:

```cpp
unsigned int lights_index = glGetUniformBlockIndex(shaderA.ID, "Lights");
glUniformBlockBinding(shaderA.ID, lights_index, 2);
```

Note that we have to repeat this process for **each** shader.

From OpenGL version 4.2 and onwards it is also possible to store the binding point of a uniform block explicitly in the shader by adding another layout specifier, saving us the calls to glGetUniformBlockIndex and glUniformBlockBinding. The following code sets the binding point of the Lights uniform block explicitly:

```cpp
layout(std140, binding = 2) uniform Lights { ... };
```

Then we also need to bind the uniform buffer object to the same binding point and this can be accomplished with either glBindBufferBase or glBindBufferRange.

```cpp
glBindBufferBase(GL_UNIFORM_BUFFER, 2, uboExampleBlock);
// or
glBindBufferRange(GL_UNIFORM_BUFFER, 2, uboExampleBlock, 0, 152);
```

The function glBindbufferBase expects a target, a binding point index and a uniform buffer object. This function links uboExampleBlock to binding point 2; from this point on, both sides of the binding point are linked. You can also use glBindBufferRange that expects an extra offset and size parameter - this way you can bind only a specific range of the uniform buffer to a binding point. Using glBindBufferRange you could have multiple different uniform blocks linked to a single uniform buffer object.

Now that everything is set up, we can start adding data to the uniform buffer. We could add all the data as a single byte array, or update parts of the buffer whenever we feel like it using `glBufferSubData`. To update the uniform variable `boolean` we could update the uniform buffer object as follows:

```cpp
glBindBuffer(GL_UNIFORM_BUFFER, uboExampleBlock);
int b = true; // bools in GLSL are defined as 4 bytes, so store as integer
glBufferSubData(GL_UNIFORM_BUFFER, 144, 4, &b);
glBindBuffer(GL_UNIFORM_BUFFER, 0);
```

And the same procedure applies for all the other uniform variables inside the uniform block, but with different range arguments.

29.8 A simple example

So let's demonstrate a real example of uniform buffer objects. If we look back at all the previous code samples we've continually been using 3 matrices: the projection, view and model matrix. Of all those matrices, only the model matrix changes frequently. If we have multiple shaders that use this same set of matrices, we'd probably be better off using uniform buffer objects.

We're going to store the projection and view matrix in a uniform block called `Matrices`. We're not going to store the model matrix in there since the model matrix tends to change frequently between shaders, so we wouldn't really benefit from uniform buffer objects.

```glsl
#version 330 core
layout (location = 0) in vec3 aPos;

layout (std140) uniform Matrices
{
    mat4 projection;
    mat4 view;
};
uniform mat4 model;

void main()
{
    gl_Position = projection * view * model * vec4(aPos, 1.0);
}
```

Not much going on here, except that we now use a uniform block with a std140 layout. What we're going to do in our sample application is display 4 cubes where each cube is displayed with a different shader program. Each of the 4 shader programs uses the same vertex shader, but has a unique fragment shader that only outputs a single color that differs per shader.

First, we set the uniform block of the vertex shaders equal to binding point 0. Note that we have to do this for each shader:

```cpp
unsigned int red    = glGetUniformBlockIndex(shaderRed.ID,    "Matrices");
unsigned int green  = glGetUniformBlockIndex(shaderGreen.ID,  "Matrices");
unsigned int blue   = glGetUniformBlockIndex(shaderBlue.ID,   "Matrices");
unsigned int yellow = glGetUniformBlockIndex(shaderYellow.ID, "Matrices");

glUniformBlockBinding(shaderRed.ID,    red,    0);
glUniformBlockBinding(shaderGreen.ID,  green,  0);
glUniformBlockBinding(shaderBlue.ID,   blue,   0);
glUniformBlockBinding(shaderYellow.ID, yellow, 0);
```

Next we create the actual uniform buffer object and bind that buffer to binding point 0:

```
unsigned int uboMatrices
glGenBuffers(1, &uboMatrices);

glBindBuffer(GL_UNIFORM_BUFFER, uboMatrices);
glBufferData(GL_UNIFORM_BUFFER, 2*sizeof(glm::mat4), NULL, GL_STATIC_DRAW);
glBindBuffer(GL_UNIFORM_BUFFER, 0);

glBindBufferRange(GL_UNIFORM_BUFFER, 0, uboMatrices, 0,
                 2 * sizeof(glm::mat4));
```

First we allocate enough memory for our buffer which is equal to 2 times the size of `glm::mat4`. The size of GLM's matrix types correspond directly to `mat4` in GLSL. Then we link a specific range of the buffer, in this case the entire buffer, to binding point 0.

Now all that's left to do is fill the buffer. If we keep the *field of view* value constant of the projection matrix (so no more camera zoom) we only have to update it once in our application - this means we only have to insert this into the buffer only once as well. Because we already allocated enough memory in the buffer object we can use `glBufferSubData` to store the projection matrix before we enter the render loop:

```
glm::mat4 projection = glm::perspective(glm::radians(45.0f), (float)width /
                                        (float)height, 0.1f, 100.0f);
glBindBuffer(GL_UNIFORM_BUFFER, uboMatrices);
glBufferSubData(GL_UNIFORM_BUFFER, 0, sizeof(glm::mat4),
                glm::value_ptr(projection));
glBindBuffer(GL_UNIFORM_BUFFER, 0);
```

Here we store the first half of the uniform buffer with the projection matrix. Then before we render the objects each frame we update the second half of the buffer with the view matrix:

```
glm::mat4 view = camera.GetViewMatrix();
glBindBuffer(GL_UNIFORM_BUFFER, uboMatrices);
glBufferSubData(GL_UNIFORM_BUFFER, sizeof(glm::mat4), sizeof(glm::mat4),
                glm::value_ptr(view));
glBindBuffer(GL_UNIFORM_BUFFER, 0);
```

And that's it for uniform buffer objects. Each vertex shader that contains a `Matrices` uniform block will now contain the data stored in `uboMatrices`. So if we now were to draw 4 cubes using 4 different shaders, their projection and view matrix should be the same:

```
glBindVertexArray(cubeVAO);
shaderRed.use();
glm::mat4 model = glm::mat4(1.0f);
model = glm::translate(model, glm::vec3(-0.75f, 0.75f, 0.0f)); // top-left
shaderRed.setMat4("model", model);
glDrawArrays(GL_TRIANGLES, 0, 36);
// ... draw Green Cube
// ... draw Blue Cube
// ... draw Yellow Cube
```

The only uniform we still need to set is the `model` uniform. Using uniform buffer objects in a scenario like this saves us from quite a few uniform calls per shader. The result looks something like this:

Each of the cubes is moved to one side of the window by translating the model matrix and, thanks to the different fragment shaders, their colors differ per object. This is a relatively simple scenario of where we could use uniform buffer objects, but any large rendering application can have over hundreds of shader programs active which is where uniform buffer objects really start to shine.

You can find the full source code of the uniform example application at `/src/4.advanced_opengl/8.advanced_glsl_ubo/`.

Uniform buffer objects have several advantages over single uniforms. First, setting a lot of uniforms at once is faster than setting multiple uniforms one at a time. Second, if you want to change the same uniform over several shaders, it is much easier to change a uniform once in a uniform buffer. One last advantage that is not immediately apparent is that you can use a lot more uniforms in shaders using uniform buffer objects. OpenGL has a limit to how much uniform data it can handle which can be queried with `GL_MAX_VERTEX_UNIFORM_COMPONENTS`. When using uniform buffer objects, this limit is much higher. So whenever you reach a maximum number of uniforms (when doing skeletal animation for example) there's always uniform buffer objects.

30. Geometry Shader

Between the vertex and the fragment shader there is an optional shader stage called the geometry shader. A geometry shader takes as input a set of vertices that form a single primitive e.g. a point or a triangle. The geometry shader can then transform these vertices as it sees fit before sending them to the next shader stage. What makes the geometry shader interesting is that it is able to convert the original primitive (set of vertices) to completely different primitives, possibly generating more vertices than were initially given.

We're going to throw you right into the deep by showing you an example of a geometry shader:

```glsl
#version 330 core
layout (points) in;
layout (line_strip, max_vertices = 2) out;

void main() {
    gl_Position = gl_in[0].gl_Position + vec4(-0.1, 0.0, 0.0, 0.0);
    EmitVertex();

    gl_Position = gl_in[0].gl_Position + vec4( 0.1, 0.0, 0.0, 0.0);
    EmitVertex();

    EndPrimitive();
}
```

At the start of a geometry shader we need to declare the type of primitive input we're receiving from the vertex shader. We do this by declaring a layout specifier in front of the `in` keyword. This input layout qualifier can take any of the following primitive values:

- `points`: when drawing `GL_POINTS` primitives (1).
- `lines`: when drawing `GL_LINES` or `GL_LINE_STRIP` (2).
- `lines_adjacency`: `GL_LINES_ADJACENCY` or `GL_LINE_STRIP_ADJACENCY` (4).
- `triangles`: `GL_TRIANGLES`, `GL_TRIANGLE_STRIP` or `GL_TRIANGLE_FAN` (3).
- `triangles_adjacency` : `GL_TRIANGLES_ADJACENCY` or `GL_TRIANGLE_STRIP_ADJACENCY` (6).

These are almost all the rendering primitives we're able to give to rendering calls like `glDrawArrays`. If we'd chosen to draw vertices as `GL_TRIANGLES` we should set the input qualifier to `triangles`. The number within the parenthesis represents the minimal number of vertices a single primitive contains.

We also need to specify a primitive type that the geometry shader will output and we do this via a layout specifier in front of the `out` keyword. Like the input layout qualifier, the output layout qualifier can take several primitive values:

- `points`
- `line_strip`
- `triangle_strip`

With just these 3 output specifiers we can create almost any shape we want from the input primitives. To generate a single triangle for example we'd specify `triangle_strip` as the output and output 3 vertices.

The geometry shader also expects us to set a maximum number of vertices it outputs (if you exceed this number, OpenGL won't draw the *extra* vertices) which we can also do within the layout qualifier of the `out` keyword. In this particular case we're going to output a `line_strip` with a maximum number of 2 vertices.

In case you're wondering what a line strip is: a line strip binds together a set of points to form one continuous line between them with a minimum of 2 points. Each extra point results in a new line between the new point and the previous point as you can see in the following image with 5 point vertices:

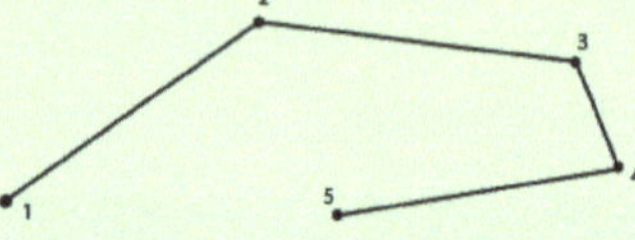

To generate meaningful results we need some way to retrieve the output from the previous shader stage. GLSL gives us a built-in variable called `gl_in` that internally (probably) looks something like this:

```glsl
in gl_Vertex
{
    vec4  gl_Position;
    float gl_PointSize;
    float gl_ClipDistance[];
} gl_in[];
```

Here it is declared as an interface block (as discussed in the previous chapter) that contains a few interesting variables of which the most interesting one is `gl_Position` that contains the vector we set as the vertex shader's output.

Note that it is declared as an array, because most render primitives contain more than 1 vertex. The geometry shader receives **all** vertices of a primitive as its input.

Using the vertex data from the vertex shader stage we can generate new data with 2 geometry shader functions called `EmitVertex` and `EndPrimitive`. The geometry shader expects you to generate/output at least one of the primitives you specified as output. In our case we want to at least generate one line strip primitive.

```glsl
#version 330 core
layout (points) in;
layout (line_strip, max_vertices = 2) out;

void main() {
    gl_Position = gl_in[0].gl_Position + vec4(-0.1, 0.0, 0.0, 0.0);
    EmitVertex();

    gl_Position = gl_in[0].gl_Position + vec4( 0.1, 0.0, 0.0, 0.0);
    EmitVertex();

    EndPrimitive();
}
```

Each time we call `EmitVertex`, the vector currently set to `gl_Position` is added to the output primitive. Whenever `EndPrimitive` is called, all emitted vertices for this primitive are combined into the specified output render primitive. By repeatedly calling `EndPrimitive`, after one or more `EmitVertex` calls, multiple primitives can be generated. This particular case emits two vertices that were translated by a small offset from the original vertex position and then calls `EndPrimitive`, combining the two vertices into a single line strip of 2 vertices.

Now that you (sort of) know how geometry shaders work you can probably guess what this geometry shader does. This geometry shader takes a point primitive as its input and creates a horizontal line primitive with the input point at its center. If we were to render this it looks something like this:

Not very impressive yet, but it's interesting to consider that this output was generated using just the following render call:

```
glDrawArrays(GL_POINTS, 0, 4);
```

While this is a relatively simple example, it does show you how we can use geometry shaders to (dynamically) generate new shapes on the fly. Later in this chapter we'll discuss a few interesting effects that we can create using geometry shaders, but for now we're going to start with a simple example.

30.1 Using geometry shaders

To demonstrate the use of a geometry shader we're going to render a really simple scene where we draw 4 points on the z-plane in normalized device coordinates. The coordinates of the points are:

```
float points[] = {
    -0.5f,  0.5f, // top-left
     0.5f,  0.5f, // top-right
     0.5f, -0.5f, // bottom-right
    -0.5f, -0.5f  // bottom-left
};
```

The vertex shader needs to draw the points on the z-plane so we'll create a basic vertex shader:

```
#version 330 core
layout (location = 0) in vec2 aPos;

void main()
{
    gl_Position = vec4(aPos.x, aPos.y, 0.0, 1.0);
}
```

And we'll output the color green for all points which we code directly in the fragment shader:

```glsl
#version 330 core
out vec4 FragColor;

void main()
{
    FragColor = vec4(0.0, 1.0, 0.0, 1.0);
}
```

Generate a VAO and a VBO for the points' vertex data and then draw them via `glDrawArrays`:

```cpp
shader.use();
glBindVertexArray(VAO);
glDrawArrays(GL_POINTS, 0, 4);
```

The result is a dark scene with 4 (difficult to see) green points:

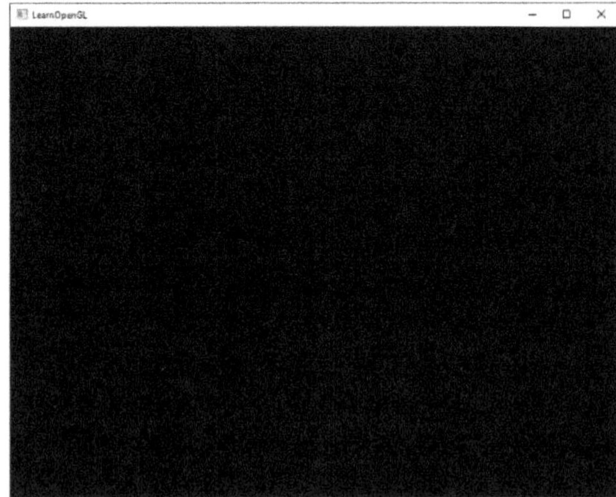

But didn't we already learn to do all this? Yes, and now we're going to spice this little scene up by adding geometry shader magic to the scene.

For learning purposes we're first going to create what is called a pass-through geometry shader that takes a point primitive as its input and *passes* it to the next shader unmodified:

```glsl
#version 330 core
layout (points) in;
layout (points, max_vertices = 1) out;

void main() {
    gl_Position = gl_in[0].gl_Position;
    EmitVertex();
    EndPrimitive();
}
```

By now this geometry shader should be fairly easy to understand. It simply emits the unmodified vertex position it received as input and generates a point primitive.

A geometry shader needs to be compiled and linked to a program just like the vertex and fragment shader, but this time we'll create the shader using `GL_GEOMETRY_SHADER` as the shader type:

```
geometryShader = glCreateShader(GL_GEOMETRY_SHADER);
glShaderSource(geometryShader, 1, &gShaderCode, NULL);
glCompileShader(geometryShader);
[...]
glAttachShader(program, geometryShader);
glLinkProgram(program);
```

The shader compilation code is the same as the vertex and fragment shaders. Be sure to check for compile or linking errors!

If you'd now compile and run you should be looking at a result that looks a bit like this:

It's exactly the same as without the geometry shader! It's a bit dull, I'll admit that, but the fact that we were still able to draw the points means that the geometry shader works, so now it's time for the more funky stuff!

30.2 Let's build houses

Drawing points and lines isn't **that** interesting so we're going to get a little creative by using the geometry shader to draw a house for us at the location of each point. We can accomplish this by setting the output of the geometry shader to triangle_strip and draw a total of three triangles: two for the square house and one for the roof.

A triangle strip in OpenGL is a more efficient way to draw triangles with fewer vertices. After the first triangle is drawn, each subsequent vertex generates another triangle next to the first triangle: every 3 adjacent vertices will form a triangle. If we have a total of 6 vertices that form a triangle strip we'd get the following triangles: (1,2,3), (2,3,4), (3,4,5) and (4,5,6); forming a total of 4 triangles. A triangle strip needs at least 3 vertices and will generate N-2 triangles; with 6 vertices we created 6-2 = 4 triangles. The following image illustrates this:

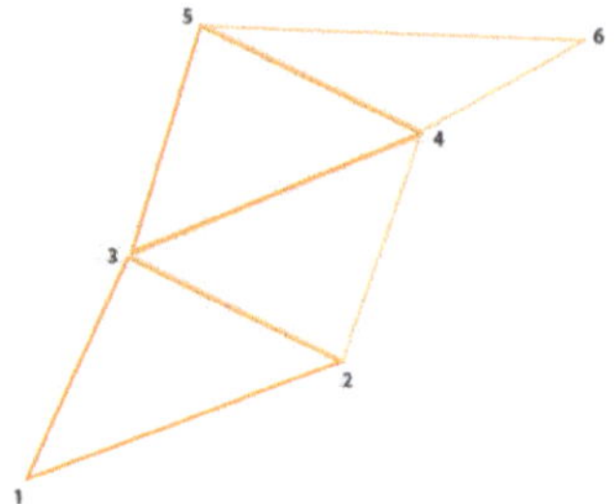

Using a triangle strip as the output of the geometry shader we can easily create the house shape we're after by generating 3 adjacent triangles in the correct order. The following image shows in what order we need to draw what vertices to get the triangles we need with the blue dot being the input point:

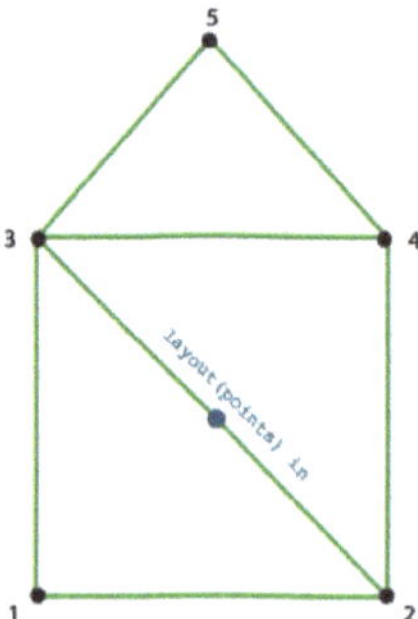

This translates to the following geometry shader:

```glsl
#version 330 core
layout (points) in;
layout (triangle_strip, max_vertices = 5) out;

void build_house(vec4 position)
{
    gl_Position = position + vec4(-0.2, -0.2, 0.0, 0.0); // 1:bottom-left
    EmitVertex();
    gl_Position = position + vec4( 0.2, -0.2, 0.0, 0.0); // 2:bottom-right
    EmitVertex();
    gl_Position = position + vec4(-0.2,  0.2, 0.0, 0.0); // 3:top-left
    EmitVertex();
    gl_Position = position + vec4( 0.2,  0.2, 0.0, 0.0); // 4:top-right
    EmitVertex();
    gl_Position = position + vec4( 0.0,  0.4, 0.0, 0.0); // 5:top
    EmitVertex();
    EndPrimitive();
}

void main() {
    build_house(gl_in[0].gl_Position);
}
```

This geometry shader generates 5 vertices, with each vertex being the point's position plus an offset to form one large triangle strip. The resulting primitive is then rasterized and the fragment shader runs on the entire triangle strip, resulting in a green house for each point we've rendered:

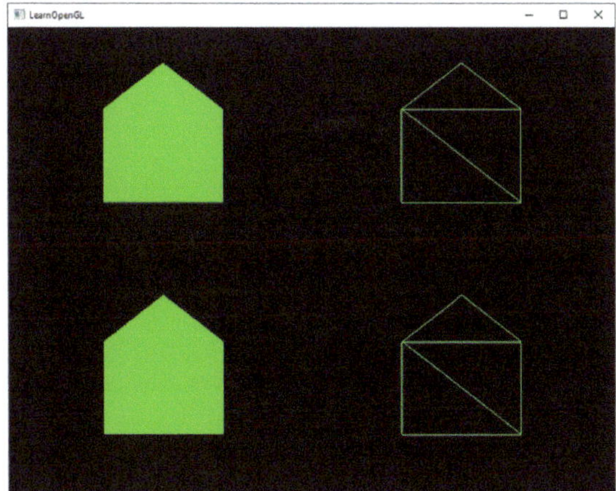

You can see that each house indeed consists of 3 triangles - all drawn using a single point in space. The green houses do look a bit boring though, so let's liven it up a bit by giving each house a unique color. To do this we're going to add an extra vertex attribute in the vertex shader with color information per vertex and direct it to the geometry shader that further forwards it to the fragment shader.

The updated vertex data is given below:

```
float points[] = {
    -0.5f,  0.5f, 1.0f, 0.0f, 0.0f, // top-left
     0.5f,  0.5f, 0.0f, 1.0f, 0.0f, // top-right
     0.5f, -0.5f, 0.0f, 0.0f, 1.0f, // bottom-right
    -0.5f, -0.5f, 1.0f, 1.0f, 0.0f  // bottom-left
};
```

Then we update the vertex shader to forward the color attribute to the geometry shader using an interface block:

```
#version 330 core
layout (location = 0) in vec2 aPos;
layout (location = 1) in vec3 aColor;

out VS_OUT {
    vec3 color;
} vs_out;

void main()
{
    gl_Position = vec4(aPos.x, aPos.y, 0.0, 1.0);
    vs_out.color = aColor;
}
```

Then we also need to declare the same interface block (with a different interface name) in the geometry shader:

```
in VS_OUT {
    vec3 color;
} gs_in[];
```

Because the geometry shader acts on a set of vertices as its input, its input data from the vertex shader is always represented as arrays of vertex data even though we only have a single vertex right now.

> We don't necessarily have to use interface blocks to transfer data to the geometry shader. We could have also written it as:
>
> ```
> in vec3 outColor[];
> ```
>
> This works if the vertex shader forwarded the color vector as `out vec3 outColor`. However, interface blocks are easier to work with in shaders like the geometry shader. In practice, geometry shader inputs can get quite large and grouping them in one large interface block array makes a lot more sense.

We should also declare an output color vector for the next fragment shader stage:

```
out vec3 fColor;
```

Because the fragment shader expects only a single (interpolated) color it doesn't make sense to forward multiple colors. The `fColor` vector is thus not an array, but a single vector. When emitting a vertex, that vertex will store the last stored value in `fColor` as that vertex's output value. For the houses, we can fill `fColor` once with the color from the vertex shader before the first vertex is emitted to color the entire house:

```
fColor = gs_in[0].color; // gs_in[0] since there's only one input vertex
gl_Position = position + vec4(-0.2, -0.2, 0.0, 0.0); // 1:bottom-left
EmitVertex();
gl_Position = position + vec4( 0.2, -0.2, 0.0, 0.0); // 2:bottom-right
EmitVertex();
gl_Position = position + vec4(-0.2,  0.2, 0.0, 0.0); // 3:top-left
EmitVertex();
gl_Position = position + vec4( 0.2,  0.2, 0.0, 0.0); // 4:top-right
EmitVertex();
gl_Position = position + vec4( 0.0,  0.4, 0.0, 0.0); // 5:top
EmitVertex();
EndPrimitive();
```

All the emitted vertices will have the last stored value in `fColor` embedded into their data, which is equal to the input vertex's color as we defined in its attributes. All the houses will now have a color of their own:

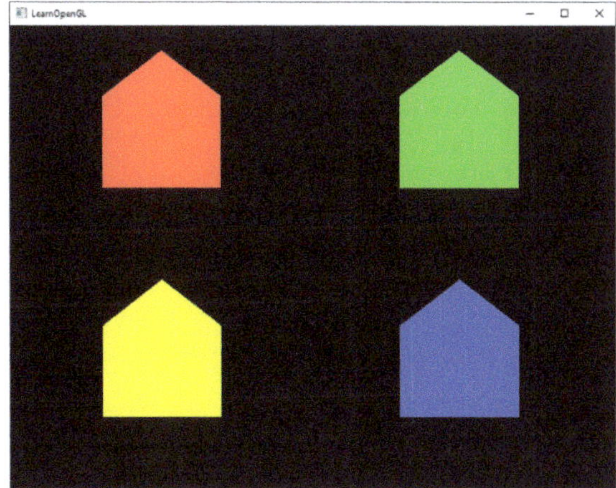

Just for fun we could also pretend it's winter and give their roofs a little snow by giving the last vertex a color of its own:

```
fColor = gs_in[0].color;
gl_Position = position + vec4(-0.2, -0.2, 0.0, 0.0); // 1:bottom-left
EmitVertex();
gl_Position = position + vec4( 0.2, -0.2, 0.0, 0.0); // 2:bottom-right
EmitVertex();
gl_Position = position + vec4(-0.2, 0.2, 0.0, 0.0);  // 3:top-left
EmitVertex();
gl_Position = position + vec4( 0.2, 0.2, 0.0, 0.0);  // 4:top-right
EmitVertex();
gl_Position = position + vec4( 0.0, 0.4, 0.0, 0.0);  // 5:top
fColor = vec3(1.0, 1.0, 1.0);
EmitVertex();
EndPrimitive();
```

The result now looks something like this:

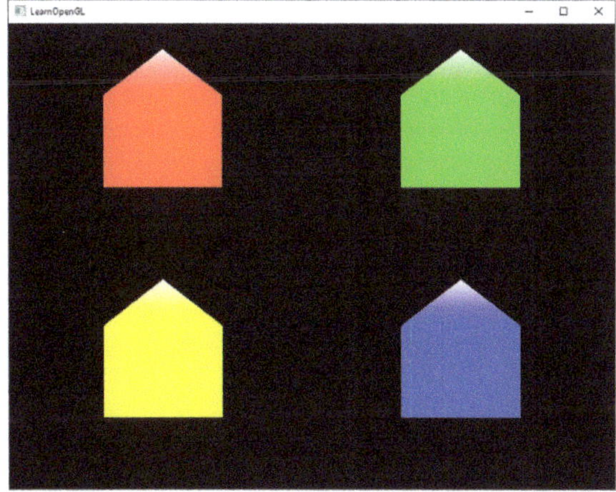

You can compare your source code with the OpenGL code at `/src/4.advanced_opengl/9.1.geometry_shader_houses/`.

You can see that with geometry shaders you can get pretty creative, even with the simplest primitives. Because the shapes are generated dynamically on the ultra-fast hardware of your GPU this can be a lot more powerful than defining these shapes yourself within vertex buffers. Geometry shaders are a great tool for simple (often-repeating) shapes, like cubes in a voxel world or grass leaves on a large outdoor field.

30.3 Exploding objects

While drawing houses is fun and all, it's not something we're going to use that much. That's why we're now going to take it up one notch and explode objects! That is something we're also probably not going to use that much either, but it's definitely fun to do!

When we say *exploding* an object we're not actually going to blow up our precious bundled sets of vertices, but we're going to move each triangle along the direction of their normal vector over a small period of time. The effect is that the entire object's triangles seem to *explode*. The effect of exploding triangles on the backpack model looks a bit like this:

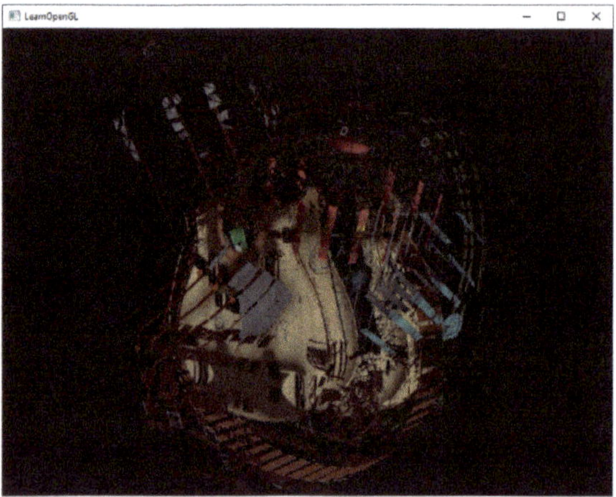

The great thing about such a geometry shader effect is that it works on all objects, regardless of their complexity.

Because we're going to translate each vertex into the direction of the triangle's normal vector we first need to calculate this normal vector. What we need to do is calculate a vector that is perpendicular to the surface of a triangle, using just the 3 vertices we have access to. You may remember from the *Transformations* chapter that we can retrieve a vector perpendicular to two other vectors using the cross product. If we were to retrieve two vectors a and b that are parallel to the surface of a triangle we can retrieve its normal vector by doing a cross product on those vectors. The following geometry shader function does exactly this to retrieve the normal vector using 3 input vertex coordinates:

```glsl
vec3 GetNormal()
{
    vec3 a = vec3(gl_in[0].gl_Position) - vec3(gl_in[1].gl_Position);
    vec3 b = vec3(gl_in[2].gl_Position) - vec3(gl_in[1].gl_Position);
    return normalize(cross(a, b));
}
```

Here we retrieve two vectors a and b that are parallel to the surface of the triangle using vector subtraction. Subtracting two vectors from each other results in a vector that is the difference of the two vectors. Since all 3 points lie on the triangle plane, subtracting any of its vectors from each other results in a vector parallel to the plane. Do note that if we switched `a` and `b` in the `cross` function we'd get a normal vector that points in the opposite direction - order is important here!

Now that we know how to calculate a normal vector we can create an `explode` function that takes this normal vector along with a vertex position vector. The function returns a new vector that translates the position vector along the direction of the normal vector:

```glsl
vec4 explode(vec4 position, vec3 normal)
{
    float magnitude = 2.0;
    vec3 direction = normal * ((sin(time) + 1.0) / 2.0) * magnitude;
    return position + vec4(direction, 0.0);
}
```

The function itself shouldn't be too complicated. The `sin` function receives a `time` uniform variable as its argument that, based on the time, returns a value between -1.0 and 1.0. Because we don't want to *implode* the object we transform the sin value to the $[0, 1]$ range. The resulting value is then used to scale the `normal` vector and the resulting `direction` vector is added to the position vector.

The complete geometry shader for the explode effect, while drawing a model loaded using our model loader, looks a bit like this:

```glsl
#version 330 core
layout (triangles) in;
layout (triangle_strip, max_vertices = 3) out;

in VS_OUT {
    vec2 texCoords;
} gs_in[];

out vec2 TexCoords;

uniform float time;

vec4 explode(vec4 position, vec3 normal) { ... }

vec3 GetNormal() { ... }

void main() {
    vec3 normal = GetNormal();

    gl_Position = explode(gl_in[0].gl_Position, normal);
    TexCoords = gs_in[0].texCoords;
    EmitVertex();
    gl_Position = explode(gl_in[1].gl_Position, normal);
    TexCoords = gs_in[1].texCoords;
    EmitVertex();
    gl_Position = explode(gl_in[2].gl_Position, normal);
    TexCoords = gs_in[2].texCoords;
    EmitVertex();
    EndPrimitive();
}
```

Note that we're also outputting the appropriate texture coordinates before emitting a vertex.

Also don't forget to actually set the `time` uniform in your OpenGL code:

```
shader.setFloat("time", glfwGetTime());
```

The result is a 3D model that seems to continually explode its vertices over time after which it returns to normal again. Although not exactly super useful, it does show you a more advanced use of the geometry shader. You can compare your source code with the complete source code at `/src/4.advanced_opengl/9.2.geometry_shader_exploding/`.

30.4 Visualizing normal vectors

To shake things up we're going to now discuss an example of using the geometry shader that is actually useful: visualizing the normal vectors of any object. When programming lighting shaders you will eventually run into weird visual outputs of which the cause is hard to determine. A common cause of lighting errors is incorrect normal vectors. Either caused by incorrectly loading vertex data, improperly specifying them as vertex attributes, or by incorrectly managing them in the shaders. What we want is some way to detect if the normal vectors we supplied are correct. A great way to determine if your normal vectors are correct is by visualizing them, and it just so happens that the geometry shader is an extremely useful tool for this purpose.

The idea is as follows: we first draw the scene as normal without a geometry shader and then we draw the scene a second time, but this time only displaying normal vectors that we generate via a geometry shader. The geometry shader takes as input a triangle primitive and generates 3 lines from them in the directions of their normal - one normal vector for each vertex. In code it'll look something like this:

```
shader.use();
DrawScene();
normalDisplayShader.use();
DrawScene();
```

This time we're creating a geometry shader that uses the vertex normals supplied by the model instead of generating it ourself. To accommodate for scaling and rotations (due to the view and model matrix) we'll transform the normals with a normal matrix. The geometry shader receives its position vectors as view-space coordinates so we should also transform the normal vectors to the same space. This can all be done in the vertex shader:

```glsl
#version 330 core
layout (location = 0) in vec3 aPos;
layout (location = 1) in vec3 aNormal;

out VS_OUT {
    vec3 normal;
} vs_out;

uniform mat4 view;
uniform mat4 model;

void main()
{
    gl_Position = view * model * vec4(aPos, 1.0);
    mat3 normalMatrix = mat3(transpose(inverse(view * model)));
    vs_out.normal = normalize(vec3(vec4(normalMatrix * aNormal, 0.0)));
}
```

The transformed view-space normal vector is then passed to the next shader stage via an interface block. The geometry shader then takes each vertex (with a position and a normal vector) and draws a normal vector from each position vector:

```glsl
#version 330 core
layout (triangles) in;
layout (line_strip, max_vertices = 6) out;

in VS_OUT {
    vec3 normal;
} gs_in[];

const float MAGNITUDE = 0.4;

uniform mat4 projection;

void GenerateLine(int index)
{
    gl_Position = projection * gl_in[index].gl_Position;
    EmitVertex();
    gl_Position = projection * (gl_in[index].gl_Position +
                               vec4(gs_in[index].normal, 0.0) * MAGNITUDE);
    EmitVertex();
    EndPrimitive();
}

void main()
{
    GenerateLine(0); // first vertex normal
    GenerateLine(1); // second vertex normal
    GenerateLine(2); // third vertex normal
}
```

The contents of geometry shaders like these should be self-explanatory by now. Note that we're multiplying the normal vector by a `MAGNITUDE` vector to restrain the size of the displayed normal vectors (otherwise they'd be a bit too large).

Since visualizing normals are mostly used for debugging purposes we can just display them as mono-colored lines (or super-fancy lines if you feel like it) with the help of the fragment shader:

```glsl
#version 330 core
out vec4 FragColor;

void main()
{
    FragColor = vec4(1.0, 1.0, 0.0, 1.0);
}
```

Now rendering your model with normal shaders first and then with the special *normal-visualizing* shader you'll see something like this:

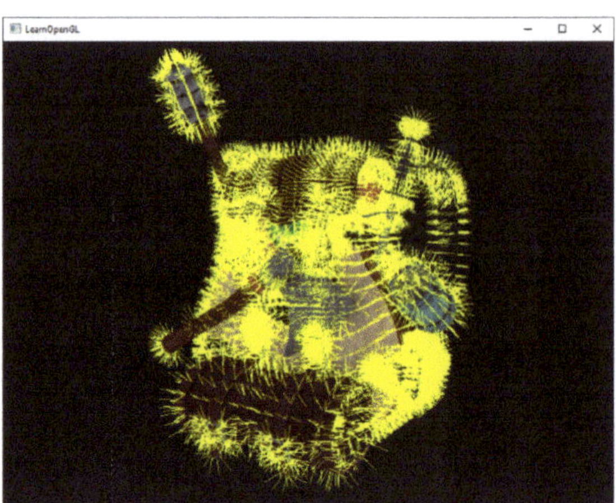

Apart from the fact that our backpack now looks a bit hairy, it gives us a really useful method for determining if the normal vectors of a model are indeed correct. You can imagine that geometry shaders like this could also be used for adding fur to objects.

You can find the OpenGL's source code at `/src/4.advanced_opengl/9.3.geometry_shader_normals/`.

31. Instancing

Say you have a scene where you're drawing a lot of models where most of these models contain the same set of vertex data, but with different world transformations. Think of a scene filled with grass leaves: each grass leave is a small model that consists of only a few triangles. You'll probably want to draw quite a few of them and your scene may end up with thousands or maybe tens of thousands of grass leaves that you need to render each frame. Because each leaf is only a few triangles, the leaf is rendered almost instantly. However, the thousands of render calls you'll have to make will drastically reduce performance.

If we were to actually render such a large amount of objects it will look a bit like this in code:

```cpp
for(unsigned int i = 0; i < amount_of_models_to_draw; i++)
{
    DoSomePreparations(); // bind VAO, bind textures, set uniforms etc.
    glDrawArrays(GL_TRIANGLES, 0, amount_of_vertices);
}
```

When drawing many instances of your model like this you'll quickly reach a performance bottleneck because of the many draw calls. Compared to rendering the actual vertices, telling the GPU to render your vertex data with functions like `glDrawArrays` or `glDrawElements` eats up quite some performance since OpenGL must make necessary preparations before it can draw your vertex data (like telling the GPU which buffer to read data from, where to find vertex attributes and all this over the relatively slow CPU to GPU bus). So even though rendering your vertices is super fast, giving your GPU the commands to render them isn't.

It would be much more convenient if we could send data over to the GPU once, and then tell OpenGL to draw multiple objects using this data with a single drawing call. Enter instancing.

Instancing is a technique where we draw many (equal mesh data) objects at once with a single render call, saving us all the CPU -> GPU communications each time we need to render an object. To render using instancing all we need to do is change the render calls `glDrawArrays` and `glDrawElements` to `glDrawArraysInstanced` and `glDrawElementsInstanced` respectively. These *instanced* versions of the classic rendering functions take an extra parameter called the instance count that sets the number of instances we want to render. We sent all the required data to the GPU once, and then tell the GPU how it should draw all these instances with a single call. The GPU then renders all these instances without having to continually communicate with the CPU.

By itself this function is a bit useless. Rendering the same object a thousand times is of no use to us since each of the rendered objects is rendered exactly the same and thus also at the same location; we would only see one object! For this reason GLSL added another built-in variable in the vertex shader called `gl_InstanceID`.

When drawing with one of the instanced rendering calls, `gl_InstanceID` is incremented for each instance being rendered starting from 0. If we were to render the 43th instance for example, `gl_InstanceID` would have the value 42 in the vertex shader. Having a unique value per instance means we could now for example index into a large array of position values to position each instance at a different location in the world.

To get a feel for instanced drawing we're going to demonstrate a simple example that renders a hundred 2D quads in normalized device coordinates with just one render call. We accomplish this by uniquely positioning each instanced quad by indexing a uniform array of 100 offset vectors. The result is a neatly organized grid of quads that fill the entire window:

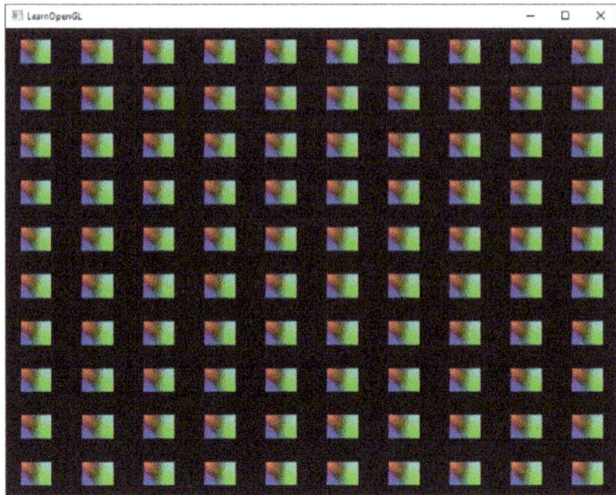

Each quad consists of 2 triangles with a total of 6 vertices. Each vertex contains a 2D NDC position vector and a color vector. Below is the vertex data used for this example - the triangles are small enough to properly fit the screen when there's a 100 of them:

```
float quadVertices[] = {
    // positions    // colors
    -0.05f,  0.05f, 1.0f, 0.0f, 0.0f,
     0.05f, -0.05f, 0.0f, 1.0f, 0.0f,
    -0.05f, -0.05f, 0.0f, 0.0f, 1.0f,

    -0.05f,  0.05f, 1.0f, 0.0f, 0.0f,
     0.05f, -0.05f, 0.0f, 1.0f, 0.0f,
     0.05f,  0.05f, 0.0f, 1.0f, 1.0f
};
```

The quads are colored in the fragment shader that receives a color vector from the vertex shader and sets it as its output:

```
#version 330 core
out vec4 FragColor;

in vec3 fColor;

void main()
{
    FragColor = vec4(fColor, 1.0);
}
```

Nothing new so far, but at the vertex shader it's starting to get interesting:

```
#version 330 core
layout (location = 0) in vec2 aPos;
layout (location = 1) in vec3 aColor;

out vec3 fColor;

uniform vec2 offsets[100];

void main()
{
```

```glsl
    vec2 offset = offsets[gl_InstanceID];
    gl_Position = vec4(aPos + offset, 0.0, 1.0);
    fColor = aColor;
}
```

Here we defined a uniform array called `offsets` that contain a total of `100` offset vectors. Within the vertex shader we retrieve an offset vector for each instance by indexing the `offsets` array using `gl_InstanceID`. If we now were to draw `100` quads with instanced drawing we'd get `100` quads located at different positions.

We do need to actually set the offset positions that we calculate in a nested for-loop before we enter the render loop:

```cpp
glm::vec2 translations[100];
int index = 0;
float offset = 0.1f;
for(int y = -10; y < 10; y += 2)
{
    for(int x = -10; x < 10; x += 2)
    {
        glm::vec2 translation;
        translation.x = (float)x / 10.0f + offset;
        translation.y = (float)y / 10.0f + offset;
        translations[index++] = translation;
    }
}
```

Here we create a set of `100` translation vectors that contains an offset vector for all positions in a 10x10 grid. In addition to generating the `translations` array, we'd also need to transfer the data to the vertex shader's uniform array:

```cpp
shader.use();
for(unsigned int i = 0; i < 100; i++)
{
    shader.setVec2(("offsets["+std::to_string(i)+"]"), translations[i]);
}
```

Within this snippet of code we transform the for-loop counter `i` to a `string` to dynamically create a location string for querying the uniform location. For each item in the `offsets` uniform array we then set the corresponding translation vector.

Now that all the preparations are finished we can start rendering the quads. To draw via instanced rendering we call `glDrawArraysInstanced` or `glDrawElementsInstanced`. Since we're not using an element index buffer we're going to call the `glDrawArrays` version:

```cpp
glBindVertexArray(quadVAO);
glDrawArraysInstanced(GL_TRIANGLES, 0, 6, 100);
```

The parameters of `glDrawArraysInstanced` are exactly the same as `glDrawArrays` except the last parameter that sets the number of instances we want to draw. Since we want to display `100` quads in a 10x10 grid we set it equal to `100`. Running the code should now give you the familiar image of `100` colorful quads.

31.1 Instanced arrays

While the previous implementation works fine for this specific use case, whenever we are rendering a lot more than 100 instances (which is quite common) we will eventually hit a limit[1] on the amount of uniform data we can send to the shaders. One alternative option is known as instanced arrays. Instanced arrays are defined as a vertex attribute (allowing us to store much more data) that are updated per instance instead of per vertex.

With vertex attributes, at the start of each run of the vertex shader, the GPU will retrieve the next set of vertex attributes that belong to the current vertex. When defining a vertex attribute as an instanced array however, the vertex shader only updates the content of the vertex attribute per instance. This allows us to use the standard vertex attributes for data per vertex and use the instanced array for storing data that is unique per instance.

To give you an example of an instanced array we're going to take the previous example and convert the offset uniform array to an instanced array. We'll have to update the vertex shader by adding another vertex attribute:

```glsl
#version 330 core
layout (location = 0) in vec2 aPos;
layout (location = 1) in vec3 aColor;
layout (location = 2) in vec2 aOffset;

out vec3 fColor;

void main()
{
    gl_Position = vec4(aPos + aOffset, 0.0, 1.0);
    fColor = aColor;
}
```

We no longer use `gl_InstanceID` and can directly use the `offset` attribute without first indexing into a large uniform array.

Because an instanced array is a vertex attribute, just like the `position` and `color` variables, we need to store its content in a vertex buffer object and configure its attribute pointer. We're first going to store the `translations` array (from the previous section) in a new buffer object:

```cpp
unsigned int instanceVBO;
glGenBuffers(1, &instanceVBO);
glBindBuffer(GL_ARRAY_BUFFER, instanceVBO);
glBufferData(GL_ARRAY_BUFFER, sizeof(glm::vec2) * 100, &translations[0],
             GL_STATIC_DRAW);
glBindBuffer(GL_ARRAY_BUFFER, 0);
```

Then we also need to set its vertex attribute pointer and enable the vertex attribute:

```cpp
glEnableVertexAttribArray(2);
glBindBuffer(GL_ARRAY_BUFFER, instanceVBO);
glVertexAttribPointer(2, 2, GL_FLOAT, GL_FALSE, 2*sizeof(float), (void*)0);
glBindBuffer(GL_ARRAY_BUFFER, 0);
glVertexAttribDivisor(2, 1);
```

What makes this code interesting is the last line where we call `glVertexAttribDivisor`. This function tells OpenGL **when** to update the content of a vertex attribute to the next element. Its

---

[1] www.khronos.org/opengl/wiki/GLSL_Uniform#Implementation_limits

first parameter is the vertex attribute in question and the second parameter the attribute divisor. By default, the attribute divisor is 0 which tells OpenGL to update the content of the vertex attribute each iteration of the vertex shader. By setting this attribute to 1 we're telling OpenGL that we want to update the content of the vertex attribute when we start to render a new instance. By setting it to 2 we'd update the content every 2 instances and so on. By setting the attribute divisor to 1 we're effectively telling OpenGL that the vertex attribute at attribute location 2 is an instanced array.

If we now were to render the quads again with `glDrawArraysInstanced` we'd get the following output:

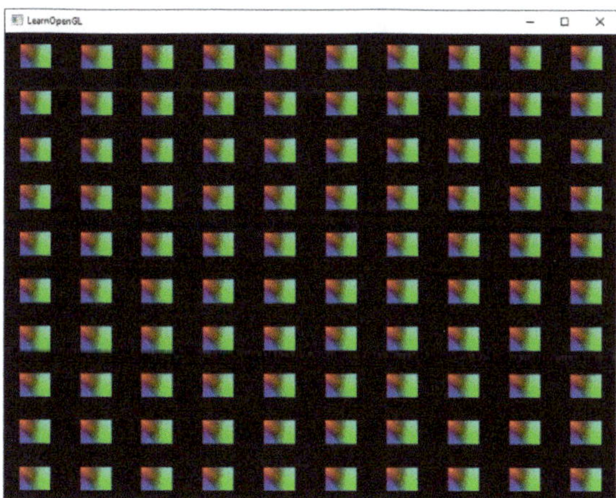

This is exactly the same as the previous example, but now with instanced arrays, which allows us to pass a lot more data (as much as memory allows us) to the vertex shader for instanced drawing.

For fun we could slowly downscale each quad from top-right to bottom-left using `gl_InstanceID` again, because why not?

```
void main()
{
    vec2 pos = aPos * (gl_InstanceID / 100.0);
    gl_Position = vec4(pos + aOffset, 0.0, 1.0);
    fColor = aColor;
}
```

The result is that the first instances of the quads are drawn extremely small and the further we're in the process of drawing the instances, the closer `gl_InstanceID` gets to 100 and thus the more the quads regain their original size. It's perfectly legal to use instanced arrays together with `gl_InstanceID` like this.

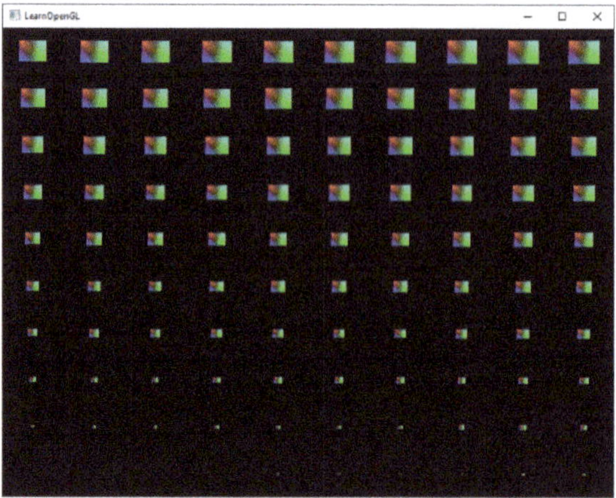

If you're still a bit unsure about how instanced rendering works or want to see how everything fits together you can find the full source code of the application at `/src/4.advanced_opengl/10.1.instancing_quads/`.

While fun and all, these examples aren't really good examples of instancing. Yes, they do give you an easy overview of how instancing works, but instancing gets most of its power when drawing an enormous amount of similar objects. For that reason we're going to venture into space.

31.2 An asteroid field

Imagine a scene where we have one large planet that's at the center of a large asteroid ring. Such an asteroid ring could contain thousands or tens of thousands of rock formations and quickly becomes un-renderable on any decent graphics card. This scenario proves itself particularly useful for instanced rendering, since all the asteroids can be represented with a single model. Each single asteroid then gets its variation from a transformation matrix unique to each asteroid.

To demonstrate the impact of instanced rendering we're first going to render a scene of asteroids hovering around a planet *without* instanced rendering. The scene will contain a large planet model (that can be downloaded from `learnopengl.com/data/models/planet.zip`) and a large set of asteroid rocks that we properly position around the planet. The asteroid rock model can be downloaded at `learnopengl.com/data/models/rock.zip`.

Within the code samples we load the models using the model loader we've previously defined in the *Model Loading* chapters.

To achieve the effect we're looking for we'll be generating a model transformation matrix for each asteroid. The transformation matrix first translates the rock somewhere in the asteroid ring - then we'll add a small random displacement value to the offset to make the ring look more natural. From there we also apply a random scale and a random rotation. The result is a transformation matrix that translates each asteroid somewhere around the planet while also giving it a more natural and unique look compared to the other asteroids.

```cpp
unsigned int amount = 1000;
glm::mat4 *modelMatrices;
modelMatrices = new glm::mat4[amount];
srand(glfwGetTime()); // initialize random seed
float radius = 50.0;
float offset = 2.5f;
```

```cpp
for(unsigned int i = 0; i < amount; i++)
{
    glm::mat4 model = glm::mat4(1.0f);
    // 1. translation: displace along circle with radius [-offset, offset]
    float angle = (float)i / (float)amount * 360.0f;
    float displacement = (rand() % (int)(2 * offset * 100)) / 100.0f -
                         offset;
    float x = sin(angle) * radius + displacement;
    displacement = (rand() % (int)(2 * offset * 100)) / 100.0f - offset;
    float y = displacement * 0.4f; // keep height of field smaller than x/z
    displacement = (rand() % (int)(2 * offset * 100)) / 100.0f - offset;
    float z = cos(angle) * radius + displacement;
    model = glm::translate(model, glm::vec3(x, y, z));

    // 2. scale: scale between 0.05 and 0.25f
    float scale = (rand() % 20) / 100.0f + 0.05;
    model = glm::scale(model, glm::vec3(scale));

    // 3. rotation: add random rotation around a (semi)random rotation axis
    float rotAngle = (rand() % 360);
    model = glm::rotate(model, rotAngle, glm::vec3(0.4f, 0.6f, 0.8f));

    // 4. now add to list of matrices
    modelMatrices[i] = model;
}
```

This piece of code may look a little daunting, but we basically transform the x and z position of the asteroid along a circle with a radius defined by `radius` and randomly displace each asteroid a little around the circle by `-offset` and `offset`. We give the `y` displacement less of an impact to create a more flat asteroid ring. Then we apply scale and rotation transformations and store the resulting transformation matrix in `modelMatrices` that is of size `amount`. Here we generate `1000` model matrices, one per asteroid.

After loading the planet and rock models and compiling a set of shaders, the rendering code then looks a bit like this:

```cpp
// draw planet
shader.use();
glm::mat4 model = glm::mat4(1.0f);
model = glm::translate(model, glm::vec3(0.0f, -3.0f, 0.0f));
model = glm::scale(model, glm::vec3(4.0f, 4.0f, 4.0f));
shader.setMat4("model", model);
planet.Draw(shader);

// draw meteorites
for(unsigned int i = 0; i < amount; i++)
{
    shader.setMat4("model", modelMatrices[i]);
    rock.Draw(shader);
}
```

First we draw the planet model, that we translate and scale a bit to accommodate the scene, and then we draw a number of rock models equal to the `amount` of transformations we generated previously. Before we draw each rock however, we first set the corresponding model transformation matrix within the shader.

The result is then a space-like scene where we can see a natural-looking asteroid ring around a planet:

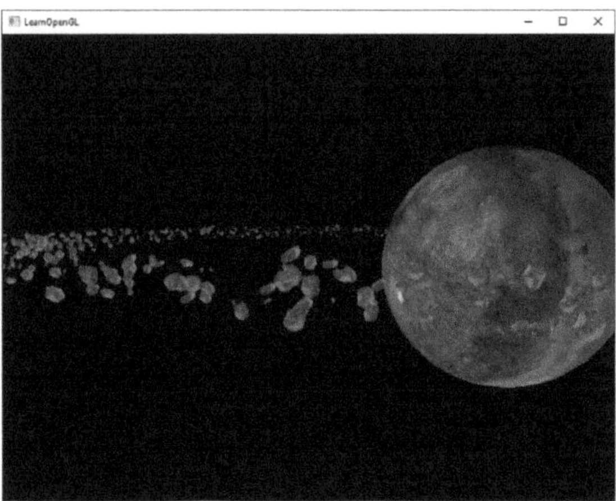

This scene contains a total of `1001` rendering calls per frame of which `1000` are of the rock model. You can find the source code for this scene at `/src/4.advanced_opengl/10.2.asteroids/`.

As soon as we start to increase this number we will quickly notice that the scene stops running smoothly and the number of frames we're able to render per second reduces drastically. As soon as we set `amount` to something close to `2000` the scene already becomes so slow on our GPU that it becomes difficult to move around.

Let's now try to render the same scene, but this time with instanced rendering. We first need to adjust the vertex shader a little:

```glsl
#version 330 core
layout (location = 0) in vec3 aPos;
layout (location = 2) in vec2 aTexCoords;
layout (location = 3) in mat4 instanceMatrix;

out vec2 TexCoords;

uniform mat4 projection;
uniform mat4 view;

void main()
{
    gl_Position = projection * view * instanceMatrix * vec4(aPos, 1.0);
    TexCoords = aTexCoords;
}
```

We're no longer using a model uniform variable, but instead declare a `mat4` as a vertex attribute so we can store an instanced array of transformation matrices. However, when we declare a datatype as a vertex attribute that is greater than a `vec4` things work a bit differently. The maximum amount of data allowed for a vertex attribute is equal to a `vec4`. Because a `mat4` is basically 4 `vec4`s, we have to reserve 4 vertex attributes for this specific matrix. Because we assigned it a location of 3, the columns of the matrix will have vertex attribute locations of 3, 4, 5, and 6.

We then have to set each of the attribute pointers of those 4 vertex attributes and configure them as instanced arrays:

```cpp
// vertex buffer object
unsigned int buffer;
glGenBuffers(1, &buffer);
glBindBuffer(GL_ARRAY_BUFFER, buffer);
glBufferData(GL_ARRAY_BUFFER, amount * sizeof(glm::mat4),
             &modelMatrices[0], GL_STATIC_DRAW);

for(unsigned int i = 0; i < rock.meshes.size(); i++)
{
    unsigned int VAO = rock.meshes[i].VAO;
    glBindVertexArray(VAO);
    // vertex attributes
    std::size_t v4s = sizeof(glm::vec4);
    glEnableVertexAttribArray(3);
    glVertexAttribPointer(3, 4, GL_FLOAT, GL_FALSE, 4*v4s, (void*)0);
    glEnableVertexAttribArray(4);
    glVertexAttribPointer(4, 4, GL_FLOAT, GL_FALSE, 4*v4s, (void*)(1*v4s));
    glEnableVertexAttribArray(5);
    glVertexAttribPointer(5, 4, GL_FLOAT, GL_FALSE, 4*v4s, (void*)(2*v4s));
    glEnableVertexAttribArray(6);
    glVertexAttribPointer(6, 4, GL_FLOAT, GL_FALSE, 4*v4s, (void*)(3*v4s));

    glVertexAttribDivisor(3, 1);
    glVertexAttribDivisor(4, 1);
    glVertexAttribDivisor(5, 1);
    glVertexAttribDivisor(6, 1);

    glBindVertexArray(0);
}
```

Note that we cheated a little by declaring the `VAO` variable of the `Mesh` as a public variable instead of a private variable so we could access its vertex array object. This is not the cleanest solution, but just a simple modification to suit this example. Aside from the little hack, this code should be clear. We're basically declaring how OpenGL should interpret the buffer for each of the matrix's vertex attributes and that each of those vertex attributes is an instanced array.

Next we take the `VAO` of the mesh(es) again and this time draw using `glDrawElementsInstanced`:

```cpp
// draw meteorites
instanceShader.use();
for(unsigned int i = 0; i < rock.meshes.size(); i++)
{
    glBindVertexArray(rock.meshes[i].VAO);
    glDrawElementsInstanced(GL_TRIANGLES, rock.meshes[i].indices.size(),
                            GL_UNSIGNED_INT, 0, amount);
}
```

Here we draw the same `amount` of asteroids as the previous example, but this time with instanced rendering. The results should be exactly the same, but once we increase the `amount` you'll really start to see the power of instanced rendering. Without instanced rendering we were able to smoothly render around `1000` to `1500` asteroids. With instanced rendering we can now set this value to `100000`. This, with the rock model having `576` vertices, would equal around `57` million vertices drawn each frame without significant performance drops; and only 2 draw calls!

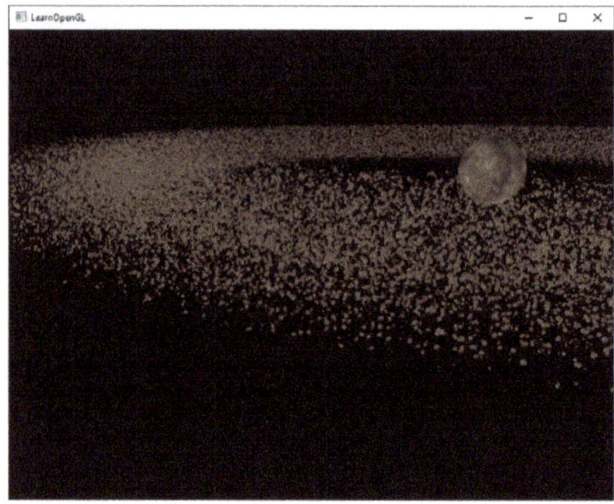

This image was rendered with `100000` asteroids with a radius of `150.0f` and an offset equal to `25.0f`. You can find the source code of the instanced rendering demo at `/src/4.advanced_opengl/10.3.asteroids_instanced/`.

On different machines an asteroid count of `100000` may be a bit too high, so try tweaking the values till you reach an acceptable framerate.

As you can see, with the right type of environments, instanced rendering can make an enormous difference to the rendering capabilities of your application. For this reason, instanced rendering is commonly used for grass, flora, particles, and scenes like this - basically any scene with many repeating shapes can benefit from instanced rendering.

32. Anti Aliasing

Somewhere in your adventurous rendering journey you probably came across some jagged saw-like patterns along the edges of your models. The reason these jagged edges appear is due to how the rasterizer transforms the vertex data into actual fragments behind the scene. An example of what these jagged edges look like can already be seen when drawing a simple cube:

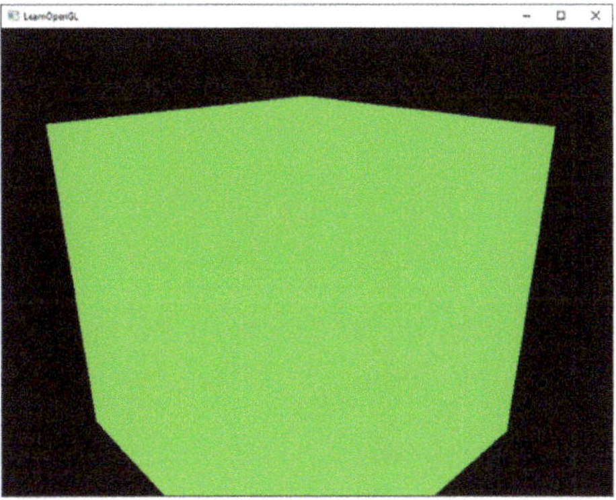

While not immediately visible, if you take a closer look at the edges of the cube you'll see a jagged pattern. If we zoom in you'd see the following:

This is clearly not something we want in a final version of an application. This effect, of clearly seeing the pixel formations an edge is composed of, is called aliasing. There are quite a few techniques out there called anti-aliasing techniques that fight this aliasing behavior by producing *smoother* edges.

At first we had a technique called super sample anti-aliasing (SSAA) that temporarily uses a much higher resolution render buffer to render the scene in (super sampling). Then when the full scene is rendered, the resolution is downsampled back to the normal resolution. This *extra* resolution was used to prevent these jagged edges. While it did provide us with a solution to the aliasing problem, it came with a major performance drawback since we have to draw **a lot** more fragments than usual. This technique therefore only had a short glory moment.

This technique did give birth to a more modern technique called multisample anti-aliasing or MSAA that borrows from the concepts behind SSAA while implementing a much more efficient approach. In this chapter we'll be extensively discussing this MSAA technique that is built-in in OpenGL.

32.1 Multisampling

To understand what multisampling is and how it works into solving the aliasing problem we first need to delve a bit further into the inner workings of OpenGL's rasterizer.

The rasterizer is the combination of all algorithms and processes that sit between your final processed vertices and the fragment shader. The rasterizer takes all vertices belonging to a single primitive and transforms this to a set of fragments. Vertex coordinates can theoretically have any coordinate, but fragments can't since they are bound by the resolution of your screen. There will almost never be a one-on-one mapping between vertex coordinates and fragments, so the rasterizer has to determine in some way what fragment/screen-coordinate each specific vertex will end up at.

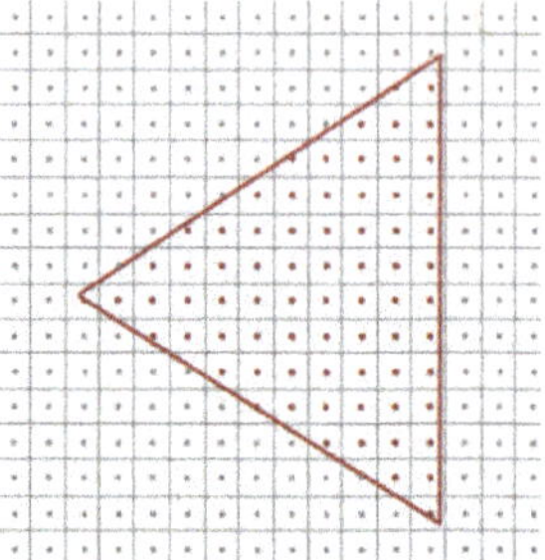

Here we see a grid of screen pixels where the center of each pixel contains a sample point that is used to determine if a pixel is covered by the triangle. The red sample points are covered by the triangle and a fragment will be generated for that covered pixel. Even though some parts of the triangle edges still enter certain screen pixels, the pixel's sample point is not covered by the inside of the triangle so this pixel won't be influenced by any fragment shader.

You can probably already figure out the origin of aliasing right now. The complete rendered version of the triangle would look like this on your screen:

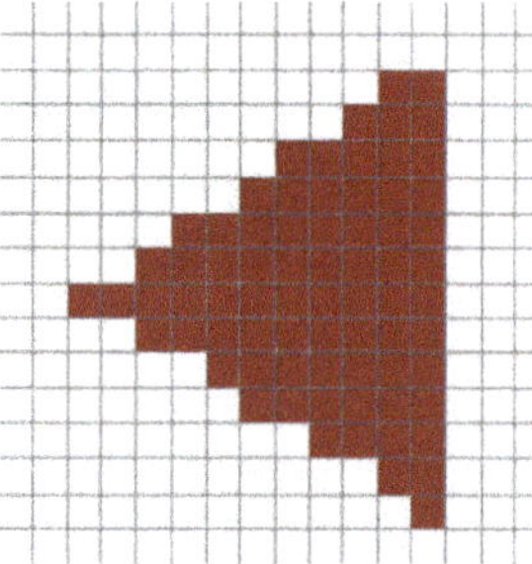

Due to the limited amount of screen pixels, some pixels will be rendered along an edge and some won't. The result is that we're rendering primitives with non-smooth edges giving rise to the jagged edges we've seen before.

What multisampling does, is not use a single sampling point for determining coverage of the triangle, but multiple sample points (guess where it got its name from). Instead of a single sample point at the center of each pixel we're going to place 4 subsamples in a general pattern and use those to determine pixel coverage.

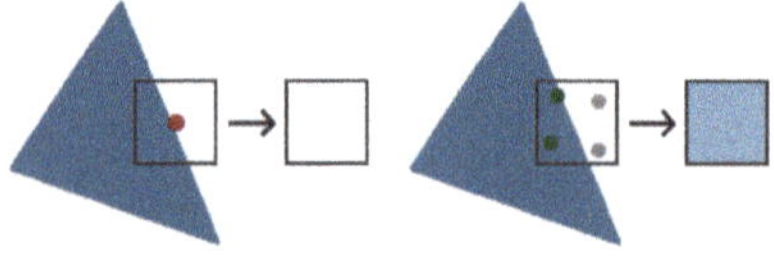

The left side of the image shows how we would normally determine the coverage of a triangle. This specific pixel won't run a fragment shader (and thus remains blank) since its sample point wasn't covered by the triangle. The right side of the image shows a multisampled version where each pixel contains 4 sample points. Here we can see that only 2 of the sample points cover the triangle.

The amount of sample points can be any number we'd like with more samples giving us better coverage precision.

This is where multisampling becomes interesting. We determined that 2 subsamples were covered by the triangle so the next step is to determine a color for this specific pixel. Our initial guess would be that we run the fragment shader for each covered subsample and later average the colors of each subsample per pixel. In this case we'd run the fragment shader twice on the interpolated vertex data at each subsample and store the resulting color in those sample points. This is (fortunately) **not** how it works, because this would mean we need to run a lot more fragment shaders than without multisampling, drastically reducing performance.

How MSAA really works is that the fragment shader is only run **once** per pixel (for each primitive) regardless of how many subsamples the triangle covers; the fragment shader runs with the vertex data interpolated to the **center** of the pixel. MSAA then uses a much larger depth/stencil (not color) buffer to determine subsample coverage. The number of subsamples covered determines how much the pixel color contributes to the framebuffer. Because only 2 of the 4 samples were covered in the previous image, half of the triangle's color is mixed with the framebuffer color (in this case the clear color) resulting in a light blue-ish color.

The result is a higher resolution buffer (with higher resolution depth/stencil) where all the primitive edges now produce a smoother pattern. Let's see what multisampling looks like when we determine the coverage of the earlier triangle:

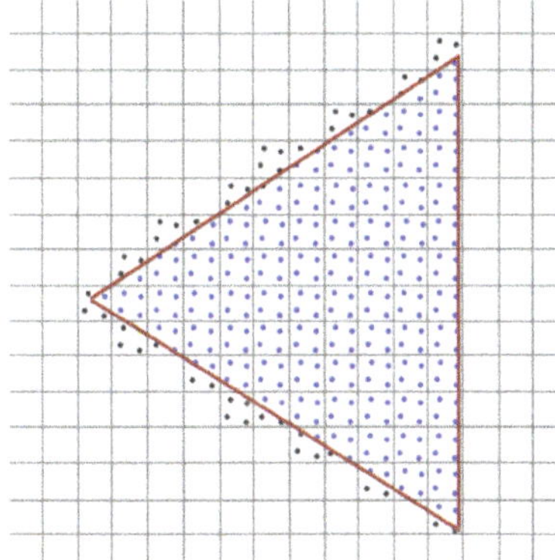

Here each pixel contains 4 subsamples (the irrelevant samples were hidden) where the blue subsamples are covered by the triangle and the gray sample points aren't. Within the inner region of the triangle all pixels will run the fragment shader once where its color output is stored directly in the framebuffer (assuming no blending). At the inner edges of the triangle however not all subsamples will be covered so the result of the fragment shader won't fully contribute to the framebuffer. Based on the number of covered samples, more or less of the triangle fragment's color ends up at that pixel.

For each pixel, the less subsamples are part of the triangle, the less it takes the color of the triangle. If we were to fill in the actual pixel colors we get the following image:

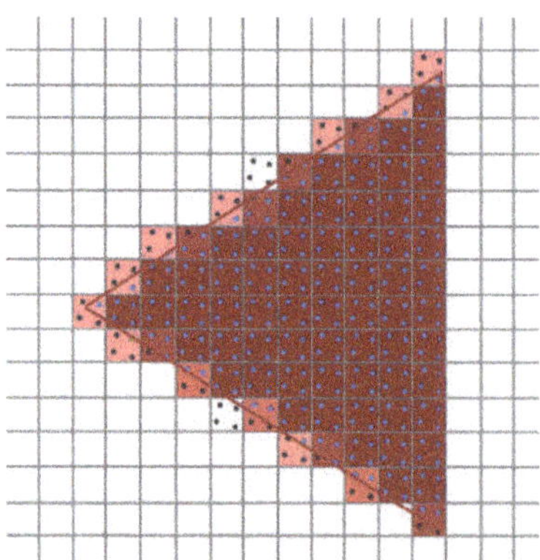

The hard edges of the triangle are now surrounded by colors slightly lighter than the actual edge color, which causes the edge to appear smooth when viewed from a distance.

Depth and stencil values are stored per subsample and, even though we only run the fragment shader once, color values are stored per subsample as well for the case of multiple triangles overlapping a single pixel. For depth testing the vertex's depth value is interpolated to each subsample before running the depth test, and for stencil testing we store the stencil values per subsample. This does mean that the size of the buffers are now increased by the amount of subsamples per pixel.

What we've discussed so far is a basic overview of how multisampled anti-aliasing works behind the scenes. The actual logic behind the rasterizer is a bit more complicated, but this brief description should be enough to understand the concept and logic behind multisampled anti-aliasing; enough to delve into the practical aspects.

32.2 MSAA in OpenGL

If we want to use MSAA in OpenGL we need to use a buffer that is able to store more than one sample value per pixel. We need a new type of buffer that can store a given amount of multisamples and this is called a multisample buffer.

Most windowing systems are able to provide us a multisample buffer instead of a default buffer. GLFW also gives us this functionality and all we need to do is *hint* GLFW that we'd like to use a multisample buffer with N samples instead of a normal buffer by calling `glfwWindowHint` before creating the window:

```
glfwWindowHint(GLFW_SAMPLES, 4);
```

When we now call `glfwCreateWindow` we create a rendering window, but this time with a buffer containing 4 subsamples per screen coordinate. This does mean that the size of the buffer is increased by 4.

Now that we asked GLFW for multisampled buffers we need to enable multisampling by calling `glEnable` with `GL_MULTISAMPLE`. On most OpenGL drivers, multisampling is enabled by default so this call is then a bit redundant, but it's usually a good idea to enable it anyways. This way all OpenGL implementations have multisampling enabled.

```
glEnable(GL_MULTISAMPLE);
```

Because the actual multisampling algorithms are implemented in the rasterizer in your OpenGL drivers there's not much else we need to do. If we now were to render the green cube from the start of this chapter we should see smoother edges:

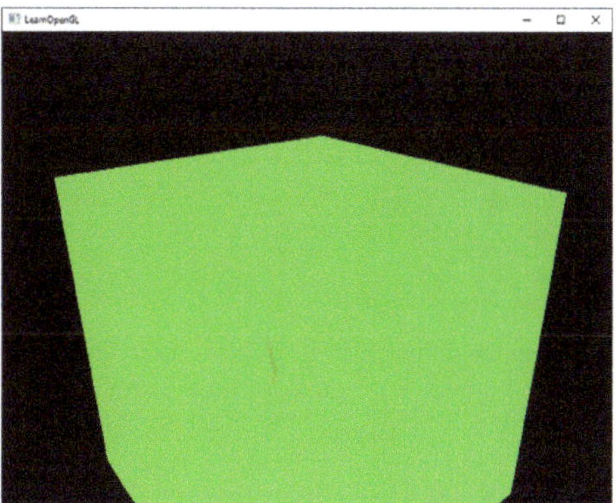

The cube does indeed look a lot smoother and the same will apply for any other object you're drawing in your scene. You can find the source code for this simple example at `/src/4.advanced_opengl/11.1.anti_aliasing_msaa/`.

32.3 Off-screen MSAA

Because GLFW takes care of creating the multisampled buffers, enabling MSAA is quite easy. If we want to use our own framebuffers however, we have to generate the multisampled buffers ourselves; now we **do** need to take care of creating multisampled buffers.

There are two ways we can create multisampled buffers to act as attachments for framebuffers: texture attachments and renderbuffer attachments. Quite similar to normal attachments like we've discussed in the *Framebuffers* chapter.

32.3.1 Multisampled texture attachments

To create a texture that supports storage of multiple sample points we use `glTexImage2DMultisample` instead of `glTexImage2D` that accepts `GL_TEXTURE_2D_MULTISAPLE` as its texture target:

```
glBindTexture(GL_TEXTURE_2D_MULTISAMPLE, tex);
glTexImage2DMultisample(GL_TEXTURE_2D_MULTISAMPLE, samples, GL_RGB,
                        width, height, GL_TRUE);
glBindTexture(GL_TEXTURE_2D_MULTISAMPLE, 0);
```

The second argument sets the number of samples we'd like the texture to have. If the last argument is set to `GL_TRUE`, the image will use identical sample locations and the same number of subsamples for each texel.

To attach a multisampled texture to a framebuffer we use `glFramebufferTexture2D`, but this time with `GL_TEXTURE_2D_MULTISAMPLE` as the texture type:

```
glFramebufferTexture2D(GL_FRAMEBUFFER, GL_COLOR_ATTACHMENT0,
                       GL_TEXTURE_2D_MULTISAMPLE, tex, 0);
```

The currently bound framebuffer now has a multisampled color buffer in the form of a texture image.

32.3.2 Multisampled renderbuffer objects

Like textures, creating a multisampled renderbuffer object isn't difficult. It is even quite easy since all we need to change is `glRenderbufferStorage` to `glRenderbufferStorageMultisample` when we configure the (currently bound) renderbuffer's memory storage:

```
glRenderbufferStorageMultisample(GL_RENDERBUFFER, 4, GL_DEPTH24_STENCIL8,
                                 width, height);
```

The one thing that changed here is the extra second parameter where we set the amount of samples we'd like to use; 4 in this particular case.

32.3.3 Render to multisampled framebuffer

Rendering to a multisampled framebuffer is straightforward. Whenever we draw anything while the framebuffer object is bound, the rasterizer will take care of all the multisample operations. However, because a multisampled buffer is a bit special, we can't directly use the buffer for other operations like sampling it in a shader.

A multisampled image contains much more information than a normal image so what we need to do is downscale or resolve the image. Resolving a multisampled framebuffer is generally done through `glBlitFramebuffer` that copies a region from one framebuffer to the other while also resolving any multisampled buffers.

`glBlitFramebuffer` transfers a given source region defined by 4 screen-space coordinates to a given target region also defined by 4 screen-space coordinates. You may remember from the *Framebuffers* chapter that if we bind to GL_FRAMEBUFFER we're binding to both the read and draw framebuffer targets. We could also bind to those targets individually by binding framebuffers to GL_READ_FRAMEBUFFER and GL_DRAW_FRAMEBUFFER respectively. The `glBlitFramebuffer` function reads from those two targets to determine which is the source and which is the target framebuffer. We could then transfer the multisampled framebuffer output to the actual screen by blitting the image to the default framebuffer like so:

```
glBindFramebuffer(GL_READ_FRAMEBUFFER, multisampledFBO);
glBindFramebuffer(GL_DRAW_FRAMEBUFFER, 0);
glBlitFramebuffer(0, 0, width, height, 0, 0, width, height,
                  GL_COLOR_BUFFER_BIT, GL_NEAREST);
```

If we then were to render the same application we should get the same output: a lime-green cube displayed with MSAA and again showing significantly less jagged edges:

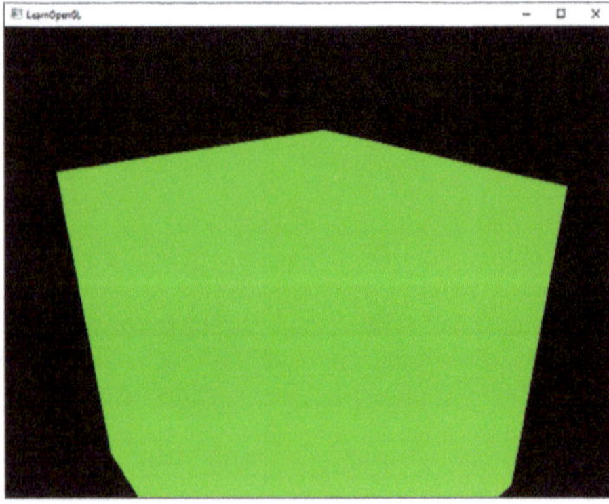

You can find the source code at `/src/4.advanced_opengl/11.2.anti_aliasing_offscreen/`.

But what if we wanted to use the texture result of a multisampled framebuffer to do stuff like post-processing? We can't directly use the multisampled texture(s) in the fragment shader. What we can do however is blit the multisampled buffer(s) to a different FBO with a non-multisampled texture attachment. We then use this ordinary color attachment texture for post-processing, effectively post-processing an image rendered via multisampling. This does mean we have to generate a new FBO that acts solely as an intermediate framebuffer object to resolve the multisampled buffer into; a normal 2D texture we can use in the fragment shader. This process looks a bit like this in pseudocode:

```cpp
unsigned int msFBO = CreateFBOWithMultiSampledAttachments();
// then create another FBO with a normal texture color attachment
[...]
glFramebufferTexture2D(GL_FRAMEBUFFER, GL_COLOR_ATTACHMENT0,
                       GL_TEXTURE_2D, screenTexture, 0);
[...]
while(!glfwWindowShouldClose(window))
{
    [...]

    glBindFramebuffer(msFBO);
    ClearFrameBuffer();
    DrawScene();
    // now resolve multisampled buffer(s) into intermediate FBO
    glBindFramebuffer(GL_READ_FRAMEBUFFER, msFBO);
    glBindFramebuffer(GL_DRAW_FRAMEBUFFER, intermediateFBO);
    glBlitFramebuffer(0, 0, width, height, 0, 0, width, height,
                      GL_COLOR_BUFFER_BIT, GL_NEAREST);
    // now scene is stored in 2D texture, use that for post-processing
    glBindFramebuffer(GL_FRAMEBUFFER, 0);
    ClearFramebuffer();
    glBindTexture(GL_TEXTURE_2D, screenTexture);
    DrawPostProcessingQuad();

    [...]
}
```

If we then implement this into the post-processing code of the *Framebuffers* chapter we're able to create all kinds of cool post-processing effects on a texture of a scene with (almost) no jagged edges. With a grayscale postprocessing filter applied it'll look something like this:

> Because the screen texture is a normal (non-multisampled) texture again, some post-processing filters like *edge-detection* will introduce jagged edges again. To accommodate for this you could blur the texture afterwards or create your own anti-aliasing algorithm.

You can see that when we want to combine multisampling with off-screen rendering we need to take care of some extra steps. The steps are worth the extra effort though since multisampling significantly boosts the visual quality of your scene. Do note that enabling multisampling can noticeably reduce performance the more samples you use.

32.4 Custom Anti-Aliasing algorithm

It is possible to directly pass a multisampled texture image to a fragment shader instead of first resolving it. GLSL gives us the option to sample the texture image per subsample so we can create our own custom anti-aliasing algorithms.

To get a texture value per subsample you'd have to define the texture uniform sampler as a `sampler2DMS` instead of the usual `sampler2D`:

```glsl
uniform sampler2DMS screenTextureMS;
```

Using the `texelFetch` function it is then possible to retrieve the color value per sample:

```glsl
vec4 colorSample = texelFetch(screenTextureMS, TexCoords, 3); // 4th sample
```

We won't go into the details of creating custom anti-aliasing techniques here, but this may be enough to get started on building one yourself.

Advanced Lighting

33. Advanced Lighting

In the *Lighting* chapters we briefly introduced the Phong lighting model to bring a basic amount of realism into our scenes. The Phong model looks nice, but has a few nuances we'll focus on in this chapter.

33.1 Blinn-Phong

Phong lighting is a great and very efficient approximation of lighting, but its specular reflections break down in certain conditions, specifically when the shininess property is low resulting in a large (rough) specular area. The image below shows what happens when we use a specular shininess exponent of `1.0` on a flat textured plane:

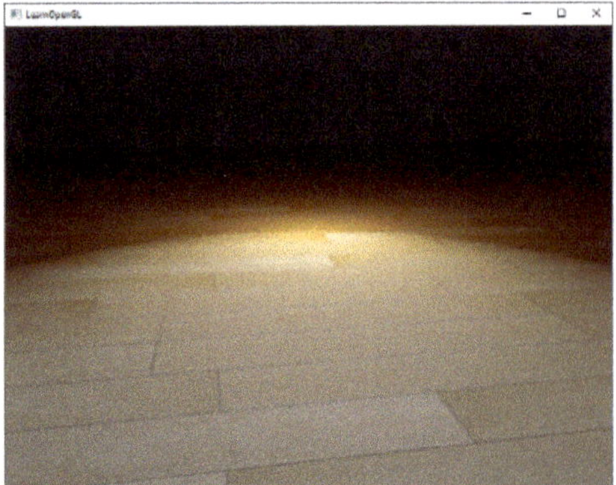

You can see at the edges that the specular area is immediately cut off. The reason this happens is because the angle between the view and reflection vector doesn't go over 90 degrees. If the angle is larger than 90 degrees, the resulting dot product becomes negative and this results in a specular exponent of `0.0`. You're probably thinking this won't be a problem since we shouldn't get any light with angles higher than 90 degrees anyways, right?

Wrong, this only applies to the diffuse component where an angle higher than 90 degrees between the normal and light source means the light source is below the lighted surface and thus the light's diffuse contribution should equal `0.0`. However, with specular lighting we're not measuring the angle between the light source and the normal, but between the view and reflection vector. Take a look at the following two images:

Here the issue should become apparent. The left image shows Phong reflections as familiar, with θ being less than 90 degrees. In the right image we can see that the angle θ between the view and reflection vector is larger than 90 degrees which as a result nullifies the specular contribution. This generally isn't a problem since the view direction is far from the reflection direction, but if we use a low specular exponent the specular radius is large enough to have a contribution under these conditions. Since we're nullifying this contribution at angles larger than 90 degrees we get the artifact as seen in the first image.

In 1977 the Blinn-Phong shading model was introduced by James F. Blinn as an extension to the Phong shading we've used so far. The Blinn-Phong model is largely similar, but approaches the specular model slightly different which as a result overcomes our problem. Instead of relying on a reflection vector we're using a so called halfway vector that is a unit vector exactly halfway between the view direction and the light direction. The closer this halfway vector aligns with the surface's normal vector, the higher the specular contribution.

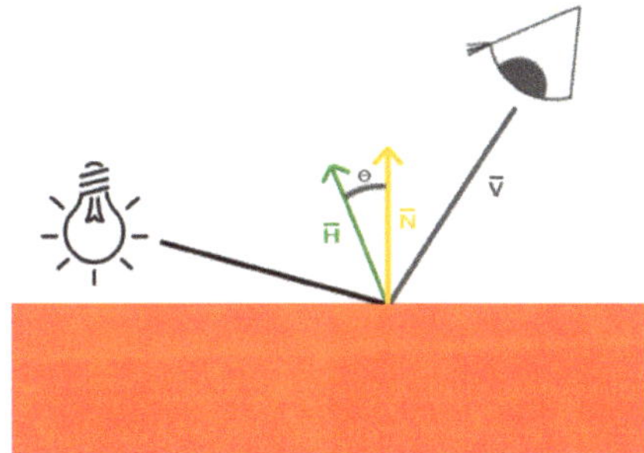

When the view direction is perfectly aligned with the (now imaginary) reflection vector, the halfway vector aligns perfectly with the normal vector. The closer the view direction is to the original reflection direction, the stronger the specular highlight.

Here you can see that whatever direction the viewer looks from, the angle between the halfway vector and the surface normal never exceeds 90 degrees (unless the light is far below the surface of course). The results are slightly different from Phong reflections, but generally more visually plausible, especially with low specular exponents. The Blinn-Phong shading model is also the exact shading model used in the earlier fixed function pipeline of OpenGL.

Getting the halfway vector is easy, we add the light's direction vector and view vector together and normalize the result:

$$\bar{H} = \frac{\bar{L}+\bar{V}}{||\bar{L}+\bar{V}||}$$

This translates to GLSL code as follows:

```glsl
vec3 lightDir   = normalize(lightPos - FragPos);
vec3 viewDir    = normalize(viewPos - FragPos);
vec3 halfwayDir = normalize(lightDir + viewDir);
```

Then the actual calculation of the specular term becomes a clamped dot product between the surface normal and the halfway vector to get the cosine angle between them that we again raise to a specular shininess exponent:

```glsl
float spec = pow(max(dot(normal, halfwayDir), 0.0), shininess);
vec3 specular = lightColor * spec;
```

And there is nothing more to Blinn-Phong than what we just described. The only difference between Blinn-Phong and Phong specular reflection is that we now measure the angle between the normal and halfway vector instead of the angle between the view and reflection vector.

With the introduction of the halfway vector we should no longer have the specular cutoff issue of Phong shading. The image below shows the specular area of both methods with a specular exponent of 0.5:

Another subtle difference between Phong and Blinn-Phong shading is that the angle between the halfway vector and the surface normal is often shorter than the angle between the view and reflection vector. As a result, to get visuals similar to Phong shading the specular shininess exponent has to be set a bit higher. A general rule of thumb is to set it between 2 and 4 times the Phong shininess exponent.

Below is a comparison between both specular reflection models with the Phong exponent set to 8.0 and the Blinn-Phong component set to 32.0:

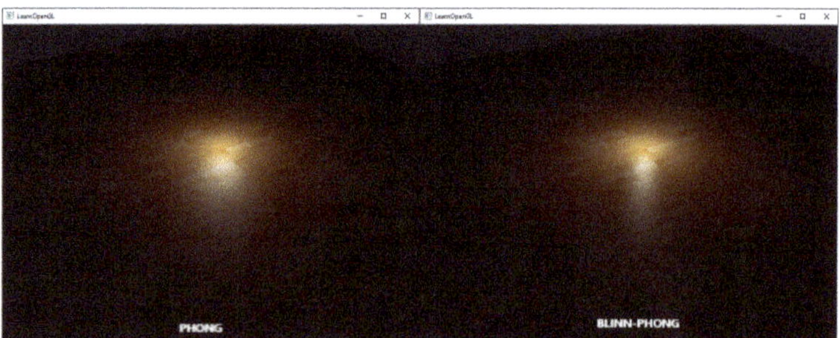

You can see that the Blinn-Phong specular exponent is bit sharper compared to Phong. It usually requires a bit of tweaking to get similar results as to what you previously had with Phong shading. It's worth it though as Blinn-Phong shading is generally more realistic compared to default Phong shading.

Here we used a simple fragment shader that switches between regular Phong reflections and Blinn-Phong reflections:

```glsl
void main()
{
    [...]
    float spec = 0.0;
    if(blinn)
    {
        vec3 halfwayDir = normalize(lightDir + viewDir);
        spec = pow(max(dot(normal, halfwayDir), 0.0), 16.0);
    }
    else
    {
        vec3 reflectDir = reflect(-lightDir, normal);
```

```
            spec = pow(max(dot(viewDir, reflectDir), 0.0), 8.0);
        }
}
```

You can find the source code for the simple demo at `/src/5.advanced_lighting/1.advanced_lighting/`. By pressing the `b` key, the demo switches from Phong to Blinn-Phong lighting and vica versa.

34. Gamma Correction

As soon as we compute the final pixel colors of the scene we will have to display them on a monitor. In the old days of digital imaging most monitors were cathode-ray tube (CRT) monitors. These monitors had the physical property that twice the input voltage did not result in twice the amount of brightness. Doubling the input voltage resulted in a brightness equal to an exponential relationship of roughly 2.2 known as the gamma of a monitor. This happens to (coincidently) also closely match how human beings measure brightness as brightness is also displayed with a similar (inverse) power relationship. To better understand what this all means take a look at the following image:

The top line looks like the correct brightness scale to the human eye, doubling the brightness (from 0.1 to 0.2 for example) does indeed look like it's twice as bright with nice consistent differences. However, when we're talking about the physical brightness of light e.g. amount of photons leaving a light source, the bottom scale actually displays the correct brightness. At the bottom scale, doubling the brightness returns the correct physical brightness, but since our eyes perceive brightness differently (more susceptible to changes in dark colors) it looks weird.

Because the human eyes prefer to see brightness colors according to the top scale, monitors (still today) use a power relationship for displaying output colors so that the original physical brightness colors are mapped to the non-linear brightness colors in the top scale.

This non-linear mapping of monitors does output more pleasing brightness results for our eyes, but when it comes to rendering graphics there is one issue: all the color and brightness options we configure in our applications are based on what we perceive from the monitor and thus all the options are actually non-linear brightness/color options. Take a look at the graph below:

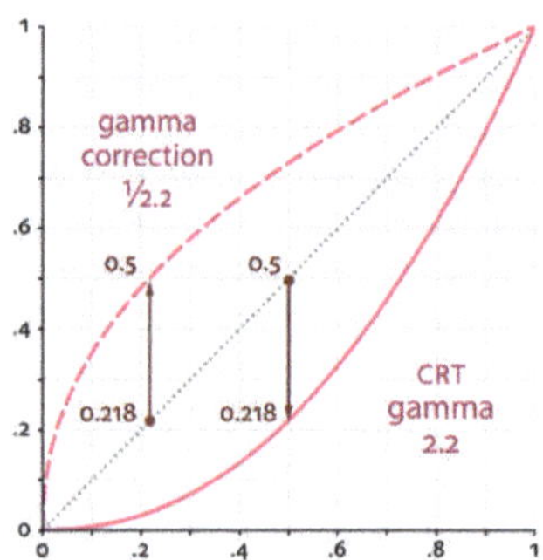

The dotted line represents color/light values in linear space and the solid line represents the color space that monitors display. If we double a color in linear space, its result is indeed double the value. For instance, take a light's color vector $(0.5, 0.0, 0.0)$ which represents a semi-dark red light. If we would double this light in linear space it would become $(1.0, 0.0, 0.0)$ as you can see in the graph. However, the original color gets displayed on the monitor as $(0.218, 0.0, 0.0)$ as you can see from the graph. Here's where the issues start to rise: once we double the dark-red light in linear space, it actually becomes more than 4.5 times as bright on the monitor!

Up until this chapter we have assumed we were working in linear space, but we've actually been working in the monitor's output space so all colors and lighting variables we configured weren't physically correct, but merely looked (sort of) right on our monitor. For this reason, we (and artists) generally set lighting values way brighter than they should be (since the monitor darkens them) which as a result makes most linear-space calculations incorrect. Note that the monitor (CRT) and linear graph both start and end at the same position; it is the intermediate values that are darkened by the display.

Because colors are configured based on the display's output, all intermediate (lighting) calculations in linear-space are physically incorrect. This becomes more obvious as more advanced lighting algorithms are in place, as you can see in the image below:

You can see that with gamma correction, the (updated) color values work more nicely together and darker areas show more details. Overall, a better image quality with a few small modifications.

Without properly correcting this monitor gamma, the lighting looks wrong and artists will have a hard time getting realistic and good-looking results. The solution is to apply gamma correction.

34.1 Gamma correction

The idea of gamma correction is to apply the inverse of the monitor's gamma to the final output color before displaying to the monitor. Looking back at the gamma curve graph earlier this chapter we see another *dashed* line that is the inverse of the monitor's gamma curve. We multiply each of the linear output colors by this inverse gamma curve (making them brighter) and as soon as the colors are displayed on the monitor, the monitor's gamma curve is applied and the resulting colors become linear. We effectively brighten the intermediate colors so that as soon as the monitor darkens them, it balances all out.

Let's give another example. Say we again have the dark-red color $(0.5, 0.0, 0.0)$. Before displaying this color to the monitor we first apply the gamma correction curve to the color value. Linear colors displayed by a monitor are roughly scaled to a power of 2.2 so the inverse requires scaling the colors by a power of $1/2.2$. The gamma-corrected dark-red color thus becomes $(0.5, 0.0, 0.0)^{1/2.2} = (0.5, 0.0, 0.0)^{0.45} = (0.73, 0.0, 0.0)$. The corrected colors are then fed to the monitor and as a result the color is displayed as $(0.73, 0.0, 0.0)^{2.2} = (0.5, 0.0, 0.0)$. You can see that by using gamma-correction, the monitor now finally displays the colors as we linearly set them in the application.

> A gamma value of 2.2 is a default gamma value that roughly estimates the average gamma of most displays. The color space as a result of this gamma of 2.2 is called the sRGB color space (not 100% exact, but close). Each monitor has their own gamma curves, but a gamma value of 2.2 gives good results on most monitors. For this reason, games often allow players to change the game's gamma setting as it varies slightly per monitor.

There are two ways to apply gamma correction to your scene:

- By using OpenGL's built-in sRGB framebuffer support.

- By doing the gamma correction ourselves in the fragment shader(s).

The first option is probably the easiest, but also gives you less control. By enabling `GL_FRAMEBU FFER_SRGB` you tell OpenGL that each subsequent drawing command should first gamma correct colors (from the sRGB color space) before storing them in color buffer(s). The sRGB is a color space that roughly corresponds to a gamma of 2.2 and a standard for most devices. After enabling `GL_FRAMEBUFFER_SRGB`, OpenGL automatically performs gamma correction after each fragment shader run to all subsequent framebuffers, including the default framebuffer.

Enabling `GL_FRAMEBUFFER_SRGB` is as simple as calling `glEnable`:

```
glEnable(GL_FRAMEBUFFER_SRGB);
```

From now on your rendered images will be gamma corrected and as this is done by the hardware it is completely free. Something you should keep in mind with this approach (and the other approach) is that gamma correction (also) transforms the colors from linear space to non-linear space so it is very important you only do gamma correction at the last and final step. If you gamma-correct your colors before the final output, all subsequent operations on those colors will operate on incorrect values. For instance, if you use multiple framebuffers you probably want intermediate results passed in between framebuffers to remain in linear-space and only have the last framebuffer apply gamma correction before being sent to the monitor.

The second approach requires a bit more work, but also gives us complete control over the gamma operations. We apply gamma correction at the end of each relevant fragment shader run so the final colors end up gamma corrected before being sent out to the monitor:

```
void main()
{
    // do super fancy lighting in linear space
    [...]
    // apply gamma correction
    float gamma = 2.2;
    FragColor.rgb = pow(fragColor.rgb, vec3(1.0/gamma));
}
```

The last line of code effectively raises each individual color component of `fragColor` to `1.0/gamma`, correcting the output color of this fragment shader run.

An issue with this approach is that in order to be consistent you have to apply gamma correction to each fragment shader that contributes to the final output. If you have a dozen fragment shaders for multiple objects, you have to add the gamma correction code to each of these shaders. An easier solution would be to introduce a post-processing stage in your render loop and apply gamma correction on the post-processed quad as a final step which you'd only have to do once.

That one line represents the technical implementation of gamma correction. Not all too impressive, but there are a few extra things you have to consider when doing gamma correction.

34.2 sRGB textures

Because monitors display colors with gamma applied, whenever you draw, edit, or paint a picture on your computer you are picking colors based on what you see on the monitor. This effectively means all the pictures you create or edit are not in linear space, but in sRGB space e.g. doubling a dark-red color on your screen based on perceived brightness, does not equal double the red component.

As a result, when texture artists create art by eye, all the textures' values are in sRGB space so if we use those textures as they are in our rendering application we have to take this into account. Before we knew about gamma correction this wasn't really an issue, because the textures looked good in sRGB space which is the same space we worked in; the textures were displayed exactly as they are which was fine. However, now that we're displaying everything in linear space, the texture colors will be off as the following image shows:

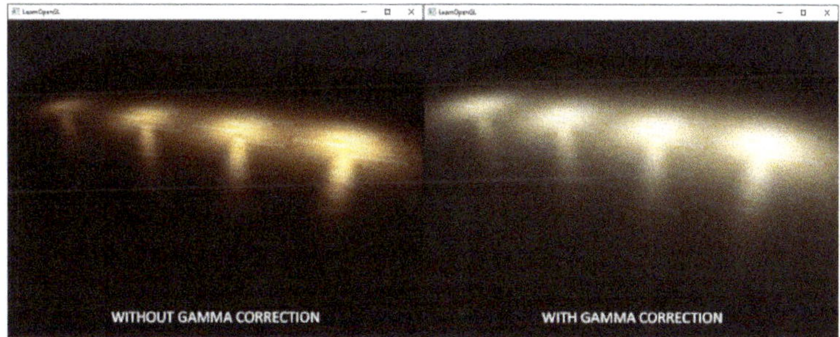

The texture image is way too bright and this happens because it is actually gamma corrected twice! Think about it, when we create an image based on what we see on the monitor, we effectively gamma correct the color values of an image so that it looks right on the monitor. Because we then again gamma correct in the renderer, the image ends up way too bright.

To fix this issue we have to make sure texture artists work in linear space. However, since it's easier to work in sRGB space and most tools don't even properly support linear texturing, this is probably not the preferred solution.

The other solution is to re-correct or transform these sRGB textures to linear space before doing any calculations on their color values. We can do this as follows:

```
float gamma = 2.2;
vec3 diffuseColor = pow(texture(diffuse, texCoords).rgb, vec3(gamma));
```

To do this for each texture in sRGB space is quite troublesome though. Luckily OpenGL gives us yet another solution to our problems by giving us the GL_SRGB and GL_SRGB_ALPHA internal texture formats.

If we create a texture in OpenGL with any of these two sRGB texture formats, OpenGL will automatically correct the colors to linear-space as soon as we use them, allowing us to properly work in linear space. We can specify a texture as an sRGB texture as follows:

```
glTexImage2D(GL_TEXTURE_2D, 0, GL_SRGB, width, height, 0, GL_RGB,
             GL_UNSIGNED_BYTE, image);
```

If you also want to include alpha components in your texture you'll have to specify the texture's internal format as GL_SRGB_ALPHA.

You should be careful when specifying your textures in sRGB space as not all textures will actually be in sRGB space. Textures used for coloring objects (like diffuse textures) are almost always in sRGB space. Textures used for retrieving lighting parameters (like specular maps and normal maps) are almost always in linear space, so if you were to configure these as sRGB textures the lighting will look odd. Be careful in which textures you specify as sRGB.

With our diffuse textures specified as sRGB textures you get the visual output you'd expect again, but this time everything is gamma corrected only once.

34.3 Attenuation

Something else that's different with gamma correction is lighting attenuation. In the real physical world, lighting attenuates closely inversely proportional to the squared distance from a light source. In normal English it simply means that the light strength is reduced over the distance to the light source squared, like below:

```
float attenuation = 1.0 / (distance * distance);
```

However, when using this equation the attenuation effect is usually way too strong, giving lights a small radius that doesn't look physically right. For that reason other attenuation functions were used (like we discussed in the *Basic Lighting* chapter) that give much more control, or the linear equivalent is used:

```
float attenuation = 1.0 / distance;
```

The linear equivalent gives more plausible results compared to its quadratic variant without gamma correction, but when we enable gamma correction the linear attenuation looks too weak and the physically correct quadratic attenuation suddenly gives the better results. The image below shows the differences:

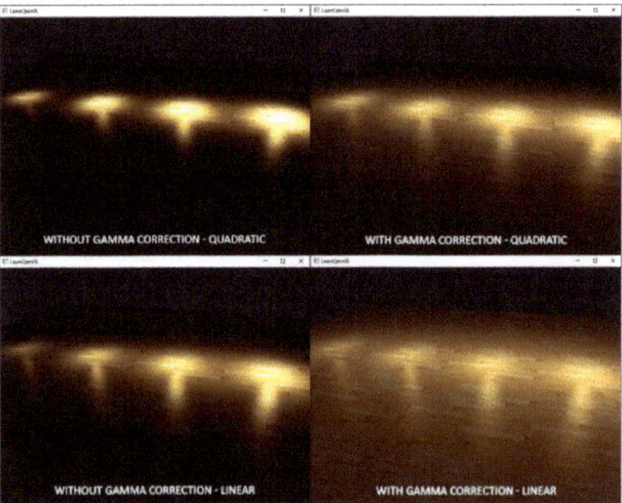

The cause of this difference is that light attenuation functions change brightness, and as we weren't visualizing our scene in linear space we chose the attenuation functions that looked best on our monitor, but weren't physically correct. Think of the squared attenuation function: if we were to use this function without gamma correction, the attenuation function effectively becomes: $(1.0/distance^2)^{2.2}$ when displayed on a monitor. This creates a much larger attenuation from what we originally anticipated. This also explains why the linear equivalent makes much more sense without gamma correction as this effectively becomes $(1.0/distance)^{2.2} = 1.0/distance^{2.2}$ which resembles its physical equivalent a lot more.

> The more advanced attenuation function we discussed in the *Basic Lighting* chapter still has its place in gamma corrected scenes as it gives more control over the exact attenuation (but of course requires different parameters in a gamma corrected scene).

You can find the source code of this simple demo scene at `/src/5.advanced_lighting/ 2.gamma_correction/`. By pressing the spacebar we switch between a gamma corrected and un-corrected scene with both scenes using their texture and attenuation equivalents. It's not the most impressive demo, but it does show how to actually apply all techniques.

To summarize, gamma correction allows us to do all our shader/lighting calculations in linear space. Because linear space makes sense in the physical world, most physical equations now actually give good results (like real light attenuation). The more advanced your lighting becomes, the easier it is to get good looking (and realistic) results with gamma correction. That is also why it's advised to only really tweak your lighting parameters as soon as you have gamma correction in place.

34.4 Additional resources

- `blog.johnnovak.net/2016/09/21/what-every-coder-should-know-abo ut-gamma/`: a well written in-depth article by John Novak about gamma correction.
- `www.cambridgeincolour.com/tutorials/gamma-correction.htm`: more about gamma and gamma correction.
- `blog.wolfire.com/2010/02/Gamma-correct-lighting`: blog post by David Rosen about the benefit of gamma correction in graphics rendering.
- `renderwonk.com/blog/index.php/archive/adventures-with-gamma-c orrect-rendering/`: some extra practical considerations.

35. Shadow Mapping

Shadows are a result of the absence of light due to occlusion. When a light source's light rays do not hit an object because it gets occluded by some other object, the object is in shadow. Shadows add a great deal of realism to a lit scene and make it easier for a viewer to observe spatial relationships between objects. They give a greater sense of depth to our scene and objects. For example, take a look at the following image of a scene with and without shadows:

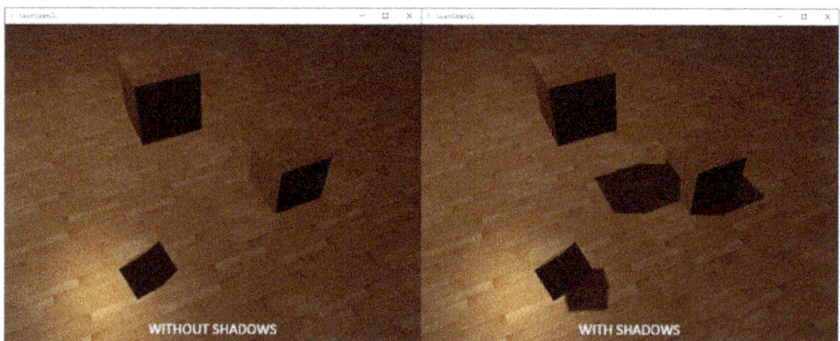

You can see that with shadows it becomes much more obvious how the objects relate to each other. For instance, the fact that one of the cubes is floating above the others is only really noticeable when we have shadows.

Shadows are a bit tricky to implement though, specifically because in current real-time (rasterized graphics) research a perfect shadow algorithm hasn't been developed yet. There are several good shadow approximation techniques, but they all have their little quirks and annoyances which we have to take into account.

One technique used by most videogames that gives decent results and is relatively easy to implement is shadow mapping. Shadow mapping is not too difficult to understand, doesn't cost too much in performance and quite easily extends into more advanced algorithms (like omnidirectional shadow maps and cascaded shadow maps).

35.1 Shadow mapping

The idea behind shadow mapping is quite simple: we render the scene from the light's point of view and everything we see from the light's perspective is lit and everything we can't see must be in shadow. Imagine a floor section with a large box between itself and a light source. Since the light source will see this box and not the floor section when looking in its direction that specific floor section should be in shadow.

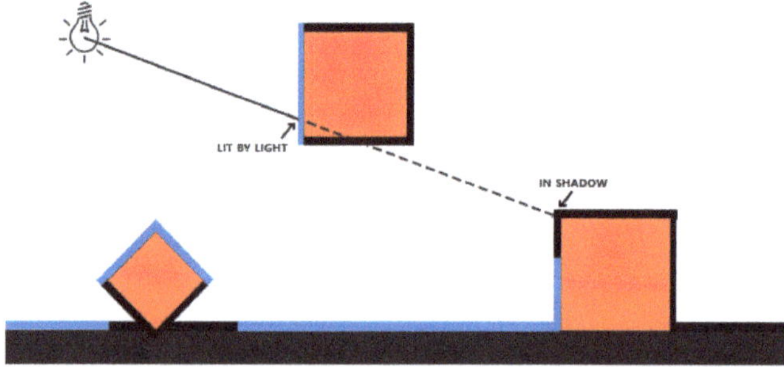

Here all the blue lines represent the fragments that the light source can see. The occluded fragments are shown as black lines: these are rendered as being shadowed. If we were to draw a line or ray from the light source to a fragment on the right-most box we can see the ray first hits the floating container before hitting the right-most container. As a result, the floating container's fragment is lit and the right-most container's fragment is not lit and thus in shadow.

We want to get the point on the ray where it first hit an object and compare this *closest point* to other points on this ray. We then do a basic test to see if a test point's ray position is further down the ray than the closest point and if so, the test point must be in shadow. Iterating through possibly thousands of light rays from such a light source is an extremely inefficient approach and doesn't lend itself too well for real-time rendering. We can do something similar, but without casting light rays. Instead, we use something we're quite familiar with: the depth buffer.

You may remember from the *Depth Testing* chapter that a value in the depth buffer corresponds to the depth of a fragment clamped to [0,1] from the camera's point of view. What if we were to render the scene from the light's perspective and store the resulting depth values in a texture? This way, we can sample the closest depth values as seen from the light's perspective. After all, the depth values show the first fragment visible from the light's perspective. We store all these depth values in a texture that we call a depth map or shadow map.

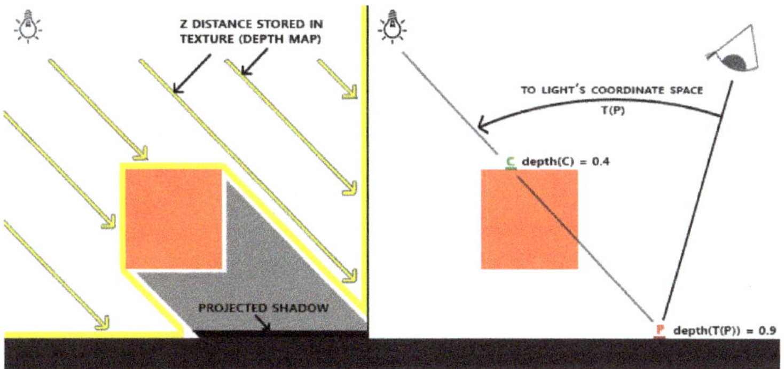

The left image shows a directional light source (all light rays are parallel) casting a shadow on the surface below the cube. Using the depth values stored in the depth map we find the closest point and use that to determine whether fragments are in shadow. We create the depth map by rendering the scene (from the light's perspective) using a view and projection matrix specific to that light source. This projection and view matrix together form a transformation T that transforms any 3D position to the light's (visible) coordinate space.

> A directional light doesn't have a position as it's modelled to be infinitely far away. However, for the sake of shadow mapping we need to render the scene from a light's perspective and thus render the scene from a position somewhere along the lines of the light direction.

In the right image we see the same directional light and the viewer. We render a fragment at point $\bar{P}$ for which we have to determine whether it is in shadow. To do this, we first transform point $\bar{P}$ to the light's coordinate space using T. Since point $\bar{P}$ is now as seen from the light's perspective, its z coordinate corresponds to its depth which in this example is 0.9. Using point $\bar{P}$ we can also index the depth/shadow map to obtain the closest visible depth from the light's perspective, which is at point $\bar{C}$ with a sampled depth of 0.4. Since indexing the depth map returns a depth smaller than the depth at point $\bar{P}$ we can conclude point $\bar{P}$ is occluded and thus in shadow.

Shadow mapping therefore consists of two passes: first we render the depth map, and in the second pass we render the scene as normal and use the generated depth map to calculate whether fragments are in shadow. It may sound a bit complicated, but as soon as we walk through the technique step-by-step it'll likely start to make sense.

35.2 The depth map

The first pass requires us to generate a depth map. The depth map is the depth texture as rendered from the light's perspective that we'll be using for testing for shadows. Because we need to store the rendered result of a scene into a texture we're going to need framebuffers again.

First we'll create a framebuffer object for rendering the depth map:

```
unsigned int depthMapFBO;
glGenFramebuffers(1, &depthMapFBO);
```

Next we create a 2D texture that we'll use as the framebuffer's depth buffer:

```
const unsigned int SHADOW_WIDTH = 1024, SHADOW_HEIGHT = 1024;

unsigned int depthMap;
glGenTextures(1, &depthMap);
glBindTexture(GL_TEXTURE_2D, depthMap);
glTexImage2D(GL_TEXTURE_2D, 0, GL_DEPTH_COMPONENT, SHADOW_WIDTH,
             SHADOW_HEIGHT, 0, GL_DEPTH_COMPONENT, GL_FLOAT, NULL);
glTexParameteri(GL_TEXTURE_2D, GL_TEXTURE_MIN_FILTER, GL_NEAREST);
glTexParameteri(GL_TEXTURE_2D, GL_TEXTURE_MAG_FILTER, GL_NEAREST);
glTexParameteri(GL_TEXTURE_2D, GL_TEXTURE_WRAP_S, GL_REPEAT);
glTexParameteri(GL_TEXTURE_2D, GL_TEXTURE_WRAP_T, GL_REPEAT);
```

Generating the depth map shouldn't look too complicated. Because we only care about depth values we specify the texture's formats as `GL_DEPTH_COMPONENT`. We also give the texture a width and height of `1024`: this is the resolution of the depth map.

With the generated depth texture we can attach it as the framebuffer's depth buffer:

```
glBindFramebuffer(GL_FRAMEBUFFER, depthMapFBO);
glFramebufferTexture2D(GL_FRAMEBUFFER, GL_DEPTH_ATTACHMENT, GL_TEXTURE_2D,
                       depthMap, 0);
glDrawBuffer(GL_NONE);
glReadBuffer(GL_NONE);
glBindFramebuffer(GL_FRAMEBUFFER, 0);
```

We only need the depth information when rendering the scene from the light's perspective so there is no need for a color buffer. A framebuffer object however is not complete without a color buffer so we need to explicitly tell OpenGL we're not going to render any color data. We do this by setting both the read and draw buffer to `GL_NONE` with `glDrawBuffer` and `glReadbuffer`.

With a properly configured framebuffer that renders depth values to a texture we can start the first pass: generate the depth map. When combined with the second pass, the complete rendering stage will look a bit like this:

```
// 1. first render to depth map
glViewport(0, 0, SHADOW_WIDTH, SHADOW_HEIGHT);
glBindFramebuffer(GL_FRAMEBUFFER, depthMapFBO);
    glClear(GL_DEPTH_BUFFER_BIT);
    ConfigureShaderAndMatrices();
```

```
    RenderScene();
glBindFramebuffer(GL_FRAMEBUFFER, 0);
// 2. then render scene as normal with shadow mapping (using depth map)
glViewport(0, 0, SCR_WIDTH, SCR_HEIGHT);
glClear(GL_COLOR_BUFFER_BIT | GL_DEPTH_BUFFER_BIT);
ConfigureShaderAndMatrices();
glBindTexture(GL_TEXTURE_2D, depthMap);
RenderScene();
```

This code left out some details, but it'll give you the general idea of shadow mapping. What is important to note here are the calls to `glViewport`. Because shadow maps often have a different resolution compared to what we originally render the scene in (usually the window resolution), we need to change the viewport parameters to accommodate for the size of the shadow map. If we forget to update the viewport parameters, the resulting depth map will be either incomplete or too small.

35.2.1 Light space transform

An unknown in the previous snippet of code is the `ConfigureShaderAndMatrices` function. In the second pass this is business as usual: make sure proper projection and view matrices are set, and set the relevant model matrices per object. However, in the first pass we need to use a different projection and view matrix to render the scene from the light's point of view.

Because we're modelling a directional light source, all its light rays are parallel. For this reason, we're going to use an orthographic projection matrix for the light source where there is no perspective deform:

```
float near_plane = 1.0f, far_plane = 7.5f;
glm::mat4 lightProjection = glm::ortho(-10.0f, 10.0f, -10.0f, 10.0f,
                                       near_plane, far_plane);
```

Here is an example orthographic projection matrix as used in this chapter's demo scene. Because a projection matrix indirectly determines the range of what is visible (e.g. what is not clipped) you want to make sure the size of the projection frustum correctly contains the objects you want to be in the depth map. When objects or fragments are not in the depth map they will not produce shadows.

To create a view matrix to transform each object so they're visible from the light's point of view, we're going to use the infamous `glm::lookAt` function; this time with the light source's position looking at the scene's center.

```
glm::mat4 lightView = glm::lookAt(glm::vec3(-2.0f, 4.0f, -1.0f),
                                  glm::vec3( 0.0f, 0.0f,  0.0f),
                                  glm::vec3( 0.0f, 1.0f,  0.0f));
```

Combining these two gives us a light space transformation matrix that transforms each world-space vector into the space as visible from the light source; exactly what we need to render the depth map.

```
glm::mat4 lightSpaceMatrix = lightProjection * lightView;
```

This `lightSpaceMatrix` is the transformation matrix that we earlier denoted as T. With this `lightSpaceMatrix`, we can render the scene as usual as long as we give each shader the light-space equivalents of the projection and view matrices. However, we only care about depth values and not all the expensive fragment (lighting) calculations. To save performance we're going to use a different, but much simpler shader for rendering to the depth map.

35.2.2 Render to depth map

When we render the scene from the light's perspective we'd much rather use a simple shader that only transforms the vertices to light space and not much more. For such a simple shader called `simpleDepthShader` we'll use the following vertex shader:

```glsl
#version 330 core
layout (location = 0) in vec3 aPos;

uniform mat4 lightSpaceMatrix;
uniform mat4 model;

void main()
{
    gl_Position = lightSpaceMatrix * model * vec4(aPos, 1.0);
}
```

This vertex shader takes a per-object model, a vertex, and transforms all vertices to light space using `lightSpaceMatrix`.

Since we have no color buffer and disabled the draw and read buffers, the resulting fragments do not require any processing so we can simply use an empty fragment shader:

```glsl
#version 330 core

void main()
{
    // gl_FragDepth = gl_FragCoord.z;
}
```

This empty fragment shader does no processing whatsoever, and at the end of its run the depth buffer is updated. We could explicitly set the depth by uncommenting its one line, but this is effectively what happens behind the scene anyways.

Rendering the depth/shadow map now effectively becomes:

```cpp
simpleDepthShader.use();
glUniformMatrix4fv(lightSpaceMatrixLocation, 1, GL_FALSE,
                   glm::value_ptr(lightSpaceMatrix));

glViewport(0, 0, SHADOW_WIDTH, SHADOW_HEIGHT);
glBindFramebuffer(GL_FRAMEBUFFER, depthMapFBO);
    glClear(GL_DEPTH_BUFFER_BIT);
    RenderScene(simpleDepthShader);
glBindFramebuffer(GL_FRAMEBUFFER, 0);
```

Here the `RenderScene` function takes a shader program, calls all relevant drawing functions and sets the corresponding model matrices where necessary.

The result is a nicely filled depth buffer holding the closest depth of each visible fragment from the light's perspective. By rendering this texture onto a 2D quad that fills the screen (similar to what we did in the post-processing section at the end of the *Framebuffers* chapter) we get something like this:

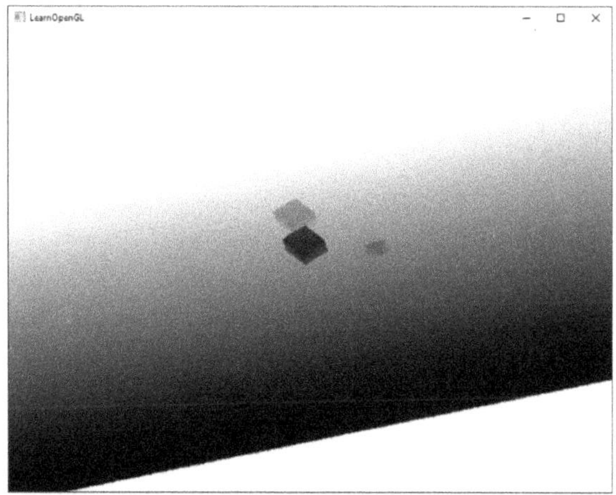

For rendering the depth map onto a quad we used the following fragment shader:

```glsl
#version 330 core
out vec4 FragColor;

in vec2 TexCoords;

uniform sampler2D depthMap;

void main()
{
    float depthValue = texture(depthMap, TexCoords).r;
    FragColor = vec4(vec3(depthValue), 1.0);
}
```

Note that there are some subtle changes when displaying depth using a perspective projection matrix instead of an orthographic projection matrix as depth is non-linear when using perspective projection. At the end of this chapter we'll discuss some of these subtle differences.

You can find the source code for rendering a scene to a depth map at `/src/5.advanced_lighting/3.1.1.shadow_mapping_depth/`.

35.3 Rendering shadows

With a properly generated depth map we can start rendering the actual shadows. The code to check if a fragment is in shadow is (quite obviously) executed in the fragment shader, but we do the light-space transformation in the vertex shader:

```glsl
#version 330 core
layout (location = 0) in vec3 aPos;
layout (location = 1) in vec3 aNormal;
layout (location = 2) in vec2 aTexCoords;

out VS_OUT {
    vec3 FragPos;
    vec3 Normal;
    vec2 TexCoords;
    vec4 FragPosLightSpace;
} vs_out;
```

```glsl
uniform mat4 projection;
uniform mat4 view;
uniform mat4 model;
uniform mat4 lightSpaceMatrix;

void main()
{
    vs_out.FragPos = vec3(model * vec4(aPos, 1.0));
    vs_out.Normal = transpose(inverse(mat3(model))) * aNormal;
    vs_out.TexCoords = aTexCoords;
    vs_out.FragPosLightSpace = lightSpaceMatrix * vec4(vs_out.FragPos, 1.0);
    gl_Position = projection * view * vec4(vs_out.FragPos, 1.0);
}
```

What is new here is the extra output vector `FragPosLightSpace`. We take the same
`lightSpaceMatrix` (used to transform vertices to light space in the depth map stage) and
transform the world-space vertex position to light space for use in the fragment shader.

The main fragment shader we'll use to render the scene uses the Blinn-Phong lighting model.
Within the fragment shader we then calculate a `shadow` value that is either `1.0` when the fragment
is in shadow or `0.0` when not in shadow. The resulting `diffuse` and `specular` components are
then multiplied by this shadow component. Because shadows are rarely completely dark (due to
light scattering) we leave the `ambient` component out of the shadow multiplications.

```glsl
#version 330 core
out vec4 FragColor;

in VS_OUT {
    vec3 FragPos;
    vec3 Normal;
    vec2 TexCoords;
    vec4 FragPosLightSpace;
} fs_in;

uniform sampler2D diffuseTexture;
uniform sampler2D shadowMap;

uniform vec3 lightPos;
uniform vec3 viewPos;

float ShadowCalculation(vec4 fragPosLightSpace)
{
    [...]
}

void main()
{
    vec3 color = texture(diffuseTexture, fs_in.TexCoords).rgb;
    vec3 normal = normalize(fs_in.Normal);
    vec3 lightColor = vec3(1.0);
    // ambient
    vec3 ambient = 0.15 * color;
    // diffuse
    vec3 lightDir = normalize(lightPos - fs_in.FragPos);
    float diff = max(dot(lightDir, normal), 0.0);
    vec3 diffuse = diff * lightColor;
    // specular
    vec3 viewDir = normalize(viewPos - fs_in.FragPos);
    float spec = 0.0;
    vec3 halfwayDir = normalize(lightDir + viewDir);
```

```glsl
    spec = pow(max(dot(normal, halfwayDir), 0.0), 64.0);
    vec3 specular = spec * lightColor;
    // calculate shadow
    float shadow = ShadowCalculation(fs_in.FragPosLightSpace);
    vec3 lighting = (ambient + (1.0 - shadow) * (diffuse + specular)) *
                    color;

    FragColor = vec4(lighting, 1.0);
}
```

The fragment shader is largely a copy from what we used in the Advanced Lighting chapter, but with an added shadow calculation. We declared a function `ShadowCalculation` that does most of the shadow work. At the end of the fragment shader, we multiply the diffuse and specular contributions by the inverse of the `shadow` component e.g. how much the fragment is *not* in shadow. This fragment shader takes as extra input the light-space fragment position and the depth map generated from the first render pass.

The first thing to do to check whether a fragment is in shadow, is transform the light-space fragment position in clip-space to normalized device coordinates. When we output a clip-space vertex position to `gl_Position` in the vertex shader, OpenGL automatically does a perspective divide e.g. transform clip-space coordinates in the range $[-w,w]$ to $[-1,1]$ by dividing the x, y and z component by the vector's w component. As the clip-space `FragPosLightSpace` is not passed to the fragment shader through `gl_Position`, we have to do this perspective divide ourselves:

```glsl
float ShadowCalculation(vec4 fragPosLightSpace)
{
    // perform perspective divide
    vec3 projCoords = fragPosLightSpace.xyz / fragPosLightSpace.w;
    [...]
}
```

This returns the fragment's light-space position in the range $[-1,1]$.

When using an orthographic projection matrix the w component of a vertex remains untouched so this step is actually quite meaningless. However, it is necessary when using perspective projection so keeping this line ensures it works with both projection matrices.

Because the depth from the depth map is in the range $[0,1]$ and we also want to use `projCoords` to sample from the depth map, we transform the NDC coordinates to the range $[0,1]$:

```glsl
projCoords = projCoords * 0.5 + 0.5;
```

With these projected coordinates we can sample the depth map as the resulting $[0,1]$ coordinates from `projCoords` directly correspond to the transformed NDC coordinates from the first render pass. This gives us the closest depth from the light's point of view:

```glsl
float closestDepth = texture(shadowMap, projCoords.xy).r;
```

To get the current depth at this fragment we simply retrieve the projected vector's z coordinate which equals the depth of this fragment from the light's perspective.

```glsl
float currentDepth = projCoords.z;
```

The actual comparison is then simply a check whether `currentDepth` is higher than `closestDepth` and if so, the fragment is in shadow:

```glsl
float shadow = currentDepth > closestDepth ? 1.0 : 0.0;
```

The complete `ShadowCalculation` function then becomes:

```glsl
float ShadowCalculation(vec4 fragPosLightSpace)
{
    // perform perspective divide
    vec3 projCoords = fragPosLightSpace.xyz / fragPosLightSpace.w;
    // transform to [0,1] range
    projCoords = projCoords * 0.5 + 0.5;
    // get closest depth value from light's perspective (using
    // [0,1] range fragPosLight as coords)
    float closestDepth = texture(shadowMap, projCoords.xy).r;
    // get depth of current fragment from light's perspective
    float currentDepth = projCoords.z;
    // check whether current frag pos is in shadow
    float shadow = currentDepth > closestDepth ? 1.0 : 0.0;

    return shadow;
}
```

Activating this shader, binding the proper textures, and activating the default projection and view matrices in the second render pass should give you a result similar to the image below:

If you did things right you should indeed see (albeit with quite a few artifacts) shadows on the floor and the cubes. You can find the source code of the demo application at `/src/5.advanced_lighting/3.1.2.shadow_mapping_base/`.

35.4 Improving shadow maps

We managed to get the basics of shadow mapping working, but as you can we're not there yet due to several (clearly visible) artifacts related to shadow mapping we need to fix. We'll focus on fixing these artifacts in the next sections.

35.4.1 Shadow acne

It is obvious something is wrong from the previous image. A closer zoom shows us a very obvious Moiré-like pattern:

We can see a large part of the floor quad rendered with obvious black lines in an alternating fashion. This shadow mapping artifact is called shadow acne and can be explained by the following image:

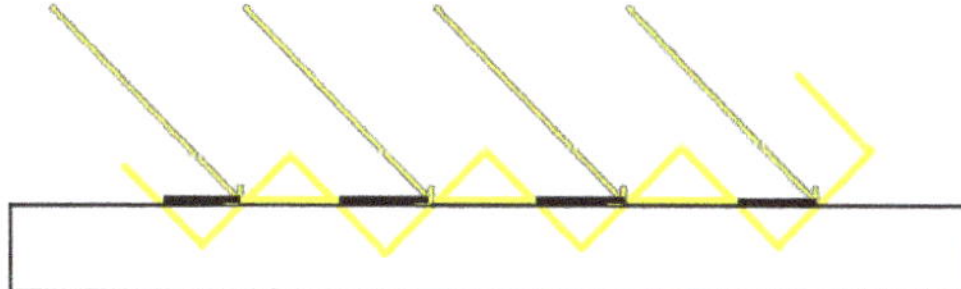

Because the shadow map is limited by resolution, multiple fragments can sample the same value from the depth map when they're relatively far away from the light source. The image shows the floor where each yellow tilted panel represents a single texel of the depth map. As you can see, several fragments sample the same depth sample.

While this is generally okay, it becomes an issue when the light source looks at an angle towards the surface as in that case the depth map is also rendered from an angle. Several fragments then access the same tilted depth texel while some are above and some below the floor; we get a shadow discrepancy. Because of this, some fragments are considered to be in shadow and some are not, giving the striped pattern from the image.

We can solve this issue with a small little hack called a shadow bias where we simply offset the depth of the surface (or the shadow map) by a small bias amount such that the fragments are not incorrectly considered below the surface.

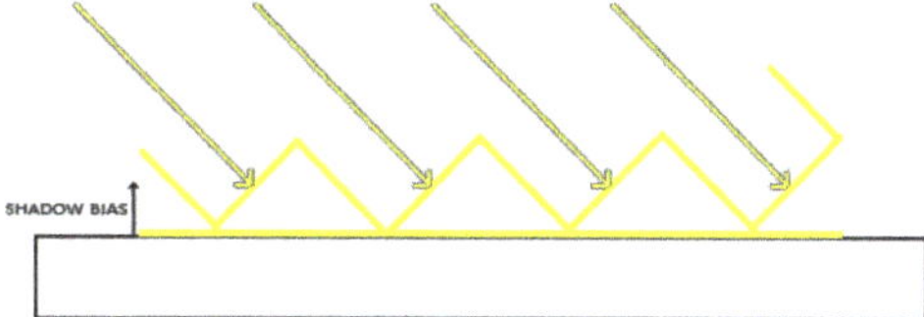

With the bias applied, all the samples get a depth smaller than the surface's depth and thus the entire surface is correctly lit without any shadows. We can implement such a bias as follows:

```
float bias = 0.005;
float shadow = currentDepth - bias > closestDepth ? 1.0 : 0.0;
```

A shadow bias of 0.005 solves the issues of our scene by a large extent, but you can imagine the bias value is highly dependent on the angle between the light source and the surface. If the surface would have a steep angle to the light source, the shadows may still display shadow acne. A more solid approach would be to change the amount of bias based on the surface angle towards the light: something we can solve with the dot product:

```
float bias = max(0.05 * (1.0 - dot(normal, lightDir)), 0.005);
```

Here we have a maximum bias of 0.05 and a minimum of 0.005 based on the surface's normal and light direction. This way, surfaces like the floor that are almost perpendicular to the light source get a small bias, while surfaces like the cube's side-faces get a much larger bias. The following image shows the same scene but now with a shadow bias:

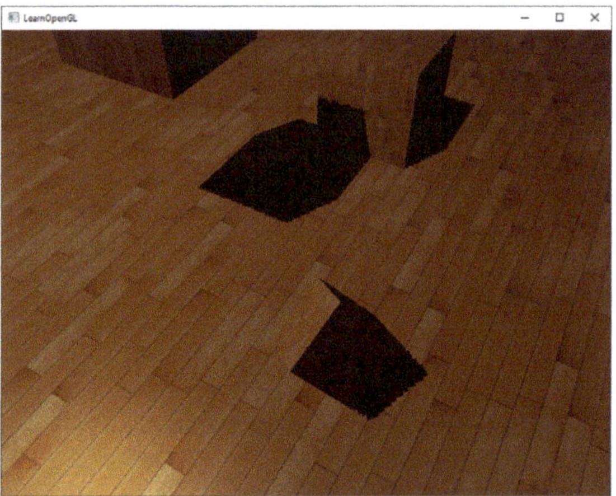

Choosing the correct bias value(s) requires some tweaking as this will be different for each scene, but most of the time it's simply a matter of slowly incrementing the bias until all acne is removed.

35.4.2 Peter panning

A disadvantage of using a shadow bias is that you're applying an offset to the actual depth of objects. As a result, the bias may become large enough to see a visible offset of shadows compared to the actual object locations as you can see below (with an exaggerated bias value):

This shadow artifact is called peter panning since objects seem slightly *detached* from their shadows. We can use a little trick to solve most of the peter panning issue by using front face culling when rendering the depth map. You may remember from the *Face Culling* chapter that OpenGL by default culls back-faces. By telling OpenGL we want to cull front faces during the shadow map stage we're switching that order around.

Because we only need depth values for the depth map it shouldn't matter for solid objects whether we take the depth of their front faces or their back faces. Using their back face depths doesn't give wrong results as it doesn't matter if we have shadows inside objects; we can't see there anyways.

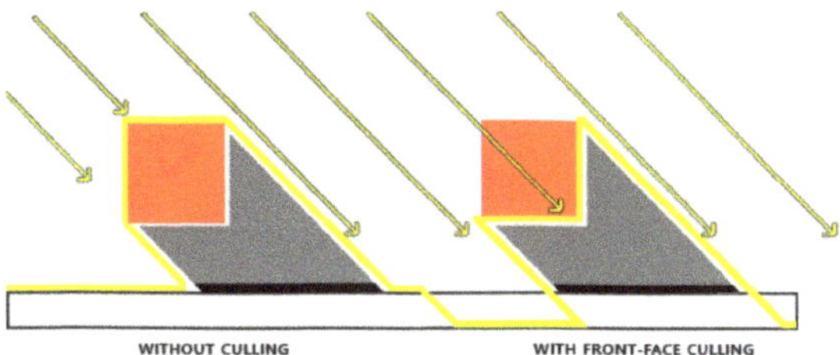

To fix peter panning we cull all front faces during the shadow map generation. Note that you need to enable GL_CULL_FACE first.

```
glCullFace(GL_FRONT);
RenderSceneToDepthMap();
glCullFace(GL_BACK); // don't forget to reset original culling face
```

This effectively solves the peter panning issues, but **only for solid** objects that actually have an inside without openings. In our scene for example, this works perfectly fine on the cubes. However, on the floor it won't work as well as culling the front face completely removes the floor from the equation. The floor is a single plane and would thus be completely culled. If one wants to solve peter panning with this trick, care has to be taken to only cull the front faces of objects where it makes sense.

Another consideration is that objects that are close to the shadow receiver (like the distant cube) may still give incorrect results. However, with normal bias values you can generally avoid peter panning.

35.4.3 Over sampling

Another visual discrepancy which you may like or dislike is that regions outside the light's visible frustum are considered to be in shadow while they're (usually) not. This happens because projected coordinates outside the light's frustum are higher than 1.0 and will thus sample the depth texture outside its default range of [0,1]. Based on the texture's wrapping method, we will get incorrect depth results not based on the real depth values from the light source.

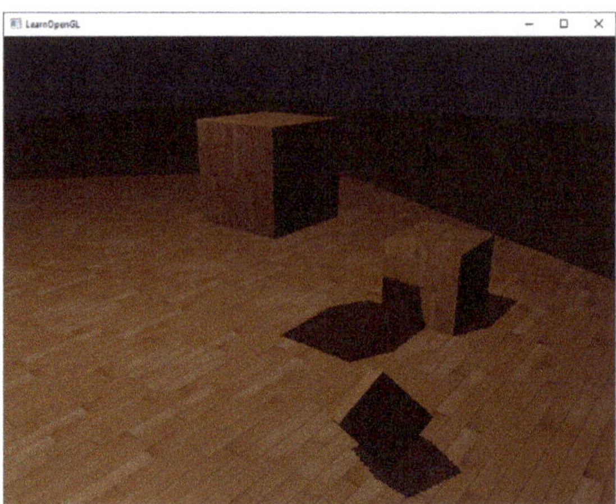

You can see in the image that there is some sort of imaginary region of light, and a large part outside this area is in shadow; this area represents the size of the depth map projected onto the floor. The reason this happens is that we earlier set the depth map's wrapping options to `GL_REPEAT`.

What we'd rather have is that all coordinates outside the depth map's range have a depth of `1.0` which as a result means these coordinates will never be in shadow (as no object will have a depth larger than `1.0`). We can do this by configuring a texture border color and set the depth map's texture wrap options to `GL_CLAMP_TO_BORDER`:

```cpp
glTexParameteri(GL_TEXTURE_2D, GL_TEXTURE_WRAP_S, GL_CLAMP_TO_BORDER);
glTexParameteri(GL_TEXTURE_2D, GL_TEXTURE_WRAP_T, GL_CLAMP_TO_BORDER);
float borderColor[] = { 1.0f, 1.0f, 1.0f, 1.0f };
glTexParameterfv(GL_TEXTURE_2D, GL_TEXTURE_BORDER_COLOR, borderColor);
```

Now whenever we sample outside the depth map's [0,1] coordinate range, the `texture` function will always return a depth of `1.0`, producing a `shadow` value of `0.0`. The result now looks more plausible:

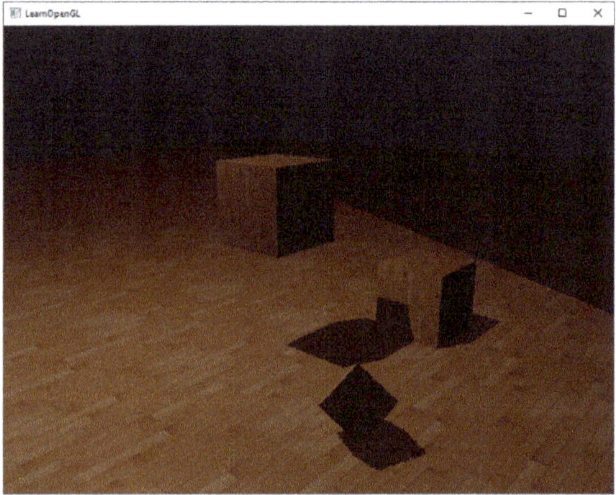

There seems to still be one part showing a dark region. Those are the coordinates outside the far plane of the light's orthographic frustum. You can see that this dark region always occurs at the far end of the light source's frustum by looking at the shadow directions.

A light-space projected fragment coordinate is further than the light's far plane when its z coordinate is larger than `1.0`. In that case the `GL_CLAMP_TO_BORDER` wrapping method doesn't work anymore as we compare the coordinate's z component with the depth map values; this always returns true for z larger than `1.0`.

The fix for this is also relatively easy as we simply force the `shadow` value to `0.0` whenever the projected vector's z coordinate is larger than `1.0`:

```glsl
float ShadowCalculation(vec4 fragPosLightSpace)
{
    [...]
    if(projCoords.z > 1.0)
        shadow = 0.0;

    return shadow;
}
```

Checking the far plane and clamping the depth map to a manually specified border color solves the over-sampling of the depth map. This finally gives us the result we are looking for:

The result of all this does mean that we only have shadows where the projected fragment coordinates sit inside the depth map range so anything outside the light frustum will have no visible shadows. As games usually make sure this only occurs in the distance it is a much more plausible effect than the obvious black regions we had before.

35.5 PCF

The shadows right now are a nice addition to the scenery, but it's still not exactly what we want. If you were to zoom in on the shadows the resolution dependency of shadow mapping quickly becomes apparent.

Because the depth map has a fixed resolution, the depth frequently usually spans more than one fragment per texel. As a result, multiple fragments sample the same depth value from the depth map and come to the same shadow conclusions, which produces these jagged blocky edges.

You can reduce these blocky shadows by increasing the depth map resolution, or by trying to fit the light frustum as closely to the scene as possible.

Another (partial) solution to these jagged edges is called PCF, or percentage-closer filtering, which is a term that hosts many different filtering functions that produce *softer* shadows, making them appear less blocky or hard. The idea is to sample more than once from the depth map, each time with slightly different texture coordinates. For each individual sample we check whether it is in shadow or not. All the sub-results are then combined and averaged and we get a nice soft looking shadow.

One simple implementation of PCF is to simply sample the surrounding texels of the depth map and average the results:

```glsl
float shadow = 0.0;
vec2 texelSize = 1.0 / textureSize(shadowMap, 0);
for(int x = -1; x <= 1; ++x)
{
    for(int y = -1; y <= 1; ++y)
    {
        float pcfDepth = texture(shadowMap, projCoords.xy + vec2(x, y) *
                                 texelSize).r;
        shadow += currentDepth - bias > pcfDepth ? 1.0 : 0.0;
    }
}
shadow /= 9.0;
```

Here `textureSize` returns a `vec2` of the width and height of the given sampler texture at mipmap level 0. 1 divided over this returns the size of a single texel that we use to offset the texture coordinates, making sure each new sample samples a different depth value. Here we sample 9 values around the projected coordinate's x and y value, test for shadow occlusion, and finally average the results by the total number of samples taken.

By using more samples and/or varying the `texelSize` variable you can increase the quality of the soft shadows. Below you can see the shadows with simple PCF applied:

From a distance the shadows look a lot better and less hard. If you zoom in you can still see the resolution artifacts of shadow mapping, but in general this gives good results for most applications.

You can find the complete source code of the example at `/src/5.advanced_lighting/3.1.3.shadow_mapping/`.

There is actually much more to PCF and quite a few techniques to considerably improve the quality of soft shadows, but for the sake of this chapter's length we'll leave that for a later discussion.

35.6 Orthographic vs projection

There is a difference between rendering the depth map with an orthographic or a projection matrix. An orthographic projection matrix does not deform the scene with perspective so all view/light rays are parallel. This makes it a great projection matrix for directional lights. A perspective projection matrix however does deform all vertices based on perspective which gives different results. The following image shows the different shadow regions of both projection methods:

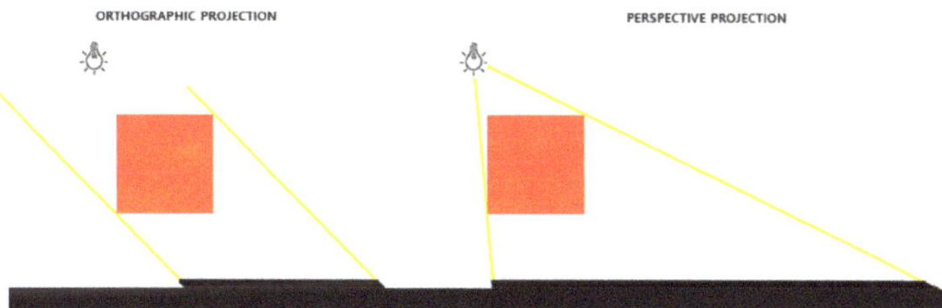

Perspective projections make most sense for light sources that have actual locations, unlike directional lights. Perspective projections are most often used with spotlights and point lights, while orthographic projections are used for directional lights.

Another subtle difference with using a perspective projection matrix is that visualizing the depth buffer will often give an almost completely white result. This happens because with perspective projection the depth is transformed to non-linear depth values with most of its noticeable range close to the near plane. To be able to properly view the depth values as we did with the orthographic projection you first want to transform the non-linear depth values to linear as we discussed in the *Depth Testing* chapter:

```glsl
#version 330 core
out vec4 FragColor;

in vec2 TexCoords;

uniform sampler2D depthMap;
uniform float near_plane;
```

```glsl
uniform float far_plane;

float LinearizeDepth(float depth)
{
    float z = depth * 2.0 - 1.0; // Back to NDC
    return (2.0 * near_plane * far_plane) / (far_plane + near_plane -
        z * (far_plane - near_plane));
}

void main()
{
    float depthValue = texture(depthMap, TexCoords).r;
    FragColor = vec4(vec3(LinearizeDepth(depthValue) / far_plane), 1.0);
    // FragColor = vec4(vec3(depthValue), 1.0); // orthographic
}
```

This shows depth values similar to what we've seen with orthographic projection. Note that this is only useful for debugging; the depth checks remain the same with orthographic or projection matrices as the relative depths do not change.

35.7 Additional resources

- `www.opengl-tutorial.org/intermediate-tutorials/tutorial-16-shadow-mapping/`: similar shadow mapping tutorial by opengl-tutorial.org with a few extra notes.
- `ogldev.atspace.co.uk/www/tutorial23/tutorial23.html`: another shadow mapping tutorial by ogldev.
- `www.youtube.com/watch?v=EsccgeUpdsM`: a 3-part YouTube tutorial by TheBennyBox on shadow mapping and its implementation.
- `msdn.microsoft.com/en-us/library/windows/desktop/ee416324%28v=vs.85%29.aspx`: a great article by Microsoft listing a large number of techniques to improve the quality of shadow maps.

36. Point Shadows

In the last chapter we learned to create dynamic shadows with shadow mapping. It works great, but it's mostly suited for directional (or spot) lights as the shadows are generated only in the direction of the light source. It is therefore also known as directional shadow mapping as the depth (or shadow) map is generated from only the direction the light is looking at.

What this chapter will focus on is the generation of dynamic shadows in all surrounding directions. The technique we're using is perfect for point lights as a real point light would cast shadows in all directions. This technique is known as point (light) shadows or more formerly as omnidirectional shadow maps.

> This chapter builds upon the previous *Shadow Mapping* chapter so unless you're familiar with traditional shadow mapping it is advised to read that chapter first.

The technique is mostly similar to directional shadow mapping: we generate a depth map from the light's perspective(s), sample the depth map based on the current fragment position, and compare each fragment with the stored depth value to see whether it is in shadow. The main difference between directional shadow mapping and omnidirectional shadow mapping is the depth map we use.

The depth map we need requires rendering a scene from all surrounding directions of a point light and as such a normal 2D depth map won't work; what if we were to use a cubemap instead? Because a cubemap can store full environment data with only 6 faces, it is possible to render the entire scene to each of the faces of a cubemap and sample these as the point light's surrounding depth values.

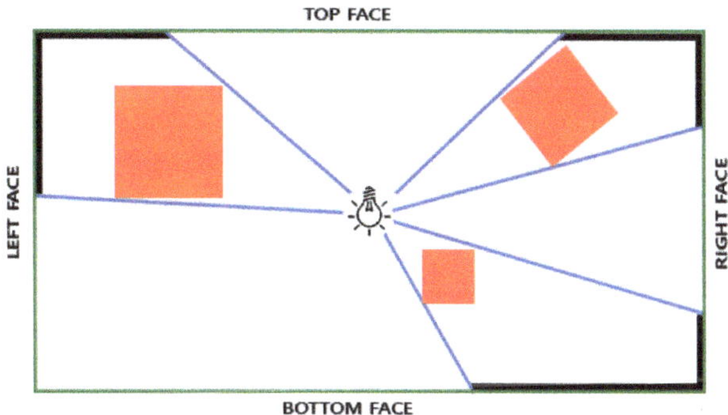

The generated depth cubemap is then passed to the lighting fragment shader that samples the cubemap with a direction vector to obtain the closest depth (from the light's perspective) at that fragment. Most of the complicated stuff we've already discussed in the shadow mapping chapter. What makes this technique a bit more difficult is the depth cubemap generation.

36.1 Generating the depth cubemap

To create a cubemap of a light's surrounding depth values we have to render the scene 6 times: once for each face. One (quite obvious) way to do this, is render the scene 6 times with 6 different view matrices, each time attaching a different cubemap face to the framebuffer object. This would look something like this:

```
for(unsigned int i = 0; i < 6; i++)
{
    GLenum face = GL_TEXTURE_CUBE_MAP_POSITIVE_X + i;
    glFramebufferTexture2D(GL_FRAMEBUFFER, GL_DEPTH_ATTACHMENT, face,
                           depthCubemap, 0);
    BindViewMatrix(lightViewMatrices[i]);
    RenderScene();
}
```

This can be quite expensive though as a lot of render calls are necessary for this single depth map. In this chapter we're going to use an alternative (more organized) approach using a little trick in the geometry shader that allows us to build the depth cubemap with just a single render pass.

First, we'll need to create a cubemap:

```
unsigned int depthCubemap;
glGenTextures(1, &depthCubemap);
```

And assign each of the single cubemap faces a 2D depth-valued texture image:

```
const unsigned int SHADOW_WIDTH = 1024, SHADOW_HEIGHT = 1024;
glBindTexture(GL_TEXTURE_CUBE_MAP, depthCubemap);
for (unsigned int i = 0; i < 6; ++i)
    glTexImage2D(GL_TEXTURE_CUBE_MAP_POSITIVE_X + i, 0, GL_DEPTH_COMPONENT,
                 SHADOW_WIDTH, SHADOW_HEIGHT, 0, GL_DEPTH_COMPONENT,
                 GL_FLOAT, NULL);
```

And don't forget to set the texture parameters:

```
glTexParameteri(GL_TEXTURE_CUBE_MAP, GL_TEXTURE_MAG_FILTER, GL_NEAREST);
glTexParameteri(GL_TEXTURE_CUBE_MAP, GL_TEXTURE_MIN_FILTER, GL_NEAREST);
glTexParameteri(GL_TEXTURE_CUBE_MAP, GL_TEXTURE_WRAP_S, GL_CLAMP_TO_EDGE);
glTexParameteri(GL_TEXTURE_CUBE_MAP, GL_TEXTURE_WRAP_T, GL_CLAMP_TO_EDGE);
glTexParameteri(GL_TEXTURE_CUBE_MAP, GL_TEXTURE_WRAP_R, GL_CLAMP_TO_EDGE);
```

Normally we'd attach a single face of a cubemap texture to the framebuffer object and render the scene 6 times, each time switching the depth buffer target of the framebuffer to a different cubemap face. Since we're going to use a geometry shader, that allows us to render to all faces in a single pass, we can directly attach the cubemap as a framebuffer's depth attachment with `glFramebufferTexture`:

```
glBindFramebuffer(GL_FRAMEBUFFER, depthMapFBO);
glFramebufferTexture(GL_FRAMEBUFFER, GL_DEPTH_ATTACHMENT, depthCubemap, 0);
glDrawBuffer(GL_NONE);
glReadBuffer(GL_NONE);
glBindFramebuffer(GL_FRAMEBUFFER, 0);
```

Again, note the call to `glDrawBuffer` and `glReadBuffer`: we only care about depth values when generating a depth cubemap so we have to explicitly tell OpenGL this framebuffer object does not render to a color buffer.

With omnidirectional shadow maps we have two render passes: first, we generate the depth cubemap and second, we use the depth cubemap in the normal render pass to add shadows to the scene. This process looks a bit like this:

```cpp
// 1. first render to depth cubemap
glViewport(0, 0, SHADOW_WIDTH, SHADOW_HEIGHT);
glBindFramebuffer(GL_FRAMEBUFFER, depthMapFBO);
    glClear(GL_DEPTH_BUFFER_BIT);
    ConfigureShaderAndMatrices();
    RenderScene();
glBindFramebuffer(GL_FRAMEBUFFER, 0);
// 2. then render scene as normal with shadow mapping (using depth cubemap)
glViewport(0, 0, SCR_WIDTH, SCR_HEIGHT);
glClear(GL_COLOR_BUFFER_BIT | GL_DEPTH_BUFFER_BIT);
ConfigureShaderAndMatrices();
glBindTexture(GL_TEXTURE_CUBE_MAP, depthCubemap);
RenderScene();
```

The process is exactly the same as with default shadow mapping, although this time we render to and use a cubemap depth texture compared to a 2D depth texture.

36.1.1 Light space transform

With the framebuffer and cubemap set, we need some way to transform all the scene's geometry to the relevant light spaces in all 6 directions of the light. Just like in the *Shadow Mapping* chapter, we're going to need a light space transformation matrix T, but this time one for each face.

Each light space transformation matrix contains both a projection and a view matrix. For the projection matrix we're going to use a perspective projection matrix; the light source represents a point in space so perspective projection makes most sense. Each light space transformation matrix uses the same projection matrix:

```cpp
float aspect = (float)SHADOW_WIDTH/(float)SHADOW_HEIGHT;
float near = 1.0f;
float far = 25.0f;
glm::mat4 shadowProj = glm::perspective(glm::radians(90.0f), aspect,
                                        near, far);
```

Important to note here is the field of view parameter of `glm::perspective` that we set to 90 degrees. By setting this to 90 degrees we make sure the viewing field is exactly large enough to fill a single face of the cubemap such that all faces align correctly to each other at the edges.

As the projection matrix does not change per direction we can re-use it for each of the 6 transformation matrices. We do need a different view matrix per direction. With `glm::lookAt` we create 6 view directions, each looking at one face direction of the cubemap in the order: right, left, top, bottom, near and far.

```cpp
std::vector<glm::mat4> shadowTransforms;
shadowTransforms.push_back(shadowProj *
                glm::lookAt(lightPos, lightPos + glm::vec3( 1.0, 0.0, 0.0)
                , glm::vec3(0.0,-1.0, 0.0)));
shadowTransforms.push_back(shadowProj *
                glm::lookAt(lightPos, lightPos + glm::vec3(-1.0, 0.0, 0.0)
                , glm::vec3(0.0,-1.0, 0.0)));
shadowTransforms.push_back(shadowProj *
                glm::lookAt(lightPos, lightPos + glm::vec3( 0.0, 1.0, 0.0)
                , glm::vec3(0.0, 0.0, 1.0)));
shadowTransforms.push_back(shadowProj *
                glm::lookAt(lightPos, lightPos + glm::vec3( 0.0,-1.0, 0.0)
                , glm::vec3(0.0, 0.0,-1.0)));
shadowTransforms.push_back(shadowProj *
```

```
                     glm::lookAt(lightPos, lightPos + glm::vec3( 0.0, 0.0, 1.0)
                     , glm::vec3(0.0,-1.0, 0.0)));
shadowTransforms.push_back(shadowProj *
                     glm::lookAt(lightPos, lightPos + glm::vec3( 0.0, 0.0,-1.0)
                     , glm::vec3(0.0,-1.0, 0.0)));
```

Here we create 6 view matrices and multiply them with the projection matrix to get a total of 6 different light space transformation matrices. The `target` parameter of `glm::lookAt` each looks into the direction of a single cubemap face.

These transformation matrices are sent to the shaders that render the depth into the cubemap.

36.1.2 Depth shaders

To render depth values to a depth cubemap we're going to need a total of three shaders: a vertex and fragment shader, and a geometry shader in between.

The geometry shader will be the shader responsible for transforming all world-space vertices to the 6 different light spaces. Therefore, the vertex shader simply transforms vertices to world-space and directs them to the geometry shader:

```glsl
#version 330 core
layout (location = 0) in vec3 aPos;

uniform mat4 model;

void main()
{
    gl_Position = model * vec4(aPos, 1.0);
}
```

The geometry shader will take as input 3 triangle vertices and a uniform array of light space transformation matrices. The geometry shader is responsible for transforming the vertices to the light spaces; this is also where it gets interesting.

The geometry shader has a built-in variable called `gl_Layer` that specifies which cubemap face to emit a primitive to. When left alone, the geometry shader just sends its primitives further down the pipeline as usual, but when we update this variable we can control to which cubemap face we render to for each primitive. This of course only works when we have a cubemap texture attached to the active framebuffer.

```glsl
#version 330 core
layout (triangles) in;
layout (triangle_strip, max_vertices=18) out;

uniform mat4 shadowMatrices[6];

out vec4 FragPos; // FragPos from GS (output per emitvertex)

void main()
{
    for(int face = 0; face < 6; ++face)
    {
        gl_Layer = face; // built-in variable: to which face we render.
        for(int i = 0; i < 3; ++i) // for each triangle vertex
        {
            FragPos = gl_in[i].gl_Position;
            gl_Position = shadowMatrices[face] * FragPos;
```

```
            EmitVertex();
        }
        EndPrimitive();
    }
}
```

This geometry shader is relatively straightforward. We take as input a triangle, and output a total of 6 triangles (6 * 3 equals 18 vertices). In the `main` function we iterate over 6 cubemap faces where we specify each face as the output face by storing the face integer into `gl_Layer`. We then generate the output triangles by transforming each world-space input vertex to the relevant light space by multiplying `FragPos` with the face's light-space transformation matrix. Note that we also sent the resulting `FragPos` variable to the fragment shader that we'll need to calculate a depth value.

In the last chapter we used an empty fragment shader and let OpenGL figure out the depth values of the depth map. This time we're going to calculate our own (linear) depth as the linear distance between each closest fragment position and the light source's position. Calculating our own depth values makes the later shadow calculations a bit more intuitive.

```glsl
#version 330 core
in vec4 FragPos;

uniform vec3 lightPos;
uniform float far_plane;

void main()
{
    // get distance between fragment and light source
    float lightDistance = length(FragPos.xyz - lightPos);

    // map to [0;1] range by dividing by far_plane
    lightDistance = lightDistance / far_plane;

    // write this as modified depth
    gl_FragDepth = lightDistance;
}
```

The fragment shader takes as input the `FragPos` from the geometry shader, the light's position vector, and the frustum's far plane value. Here we take the distance between the fragment and the light source, map it to the [0,1] range and write it as the fragment's depth value.

Rendering the scene with these shaders and the cubemap-attached framebuffer object active should give you a completely filled depth cubemap for the second pass's shadow calculations.

36.2 Omnidirectional shadow maps

With everything set up it is time to render the actual omnidirectional shadows. The procedure is similar to the directional shadow mapping chapter, although this time we bind a cubemap texture instead of a 2D texture and also pass the light projection's far plane variable to the shaders.

```cpp
glViewport(0, 0, SCR_WIDTH, SCR_HEIGHT);
glClear(GL_COLOR_BUFFER_BIT | GL_DEPTH_BUFFER_BIT);
shader.use();
// ... send uniforms to shader (including light's far_plane value)
glActiveTexture(GL_TEXTURE0);
glBindTexture(GL_TEXTURE_CUBE_MAP, depthCubemap);
// ... bind other textures
```

```
RenderScene();
```

Here the `renderScene` function renders a few cubes in a large cube room scattered around a light source at the center of the scene.

The vertex and fragment shader are mostly similar to the original shadow mapping shaders: the difference being that the fragment shader no longer requires a fragment position in light space as we can now sample the depth values with a direction vector.

Because of this, the vertex shader doesn't needs to transform its position vectors to light space so we can remove the `FragPosLightSpace` variable:

```glsl
#version 330 core
layout (location = 0) in vec3 aPos;
layout (location = 1) in vec3 aNormal;
layout (location = 2) in vec2 aTexCoords;

out vec2 TexCoords;

out VS_OUT {
    vec3 FragPos;
    vec3 Normal;
    vec2 TexCoords;
} vs_out;

uniform mat4 projection;
uniform mat4 view;
uniform mat4 model;

void main()
{
    vs_out.FragPos = vec3(model * vec4(aPos, 1.0));
    vs_out.Normal = transpose(inverse(mat3(model))) * aNormal;
    vs_out.TexCoords = aTexCoords;
    gl_Position = projection * view * model * vec4(aPos, 1.0);
}
```

The fragment shader's Blinn-Phong lighting code is exactly the same as we had before with a shadow multiplication at the end:

```glsl
#version 330 core
out vec4 FragColor;

in VS_OUT {
    vec3 FragPos;
    vec3 Normal;
    vec2 TexCoords;
} fs_in;

uniform sampler2D diffuseTexture;
uniform samplerCube depthMap;

uniform vec3 lightPos;
uniform vec3 viewPos;

uniform float far_plane;

float ShadowCalculation(vec3 fragPos)
{
```

```glsl
    [...]
}

void main()
{
    vec3 color = texture(diffuseTexture, fs_in.TexCoords).rgb;
    vec3 normal = normalize(fs_in.Normal);
    vec3 lightColor = vec3(0.3);
    // ambient
    vec3 ambient = 0.3 * color;
    // diffuse
    vec3 lightDir = normalize(lightPos - fs_in.FragPos);
    float diff = max(dot(lightDir, normal), 0.0);
    vec3 diffuse = diff * lightColor;
    // specular
    vec3 viewDir = normalize(viewPos - fs_in.FragPos);
    vec3 reflectDir = reflect(-lightDir, normal);
    float spec = 0.0;
    vec3 halfwayDir = normalize(lightDir + viewDir);
    spec = pow(max(dot(normal, halfwayDir), 0.0), 64.0);
    vec3 specular = spec * lightColor;
    // calculate shadow
    float shadow = ShadowCalculation(fs_in.FragPos);
    vec3 lighting = (ambient + (1.0 - shadow) * (diffuse + specular)) *
                    color;

    FragColor = vec4(lighting, 1.0);
}
```

There are a few subtle differences: the lighting code is the same, but we now have a `samplerCube` uniform and the `ShadowCalculation` function takes the current fragment's position as its argument instead of the fragment position in light space. We now also include the light frustum's `far_plane` value that we'll later need.

The biggest difference is in the content of the `ShadowCalculation` function that now samples depth values from a cubemap instead of a 2D texture. Let's discuss its content step by step.

The first thing we have to do is retrieve the depth of the cubemap. You may remember from the cubemap section of this chapter that we stored the depth as the linear distance between the fragment and the light position; we're taking a similar approach here:

```glsl
float ShadowCalculation(vec3 fragPos)
{
    vec3 fragToLight = fragPos - lightPos;
    float closestDepth = texture(depthMap, fragToLight).r;
}
```

Here we take the difference vector between the fragment's position and the light's position and use that vector as a direction vector to sample the cubemap. The direction vector doesn't need to be a unit vector to sample from a cubemap so there's no need to normalize it. The resulting `closestDepth` value is the normalized depth value between the light source and its closest visible fragment.

The `closestDepth` value is currently in the range [0,1] so we first transform it back to [0,far_plane] by multiplying it with `far_plane`.

```glsl
closestDepth *= far_plane;
```

Next we retrieve the depth value between the current fragment and the light source, which we can easily obtain by taking the length of `fragToLight` due to how we calculated depth values in the cubemap:

```
float currentDepth = length(fragToLight);
```

This returns a depth value in the same (or larger) range as `closestDepth`.

Now we can compare both depth values to see which is closer than the other and determine whether the current fragment is in shadow. We also include a shadow bias so we don't get shadow acne as discussed in the previous chapter.

```
float bias = 0.05;
float shadow = currentDepth - bias > closestDepth ? 1.0 : 0.0;
```

The complete `ShadowCalculation` then becomes:

```glsl
float ShadowCalculation(vec3 fragPos)
{
    // get vector between fragment position and light position
    vec3 fragToLight = fragPos - lightPos;
    // use the light to fragment vector to sample from the depth map
    float closestDepth = texture(depthMap, fragToLight).r;
    // it is currently in linear range between [0,1].
    // re-transform back to original value
    closestDepth *= far_plane;
    // now get current linear depth as the length between the
    // fragment and light position
    float currentDepth = length(fragToLight);
    // now test for shadows
    float bias = 0.05;
    float shadow = currentDepth - bias > closestDepth ? 1.0 : 0.0;

    return shadow;
}
```

With these shaders we already get pretty good shadows and this time in all surrounding directions from a point light. With a point light positioned at the center of a simple scene it'll look a bit like this:

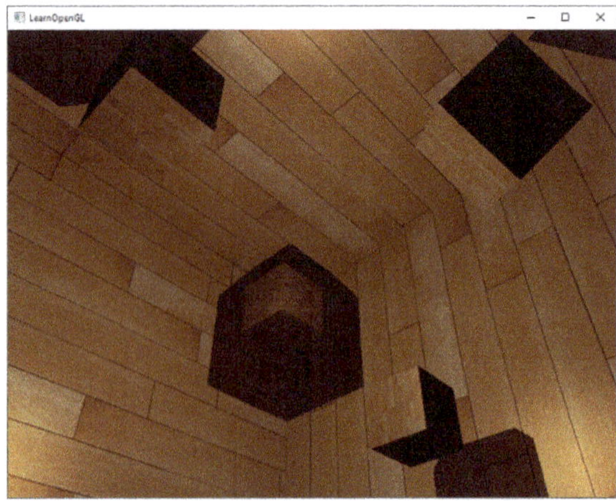

You can find the source code of this demo at `/src/5.advanced_lighting/3.2.1.point_shadows/`.

36.2.1 Visualizing cubemap depth buffer

If you're somewhat like me you probably didn't get this right on the first try so it makes sense to do some debugging, with one of the obvious checks being validating whether the depth map was built correctly. A simple trick to visualize the depth buffer is to take the `closestDepth` variable in the `ShadowCalculation` function and display that variable as:

```
FragColor = vec4(vec3(closestDepth / far_plane), 1.0);
```

The result is a grayed out scene where each color represents the linear depth values of the scene:

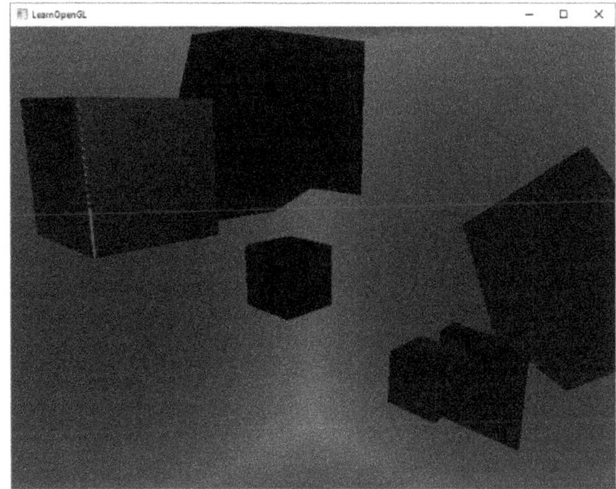

You can also see the to-be shadowed regions on the outside wall. If it looks somewhat similar, you know the depth cubemap was properly generated.

36.3 PCF

Since omnidirectional shadow maps are based on the same principles of traditional shadow mapping it also has the same resolution dependent artifacts. If you zoom in close enough you can again see jagged edges. Percentage-closer filtering or PCF allows us to smooth out these jagged edges by filtering multiple samples around the fragment position and average the results.

If we take the same simple PCF filter of the previous chapter and add a third dimension we get:

```
float shadow = 0.0;
float bias   = 0.05;
float samples = 4.0;
float offset = 0.1;
for(float x = -offset; x < offset; x += offset / (samples * 0.5))
{
    for(float y = -offset; y < offset; y += offset / (samples * 0.5))
    {
        for(float z = -offset; z < offset; z += offset / (samples * 0.5))
        {
            float closestDepth = texture(depthMap, fragToLight +
                                         vec3(x, y, z)).r;
            closestDepth *= far_plane; // undo mapping [0;1]
```

```
            if(currentDepth - bias > closestDepth)
                shadow += 1.0;
        }
    }
}
shadow /= (samples * samples * samples);
```

The code isn't that different from the traditional shadow mapping code. We calculate and add
texture offsets dynamically for each axis based on a fixed number of samples. For each sample we
repeat the original shadow process on the offsetted sample direction and average the results at the
end.

The shadows now look more soft and smooth and give more plausible results.

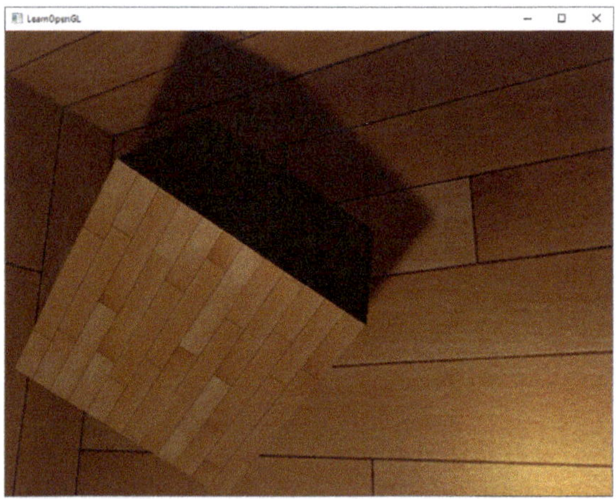

However, with `samples` set to `4.0` we take a total of `64` samples each fragment which is a
lot!

As most of these samples are redundant in that they sample close to the original direction vector
it may make more sense to only sample in perpendicular directions of the sample direction vector.
However as there is no (easy) way to figure out which sub-directions are redundant this becomes
difficult. One trick we can use is to take an array of offset directions that are all roughly separable
e.g. each of them points in completely different directions. This will significantly reduce the number
of sub-directions that are close together. Below we have such an array of a maximum of `20` offset
directions:

```
vec3 sampleOffsetDirections[20] = vec3[]
(
   vec3( 1,  1,  1), vec3( 1, -1,  1), vec3(-1, -1,  1), vec3(-1, 1,  1),
   vec3( 1,  1, -1), vec3( 1, -1, -1), vec3(-1, -1, -1), vec3(-1, 1, -1),
   vec3( 1,  1,  0), vec3( 1, -1,  0), vec3(-1, -1,  0), vec3(-1, 1,  0),
   vec3( 1,  0,  1), vec3(-1,  0,  1), vec3( 1,  0, -1), vec3(-1, 0, -1),
   vec3( 0,  1,  1), vec3( 0, -1,  1), vec3( 0, -1, -1), vec3( 0, 1, -1)
);
```

From this we can adapt the PCF algorithm to take a fixed amount of samples from `sampleOffs
etDirections` and use these to sample the cubemap. The advantage here is that we need a lot
less samples to get visually similar results.

```glsl
float shadow = 0.0;
float bias = 0.15;
int samples = 20;
float viewDistance = length(viewPos - fragPos);
float diskRadius = 0.05;
for(int i = 0; i < samples; ++i)
{
    float closestDepth = texture(depthMap, fragToLight +
                         sampleOffsetDirections[i] * diskRadius).r;
    closestDepth *= far_plane; // undo mapping [0;1]
    if(currentDepth - bias > closestDepth)
        shadow += 1.0;
}
shadow /= float(samples);
```

Here we add multiple offsets, scaled by some `diskRadius`, around the original `fragToLight` direction vector to sample from the cubemap.

Another interesting trick we can apply here is that we can change `diskRadius` based on the distance of the viewer to the fragment, making the shadows softer when far away and sharper when close by.

```glsl
float diskRadius = (1.0 + (viewDistance / far_plane)) / 25.0;
```

The results of the updated PCF algorithm gives just as good, if not better, results of soft shadows:

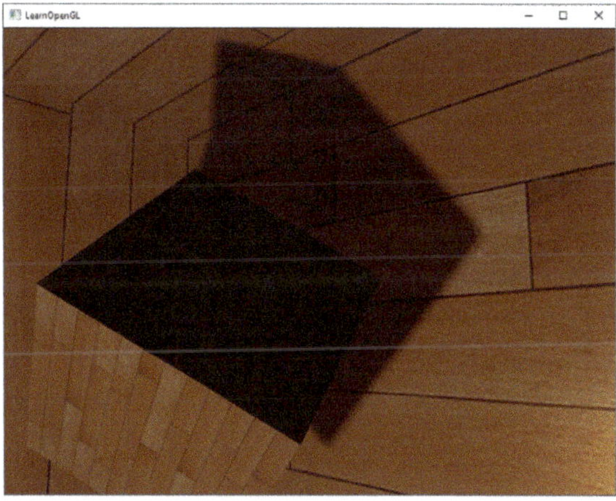

Of course, the `bias` we add to each sample is highly based on context and will always require tweaking based on the scene you're working with. Play around with all the values and see how they affect the scene.

You can find the final code at `/src/5.advanced_lighting/3.2.2.point_shadows_soft/`.

I should mention that using geometry shaders to generate a depth map isn't necessarily faster than rendering the scene 6 times for each face. Using a geometry shader like this has its own performance penalties that may outweigh the performance gain of using one in the first place. This of course depends on the type of environment, the specific video card drivers, and plenty of other factors. So if you really care about pushing the most out of your system, make sure to profile both methods and select the more efficient one for your scene.

36.4 Additional resources

- `www.sunandblackcat.com/tipFullView.php?l=eng&topicid=36`: omnidirectional shadow mapping tutorial by sunandblackcat.
- `ogldev.atspace.co.uk/www/tutorial43/tutorial43.html`: omnidirectional shadow mapping tutorial by ogldev.
- `www.cg.tuwien.ac.at/~husky/RTR/OmnidirShadows-whyCaps.pdf`: a nice set of slides about omnidirectional shadow mapping by Peter Houska.

37. Normal Mapping

All of our scenes are filled with meshes, each consisting of hundreds or maybe thousands of triangles. We boosted the realism by wrapping 2D textures on these flat triangles, hiding the fact that the polygons are just tiny flat triangles. Textures help, but when you take a good close look at the meshes it is still quite easy to see the underlying flat surfaces. Most real-life surface aren't flat however and exhibit a lot of (bumpy) details.

For instance, take a brick surface. A brick surface is quite a rough surface and obviously not completely flat: it contains sunken cement stripes and a lot of detailed little holes and cracks. If we were to view such a brick surface in a lit scene the immersion gets easily broken. Below we can see a brick texture applied to a flat surface lit by a point light.

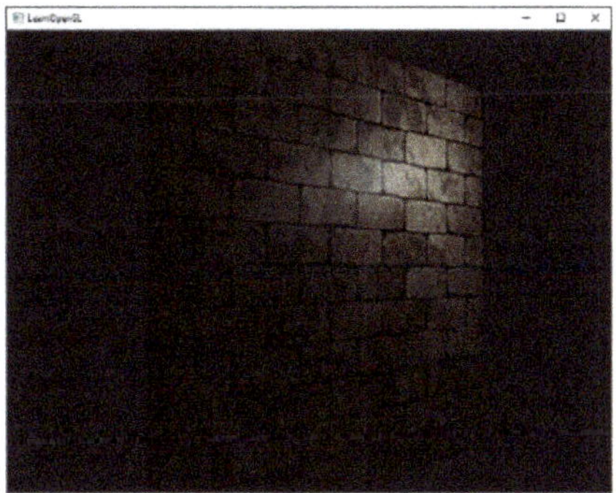

The lighting doesn't take any of the small cracks and holes into account and completely ignores the deep stripes between the bricks; the surface looks perfectly flat. We can partly fix the flat look by using a specular map to pretend some surfaces are less lit due to depth or other details, but that's more of a hack than a real solution. What we need is some way to inform the lighting system about all the little depth-like details of the surface.

If we think about this from a light's perspective: how comes the surface is lit as a completely flat surface? The answer is the surface's normal vector. From the lighting technique's point of view, the only way it determines the shape of an object is by its perpendicular normal vector. The brick surface only has a single normal vector, and as a result the surface is uniformly lit based on this normal vector's direction. What if we, instead of a per-surface normal that is the same for each fragment, use a per-fragment normal that is different for each fragment? This way we can slightly deviate the normal vector based on a surface's little details; this gives the illusion the surface is a lot more complex:

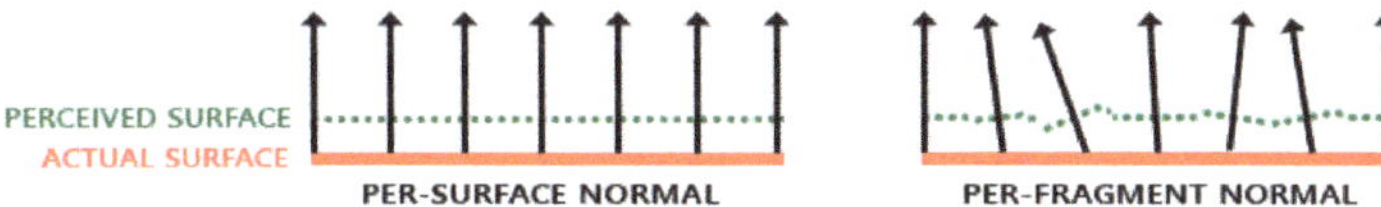

By using per-fragment normals we can trick the lighting into believing a surface consists of tiny little planes (perpendicular to the normal vectors) giving the surface an enormous boost in detail. This technique to use per-fragment normals compared to per-surface normals is called normal mapping or bump mapping. Applied to the brick plane it looks a bit like this:

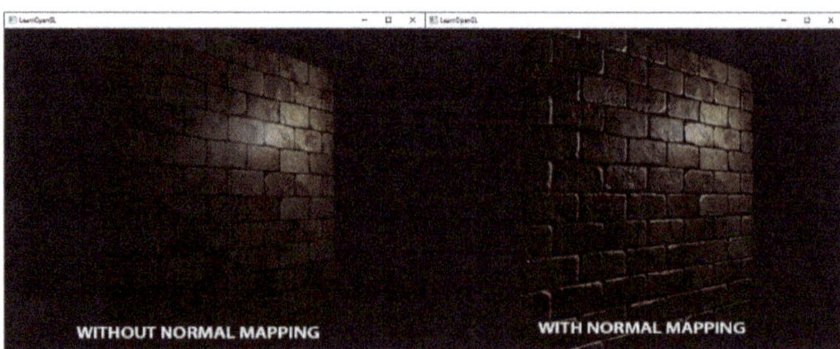

As you can see, it gives an enormous boost in detail and for a relatively low cost. Since we only change the normal vectors per fragment there is no need to change the lighting equation. We now pass a per-fragment normal, instead of an interpolated surface normal, to the lighting algorithm. The lighting then does the rest.

37.1 Normal mapping

To get normal mapping to work we're going to need a per-fragment normal. Similar to what we did with diffuse and specular maps we can use a 2D texture to store per-fragment normal data. This way we can sample a 2D texture to get a normal vector for that specific fragment.

While normal vectors are geometric entities and textures are generally only used for color information, storing normal vectors in a texture may not be immediately obvious. If you think about color vectors in a texture they are represented as a 3D vector with an r, g, and b component. We can similarly store a normal vector's x, y and z component in the respective color components. Normal vectors range between -1 and 1 so they're first mapped to $[0,1]$:

```
vec3 rgb_normal = normal * 0.5 + 0.5; // transforms from [-1,1] to [0,1]
```

With normal vectors transformed to an RGB color component like this, we can store a per-fragment normal derived from the shape of a surface onto a 2D texture. An example normal map of the brick surface at the start of this chapter is shown below:

This (and almost all normal maps you find online) will have a blue-ish tint. This is because the normals are all closely pointing outwards towards the positive z-axis $(0, 0, 1)$: a blue-ish color. The deviations in color represent normal vectors that are slightly offset from the general positive z direction, giving a sense of depth to the texture. For example, you can see that at the top of each brick the color tends to be more greenish, which makes sense as the top side of a brick would have normals pointing more in the positive y direction $(0, 1, 0)$ which happens to be the color green!

With a simple plane, looking at the positive z-axis, we can take a diffuse texture[1] and a normal map[2] to render the image from the previous section. Note that the linked normal map is different from the one shown above. The reason for this is that OpenGL reads texture coordinates with the y (or v) coordinate reversed from how textures are generally created. The linked normal map thus has its y (or green) component inversed (you can see the green colors are now pointing downwards); if you fail to take this into account, the lighting will be incorrect. Load both textures, bind them to the proper texture units, and render a plane with the following changes in the lighting fragment shader:

```glsl
uniform sampler2D normalMap;

void main()
{
    // obtain normal from normal map in range [0,1]
    normal = texture(normalMap, fs_in.TexCoords).rgb;
    // transform normal vector to range [-1,1]
    normal = normalize(normal * 2.0 - 1.0);

    [...]
    // proceed with lighting as normal
}
```

Here we reverse the process of mapping normals to RGB colors by remapping the sampled normal color from [0,1] back to [-1,1] and then use the sampled normal vectors for the upcoming lighting calculations. In this case we used a Blinn-Phong shader.

By slowly moving the light source over time you really get a sense of depth using the normal map. Running this normal mapping example gives the exact results as shown at the start of this chapter:

There is one issue however that greatly limits this use of normal maps. The normal map we used had normal vectors that all pointed somewhat in the positive z direction. This worked because the plane's surface normal was also pointing in the positive z direction. However, what would happen if we used the same normal map on a plane laying on the ground with a surface normal vector pointing in the positive y direction?

---

[1] learnopengl.com/img/textures/brickwall.jpg
[2] learnopengl.com/img/textures/brickwall_normal.jpg

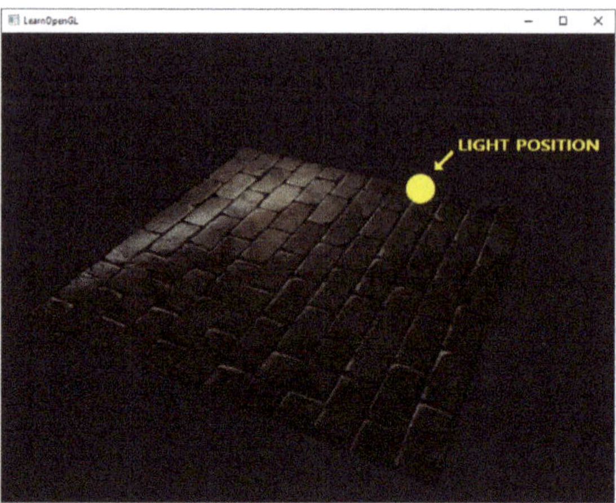

The lighting doesn't look right! This happens because the sampled normals of this plane still roughly point in the positive z direction even though they should mostly point in the positive y direction. As a result, the lighting thinks the surface's normals are the same as before when the plane was pointing towards the positive z direction; the lighting is incorrect. The image below shows what the sampled normals approximately look like on this surface:

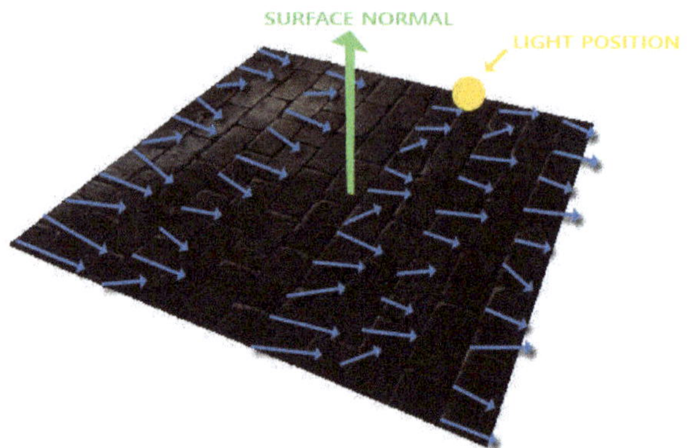

You can see that all the normals point somewhat in the positive z direction even though they should be pointing towards the positive y direction. One solution to this problem is to define a normal map for each possible direction of the surface; in the case of a cube we would need 6 normal maps. However, with advanced meshes that can have more than hundreds of possible surface directions this becomes an infeasible approach.

A different solution exists that does all the lighting in a different coordinate space: a coordinate space where the normal map vectors always point towards the positive z direction; all other lighting vectors are then transformed relative to this positive z direction. This way we can always use the same normal map, regardless of orientation. This coordinate space is called tangent space.

37.2 Tangent space

Normal vectors in a normal map are expressed in tangent space where normals always point roughly in the positive z direction. Tangent space is a space that's local to the surface of a triangle: the normals are relative to the local reference frame of the individual triangles. Think of it as the local space of the normal map's vectors; they're all defined pointing in the positive z direction regardless of the final transformed direction. Using a specific matrix we can then transform normal vectors from this *local* tangent space to world or view coordinates, orienting them along the final mapped surface's direction.

Let's say we have the incorrect normal mapped surface from the previous section looking in the positive y direction. The normal map is defined in tangent space, so one way to solve the problem is to calculate a matrix to transform normals from tangent space to a different space such that they're aligned with the surface's normal direction: the normal vectors are then all pointing roughly in the positive y direction. The great thing about tangent space is that we can calculate this matrix for any type of surface so that we can properly align the tangent space's z direction to the surface's normal direction.

Such a matrix is called a TBN matrix where the letters depict a Tangent, Bitangent and Normal vector. These are the vectors we need to construct this matrix. To construct such a *change-of-basis* matrix, that transforms a tangent-space vector to a different coordinate space, we need three perpendicular vectors that are aligned along the surface of a normal map: an up, right, and forward vector; similar to what we did in the *Camera* chapter.

We already know the up vector, which is the surface's normal vector. The right and forward vector are the tangent and bitangent vector respectively. The following image of a surface shows all three vectors on a surface:

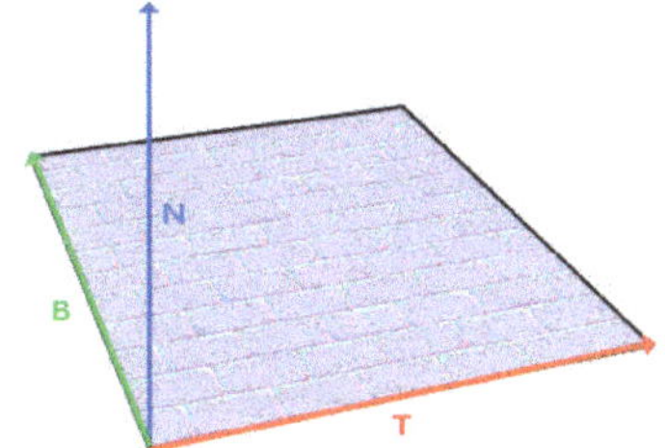

Calculating the tangent and bitangent vectors is not as straightforward as the normal vector. We can see from the image that the direction of the normal map's tangent and bitangent vector align with the direction in which we define a surface's texture coordinates. We'll use this fact to calculate tangent and bitangent vectors for each surface. Retrieving them does require a bit of math; take a look at the following image:

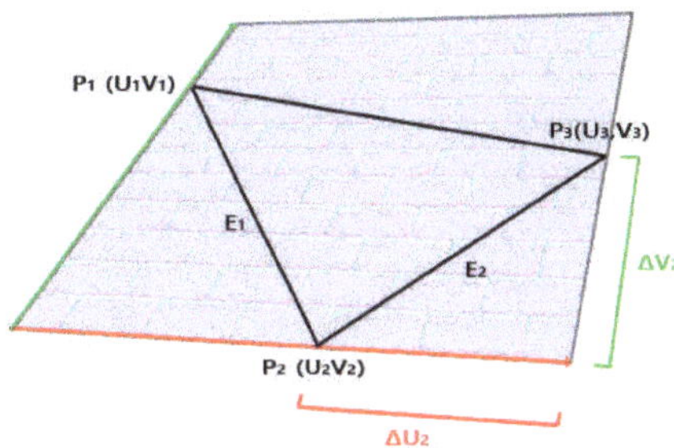

From the image we can see that the texture coordinate differences of an edge E_2 of a triangle (denoted as ΔU_2 and ΔV_2) are expressed in the same direction as the tangent vector T and bitangent vector B. Because of this we can write both displayed edges E_1 and E_2 of the triangle as a linear combination of the tangent vector T and the bitangent vector B:

$$E_1 = \Delta U_1 T + \Delta V_1 B$$
$$E_2 = \Delta U_2 T + \Delta V_2 B$$

Which we can also write as:

$$(E_{1x}, E_{1y}, E_{1z}) = \Delta U_1 (T_x, T_y, T_z) + \Delta V_1 (B_x, B_y, B_z)$$
$$(E_{2x}, E_{2y}, E_{2z}) = \Delta U_2 (T_x, T_y, T_z) + \Delta V_2 (B_x, B_y, B_z)$$

We can calculate E as the difference vector between two triangle positions, and ΔU and ΔV as their texture coordinate differences. We're then left with two unknowns (tangent T and bitangent B) and two equations. You may remember from your algebra classes that this allows us to solve for T and B.

The last equation allows us to write it in a different form: that of matrix multiplication:

$$\begin{bmatrix} E_{1x} & E_{1y} & E_{1z} \\ E_{2x} & E_{2y} & E_{2z} \end{bmatrix} = \begin{bmatrix} \Delta U_1 & \Delta V_1 \\ \Delta U_2 & \Delta V_2 \end{bmatrix} \begin{bmatrix} T_x & T_y & T_z \\ B_x & B_y & B_z \end{bmatrix}$$

Try to visualize the matrix multiplications in your head and confirm that this is indeed the same equation. An advantage of rewriting the equations in matrix form is that solving for T and B is easier to understand. If we multiply both sides of the equations by the inverse of the $\Delta U \Delta V$ matrix we get:

$$\begin{bmatrix} \Delta U_1 & \Delta V_1 \\ \Delta U_2 & \Delta V_2 \end{bmatrix}^{-1} \begin{bmatrix} E_{1x} & E_{1y} & E_{1z} \\ E_{2x} & E_{2y} & E_{2z} \end{bmatrix} = \begin{bmatrix} T_x & T_y & T_z \\ B_x & B_y & B_z \end{bmatrix}$$

This allows us to solve for T and B. This does require us to calculate the inverse of the delta texture coordinate matrix. I won't go into the mathematical details of calculating a matrix' inverse, but it roughly translates to 1 over the determinant of the matrix, multiplied by its adjugate matrix:

$$\begin{bmatrix} T_x & T_y & T_z \\ B_x & B_y & B_z \end{bmatrix} = \frac{1}{\Delta U_1 \Delta V_2 - \Delta U_2 \Delta V_1} \begin{bmatrix} \Delta V_2 & -\Delta V_1 \\ -\Delta U_2 & \Delta U_1 \end{bmatrix} \begin{bmatrix} E_{1x} & E_{1y} & E_{1z} \\ E_{2x} & E_{2y} & E_{2z} \end{bmatrix}$$

This final equation gives us a formula for calculating the tangent vector T and bitangent vector B from a triangle's two edges and its texture coordinates.

Don't worry if you do not fully understand the mathematics behind this. As long as you understand that we can calculate tangents and bitangents from a triangle's vertices and its texture coordinates (since texture coordinates are in the same space as tangent vectors) you're halfway there.

37.2.1 Manual calculation of tangents and bitangents

In the previous demo we had a simple normal mapped plane facing the positive z direction. This time we want to implement normal mapping using tangent space so we can orient this plane however we want and normal mapping would still work. Using the previously discussed mathematics we're going to manually calculate this surface's tangent and bitangent vectors.

Let's assume the plane is built up from the following vectors (with 1, 2, 3 and 1, 3, 4 as its two triangles):

```cpp
// positions
glm::vec3 pos1(-1.0,  1.0,  0.0);
glm::vec3 pos2(-1.0, -1.0,  0.0);
glm::vec3 pos3( 1.0, -1.0,  0.0);
glm::vec3 pos4( 1.0,  1.0,  0.0);
// texture coordinates
glm::vec2 uv1(0.0,  1.0);
glm::vec2 uv2(0.0,  0.0);
glm::vec2 uv3(1.0,  0.0);
glm::vec2 uv4(1.0,  1.0);
// normal vector
glm::vec3 nm(0.0,  0.0,  1.0);
```

We first calculate the first triangle's edges and delta UV coordinates:

```cpp
glm::vec3 edge1 = pos2 - pos1;
glm::vec3 edge2 = pos3 - pos1;
glm::vec2 deltaUV1 = uv2 - uv1;
glm::vec2 deltaUV2 = uv3 - uv1;
```

With the required data for calculating tangents and bitangents we can start following the equation from the previous section:

```cpp
float f = 1.0f / (deltaUV1.x * deltaUV2.y - deltaUV2.x * deltaUV1.y);

tangent1.x = f * (deltaUV2.y * edge1.x - deltaUV1.y * edge2.x);
tangent1.y = f * (deltaUV2.y * edge1.y - deltaUV1.y * edge2.y);
tangent1.z = f * (deltaUV2.y * edge1.z - deltaUV1.y * edge2.z);

bitangent1.x = f * (-deltaUV2.x * edge1.x + deltaUV1.x * edge2.x);
bitangent1.y = f * (-deltaUV2.x * edge1.y + deltaUV1.x * edge2.y);
bitangent1.z = f * (-deltaUV2.x * edge1.z + deltaUV1.x * edge2.z);

[...] // similar procedure for plane's second triangle
```

Here we first pre-calculate the fractional part of the equation as `f` and then for each vector component we do the corresponding matrix multiplication multiplied by `f`. If you compare this code with the final equation you can see it is a direct translation. Because a triangle is always a flat shape, we only need to calculate a single tangent/bitangent pair per triangle as they will be the same for each of the triangle's vertices.

The resulting tangent and bitangent vector should have a value of $(1,0,0)$ and $(0,1,0)$ respectively that together with the normal $(0,0,1)$ forms an orthogonal **TBN** matrix. Visualized on the plane, the TBN vectors would look like this:

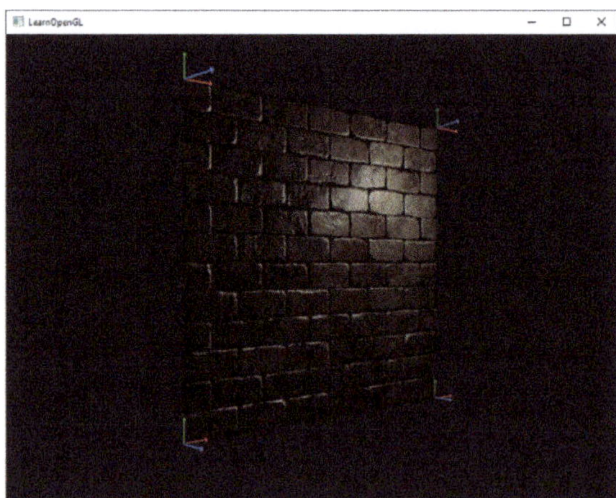

With tangent and bitangent vectors defined per vertex we can start implementing *proper* normal mapping.

37.2.2 Tangent space normal mapping

To get normal mapping working, we first have to create a TBN matrix in the shaders. To do that, we pass the earlier calculated tangent and bitangent vectors to the vertex shader as vertex attributes:

```glsl
#version 330 core
layout (location = 0) in vec3 aPos;
layout (location = 1) in vec3 aNormal;
layout (location = 2) in vec2 aTexCoords;
layout (location = 3) in vec3 aTangent;
layout (location = 4) in vec3 aBitangent;
```

Then within the vertex shader's `main` function we create the TBN matrix:

```glsl
void main()
{
    [...]
    vec3 T = normalize(vec3(model * vec4(aTangent,   0.0)));
    vec3 B = normalize(vec3(model * vec4(aBitangent, 0.0)));
    vec3 N = normalize(vec3(model * vec4(aNormal,    0.0)));
    mat3 TBN = mat3(T, B, N);
}
```

Here we first transform all the TBN vectors to the coordinate system we'd like to work in, which in this case is world-space as we multiply them with the `model` matrix. Then we create the actual TBN matrix by directly supplying `mat3`'s constructor with the relevant vectors. Note that if we want to be really precise, we would multiply the TBN vectors with the normal matrix as we only care about the orientation of the vectors.

> Technically there is no need for the `bitangent` variable in the vertex shader. All three TBN vectors are perpendicular to each other so we can calculate the `bitangent` ourselves in the vertex shader by taking the cross product of the `T` and `N` vector: `vec3 B = cross(N, T);`

So now that we have a TBN matrix, how are we going to use it? There are two ways we can use a TBN matrix for normal mapping, and we'll demonstrate both of them:

1. We take the TBN matrix that transforms any vector from tangent to world space, give it to the fragment shader, and transform the sampled normal from tangent space to world space using the TBN matrix; the normal is then in the same space as the other lighting variables.
2. We take the inverse of the TBN matrix that transforms any vector from world space to tangent space, and use this matrix to transform not the normal, but the other relevant lighting variables to tangent space; the normal is then again in the same space as the other lighting variables.

Let's review the first case. The normal vector we sample from the normal map is expressed in tangent space whereas the other lighting vectors (light and view direction) are expressed in world space. By passing the TBN matrix to the fragment shader we can multiply the sampled tangent space normal with this TBN matrix to transform the normal vector to the same reference space as the other lighting vectors. This way, all the lighting calculations (specifically the dot product) make sense.

Sending the TBN matrix to the fragment shader is easy:

```glsl
out VS_OUT {
    vec3 FragPos;
    vec2 TexCoords;
    mat3 TBN;
} vs_out;

void main()
{
    [...]
    vs_out.TBN = mat3(T, B, N);
}
```

In the fragment shader we similarly take a `mat3` as an input variable:

```glsl
in VS_OUT {
    vec3 FragPos;
    vec2 TexCoords;
    mat3 TBN;
} fs_in;
```

With this TBN matrix we can now update the normal mapping code to include the tangent-to-world space transformation:

```glsl
normal = texture(normalMap, fs_in.TexCoords).rgb;
normal = normal * 2.0 - 1.0;
normal = normalize(fs_in.TBN * normal);
```

Because the resulting `normal` is now in world space, there is no need to change any of the other fragment shader code as the lighting code assumes the normal vector to be in world space.

Let's also review the second case, where we take the inverse of the TBN matrix to transform all relevant world-space vectors to the space the sampled normal vectors are in: tangent space. The construction of the TBN matrix remains the same, but we first invert the matrix before sending it to the fragment shader:

```glsl
vs_out.TBN = transpose(mat3(T, B, N));
```

Note that we use the `transpose` function instead of the `inverse` function here. A great property of orthogonal matrices (each axis is a perpendicular unit vector) is that the transpose of an orthogonal matrix equals its inverse. This is a great property as `inverse` is expensive and a transpose isn't.

Within the fragment shader we do not transform the normal vector, but we transform the other relevant vectors to tangent space, namely the `lightDir` and `viewDir` vectors. That way, each vector is in the same coordinate space: tangent space.

```
void main()
{
    vec3 normal = texture(normalMap, fs_in.TexCoords).rgb;
    normal = normalize(normal * 2.0 - 1.0);

    vec3 lightDir = fs_in.TBN * normalize(lightPos - fs_in.FragPos);
    vec3 viewDir  = fs_in.TBN * normalize(viewPos - fs_in.FragPos);
    [...]
}
```

The second approach looks like more work and also requires matrix multiplications in the fragment shader, so why would we bother with the second approach?

Well, transforming vectors from world to tangent space has an added advantage in that we can transform all the relevant lighting vectors to tangent space in the vertex shader instead of in the fragment shader. This works, because `lightPos` and `viewPos` don't update every fragment run, and for `fs_in.FragPos` we can calculate its tangent-space position in the vertex shader and let fragment interpolation do its work. There is effectively no need to transform a vector to tangent space in the fragment shader, while it is necessary with the first approach as sampled normal vectors are specific to each fragment shader run.

So instead of sending the inverse of the TBN matrix to the fragment shader, we send a tangent-space light position, view position, and vertex position to the fragment shader. This saves us from having to do matrix multiplications in the fragment shader. This is a nice optimization as the vertex shader runs considerably less often than the fragment shader. This is also the reason why this approach is often the preferred approach.

```
out VS_OUT {
    vec3 FragPos;
    vec2 TexCoords;
    vec3 TangentLightPos;
    vec3 TangentViewPos;
    vec3 TangentFragPos;
} vs_out;

uniform vec3 lightPos;
uniform vec3 viewPos;

[...]

void main()
{
    [...]
    mat3 TBN = transpose(mat3(T, B, N));
    vs_out.TangentLightPos = TBN * lightPos;
    vs_out.TangentViewPos  = TBN * viewPos;
    vs_out.TangentFragPos  = TBN * vec3(model * vec4(aPos, 0.0));
}
```

In the fragment shader we then use these new input variables to calculate lighting in tangent space. As the normal vector is already in tangent space, the lighting makes sense.

With normal mapping applied in tangent space, we should get similar results to what we had at the start of this chapter. This time however, we can orient our plane in any way we'd like and the lighting would still be correct:

```cpp
glm::mat4 model = glm::mat4(1.0f);
model = glm::rotate(model, (float)glfwGetTime() * -10.0f,
                    glm::normalize(glm::vec3(1.0, 0.0, 1.0)));
shader.setMat4("model", model);
RenderQuad();
```

Which indeed looks like proper normal mapping:

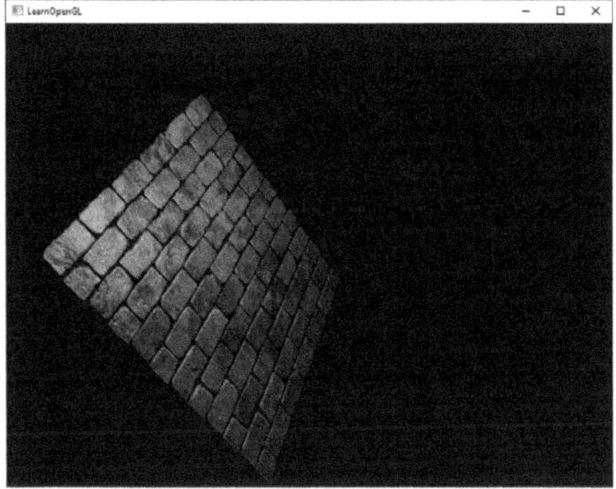

You can find the source code at `/src/5.advanced_lighting/4.normal_mapping/`.

37.3 Complex objects

We've demonstrated how we can use normal mapping, together with tangent space transformations, by manually calculating the tangent and bitangent vectors. Luckily for us, having to manually calculate these tangent and bitangent vectors is not something we do too often. Most of the time you implement it once in a custom model loader, or in our case with a model loader using Assimp.

Assimp has a very useful configuration bit we can set when loading a model called `aiProcess_CalcTangentSpace`. When the `aiProcess_CalcTangentSpace` bit is supplied to Assimp's `ReadFile` function, Assimp calculates smooth tangent and bitangent vectors for each of the loaded vertices, similarly to how we did it in this chapter.

```cpp
const aiScene *scene = importer.ReadFile(
    path, aiProcess_Triangulate | aiProcess_FlipUVs |
    aiProcess_CalcTangentSpace
);
```

Within Assimp we can then retrieve the calculated tangents via:

```
vector.x = mesh->mTangents[i].x;
vector.y = mesh->mTangents[i].y;
vector.z = mesh->mTangents[i].z;
vertex.Tangent = vector;
```

Then you'll have to update the model loader to also load normal maps from a textured model. The wavefront object format (.obj) exports normal maps slightly different from Assimp's conventions as `aiTextureType_NORMAL` doesn't load normal maps, while `aiTextureType_HEIGHT` does:

```
vector<Texture> normalMaps = loadMaterialTextures(material,
                            aiTextureType_HEIGHT, "texture_normal");
```

Of course, this is different for each type of loaded model and file format.

Running the application on a model with specular and normal maps, using an updated model loader, gives the following result:

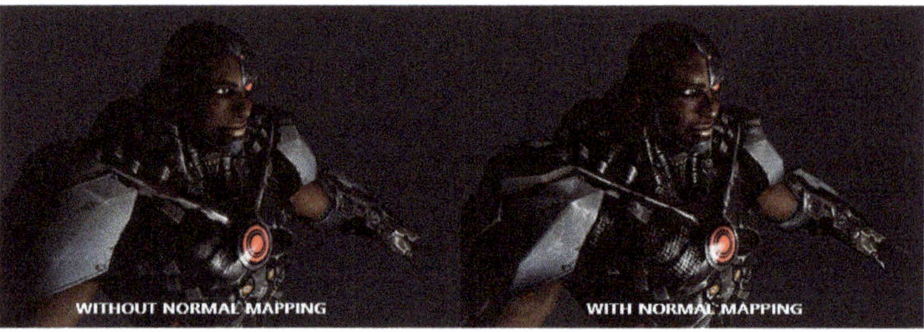

As you can see, normal mapping boosts the detail of an object by an incredible amount without too much extra cost.

Using normal maps is also a great way to boost performance. Before normal mapping, you had to use a large number of vertices to get a high number of detail on a mesh. With normal mapping, we can get the same level of detail on a mesh using a lot less vertices. The image below from Paolo Cignoni shows a nice comparison of both methods:

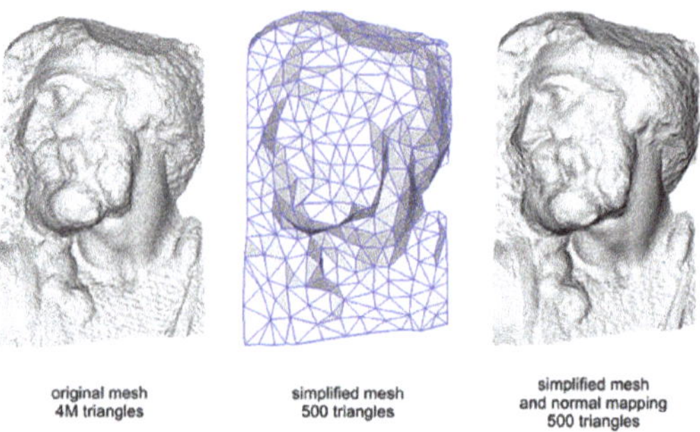

The details on both the high-vertex mesh and the low-vertex mesh with normal mapping are almost indistinguishable. So normal mapping doesn't only look nice, it's a great tool to replace high-vertex meshes with low-vertex meshes without losing (too much) detail.

37.4 **One last thing**

There is one last trick left to discuss that slightly improves quality without too much extra cost.

When tangent vectors are calculated on larger meshes that share a considerable amount of vertices, the tangent vectors are generally averaged to give nice and smooth results. A problem with this approach is that the three TBN vectors could end up non-perpendicular, which means the resulting TBN matrix would no longer be orthogonal. Normal mapping would only be slightly off with a non-orthogonal TBN matrix, but it's still something we can improve.

Using a mathematical trick called the Gram-Schmidt process, we can re-orthogonalize the TBN vectors such that each vector is again perpendicular to the other vectors. Within the vertex shader we would do it like this:

```glsl
vec3 T = normalize(vec3(model * vec4(aTangent, 0.0)));
vec3 N = normalize(vec3(model * vec4(aNormal, 0.0)));
// re-orthogonalize T with respect to N
T = normalize(T - dot(T, N) * N);
// then retrieve perpendicular vector B with the cross product of T and N
vec3 B = cross(N, T);

mat3 TBN = mat3(T, B, N)
```

This, albeit by a little, generally improves the normal mapping results with a little extra cost. Take a look at the end of the *Normal Mapping Mathematics* video in the additional resources for a great explanation of how this process actually works.

37.5 **Additional resources**

- `ogldev.atspace.co.uk/www/tutorial26/tutorial26.html`: normal mapping tutorial by ogldev.
- `www.youtube.com/watch?v=LIOPYmknj5Q`: a nice video tutorial of how normal mapping works by TheBennyBox.
- `www.youtube.com/watch?v=4FaWLgsctqY`: a similar video by TheBennyBox about the mathematics behind normal mapping.
- `www.opengl-tutorial.org/intermediate-tutorials/tutorial-13-normal-mapping/`: normal mapping tutorial by opengl-tutorial.org.

38. Parallax Mapping

Parallax mapping is a technique similar to normal mapping, but based on different principles. Just like normal mapping it is a technique that significantly boosts a textured surface's detail and gives it a sense of depth. While also an illusion, parallax mapping is a lot better in conveying a sense of depth and together with normal mapping gives incredibly realistic results. While parallax mapping isn't necessarily a technique directly related to (advanced) lighting, I'll still discuss it here as the technique is a logical follow-up of normal mapping. Note that getting an understanding of normal mapping, specifically tangent space, is strongly advised before learning parallax mapping.

Parallax mapping is closely related to the family of displacement mapping techniques that *displace* or *offset* vertices based on geometrical information stored inside a texture. One way to do this, is to take a plane with roughly 1000 vertices and displace each of these vertices based on a value in a texture that tells us the height of the plane at that specific area. Such a texture that contains height values per texel is called a height map. An example height map derived from the geometric properties of a simple brick surface looks a bit like this:

When spanned over a plane, each vertex is displaced based on the sampled height value in the height map, transforming a flat plane to a rough bumpy surface based on a material's geometric properties. For instance, taking a flat plane displaced with the above heightmap results in the following image:

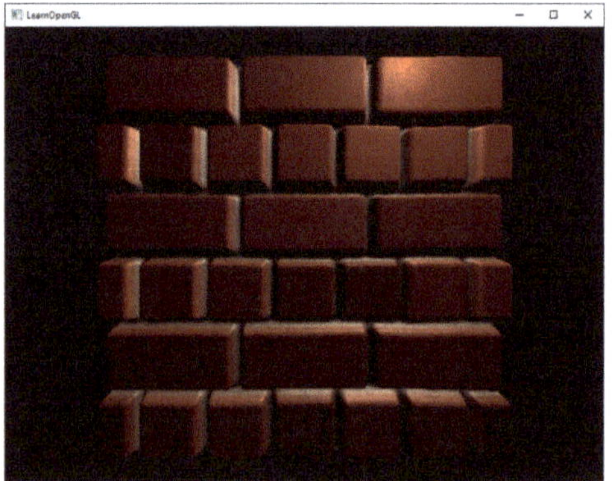

A problem with displacing vertices this way is that a plane needs to contain a huge amount of triangles to get a realistic displacement, otherwise the displacement looks too blocky. As each flat surface may then require over 10000 vertices this quickly becomes computationally infeasible. What if we could somehow achieve similar realism without the need of extra vertices? In fact, what if I were to tell you that the previously shown displaced surface is actually rendered with only 2 triangles. This brick surface shown is rendered with parallax mapping, a displacement mapping technique that doesn't require extra vertex data to convey depth, but (similar to normal mapping) uses a clever technique to trick the user.

The idea behind parallax mapping is to alter the texture coordinates in such a way that it looks like a fragment's surface is higher or lower than it actually is, all based on the view direction and a heightmap. To understand how it works, take a look at the following image of our brick surface:

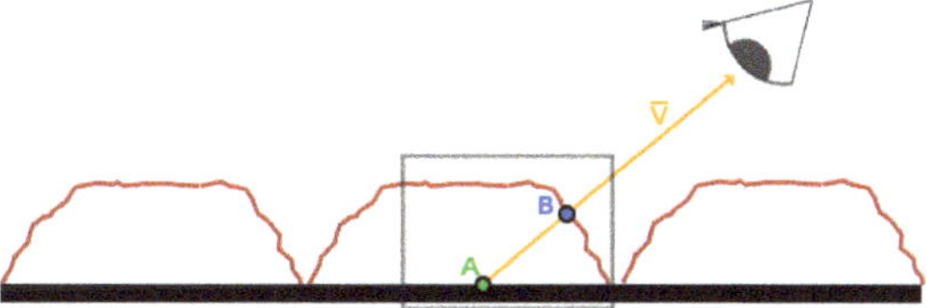

Here the rough red line represents the values in the heightmap as the geometric surface representation of the brick surface and the vector $\bar{V}$ represents the surface to view direction (`viewDir`). If the plane would have actual displacement, the viewer would see the surface at point B. However, as our plane has no actual displacement the view direction is calculated from point A as we'd expect. Parallax mapping aims to offset the texture coordinates at fragment position A in such a way that we get texture coordinates at point B. We then use the texture coordinates at point B for all subsequent texture samples, making it look like the viewer is actually looking at point B.

The trick is to figure out how to get the texture coordinates at point B from point A. Parallax mapping tries to solve this by scaling the fragment-to-view direction vector $\bar{V}$ by the height at fragment A. So we're scaling the length of $\bar{V}$ to be equal to a sampled value from the heightmap $H(A)$ at fragment position A. The image below shows this scaled vector $\bar{P}$:

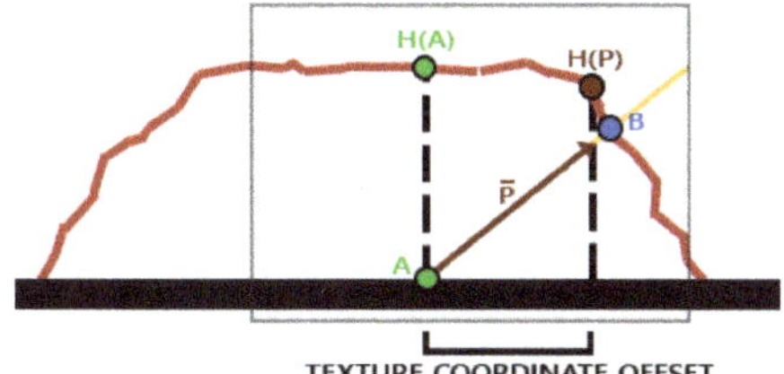

We then take this vector $\bar{P}$ and take its vector coordinates that align with the plane as the texture coordinate offset. This works because vector $\bar{P}$ is calculated using a height value from the heightmap. So the higher a fragment's height, the more it effectively gets displaced.

This little trick gives good results most of the time, but it is still a really crude approximation to get to point B. When heights change rapidly over a surface the results tend to look unrealistic as the vector $\bar{P}$ will not end up close to B as you can see below:

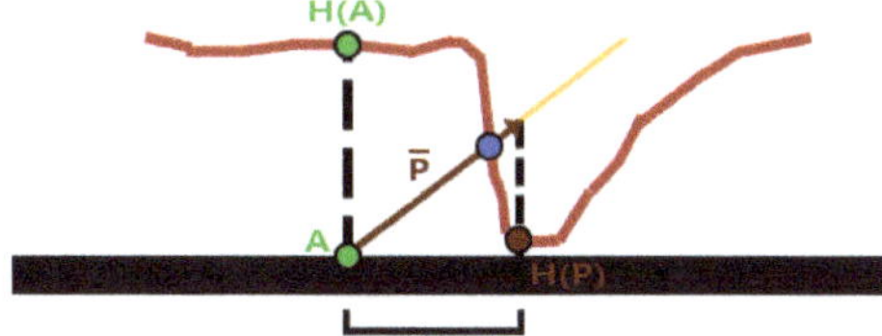

Another issue with parallax mapping is that it's difficult to figure out which coordinates to retrieve from $\bar{P}$ when the surface is arbitrarily rotated in some way. We'd rather do this in a different coordinate space where the x and y component of vector $\bar{P}$ always align with the texture's surface. If you've followed along in the previous chapter you probably guessed how we can accomplish this.

And yes, we would like to do parallax mapping in tangent space.

By transforming the fragment-to-view direction vector $\bar{V}$ to tangent space, the transformed $\bar{P}$ vector will have its x and y component aligned to the surface's tangent and bitangent vectors. As the tangent and bitangent vectors are pointing in the same direction as the surface's texture coordinates we can take the x and y components of $\bar{P}$ as the texture coordinate offset, regardless of the surface's orientation.

But enough about the theory, let's get our feet wet and start implementing actual parallax mapping.

38.1 Parallax mapping

For parallax mapping we're going to use a simple 2D plane for which we calculated its tangent and bitangent vectors before sending it to the GPU; similar to what we did in the normal mapping chapter. Onto the plane we're going to attach a diffuse texture[1], a normal map[2], and a displacement map[3] that you can download from their urls. For this example we're going to use parallax mapping in conjunction with normal mapping. Because parallax mapping gives the illusion of displacing a surface, the illusion breaks when the lighting doesn't match. As normal maps are often generated from heightmaps, using a normal map together with the heightmap makes sure the lighting is in place with the displacement.

You may have already noted that the displacement map linked above is the inverse of the heightmap shown at the start of this chapter. With parallax mapping it makes more sense to use the inverse of the heightmap as it's easier to fake depth than height on flat surfaces. This slightly changes how we perceive parallax mapping as shown below:

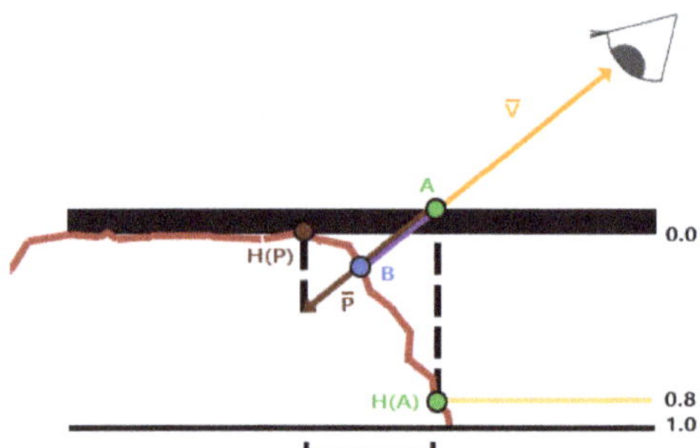

We again have a points A and B, but this time we obtain vector $\bar{P}$ by **subtracting** vector $\bar{V}$ from the texture coordinates at point A. We can obtain depth values instead of height values by subtracting the sampled heightmap values from 1.0 in the shaders, or by simply inversing its texture values in image-editing software as we did with the depthmap linked above.

Parallax mapping is implemented in the fragment shader as the displacement effect is different all over a triangle's surface. In the fragment shader we're then going to need to calculate the fragment-to-view direction vector $\bar{V}$ so we need the view position and a fragment position in tangent space. In the normal mapping chapter we already had a vertex shader that sends these vectors in tangent space so we can take an exact copy of that chapter's vertex shader:

[1]learnopengl.com/img/textures/bricks2.jpg
[2]learnopengl.com/img/textures/bricks2_normal.jpg
[3]learnopengl.com/img/textures/bricks2_disp.jpg

```glsl
#version 330 core
layout (location = 0) in vec3 aPos;
layout (location = 1) in vec3 aNormal;
layout (location = 2) in vec2 aTexCoords;
layout (location = 3) in vec3 aTangent;
layout (location = 4) in vec3 aBitangent;

out VS_OUT {
    vec3 FragPos;
    vec2 TexCoords;
    vec3 TangentLightPos;
    vec3 TangentViewPos;
    vec3 TangentFragPos;
} vs_out;

uniform mat4 projection;
uniform mat4 view;
uniform mat4 model;

uniform vec3 lightPos;
uniform vec3 viewPos;

void main()
{
    gl_Position     = projection * view * model * vec4(aPos, 1.0);
    vs_out.FragPos = vec3(model * vec4(aPos, 1.0));
    vs_out.TexCoords = aTexCoords;

    vec3 T = normalize(mat3(model) * aTangent);
    vec3 B = normalize(mat3(model) * aBitangent);
    vec3 N = normalize(mat3(model) * aNormal);
    mat3 TBN = transpose(mat3(T, B, N));

    vs_out.TangentLightPos = TBN * lightPos;
    vs_out.TangentViewPos  = TBN * viewPos;
    vs_out.TangentFragPos  = TBN * vs_out.FragPos;
}
```

Within the fragment shader we then implement the parallax mapping logic. The fragment shader looks a bit like this:

```glsl
#version 330 core
out vec4 FragColor;

in VS_OUT {
    vec3 FragPos;
    vec2 TexCoords;
    vec3 TangentLightPos;
    vec3 TangentViewPos;
    vec3 TangentFragPos;
} fs_in;

uniform sampler2D diffuseMap;
uniform sampler2D normalMap;
uniform sampler2D depthMap;

uniform float height_scale;

vec2 ParallaxMapping(vec2 texCoords, vec3 viewDir);
```

```glsl
void main()
{
    // offset texture coordinates with Parallax Mapping
    vec3 viewDir = normalize(fs_in.TangentViewPos - fs_in.TangentFragPos);
    vec2 texCoords = ParallaxMapping(fs_in.TexCoords, viewDir);

    // then sample textures with new texture coords
    vec3 diffuse = texture(diffuseMap, texCoords);
    vec3 normal = texture(normalMap, texCoords);
    normal = normalize(normal * 2.0 - 1.0);
    // proceed with lighting code
    [...]
}
```

We defined a function called `ParallaxMapping` that takes as input the fragment's texture coordinates and the fragment-to-view direction $\bar{V}$ in tangent space. The function returns the displaced texture coordinates. We then use these *displaced* texture coordinates as the texture coordinates for sampling the diffuse and normal map. As a result, the fragment's diffuse and normal vector correctly corresponds to the surface's displaced geometry.

Let's take a look inside the `ParallaxMapping` function:

```glsl
vec2 ParallaxMapping(vec2 texCoords, vec3 viewDir)
{
    float height = texture(depthMap, texCoords).r;
    vec2 p = viewDir.xy / viewDir.z * (height * height_scale);
    return texCoords - p;
}
```

This relatively simple function is a direct translation of what we've discussed so far. We take the original texture coordinates `texCoords` and use these to sample the height (or depth) from the `depthMap` at the current fragment A as $H(A)$. We then calculate $\bar{P}$ as the x and y component of the tangent-space `viewDir` vector divided by its z component and scaled by $H(A)$. We also introduced a `height_scale` uniform for some extra control as the parallax effect is usually too strong without an extra scale parameter. We then subtract this vector $\bar{P}$ from the texture coordinates to get the final displaced texture coordinates.

What is interesting to note here is the division of `viewDir.xy` by `viewDir.z`. As the `viewDir` vector is normalized, `viewDir.z` will be somewhere in the range between `0.0` and `1.0`. When `viewDir` is largely parallel to the surface, its z component is close to `0.0` and the division returns a much larger vector $\bar{P}$ compared to when `viewDir` is largely perpendicular to the surface. We're adjusting the size of $\bar{P}$ in such a way that it offsets the texture coordinates at a larger scale when looking at a surface from an angle compared to when looking at it from the top; this gives more realistic results at angles. Some prefer to leave the division by `viewDir.z` out of the equation as default Parallax Mapping could produce undesirable results at angles; the technique is then called Parallax Mapping with Offset Limiting. Choosing which technique to pick is usually a matter of personal preference.

The resulting texture coordinates are then used to sample the other textures (diffuse and normal) and this gives a very neat displaced effect as you can see below with a `height_scale` of roughly `0.1`:

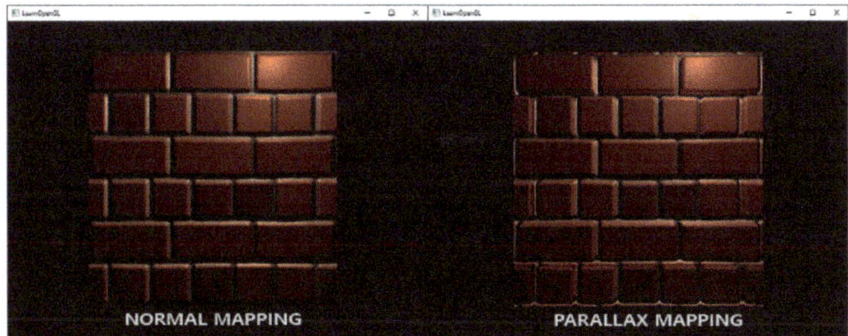

Here you can see the difference between normal mapping and parallax mapping combined with normal mapping. Because parallax mapping tries to simulate depth it is actually possible to have bricks overlap other bricks based on the direction you view them.

You can still see a few weird border artifacts at the edge of the parallax mapped plane. This happens because at the edges of the plane the displaced texture coordinates can oversample outside the range [0, 1]. This gives unrealistic results based on the texture's wrapping mode(s). A cool trick to solve this issue is to discard the fragment whenever it samples outside the default texture coordinate range:

```
texCoords = ParallaxMapping(fs_in.TexCoords, viewDir);
if(texCoords.x > 1.0 || texCoords.y > 1.0 || texCoords.x < 0.0 ||
   texCoords.y < 0.0)
     discard;
```

All fragments with (displaced) texture coordinates outside the default range are discarded and Parallax Mapping then gives proper result around the edges of a surface. Note that this trick doesn't work on all types of surfaces, but when applied to a plane it gives great results:

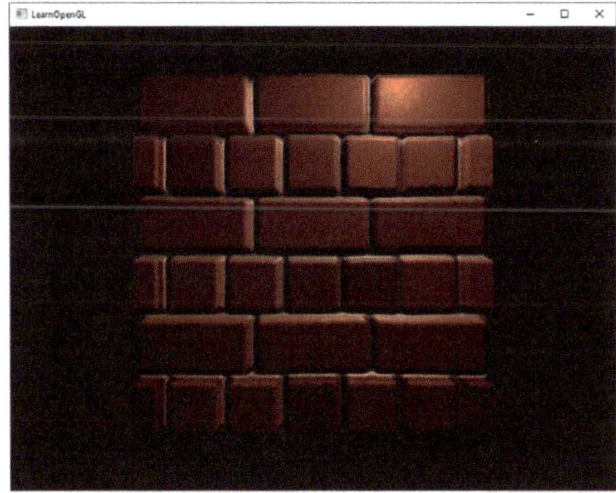

You can find the source code at `/src/5.advanced_lighting/5.1.parallax_mappi ng/`.

It looks great and is quite fast as well as we only need a single extra texture sample for parallax mapping to work. It does come with a few issues though as it sort of breaks down when looking at it from an angle (similar to normal mapping) and gives incorrect results with steep height changes, as you can see below:

The reason that it doesn't work properly at times is that it's just a crude approximation of displacement mapping. There are some extra tricks however that still allows us to get almost perfect results with steep height changes, even when looking at an angle. For instance, what if we instead of one sample take multiple samples to find the closest point to B?

38.2 Steep Parallax Mapping

Steep Parallax Mapping is an extension on top of Parallax Mapping in that it uses the same principles, but instead of 1 sample it takes multiple samples to better pinpoint vector $\bar{P}$ to B. This gives much better results, even with steep height changes, as the accuracy of the technique is improved by the number of samples.

The general idea of Steep Parallax Mapping is that it divides the total depth range into multiple layers of the same height/depth. For each of these layers we sample the depthmap, shifting the texture coordinates along the direction of $\bar{P}$, until we find a sampled depth value that is less than the depth value of the current layer. Take a look at the following image:

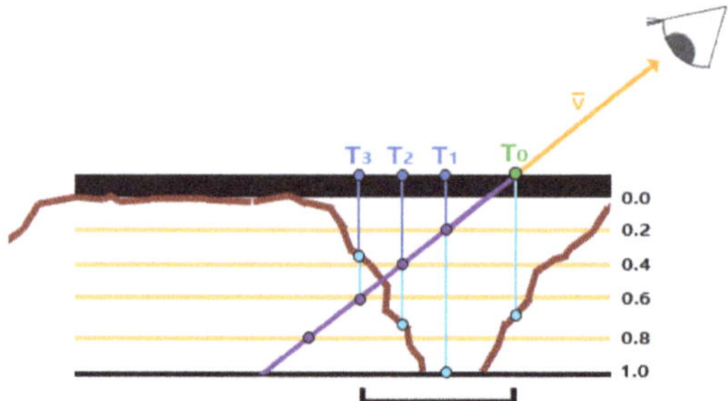

We traverse the depth layers from the top down and for each layer we compare its depth value to the depth value stored in the depthmap. If the layer's depth value is less than the depthmap's value it means this layer's part of vector $\bar{P}$ is not below the surface. We continue this process until the layer's depth is higher than the value stored in the depthmap: this point is then below the (displaced) geometric surface.

In this example we can see that the depthmap value at the second layer (D(2) = 0.73) is lower than the second layer's depth value `0.4` so we continue. In the next iteration, the layer's depth value `0.6` is higher than the depthmap's sampled depth value (D(3) = 0.37). We can thus assume vector $\bar{P}$ at the third layer to be the most viable position of the displaced geometry. We then take the texture coordinate offset T_3 from vector $\bar{P}_3$ to displace the fragment's texture coordinates. You can see how the accuracy increases with more depth layers.

To implement this technique we only have to change the `ParallaxMapping` function as we already have all the variables we need:

```glsl
vec2 ParallaxMapping(vec2 texCoords, vec3 viewDir)
{
    // number of depth layers
    const float numLayers = 10;
    // calculate the size of each layer
    float layerDepth = 1.0 / numLayers;
    // depth of current layer
    float currentLayerDepth = 0.0;
    // amount to shift the texture coordinates per layer (from vector P)
    vec2 P = viewDir.xy * height_scale;
    vec2 deltaTexCoords = P / numLayers;

    [...]
}
```

Here we first set things up: we specify the number of layers, calculate the depth offset of each layer, and finally calculate the texture coordinate offset that we have to shift along the direction of $\bar{P}$ per layer.

We then iterate through all the layers, starting from the top, until we find a depthmap value less than the layer's depth value:

```glsl
// get initial values
vec2 currentTexCoords     = texCoords;
float currentDepthMapValue = texture(depthMap, currentTexCoords).r;

while(currentLayerDepth < currentDepthMapValue)
{
    // shift texture coordinates along direction of P
    currentTexCoords -= deltaTexCoords;
    // get depthmap value at current texture coordinates
    currentDepthMapValue = texture(depthMap, currentTexCoords).r;
    // get depth of next layer
    currentLayerDepth += layerDepth;
}

return currentTexCoords;
```

Here we loop over each depth layer and stop until we find the texture coordinate offset along vector $\bar{P}$ that first returns a depth that's below the (displaced) surface. The resulting offset is subtracted from the fragment's texture coordinates to get a final displaced texture coordinate vector, this time with much more accuracy compared to traditional parallax mapping.

With around 10 samples the brick surface already looks more viable even when looking at it from an angle, but steep parallax mapping really shines when having a complex surface with steep height changes; like the earlier displayed wooden toy surface:

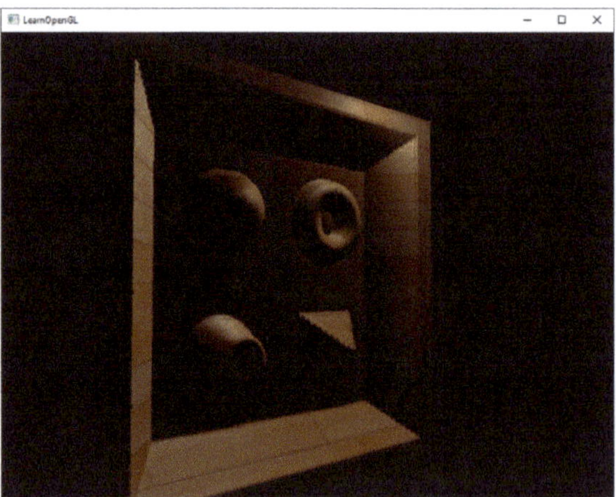

We can improve the algorithm a bit by exploiting one of Parallax Mapping's properties. When looking straight onto a surface there isn't much texture displacement going on while there is a lot of displacement when looking at a surface from an angle (visualize the view direction on both cases). By taking less samples when looking straight at a surface and more samples when looking at an angle we only sample the necessary amount:

```glsl
const float minLayers = 8.0;
const float maxLayers = 32.0;
float numLayers = mix(maxLayers, minLayers, max(dot(vec3(0.0, 0.0, 1.0),
                                                viewDir), 0.0));
```

Here we take the dot product of `viewDir` and the positive z direction and use its result to align the number of samples to `minLayers` or `maxLayers` based on the angle we're looking towards a surface (note that the positive z direction equals the surface's normal vector in tangent space). If we were to look at a direction parallel to the surface we'd use a total of 32 layers.

You can find the updated source code at `/src/5.advanced_lighting/5.2.steep_parallax_mapping/`. You can also find the wooden toy box surface textures here: diffuse[1], normal[2], and displacement[3].

Steep Parallax Mapping also comes with its problems though. Because the technique is based on a finite number of samples, we get aliasing effects and the clear distinctions between layers can easily be spotted:

---

[1]learnopengl.com/img/textures/wood.png
[2]learnopengl.com/img/textures/toy_box_normal.png
[3]learnopengl.com/img/textures/toy_box_disp.png

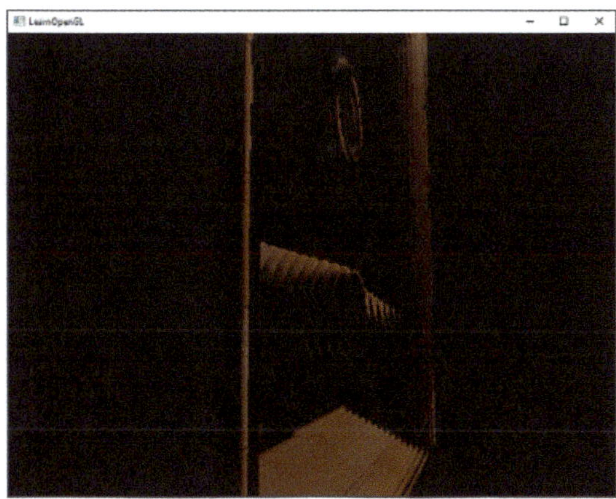

We can reduce the issue by taking a larger number of samples, but this quickly becomes too heavy a burden on performance. There are several approaches that aim to fix this issue by not taking the first position that's below the (displaced) surface, but by *interpolating* between the position's two closest depth layers to find a much closer match to B.

Two of the more popular of these approaches are called Relief Parallax Mapping and Parallax Occlusion Mapping of which Relief Parallax Mapping gives the most accurate results, but is also more performance heavy compared to Parallax Occlusion Mapping. Because Parallax Occlusion Mapping gives almost the same results as Relief Parallax Mapping and is also more efficient it is often the preferred approach.

38.3 Parallax Occlusion Mapping

Parallax Occlusion Mapping is based on the same principles as Steep Parallax Mapping, but instead of taking the texture coordinates of the first depth layer after a collision, we're going to linearly interpolate between the depth layer after and before the collision. We base the weight of the linear interpolation on how far the surface's height is from the depth layer's value of both layers. Take a look at the following picture to get a grasp of how it works:

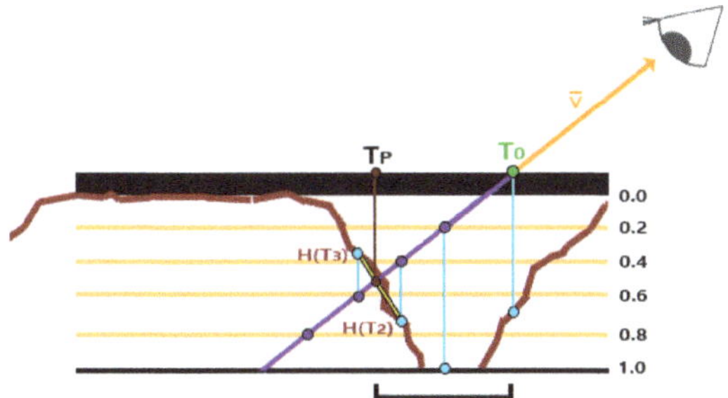

As you can see, it's largely similar to Steep Parallax Mapping with as an extra step the linear interpolation between the two depth layers' texture coordinates surrounding the intersected point. This is again an approximation, but significantly more accurate than Steep Parallax Mapping.

The code for Parallax Occlusion Mapping is an extension on top of Steep Parallax Mapping and not too difficult:

```glsl
[...] // steep parallax mapping code here

// get texture coordinates before collision (reverse operations)
vec2 prevTexCoords = currentTexCoords + deltaTexCoords;

// get depth after and before collision for linear interpolation
float afterDepth  = currentDepthMapValue - currentLayerDepth;
float beforeDepth = texture(depthMap, prevTexCoords).r - currentLayerDepth
    + layerDepth;

// interpolation of texture coordinates
float weight = afterDepth / (afterDepth - beforeDepth);
vec2 finalTexCoords = prevTexCoords * weight + currentTexCoords * (1.0 -
    weight);

return finalTexCoords;
```

After we found the depth layer after intersecting the (displaced) surface geometry, we also retrieve the texture coordinates of the depth layer before intersection. Then we calculate the distance of the (displaced) geometry's depth from the corresponding depth layers and interpolate between these two values. The linear interpolation is a basic interpolation between both layer's texture coordinates. The function then finally returns the final interpolated texture coordinates.

Parallax Occlusion Mapping gives surprisingly good results and although some slight artifacts and aliasing issues are still visible, it's a generally a good trade-off and only really visible when heavily zoomed in or looking at very steep angles.

You can find the source code at `/src/5.advanced_lighting/5.3.parallax_occlu sion_mapping/`.

Parallax Mapping is a great technique to boost the detail of your scene, but does come with a few artifacts you'll have to consider when using it. Most often, parallax mapping is used on floor or wall-like surfaces where it's not as easy to determine the surface's outline and the viewing angle is most often roughly perpendicular to the surface. This way, the artifacts of Parallax Mapping aren't as noticeable and make it an incredibly interesting technique for boosting your objects' details.

38.4 Additional resources

- `sunandblackcat.com/tipFullView.php?topicid=28`: great parallax mapping tutorial by sunandblackcat.com.
- `www.youtube.com/watch?v=xvOT62L-fQI`: a nice video tutorial of how parallax mapping works by TheBennyBox.

39. HDR

Brightness and color values, by default, are clamped between `0.0` and `1.0` when stored into a framebuffer. This, at first seemingly innocent, statement caused us to always specify light and color values somewhere in this range, trying to make them fit into the scene. This works oké and gives decent results, but what happens if we walk in a really bright area with multiple bright light sources that as a total sum exceed `1.0`? The answer is that all fragments that have a brightness or color sum over `1.0` get clamped to `1.0`, which isn't pretty to look at:

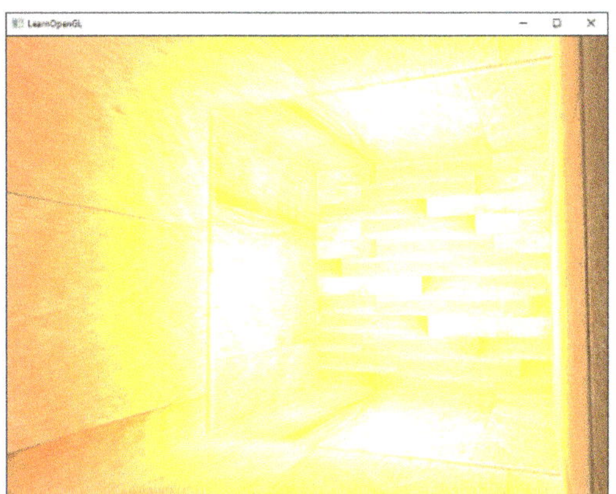

Due to a large number of fragments' color values getting clamped to `1.0`, each of the bright fragments have the exact same white color value in large regions, losing a significant amount of detail and giving it a fake look.

A solution to this problem would be to reduce the strength of the light sources and ensure no area of fragments in your scene ends up brighter than `1.0`; this is not a good solution as this forces you to use unrealistic lighting parameters. A better approach is to allow color values to temporarily exceed `1.0` and transform them back to the original range of `0.0` and `1.0` as a final step, but without losing detail.

Monitors (non-HDR) are limited to display colors in the range of `0.0` and `1.0`, but there is no such limitation in lighting equations. By allowing fragment colors to exceed `1.0` we have a much higher range of color values available to work in known as high dynamic range (HDR). With high dynamic range, bright things can be really bright, dark things can be really dark, and details can be seen in both.

High dynamic range was originally only used for photography where a photographer takes multiple pictures of the same scene with varying exposure levels, capturing a large range of color values. Combining these forms a HDR image where a large range of details are visible based on the combined exposure levels, or a specific exposure it is viewed with. For instance, the following image (credits to Colin Smith) shows a lot of detail at brightly lit regions with a low exposure (look at the window), but these details are gone with a high exposure. However, a high exposure now reveals a great amount of detail at darker regions that weren't previously visible.

This is also very similar to how the human eye works and the basis of high dynamic range rendering. When there is little light, the human eye adapts itself so the darker parts become more visible and similarly for bright areas. It's like the human eye has an automatic exposure slider based on the scene's brightness.

High dynamic range rendering works a bit like that. We allow for a much larger range of color values to render to, collecting a large range of dark and bright details of a scene, and at the end we transform all the HDR values back to the low dynamic range (LDR) of [0.0, 1.0]. This process of converting HDR values to LDR values is called tone mapping and a large collection of tone mapping algorithms exist that aim to preserve most HDR details during the conversion process. These tone mapping algorithms often involve an exposure parameter that selectively favors dark or bright regions.

When it comes to real-time rendering, high dynamic range allows us to not only exceed the LDR range of [0.0, 1.0] and preserve more detail, but also gives us the ability to specify a light source's intensity by their *real* intensities. For instance, the sun has a much higher intensity than something like a flashlight so why not configure the sun as such (e.g. a diffuse brightness of 100.0). This allows us to more properly configure a scene's lighting with more realistic lighting parameters, something that wouldn't be possible with LDR rendering as they'd then directly get clamped to 1.0.

As (non-HDR) monitors only display colors in the range between 0.0 and 1.0 we do need to transform the currently high dynamic range of color values back to the monitor's range. Simply re-transforming the colors back with a simple average wouldn't do us much good as brighter areas then become a lot more dominant. What we can do, is use different equations and/or curves to transform the HDR values back to LDR that give us complete control over the scene's brightness. This is the process earlier denoted as tone mapping and the final step of HDR rendering.

39.1 Floating point framebuffers

To implement high dynamic range rendering we need some way to prevent color values getting clamped after each fragment shader run. When framebuffers use a normalized fixed-point color format (like `GL_RGB`) as their color buffer's internal format, OpenGL automatically clamps the values between 0.0 and 1.0 before storing them in the framebuffer. This operation holds for most types of framebuffer formats, except for floating point formats.

When the internal format of a framebuffer's color buffer is specified as `GL_RGB16F`, `GL_RGBA16F`, `GL_RGB32F`, or `GL_RGBA32F` the framebuffer is known as a floating point framebuffer that can store floating point values outside the default range of 0.0 and 1.0. This is perfect for rendering in high dynamic range!

To create a floating point framebuffer the only thing we need to change is its color buffer's internal format parameter:

```cpp
glBindTexture(GL_TEXTURE_2D, colorBuffer);
glTexImage2D(GL_TEXTURE_2D, 0, GL_RGBA16F, SCR_WIDTH, SCR_HEIGHT, 0,
             GL_RGBA, GL_FLOAT, NULL);
```

The default framebuffer of OpenGL (by default) only takes up 8 bits per color component. With a floating point framebuffer with 32 bits per color component (when using `GL_RGB32F` or `GL_RGBA32F`) we're using 4 times more memory for storing color values. As 32 bits isn't really necessary (unless you need a high level of precision) using `GL_RGBA16F` will suffice.

With a floating point color buffer attached to a framebuffer we can now render the scene into this framebuffer knowing color values won't get clamped between 0.0 and 1.0. In this chapter's example demo we first render a lit scene into the floating point framebuffer and then display the framebuffer's color buffer on a screen-filled quad; it'll look a bit like this:

```cpp
glBindFramebuffer(GL_FRAMEBUFFER, hdrFBO);
    glClear(GL_COLOR_BUFFER_BIT | GL_DEPTH_BUFFER_BIT);
    // [...] render (lit) scene
glBindFramebuffer(GL_FRAMEBUFFER, 0);

// now render hdr color buffer to 2D screen-filling quad w/ tone mapping
hdrShader.use();
glActiveTexture(GL_TEXTURE0);
glBindTexture(GL_TEXTURE_2D, hdrColorBufferTexture);
RenderQuad();
```

Here a scene's color values are filled into a floating point color buffer which can contain any arbitrary color value, possibly exceeding 1.0. For this chapter, a simple demo scene was created with a large stretched cube acting as a tunnel with four point lights, one being extremely bright positioned at the tunnel's end:

```cpp
std::vector<glm::vec3> lightColors;
lightColors.push_back(glm::vec3(200.0f, 200.0f, 200.0f));
lightColors.push_back(glm::vec3(0.1f, 0.0f, 0.0f));
lightColors.push_back(glm::vec3(0.0f, 0.0f, 0.2f));
lightColors.push_back(glm::vec3(0.0f, 0.1f, 0.0f));
```

Rendering to a floating point framebuffer is exactly the same as we would normally render into a framebuffer. What is new is `hdrShader`'s fragment shader that renders the final 2D quad with the floating point color buffer texture attached. Let's first define a simple pass-through fragment shader:

```glsl
#version 330 core
out vec4 FragColor;

in vec2 TexCoords;

uniform sampler2D hdrBuffer;

void main()
{
    vec3 hdrColor = texture(hdrBuffer, TexCoords).rgb;
    FragColor = vec4(hdrColor, 1.0);
}
```

Here we directly sample the floating point color buffer and use its color value as the fragment shader's output. However, as the 2D quad's output is directly rendered into the default framebuffer, all the fragment shader's output values will still end up clamped between 0.0 and 1.0 even though we have several values in the floating point color texture exceeding 1.0.

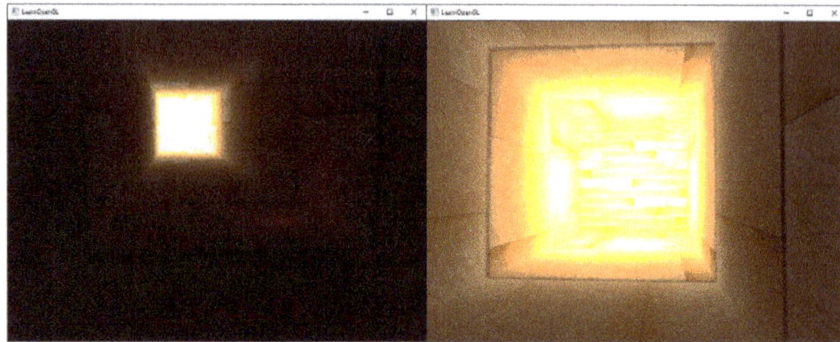

It becomes clear the intense light values at the end of the tunnel are clamped to `1.0` as a large portion of it is completely white, effectively losing all lighting details in the process. As we directly write HDR values to an LDR output buffer it is as if we have no HDR enabled in the first place. What we need to do is transform all the floating point color values into the `0.0 - 1.0` range without losing any of its details. We need to apply a process called tone mapping.

39.2 Tone mapping

Tone mapping is the process of transforming floating point color values to the expected $[0.0, 1.0]$ range known as low dynamic range without losing too much detail, often accompanied with a specific stylistic color balance.

One of the more simple tone mapping algorithms is Reinhard tone mapping that involves dividing the entire HDR color values to LDR color values. The Reinhard tone mapping algorithm evenly balances out all brightness values onto LDR. We include Reinhard tone mapping into the previous fragment shader and also add a gamma correction filter for good measure (including the use of sRGB textures):

```glsl
void main()
{
    const float gamma = 2.2;
    vec3 hdrColor = texture(hdrBuffer, TexCoords).rgb;

    // reinhard tone mapping
    vec3 mapped = hdrColor / (hdrColor + vec3(1.0));
    // gamma correction
    mapped = pow(mapped, vec3(1.0 / gamma));

    FragColor = vec4(mapped, 1.0);
}
```

With Reinhard tone mapping applied we no longer lose any detail at the bright areas of our scene. It does tend to slightly favor brighter areas, making darker regions seem less detailed and distinct:

Here you can again see details at the end of the tunnel as the wood texture pattern becomes visible again. With this relatively simple tone mapping algorithm we can properly see the entire range of HDR values stored in the floating point framebuffer, giving us precise control over the scene's lighting without losing details.

> Note that we could also directly tone map at the end of our lighting shader, not needing any floating point framebuffer at all! However, as scenes get more complex you'll frequently find the need to store intermediate HDR results as floating point buffers so this is a good exercise.

Another interesting use of tone mapping is to allow the use of an exposure parameter. You probably remember from the introduction that HDR images contain a lot of details visible at different exposure levels. If we have a scene that features a day and night cycle it makes sense to use a lower exposure at daylight and a higher exposure at night time, similar to how the human eye adapts. With such an exposure parameter it allows us to configure lighting parameters that work both at day and night under different lighting conditions as we only have to change the exposure parameter.

A relatively simple exposure tone mapping algorithm looks as follows:

```glsl
uniform float exposure;

void main()
{
    const float gamma = 2.2;
    vec3 hdrColor = texture(hdrBuffer, TexCoords).rgb;

    // exposure tone mapping
    vec3 mapped = vec3(1.0) - exp(-hdrColor * exposure);
    // gamma correction
    mapped = pow(mapped, vec3(1.0 / gamma));

    FragColor = vec4(mapped, 1.0);
}
```

Here we defined an `exposure` uniform that defaults at 1.0 and allows us to more precisely specify whether we'd like to focus more on dark or bright regions of the HDR color values. For instance, with high exposure values the darker areas of the tunnel show significantly more detail. In contrast, a low exposure largely removes the dark region details, but allows us to see more detail in the bright areas of a scene. Take a look at the image below to see the tunnel at multiple exposure levels:

This image clearly shows the benefit of high dynamic range rendering. By changing the exposure level we get to see a lot of details of our scene, that would've been otherwise lost with low dynamic range rendering. Take the end of the tunnel for example. With a normal exposure the wood structure is barely visible, but with a low exposure the detailed wooden patterns are clearly visible. The same holds for the wooden patterns close by that are more visible with a high exposure.

You can find the source code of the demo at `/src/5.advanced_lighting/6.hdr/`.

39.2.1 More HDR

The two tone mapping algorithms shown are only a few of a large collection of (more advanced) tone mapping algorithms of which each has their own strengths and weaknesses. Some tone mapping algorithms favor certain colors/intensities above others and some algorithms display both the low and high exposure colors at the same time to create more colorful and detailed images. There is also a collection of techniques known as automatic exposure adjustment or eye adaptation techniques that determine the brightness of the scene in the previous frame and (slowly) adapt the exposure parameter such that the scene gets brighter in dark areas or darker in bright areas mimicking the human eye.

The real benefit of HDR rendering really shows itself in large and complex scenes with heavy lighting algorithms. As it is difficult to create such a complex demo scene for teaching purposes while keeping it accessible, the chapter's demo scene is small and lacks detail. While relatively simple it does show some of the benefits of HDR rendering: no details are lost in high and dark regions as they can be restored with tone mapping, the addition of multiple lights doesn't cause clamped regions, and light values can be specified by real brightness values not being limited by LDR values. Furthermore, HDR rendering also makes several other interesting effects more feasible and realistic; one of these effects is bloom that we'll discuss in the next chapter.

39.3 Additional resources

- `gamedev.stackexchange.com/questions/62836/does-hdr-rendering-have-any-benefits-if-bloom-wont-be-applied`: a stackexchange question that features a great lengthy answer describing some of the benefits of HDR rendering.
- `photo.stackexchange.com/questions/7630/what-is-tone-mapping-how-does-it-relate-to-hdr`: another interesting answer with great reference images to explain tone mapping.

40. Bloom

Bright light sources and brightly lit regions are often difficult to convey to the viewer as the intensity range of a monitor is limited. One way to distinguish bright light sources on a monitor is by making them glow; the light then *bleeds* around the light source. This effectively gives the viewer the illusion these light sources or bright regions are intensely bright.

This light bleeding, or glow effect, is achieved with a post-processing effect called Bloom. Bloom gives all brightly lit regions of a scene a glow-like effect. An example of a scene with and without glow can be seen below (image courtesy of Epic Games):

Bloom gives noticeable visual cues about the brightness of objects. When done in a subtle fashion (which some games drastically fail to do) Bloom significantly boosts the lighting of your scene and allows for a large range of dramatic effects.

Bloom works best in combination with HDR rendering. A common misconception is that HDR is the same as Bloom as many people use the terms interchangeably. They are however completely different techniques used for different purposes. It is possible to implement Bloom with default 8-bit precision framebuffers, just as it is possible to use HDR without the Bloom effect. It is simply that HDR makes Bloom more effective to implement (as we'll later see).

To implement Bloom, we render a lit scene as usual and extract both the scene's HDR color buffer and an image of the scene with only its bright regions visible. This extracted brightness image is then blurred and the result added on top of the original HDR scene image.

Let's illustrate this process in a step by step fashion. We render a scene filled with 4 bright light sources, visualized as colored cubes. The colored light cubes have a brightness values between `1.5` and `15.0`. If we were to render this to an HDR color buffer the scene looks as follows:

We take this HDR color buffer texture and extract all the fragments that exceed a certain brightness. This gives us an image that only show the bright colored regions as their fragment intensities exceeded a certain threshold:

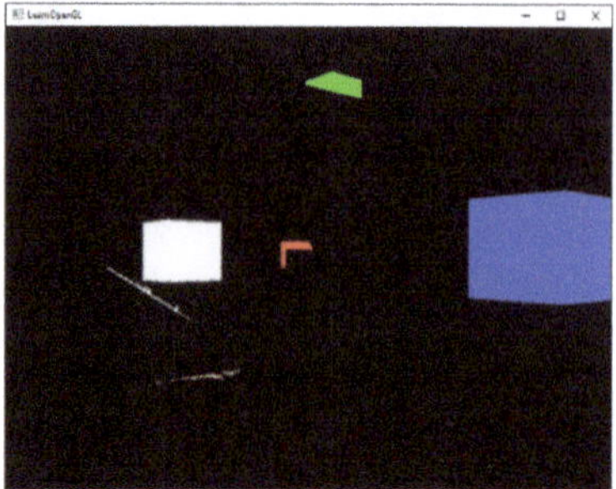

We then take this thresholded brightness texture and blur the result. The strength of the bloom effect is largely determined by the range and strength of the blur filter used.

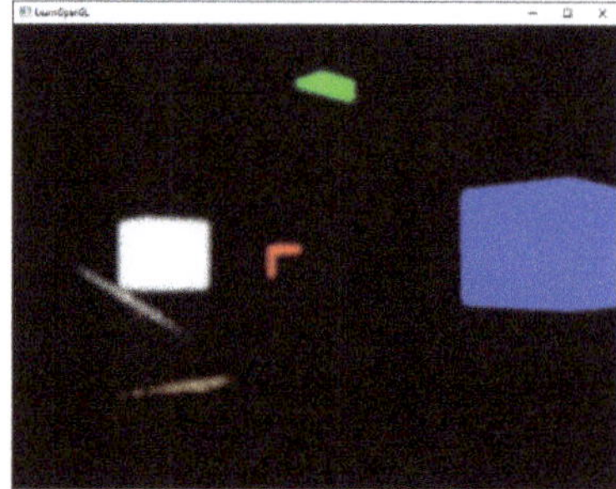

The resulting blurred texture is what we use to get the glow or light-bleeding effect. This blurred texture is added on top of the original HDR scene texture. Because the bright regions are extended in both width and height due to the blur filter, the bright regions of the scene appear to glow or *bleed* light.

Bloom by itself isn't a complicated technique, but difficult to get exactly right. Most of its visual quality is determined by the quality and type of blur filter used for blurring the extracted brightness regions. Simply tweaking the blur filter can drastically change the quality of the Bloom effect.

Following these steps gives us the Bloom post-processing effect. The next image briefly summarizes the required steps for implementing Bloom:

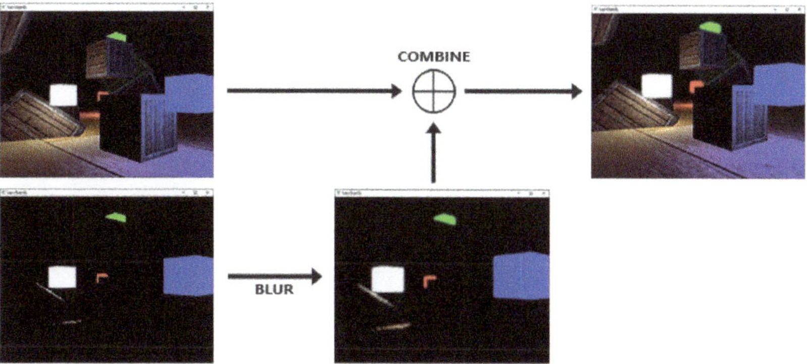

The first step requires us to extract all the bright colors of a scene based on some threshold. Let's first delve into that.

40.1 Extracting bright color

The first step requires us to extract two images from a rendered scene. We could render the scene twice, both rendering to a different framebuffer with different shaders, but we can also use a neat little trick called Multiple Render Targets (MRT) that allows us to specify more than one fragment shader output; this gives us the option to extract the first two images in a single render pass. By specifying a layout location specifier before a fragment shader's output we can control to which color buffer a fragment shader writes to:

```glsl
layout (location = 0) out vec4 FragColor;
layout (location = 1) out vec4 BrightColor;
```

This only works if we actually have multiple buffers to write to. As a requirement for using multiple fragment shader outputs we need multiple color buffers attached to the currently bound framebuffer object. You may remember from the *Framebuffers* chapter that we can specify a color attachment number when linking a texture as a framebuffer's color buffer. Up until now we've always used GL_COLOR_ATTACHMENT0, but by also using GL_COLOR_ATTACHMENT1 we can have two color buffers attached to a framebuffer object:

```cpp
// set up floating point framebuffer to render scene to
unsigned int hdrFBO;
glGenFramebuffers(1, &hdrFBO);
glBindFramebuffer(GL_FRAMEBUFFER, hdrFBO);
unsigned int colorBuffers[2];
glGenTextures(2, colorBuffers);
for (unsigned int i = 0; i < 2; i++)
{
    glBindTexture(GL_TEXTURE_2D, colorBuffers[i]);
    glTexImage2D(GL_TEXTURE_2D, 0, GL_RGBA16F, SCR_WIDTH, SCR_HEIGHT, 0,
                 GL_RGBA, GL_FLOAT, NULL);
    glTexParameteri(GL_TEXTURE_2D, GL_TEXTURE_MIN_FILTER, GL_LINEAR);
    glTexParameteri(GL_TEXTURE_2D, GL_TEXTURE_MAG_FILTER, GL_LINEAR);
    glTexParameteri(GL_TEXTURE_2D, GL_TEXTURE_WRAP_S, GL_CLAMP_TO_EDGE);
    glTexParameteri(GL_TEXTURE_2D, GL_TEXTURE_WRAP_T, GL_CLAMP_TO_EDGE);
    // attach texture to framebuffer
    glFramebufferTexture2D(GL_FRAMEBUFFER, GL_COLOR_ATTACHMENT0 + i,
                           GL_TEXTURE_2D, colorBuffers[i], 0);
}
```

We do have to explicitly tell OpenGL we're rendering to multiple color buffers via `glDrawBuff ers`. OpenGL, by default, only renders to a framebuffer's first color attachment, ignoring all others. We can do this by passing an array of color attachment enums that we'd like to render to in subsequent operations:

```cpp
unsigned int attachments[2] = {GL_COLOR_ATTACHMENT0, GL_COLOR_ATTACHMENT1};
glDrawBuffers(2, attachments);
```

When rendering into this framebuffer, whenever a fragment shader uses the layout location specifier, the respective color buffer is used to render the fragment to. This is great as this saves us an extra render pass for extracting bright regions as we can now directly extract them from the to-be-rendered fragment:

```glsl
#version 330 core
layout (location = 0) out vec4 FragColor;
layout (location = 1) out vec4 BrightColor;

[...]

void main()
{
    [...] // first do normal lighting calculations and output results
    FragColor = vec4(lighting, 1.0);
    // if fragment output is higher than threshold, output brightness color
    float brightness = dot(FragColor.rgb, vec3(0.2126, 0.7152, 0.0722));
    if(brightness > 1.0)
        BrightColor = vec4(FragColor.rgb, 1.0);
    else
        BrightColor = vec4(0.0, 0.0, 0.0, 1.0);
}
```

Here we first calculate lighting as normal and pass it to the first fragment shader's output variable `FragColor`. Then we use what is currently stored in `FragColor` to determine if its brightness exceeds a certain threshold. We calculate the brightness of a fragment by properly transforming it to grayscale first (by taking the dot product of both vectors we effectively multiply each individual component of both vectors and add the results together). If the brightness exceeds a certain threshold, we output the color to the second color buffer. We do the same for the light cubes.

This also shows why Bloom works incredibly well with HDR rendering. Because we render in high dynamic range, color values can exceed `1.0` which allows us to specify a brightness threshold outside the default range, giving us much more control over what is considered bright. Without HDR we'd have to set the threshold lower than `1.0`, which is still possible, but regions are much quicker considered bright. This sometimes leads to the glow effect becoming too dominant (think of white glowing snow for example).

With these two color buffers we have an image of the scene as normal, and an image of the extracted bright regions; all generated in a single render pass.

With an image of the extracted bright regions we now need to blur the image. We can do this with a simple box filter as we've done in the post-processing section of the framebufers chapter, but we'd rather use a more advanced (and better-looking) blur filter called Gaussian blur.

40.2 Gaussian blur

In the post-processing chapter's blur we took the average of all surrounding pixels of an image. While it does give us an easy blur, it doesn't give the best results. A Gaussian blur is based on the Gaussian curve which is commonly described as a *bell-shaped curve* giving high values close to its center that gradually wear off over distance. The Gaussian curve can be mathematically represented in different forms, but generally has the following shape:

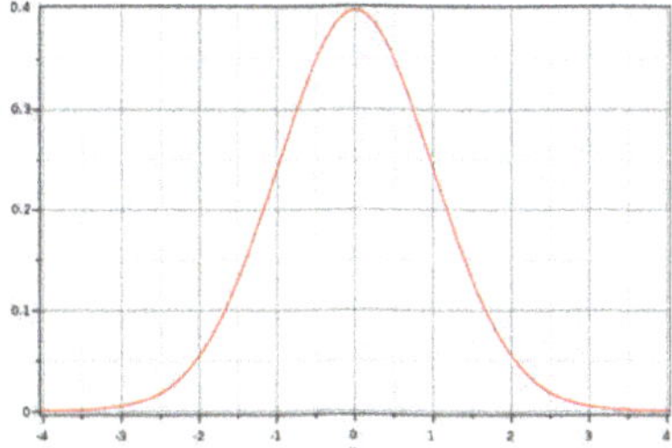

As the Gaussian curve has a larger area close to its center, using its values as weights to blur an image give more natural results as samples close by have a higher precedence. If we for instance sample a 32x32 box around a fragment, we use progressively smaller weights the larger the distance to the fragment; this gives a better and more realistic blur which is known as a Gaussian blur.

To implement a Gaussian blur filter we'd need a two-dimensional box of weights that we can obtain from a 2 dimensional Gaussian curve equation. The problem with this approach however is that it quickly becomes extremely heavy on performance. Take a blur kernel of 32 by 32 for example, this would require us to sample a texture a total of 1024 times for each fragment!

Luckily for us, the Gaussian equation has a very neat property that allows us to separate the two-dimensional equation into two smaller one-dimensional equations: one that describes the horizontal weights and the other that describes the vertical weights. We'd then first do a horizontal blur with the horizontal weights on the scene texture, and then on the resulting texture do a vertical blur. Due to this property the results are exactly the same, but this time saving us an incredible amount of performance as we'd now only have to do 32 + 32 samples compared to 1024! This is known as two-pass Gaussian blur.

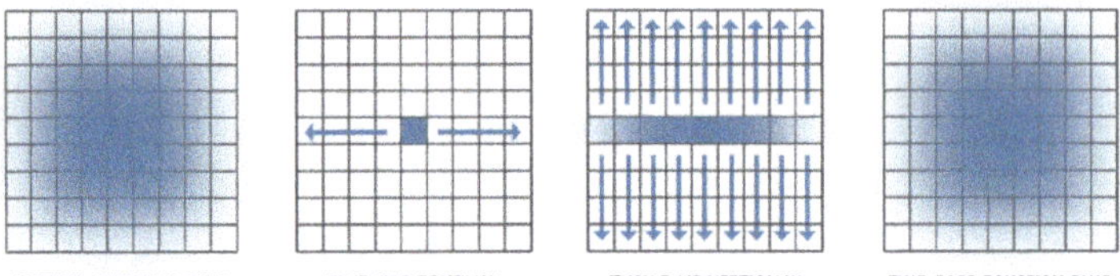

This does mean we need to blur an image at least two times and this works best with the use of framebuffer objects. Specifically for the two-pass Gaussian blur we're going to implement *ping-pong* framebuffers. That is a pair of framebuffers where we render and swap, a given number of times, the other framebuffer's color buffer into the current framebuffer's color buffer with an alternating shader effect. We basically continuously switch the framebuffer to render to and the texture to draw with. This allows us to first blur the scene's texture in the first framebuffer, then blur the first framebuffer's color buffer into the second framebuffer, and then the second framebuffer's color buffer into the first, and so on.

Before we delve into the framebuffers let's first discuss the Gaussian blur's fragment shader:

```glsl
#version 330 core
out vec4 FragColor;

in vec2 TexCoords;

uniform sampler2D image;

uniform bool horizontal;
uniform float weight[5] = float[] (0.227027, 0.1945946, 0.1216216,
                                   0.054054, 0.016216);

void main()
{
    vec2 tex_offset = 1.0 / textureSize(image, 0); // size of single texel
    vec3 result = texture(image, TexCoords).rgb * weight[0]; // this
      fragment
    if(horizontal)
    {
        for(int i = 1; i < 5; ++i)
        {
            result += texture(image, TexCoords +
                    vec2(tex_offset.x * i, 0.0)).rgb * weight[i];
            result += texture(image, TexCoords -
                    vec2(tex_offset.x * i, 0.0)).rgb * weight[i];
        }
    }
    else
    {
        for(int i = 1; i < 5; ++i)
        {
            result += texture(image, TexCoords +
                    vec2(0.0, tex_offset.y * i)).rgb * weight[i];
            result += texture(image, TexCoords -
                    vec2(0.0, tex_offset.y * i)).rgb * weight[i];
        }
    }
    FragColor = vec4(result, 1.0);
}
```

Here we take a relatively small sample of Gaussian weights that we each use to assign a specific weight to the horizontal or vertical samples around the current fragment. You can see that we split the blur filter into a horizontal and vertical section based on whatever value we set the `horizontal` uniform. We base the offset distance on the exact size of a texel obtained by the division of `1.0` over the size of the texture (a `vec2` from `textureSize`).

For blurring an image we create two basic framebuffers, each with only a color buffer texture:

```cpp
unsigned int pingpongFBO[2];
unsigned int pingpongBuffer[2];
glGenFramebuffers(2, pingpongFBO);
glGenTextures(2, pingpongBuffer);
for (unsigned int i = 0; i < 2; i++)
{
    glBindFramebuffer(GL_FRAMEBUFFER, pingpongFBO[i]);
    glBindTexture(GL_TEXTURE_2D, pingpongBuffer[i]);
    glTexImage2D(GL_TEXTURE_2D, 0, GL_RGBA16F, SCR_WIDTH, SCR_HEIGHT, 0,
                 GL_RGBA, GL_FLOAT, NULL);
    glTexParameteri(GL_TEXTURE_2D, GL_TEXTURE_MIN_FILTER, GL_LINEAR);
    glTexParameteri(GL_TEXTURE_2D, GL_TEXTURE_MAG_FILTER, GL_LINEAR);
    glTexParameteri(GL_TEXTURE_2D, GL_TEXTURE_WRAP_S, GL_CLAMP_TO_EDGE);
    glTexParameteri(GL_TEXTURE_2D, GL_TEXTURE_WRAP_T, GL_CLAMP_TO_EDGE);
    glFramebufferTexture2D(GL_FRAMEBUFFER, GL_COLOR_ATTACHMENT0,
                           GL_TEXTURE_2D, pingpongBuffer[i], 0);
}
```

Then after we've obtained an HDR texture and an extracted brightness texture, we first fill one of the ping-pong framebuffers with the brightness texture and then blur the image 10 times (5 times horizontally and 5 times vertically):

```cpp
bool horizontal = true, first_iteration = true;
int amount = 10;
shaderBlur.use();
for (unsigned int i = 0; i < amount; i++)
{
    glBindFramebuffer(GL_FRAMEBUFFER, pingpongFBO[horizontal]);
    shaderBlur.setInt("horizontal", horizontal);
    glBindTexture(GL_TEXTURE_2D, first_iteration ?
                  colorBuffers[1] : pingpongBuffers[!horizontal]);
    RenderQuad();
    horizontal = !horizontal;
    if (first_iteration)
        first_iteration = false;
}
glBindFramebuffer(GL_FRAMEBUFFER, 0);
```

Each iteration we bind one of the two framebuffers based on whether we want to blur horizontally or vertically and bind the other framebuffer's color buffer as the texture to blur. The first iteration we specifically bind the texture we'd like to blur (`brightnessTexture`) as both color buffers would else end up empty. By repeating this process 10 times, the brightness image ends up with a complete Gaussian blur that was repeated 5 times. This construct allows us to blur any image as often as we'd like; the more Gaussian blur iterations, the stronger the blur.

By blurring the extracted brightness texture 5 times, we get a properly blurred image of all bright regions of a scene.

The last step to complete the Bloom effect is to combine this blurred brightness texture with the original scene's HDR texture.

40.3 Blending both textures

With the scene's HDR texture and a blurred brightness texture of the scene we only need to combine the two to achieve the infamous Bloom or glow effect. In the final fragment shader (largely similar to the one we used in the *HDR* chapter) we additively blend both textures:

```glsl
#version 330 core
out vec4 FragColor;

in vec2 TexCoords;

uniform sampler2D scene;
uniform sampler2D bloomBlur;
uniform float exposure;

void main()
{
    const float gamma = 2.2;
    vec3 hdrColor = texture(scene, TexCoords).rgb;
    vec3 bloomColor = texture(bloomBlur, TexCoords).rgb;
    hdrColor += bloomColor; // additive blending
    // tone mapping
    vec3 result = vec3(1.0) - exp(-hdrColor * exposure);
    // also gamma correct while we're at it
    result = pow(result, vec3(1.0 / gamma));
    FragColor = vec4(result, 1.0);
}
```

Interesting to note here is that we add the Bloom effect before we apply tone mapping. This way, the added brightness of bloom is also softly transformed to LDR range with better relative lighting as a result.

With both textures added together, all bright areas of our scene now get a proper glow effect:

The colored cubes now appear much more bright and give a better illusion as light emitting objects. This is a relatively simple scene so the Bloom effect isn't too impressive here, but in well lit scenes it can make a significant difference when properly configured. You can find the source code of this simple demo at `/src/5.advanced_lighting/7.bloom/`.

For this chapter we used a relatively simple Gaussian blur filter where we only take 5 samples in each direction. By taking more samples along a larger radius or repeating the blur filter an extra number of times we can improve the blur effect. As the quality of the blur directly correlates to the quality of the Bloom effect, improving the blur step can make a significant improvement. Some of these improvements combine blur filters with varying sized blur kernels or use multiple Gaussian curves to selectively combine weights. The additional resources from Kalogirou and Epic Games discuss how to significantly improve the Bloom effect by improving the Gaussian blur.

40.4 Additional resources

- `rastergrid.com/blog/2010/09/efficient-gaussian-blur-with-linear-sampling/`: describes the Gaussian blur very well and how to improve its performance using OpenGL's bilinear texture sampling.
- `udk-legacy.unrealengine.com/udk/Three/Bloom.html`: article from Epic Games about improving the Bloom effect by combining multiple Gaussian curves for its weights.
- `kalogirou.net/2006/05/20/how-to-do-good-bloom-for-hdr-rendering/`: Article from Kalogirou that describes how to improve the Bloom effect using a better Gaussian blur method.

41. Deferred Shading

The way we did lighting so far was called forward rendering or forward shading. A straightforward approach where we render an object and light it according to all light sources in a scene. We do this for every object individually for each object in the scene. While quite easy to understand and implement it is also quite heavy on performance as each rendered object has to iterate over each light source for every rendered fragment, which is a lot! Forward rendering also tends to waste a lot of fragment shader runs in scenes with a high depth complexity (multiple objects cover the same screen pixel) as fragment shader outputs are overwritten.

Deferred shading or deferred rendering aims to overcome these issues by drastically changing the way we render objects. This gives us several new options to significantly optimize scenes with large numbers of lights, allowing us to render hundreds (or even thousands) of lights with an acceptable framerate. The following image is a scene with 1847 point lights rendered with deferred shading (image courtesy of Hannes Nevalainen); something that wouldn't be possible with forward rendering.

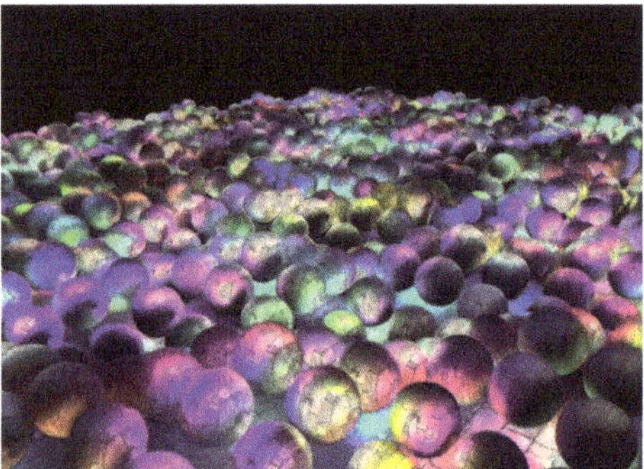

Deferred shading is based on the idea that we *defer* or *postpone* most of the heavy rendering (like lighting) to a later stage. Deferred shading consists of two passes: in the first pass, called the geometry pass, we render the scene once and retrieve all kinds of geometrical information from the objects that we store in a collection of textures called the G-buffer; think of position vectors, color vectors, normal vectors, and/or specular values. The geometric information of a scene stored in the G-buffer is then later used for (more complex) lighting calculations. Below is the content of a G-buffer of a single frame:

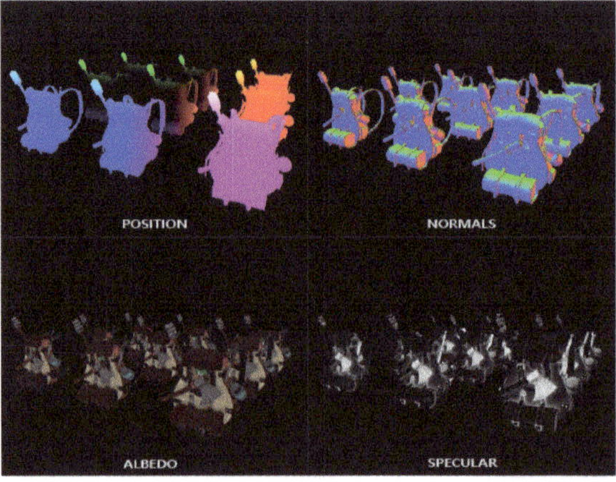

We use the textures from the G-buffer in a second pass called the lighting pass where we render a screen-filled quad and calculate the scene's lighting for each fragment using the geometrical information stored in the G-buffer; pixel by pixel we iterate over the G-buffer. Instead of taking each object all the way from the vertex shader to the fragment shader, we decouple its advanced fragment processes to a later stage. The lighting calculations are exactly the same, but this time we take all required input variables from the corresponding G-buffer textures, instead of the vertex shader (plus some uniform variables).

The image below nicely illustrates the process of deferred shading.

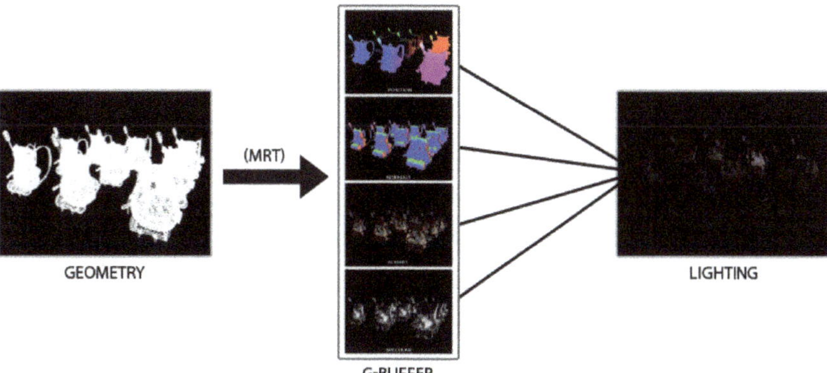

A major advantage of this approach is that whatever fragment ends up in the G-buffer is the actual fragment information that ends up as a screen pixel. The depth test already concluded this fragment to be the last and top-most fragment. This ensures that for each pixel we process in the lighting pass, we only calculate lighting once. Furthermore, deferred rendering opens up the possibility for further optimizations that allow us to render a much larger amount of light sources compared to forward rendering.

It also comes with some disadvantages though as the G-buffer requires us to store a relatively large amount of scene data in its texture color buffers. This eats memory, especially since scene data like position vectors require a high precision. Another disadvantage is that it doesn't support blending (as we only have information of the top-most fragment) and MSAA no longer works. There are several workarounds for this that we'll get to at the end of the chapter.

Filling the G-buffer (in the geometry pass) isn't too expensive as we directly store object information like position, color, or normals into a framebuffer with a small or zero amount of processing. By using multiple render targets (MRT) we can even do all of this in a single render pass.

41.1 The G-buffer

The G-buffer is the collective term of all textures used to store lighting-relevant data for the final lighting pass. Let's take this moment to briefly review all the data we need to light a fragment with forward rendering:

- A 3D world-space **position** vector to calculate the (interpolated) fragment position variable used for `lightDir` and `viewDir`.
- An RGB diffuse **color** vector also known as albedo.
- A 3D **normal** vector for determining a surface's slope.
- A **specular intensity** float.
- All light source position and color vectors.
- The player or viewer's position vector.

With these (per-fragment) variables at our disposal we are able to calculate the (Blinn-)Phong lighting we're accustomed to. The light source positions and colors, and the player's view position, can be configured using uniform variables, but the other variables are all fragment specific. If we can somehow pass the exact same data to the final deferred lighting pass we can calculate the same lighting effects, even though we're rendering fragments of a 2D quad.

There is no limit in OpenGL to what we can store in a texture so it makes sense to store all per-fragment data in one or multiple screen-filled textures of the G-buffer and use these later in the lighting pass. As the G-buffer textures will have the same size as the lighting pass's 2D quad, we get the exact same fragment data we'd had in a forward rendering setting, but this time in the lighting pass; there is a one on one mapping.

In pseudocode the entire process will look a bit like this:

```cpp
while(...) // render loop
{
    // 1. geometry pass: render all geometric/color data to g-buffer
    glBindFramebuffer(GL_FRAMEBUFFER, gBuffer);
    glClearColor(0.0, 0.0, 0.0, 1.0); // black so it won't leak in g-buffer
    glClear(GL_COLOR_BUFFER_BIT | GL_DEPTH_BUFFER_BIT);
    gBufferShader.use();
    for(Object obj : Objects)
    {
        ConfigureShaderTransformsAndUniforms();
        obj.Draw();
    }
    // 2. lighting pass: use g-buffer to calculate the scene's lighting
    glBindFramebuffer(GL_FRAMEBUFFER, 0);
    lightingPassShader.use();
    BindAllGBufferTextures();
    SetLightingUniforms();
    RenderQuad();
}
```

The data we'll need to store of each fragment is a **position** vector, a **normal** vector, a **color** vector, and a **specular intensity** value. In the geometry pass we need to render all objects of the scene and store these data components in the G-buffer. We can again use multiple render targets to render to multiple color buffers in a single render pass; this was briefly discussed in the *Bloom* chapter.

For the geometry pass we'll need to initialize a framebuffer object that we'll call `gBuffer` that has multiple color buffers attached and a single depth renderbuffer object. For the position and normal texture we'd preferably use a high-precision texture (16 or 32-bit float per component). For the albedo and specular values we'll be fine with the default texture precision (8-bit precision per component). Note that we use `GL_RGBA16F` over `GL_RGB16F` as GPUs generally prefer 4-component formats over 3-component formats due to byte alignment; some drivers may fail to complete the framebuffer otherwise.

```cpp
unsigned int gBuffer;
glGenFramebuffers(1, &gBuffer);
glBindFramebuffer(GL_FRAMEBUFFER, gBuffer);
unsigned int gPosition, gNormal, gColorSpec;

// - position color buffer
glGenTextures(1, &gPosition);
glBindTexture(GL_TEXTURE_2D, gPosition);
glTexImage2D(GL_TEXTURE_2D, 0, GL_RGBA16F, SCR_WIDTH, SCR_HEIGHT, 0,
```

```cpp
                GL_RGBA, GL_FLOAT, NULL);
glTexParameteri(GL_TEXTURE_2D, GL_TEXTURE_MIN_FILTER, GL_NEAREST);
glTexParameteri(GL_TEXTURE_2D, GL_TEXTURE_MAG_FILTER, GL_NEAREST);
glFramebufferTexture2D(GL_FRAMEBUFFER, GL_COLOR_ATTACHMENT0, GL_TEXTURE_2D,
                    gPosition, 0);

// - normal color buffer
glGenTextures(1, &gNormal);
glBindTexture(GL_TEXTURE_2D, gNormal);
glTexImage2D(GL_TEXTURE_2D, 0, GL_RGBA16F, SCR_WIDTH, SCR_HEIGHT, 0,
            GL_RGBA, GL_FLOAT, NULL);
glTexParameteri(GL_TEXTURE_2D, GL_TEXTURE_MIN_FILTER, GL_NEAREST);
glTexParameteri(GL_TEXTURE_2D, GL_TEXTURE_MAG_FILTER, GL_NEAREST);
glFramebufferTexture2D(GL_FRAMEBUFFER, GL_COLOR_ATTACHMENT1, GL_TEXTURE_2D,
                    gNormal, 0);

// - color + specular color buffer
glGenTextures(1, &gAlbedoSpec);
glBindTexture(GL_TEXTURE_2D, gAlbedoSpec);
glTexImage2D(GL_TEXTURE_2D, 0, GL_RGBA, SCR_WIDTH, SCR_HEIGHT, 0,
            GL_RGBA, GL_UNSIGNED_BYTE, NULL);
glTexParameteri(GL_TEXTURE_2D, GL_TEXTURE_MIN_FILTER, GL_NEAREST);
glTexParameteri(GL_TEXTURE_2D, GL_TEXTURE_MAG_FILTER, GL_NEAREST);
glFramebufferTexture2D(GL_FRAMEBUFFER, GL_COLOR_ATTACHMENT2, GL_TEXTURE_2D,
                    gAlbedoSpec, 0);

// - tell OpenGL which color attachments we'll use (of this framebuffer)
unsigned int attachments[3] = { GL_COLOR_ATTACHMENT0, GL_COLOR_ATTACHMENT1,
    GL_COLOR_ATTACHMENT2 };
glDrawBuffers(3, attachments);

// then also add render buffer object as depth buffer and check for
    completeness.
[...]
```

Since we use multiple render targets, we have to explicitly tell OpenGL which of the color buffers associated with GBuffer we'd like to render to with glDrawBuffers. Also interesting to note here is we combine the color and specular intensity data in a single RGBA texture; this saves us from having to declare an additional color buffer texture. As your deferred shading pipeline gets more complex and needs more data you'll quickly find new ways to combine data in individual textures.

Next we need to render into the G-buffer. Assuming each object has a diffuse, normal, and specular texture we'd use something like the following fragment shader to render into the G-buffer:

```glsl
#version 330 core
layout (location = 0) out vec3 gPosition;
layout (location = 1) out vec3 gNormal;
layout (location = 2) out vec4 gAlbedoSpec;

in vec2 TexCoords;
in vec3 FragPos;
in vec3 Normal;

uniform sampler2D texture_diffuse1;
uniform sampler2D texture_specular1;

void main()
{
    // store the fragment position vector in the first gbuffer texture
```

```glsl
    gPosition = FragPos;
    // also store the per-fragment normals into the gbuffer
    gNormal = normalize(Normal);
    // and the diffuse per-fragment color
    gAlbedoSpec.rgb = texture(texture_diffuse1, TexCoords).rgb;
    // store specular intensity in gAlbedoSpec's alpha component
    gAlbedoSpec.a = texture(texture_specular1, TexCoords).r;
}
```

As we use multiple render targets, the layout specifier tells OpenGL to which color buffer of the active framebuffer we render to. Note that we do not store the specular intensity into a single color buffer texture as we can store its single float value in the alpha component of one of the other color buffer textures.

Keep in mind that with lighting calculations it is extremely important to keep all relevant variables in the same coordinate space. In this case we store (and calculate) all variables in world-space.

If we'd now were to render a large collection of backpack objects into the `gBuffer` framebuffer and visualize its content by projecting each color buffer one by one onto a screen-filled quad we'd see something like this:

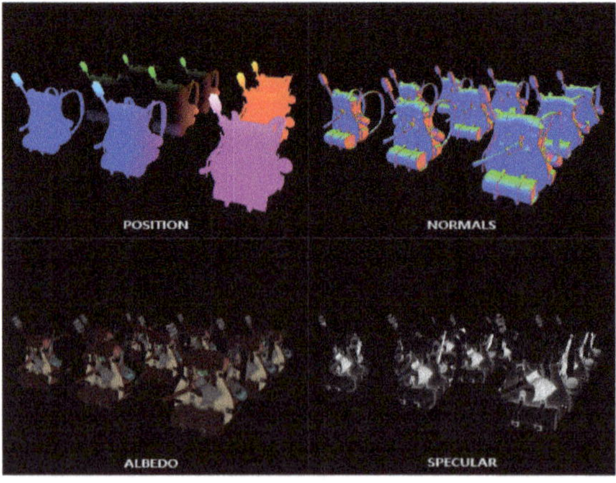

Try to visualize that the world-space position and normal vectors are indeed correct. For instance, the normal vectors pointing to the right would be more aligned to a red color, similarly for position vectors that point from the scene's origin to the right. As soon as you're satisfied with the content of the G-buffer it's time to move to the next step: the lighting pass.

41.2 The deferred lighting pass

With a large collection of fragment data in the G-Buffer at our disposal we have the option to completely calculate the scene's final lit colors. We do this by iterating over each of the G-Buffer textures pixel by pixel and use their content as input to the lighting algorithms. Because the G-buffer texture values all represent the final transformed fragment values we only have to do the expensive lighting operations once per pixel. This is especially useful in complex scenes where we'd easily invoke multiple expensive fragment shader calls per pixel in a forward rendering setting.

For the lighting pass we're going to render a 2D screen-filled quad (a bit like a post-processing effect) and execute an expensive lighting fragment shader on each pixel:

```cpp
glClear(GL_COLOR_BUFFER_BIT | GL_DEPTH_BUFFER_BIT);
glActiveTexture(GL_TEXTURE0);
glBindTexture(GL_TEXTURE_2D, gPosition);
glActiveTexture(GL_TEXTURE1);
glBindTexture(GL_TEXTURE_2D, gNormal);
glActiveTexture(GL_TEXTURE2);
glBindTexture(GL_TEXTURE_2D, gAlbedoSpec);
// also send light relevant uniforms
shaderLightingPass.use();
SendAllLightUniformsToShader(shaderLightingPass);
shaderLightingPass.setVec3("viewPos", camera.Position);
RenderQuad();
```

We bind all relevant textures of the G-buffer before rendering and also send the lighting-relevant uniform variables to the shader.

The fragment shader of the lighting pass is largely similar to the lighting chapter shaders we've used so far. What is new is the method in which we obtain the lighting's input variables, which we now directly sample from the G-buffer:

```glsl
#version 330 core
out vec4 FragColor;
in vec2 TexCoords;

uniform sampler2D gPosition;
uniform sampler2D gNormal;
uniform sampler2D gAlbedoSpec;

struct Light {
    vec3 Position;
    vec3 Color;
};
const int NR_LIGHTS = 32;
uniform Light lights[NR_LIGHTS];
uniform vec3 viewPos;

void main()
{
    // retrieve data from G-buffer
    vec3 FragPos = texture(gPosition, TexCoords).rgb;
    vec3 Normal = texture(gNormal, TexCoords).rgb;
    vec3 Albedo = texture(gAlbedoSpec, TexCoords).rgb;
    float Specular = texture(gAlbedoSpec, TexCoords).a;

    // then calculate lighting as usual
    vec3 lighting = Albedo * 0.1; // hard-coded ambient component
    vec3 viewDir = normalize(viewPos - FragPos);
    for(int i = 0; i < NR_LIGHTS; ++i)
    {
        // diffuse
        vec3 lightDir = normalize(lights[i].Position - FragPos);
        vec3 diffuse = max(dot(Normal, lightDir), 0.0) * Albedo *
                       lights[i].Color;
        lighting += diffuse;
    }

    FragColor = vec4(lighting, 1.0);
}
```

The lighting pass shader accepts 3 uniform textures that represent the G-buffer and hold all the data we've stored in the geometry pass. If we were to sample these with the current fragment's texture coordinates we'd get the exact same fragment values as if we were rendering the geometry directly. Note that we retrieve both the `Albedo` color and the `Specular` intensity from the single `gAlbedoSpec` texture.

As we now have the per-fragment variables (and the relevant uniform variables) necessary to calculate Blinn-Phong lighting, we don't have to make any changes to the lighting code. The only thing we change in deferred shading here is the method of obtaining lighting input variables.

Running a simple demo with a total of 32 small lights looks a bit like this:

One of the disadvantages of deferred shading is that it is not possible to do blending as all values in the G-buffer are from single fragments, and blending operates on the combination of multiple fragments. Another disadvantage is that deferred shading forces you to use the same lighting algorithm for most of your scene's lighting; you can somehow alleviate this a bit by including more material-specific data in the G-buffer.

To overcome these disadvantages (especially blending) we often split the renderer into two parts: one deferred rendering part, and the other a forward rendering part specifically meant for blending or special shader effects not suited for a deferred rendering pipeline. To illustrate how this works, we'll render the light sources as small cubes using a forward renderer as the light cubes require a special shader (simply output a single light color).

41.3 Combining deferred rendering with forward rendering

Say we want to render each of the light sources as a 3D cube positioned at the light source's position emitting the color of the light. A first idea that comes to mind is to simply forward render all the light sources on top of the deferred lighting quad at the end of the deferred shading pipeline. So basically render the cubes as we'd normally do, but only after we've finished the deferred rendering operations. In code this will look a bit like this:

```
// deferred lighting pass
[...]
RenderQuad();

// now render all light cubes with forward rendering as we'd normally do
shaderLightBox.use();
```

```cpp
shaderLightBox.setMat4("projection", projection);
shaderLightBox.setMat4("view", view);
for (unsigned int i = 0; i < lightPositions.size(); i++)
{
    model = glm::mat4(1.0f);
    model = glm::translate(model, lightPositions[i]);
    model = glm::scale(model, glm::vec3(0.25f));
    shaderLightBox.setMat4("model", model);
    shaderLightBox.setVec3("lightColor", lightColors[i]);
    RenderCube();
}
```

However, these rendered cubes do not take any of the stored geometry depth of the deferred renderer into account and are, as a result, always rendered on top of the previously rendered objects; this isn't the result we were looking for.

What we need to do, is first copy the depth information stored in the geometry pass into the default framebuffer's depth buffer and only then render the light cubes. This way the light cubes' fragments are only rendered when on top of the previously rendered geometry.

We can copy the content of a framebuffer to the content of another framebuffer with the help of `glBlitFramebuffer`, a function we also used in the *Anti Aliasing* chapter to resolve multisampled framebuffers. The `glBlitFramebuffer` function allows us to copy a user-defined region of a framebuffer to a user-defined region of another framebuffer.

We stored the depth of all the objects rendered in the deferred geometry pass in the `gBuffer` FBO. If we were to copy the content of its depth buffer to the depth buffer of the default framebuffer, the light cubes would then render as if all of the scene's geometry was rendered with forward rendering. As briefly explained in the anti-aliasing chapter, we have to specify a framebuffer as the read framebuffer and similarly specify a framebuffer as the write framebuffer:

```cpp
glBindFramebuffer(GL_READ_FRAMEBUFFER, gBuffer);
glBindFramebuffer(GL_DRAW_FRAMEBUFFER, 0); // write to default framebuffer
glBlitFramebuffer(0, 0, SCR_WIDTH, SCR_HEIGHT, 0, 0, SCR_WIDTH, SCR_HEIGHT,
                  GL_DEPTH_BUFFER_BIT, GL_NEAREST);
glBindFramebuffer(GL_FRAMEBUFFER, 0);
// now render light cubes as before
[...]
```

Here we copy the entire read framebuffer's depth buffer content to the default framebuffer's depth buffer; this can similarly be done for color buffers and stencil buffers. If we then render the light cubes, the cubes indeed render correctly over the scene's geometry:

You can find the full source code of the demo at `/src/5.advanced_lighting/8.1.deferred_shading/`.

With this approach we can easily combine deferred shading with forward shading. This is great as we can now still apply blending and render objects that require special shader effects, something that isn't possible in a pure deferred rendering context.

41.4　A larger number of lights

What deferred rendering is often praised for, is its ability to render an enormous amount of light sources without a heavy cost on performance. Deferred rendering by itself doesn't allow for a very large amount of light sources as we'd still have to calculate each fragment's lighting component for each of the scene's light sources. What makes a large amount of light sources possible is a very neat optimization we can apply to the deferred rendering pipeline: that of light volumes.

Normally when we render a fragment in a large lit scene we'd calculate the contribution of **each** light source in a scene, regardless of their distance to the fragment. A large portion of these light sources will never reach the fragment, so why waste all these lighting computations?

The idea behind light volumes is to calculate the radius, or volume, of a light source i.e. the area where its light is able to reach fragments. As most light sources use some form of attenuation, we can use that to calculate the maximum distance or radius their light is able to reach. We then only do the expensive lighting calculations if a fragment is inside one or more of these light volumes. This can save us a considerable amount of computation as we now only calculate lighting where it's necessary.

The trick to this approach is mostly figuring out the size or radius of the light volume of a light source.

41.4.1　Calculating a light's volume or radius

To obtain a light's volume radius we have to solve the attenuation equation for when its light contribution becomes `0.0`. For the attenuation function we'll use the function introduced in the *Light Casters* chapter:

$$F_{\text{light}} = \frac{I}{K_c + K_1 * d + K_q * d^2}$$

What we want to do is solve this equation for when F_{light} is `0.0`. However, this equation will never exactly reach the value `0.0`, so there won't be a solution. What we can do however, is not solve the equation for `0.0`, but solve it for a brightness value that is close to `0.0` but still perceived as dark. The brightness value of $5/256$ would be acceptable for this chapter's demo scene; divided by 256 as the default 8-bit framebuffer can only display that many intensities per component.

> The attenuation function used is mostly dark in its visible range. If we were to limit it to an even darker brightness than $5/256$, the light volume would become too large and thus less effective. As long as a user cannot see a sudden cut-off of a light source at its volume borders we'll be fine. Of course this always depends on the type of scene; a higher brightness threshold results in smaller light volumes and thus a better efficiency, but can produce noticeable artifacts where lighting seems to break at a volume's borders.

The attenuation equation we have to solve becomes:

$$\frac{5}{256} = \frac{I_{\text{max}}}{Attenuation}$$

Here I_{max} is the light source's brightest color component. We use a light source's brightest color component as solving the equation for a light's brightest intensity value best reflects the ideal light volume radius.

From here on we continue solving the equation:

$$\frac{5}{256} * Attenuation = I_{\text{max}}$$

$$5 * Attenuation = I_{\text{max}} * 256$$

$$Attenuation = I_{\text{max}} * \frac{256}{5}$$

$$K_c + K_1 * d + K_q * d^2 = I_{\text{max}} * \frac{256}{5}$$

$$K_q * d^2 + K_1 * d + K_c - I_{\text{max}} * \frac{256}{5} = 0$$

The last equation is an equation of the form $ax^2 + bx + c = 0$, which we can solve using the quadratic equation:

$$x = \frac{-K_1 + \sqrt{K_1^2 - 4 * K_q * (K_c - I_{\text{max}} * \frac{256}{5})}}{2 * K_q}$$

This gives us a general equation that allows us to calculate x i.e. the light volume's radius for the light source given a constant, linear, and quadratic parameter:

```cpp
float constant  = 1.0;
float linear    = 0.7;
float quadratic = 1.8;
float lightMax  = std::fmaxf(std::fmaxf(lightColor.r, lightColor.g),
                    lightColor.b);
float radius = (-linear + std::sqrtf(linear * linear - 4 * quadratic *
                (constant - (256.0 / 5.0) * lightMax))) / (2 * quadratic);
```

We calculate this radius for each light source of the scene and use it to only calculate lighting for that light source if a fragment is inside the light source's volume. Below is the updated lighting pass fragment shader that takes the calculated light volumes into account. Note that this approach is merely done for teaching purposes and not viable in a practical setting as we'll soon discuss:

```glsl
struct Light {
    [...]
    float Radius;
};

void main()
{
    [...]
    for(int i = 0; i < NR_LIGHTS; ++i)
    {
        // calculate distance between light source and current fragment
        float distance = length(lights[i].Position - FragPos);
        if(distance < lights[i].Radius)
        {
            // do expensive lighting
            [...]
        }
    }
}
```

The results are exactly the same as before, but this time each light only calculates lighting for the light sources in which volume it resides.

You can find the final source code of the demo at `/src/5.advanced_lighting/8.2. deferred_shading_volumes/`.

41.4.2 How we really use light volumes

The fragment shader shown above doesn't really work in practice and only illustrates how we can *sort of* use a light's volume to reduce lighting calculations. The reality is that your GPU and GLSL are pretty bad at optimizing loops and branches. The reason for this is that shader execution on the GPU is highly parallel and most architectures have a requirement that for large collection of threads they need to run the exact same shader code for it to be efficient. This often means that a shader is run that executes **all** branches of an `if` statement to ensure the shader runs are the same for that group of threads, making our previous *radius check* optimization completely useless; we'd still calculate lighting for all light sources!

The appropriate approach to using light volumes is to render actual spheres, scaled by the light volume radius. The centers of these spheres are positioned at the light source's position, and as it is scaled by the light volume radius the sphere exactly encompasses the light's visible volume. This is where the trick comes in: we use the deferred lighting shader for rendering the spheres. As a rendered sphere produces fragment shader invocations that exactly match the pixels the light source affects, we only render the relevant pixels and skip all other pixels. The image below illustrates this:

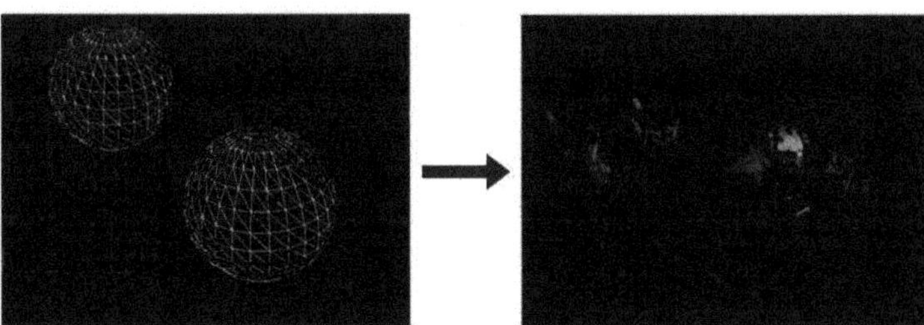

This is done for each light source in the scene, and the resulting fragments are additively blended together. The result is then the exact same scene as before, but this time rendering only the relevant fragments per light source. This effectively reduces the computations from `nr_objects * nr_lights` to `nr_objects + nr_lights`, which makes it incredibly efficient in scenes with a large number of lights. This approach is what makes deferred rendering so suitable for rendering a large number of lights.

There is still an issue with this approach: face culling should be enabled (otherwise we'd render a light's effect twice) and when it is enabled the user may enter a light source's volume after which the volume isn't rendered anymore (due to back-face culling), removing the light source's influence; we can solve that by only rendering the spheres' back faces.

Rendering light volumes does take its toll on performance, and while it is generally much faster than normal deferred shading for rendering a large number of lights, there's still more we can optimize. Two other popular (and more efficient) extensions on top of deferred shading exist called deferred lighting and tile-based deferred shading. These are even more efficient at rendering large amounts of light and also allow for relatively efficient MSAA.

41.5 Deferred rendering vs forward rendering

By itself (without light volumes), deferred shading is a nice optimization as each pixel only runs a single fragment shader, compared to forward rendering where we'd often run the fragment shader multiple times per pixel. Deferred rendering does come with a few disadvantages though: a large memory overhead, no MSAA, and blending still has to be done with forward rendering.

When you have a small scene and not too many lights, deferred rendering is not necessarily faster and sometimes even slower as the overhead then outweighs the benefits of deferred rendering. In more complex scenes, deferred rendering quickly becomes a significant optimization; especially with the more advanced optimization extensions. In addition, some render effects (especially post-processing effects) become cheaper on a deferred render pipeline as a lot of scene inputs are already available from the g-buffer.

As a final note I'd like to mention that basically all effects that can be accomplished with forward rendering can also be implemented in a deferred rendering context; this often only requires a small translation step. For instance, if we want to use normal mapping in a deferred renderer, we'd change the geometry pass shaders to output a world-space normal extracted from a normal map (using a TBN matrix) instead of the surface normal; the lighting calculations in the lighting pass don't need to change at all. And if you want parallax mapping to work, you'd want to first displace the texture coordinates in the geometry pass before sampling an object's diffuse, specular, and normal textures. Once you understand the idea behind deferred rendering, it's not too difficult to get creative.

41.6 Additional resources

- `ogldev.atspace.co.uk/www/tutorial35/tutorial35.html`: a three-part deferred shading tutorial by OGLDev.
- `software.intel.com/sites/default/files/m/d/4/1/d/8/lauritzen_deferred_shading_siggraph_2010.pdf`: slides by Andrew Lauritzen discussing high-level tile-based deferred shading and deferred lighting.

42. SSAO

We've briefly touched the topic in the basic lighting chapter: ambient lighting. Ambient lighting is a fixed light constant we add to the overall lighting of a scene to simulate the scattering of light. In reality, light scatters in all kinds of directions with varying intensities so the indirectly lit parts of a scene should also have varying intensities. One type of indirect lighting approximation is called ambient occlusion that tries to approximate indirect lighting by darkening creases, holes, and surfaces that are close to each other. These areas are largely occluded by surrounding geometry and thus light rays have fewer places to escape to, hence the areas appear darker. Take a look at the corners and creases of your room to see that the light there seems just a little darker.

Below is an example image of a scene with and without ambient occlusion. Notice how especially between the creases, the (ambient) light is more occluded:

While not an incredibly obvious effect, the image with ambient occlusion enabled does feel a lot more realistic due to these small occlusion-like details, giving the entire scene a greater feel of depth.

Ambient occlusion techniques are expensive as they have to take surrounding geometry into account. One could shoot a large number of rays for each point in space to determine its amount of occlusion, but that quickly becomes computationally infeasible for real-time solutions. In 2007, Crytek published a technique called screen-space ambient occlusion (SSAO) for use in their title *Crysis*. The technique uses a scene's depth buffer in screen-space to determine the amount of occlusion instead of real geometrical data. This approach is incredibly fast compared to real ambient occlusion and gives plausible results, making it the de-facto standard for approximating real-time ambient occlusion.

The basics behind screen-space ambient occlusion are simple: for each fragment on a screen-filled quad we calculate an occlusion factor based on the fragment's surrounding depth values. The occlusion factor is then used to reduce or nullify the fragment's ambient lighting component. The occlusion factor is obtained by taking multiple depth samples in a sphere sample kernel surrounding the fragment position and compare each of the samples with the current fragment's depth value. The number of samples that have a higher depth value than the fragment's depth represents the occlusion factor.

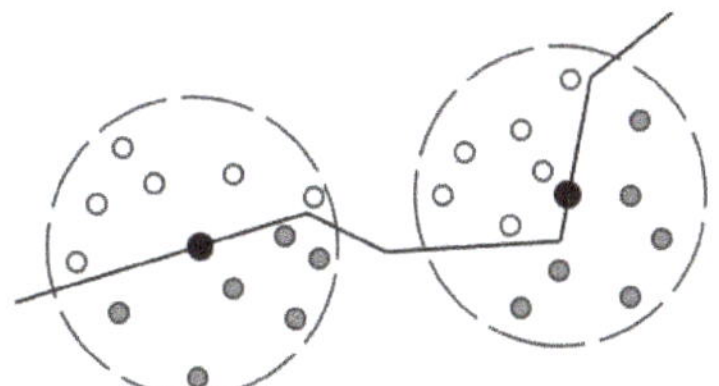

Each of the gray depth samples that are inside geometry contribute to the total occlusion factor; the more samples we find inside geometry, the less ambient lighting the fragment should eventually receive.

It is clear the quality and precision of the effect directly relates to the number of surrounding samples we take. If the sample count is too low, the precision drastically reduces and we get an artifact called banding; if it is too high, we lose performance. We can reduce the amount of samples we have to test by introducing some randomness into the sample kernel. By randomly rotating the sample kernel each fragment we can get high quality results with a much smaller amount of samples. This does come at a price as the randomness introduces a noticeable noise pattern that we'll have to fix by blurring the results. Below is an image (courtesy of `john-chapman-graphics.blogspot.com/`) showcasing the banding effect and the effect randomness has on the results:

As you can see, even though we get noticeable banding on the SSAO results due to a low sample count, by introducing some randomness the banding effects are completely gone.

The SSAO method developed by Crytek had a certain visual style. Because the sample kernel used was a sphere, it caused flat walls to look gray as half of the kernel samples end up being in the surrounding geometry. Below is an image of Crysis's screen-space ambient occlusion that clearly portrays this gray feel:

For that reason we won't be using a sphere sample kernel, but rather a hemisphere sample kernel oriented along a surface's normal vector.

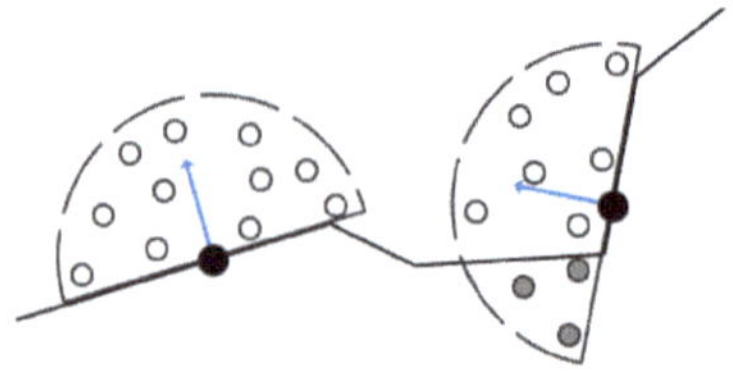

By sampling around this normal-oriented hemisphere we do not consider the fragment's underlying geometry to be a contribution to the occlusion factor. This removes the gray-feel of ambient occlusion and generally produces more realistic results. This chapter's technique is based on this normal-oriented hemisphere method and a slightly modified version of John Chapman's brilliant SSAO tutorial[1].

42.1 Sample buffers

SSAO requires geometrical info as we need some way to determine the occlusion factor of a fragment. For each fragment, we're going to need the following data:

- A per-fragment **position** vector.
- A per-fragment **normal** vector.
- A per-fragment **albedo** color.
- A **sample kernel**.
- A per-fragment **random rotation** vector used to rotate the sample kernel.

Using a per-fragment view-space position we can orient a sample hemisphere kernel around the fragment's view-space surface normal and use this kernel to sample the position buffer texture at varying offsets. For each per-fragment kernel sample we compare its depth with its depth in the position buffer to determine the amount of occlusion. The resulting occlusion factor is then used to limit the final ambient lighting component. By also including a per-fragment rotation vector we can significantly reduce the number of samples we'll need to take as we'll soon see.

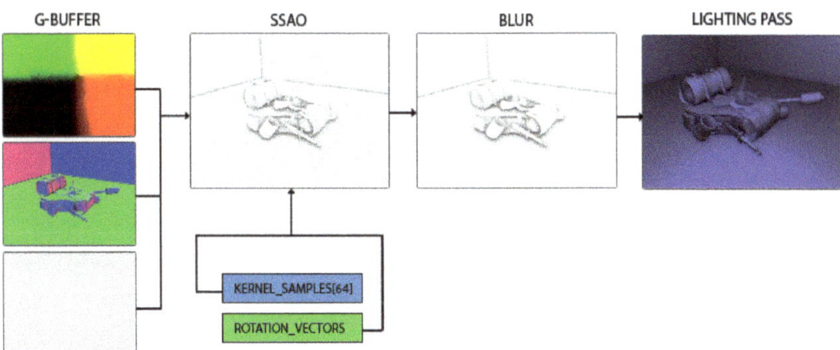

As SSAO is a screen-space technique we calculate its effect on each fragment on a screen-filled 2D quad. This does mean we have no geometrical information of the scene. What we could do, is render the geometrical per-fragment data into screen-space textures that we then later send to the SSAO shader so we have access to the per-fragment geometrical data. If you've followed along with the previous chapter you'll realize this looks quite like a deferred renderer's G-buffer setup. For that reason SSAO is perfectly suited in combination with deferred rendering as we already have the position and normal vectors in the G-buffer.

In this chapter we're going to implement SSAO on top of a slightly simplified version of the deferred renderer from the previous chapter. If you're not sure what deferred shading is, be sure to first read up on that.

As we should have per-fragment position and normal data available from the scene objects, the

---

[1] john-chapman-graphics.blogspot.nl/2013/01/ssao-tutorial.html

fragment shader of the geometry stage is fairly simple:

```glsl
#version 330 core
layout (location = 0) out vec4 gPosition;
layout (location = 1) out vec3 gNormal;
layout (location = 2) out vec4 gAlbedoSpec;

in vec2 TexCoords;
in vec3 FragPos;
in vec3 Normal;

void main()
{
    // store the fragment position vector in the first gbuffer texture
    gPosition = FragPos;
    // also store the per-fragment normals into the gbuffer
    gNormal = normalize(Normal);
    // and the diffuse per-fragment color, ignore specular
    gAlbedoSpec.rgb = vec3(0.95);
}
```

Since SSAO is a screen-space technique where occlusion is calculated from the visible view, it makes sense to implement the algorithm in view-space. Therefore, `FragPos` and `Normal` as supplied by the geometry stage's vertex shader are transformed to view space (multiplied by the view matrix as well).

> It is possible to reconstruct the position vectors from depth values alone, using some clever tricks as Matt Pettineo described in his blog[a]. This requires a few extra calculations in the shaders, but saves us from having to store position data in the G-buffer (which costs a lot of memory). For the sake of a more simple example, we'll leave these optimizations out of the chapter.
>
> ---
> [a]mynameismjp.wordpress.com/2010/09/05/position-from-depth-3/

The `gPosition` color buffer texture is configured as follows:

```cpp
glGenTextures(1, &gPosition);
glBindTexture(GL_TEXTURE_2D, gPosition);
glTexImage2D(GL_TEXTURE_2D, 0, GL_RGBA16F, SCR_WIDTH, SCR_HEIGHT, 0,
             GL_RGBA, GL_FLOAT, NULL);
glTexParameteri(GL_TEXTURE_2D, GL_TEXTURE_MIN_FILTER, GL_NEAREST);
glTexParameteri(GL_TEXTURE_2D, GL_TEXTURE_MAG_FILTER, GL_NEAREST);
glTexParameteri(GL_TEXTURE_2D, GL_TEXTURE_WRAP_S, GL_CLAMP_TO_EDGE);
glTexParameteri(GL_TEXTURE_2D, GL_TEXTURE_WRAP_T, GL_CLAMP_TO_EDGE);
```

This gives us a position texture that we can use to obtain depth values for each of the kernel samples. Note that we store the positions in a floating point data format; this way position values aren't clamped to [0.0,1.0] and we need the higher precision. Also note the texture wrapping method of `GL_CLAMP_TO_EDGE`. This ensures we don't accidentally oversample position/depth values in screen-space outside the texture's default coordinate region.

Next, we need the actual hemisphere sample kernel and some method to randomly rotate it.

42.2 **Normal-oriented hemisphere**

We need to generate a number of samples oriented along the normal of a surface. As we briefly discussed at the start of this chapter, we want to generate samples that form a hemisphere. As it is difficult nor plausible to generate a sample kernel for each surface normal direction, we're going to generate a sample kernel in tangent space, with the normal vector pointing in the positive z direction.

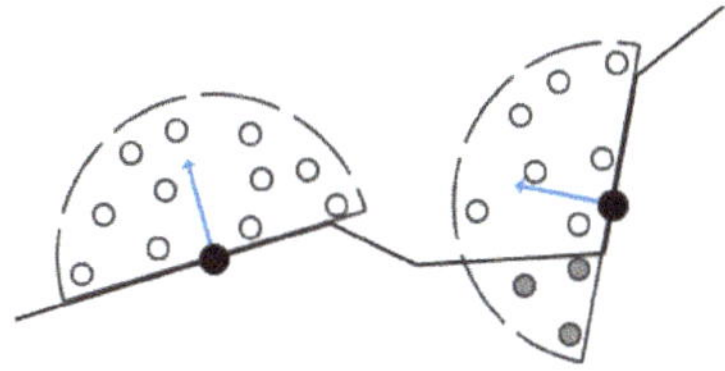

Assuming we have a unit hemisphere, we can obtain a sample kernel with a maximum of 64 sample values as follows:

```cpp
std::uniform_real_distribution<float> randomFloats(0.0, 1.0);
std::default_random_engine generator;
std::vector<glm::vec3> ssaoKernel;
for (unsigned int i = 0; i < 64; ++i)
{
    glm::vec3 sample(
        randomFloats(generator) * 2.0 - 1.0,
        randomFloats(generator) * 2.0 - 1.0,
        randomFloats(generator)
    );
    sample = glm::normalize(sample);
    sample *= randomFloats(generator);
    ssaoKernel.push_back(sample);
}
```

We vary the x and y direction in tangent space between -1.0 and 1.0, and vary the z direction of the samples between 0.0 and 1.0 (if we varied the z direction between -1.0 and 1.0 as well we'd have a sphere sample kernel). As the sample kernel will be oriented along the surface normal, the resulting sample vectors will all end up in the hemisphere.

Currently, all samples are randomly distributed in the sample kernel, but we'd rather place a larger weight on occlusions close to the actual fragment. We want to distribute more kernel samples closer to the origin. We can do this with an accelerating interpolation function:

```cpp
    float scale = (float)i / 64.0;
    scale = lerp(0.1f, 1.0f, scale * scale);
    sample *= scale;
    ssaoKernel.push_back(sample);
}
```

Where `lerp` is defined as:

```cpp
float lerp(float a, float b, float f)
{
    return a + f * (b - a);
}
```

This gives us a kernel distribution that places most samples closer to its origin.

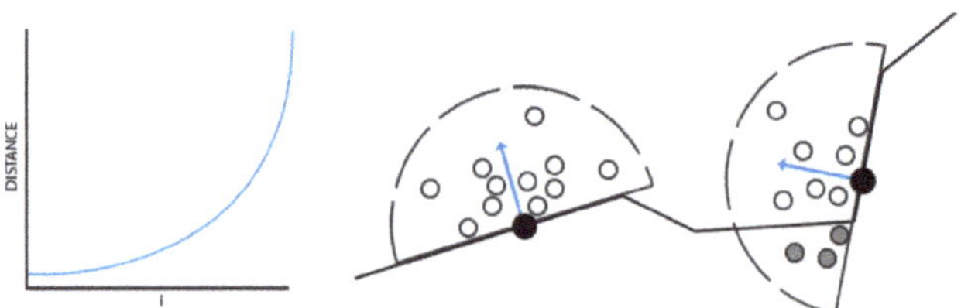

Each of the kernel samples will be used to offset the view-space fragment position to sample surrounding geometry. We do need quite a lot of samples in view-space in order to get realistic results, which may be too heavy on performance. However, if we can introduce some semi-random rotation/noise on a per-fragment basis, we can significantly reduce the number of samples required.

42.3 Random kernel rotations

By introducing some randomness onto the sample kernels we largely reduce the number of samples necessary to get good results. We could create a random rotation vector for each fragment of a scene, but that quickly eats up memory. It makes more sense to create a small texture of random rotation vectors that we tile over the screen.

We create a 4x4 array of random rotation vectors oriented around the tangent-space surface normal:

```cpp
std::vector<glm::vec3> ssaoNoise;
for (unsigned int i = 0; i < 16; i++)
{
    glm::vec3 noise(
        randomFloats(generator) * 2.0 - 1.0,
        randomFloats(generator) * 2.0 - 1.0,
        0.0f);
    ssaoNoise.push_back(noise);
}
```

As the sample kernel is oriented along the positive z direction in tangent space, we leave the z component at 0.0 so we rotate around the z axis.

We then create a 4x4 texture that holds the random rotation vectors; make sure to set its wrapping method to GL_REPEAT so it properly tiles over the screen.

```cpp
unsigned int noiseTexture;
glGenTextures(1, &noiseTexture);
glBindTexture(GL_TEXTURE_2D, noiseTexture);
glTexImage2D(GL_TEXTURE_2D, 0, GL_RGBA16F, 4, 4, 0, GL_RGB, GL_FLOAT,
            &ssaoNoise[0]);
glTexParameteri(GL_TEXTURE_2D, GL_TEXTURE_MIN_FILTER, GL_NEAREST);
glTexParameteri(GL_TEXTURE_2D, GL_TEXTURE_MAG_FILTER, GL_NEAREST);
glTexParameteri(GL_TEXTURE_2D, GL_TEXTURE_WRAP_S, GL_REPEAT);
glTexParameteri(GL_TEXTURE_2D, GL_TEXTURE_WRAP_T, GL_REPEAT);
```

We now have all the relevant input data we need to implement SSAO.

42.4 The SSAO shader

The SSAO shader runs on a 2D screen-filled quad that calculates the occlusion value for each of its fragments. As we need to store the result of the SSAO stage (for use in the final lighting shader), we create yet another framebuffer object:

```cpp
unsigned int ssaoFBO;
glGenFramebuffers(1, &ssaoFBO);
glBindFramebuffer(GL_FRAMEBUFFER, ssaoFBO);

unsigned int ssaoColorBuffer;
glGenTextures(1, &ssaoColorBuffer);
glBindTexture(GL_TEXTURE_2D, ssaoColorBuffer);
glTexImage2D(GL_TEXTURE_2D, 0, GL_RED, SCR_WIDTH, SCR_HEIGHT, 0, GL_RED,
             GL_FLOAT, NULL);
glTexParameteri(GL_TEXTURE_2D, GL_TEXTURE_MIN_FILTER, GL_NEAREST);
glTexParameteri(GL_TEXTURE_2D, GL_TEXTURE_MAG_FILTER, GL_NEAREST);

glFramebufferTexture2D(GL_FRAMEBUFFER, GL_COLOR_ATTACHMENT0, GL_TEXTURE_2D,
                       ssaoColorBuffer, 0);
```

As the ambient occlusion result is a single grayscale value we'll only need a texture's red component, so we set the color buffer's internal format to `GL_RED`.

The complete process for rendering SSAO then looks a bit like this:

```cpp
// geometry pass: render stuff into G-buffer
glBindFramebuffer(GL_FRAMEBUFFER, gBuffer);
    [...]
glBindFramebuffer(GL_FRAMEBUFFER, 0);

// use G-buffer to render SSAO texture
glBindFramebuffer(GL_FRAMEBUFFER, ssaoFBO);
    glClear(GL_COLOR_BUFFER_BIT);
    glActiveTexture(GL_TEXTURE0);
    glBindTexture(GL_TEXTURE_2D, gPosition);
    glActiveTexture(GL_TEXTURE1);
    glBindTexture(GL_TEXTURE_2D, gNormal);
    glActiveTexture(GL_TEXTURE2);
    glBindTexture(GL_TEXTURE_2D, noiseTexture);
    shaderSSAO.use();
    SendKernelSamplesToShader();
    shaderSSAO.setMat4("projection", projection);
    RenderQuad();
glBindFramebuffer(GL_FRAMEBUFFER, 0);

// lighting pass: render scene lighting
glClear(GL_COLOR_BUFFER_BIT | GL_DEPTH_BUFFER_BIT);
shaderLightingPass.use();
[...]
glActiveTexture(GL_TEXTURE3);
glBindTexture(GL_TEXTURE_2D, ssaoColorBuffer);
[...]
RenderQuad();
```

The `shaderSSAO` shader takes as input the relevant G-buffer textures, the noise texture, and the normal-oriented hemisphere kernel samples:

```glsl
#version 330 core
out float FragColor;

in vec2 TexCoords;

uniform sampler2D gPosition;
uniform sampler2D gNormal;
uniform sampler2D texNoise;

uniform vec3 samples[64];
uniform mat4 projection;

// tile noise texture over screen, based on screen dimensions / noise size
const vec2 noiseScale = vec2(800.0/4.0, 600.0/4.0); // screen = 800x600

void main()
{
    [...]
}
```

Interesting to note here is the `noiseScale` variable. We want to tile the noise texture all over the screen, but as the `TexCoords` vary between `0.0` and `1.0`, the `texNoise` texture won't tile at all. So we'll calculate the required amount to scale `TexCoords` by dividing the screen's dimensions by the noise texture size.

```glsl
vec3 fragPos   = texture(gPosition, TexCoords).xyz;
vec3 normal    = texture(gNormal, TexCoords).rgb;
vec3 randomVec = texture(texNoise, TexCoords * noiseScale).xyz;
```

As we set the tiling parameters of `texNoise` to `GL_REPEAT`, the random values will be repeated all over the screen. Together with the `fragPos` and `normal` vector, we then have enough data to create a TBN matrix that transforms any vector from tangent-space to view-space:

```glsl
vec3 tangent   = normalize(randomVec - normal * dot(randomVec, normal));
vec3 bitangent = cross(normal, tangent);
mat3 TBN       = mat3(tangent, bitangent, normal);
```

Using a process called the Gramm-Schmidt process we create an orthogonal basis, each time slightly tilted based on the value of `randomVec`. Note that because we use a random vector for constructing the tangent vector, there is no need to have the TBN matrix exactly aligned to the geometry's surface, thus no need for per-vertex tangent (and bitangent) vectors.

Next we iterate over each of the kernel samples, transform the samples from tangent to view-space, add them to the current fragment position, and compare the fragment position's depth with the sample depth stored in the view-space position buffer. Let's discuss this in a step-by-step fashion:

```glsl
float occlusion = 0.0;
for(int i = 0; i < kernelSize; ++i)
{
    // get sample position
    vec3 sample = TBN * samples[i]; // from tangent to view-space
    sample = fragPos + sample * radius;

    [...]
}
```

Here `kernelSize` and `radius` are variables that we can use to tweak the effect; in this case a value of `64` and `0.5` respectively. For each iteration we first transform the respective sample to view-space. We then add the view-space kernel offset sample to the view-space fragment position. Then we multiply the offset sample by `radius` to increase (or decrease) the effective sample radius of SSAO.

Next we want to transform `sample` to screen-space so we can sample the position/depth value of `sample` as if we were rendering its position directly to the screen. As the vector is currently in view-space, we'll transform it to clip-space first using the `projection` matrix uniform:

```glsl
vec4 offset = vec4(sample, 1.0);
offset      = projection * offset;    // from view to clip-space
offset.xyz /= offset.w;               // perspective divide
offset.xyz = offset.xyz * 0.5 + 0.5;  // transform to range 0.0 - 1.0
```

After the variable is transformed to clip-space, we perform the perspective divide step by dividing its `xyz` components with its `w` component. The resulting normalized device coordinates are then transformed to the [`0.0, 1.0`] range so we can use them to sample the position texture:

```glsl
float sampleDepth = texture(gPosition, offset.xy).z;
```

We use the `offset` vector's `x` and `y` component to sample the position texture to retrieve the depth (or z value) of the sample position as seen from the viewer's perspective (the first non-occluded visible fragment). We then check if the sample's current depth value is larger than the stored depth value and if so, we add to the final contribution factor:

```glsl
occlusion += (sampleDepth >= sample.z + bias ? 1.0 : 0.0);
```

Note that we add a small `bias` here to the original fragment's depth value (set to `0.025` in this example). A bias isn't always necessary, but it helps visually tweak the SSAO effect and solves acne effects that may occur based on the scene's complexity.

We're not completely finished yet as there is still a small issue we have to take into account. Whenever a fragment is tested for ambient occlusion that is aligned close to the edge of a surface, it will also consider depth values of surfaces far behind the test surface; these values will (incorrectly) contribute to the occlusion factor. We can solve this by introducing a range check as the following image (courtesy of `john-chapman-graphics.blogspot.com/`) illustrates:

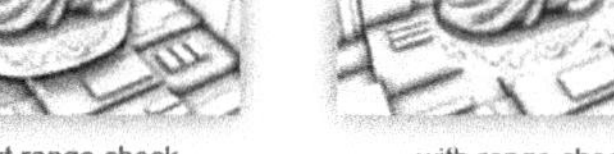

We introduce a range check that makes sure a fragment contributes to the occlusion factor if its depth values is within the sample's radius. We change the last line to:

```
float rangeCheck = smoothstep(0.0, 1.0, radius /
                   abs(fragPos.z - sampleDepth));
occlusion += (sampleDepth >= sample.z + bias ? 1.0 : 0.0) * rangeCheck;
```

Here we used GLSL's `smoothstep` function that smoothly interpolates its third parameter between the first and second parameter's range, returning `0.0` if less than or equal to its first parameter and `1.0` if equal or higher to its second parameter. If the depth difference ends up between `radius`, its value gets smoothly interpolated between `0.0` and `1.0` by the following curve:

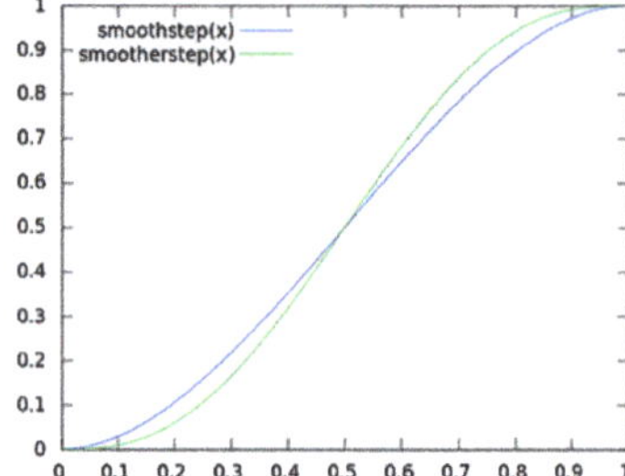

If we were to use a hard cut-off range check that would abruptly remove occlusion contributions if the depth values are outside `radius`, we'd see obvious (unattractive) borders at where the range check is applied.

As a final step we normalize the occlusion contribution by the size of the kernel and output the results. Note that we subtract the occlusion factor from `1.0` so we can directly use the occlusion factor to scale the ambient lighting component.

```
}
occlusion = 1.0 - (occlusion / kernelSize);
FragColor = occlusion;
```

If we'd imagine a scene where our favorite backpack model is taking a little nap, the ambient occlusion shader produces the following texture:

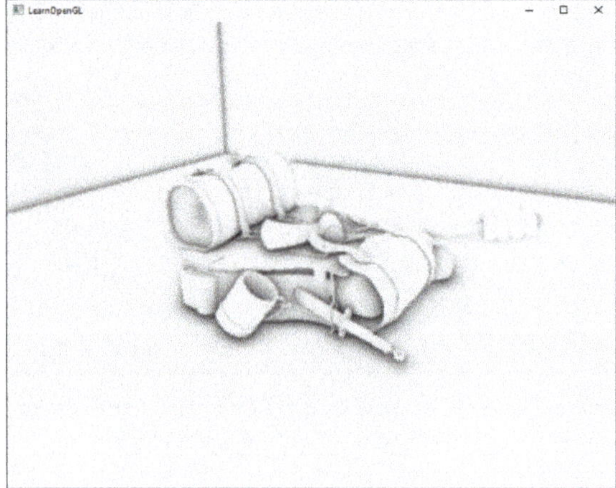

As we can see, ambient occlusion gives a great sense of depth. With just the ambient occlusion texture we can already clearly see the model is indeed laying on the floor, instead of hovering slightly above it.

It still doesn't look perfect, as the repeating pattern of the noise texture is clearly visible. To create a smooth ambient occlusion result we need to blur the ambient occlusion texture.

42.5 **Ambient occlusion blur**

Between the SSAO pass and the lighting pass, we first want to blur the SSAO texture. So let's create yet another framebuffer object for storing the blur result:

```cpp
unsigned int ssaoBlurFBO, ssaoColorBufferBlur;
glGenFramebuffers(1, &ssaoBlurFBO);
glBindFramebuffer(GL_FRAMEBUFFER, ssaoBlurFBO);
glGenTextures(1, &ssaoColorBufferBlur);
glBindTexture(GL_TEXTURE_2D, ssaoColorBufferBlur);
glTexImage2D(GL_TEXTURE_2D, 0, GL_RED, SCR_WIDTH, SCR_HEIGHT, 0, GL_RED,
        GL_FLOAT, NULL);
glTexParameteri(GL_TEXTURE_2D, GL_TEXTURE_MIN_FILTER, GL_NEAREST);
glTexParameteri(GL_TEXTURE_2D, GL_TEXTURE_MAG_FILTER, GL_NEAREST);
glFramebufferTexture2D(GL_FRAMEBUFFER, GL_COLOR_ATTACHMENT0, GL_TEXTURE_2D,
                ssaoColorBufferBlur, 0);
```

Because the tiled random vector texture gives us a consistent randomness, we can use this property to our advantage to create a simple blur shader:

```glsl
#version 330 core
out float FragColor;

in vec2 TexCoords;

uniform sampler2D ssaoInput;

void main() {
    vec2 texelSize = 1.0 / vec2(textureSize(ssaoInput, 0));
    float result = 0.0;
    for (int x = -2; x < 2; ++x)
    {
        for (int y = -2; y < 2; ++y)
        {
            vec2 offset = vec2(float(x), float(y)) * texelSize;
            result += texture(ssaoInput, TexCoords + offset).r;
        }
    }
    FragColor = result / (4.0 * 4.0);
}
```

Here we traverse the surrounding SSAO texels between `-2.0` and `2.0`, sampling the SSAO texture an amount identical to the noise texture's dimensions. We offset each texture coordinate by the exact size of a single texel using `textureSize` that returns a `vec2` of the given texture's dimensions. We average the obtained results to get a simple, but effective blur:

And there we go, a texture with per-fragment ambient occlusion data; ready for use in the lighting pass.

42.6 Applying ambient occlusion

Applying the occlusion factors to the lighting equation is incredibly easy: all we have to do is multiply the per-fragment ambient occlusion factor to the lighting's ambient component and we're done. If we take the Blinn-Phong deferred lighting shader of the previous chapter and adjust it a bit, we get the following fragment shader:

```glsl
#version 330 core
out vec4 FragColor;

in vec2 TexCoords;

uniform sampler2D gPosition;
uniform sampler2D gNormal;
uniform sampler2D gAlbedo;
uniform sampler2D ssao;

struct Light {
    vec3 Position;
    vec3 Color;

    float Linear;
    float Quadratic;
    float Radius;
};
uniform Light light;

void main()
{
    // retrieve data from gbuffer
    vec3 FragPos = texture(gPosition, TexCoords).rgb;
    vec3 Normal = texture(gNormal, TexCoords).rgb;
    vec3 Diffuse = texture(gAlbedo, TexCoords).rgb;
    float AmbientOcclusion = texture(ssao, TexCoords).r;

    // blinn-phong (in view-space)
    vec3 ambient = vec3(0.3 * Diffuse * AmbientOcclusion); // add occlusion
    vec3 lighting = ambient;
    vec3 viewDir = normalize(-FragPos); // viewpos is (0.0.0) in view-space
```

```glsl
    // diffuse
    vec3 lightDir = normalize(light.Position - FragPos);
    vec3 diffuse = max(dot(Normal, lightDir), 0.0) * Diffuse * light.Color;
    // specular
    vec3 halfwayDir = normalize(lightDir + viewDir);
    float spec = pow(max(dot(Normal, halfwayDir), 0.0), 8.0);
    vec3 specular = light.Color * spec;
    // attenuation
    float dist = length(light.Position - FragPos);
    float attenuation = 1.0 / (1.0 + light.Linear * dist + light.Quadratic
    * dist * dist);
    diffuse *= attenuation;
    specular *= attenuation;
    lighting += diffuse + specular;

    FragColor = vec4(lighting, 1.0);
}
```

The only thing (aside from the change to view-space) we really changed is the multiplication of
the scene's ambient component by `AmbientOcclusion`. With a single blue-ish point light in the
scene we'd get the following result:

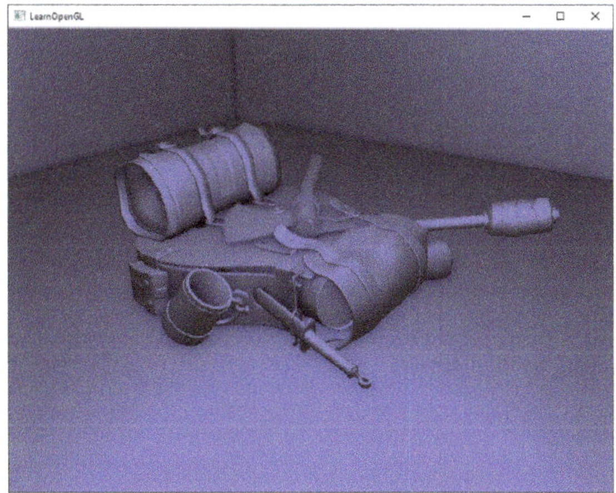

You can find the full source code of the demo scene at `/src/5.advanced_lighting/9.
ssao/`.

Screen-space ambient occlusion is a highly customizable effect that relies heavily on tweaking
its parameters based on the type of scene. There is no perfect combination of parameters for every
type of scene. Some scenes only work with a small radius, while other scenes require a larger radius
and a larger sample count for them to look realistic. The current demo uses 64 samples, which is a
bit much; play around with a smaller kernel size and try to get good results.

Some parameters you can tweak (by using uniforms for example): kernel size, radius, bias,
and/or the size of the noise kernel. You can also raise the final occlusion value to a user-defined
power to increase its strength:

```glsl
occlusion = 1.0 - (occlusion / kernelSize);
FragColor = pow(occlusion, power);
```

Play around with different scenes and different parameters to appreciate the customizability of SSAO.

Even though SSAO is a subtle effect that isn't too clearly noticeable, it adds a great deal of realism to properly lit scenes and is definitely a technique you'd want to have in your toolkit.

42.7 Additional resources

- `john-chapman-graphics.blogspot.nl/2013/01/ssao-tutorial.html`: excellent SSAO tutorial by John Chapman; a large portion of this chapter's code and techniques are based of his article.
- `mtnphil.wordpress.com/2013/06/26/know-your-ssao-artifacts/`: great article about improving SSAO specific artifacts.
- `ogldev.atspace.co.uk/www/tutorial46/tutorial46.html`: extension tutorial on top of SSAO from OGLDev about reconstructing position vectors from depth alone, saving us from storing the expensive position vectors in the G-buffer.

VI

PBR

43. Theory

PBR, or more commonly known as physically based rendering, is a collection of render techniques that are more or less based on the same underlying theory that more closely matches that of the physical world. As physically based rendering aims to mimic light in a physically plausible way, it generally looks more realistic compared to our original lighting algorithms like Phong and Blinn-Phong. Not only does it look better, as it closely approximates actual physics, we (and especially the artists) can author surface materials based on physical parameters without having to resort to cheap hacks and tweaks to make the lighting look right. One of the bigger advantages of authoring materials based on physical parameters is that these materials will look correct regardless of lighting conditions; something that is not true in non-PBR pipelines.

Physically based rendering is still nonetheless an approximation of reality (based on the principles of physics) which is why it's not called physical shading, but physically *based* shading. For a PBR lighting model to be considered physically based, it has to satisfy the following 3 conditions (don't worry, we'll get to them soon enough):

1. Be based on the microfacet surface model.
2. Be energy conserving.
3. Use a physically based BRDF.

In the next PBR chapters we'll be focusing on the PBR approach as originally explored by Disney and adopted for real-time display by Epic Games. Their approach, based on the metallic workflow, is decently documented, widely adopted on most popular engines, and looks visually amazing. By the end of these chapters we'll have something that looks like this:

Keep in mind, the topics in these chapters are rather advanced so it is advised to have a good understanding of OpenGL and shader lighting. Some of the more advanced knowledge you'll need for this series are: *Framebuffers*, *Cubemaps*, *Gamma Correction*, *HDR*, and *Normal Mapping*. We'll also delve into some advanced mathematics, but I'll do my best to explain the concepts as clear as possible.

43.1 The microfacet model

All the PBR techniques are based on the theory of microfacets. The theory describes that any surface at a microscopic scale can be described by tiny little perfectly reflective mirrors called microfacets. Depending on the roughness of a surface, the alignment of these tiny little mirrors can differ quite a lot:

The rougher a surface is, the more chaotically aligned each microfacet will be along the surface. The effect of these tiny-like mirror alignments is, that when specifically talking about specular lighting/reflection, the incoming light rays are more likely to scatter along completely different directions on rougher surfaces, resulting in a more widespread specular reflection. In contrast, on a smooth surface the light rays are more likely to reflect in roughly the same direction, giving us smaller and sharper reflections:

No surface is completely smooth on a microscopic level, but seeing as these microfacets are small enough that we can't make a distinction between them on a per-pixel basis, we statistically approximate the surface's microfacet roughness given a roughness parameter. Based on the roughness of a surface, we can calculate the ratio of microfacets roughly aligned to some vector h. This vector h is the halfway vector that sits halfway between the light l and view v vector. We've discussed the halfway vector before in the *Advanced Lighting* chapter which is calculated as the sum of l and v divided by its length:

$$h = \frac{l+v}{\|l+v\|}$$

The more the microfacets are aligned to the halfway vector, the sharper and stronger the specular reflection. Together with a roughness parameter that varies between 0 and 1, we can statistically approximate the alignment of the microfacets:

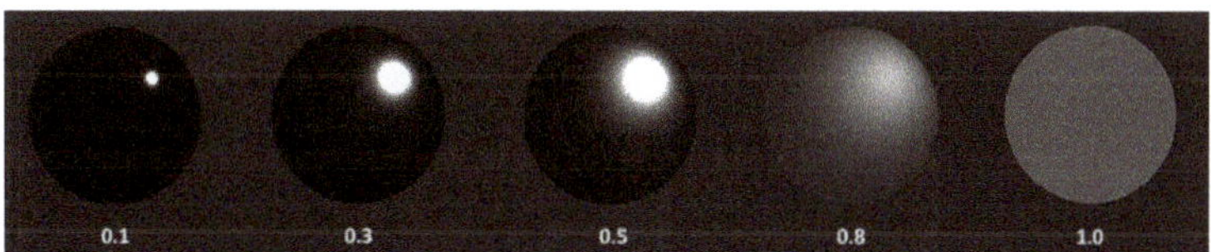

We can see that higher roughness values display a much larger specular reflection shape, in contrast with the smaller and sharper specular reflection shape of smooth surfaces.

43.2 Energy conservation

The microfacet approximation employs a form of energy conservation: outgoing light energy should never exceed the incoming light energy (excluding emissive surfaces). Looking at the above image we see the specular reflection area increase, but also its brightness decrease at increasing roughness levels. If the specular intensity were to be the same at each pixel (regardless of the size of the specular shape) the rougher surfaces would emit much more energy, violating the energy conservation principle. This is why we see specular reflections more intensely on smooth surfaces and more dimly on rough surfaces.

For energy conservation to hold, we need to make a clear distinction between diffuse and specular light. The moment a light ray hits a surface, it gets split in both a refraction part and a reflection part. The reflection part is light that directly gets reflected and doesn't enter the surface; this is what we know as specular lighting. The refraction part is the remaining light that enters the surface and gets absorbed; this is what we know as diffuse lighting.

There are some nuances here as refracted light doesn't immediately get absorbed by touching the surface. From physics, we know that light can be modeled as a beam of energy that keeps moving forward until it loses all of its energy; the way a light beam loses energy is by collision. Each material consists of tiny little particles that can collide with the light ray as illustrated in the following image. The particles absorb some, or all, of the light's energy at each collision which is converted into heat.

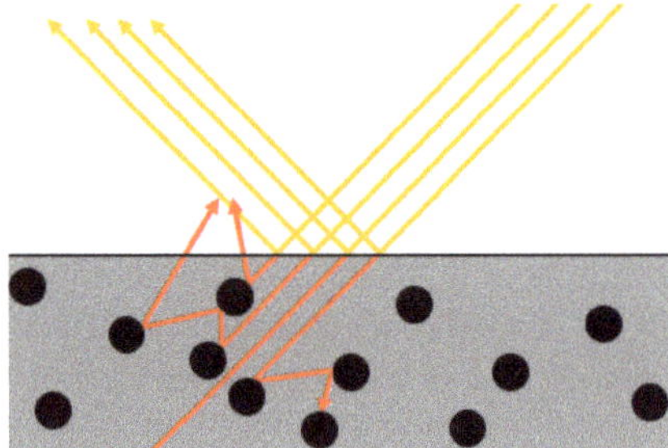

Generally, not all energy is absorbed and the light will continue to scatter in a (mostly) random direction at which point it collides with other particles until its energy is depleted or it leaves the surface again. Light rays re-emerging out of the surface contribute to the surface's observed (diffuse) color. In physically based rendering however, we make the simplifying assumption that all refracted light gets absorbed and scattered at a very small area of impact, ignoring the effect of scattered light rays that would've exited the surface at a distance. Specific shader techniques that do take this into account are known as subsurface scattering techniques that significantly improve the visual quality on materials like skin, marble, or wax, but come at the price of performance.

An additional subtlety when it comes to reflection and refraction are surfaces that are metallic. Metallic surfaces react different to light compared to non-metallic surfaces (also known as dielectrics). Metallic surfaces follow the same principles of reflection and refraction, but **all** refracted light gets directly absorbed without scattering. This means metallic surfaces only leave reflected or specular light; metallic surfaces show no diffuse colors. Because of this apparent distinction between metals and dielectrics, they're both treated differently in the PBR pipeline which we'll delve into further down the chapter.

This distinction between reflected and refracted light brings us to another observation regarding energy preservation: they're **mutually exclusive**. Whatever light energy gets reflected will no longer be absorbed by the material itself. Thus, the energy left to enter the surface as refracted light is directly the resulting energy after we've taken reflection into account.

We preserve this energy conserving relation by first calculating the specular fraction that amounts the percentage the incoming light's energy is reflected. The fraction of refracted light is then directly calculated from the specular fraction as:

```
float kS = calculateSpecularComponent(...); // reflection/specular fraction
float kD = 1.0 - kS;                         // refraction/diffuse fraction
```

This way we know both the amount the incoming light reflects and the amount the incoming light refracts, while adhering to the energy conservation principle. Given this approach, it is impossible for both the refracted/diffuse and reflected/specular contribution to exceed 1.0, thus ensuring the sum of their energy never exceeds the incoming light energy. Something we did not take into account in the previous lighting chapters.

43.3 **The reflectance equation**

This brings us to something called the rendering equation[1], an elaborate equation some very smart
folks out there came up with that is currently the best model we have for simulating the visuals of
light. Physically based rendering strongly follows a more specialized version of the render equation
known as the reflectance equation. To properly understand PBR, it's important to first build a solid
understanding of the reflectance equation:

$$L_o(p, \omega_o) = \int_\Omega f_r(p, \omega_i, \omega_o) L_i(p, \omega_i) n \cdot \omega_i d\omega_i$$

The reflectance equation appears daunting at first, but as we'll dissect it you'll see it slowly starts
to makes sense. To understand the equation, we have to delve into a bit of radiometry. Radiometry is
the measurement of electromagnetic radiation, including visible light. There are several radiometric
quantities we can use to measure light over surfaces and directions, but we will only discuss a single
one that's relevant to the reflectance equation known as radiance, denoted here as L. Radiance is
used to quantify the magnitude or strength of light coming from a single direction. It's a bit tricky
to understand at first as radiance is a combination of multiple physical quantities so we'll focus on
those first:

Radiant flux: radiant flux Φ is the transmitted energy of a light source measured in Watts. Light
is a collective sum of energy over multiple different wavelengths, each wavelength associated with
a particular (visible) color. The emitted energy of a light source can therefore be thought of as a
function of all its different wavelengths. Wavelengths between 390nm to 700nm (nanometers) are
considered part of the visible light spectrum i.e. wavelengths the human eye is able to perceive.
Below you'll find an image of the different energies per wavelength of daylight:

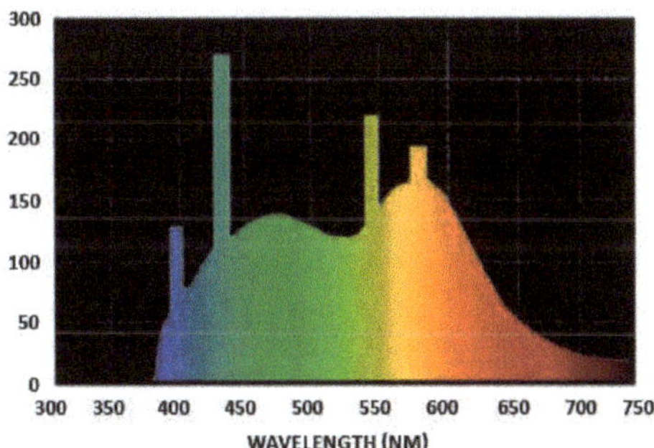

The radiant flux measures the total area of this function of different wavelengths. Directly taking
this measure of wavelengths as input is slightly impractical so we often make the simplification
of representing radiant flux, not as a function of varying wavelength strengths, but as a light color
triplet encoded as RGB (or as we'd commonly call it: light color). This encoding does come at quite
a loss of information, but this is generally negligible for visual aspects.

---

[1]en.wikipedia.org/wiki/Rendering_equation

Solid angle: the solid angle, denoted as ω, tells us the size or area of a shape projected onto a unit sphere. The area of the projected shape onto this unit sphere is known as the solid angle; you can visualize the solid angle as a direction with volume:

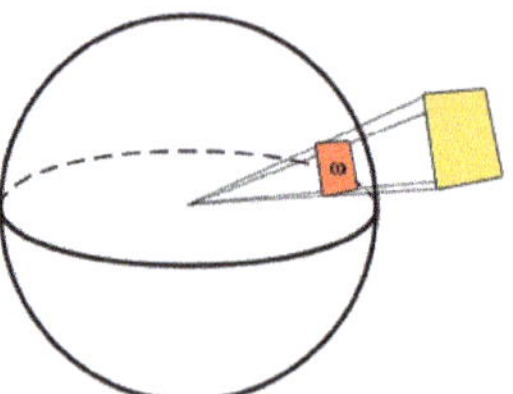

Think of being an observer at the center of this unit sphere and looking in the direction of the shape; the size of the silhouette you make out of it is the solid angle.

Radiant intensity: radiant intensity measures the amount of radiant flux per solid angle, or the strength of a light source over a projected area onto the unit sphere. For instance, given an omnidirectional light that radiates equally in all directions, the radiant intensity can give us its energy over a specific area (solid angle):

The equation to describe the radiant intensity is defined as follows:

$$I = \frac{d\Phi}{d\omega}$$

Where I is the radiant flux Φ over the solid angle ω.

With knowledge of radiant flux, radiant intensity, and the solid angle, we can finally describe the equation for **radiance**. Radiance is described as the total observed energy in an area A over the solid angle ω of a light of radiant intensity Φ:

$$L = \frac{d^2\Phi}{dA\,d\omega\cos\theta}$$

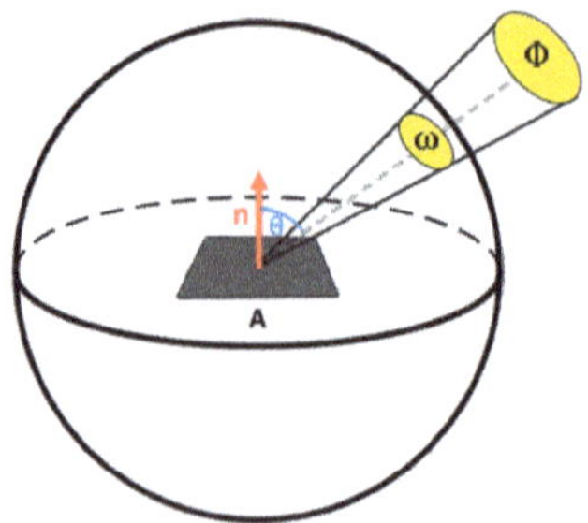

Radiance is a radiometric measure of the amount of light in an area, scaled by the incident (or incoming) angle θ of the light to the surface's normal as $\cos\theta$: light is weaker the less it directly radiates onto the surface, and strongest when it is directly perpendicular to the surface. This is similar to our perception of diffuse lighting from the *Basic Lighting* chapter as $\cos\theta$ directly corresponds to the dot product between the light's direction vector and the surface normal:

```
float cosTheta = dot(lightDir, N);
```

The radiance equation is quite useful as it contains most physical quantities we're interested in. If we consider the solid angle ω and the area A to be infinitely small, we can use radiance to measure the flux of a single ray of light hitting a single point in space. This relation allows us to calculate the radiance of a single light ray influencing a single (fragment) point; we effectively translate the solid angle ω into a direction vector ω, and A into a point p. This way, we can directly use radiance in our shaders to calculate a single light ray's per-fragment contribution.

In fact, when it comes to radiance we generally care about **all** incoming light onto a point p, which is the sum of all radiance known as irradiance. With knowledge of both radiance and irradiance we can get back to the reflectance equation:

$$L_o(p, \omega_o) = \int_\Omega f_r(p, \omega_i, \omega_o) L_i(p, \omega_i) n \cdot \omega_i d\omega_i$$

We now know that L in the render equation represents the radiance of some point p and some incoming infinitely small solid angle ω_i which can be thought of as an incoming direction vector ω_i. Remember that $\cos\theta$ scales the energy based on the light's incident angle to the surface, which we find in the reflectance equation as $n \cdot \omega_i$. The reflectance equation calculates the sum of reflected radiance $L_o(p, \omega_o)$ of a point p in direction ω_o which is the outgoing direction to the viewer. Or to put it differently: L_o measures the reflected sum of the lights' irradiance onto point p as viewed from ω_o.

The reflectance equation is based around irradiance, which is the sum of all incoming radiance we measure light of. Not just of a single incoming light direction, but of all incoming light directions within a hemisphere Ω centered around point p. A hemisphere can be described as half a sphere aligned around a surface's normal n:

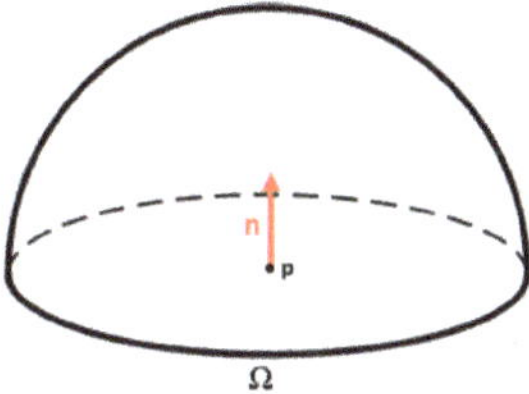

To calculate the total of values inside an area or (in the case of a hemisphere) a volume, we use a mathematical construct called an integral denoted in the reflectance equation as $\int$ over all incoming directions $d\omega_i$ within the hemisphere Ω. An integral measures the area of a function, which can either be calculated analytically or numerically. As there is no analytical solution to both the render and reflectance equation, we'll want to numerically solve the integral discretely. This translates to taking the result of small discrete steps of the reflectance equation over the hemisphere Ω and averaging their results over the step size. This is known as the Riemann sum that we can roughly visualize in code as follows:

```
int steps = 100;
float sum = 0.0f;
vec3 P      = ...;
vec3 Wo     = ...;
vec3 N      = ...;
float dW  = 1.0f / steps;
for(int i = 0; i < steps; ++i)
{
    vec3 Wi = getNextIncomingLightDir(i);
    sum += Fr(P, Wi, Wo) * L(P, Wi) * dot(N, Wi) * dW;
}
```

By scaling the steps by `dW`, the sum will equal the total area or volume of the integral function. The `dW` to scale each discrete step can be thought of as $d\omega_i$ in the reflectance equation. Mathematically $d\omega_i$ is the continuous symbol over which we calculate the integral, and while it does not directly relate to `dW` in code (as this is a discrete step of the Riemann sum), it helps to think of it this way. Keep in mind that taking discrete steps will always give us an approximation of the total area of the function. A careful reader will notice we can increase the *accuracy* of the Riemann Sum by increasing the number of steps.

The reflectance equation sums up the radiance of all incoming light directions ω_i over the hemisphere Ω scaled by f_r that hit point p and returns the sum of reflected light L_o in the viewer's direction. The incoming radiance can come from light sources as we're familiar with, or from an environment map measuring the radiance of every incoming direction as we'll discuss in the following chapters.

Now the only unknown left is the f_r symbol known as the BRDF or bidirectional reflective distribution function that scales or weighs the incoming radiance based on the surface's material properties.

43.4 BRDF

The BRDF, or bidirectional reflective distribution function, is a function that takes as input the incoming (light) direction ω_i, the outgoing (view) direction ω_o, the surface normal n, and a surface parameter a that represents the microsurface's roughness. The BRDF approximates how much each individual light ray ω_i contributes to the final reflected light of an opaque surface given its material properties. For instance, if the surface has a perfectly smooth surface (like a mirror) the BRDF function would return 0.0 for all incoming light rays ω_i except the one ray that has the same (reflected) angle as the outgoing ray ω_o at which the function returns 1.0.

A BRDF approximates the material's reflective and refractive properties based on the previously discussed microfacet theory. For a BRDF to be physically plausible it has to respect the law of energy conservation i.e. the sum of reflected light should never exceed the amount of incoming light. Technically, Blinn-Phong is considered a BRDF taking the same ω_i and ω_o as inputs. However, Blinn-Phong is not considered physically based as it doesn't adhere to the energy conservation principle. There are several physically based BRDFs out there to approximate the surface's reaction to light. However, almost all real-time PBR render pipelines use a BRDF known as the Cook-Torrance BRDF.

The Cook-Torrance BRDF contains both a diffuse and specular part:

$$f_r = k_d f_{\text{lambert}} + k_s f_{\text{cook-torrance}}$$

Here k_d is the earlier mentioned ratio of incoming light energy that gets *refracted* with k_s being the ratio that gets *reflected*. The left side of the BRDF states the diffuse part of the equation denoted here as f_{lambert}. This is known as Lambertian diffuse similar to what we used for diffuse shading, which is a constant factor denoted as:

$$f_{\text{lambert}} = \frac{c}{\pi}$$

With c being the albedo or surface color (think of the diffuse surface texture). The divide by pi is there to normalize the diffuse light as the earlier denoted integral that contains the BRDF is scaled by π (we'll get to that in the later chapters).

> You may wonder how this Lambertian diffuse relates to the diffuse lighting we've been using before: the surface color multiplied by the dot product between the surface's normal and the light direction. The dot product is still there, but moved out of the BRDF as we find $n \cdot \omega_i$ at the end of the L_o integral.

There exist different equations for the diffuse part of the BRDF which tend to look more realistic, but are also more computationally expensive. As concluded by Epic Games however, the Lambertian diffuse is sufficient enough for most real-time rendering purposes.

The specular part of the BRDF is a bit more advanced and is described as:

$$f_{\text{CookTorrance}} = \frac{DFG}{4(\omega_o \cdot n)(\omega_i \cdot n)}$$

The Cook-Torrance specular BRDF is composed three functions and a normalization factor in the denominator. Each of the D, F and G symbols represent a type of function that approximates a specific part of the surface's reflective properties. These are defined as the normal **D**istribution function, the **F**resnel equation and the **G**eometry function:

- **Normal distribution function**: approximates the amount the surface's microfacets are aligned to the halfway vector, influenced by the roughness of the surface; this is the primary function approximating the microfacets.
- **Geometry function**: describes the self-shadowing property of the microfacets. When a surface is relatively rough, the surface's microfacets can overshadow other microfacets reducing the light the surface reflects.
- **Fresnel equation**: The Fresnel equation describes the ratio of surface reflection at different surface angles.

Each of these functions are an approximation of their physics equivalents and you'll find more than one version of each that aims to approximate the underlying physics in different ways; some more realistic, others more efficient. It is perfectly fine to pick whatever approximated version of these functions you want to use. Brian Karis from Epic Games did a great deal of research in his blog[1] on the multiple types of approximations. We're going to pick the same functions used by Epic Game's Unreal Engine 4 which are the Trowbridge-Reitz GGX for D, the Fresnel-Schlick approximation for F, and the Smith's Schlick-GGX for G.

---

[1] graphicrants.blogspot.nl/2013/08/specular-brdf-reference.html

43.4.1 Normal distribution function

The normal distribution function D statistically approximates the relative surface area of microfacets exactly aligned to the (halfway) vector h. There are a multitude of NDFs that statistically approximate the general alignment of the microfacets given some roughness parameter and the one we'll be using is known as the Trowbridge-Reitz GGX:

$$NDF_{\text{GGX TR}}(n,h,\alpha) = \frac{\alpha^2}{\pi((n \cdot h)^2(\alpha^2 - 1) + 1)^2}$$

Here h is the halfway vector to measure against the surface's microfacets, with a being a measure of the surface's roughness. If we take h as the halfway vector between the surface normal and light direction over varying roughness parameters we get the following visual result:

When the roughness is low (thus the surface is smooth), a highly concentrated number of microfacets are aligned to halfway vectors over a small radius. Due to this high concentration, the NDF displays a very bright spot. On a rough surface however, where the microfacets are aligned in much more random directions, you'll find a much larger number of halfway vectors h somewhat aligned to the microfacets (but less concentrated), giving us the more grayish results.

In GLSL the Trowbridge-Reitz GGX normal distribution function translates to the following code:

```glsl
float DistributionGGX(vec3 N, vec3 H, float a)
{
    float a2     = a*a;
    float NdotH  = max(dot(N, H), 0.0);
    float NdotH2 = NdotH*NdotH;

    float nom    = a2;
    float denom  = (NdotH2 * (a2 - 1.0) + 1.0);
    denom        = PI * denom * denom;

    return nom / denom;
}
```

43.4.2 Geometry function

The geometry function statistically approximates the relative surface area where its micro surface-details overshadow each other, causing light rays to be occluded.

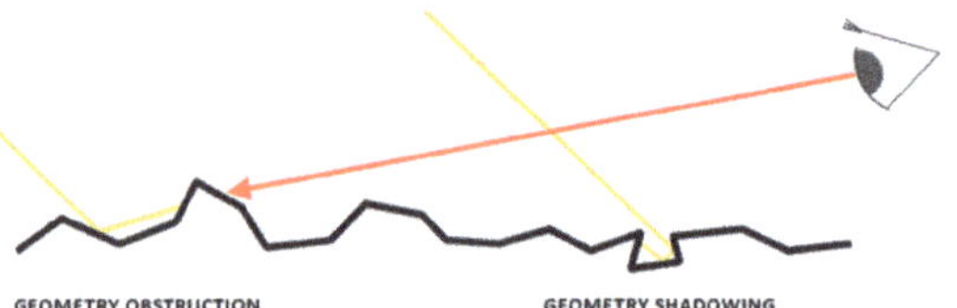

Similar to the NDF, the Geometry function takes a material's roughness parameter as input with rougher surfaces having a higher probability of overshadowing microfacets. The geometry function we will use is a combination of the GGX and Schlick-Beckmann approximation known as Schlick-GGX:

$$G_{\text{SchlickGGX}}(n, v, k) = \frac{n \cdot v}{(n \cdot v)(1 - k) + k}$$

Here k is a remapping of α based on whether we're using the geometry function for either direct lighting or IBL lighting:

$$k_{\text{direct}} = \frac{(\alpha + 1)^2}{8}$$

$$k_{\text{IBL}} = \frac{\alpha^2}{2}$$

Note that the value of α may differ based on how your engine translates roughness to α. In the following chapters we'll extensively discuss how and where this remapping becomes relevant.

To effectively approximate the geometry we need to take account of both the view direction (geometry obstruction) and the light direction vector (geometry shadowing). We can take both into account using Smith's method:

$$G(n, v, l, k) = G_{\text{sub}}(n, v, k) G_{\text{sub}}(n, l, k)$$

Using Smith's method with Schlick-GGX as G_{sub} gives the following visual appearance over varying roughness R:

The geometry function is a multiplier between [0.0, 1.0] with 1.0 (or white) measuring no microfacet shadowing, and 0.0 (or black) complete microfacet shadowing.

In GLSL the geometry function translates to the following code:

```glsl
float GeometrySchlickGGX(float NdotV, float k)
{
    float nom   = NdotV;
    float denom = NdotV * (1.0 - k) + k;

    return nom / denom;
}
float GeometrySmith(vec3 N, vec3 V, vec3 L, float k)
{
    float NdotV = max(dot(N, V), 0.0);
    float NdotL = max(dot(N, L), 0.0);
    float ggx1 = GeometrySchlickGGX(NdotV, k);
    float ggx2 = GeometrySchlickGGX(NdotL, k);

    return ggx1 * ggx2;
}
```

43.4.3 Fresnel equation

The Fresnel equation (pronounced as Freh-nel) describes the ratio of light that gets reflected over the light that gets refracted, which varies over the angle we're looking at a surface. The moment light hits a surface, based on the surface-to-view angle, the Fresnel equation tells us the percentage of light that gets reflected. From this ratio of reflection and the energy conservation principle we can directly obtain the refracted portion of light.

Every surface or material has a level of base reflectivity when looking straight at its surface, but when looking at the surface from an angle all[1] reflections become more apparent compared to the surface's base reflectivity. You can check this for yourself by looking at your (presumably) wooden/metallic desk which has a certain level of base reflectivity from a perpendicular view angle, but by looking at your desk from an almost 90 degree angle you'll see the reflections become much more apparent. All surfaces theoretically fully reflect light if seen from perfect 90-degree angles. This phenomenon is known as Fresnel and is described by the Fresnel equation.

The Fresnel equation is a rather complex equation, but luckily the Fresnel equation can be approximated using the Fresnel-Schlick approximation:

$$F_{\text{Schlick}}(h, v, F_0) = F_0 + (1 - F_0)(1 - (h \cdot v))^5$$

F_0 represents the base reflectivity of the surface, which we calculate using something called the *indices of refraction* or IOR. As you can see on a sphere surface, the more we look towards the surface's grazing angles (with the halfway-view angle reaching 90 degrees), the stronger the Fresnel and thus the reflections:

There are a few subtleties involved with the Fresnel equation. One is that the Fresnel-Schlick approximation is only really defined for dielectric or non-metal surfaces. For conductor surfaces (metals), calculating the base reflectivity with indices of refraction doesn't properly hold and we need to use a different Fresnel equation for conductors altogether. As this is inconvenient, we further approximate by pre-computing the surface's response at normal incidence (F_0) at a 0 degree angle as if looking directly onto a surface. We interpolate this value based on the view angle, as per the Fresnel-Schlick approximation, such that we can use the same equation for both metals and non-metals.

The surface's response at normal incidence, or the base reflectivity, can be found in large databases[2] with some of the more common values listed below as taken from Naty Hoffman's course notes:

---

[1] filmicworlds.com/blog/everything-has-fresnel/
[2] refractiveindex.info/

Material	F_0 **(Linear)**	F_0 **(sRGB)**
Water	(0.02, 0.02, 0.02)	(0.15, 0.15, 0.15)
Plastic / Glass (Low)	(0.03, 0.03, 0.03)	(0.21, 0.21, 0.21)
Plastic High	(0.05, 0.05, 0.05)	(0.24, 0.24, 0.24)
Glass (high) / Ruby	(0.08, 0.08, 0.08)	(0.31, 0.31, 0.31)
Diamond	(0.17, 0.17, 0.17)	(0.45, 0.45, 0.45)
Iron	(0.56, 0.57, 0.58)	(0.77, 0.78, 0.78)
Copper	(0.95, 0.64, 0.54)	(0.98, 0.82, 0.76)
Gold	(1.00, 0.71, 0.29)	(1.00, 0.86, 0.57)
Aluminium	(0.91, 0.92, 0.92)	(0.96, 0.96, 0.97)
Silver	(0.95, 0.93, 0.88)	(0.98, 0.97, 0.95)

What is interesting to observe here is that for all dielectric surfaces the base reflectivity never gets above 0.17 which is the exception rather than the rule, while for conductors the base reflectivity starts much higher and (mostly) varies between 0.5 and 1.0. Furthermore, for conductors (or metallic surfaces) the base reflectivity is tinted. This is why F_0 is presented as an RGB triplet (reflectivity at normal incidence can vary per wavelength); this is something we **only** see at metallic surfaces.

These specific attributes of metallic surfaces compared to dielectric surfaces gave rise to something called the metallic workflow. In the metallic workflow we author surface materials with an extra parameter known as metalness that describes whether a surface is either a metallic or a non-metallic surface.

> Theoretically, the metalness of a material is binary: it's either a metal or it isn't; it can't be both. However, most render pipelines allow configuring the metalness of a surface linearly between 0.0 and 1.0. This is mostly because of the lack of material texture precision. For instance, a surface having small (non-metal) dust/sand-like particles/scratches over a metallic surface is difficult to render with binary metalness values.

By pre-computing F_0 for both dielectrics and conductors we can use the same Fresnel-Schlick approximation for both types of surfaces, but we do have to tint the base reflectivity if we have a metallic surface. We generally accomplish this as follows:

```glsl
vec3 F0 = vec3(0.04);
F0      = mix(F0, surfaceColor.rgb, metalness);
```

We define a base reflectivity that is approximated for most dielectric surfaces. This is yet another approximation as F_0 is averaged around most common dielectrics. A base reflectivity of 0.04 holds for most dielectrics and produces physically plausible results without having to author an additional surface parameter. Then, based on how metallic a surface is, we either take the dielectric base reflectivity or take F_0 authored as the surface color. Because metallic surfaces absorb all refracted light they have no diffuse reflections and we can directly use the surface color texture as their base reflectivity.

In code, the Fresnel Schlick approximation translates to:

```glsl
vec3 fresnelSchlick(float cosTheta, vec3 F0)
{
    return F0 + (1.0 - F0) * pow(1.0 - cosTheta, 5.0);
}
```

With `cosTheta` being the dot product result between the surface's normal n and the halfway h (or view v) direction.

43.4.4 Cook-Torrance reflectance equation

With every component of the Cook-Torrance BRDF described, we can include the physically based BRDF into the now final reflectance equation:

$$L_o(p, \omega_o) = \int_\Omega (k_d \frac{c}{\pi} + k_s \frac{DFG}{4(\omega_o \cdot n)(\omega_i \cdot n)}) L_i(p, \omega_i) n \cdot \omega_i d\omega_i$$

This equation is not fully mathematically correct however. You may remember that the Fresnel term F represents the ratio of light that gets *reflected* on a surface. This is effectively our ratio k_s, meaning the specular (BRDF) part of the reflectance equation implicitly contains the reflectance ratio k_s. Given this, our final final reflectance equation becomes:

$$L_o(p, \omega_o) = \int_\Omega (k_d \frac{c}{\pi} + \frac{DFG}{4(\omega_o \cdot n)(\omega_i \cdot n)}) L_i(p, \omega_i) n \cdot \omega_i d\omega_i$$

This equation now completely describes a physically based render model that is generally recognized as what we commonly understand as physically based rendering, or PBR. Don't worry if you didn't yet completely understand how we'll need to fit all the discussed mathematics together in code. In the next chapters, we'll explore how to utilize the reflectance equation to get much more physically plausible results in our rendered lighting and all the bits and pieces should slowly start to fit together.

43.5 Authoring PBR materials

With knowledge of the underlying mathematical model of PBR we'll finalize the discussion by describing how artists generally author the physical properties of a surface that we can directly feed into the PBR equations. Each of the surface parameters we need for a PBR pipeline can be defined or modeled by textures. Using textures gives us per-fragment control over how each specific surface point should react to light: whether that point is metallic, rough or smooth, or how the surface responds to different wavelengths of light.

Below you'll see a list of textures you'll frequently find in a PBR pipeline together with its visual output if supplied to a PBR renderer:

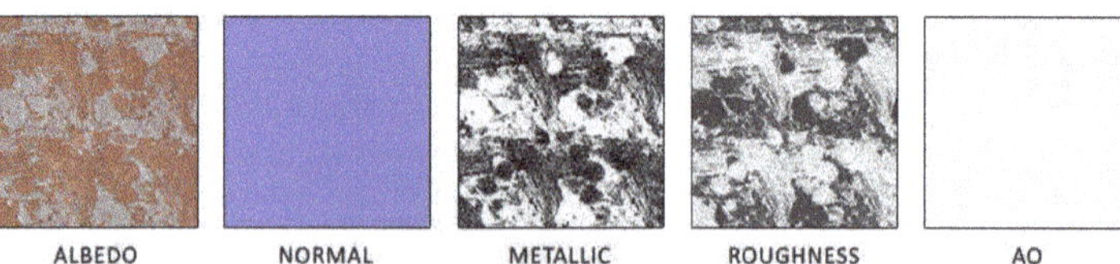

Albedo: the albedo texture specifies for each texel the color of the surface, or the base reflectivity if that texel is metallic. This is largely similar to what we've been using before as a diffuse texture, but all lighting information is extracted from the texture. Diffuse textures often have slight shadows or darkened crevices inside the image which is something you don't want in an albedo texture; it should only contain the color (or refracted absorption coefficients) of the surface.

Normal: the normal map texture is exactly as we've been using before in the *Normal Mapping* chapter. The normal map allows us to specify, per fragment, a unique normal to give the illusion that a surface is *bumpier* than its flat counterpart.

Metallic: the metallic map specifies per texel whether a texel is either metallic or it isn't. Based on how the PBR engine is set up, artists can author metalness as either grayscale values or as binary black or white.

Roughness: the roughness map specifies how rough a surface is on a per texel basis. The sampled roughness value of the roughness influences the statistical microfacet orientations of the surface. A rougher surface gets wider and blurrier reflections, while a smooth surface gets focused and clear reflections. Some PBR engines expect a smoothness map instead of a roughness map which some artists find more intuitive. These values are then translated (1.0 - smoothness) to roughness the moment they're sampled.

AO: the ambient occlusion or AO map specifies an extra shadowing factor of the surface and potentially surrounding geometry. If we have a brick surface for instance, the albedo texture should have no shadowing information inside the brick's crevices. The AO map however does specify these darkened edges as it's more difficult for light to escape. Taking ambient occlusion in account at the end of the lighting stage can significantly boost the visual quality of your scene. The ambient occlusion map of a mesh/surface is either manually generated, or pre-calculated in 3D modeling programs.

Artists set and tweak these physically based input values on a per-texel basis and can base their texture values on the physical surface properties of real-world materials. This is one of the biggest advantages of a PBR render pipeline as these physical properties of a surface remain the same, regardless of environment or lighting setup, making life easier for artists to get physically plausible results. Surfaces authored in a PBR pipeline can easily be shared among different PBR render engines, will look correct regardless of the environment they're in, and as a result look much more natural.

43.6 **Further reading**

- `blog.selfshadow.com/publications/s2013-shading-course/hoffman/s2013_pbs_physics_math_notes.pdf`: there is too much theory to fully discuss in a single article so the theory here barely scratches the surface; if you want to know more about the physics of light and how it relates to the theory of PBR **this** is the resource you want to read.
- `blog.selfshadow.com/publications/s2013-shading-course/karis/s2013_pbs_epic_notes_v2.pdf`: discusses the PBR model adopted by Epic Games in their 4th Unreal Engine installment. The PBR system we'll focus on in these chapters is based on this model of PBR.
- `www.shadertoy.com/view/4sSfzK`: great showcase of all individual PBR elements in an interactive ShaderToy demo.
- `www.marmoset.co/toolbag/learn/pbr-theory`: an introduction to PBR mostly meant for artists, but nevertheless a good read.
- `www.codinglabs.net/article_physically_based_rendering.aspx`: an

introduction to the render equation and how it relates to PBR.

- `www.codinglabs.net/article_physically_based_rendering_cook_to rrance.aspx`: an introduction to the Cook-Torrance BRDF.
- `blog.wolfire.com/2015/10/Physically-based-rendering`: an introduction to PBR by Lukas Orsvärn.
- `www.shadertoy.com/view/4sSfzK`: a great interactive shadertoy example (warning: may take a while to load) by Krzysztof Narkowi showcasing light-material interaction in a PBR fashion.

44. Lighting

In the previous chapter we laid the foundation for getting a realistic physically based renderer off the ground. In this chapter we'll focus on translating the previously discussed theory into an actual renderer that uses direct (or analytic) light sources: think of point lights, directional lights, and/or spotlights.

Let's start by re-visiting the final reflectance equation from the previous chapter:

$$L_o(p, \omega_o) = \int_\Omega (k_d \frac{c}{\pi} + \frac{DFG}{4(\omega_o \cdot n)(\omega_i \cdot n)}) L_i(p, \omega_i) n \cdot \omega_i d\omega_i$$

We now know mostly what's going on, but what still remained a big unknown is how exactly we're going to represent irradiance, the total radiance L, of the scene. We know that radiance L (as interpreted in computer graphics land) measures the radiant flux ϕ or light energy of a light source over a given solid angle ω. In our case we assumed the solid angle ω to be infinitely small in which case radiance measures the flux of a light source over a single light ray or direction vector.

Given this knowledge, how do we translate this into some of the lighting knowledge we've accumulated from previous chapters? Well, imagine we have a single point light (a light source that shines equally bright in all directions) with a radiant flux of `(23.47, 21.31, 20.79)` as translated to an RGB triplet. The radiant intensity of this light source equals its radiant flux at all outgoing direction rays. However, when shading a specific point p on a surface, of all possible incoming light directions over its hemisphere Ω, only one incoming direction vector w_i directly comes from the point light source. As we only have a single light source in our scene, assumed to be a single point in space, all other possible incoming light directions have zero radiance observed over the surface point p:

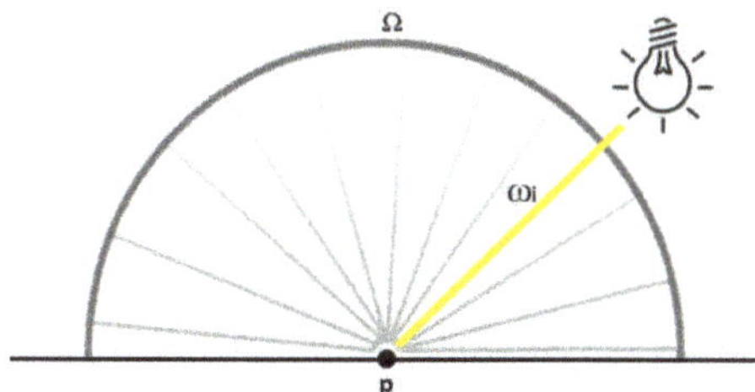

If at first, we assume that light attenuation (dimming of light over distance) does not affect the point light source, the radiance of the incoming light ray is the same regardless of where we position the light (excluding scaling the radiance by the incident angle $\cos \theta$). This, because the point light has the same radiant intensity regardless of the angle we look at it, effectively modeling its radiant intensity as its radiant flux: a constant vector `(23.47, 21.31, 20.79)`.

However, radiance also takes a position p as input and as any realistic point light source takes light attenuation into account, the radiant intensity of the point light source is scaled by some measure of the distance between point p and the light source. Then, as extracted from the original radiance equation, the result is scaled by the dot product between the surface normal n and the incoming light direction w_i.

To put this in more practical terms: in the case of a direct point light the radiance function L measures the light color, attenuated over its distance to p and scaled by $n \cdot w_i$, but only over the single light ray w_i that hits p which equals the light's direction vector from p. In code this translates to:

```glsl
vec3 lightColor     = vec3(23.47, 21.31, 20.79);
vec3 wi             = normalize(lightPos - fragPos);
float cosTheta      = max(dot(N, Wi), 0.0);
float attenuation   = calculateAttenuation(fragPos, lightPos);
vec3 radiance       = lightColor * attenuation * cosTheta;
```

Aside from the different terminology, this piece of code should be awfully familiar to you: this is exactly how we've been doing diffuse lighting so far. When it comes to direct lighting, radiance is calculated similarly to how we've calculated lighting before as only a single light direction vector contributes to the surface's radiance.

> Note that this assumption holds as point lights are infinitely small and only a single point in space. If we were to model a light that has area or volume, its radiance would be non-zero in more than one incoming light direction.

For other types of light sources originating from a single point we calculate radiance similarly. For instance, a directional light source has a constant w_i without an attenuation factor. And a spotlight would not have a constant radiant intensity, but one that is scaled by the forward direction vector of the spotlight.

This also brings us back to the integral $\int$ over the surface's hemisphere Ω . As we know beforehand the single locations of all the contributing light sources while shading a single surface point, it is not required to try and solve the integral. We can directly take the (known) number of light sources and calculate their total irradiance, given that each light source has only a single light direction that influences the surface's radiance. This makes **PBR** on direct light sources relatively simple as we effectively only have to loop over the contributing light sources. When we later take environment lighting into account, we have to take the integral into account as light can come from any direction.

44.1 A PBR surface model

Let's start by writing a fragment shader that implements the previously described **PBR** models. First, we need to take the relevant **PBR** inputs required for shading the surface:

```glsl
#version 330 core
out vec4 FragColor;
in vec2 TexCoords;
in vec3 WorldPos;
in vec3 Normal;

uniform vec3 camPos;

uniform vec3 albedo;
uniform float metallic;
uniform float roughness;
uniform float ao;
```

We take the standard inputs as calculated from a generic vertex shader and a set of constant material properties over the surface of the object.

Then at the start of the fragment shader we do the usual calculations required for any lighting algorithm:

```glsl
void main()
{
    vec3 N = normalize(Normal);
    vec3 V = normalize(camPos - WorldPos);
    [...]
}
```

44.1.1 Direct lighting

In this chapter's example demo we have a total of 4 point lights that together represent the scene's irradiance. To satisfy the reflectance equation we loop over each light source, calculate its individual radiance and sum its contribution scaled by the BRDF and the light's incident angle. We can think of the loop as solving the integral $\int$ over Ω for direct light sources. First, we calculate the relevant per-light variables:

```glsl
vec3 Lo = vec3(0.0);
for(int i = 0; i < 4; ++i)
{
    vec3 L = normalize(lightPositions[i] - WorldPos);
    vec3 H = normalize(V + L);

    float distance    = length(lightPositions[i] - WorldPos);
    float attenuation = 1.0 / (distance * distance);
    vec3 radiance     = lightColors[i] * attenuation;
    [...]
```

As we calculate lighting in linear space (we'll gamma correct at the end of the shader) we attenuate the light sources by the more physically correct inverse-square law.

> While physically correct, you may still want to use the constant-linear-quadratic attenuation equation that (while not physically correct) can offer you significantly more control over the light's energy falloff.

Then, for each light we want to calculate the full Cook-Torrance specular BRDF term:

$$\frac{DFG}{4(\omega_o \cdot n)(\omega_i \cdot n)}$$

The first thing we want to do is calculate the ratio between specular and diffuse reflection, or how much the surface reflects light versus how much it refracts light. We know from the previous chapter that the Fresnel equation calculates just that:

```glsl
vec3 fresnelSchlick(float cosTheta, vec3 F0)
{
    return F0 + (1.0 - F0) * pow(1.0 - cosTheta, 5.0);
}
```

The Fresnel-Schlick approximation expects a `F0` parameter which is known as the *surface reflection at zero incidence* or how much the surface reflects if looking directly at the surface. The `F0` varies per material and is tinted on metals as we find in large material databases. In the PBR metallic workflow we make the simplifying assumption that most dielectric surfaces look visually correct with a constant `F0` of `0.04`, while we do specify `F0` for metallic surfaces as then given by the albedo value. This translates to code as follows:

```glsl
vec3 F0 = vec3(0.04);
F0      = mix(F0, albedo, metallic);
vec3 F  = fresnelSchlick(max(dot(H, V), 0.0), F0);
```

As you can see, for non-metallic surfaces `F0` is always `0.04`. For metallic surfaces, we vary `F0` by linearly interpolating between the original `F0` and the albedo value given the `metallic` property.

Given F, the remaining terms to calculate are the normal distribution function D and the geometry function G.

In a direct PBR lighting shader their code equivalents are:

```glsl
float DistributionGGX(vec3 N, vec3 H, float roughness)
{
    float a      = roughness*roughness;
    float a2     = a*a;
    float NdotH  = max(dot(N, H), 0.0);
    float NdotH2 = NdotH*NdotH;

    float num    = a2;
    float denom  = (NdotH2 * (a2 - 1.0) + 1.0);
    denom = PI * denom * denom;

    return num / denom;
}

float GeometrySchlickGGX(float NdotV, float roughness)
{
    float r = (roughness + 1.0);
    float k = (r*r) / 8.0;

    float num = NdotV;
    float denom = NdotV * (1.0 - k) + k;

    return num / denom;
}
float GeometrySmith(vec3 N, vec3 V, vec3 L, float roughness)
{
    float NdotV = max(dot(N, V), 0.0);
    float NdotL = max(dot(N, L), 0.0);
    float ggx2 = GeometrySchlickGGX(NdotV, roughness);
    float ggx1 = GeometrySchlickGGX(NdotL, roughness);

    return ggx1 * ggx2;
}
```

What's important to note here is that in contrast to the *Theory* chapter, we pass the roughness parameter directly to these functions; this way we can make some term-specific modifications to the original roughness value. Based on observations by Disney and adopted by Epic Games, the lighting looks more correct squaring the roughness in both the geometry and normal distribution function.

With both functions defined, calculating the NDF and the G term in the reflectance loop is straightforward:

```glsl
float NDF = DistributionGGX(N, H, roughness);
float G = GeometrySmith(N, V, L, roughness);
```

This gives us enough to calculate the Cook-Torrance BRDF:

```
vec3 numerator     = NDF * G * F;
float denominator = 4.0 * max(dot(N, V), 0.0) * max(dot(N, L), 0.0);
vec3 specular      = numerator / max(denominator, 0.001);
```

Note that we constrain the denominator to `0.001` to prevent a divide by zero in case any dot product ends up `0.0`.

Now we can finally calculate each light's contribution to the reflectance equation. As the Fresnel value directly corresponds to k_S we can use `F` to denote the specular contribution of any light that hits the surface. From k_S we can then calculate the ratio of refraction k_D:

```
vec3 kS = F;
vec3 kD = vec3(1.0) - kS;

kD *= 1.0 - metallic;
```

Seeing as `kS` represents the energy of light that gets reflected, the remaining ratio of light energy is the light that gets refracted which we store as `kD`. Furthermore, because metallic surfaces don't refract light and thus have no diffuse reflections we enforce this property by nullifying `kD` if the surface is metallic. This gives us the final data we need to calculate each light's outgoing reflectance value:

```
    const float PI = 3.14159265359;

    float NdotL = max(dot(N, L), 0.0);
    Lo += (kD * albedo / PI + specular) * radiance * NdotL;
}
```

The resulting `Lo` value, or the outgoing radiance, is effectively the result of the reflectance equation's integral $\int$ over Ω. We don't really have to try and solve the integral for all possible incoming light directions as we know exactly the 4 incoming light directions that can influence the fragment. Because of this, we can directly loop over these incoming light directions e.g. the number of lights in the scene.

What's left is to add an (improvised) ambient term to the direct lighting result `Lo` and we have the final lit color of the fragment:

```
vec3 ambient = vec3(0.03) * albedo * ao;
vec3 color = ambient + Lo;
```

44.1.2 Linear and HDR rendering

So far we've assumed all our calculations to be in linear color space and to account for this we need to gamma correct at the end of the shader. Calculating lighting in linear space is incredibly important as PBR requires all inputs to be linear. Not taking this into account will result in incorrect lighting. Additionally, we want light inputs to be close to their physical equivalents such that their radiance or color values can vary wildly over a high spectrum of values. As a result, `Lo` can rapidly grow really high which then gets clamped between `0.0` and `1.0` due to the default low dynamic range (LDR) output. We fix this by taking `Lo` and tone or exposure map the high dynamic range (HDR) value correctly to LDR before gamma correction:

```glsl
color = color / (color + vec3(1.0));
color = pow(color, vec3(1.0/2.2));
```

Here we tone map the HDR color using the Reinhard operator, preserving the high dynamic range of a possibly highly varying irradiance, after which we gamma correct the color. We don't have a separate framebuffer or post-processing stage so we can directly apply both the tone mapping and gamma correction step at the end of the forward fragment shader.

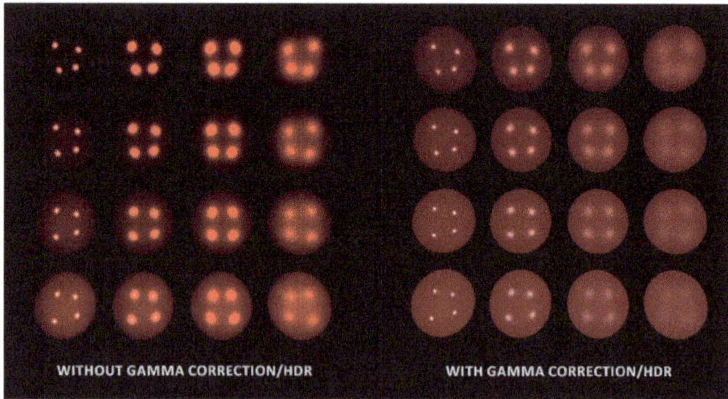

Taking both linear color space and high dynamic range into account is incredibly important in a PBR pipeline. Without these it's impossible to properly capture the high and low details of varying light intensities and your calculations end up incorrect and thus visually unpleasing.

44.1.3 Full direct lighting PBR shader

All that's left now is to pass the final tone mapped and gamma corrected color to the fragment shader's output channel and we have ourselves a direct PBR lighting shader. For completeness' sake, the complete `main` function is listed below:

```glsl
#version 330 core
out vec4 FragColor;
in vec2 TexCoords;
in vec3 WorldPos;
in vec3 Normal;

// material parameters
uniform vec3 albedo;
uniform float metallic;
uniform float roughness;
uniform float ao;

// lights
uniform vec3 lightPositions[4];
uniform vec3 lightColors[4];

uniform vec3 camPos;

const float PI = 3.14159265359;

float DistributionGGX(vec3 N, vec3 H, float roughness);
float GeometrySchlickGGX(float NdotV, float roughness);
float GeometrySmith(vec3 N, vec3 V, vec3 L, float roughness);
vec3 fresnelSchlick(float cosTheta, vec3 F0);
```

```glsl
void main()
{
  vec3 N = normalize(Normal);
  vec3 V = normalize(camPos - WorldPos);

  vec3 F0 = vec3(0.04);
  F0 = mix(F0, albedo, metallic);

  // reflectance equation
  vec3 Lo = vec3(0.0);
  for(int i = 0; i < 4; ++i)
  {
    // calculate per-light radiance
    vec3 L = normalize(lightPositions[i] - WorldPos);
    vec3 H = normalize(V + L);
    float distance    = length(lightPositions[i] - WorldPos);
    float attenuation = 1.0 / (distance * distance);
    vec3 radiance     = lightColors[i] * attenuation;

    // cook-torrance brdf
    float NDF = DistributionGGX(N, H, roughness);
    float G   = GeometrySmith(N, V, L, roughness);
    vec3 F    = fresnelSchlick(max(dot(H, V), 0.0), F0);

    vec3 kS = F;
    vec3 kD = vec3(1.0) - kS;
    kD *= 1.0 - metallic;

    vec3 numerator    = NDF * G * F;
    float denominator = 4.0 * max(dot(N, V), 0.0) * max(dot(N, L), 0.0);
    vec3 specular     = numerator / max(denominator, 0.001);

    // add to outgoing radiance Lo
    float NdotL = max(dot(N, L), 0.0);
    Lo += (kD * albedo / PI + specular) * radiance * NdotL;
  }

  vec3 ambient = vec3(0.03) * albedo * ao;
  vec3 color = ambient + Lo;

  color = color / (color + vec3(1.0));
  color = pow(color, vec3(1.0/2.2));

  FragColor = vec4(color, 1.0);
}
```

Hopefully, with the theory from the previous chapter and the knowledge of the reflectance equation this shader shouldn't be as daunting anymore. If we take this shader, 4 point lights, and quite a few spheres where we vary both their metallic and roughness values on their vertical and horizontal axis respectively, we'd get something like this:

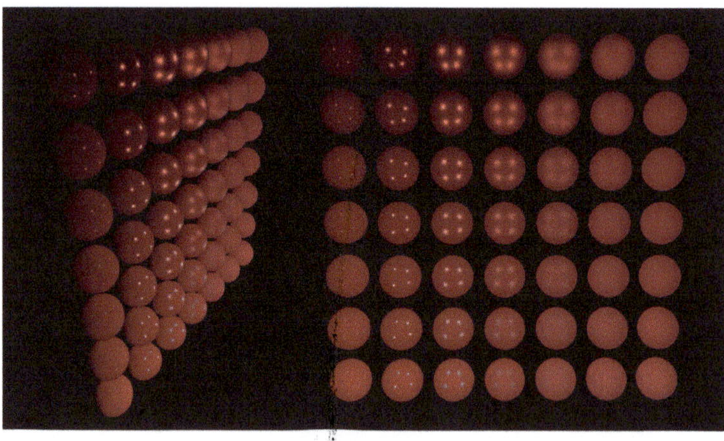

From bottom to top the metallic value ranges from `0.0` to `1.0`, with roughness increasing left to right from `0.0` to `1.0`. You can see that by only changing these two simple to understand parameters we can already display a wide array of different materials.

You can find the full source code of the demo at `/src/6.pbr/1.1.lighting/`.

44.2 Textured PBR

Extending the system to now accept its surface parameters as textures instead of uniform values gives us per-fragment control over the surface material's properties:

```glsl
[...]
uniform sampler2D albedoMap;
uniform sampler2D normalMap;
uniform sampler2D metallicMap;
uniform sampler2D roughnessMap;
uniform sampler2D aoMap;

void main()
{
    vec3 albedo     = pow(texture(albedoMap, TexCoords).rgb, 2.2);
    vec3 normal     = getNormalFromNormalMap();
    float metallic  = texture(metallicMap, TexCoords).r;
    float roughness = texture(roughnessMap, TexCoords).r;
    float ao        = texture(aoMap, TexCoords).r;
    [...]
}
```

Note that the albedo textures that come from artists are generally authored in sRGB space which is why we first convert them to linear space before using albedo in our lighting calculations. Based on the system artists use to generate ambient occlusion maps you may also have to convert these from sRGB to linear space as well. Metallic and roughness maps are almost always authored in linear space.

Replacing the material properties of the previous set of spheres with textures, already shows a major visual improvement over the previous lighting algorithms we've used:

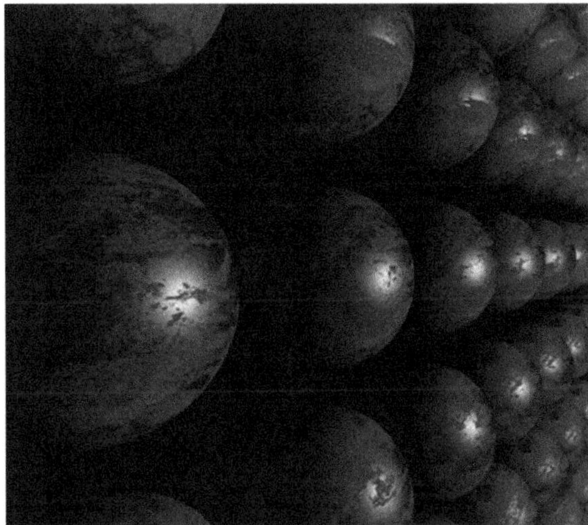

You can find the full source code of the textured demo at `/src/6.pbr/1.2.lighting_textured/lighting_textured.cpp` and the texture set used at `freepbr.com/materials/rusted-iron-pbr-metal-material-alt/` (with a white ao map). Keep in mind that metallic surfaces tend to look too dark in direct lighting environments as they don't have diffuse reflectance. They do look more correct when taking the environment's specular ambient lighting into account, which is what we'll focus on in the next chapters.

While not as visually impressive as some of the PBR render demos you find out there, given that we don't yet have image based lighting built in, the system we have now is still a physically based renderer, and even without IBL you'll see your lighting look a lot more realistic.

45. Diffuse irradiance

IBL, or image based lighting, is a collection of techniques to light objects, not by direct analytical lights as in the previous chapter, but by treating the surrounding environment as one big light source. This is generally accomplished by manipulating a cubemap environment map (taken from the real world or generated from a 3D scene) such that we can directly use it in our lighting equations: treating each cubemap texel as a light emitter. This way we can effectively capture an environment's global lighting and general feel, giving objects a better sense of *belonging* in their environment.

As image based lighting algorithms capture the lighting of some (global) environment, its input is considered a more precise form of ambient lighting, even a crude approximation of global illumination. This makes IBL interesting for **PBR** as objects look significantly more physically accurate when we take the environment's lighting into account.

To start introducing IBL into our **PBR** system let's again take a quick look at the reflectance equation:

$$L_o(p, \omega_o) = \int_\Omega (k_d \frac{c}{\pi} + k_s \frac{DFG}{4(\omega_o \cdot n)(\omega_i \cdot n)}) L_i(p, \omega_i) n \cdot \omega_i d\omega_i$$

As described before, our main goal is to solve the integral of all incoming light directions w_i over the hemisphere Ω . Solving the integral in the previous chapter was easy as we knew beforehand the exact few light directions w_i that contributed to the integral. This time however, **every** incoming light direction w_i from the surrounding environment could potentially have some radiance making it less trivial to solve the integral. This gives us two main requirements for solving the integral:

- We need some way to retrieve the scene's radiance given any direction vector w_i.
- Solving the integral needs to be fast and real-time.

Now, the first requirement is relatively easy. We've already hinted it, but one way of representing an environment or scene's irradiance is in the form of a (processed) environment cubemap. Given such a cubemap, we can visualize every texel of the cubemap as one single emitting light source. By sampling this cubemap with any direction vector w_i, we retrieve the scene's radiance from that direction.

Getting the scene's radiance given any direction vector w_i is then as simple as:

```glsl
vec3 radiance = texture(_cubemapEnvironment, w_i).rgb;
```

Still, solving the integral requires us to sample the environment map from not just one direction, but all possible directions w_i over the hemisphere Ω which is far too expensive for each fragment shader invocation. To solve the integral in a more efficient fashion we'll want to *pre-process* or pre-compute most of the computations. For this we'll have to delve a bit deeper into the reflectance equation:

$$L_o(p, \omega_o) = \int_\Omega (k_d \frac{c}{\pi} + k_s \frac{DFG}{4(\omega_o \cdot n)(\omega_i \cdot n)}) L_i(p, \omega_i) n \cdot \omega_i d\omega_i$$

Taking a good look at the reflectance equation we find that the diffuse k_d and specular k_s term of the BRDF are independent from each other and we can split the integral in two:

$$L_o(p,\omega_o) = \int_\Omega (k_d\frac{c}{\pi})L_i(p,\omega_i)n \cdot \omega_i d\omega_i + \int_\Omega (k_s\frac{DFG}{4(\omega_o \cdot n)(\omega_i \cdot n)})L_i(p,\omega_i)n \cdot \omega_i d\omega_i$$

By splitting the integral in two parts we can focus on both the diffuse and specular term individually; the focus of this chapter being on the diffuse integral.

Taking a closer look at the diffuse integral we find that the diffuse lambert term is a constant term (the color c, the refraction ratio k_d, and π are constant over the integral) and not dependent on any of the integral variables. Given this, we can move the constant term out of the diffuse integral:

$$L_o(p,\omega_o) = k_d\frac{c}{\pi}\int_\Omega L_i(p,\omega_i)n \cdot \omega_i d\omega_i$$

This gives us an integral that only depends on w_i (assuming p is at the center of the environment map). With this knowledge, we can calculate or *pre-compute* a new cubemap that stores in each sample direction (or texel) w_o the diffuse integral's result by convolution.

Convolution is applying some computation to each entry in a data set considering all other entries in the data set; the data set being the scene's radiance or environment map. Thus for every sample direction in the cubemap, we take all other sample directions over the hemisphere Ω into account.

To convolute an environment map we solve the integral for each output w_o sample direction by discretely sampling a large number of directions w_i over the hemisphere Ω and averaging their radiance. The hemisphere we build the sample directions w_i from is oriented towards the output w_o sample direction we're convoluting.

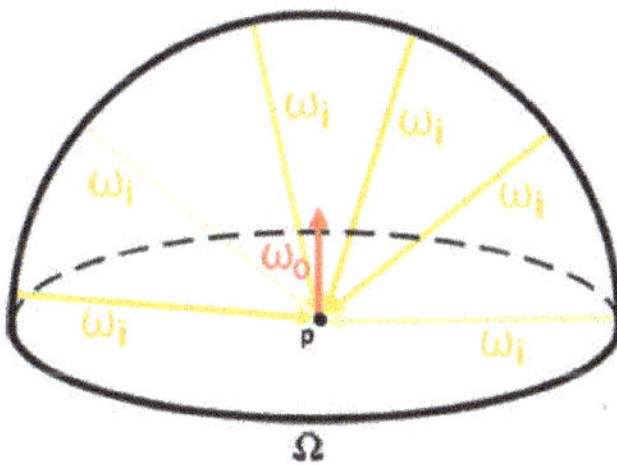

This pre-computed cubemap, that for each sample direction w_o stores the integral result, can be thought of as the pre-computed sum of all indirect diffuse light of the scene hitting some surface aligned along direction w_o. Such a cubemap is known as an irradiance map seeing as the convoluted cubemap effectively allows us to directly sample the scene's (pre-computed) irradiance from any direction w_o.

> The radiance equation also depends on a position p, which we've assumed to be at the center of the irradiance map. This does mean all diffuse indirect light must come from a single environment map which may break the illusion of reality (especially indoors). Render engines solve this by placing reflection probes all over the scene where each reflection probes calculates its own irradiance map of its surroundings. This way, the irradiance (and radiance) at position p is the interpolated irradiance between its closest reflection probes. For now, we assume we always sample the environment map from its center.

Below is an example of a cubemap environment map and its resulting irradiance map (courtesy of Wave Engine[1]), averaging the scene's radiance for every direction w_o.

By storing the convoluted result in each cubemap texel (in the direction of w_o), the irradiance map displays somewhat like an average color or lighting display of the environment. Sampling any direction from this environment map will give us the scene's irradiance in that particular direction.

45.1 PBR and HDR

We've briefly touched upon it in the previous chapter: taking the high dynamic range of your scene's lighting into account in a PBR pipeline is incredibly important. As PBR bases most of its inputs on real physical properties and measurements it makes sense to closely match the incoming light values to their physical equivalents. Whether we make educated guesses on each light's radiant flux or use their direct physical equivalent[2], the difference between a simple light bulb or the sun is significant either way. Without working in an HDR render environment it's impossible to correctly specify each light's relative intensity.

So, PBR and HDR go hand in hand, but how does it all relate to image based lighting? We've seen in the previous chapter that it's relatively easy to get PBR working in HDR. However, seeing as for image based lighting we base the environment's indirect light intensity on the color values of an environment cubemap we need some way to store the lighting's high dynamic range into an environment map.

The environment maps we've been using so far as cubemaps (used as skyboxes for instance) are in low dynamic range (LDR). We directly used their color values from the individual face images, ranged between `0.0` and `1.0`, and processed them as is. While this may work fine for visual output, when taking them as physical input parameters it's not going to work.

---

[1] www.indiedb.com/features/using-image-based-lighting-ibl
[2] en.wikipedia.org/wiki/Lumen_(unit)

45.1.1 The radiance HDR file format

Enter the radiance file format. The radiance file format (with the `.hdr` extension) stores a full cubemap with all 6 faces as floating point data. This allows us to specify color values outside the `0.0` to `1.0` range to give lights their correct color intensities. The file format also uses a clever trick to store each floating point value, not as a 32 bit value per channel, but 8 bits per channel using the color's alpha channel as an exponent (this does come with a loss of precision). This works quite well, but requires the parsing program to re-convert each color to their floating point equivalent.

There are quite a few radiance HDR environment maps freely available from sources like sIBL-archive[1] of which you can see an example below:

This may not be exactly what you were expecting, as the image appears distorted and doesn't show any of the 6 individual cubemap faces of environment maps we've seen before. This environment map is projected from a sphere onto a flat plane such that we can more easily store the environment into a single image known as an equirectangular map. This does come with a small caveat as most of the visual resolution is stored in the horizontal view direction, while less is preserved in the bottom and top directions. In most cases this is a decent compromise as with almost any renderer you'll find most of the interesting lighting and surroundings in the horizontal viewing directions.

45.1.2 HDR and stb_image.h

Loading radiance HDR images directly requires some knowledge of the file format[2] which isn't too difficult, but cumbersome nonetheless. Lucky for us, the popular one header library stb_image.h[3] supports loading radiance HDR images directly as an array of floating point values which perfectly fits our needs. With `stb_image` added to your project, loading an HDR image is now as simple as follows:

```cpp
#include "stb_image.h"
[...]

stbi_set_flip_vertically_on_load(true);
int width, height, nrComponents;
float *data = stbi_loadf("newport_loft.hdr", &width, &height,
                         &nrComponents, 0);
unsigned int hdrTexture;
if (data)
```

---

[1] www.hdrlabs.com/sibl/archive.html
[2] radsite.lbl.gov/radiance/refer/Notes/picture_format.html
[3] github.com/nothings/stb/blob/master/stb_image.h

```cpp
{
    glGenTextures(1, &hdrTexture);
    glBindTexture(GL_TEXTURE_2D, hdrTexture);
    glTexImage2D(GL_TEXTURE_2D, 0, GL_RGB16F, width, height, 0, GL_RGB,
                 GL_FLOAT, data);

    glTexParameteri(GL_TEXTURE_2D, GL_TEXTURE_WRAP_S, GL_CLAMP_TO_EDGE);
    glTexParameteri(GL_TEXTURE_2D, GL_TEXTURE_WRAP_T, GL_CLAMP_TO_EDGE);
    glTexParameteri(GL_TEXTURE_2D, GL_TEXTURE_MIN_FILTER, GL_LINEAR);
    glTexParameteri(GL_TEXTURE_2D, GL_TEXTURE_MAG_FILTER, GL_LINEAR);

    stbi_image_free(data);
}
else
{
    std::cout << "Failed to load HDR image." << std::endl;
}
```

`stb_image.h` automatically maps the HDR values to a list of floating point values: 32 bits per channel and 3 channels per color by default. This is all we need to store the equirectangular HDR environment map into a 2D floating point texture.

45.1.3 From Equirectangular to Cubemap

It is possible to use the equirectangular map directly for environment lookups, but these operations can be relatively expensive in which case a direct cubemap sample is more performant. Therefore, in this chapter we'll first convert the equirectangular image to a cubemap for further processing. Note that in the process we also show how to sample an equirectangular map as if it was a 3D environment map in which case you're free to pick whichever solution you prefer.

To convert an equirectangular image into a cubemap we need to render a (unit) cube and project the equirectangular map on all of the cube's faces from the inside and take 6 images of each of the cube's sides as a cubemap face. The vertex shader of this cube simply renders the cube as is and passes its local position to the fragment shader as a 3D sample vector:

```glsl
#version 330 core
layout (location = 0) in vec3 aPos;

out vec3 localPos;

uniform mat4 projection;
uniform mat4 view;

void main()
{
    localPos = aPos;
    gl_Position = projection * view * vec4(localPos, 1.0);
}
```

For the fragment shader, we color each part of the cube as if we neatly folded the equirectangular map onto each side of the cube. To accomplish this, we take the fragment's sample direction as interpolated from the cube's local position and then use this direction vector and some trigonometry magic (spherical to cartesian) to sample the equirectangular map as if it's a cubemap itself. We directly store the result onto the cube-face's fragment which should be all we need to do:

```glsl
#version 330 core
out vec4 FragColor;
in vec3 localPos;

uniform sampler2D equirectangularMap;

const vec2 invAtan = vec2(0.1591, 0.3183);
vec2 SampleSphericalMap(vec3 v)
{
    vec2 uv = vec2(atan(v.z, v.x), asin(v.y));
    uv *= invAtan;
    uv += 0.5;
    return uv;
}

void main()
{
    vec2 uv = SampleSphericalMap(normalize(localPos)); // normalize
    vec3 color = texture(equirectangularMap, uv).rgb;

    FragColor = vec4(color, 1.0);
}
```

If you render a cube at the center of the scene given an **HDR** equirectangular map you'll get something that looks like this:

This demonstrates that we effectively mapped an equirectangular image onto a cubic shape, but doesn't yet help us in converting the source **HDR** image to a cubemap texture. To accomplish this we have to render the same cube 6 times, looking at each individual face of the cube, while recording its visual result with a framebuffer object:

```cpp
unsigned int captureFBO, captureRBO;
glGenFramebuffers(1, &captureFBO);
glGenRenderbuffers(1, &captureRBO);

glBindFramebuffer(GL_FRAMEBUFFER, captureFBO);
glBindRenderbuffer(GL_RENDERBUFFER, captureRBO);
glRenderbufferStorage(GL_RENDERBUFFER, GL_DEPTH_COMPONENT24, 512, 512);
glFramebufferRenderbuffer(GL_FRAMEBUFFER, GL_DEPTH_ATTACHMENT,
                          GL_RENDERBUFFER, captureRBO);
```

Of course, we then also generate the corresponding cubemap color textures, pre-allocating memory for each of its 6 faces:

```cpp
unsigned int envCubemap;
glGenTextures(1, &envCubemap);
glBindTexture(GL_TEXTURE_CUBE_MAP, envCubemap);
for (unsigned int i = 0; i < 6; ++i)
{
    // note that we store each face with 16 bit floating point values
    glTexImage2D(GL_TEXTURE_CUBE_MAP_POSITIVE_X + i, 0, GL_RGB16F,
                 512, 512, 0, GL_RGB, GL_FLOAT, nullptr);
}
glTexParameteri(GL_TEXTURE_CUBE_MAP, GL_TEXTURE_WRAP_S, GL_CLAMP_TO_EDGE);
glTexParameteri(GL_TEXTURE_CUBE_MAP, GL_TEXTURE_WRAP_T, GL_CLAMP_TO_EDGE);
glTexParameteri(GL_TEXTURE_CUBE_MAP, GL_TEXTURE_WRAP_R, GL_CLAMP_TO_EDGE);
glTexParameteri(GL_TEXTURE_CUBE_MAP, GL_TEXTURE_MIN_FILTER, GL_LINEAR);
glTexParameteri(GL_TEXTURE_CUBE_MAP, GL_TEXTURE_MAG_FILTER, GL_LINEAR);
```

Then what's left to do is capture the equirectangular 2D texture onto the cubemap faces.

I won't go over the details as the code details topics previously discussed in the *Framebuffers* and *Point Shadows* chapters, but it effectively boils down to setting up 6 different view matrices (facing each side of the cube), set up a projection matrix with a fov of 90 degrees to capture the entire face, and render a cube 6 times storing the results in a floating point framebuffer:

```cpp
glm::mat4 captureProjection = glm::perspective(glm::radians(90.0f), 1.0f,
                                               0.1f, 10.0f);
glm::mat4 captureViews[] =
{
glm::lookAt(glm::vec3(0.0f, 0.0f, 0.0f), glm::vec3( 1.0f, 0.0f, 0.0f),
            glm::vec3(0.0f, -1.0f, 0.0f)),
glm::lookAt(glm::vec3(0.0f, 0.0f, 0.0f), glm::vec3(-1.0f, 0.0f, 0.0f),
            glm::vec3(0.0f, -1.0f, 0.0f)),
glm::lookAt(glm::vec3(0.0f, 0.0f, 0.0f), glm::vec3( 0.0f, 1.0f, 0.0f),
            glm::vec3(0.0f, 0.0f, 1.0f)),
glm::lookAt(glm::vec3(0.0f, 0.0f, 0.0f), glm::vec3( 0.0f, -1.0f, 0.0f),
            glm::vec3(0.0f, 0.0f, -1.0f)),
glm::lookAt(glm::vec3(0.0f, 0.0f, 0.0f), glm::vec3( 0.0f, 0.0f, 1.0f),
            glm::vec3(0.0f, -1.0f, 0.0f)),
glm::lookAt(glm::vec3(0.0f, 0.0f, 0.0f), glm::vec3( 0.0f, 0.0f, -1.0f),
            glm::vec3(0.0f, -1.0f, 0.0f))
};

// convert HDR equirectangular environment map to cubemap equivalent
equirectangularToCubemapShader.use();
equirectangularToCubemapShader.setInt("equirectangularMap", 0);
equirectangularToCubemapShader.setMat4("projection", captureProjection);
glActiveTexture(GL_TEXTURE0);
glBindTexture(GL_TEXTURE_2D, hdrTexture);

glViewport(0, 0, 512, 512); // don't forget to configure the viewport
glBindFramebuffer(GL_FRAMEBUFFER, captureFBO);
for (unsigned int i = 0; i < 6; ++i)
{
    equirectangularToCubemapShader.setMat4("view", captureViews[i]);
    glFramebufferTexture2D(GL_FRAMEBUFFER, GL_COLOR_ATTACHMENT0,
        GL_TEXTURE_CUBE_MAP_POSITIVE_X + i, envCubemap, 0);
    glClear(GL_COLOR_BUFFER_BIT | GL_DEPTH_BUFFER_BIT);

    renderCube(); // renders a 1x1 cube
```

```
}
glBindFramebuffer(GL_FRAMEBUFFER, 0);
```

We take the color attachment of the framebuffer and switch its texture target around for every face of the cubemap, directly rendering the scene into one of the cubemap's faces. Once this routine has finished (which we only have to do once), the cubemap `envCubemap` should be the cubemapped environment version of our original **HDR** image.

Let's test the cubemap by writing a very simple skybox shader to display the cubemap around us:

```glsl
#version 330 core
layout (location = 0) in vec3 aPos;

uniform mat4 projection;
uniform mat4 view;

out vec3 localPos;

void main()
{
    localPos = aPos;

    mat4 rotView = mat4(mat3(view)); // remove translation
    vec4 clipPos = projection * rotView * vec4(localPos, 1.0);

    gl_Position = clipPos.xyww;
}
```

Note the `xyww` trick here that ensures the depth value of the rendered cube fragments always end up at `1.0`, the maximum depth value, as described in the *Cubemaps* chapter. Do note that we need to change the depth comparison function to `GL_LEQUAL`:

```
glDepthFunc(GL_LEQUAL);
```

The fragment shader then directly samples the cubemap environment map using the cube's local fragment position:

```glsl
#version 330 core
out vec4 FragColor;

in vec3 localPos;

uniform samplerCube environmentMap;

void main()
{
    vec3 envColor = texture(environmentMap, localPos).rgb;

    envColor = envColor / (envColor + vec3(1.0));
    envColor = pow(envColor, vec3(1.0/2.2));

    FragColor = vec4(envColor, 1.0);
}
```

We sample the environment map using its interpolated vertex cube positions that directly correspond to the correct direction vector to sample. Seeing as the camera's translation components are ignored, rendering this shader over a cube should give you the environment map as a non-moving background. Also, as we directly output the environment map's HDR values to the default LDR framebuffer, we want to properly tone map the color values. Furthermore, almost all HDR maps are in linear color space by default so we need to apply gamma correction before writing to the default framebuffer.

Now rendering the sampled environment map over the previously rendered spheres should look something like this:

Well... it took us quite a bit of setup to get here, but we successfully managed to read an HDR environment map, convert it from its equirectangular mapping to a cubemap, and render the HDR cubemap into the scene as a skybox. Furthermore, we set up a small system to render onto all 6 faces of a cubemap, which we'll need again when convoluting the environment map. You can find the source code of the entire conversion process at `/src/6.pbr/2.1.1.ibl_irradiance_ conversion/`.

45.2 Cubemap convolution

As described at the start of the chapter, our main goal is to solve the integral for all diffuse indirect lighting given the scene's irradiance in the form of a cubemap environment map. We know that we can get the radiance of the scene $L(p, w_i)$ in a particular direction by sampling an HDR environment map in direction w_i. To solve the integral, we have to sample the scene's radiance from all possible directions within the hemisphere Ω for each fragment.

It is however computationally impossible to sample the environment's lighting from every possible direction in Ω, the number of possible directions is theoretically infinite. We can however, approximate the number of directions by taking a finite number of directions or samples, spaced uniformly or taken randomly from within the hemisphere, to get a fairly accurate approximation of the irradiance; effectively solving the integral $\int$ discretely

It is however still too expensive to do this for every fragment in real-time as the number of samples needs to be significantly large for decent results, so we want to pre-compute this. Since the orientation of the hemisphere decides where we capture the irradiance, we can pre-calculate the irradiance for every possible hemisphere orientation oriented around all outgoing directions w_o:

$$L_o(p, \omega_o) = k_d \frac{c}{\pi} \int_\Omega L_i(p, \omega_i) n \cdot \omega_i d\omega_i$$

Given any direction vector w_i in the lighting pass, we can then sample the pre-computed irradiance map to retrieve the total diffuse irradiance from direction w_i. To determine the amount of indirect diffuse (irradiant) light at a fragment surface, we retrieve the total irradiance from the hemisphere oriented around its surface normal. Obtaining the scene's irradiance is then as simple as:

```glsl
vec3 irradiance = texture(irradianceMap, N).rgb;
```

Now, to generate the irradiance map, we need to convolute the environment's lighting as converted to a cubemap. Given that for each fragment the surface's hemisphere is oriented along the normal vector N, convoluting a cubemap equals calculating the total averaged radiance of each direction w_i in the hemisphere Ω oriented along N.

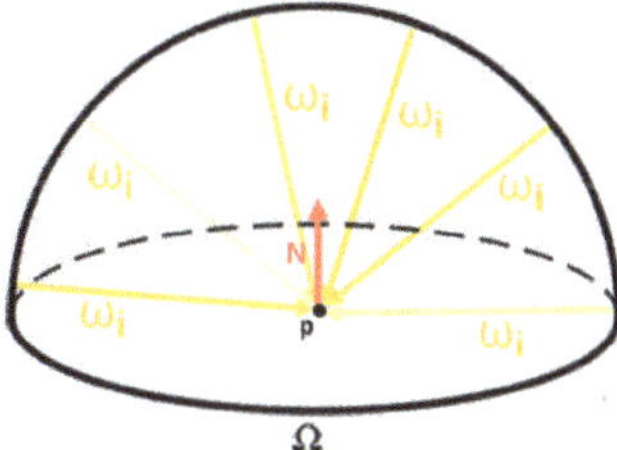

Thankfully, all of the cumbersome setup of this chapter isn't all for nothing as we can now directly take the converted cubemap, convolute it in a fragment shader, and capture its result in a new cubemap using a framebuffer that renders to all 6 face directions. As we've already set this up for converting the equirectangular environment map to a cubemap, we can take the exact same approach but use a different fragment shader:

```glsl
#version 330 core
out vec4 FragColor;
in vec3 localPos;

uniform samplerCube environmentMap;

const float PI = 3.14159265359;

void main()
{
    // the sample direction equals the hemisphere's orientation
    vec3 normal = normalize(localPos);

    vec3 irradiance = vec3(0.0);

    [...] // convolution code

    FragColor = vec4(irradiance, 1.0);
}
```

With `environmentMap` being the HDR cubemap as converted from the equirectangular HDR environment map.

There are many ways to convolute the environment map, but for this chapter we're going to generate a fixed amount of sample vectors for each cubemap texel along a hemisphere Ω oriented around the sample direction and average the results. The fixed amount of sample vectors will be uniformly spread inside the hemisphere. Note that an integral is a continuous function and discretely sampling its function given a fixed amount of sample vectors will be an approximation. The more sample vectors we use, the better we approximate the integral.

The integral $\int$ of the reflectance equation revolves around the solid angle dw which is rather difficult to work with. Instead of integrating over the solid angle dw we'll integrate over its equivalent spherical coordinates θ and ϕ.

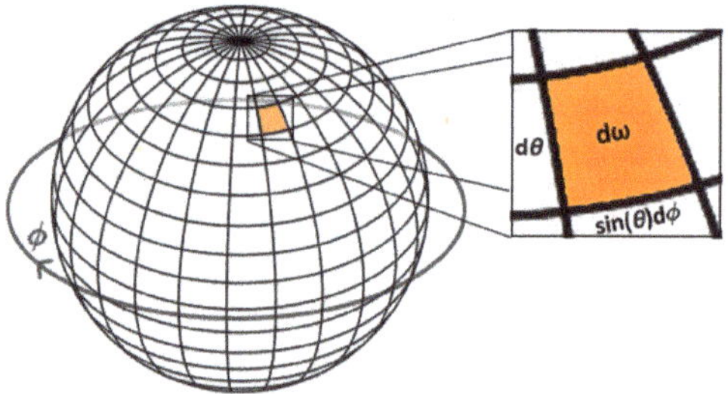

We use the polar azimuth ϕ angle to sample around the ring of the hemisphere between 0 and 2π, and use the inclination zenith θ angle between 0 and $\frac{1}{2}\pi$ to sample the increasing rings of the hemisphere. This will give us the updated reflectance integral:

$$L_o(p, \phi_o, \theta_o) = k_d \frac{c}{\pi} \int_{\phi=0}^{2\pi} \int_{\theta=0}^{\frac{1}{2}\pi} L_i(p, \phi_i, \theta_i) \cos(\theta) \sin(\theta) d\phi d\theta$$

Solving the integral requires us to take a fixed number of discrete samples within the hemisphere Ω and averaging their results. This translates the integral to the following discrete version as based on the Riemann sum[1] given $n1$ and $n2$ discrete samples on each spherical coordinate respectively:

$$L_o(p, \phi_o, \theta_o) = k_d \frac{c\pi}{n1n2} \sum_{\phi=0}^{n1} \sum_{\theta=0}^{n2} L_i(p, \phi_i, \theta_i) \cos(\theta) \sin(\theta) d\phi d\theta$$

As we sample both spherical values discretely, each sample will approximate or average an area on the hemisphere as the image before shows. Note that (due to the general properties of a spherical shape) the hemisphere's discrete sample area gets smaller the higher the zenith angle θ as the sample regions converge towards the center top. To compensate for the smaller areas, we weigh its contribution by scaling the area by $\sin\theta$.

Discretely sampling the hemisphere given the integral's spherical coordinates translates to the following fragment code:

---

[1]en.wikipedia.org/wiki/Riemann_sum

```glsl
vec3 irradiance = vec3(0.0);

vec3 up    = vec3(0.0, 1.0, 0.0);
vec3 right = cross(up, normal);
up         = cross(normal, right);

float sampleDelta = 0.025;
float nrSamples = 0.0;
for(float phi = 0.0; phi < 2.0 * PI; phi += sampleDelta)
{
    for(float theta = 0.0; theta < 0.5 * PI; theta += sampleDelta)
    {
        // spherical to cartesian (in tangent space)
        vec3 tangentSample = vec3(sin(theta) * cos(phi), sin(theta) *
                             sin(phi), cos(theta));
        // tangent space to world
        vec3 sampleVec = tangentSample.x * right + tangentSample.y * up +
                         tangentSample.z * N;

        irradiance += texture(environmentMap, sampleVec).rgb * cos(theta) *
                      sin(theta);
        nrSamples++;
    }
}
irradiance = PI * irradiance * (1.0 / float(nrSamples));
```

We specify a fixed `sampleDelta` delta value to traverse the hemisphere; decreasing or increasing the sample delta will increase or decrease the accuracy respectively.

From within both loops, we take both spherical coordinates to convert them to a 3D Cartesian sample vector, convert the sample from tangent to world space oriented around the normal, and use this sample vector to directly sample the HDR environment map. We add each sample result to `irradiance` which at the end we divide by the total number of samples taken, giving us the average sampled irradiance. Note that we scale the sampled color value by `cos(theta)` due to the light being weaker at larger angles and by `sin(theta)` to account for the smaller sample areas in the higher hemisphere areas.

Now what's left to do is to set up the OpenGL rendering code such that we can convolute the earlier captured `envCubemap`. First we create the irradiance cubemap (again, we only have to do this once before the render loop):

```cpp
unsigned int irradianceMap;
glGenTextures(1, &irradianceMap);
glBindTexture(GL_TEXTURE_CUBE_MAP, irradianceMap);
for (unsigned int i = 0; i < 6; ++i)
{
    glTexImage2D(GL_TEXTURE_CUBE_MAP_POSITIVE_X + i, 0, GL_RGB16F, 32, 32,
                 0, GL_RGB, GL_FLOAT, nullptr);
}
glTexParameteri(GL_TEXTURE_CUBE_MAP, GL_TEXTURE_WRAP_S, GL_CLAMP_TO_EDGE);
glTexParameteri(GL_TEXTURE_CUBE_MAP, GL_TEXTURE_WRAP_T, GL_CLAMP_TO_EDGE);
glTexParameteri(GL_TEXTURE_CUBE_MAP, GL_TEXTURE_WRAP_R, GL_CLAMP_TO_EDGE);
glTexParameteri(GL_TEXTURE_CUBE_MAP, GL_TEXTURE_MIN_FILTER, GL_LINEAR);
glTexParameteri(GL_TEXTURE_CUBE_MAP, GL_TEXTURE_MAG_FILTER, GL_LINEAR);
```

As the irradiance map averages all surrounding radiance uniformly it doesn't have a lot of high frequency details, so we can store the map at a low resolution (32x32) and let OpenGL's linear filtering do most of the work. Next, we re-scale the capture framebuffer to the new resolution:

```
glBindFramebuffer(GL_FRAMEBUFFER, captureFBO);
glBindRenderbuffer(GL_RENDERBUFFER, captureRBO);
glRenderbufferStorage(GL_RENDERBUFFER, GL_DEPTH_COMPONENT24, 32, 32);
```

Using the convolution shader, we render the environment map in a similar way to how we captured the environment cubemap:

```
irradianceShader.use();
irradianceShader.setInt("environmentMap", 0);
irradianceShader.setMat4("projection", captureProjection);
glActiveTexture(GL_TEXTURE0);
glBindTexture(GL_TEXTURE_CUBE_MAP, envCubemap);

glViewport(0, 0, 32, 32); // don't forget to configure the viewport
glBindFramebuffer(GL_FRAMEBUFFER, captureFBO);
for (unsigned int i = 0; i < 6; ++i)
{
    irradianceShader.setMat4("view", captureViews[i]);
    glFramebufferTexture2D(GL_FRAMEBUFFER, GL_COLOR_ATTACHMENT0,
        GL_TEXTURE_CUBE_MAP_POSITIVE_X + i, irradianceMap, 0);
    glClear(GL_COLOR_BUFFER_BIT | GL_DEPTH_BUFFER_BIT);

    renderCube();
}
glBindFramebuffer(GL_FRAMEBUFFER, 0);
```

Now after this routine we should have a pre-computed irradiance map that we can directly use for our diffuse image based lighting. To see if we successfully convoluted the environment map we'll substitute the environment map for the irradiance map as the skybox's environment sampler:

If it looks like a heavily blurred version of the environment map you've successfully convoluted the environment map.

45.3 PBR and indirect irradiance lighting

The irradiance map represents the diffuse part of the reflectance integral as accumulated from all surrounding indirect light. Seeing as the light doesn't come from direct light sources, but from the surrounding environment, we treat both the diffuse and specular indirect lighting as the ambient lighting, replacing our previously set constant term.

First, be sure to add the pre-calculated irradiance map as a cube sampler:

```
uniform samplerCube irradianceMap;
```

Given the irradiance map that holds all of the scene's indirect diffuse light, retrieving the irradiance influencing the fragment is as simple as a single texture sample given the surface normal:

```
// vec3 ambient = vec3(0.03);
vec3 ambient = texture(irradianceMap, N).rgb;
```

However, as the indirect lighting contains both a diffuse and specular part (as we've seen from the split version of the reflectance equation) we need to weigh the diffuse part accordingly. Similar to what we did in the previous chapter, we use the Fresnel equation to determine the surface's indirect reflectance ratio from which we derive the refractive (or diffuse) ratio:

```
vec3 kS = fresnelSchlick(max(dot(N, V), 0.0), F0);
vec3 kD = 1.0 - kS;
vec3 irradiance = texture(irradianceMap, N).rgb;
vec3 diffuse    = irradiance * albedo;
vec3 ambient    = (kD * diffuse) * ao;
```

As the ambient light comes from all directions within the hemisphere oriented around the normal N, there's no single halfway vector to determine the Fresnel response. To still simulate Fresnel, we calculate the Fresnel from the angle between the normal and view vector. However, earlier we used the micro-surface halfway vector, influenced by the roughness of the surface, as input to the Fresnel equation. As we currently don't take roughness into account, the surface's reflective ratio will always end up relatively high. Indirect light follows the same properties of direct light so we expect rougher surfaces to reflect less strongly on the surface edges. Because of this, the indirect Fresnel reflection strength looks off on rough non-metal surfaces (slightly exaggerated for demonstration purposes):

We can alleviate the issue by injecting a roughness term in the Fresnel-Schlick equation as described by Sébastien Lagarde[1]:

```
vec3 fresnelSchlickRoughness(float cosTheta, vec3 F0, float roughness)
{
    return F0 + (max(vec3(1.0 - roughness), F0) - F0) *
           pow(1.0 - cosTheta, 5.0);
}
```

By taking account of the surface's roughness when calculating the Fresnel response, the ambient code ends up as:

---

[1] seblagarde.wordpress.com/2011/08/17/hello-world/

```glsl
vec3 kS = fresnelSchlickRoughness(max(dot(N, V), 0.0), F0, roughness);
vec3 kD = 1.0 - kS;
vec3 irradiance = texture(irradianceMap, N).rgb;
vec3 diffuse    = irradiance * albedo;
vec3 ambient    = (kD * diffuse) * ao;
```

As you can see, the actual image based lighting computation is quite simple and only requires a single cubemap texture lookup; most of the work is in pre-computing or convoluting the irradiance map.

If we take the initial scene from the **PBR** previous chapter, where each sphere has a vertically increasing metallic and a horizontally increasing roughness value, and add the diffuse image based lighting it'll look a bit like this:

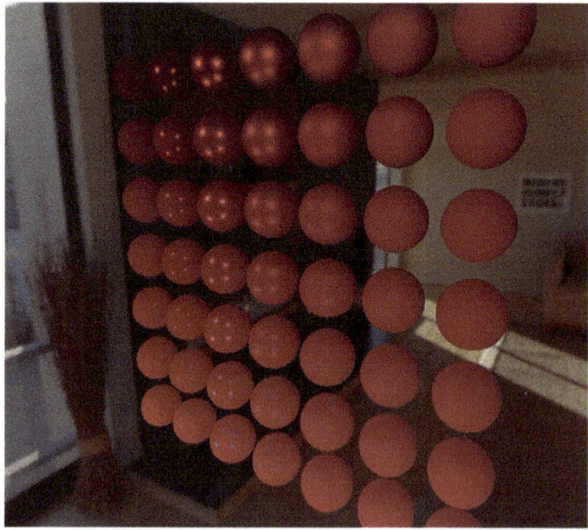

It still looks a bit weird as the more metallic spheres **require** some form of reflection to properly start looking like metallic surfaces (as metallic surfaces don't reflect diffuse light) which at the moment are only (barely) coming from the point light sources. Nevertheless, you can already tell the spheres do feel more *in place* within the environment (especially if you switch between environment maps) as the surface response reacts accordingly to the environment's ambient lighting.

You can find the complete source code of the discussed topics at `/src/6.pbr/2.1.2.ibl_ irradiance/`. In the next chapter we'll add the indirect specular part of the reflectance integral at which point we're really going to see the power of **PBR**.

45.4 Further reading

- `www.codinglabs.net/article_physically_based_rendering.aspx`: an introduction to PBR and how and why to generate an irradiance map.
- `www.scratchapixel.com/lessons/mathematics-physics-for-compute r-graphics/mathematics-of-shading`: a brief introduction by ScratchAPixel on several of the mathematics described in this tutorial, specifically on polar coordinates and integrals.

46. Specular IBL

In the previous chapter we've set up PBR in combination with image based lighting by pre-computing an irradiance map as the lighting's indirect diffuse portion. In this chapter we'll focus on the specular part of the reflectance equation:

$$L_o(p, \omega_o) = \int_\Omega (k_d \frac{c}{\pi} + \frac{DFG}{4(\omega_o \cdot n)(\omega_i \cdot n)}) L_i(p, \omega_i) n \cdot \omega_i d\omega_i$$

You'll notice that the Cook-Torrance specular portion (multiplied by kS) isn't constant over the integral and is dependent on the incoming light direction, but **also** the incoming view direction. Trying to solve the integral for all incoming light directions including all possible view directions is a combinatorial overload and way too expensive to calculate on a real-time basis. Epic Games proposed a solution where they were able to pre-convolute the specular part for real time purposes, given a few compromises, known as the split sum approximation.

The split sum approximation splits the specular part of the reflectance equation into two separate parts that we can individually convolute and later combine in the PBR shader for specular indirect image based lighting. Similar to how we pre-convoluted the irradiance map, the split sum approximation requires an HDR environment map as its convolution input. To understand the split sum approximation we'll again look at the reflectance equation, but this time focus on the specular part:

$$L_o(p, \omega_o) = \int_\Omega (k_s \frac{DFG}{4(\omega_o \cdot n)(\omega_i \cdot n)} L_i(p, \omega_i) n \cdot \omega_i d\omega_i = \int_\Omega f_r(p, \omega_i, \omega_o) L_i(p, \omega_i) n \cdot \omega_i d\omega_i$$

For the same (performance) reasons as the irradiance convolution, we can't solve the specular part of the integral in real time and expect a reasonable performance. So preferably we'd pre-compute this integral to get something like a specular IBL map, sample this map with the fragment's normal, and be done with it. However, this is where it gets a bit tricky. We were able to pre-compute the irradiance map as the integral only depended on ω_i and we could move the constant diffuse albedo terms out of the integral. This time, the integral depends on more than just ω_i as evident from the BRDF:

$$f_r(p, w_i, w_o) = \frac{DFG}{4(\omega_o \cdot n)(\omega_i \cdot n)}$$

The integral also depends on w_o, and we can't really sample a pre-computed cubemap with two direction vectors. The position p is irrelevant here as described in the previous chapter. Pre-computing this integral for every possible combination of ω_i and ω_o isn't practical in a real-time setting.

Epic Games' split sum approximation solves the issue by splitting the pre-computation into 2 individual parts that we can later combine to get the resulting pre-computed result we're after. The split sum approximation splits the specular integral into two separate integrals:

$$L_o(p, \omega_o) = \int_\Omega L_i(p, \omega_i) d\omega_i * \int_\Omega f_r(p, \omega_i, \omega_o) n \cdot \omega_i d\omega_i$$

The first part (when convoluted) is known as the pre-filtered environment map which is (similar to the irradiance map) a pre-computed environment convolution map, but this time taking roughness into account. For increasing roughness levels, the environment map is convoluted with more scattered sample vectors, creating blurrier reflections. For each roughness level we convolute, we store the sequentially blurrier results in the pre-filtered map's mipmap levels. For instance, a pre-filtered environment map storing the pre-convoluted result of 5 different roughness values in its 5 mipmap levels looks as follows:

We generate the sample vectors and their scattering amount using the normal distribution function (NDF) of the Cook-Torrance BRDF that takes as input both a normal and view direction. As we don't know beforehand the view direction when convoluting the environment map, Epic Games makes a further approximation by assuming the view direction (and thus the specular reflection direction) to be equal to the output sample direction ω_o. This translates itself to the following code:

```
vec3 N = normalize(w_o);
vec3 R = N;
vec3 V = R;
```

This way, the pre-filtered environment convolution doesn't need to be aware of the view direction. This does mean we don't get nice grazing specular reflections when looking at specular surface reflections from an angle as seen in the image below (courtesy of the *Moving Frostbite to PBR* article); this is however generally considered an acceptable compromise:

The second part of the split sum equation equals the BRDF part of the specular integral. If we pretend the incoming radiance is completely white for every direction (thus $L(p,x) = 1.0$) we can pre-calculate the BRDF's response given an input roughness and an input angle between the normal n and light direction ω_i, or $n \cdot \omega_i$. Epic Games stores the pre-computed BRDF's response to each normal and light direction combination on varying roughness values in a 2D lookup texture (LUT) known as the BRDF integration map. The 2D lookup texture outputs a scale (red) and a bias value (green) to the surface's Fresnel response giving us the second part of the split specular integral:

We generate the lookup texture by treating the horizontal texture coordinate (ranged between 0.0 and 1.0) of a plane as the BRDF's input $n \cdot \omega_i$, and its vertical texture coordinate as the input roughness value. With this BRDF integration map and the pre-filtered environment map we can combine both to get the result of the specular integral:

```glsl
float lod             = getMipLevelFromRoughness(roughness);
vec3 prefilteredColor = textureCubeLod(PrefilteredEnvMap, refVec, lod);
vec2 envBRDF          = texture2D(BRDFIntegrationMap,
                             vec2(NdotV, roughness)).xy;
vec3 indirectSpecular = prefilteredColor * (F * envBRDF.x + envBRDF.y)
```

This should give you a bit of an overview on how Epic Games' split sum approximation roughly approaches the indirect specular part of the reflectance equation. Let's now try and build the pre-convoluted parts ourselves.

46.1 Pre-filtering an HDR environment map

Pre-filtering an environment map is quite similar to how we convoluted an irradiance map. The difference being that we now account for roughness and store sequentially rougher reflections in the pre-filtered map's mip levels.

First, we need to generate a new cubemap to hold the pre-filtered environment map data. To make sure we allocate enough memory for its mip levels we call `glGenerateMipmap` as an easy way to allocate the required amount of memory:

```cpp
unsigned int prefilterMap;
glGenTextures(1, &prefilterMap);
glBindTexture(GL_TEXTURE_CUBE_MAP, prefilterMap);
for (unsigned int i = 0; i < 6; ++i)
{
    glTexImage2D(GL_TEXTURE_CUBE_MAP_POSITIVE_X + i, 0, GL_RGB16F, 128,
                 128, 0, GL_RGB, GL_FLOAT, nullptr);
}
glTexParameteri(GL_TEXTURE_CUBE_MAP, GL_TEXTURE_WRAP_S, GL_CLAMP_TO_EDGE);
glTexParameteri(GL_TEXTURE_CUBE_MAP, GL_TEXTURE_WRAP_T, GL_CLAMP_TO_EDGE);
glTexParameteri(GL_TEXTURE_CUBE_MAP, GL_TEXTURE_WRAP_R, GL_CLAMP_TO_EDGE);
glTexParameteri(GL_TEXTURE_CUBE_MAP, GL_TEXTURE_MIN_FILTER,
                GL_LINEAR_MIPMAP_LINEAR);
glTexParameteri(GL_TEXTURE_CUBE_MAP, GL_TEXTURE_MAG_FILTER, GL_LINEAR);

glGenerateMipmap(GL_TEXTURE_CUBE_MAP);
```

Note that because we plan to sample `prefilterMap`'s mipmaps you'll need to make sure its minification filter is set to `GL_LINEAR_MIPMAP_LINEAR` to enable trilinear filtering. We store the pre-filtered specular reflections in a per-face resolution of 128 by 128 at its base mip level. This is likely to be enough for most reflections, but if you have a large number of smooth materials (think of car reflections) you may want to increase the resolution.

In the previous chapter we convoluted the environment map by generating sample vectors uniformly spread over the hemisphere Ω using spherical coordinates. While this works just fine for irradiance, for specular reflections it's less efficient. When it comes to specular reflections, based on the roughness of a surface, the light reflects closely or roughly around a reflection vector r over a normal n, but (unless the surface is extremely rough) around the reflection vector nonetheless:

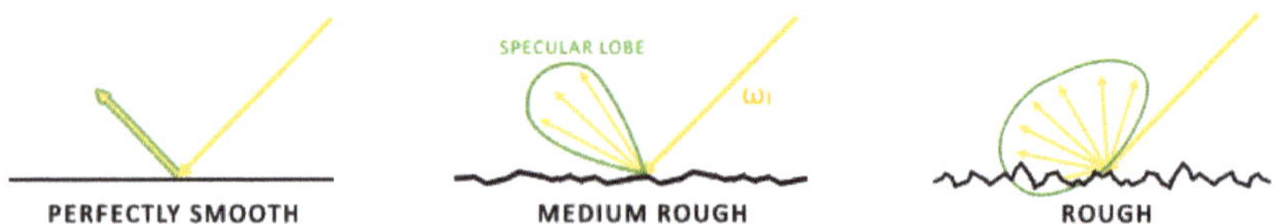

The general shape of possible outgoing light reflections is known as the specular lobe. As roughness increases, the specular lobe's size increases; and the shape of the specular lobe changes on varying incoming light directions. The shape of the specular lobe is thus highly dependent on the material.

When it comes to the microsurface model, we can imagine the specular lobe as the reflection orientation about the microfacet halfway vectors given some incoming light direction. Seeing as most light rays end up in a specular lobe reflected around the microfacet halfway vectors, it makes sense to generate the sample vectors in a similar fashion as most would otherwise be wasted. This process is known as importance sampling.

46.1.1 Monte Carlo integration and importance sampling

To fully get a grasp of importance sampling it's relevant we first delve into the mathematical construct known as Monte Carlo integration. Monte Carlo integration revolves mostly around a combination of statistics and probability theory. Monte Carlo helps us in discretely solving the problem of figuring out some statistic or value of a population without having to take **all** of the population into consideration.

For instance, let's say you want to count the average height of all citizens of a country. To get your result, you could measure **every** citizen and average their height which will give you the **exact** answer you're looking for. However, since most countries have a considerable population this isn't a realistic approach: it would take too much effort and time.

A different approach is to pick a much smaller **completely random** (unbiased) subset of this population, measure their height, and average the result. This population could be as small as a 100 people. While not as accurate as the exact answer, you'll get an answer that is relatively close to the ground truth. This is known as the law of large numbers. The idea is that if you measure a smaller set of size N of truly random samples from the total population, the result will be relatively close to the true answer and gets closer as the number of samples N increases.

Monte Carlo integration builds on this law of large numbers and takes the same approach in solving an integral. Rather than solving an integral for all possible (theoretically infinite) sample values x, simply generate N sample values randomly picked from the total population and average. As N increases, we're guaranteed to get a result closer to the exact answer of the integral:

$$O = \int_{a}^{b} f(x)dx = \frac{1}{N} \sum_{i=0}^{N-1} \frac{f(x)}{pdf(x)}$$

To solve the integral, we take N random samples over the population a to b, add them together, and divide by the total number of samples to average them. The *pdf* stands for the probability density function that tells us the probability a specific sample occurs over the total sample set. For instance, the pdf of the height of a population would look a bit like this:

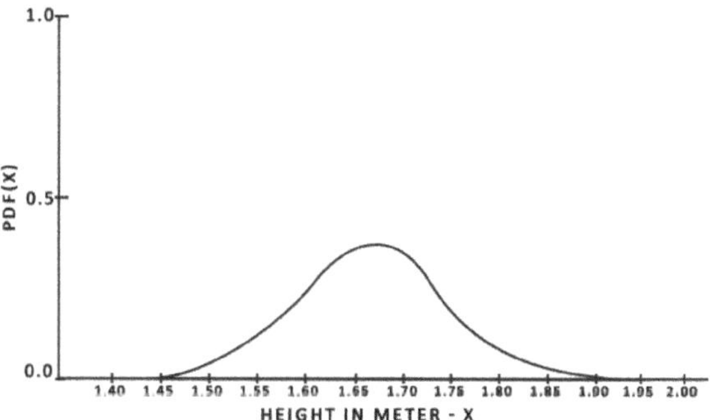

From this graph we can see that if we take any random sample of the population, there is a higher chance of picking a sample of someone of height 1.70, compared to the lower probability of the sample being of height 1.50.

When it comes to Monte Carlo integration, some samples may have a higher probability of being generated than others. This is why for any general Monte Carlo estimation we divide or multiply the sampled value by the sample probability according to a pdf. So far, in each of our cases of estimating an integral, the samples we've generated were uniform, having the exact same chance of being generated. Our estimations so far were unbiased, meaning that given an ever-increasing amount of samples we will eventually converge to the **exact** solution of the integral.

However, some Monte Carlo estimators are biased, meaning that the generated samples aren't completely random, but focused towards a specific value or direction. These biased Monte Carlo estimators have a faster rate of convergence, meaning they can converge to the exact solution at a much faster rate, but due to their biased nature it's likely they won't ever converge to the exact solution. This is generally an acceptable tradeoff, especially in computer graphics, as the exact solution isn't too important as long as the results are visually acceptable. As we'll soon see with importance sampling (which uses a biased estimator), the generated samples are biased towards specific directions in which case we account for this by multiplying or dividing each sample by its corresponding pdf.

Monte Carlo integration is quite prevalent in computer graphics as it's a fairly intuitive way to approximate continuous integrals in a discrete and efficient fashion: take any area/volume to sample over (like the hemisphere Ω), generate N amount of random samples within the area/volume, and sum and weigh every sample contribution to the final result.

Monte Carlo integration is an extensive mathematical topic and I won't delve much further into the specifics, but we'll mention that there are multiple ways of generating the *random samples*. By default, each sample is completely (pseudo)random as we're used to, but by utilizing certain properties of semi-random sequences we can generate sample vectors that are still random, but have interesting properties. For instance, we can do Monte Carlo integration on something called low-discrepancy sequences which still generate random samples, but each sample is more evenly distributed (image courtesy of James Heald):

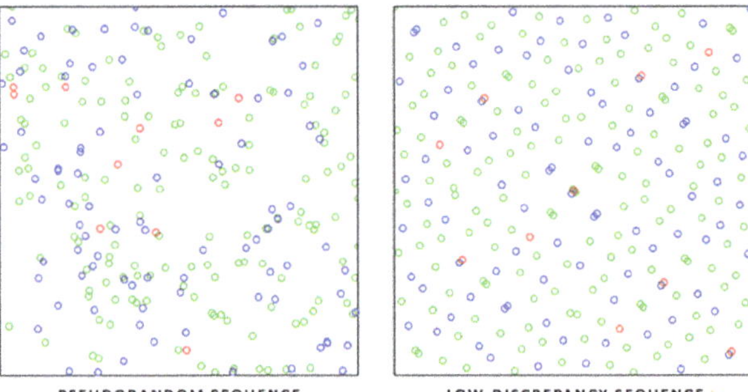

When using a low-discrepancy sequence for generating the Monte Carlo sample vectors, the process is known as Quasi-Monte Carlo integration. Quasi-Monte Carlo methods have a faster rate of convergence which makes them interesting for performance heavy applications.

Given our newly obtained knowledge of Monte Carlo and Quasi-Monte Carlo integration, there is an interesting property we can use for an even faster rate of convergence known as importance sampling. We've mentioned it before in this chapter, but when it comes to specular reflections of light, the reflected light vectors are constrained in a specular lobe with its size determined by the roughness of the surface. Seeing as any (quasi-)randomly generated sample outside the specular lobe isn't relevant to the specular integral it makes sense to focus the sample generation to within the specular lobe, at the cost of making the Monte Carlo estimator biased.

This is in essence what importance sampling is about: generate sample vectors in some region constrained by the roughness oriented around the microfacet's halfway vector. By combining Quasi-Monte Carlo sampling with a low-discrepancy sequence and biasing the sample vectors using importance sampling, we get a high rate of convergence. Because we reach the solution at a faster rate, we'll need significantly fewer samples to reach an approximation that is sufficient enough.

46.1.2 A low-discrepancy sequence

In this chapter we'll pre-compute the specular portion of the indirect reflectance equation using importance sampling given a random low-discrepancy sequence based on the Quasi-Monte Carlo method. The sequence we'll be using is known as the Hammersley Sequence as carefully described by Holger Dammertz[1]. The Hammersley sequence is based on the Van Der Corpus sequence which mirrors a decimal binary representation around its decimal point.

Given some neat bit tricks, we can quite efficiently generate the Van Der Corpus sequence in a shader program which we'll use to get a Hammersley sequence sample i over N total samples:

```glsl
float RadicalInverse_VdC(uint bits)
{
    bits = (bits << 16u) | (bits >> 16u);
    bits = ((bits & 0x55555555u) << 1u) | ((bits & 0xAAAAAAAAu) >> 1u);
    bits = ((bits & 0x33333333u) << 2u) | ((bits & 0xCCCCCCCCu) >> 2u);
    bits = ((bits & 0x0F0F0F0Fu) << 4u) | ((bits & 0xF0F0F0F0u) >> 4u);
    bits = ((bits & 0x00FF00FFu) << 8u) | ((bits & 0xFF00FF00u) >> 8u);
```

---

[1] holger.dammertz.org/stuff/notes_HammersleyOnHemisphere.html

```glsl
    return float(bits) * 2.3283064365386963e-10; // / 0x100000000
}

vec2 Hammersley(uint i, uint N)
{
    return vec2(float(i)/float(N), RadicalInverse_VdC(i));
}
```

The GLSL `Hammersley` function gives us the low-discrepancy sample `i` of the total sample set of size `N`.

Hammersley sequence without bit operator support
Not all OpenGL related drivers support bit operators (WebGL and OpenGL ES 2.0 for instance) in which case you may want to use an alternative version of the Van Der Corpus Sequence that doesn't rely on bit operators:

```glsl
float VanDerCorpus(uint n, uint base)
{
    float invBase = 1.0 / float(base);
    float denom   = 1.0;
    float result  = 0.0;

    for(uint i = 0u; i < 32u; ++i)
    {
        if(n > 0u)
        {
            denom   = mod(float(n), 2.0);
            result += denom * invBase;
            invBase = invBase / 2.0;
            n       = uint(float(n) / 2.0);
        }
    }

    return result;
}
// ----------------------------------------------------------------------
vec2 HammersleyNoBitOps(uint i, uint N)
{
    return vec2(float(i)/float(N), VanDerCorpus(i, 2u));
}
```

Note that due to GLSL loop restrictions in older hardware, the sequence loops over all possible 32 bits. This version is less performant, but does work on all hardware if you ever find yourself without bit operators.

46.1.3 GGX Importance sampling

Instead of uniformly or randomly (Monte Carlo) generating sample vectors over the integral's hemisphere Ω, we'll generate sample vectors biased towards the general reflection orientation of the microsurface halfway vector based on the surface's roughness. The sampling process will be similar to what we've seen before: begin a large loop, generate a random (low-discrepancy) sequence value, take the sequence value to generate a sample vector in tangent space, transform to world space, and sample the scene's radiance. What's different is that we now use a low-discrepancy sequence value as input to generate a sample vector:

```
const uint SAMPLE_COUNT = 4096u;
for(uint i = 0u; i < SAMPLE_COUNT; ++i)
{
    vec2 Xi = Hammersley(i, SAMPLE_COUNT);
```

Additionally, to build a sample vector, we need some way of orienting and biasing the sample vector towards the specular lobe of some surface roughness. We can take the NDF as described in the *Theory* chapter and combine the GGX NDF in the spherical sample vector process as described by Epic Games:

```
vec3 ImportanceSampleGGX(vec2 Xi, vec3 N, float roughness)
{
    float a = roughness*roughness;

    float phi = 2.0 * PI * Xi.x;
    float cosTheta = sqrt((1.0 - Xi.y) / (1.0 + (a*a - 1.0) * Xi.y));
    float sinTheta = sqrt(1.0 - cosTheta*cosTheta);

    // from spherical coordinates to cartesian coordinates
    vec3 H;
    H.x = cos(phi) * sinTheta;
    H.y = sin(phi) * sinTheta;
    H.z = cosTheta;

    // from tangent-space vector to world-space sample vector
    vec3 up = abs(N.z) < 0.999 ? vec3(0.0, 0.0, 1.0) : vec3(1.0, 0.0, 0.0);
    vec3 tangent = normalize(cross(up, N));
    vec3 bitangent = cross(N, tangent);

    vec3 sampleVec = tangent * H.x + bitangent * H.y + N * H.z;
    return normalize(sampleVec);
}
```

This gives us a sample vector somewhat oriented around the expected microsurface's halfway vector based on some input roughness and the low-discrepancy sequence value `Xi`. Note that Epic Games uses the squared roughness for better visual results as based on Disney's original PBR research.

With the low-discrepancy Hammersley sequence and sample generation defined, we can finalize the pre-filter convolution shader:

```
#version 330 core
out vec4 FragColor;
in vec3 localPos;

uniform samplerCube environmentMap;
uniform float roughness;

const float PI = 3.14159265359;

float RadicalInverse_VdC(uint bits);
vec2 Hammersley(uint i, uint N);
vec3 ImportanceSampleGGX(vec2 Xi, vec3 N, float roughness);

void main()
{
    vec3 N = normalize(localPos);
    vec3 R = N;
```

```glsl
    vec3 V = R;

    const uint SAMPLE_COUNT = 1024u;
    float totalWeight = 0.0;
    vec3 prefilteredColor = vec3(0.0);
    for(uint i = 0u; i < SAMPLE_COUNT; ++i)
    {
        vec2 Xi = Hammersley(i, SAMPLE_COUNT);
        vec3 H = ImportanceSampleGGX(Xi, N, roughness);
        vec3 L = normalize(2.0 * dot(V, H) * H - V);

        float NdotL = max(dot(N, L), 0.0);
        if(NdotL > 0.0)
        {
            prefilteredColor += texture(environmentMap, L).rgb * NdotL;
            totalWeight      += NdotL;
        }
    }
    prefilteredColor = prefilteredColor / totalWeight;

    FragColor = vec4(prefilteredColor, 1.0);
}
```

We pre-filter the environment, based on some input roughness that varies over each mipmap level of the pre-filter cubemap (from `0.0` to `1.0`), and store the result in `prefilteredColor`. The resulting `prefilteredColor` is divided by the total sample weight, where samples with less influence on the final result (for small `NdotL`) contribute less to the final weight.

46.1.4 Capturing pre-filter mipmap levels

What's left to do is let OpenGL pre-filter the environment map with different roughness values over multiple mipmap levels. This is actually fairly easy to do with the original setup of the previous chapter:

```cpp
prefilterShader.use();
prefilterShader.setInt("environmentMap", 0);
prefilterShader.setMat4("projection", captureProjection);
glActiveTexture(GL_TEXTURE0);
glBindTexture(GL_TEXTURE_CUBE_MAP, envCubemap);

glBindFramebuffer(GL_FRAMEBUFFER, captureFBO);
unsigned int maxMipLevels = 5;
for (unsigned int mip = 0; mip < maxMipLevels; ++mip)
{
    // reisze framebuffer according to mip-level size.
    unsigned int mipWidth = 128 * std::pow(0.5, mip);
    unsigned int mipHeight = 128 * std::pow(0.5, mip);
    glBindRenderbuffer(GL_RENDERBUFFER, captureRBO);
    glRenderbufferStorage(GL_RENDERBUFFER, GL_DEPTH_COMPONENT24,
                          mipWidth, mipHeight);
    glViewport(0, 0, mipWidth, mipHeight);

    float roughness = (float)mip / (float)(maxMipLevels - 1);
    prefilterShader.setFloat("roughness", roughness);
    for (unsigned int i = 0; i < 6; ++i)
    {
        prefilterShader.setMat4("view", captureViews[i]);
        glFramebufferTexture2D(GL_FRAMEBUFFER, GL_COLOR_ATTACHMENT0,
            GL_TEXTURE_CUBE_MAP_POSITIVE_X + i, prefilterMap, mip);

        glClear(GL_COLOR_BUFFER_BIT | GL_DEPTH_BUFFER_BIT);
```

```
            renderCube();
    }
}
glBindFramebuffer(GL_FRAMEBUFFER, 0);
```

The process is similar to the irradiance map convolution, but this time we scale the framebuffer's dimensions to the appropriate mipmap scale, each mip level reducing the dimensions by a scale of 2. Additionally, we specify the mip level we're rendering into in `glFramebufferTexture2D`'s last parameter and pass the roughness we're pre-filtering for to the pre-filter shader.

This should give us a properly pre-filtered environment map that returns blurrier reflections the higher mip level we access it from. If we use the pre-filtered environment cubemap in the skybox shader and forcefully sample somewhat above its first mip level like so:

```
vec3 envColor = textureLod(environmentMap, WorldPos, 1.2).rgb;
```

We get a result that indeed looks like a blurrier version of the original environment:

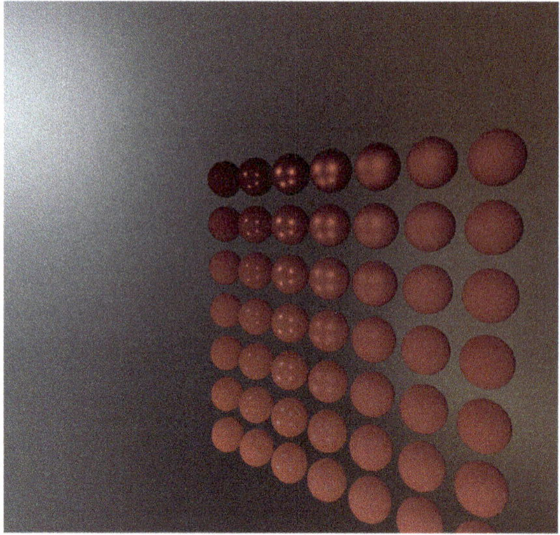

If it looks somewhat similar you've successfully pre-filtered the HDR environment map. Play around with different mipmap levels to see the pre-filter map gradually change from sharp to blurry reflections on increasing mip levels.

46.2 Pre-filter convolution artifacts

While the current pre-filter map works fine for most purposes, sooner or later you'll come across several render artifacts that are directly related to the pre-filter convolution. I'll list the most common here including how to fix them.

46.2.1 Cubemap seams at high roughness

Sampling the pre-filter map on surfaces with a rough surface means sampling the pre-filter map on some of its lower mip levels. When sampling cubemaps, OpenGL by default doesn't linearly interpolate **across** cubemap faces. Because the lower mip levels are both of a lower resolution and the pre-filter map is convoluted with a much larger sample lobe, the lack of *between-cube-face filtering* becomes quite apparent:

Luckily for us, OpenGL gives us the option to properly filter across cubemap faces by enabling `GL_TEXTURE_CUBE_MAP_SEAMLESS`:

```
glEnable(GL_TEXTURE_CUBE_MAP_SEAMLESS);
```

Simply enable this property somewhere at the start of your application and the seams will be gone.

46.2.2 Bright dots in the pre-filter convolution

Due to high frequency details and wildly varying light intensities in specular reflections, convoluting the specular reflections requires a large number of samples to properly account for the wildly varying nature of HDR environmental reflections. We already take a very large number of samples, but on some environments it may still not be enough at some of the rougher mip levels in which case you'll start seeing dotted patterns emerge around bright areas:

One option is to further increase the sample count, but this won't be enough for all environments.

As described by Chetan Jags[1] we can reduce this artifact by (during the pre-filter convolution) not directly sampling the environment map, but sampling a mip level of the environment map based on the integral's PDF and the roughness:

```cpp
float D   = DistributionGGX(NdotH, roughness);
float pdf = (D * NdotH / (4.0 * HdotV)) + 0.0001;

float resolution = 512.0; // resolution of source cubemap (per face)
float saTexel    = 4.0 * PI / (6.0 * resolution * resolution);
float saSample   = 1.0 / (float(SAMPLE_COUNT) * pdf + 0.0001);

float mipLevel = roughness == 0.0 ? 0.0 : 0.5 * log2(saSample / saTexel);
```

Don't forget to enable trilinear filtering on the environment map you want to sample its mip levels from:

```cpp
glBindTexture(GL_TEXTURE_CUBE_MAP, envCubemap);
glTexParameteri(GL_TEXTURE_CUBE_MAP, GL_TEXTURE_MIN_FILTER,
                GL_LINEAR_MIPMAP_LINEAR);
```

And let OpenGL generate the mipmaps **after** the cubemap's base texture is set:

```cpp
// convert HDR equirectangular environment map to cubemap equivalent
[...]
// then generate mipmaps
glBindTexture(GL_TEXTURE_CUBE_MAP, envCubemap);
glGenerateMipmap(GL_TEXTURE_CUBE_MAP);
```

This works surprisingly well and should remove most, if not all, dots in your pre-filter map on rougher surfaces.

46.3 Pre-computing the BRDF

With the pre-filtered environment up and running, we can focus on the second part of the split-sum approximation: the BRDF. Let's briefly review the specular split sum approximation again:

$$L_o(p, \omega_o) = \int_\Omega L_i(p, \omega_i)d\omega_i * \int_\Omega f_r(p, \omega_i, \omega_o)n \cdot \omega_i d\omega_i$$

We've pre-computed the left part of the split sum approximation in the pre-filter map over different roughness levels. The right side requires us to convolute the BRDF equation over the angle $n \cdot \omega_o$, the surface roughness, and Fresnel's F_0. This is similar to integrating the specular BRDF with a solid-white environment or a constant radiance L_i of 1.0. Convoluting the BRDF over 3 variables is a bit much, but we can try to move F_0 out of the specular BRDF equation:

$$\int_\Omega f_r(p, \omega_i, \omega_o)n \cdot \omega_i d\omega_i = \int_\Omega f_r(p, \omega_i, \omega_o)\frac{F(\omega_o, h)}{F(\omega_o, h)}n \cdot \omega_i d\omega_i$$

---

[1]chetanjags.wordpress.com/2015/08/26/image-based-lighting/

With F being the Fresnel equation. Moving the Fresnel denominator to the BRDF gives us the following equivalent equation:

$$\int_\Omega \frac{f_r(p, \omega_i, \omega_o)}{F(\omega_o, h)} F(\omega_o, h) n \cdot \omega_i d\omega_i$$

Substituting the right-most F with the Fresnel-Schlick approximation gives us:

$$\int_\Omega \frac{f_r(p, \omega_i, \omega_o)}{F(\omega_o, h)} (F_0 + (1 - F_0)(1 - \omega_o \cdot h)^5) n \cdot \omega_i d\omega_i$$

Let's replace $(1 - \omega_o \cdot h)^5$ by α to make it easier to solve for F_0:

$$\int_\Omega \frac{f_r(p, \omega_i, \omega_o)}{F(\omega_o, h)} (F_0 + (1 - F_0)\alpha) n \cdot \omega_i d\omega_i$$

$$\int_\Omega \frac{f_r(p, \omega_i, \omega_o)}{F(\omega_o, h)} (F_0 + 1 * \alpha - F_0 * \alpha) n \cdot \omega_i d\omega_i$$

$$\int_\Omega \frac{f_r(p, \omega_i, \omega_o)}{F(\omega_o, h)} (F_0 * (1 - \alpha) + \alpha) n \cdot \omega_i d\omega_i$$

Then we split the Fresnel function F over two integrals:

$$\int_\Omega \frac{f_r(p, \omega_i, \omega_o)}{F(\omega_o, h)} (F_0 * (1 - \alpha)) n \cdot \omega_i d\omega_i + \int_\Omega \frac{f_r(p, \omega_i, \omega_o)}{F(\omega_o, h)} (\alpha) n \cdot \omega_i d\omega_i$$

This way, F_0 is constant over the integral and we can take F_0 out of the integral. Next, we substitute α back to its original form giving us the final split sum BRDF equation:

$$F_0 \int_\Omega f_r(p, \omega_i, \omega_o)(1 - (1 - \omega_o \cdot h)^5) n \cdot \omega_i d\omega_i + \int_\Omega f_r(p, \omega_i, \omega_o)(1 - \omega_o \cdot h)^5 n \cdot \omega_i d\omega_i$$

The two resulting integrals represent a scale and a bias to F_0 respectively. Note that as $f_r(p, \omega_i, \omega_o)$ already contains a term for F they both cancel out, removing F from f_r.

In a similar fashion to the earlier convoluted environment maps, we can convolute the BRDF equations on their inputs: the angle between n and ω_o, and the roughness. We store the convoluted results in a 2D lookup texture (LUT) known as a BRDF integration map that we later use in our PBR lighting shader to get the final convoluted indirect specular result.

The BRDF convolution shader operates on a 2D plane, using its 2D texture coordinates directly as inputs to the BRDF convolution (`NdotV` and `roughness`). The convolution code is largely similar to the pre-filter convolution, except that it now processes the sample vector according to our

BRDF's geometry function and Fresnel-Schlick's approximation:

```glsl
vec2 IntegrateBRDF(float NdotV, float roughness)
{
    vec3 V;
    V.x = sqrt(1.0 - NdotV*NdotV);
    V.y = 0.0;
    V.z = NdotV;

    float A = 0.0;
    float B = 0.0;

    vec3 N = vec3(0.0, 0.0, 1.0);

    const uint SAMPLE_COUNT = 1024u;
    for(uint i = 0u; i < SAMPLE_COUNT; ++i)
    {
        vec2 Xi = Hammersley(i, SAMPLE_COUNT);
        vec3 H  = ImportanceSampleGGX(Xi, N, roughness);
        vec3 L  = normalize(2.0 * dot(V, H) * H - V);

        float NdotL = max(L.z, 0.0);
        float NdotH = max(H.z, 0.0);
        float VdotH = max(dot(V, H), 0.0);

        if(NdotL > 0.0)
        {
            float G = GeometrySmith(N, V, L, roughness);
            float G_Vis = (G * VdotH) / (NdotH * NdotV);
            float Fc = pow(1.0 - VdotH, 5.0);

            A += (1.0 - Fc) * G_Vis;
            B += Fc * G_Vis;
        }
    }
    A /= float(SAMPLE_COUNT);
    B /= float(SAMPLE_COUNT);
    return vec2(A, B);
}
void main()
{
    vec2 integratedBRDF = IntegrateBRDF(TexCoords.x, TexCoords.y);
    FragColor = integratedBRDF;
}
```

As you can see, the BRDF convolution is a direct translation from the mathematics to code. We take both the angle θ and the roughness as input, generate a sample vector with importance sampling, process it over the geometry and the derived Fresnel term of the BRDF, and output both a scale and a bias to F_0 for each sample, averaging them in the end.

You may recall from the *Theory* chapter that the geometry term of the BRDF is slightly different when used alongside IBL as its k variable has a slightly different interpretation:

$$k_{\text{direct}} = \frac{(\alpha + 1)^2}{8}$$

$$k_{\text{IBL}} = \frac{\alpha^2}{2}$$

Since the BRDF convolution is part of the specular IBL integral we'll use k_{IBL} for the Schlick-GGX geometry function:

```
float GeometrySchlickGGX(float NdotV, float roughness)
{
    float a = roughness;
    float k = (a * a) / 2.0;

    float nom   = NdotV;
    float denom = NdotV * (1.0 - k) + k;

    return nom / denom;
}
float GeometrySmith(vec3 N, vec3 V, vec3 L, float roughness)
{
    float NdotV = max(dot(N, V), 0.0);
    float NdotL = max(dot(N, L), 0.0);
    float ggx2 = GeometrySchlickGGX(NdotV, roughness);
    float ggx1 = GeometrySchlickGGX(NdotL, roughness);

    return ggx1 * ggx2;
}
```

Note that while k takes `a` as its parameter we didn't square `roughness` as `a` as we originally did for other interpretations of `a`; likely as `a` is squared here already. I'm not sure whether this is an inconsistency on Epic Games' part or the original Disney paper, but directly translating `roughness` to `a` gives the BRDF integration map that is identical to Epic Games' version.

Finally, to store the BRDF convolution result we'll generate a 2D texture of a 512 by 512 resolution:

```
unsigned int brdfLUTTexture;
glGenTextures(1, &brdfLUTTexture);

// pre-allocate enough memory for the LUT texture.
glBindTexture(GL_TEXTURE_2D, brdfLUTTexture);
glTexImage2D(GL_TEXTURE_2D, 0, GL_RG16F, 512, 512, 0, GL_RG, GL_FLOAT, 0);
glTexParameteri(GL_TEXTURE_2D, GL_TEXTURE_WRAP_S, GL_CLAMP_TO_EDGE);
glTexParameteri(GL_TEXTURE_2D, GL_TEXTURE_WRAP_T, GL_CLAMP_TO_EDGE);
glTexParameteri(GL_TEXTURE_2D, GL_TEXTURE_MIN_FILTER, GL_LINEAR);
glTexParameteri(GL_TEXTURE_2D, GL_TEXTURE_MAG_FILTER, GL_LINEAR);
```

Note that we use a 16-bit precision floating format as recommended by Epic Games. Be sure to set the wrapping mode to `GL_CLAMP_TO_EDGE` to prevent edge sampling artifacts.

Then, we re-use the same framebuffer object and run this shader over an NDC screen-space quad:

```
glBindFramebuffer(GL_FRAMEBUFFER, captureFBO);
glBindRenderbuffer(GL_RENDERBUFFER, captureRBO);
glRenderbufferStorage(GL_RENDERBUFFER, GL_DEPTH_COMPONENT24, 512, 512);
glFramebufferTexture2D(GL_FRAMEBUFFER, GL_COLOR_ATTACHMENT0,
                       GL_TEXTURE_2D, brdfLUTTexture, 0);

glViewport(0, 0, 512, 512);
brdfShader.use();
glClear(GL_COLOR_BUFFER_BIT | GL_DEPTH_BUFFER_BIT);
RenderQuad();
```

```
glBindFramebuffer(GL_FRAMEBUFFER, 0);
```

The convoluted BRDF part of the split sum integral should give you the following result:

With both the pre-filtered environment map and the BRDF 2D LUT we can re-construct the indirect specular integral according to the split sum approximation. The combined result then acts as the indirect or ambient specular light.

46.4 Completing the IBL reflectance

To get the indirect specular part of the reflectance equation up and running we need to stitch both parts of the split sum approximation together. Let's start by adding the pre-computed lighting data to the top of our PBR shader:

```
uniform samplerCube prefilterMap;
uniform sampler2D brdfLUT;
```

First, we get the indirect specular reflections of the surface by sampling the pre-filtered environment map using the reflection vector. Note that we sample the appropriate mip level based on the surface roughness, giving rougher surfaces *blurrier* specular reflections:

```
void main()
{
    [...]
    vec3 R = reflect(-V, N);

    const float MAX_REFLECTION_LOD = 4.0;
    vec3 prefilteredColor = textureLod(prefilterMap, R, roughness *
                                       MAX_REFLECTION_LOD).rgb;

    [...]
}
```

In the pre-filter step we only convoluted the environment map up to a maximum of 5 mip levels (0 to 4), which we denote here as MAX_REFLECTION_LOD to ensure we don't sample a mip level where there's no (relevant) data.

Then we sample from the BRDF lookup texture given the material's roughness and the angle between the normal and view vector:

```
vec3 F = FresnelSchlickRoughness(max(dot(N, V), 0.0), F0, roughness);
vec2 envBRDF = texture(brdfLUT, vec2(max(dot(N, V), 0.0), roughness)).rg;
vec3 specular = prefilteredColor * (F * envBRDF.x + envBRDF.y);
```

Given the scale and bias to F_0 (here we're directly using the indirect Fresnel result `F`) from the BRDF lookup texture, we combine this with the left pre-filter portion of the IBL reflectance equation and re-construct the approximated integral result as `specular`.

This gives us the indirect specular part of the reflectance equation. Now, combine this with the diffuse IBL part of the reflectance equation from the last chapter and we get the full **PBR** IBL result:

```glsl
vec3 F = FresnelSchlickRoughness(max(dot(N, V), 0.0), F0, roughness);

vec3 kS = F;
vec3 kD = 1.0 - kS;
kD *= 1.0 - metallic;

vec3 irradiance = texture(irradianceMap, N).rgb;
vec3 diffuse    = irradiance * albedo;

const float MAX_REFLECTION_LOD = 4.0;
vec3 prefilteredColor = textureLod(prefilterMap, R, roughness *
                                   MAX_REFLECTION_LOD).rgb;
vec2 envBRDF = texture(brdfLUT, vec2(max(dot(N, V), 0.0), roughness)).rg;
vec3 specular = prefilteredColor * (F * envBRDF.x + envBRDF.y);

vec3 ambient = (kD * diffuse + specular) * ao;
```

Note that we don't multiply `specular` by `kS` as we already have a Fresnel multiplication in there.

Now, running this exact code on the series of spheres that differ by their roughness and metallic properties, we finally get to see their true colors in the final **PBR** renderer:

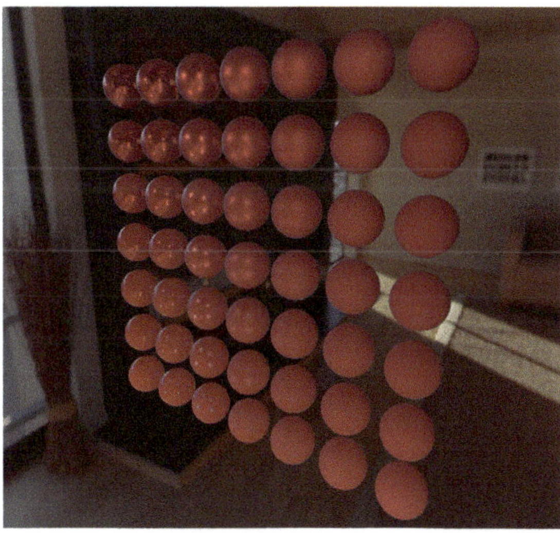

We could even go wild, and use some cool textured **PBR** materials[1]:

---

[1] freepbr.com

Or load this awesome free 3D PBR model[1] by Andrew Maximov:

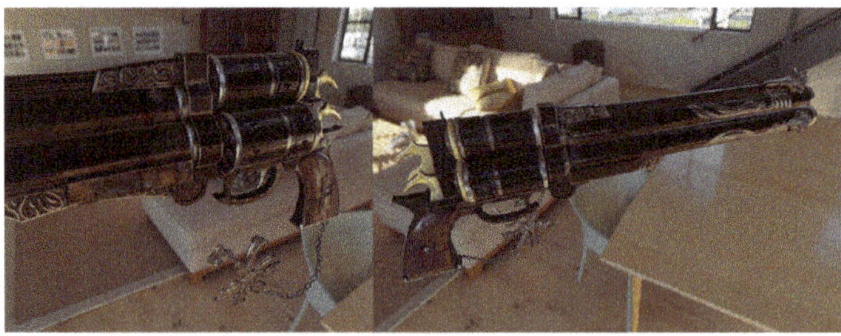

I'm sure we can all agree that our lighting now looks a lot more convincing. What's even better, is that our lighting looks physically correct regardless of which environment map we use. Below you'll see several different pre-computed HDR maps, completely changing the lighting dynamics, but still looking physically correct without changing a single lighting variable!

Well, this PBR adventure turned out to be quite a long journey. There are a lot of steps and thus a lot that could go wrong so carefully work your way through the sphere scene (`/src/6.pbr/2.2.1.ibl_specular/ibl_specular.cpp`) or the textured scene (`/src/6.pbr/2.2.2.ibl_specular_textured/ibl_specular_textured.cpp`) code samples (including all shaders) if you're stuck.

---

[1] artisaverb.info/PBT.html

46.4.1 What's next?

Hopefully, by the end of this tutorial you should have a pretty clear understanding of what PBR is about, and even have an actual PBR renderer up and running. In these tutorials, we've pre-computed all the relevant PBR image-based lighting data at the start of our application, before the render loop. This was fine for educational purposes, but not too great for any practical use of PBR. First, the pre-computation only really has to be done once, not at every startup. And second, the moment you use multiple environment maps you'll have to pre-compute each and every one of them at every startup which tends to build up.

For this reason you'd generally pre-compute an environment map into an irradiance and pre-filter map just once, and then store it on disk (note that the BRDF integration map isn't dependent on an environment map so you only need to calculate or load it once). This does mean you'll need to come up with a custom image format to store HDR cubemaps, including their mip levels. Or, you'll store (and load) it as one of the available formats (like .dds that supports storing mip levels).

Furthermore, we've described the **total** process in these tutorials, including generating the pre-computed IBL images to help further our understanding of the PBR pipeline. But, you'll be just as fine by using several great tools like cmftStudio[1] or IBLBaker[2] to generate these pre-computed maps for you.

One point we've skipped over is pre-computed cubemaps as reflection probes: cubemap interpolation and parallax correction. This is the process of placing several reflection probes in your scene that take a cubemap snapshot of the scene at that specific location, which we can then convolute as IBL data for that part of the scene. By interpolating between several of these probes based on the camera's vicinity we can achieve local high-detail image-based lighting that is simply limited by the amount of reflection probes we're willing to place. This way, the image-based lighting could correctly update when moving from a bright outdoor section of a scene to a darker indoor section for instance. I'll write a tutorial about reflection probes somewhere in the future, but for now I recommend the article by Chetan Jags below to give you a head start.

46.5 Further reading

- `blog.selfshadow.com/publications/s2013-shading-course/karis/s2013_pbs_epic_notes_v2.pdf`: explains Epic Games' split sum approximation. This is the article the IBL PBR code is based of.
- `www.trentreed.net/blog/physically-based-shading-and-image-based-lighting/`: great blog post by Trent Reed about integrating specular IBL into a PBR pipeline in real time.
- `chetanjags.wordpress.com/2015/08/26/image-based-lighting/`: very extensive write-up by Chetan Jags about specular-based image-based lighting and several of its caveats, including light probe interpolation.
- `seblagarde.files.wordpress.com/2015/07/course_notes_moving_frostbite_to_pbr_v32.pdf`: well written and in-depth overview of integrating PBR into a AAA game engine by Sébastien Lagarde and Charles de Rousiers.
- `jmonkeyengine.github.io/wiki/jme3/advanced/pbr_part3.html`: high level overview of IBL lighting and PBR by the JMonkeyEngine team.
- `placeholderart.wordpress.com/2015/07/28/implementation-notes-runtime-environment-map-filtering-for-image-based-lighting/`: extensive write-up by Padraic Hennessy about pre-filtering HDR environment maps and significantly optimizing the sample process.

---

[1] github.com/dariomancsku/cmftStudio
[2] github.com/derkreature/IBLBaker

VII In Practice

47. Debugging

Graphics programming can be a lot of fun, but it can also be a large source of frustration whenever something isn't rendering just right, or perhaps not even rendering at all! Seeing as most of what we do involves manipulating pixels, it can be difficult to figure out the cause of error whenever something doesn't work the way it's supposed to. Debugging these kinds of *visual* errors is different than what you're used to when debugging errors on the CPU. We have no console to output text to, no breakpoints to set on GLSL code, and no way of easily checking the state of GPU execution.

In this chapter we'll look into several techniques and tricks of debugging your OpenGL program. Debugging in OpenGL is not too difficult to do and getting a grasp of its techniques definitely pays out in the long run.

47.1 glGetError()

The moment you incorrectly use OpenGL (like configuring a buffer without first binding any) it will take notice and generate one or more user error flags behind the scenes. We can query these error flags using a function named `glGetError` that checks the error flag(s) set and returns an error value if OpenGL got misused:

```
GLenum glGetError();
```

The moment `glGetError` is called, it returns either an error flag or no error at all. The error codes that `glGetError` can return are listed below:

Flag	Code	Description
GL_NO_ERROR	0	No user error reported since last call to `glGetError`.
GL_INVALID_ENUM	1280	Set when an enumeration parameter is not legal.
GL_INVALID_VALUE	1281	Set when a value parameter is not legal.
GL_INVALID_OPERATION	1282	Set when the state for a command is not legal for its given parameters.
GL_STACK_OVERFLOW	1283	Set when a stack pushing operation causes a stack overflow.
GL_STACK_UNDERFLOW	1284	Set when a stack popping operation occurs while the stack is at its lowest point.
GL_OUT_OF_MEMORY	1285	Set when a memory allocation operation cannot allocate (enough) memory.
GL_INVALID_FRAMEBUFFER_OPERATION	1286	Set when reading or writing to a framebuffer that is not complete.

Within OpenGL's function documentation you can always find the error codes a function generates the moment it is incorrectly used. For instance, if you take a look at the documentation of the `glBindTexture`[1] function, you can find all the user error codes it could generate under the *Errors* section.

The moment an error flag is set, no other error flags will be reported. Furthermore, the moment `glGetError` is called it clears all error flags (or only one if on a distributed system, see note below). This means that if you call `glGetError` once at the end of each frame and it returns an error, you can't conclude this was the only error, and the source of the error could've been anywhere in the frame.

---

[1] docs.gl/gl3/glBindTexture

Note that when OpenGL runs distributedly like frequently found on X11 systems, other user error codes can still be generated as long as they have different error codes. Calling `glGetError` then only resets one of the error code flags instead of all of them. Because of this, it is recommended to call `glGetError` inside a loop.

```cpp
glBindTexture(GL_TEXTURE_2D, tex);
std::cout << glGetError() << std::endl; // returns 0 (no error)

glTexImage2D(GL_TEXTURE_3D, 0, GL_RGB, 512, 512, 0, GL_RGB,
             GL_UNSIGNED_BYTE, data);
std::cout << glGetError() << std::endl; // returns 1280 (invalid enum)

glGenTextures(-5, textures);
std::cout << glGetError() << std::endl; // returns 1281 (invalid value)

std::cout << glGetError() << std::endl; // returns 0 (no error)
```

The great thing about `glGetError` is that it makes it relatively easy to pinpoint where any error may be and to validate the proper use of OpenGL. Let's say you get a black screen and you have no idea what's causing it: is the framebuffer not properly set? Did I forget to bind a texture? By calling `glGetError` all over your codebase, you can quickly catch the first place an OpenGL error starts showing up.

By default `glGetError` only prints error numbers, which isn't easy to understand unless you've memorized the error codes. It often makes sense to write a small helper function to easily print out the error strings together with where the error check function was called:

```cpp
GLenum glCheckError_(const char *file, int line)
{
    GLenum errorCode;
    while ((errorCode = glGetError()) != GL_NO_ERROR)
    {
        std::string error;
        switch (errorCode)
        {
            case GL_INVALID_ENUM:      error = "INVALID_ENUM"; break;
            case GL_INVALID_VALUE:     error = "INVALID_VALUE"; break;
            case GL_INVALID_OPERATION: error = "INVALID_OPERATION"; break;
            case GL_STACK_OVERFLOW:    error = "STACK_OVERFLOW"; break;
            case GL_STACK_UNDERFLOW:   error = "STACK_UNDERFLOW"; break;
            case GL_OUT_OF_MEMORY:     error = "OUT_OF_MEMORY"; break;
            case GL_INVALID_FRAMEBUFFER_OPERATION:
                error = "INVALID_FRAMEBUFFER_OPERATION"; break;
        }
        std::cout << error << " | " << file << " (" << line << ")" <<
        std::endl;
    }
    return errorCode;
}
#define glCheckError() glCheckError_(__FILE__, __LINE__)
```

In case you're unaware of what the preprocessor directives `__FILE__` and `__LINE__` are: these variables get replaced during compile time with the respective file and line they were compiled in. If we decide to stick a large number of these `glCheckError` calls in our codebase it's helpful to more precisely know which `glCheckError` call returned the error.

```
glBindBuffer(GL_VERTEX_ARRAY, vbo);
glCheckError();
```

This will give us the following output:

`glGetError` doesn't help you too much as the information it returns is rather simple, but it does often help you catch typos or quickly pinpoint where in your code things went wrong; a simple but effective tool in your debugging toolkit.

47.2 Debug output

A less common, but more useful tool than `glCheckError` is an OpenGL extension called debug output that became part of core OpenGL since version 4.3. With the debug output extension, OpenGL itself will directly send an error or warning message to the user with a lot more details compared to `glCheckError`. Not only does it provide more information, it can also help you catch errors exactly where they occur by intelligently using a debugger.

> Debug output is core since OpenGL version 4.3, which means you'll find this functionality on any machine that runs OpenGL 4.3 or higher. If they're not available, its functionality can be queried from the ARB_debug_output or AMD_debug_output extension. Note that OS X does not seem to support debug output functionality (as gathered online).

In order to start using debug output we have to request a debug output context from OpenGL at our initialization process. This process varies based on whatever windowing system you use; here we will discuss setting it up on GLFW, but you can find info on other systems in the additional resources at the end of the chapter.

47.2.1 Debug output in GLFW

Requesting a debug context in GLFW is surprisingly easy as all we have to do is pass a hint to GLFW that we'd like to have a debug output context. We have to do this before we call `glfwCreateWindow`:

```
glfwWindowHint(GLFW_OPENGL_DEBUG_CONTEXT, true);
```

Once we've then initialized GLFW, we should have a debug context if we're using OpenGL version 4.3 or higher. If not, we have to take our chances and hope the system is still able to request a debug context. Otherwise we have to request debug output using its OpenGL extension(s).

> Using OpenGL in debug context can be significantly slower compared to a non-debug context, so when working on optimizations or releasing your application you want to remove GLFW's debug request hint.

To check if we successfully initialized a debug context we can query OpenGL:

```
int flags; glGetIntegerv(GL_CONTEXT_FLAGS, &flags);
if (flags & GL_CONTEXT_FLAG_DEBUG_BIT)
{
    // initialize debug output
}
```

The way debug output works is that we pass OpenGL an error logging function callback (similar to GLFW's input callbacks) and in the callback function we are free to process the OpenGL error data as we see fit; in our case we'll be displaying useful error data to the console. Below is the callback function prototype that OpenGL expects for debug output:

```
void APIENTRY glDebugOutput(GLenum source, GLenum type, unsigned int id,
                            GLenum severity, GLsizei length,
                            const char *message, const void *userParam);
```

Given the large set of data we have at our exposal, we can create a useful error printing tool like below:

```
void APIENTRY glDebugOutput(GLenum source,
                            GLenum type,
                            unsigned int id,
                            GLenum severity,
                            GLsizei length,
                            const char *message,
                            const void *userParam)
{
    // ignore non-significant error/warning codes
    if(id == 131169 || id == 131185 || id == 131218 || id == 131204) return;

    std::cout << "---------------" << std::endl;
    std::cout << "Debug message (" << id << "): " << message << std::endl;

    switch (source)
    {
        case GL_DEBUG_SOURCE_API:
          std::cout << "Source: API"; break;
        case GL_DEBUG_SOURCE_WINDOW_SYSTEM:
          std::cout << "Source: Window System"; break;
        case GL_DEBUG_SOURCE_SHADER_COMPILER:
          std::cout << "Source: Shader Compiler"; break;
        case GL_DEBUG_SOURCE_THIRD_PARTY:
          std::cout << "Source: Third Party"; break;
        case GL_DEBUG_SOURCE_APPLICATION:
          std::cout << "Source: Application"; break;
        case GL_DEBUG_SOURCE_OTHER:
          std::cout << "Source: Other"; break;
    } std::cout << std::endl;

    switch (type)
    {
        case GL_DEBUG_TYPE_ERROR:
          std::cout << "Type: Error"; break;
        case GL_DEBUG_TYPE_DEPRECATED_BEHAVIOR:
          std::cout << "Type: Deprecated Behaviour"; break;
        case GL_DEBUG_TYPE_UNDEFINED_BEHAVIOR:
          std::cout << "Type: Undefined Behaviour"; break;
        case GL_DEBUG_TYPE_PORTABILITY:
          std::cout << "Type: Portability"; break;
        case GL_DEBUG_TYPE_PERFORMANCE:
```

```cpp
            std::cout << "Type: Performance"; break;
        case GL_DEBUG_TYPE_MARKER:
            std::cout << "Type: Marker"; break;
        case GL_DEBUG_TYPE_PUSH_GROUP:
            std::cout << "Type: Push Group"; break;
        case GL_DEBUG_TYPE_POP_GROUP:
            std::cout << "Type: Pop Group"; break;
        case GL_DEBUG_TYPE_OTHER:
            std::cout << "Type: Other"; break;
    } std::cout << std::endl;

    switch (severity)
    {
        case GL_DEBUG_SEVERITY_HIGH:
            std::cout << "Severity: high"; break;
        case GL_DEBUG_SEVERITY_MEDIUM:
            std::cout << "Severity: medium"; break;
        case GL_DEBUG_SEVERITY_LOW:
            std::cout << "Severity: low"; break;
        case GL_DEBUG_SEVERITY_NOTIFICATION:
            std::cout << "Severity: notification"; break;
    } std::cout << std::endl;
    std::cout << std::endl;
}
```

Whenever debug output detects an OpenGL error, it will call this callback function and we'll be able to print out a large deal of information regarding the OpenGL error. Note that we ignore a few error codes that tend to not really display anything useful (like 131185 in NVidia drivers that tells us a buffer was successfully created).

Now that we have the callback function it's time to initialize debug output:

```cpp
if (flags & GL_CONTEXT_FLAG_DEBUG_BIT)
{
    glEnable(GL_DEBUG_OUTPUT);
    glEnable(GL_DEBUG_OUTPUT_SYNCHRONOUS);
    glDebugMessageCallback(glDebugOutput, nullptr);
    glDebugMessageControl(GL_DONT_CARE, GL_DONT_CARE, GL_DONT_CARE, 0,
      nullptr, GL_TRUE);
}
```

Here we tell OpenGL to enable debug output. The `glEnable(GL_DEBUG_SYNCRHONOUS)` call tells OpenGL to directly call the callback function the moment an error occurred.

47.2.2 Filter debug output

With `glDebugMessageControl` you can potentially filter the type(s) of errors you'd like to receive a message from. In our case we decided to not filter on any of the sources, types, or severity rates. If we wanted to only show messages from the OpenGL API, that are errors, and have a high severity, we'd configure it as follows:

```cpp
glDebugMessageControl(GL_DEBUG_SOURCE_API,
                      GL_DEBUG_TYPE_ERROR,
                      GL_DEBUG_SEVERITY_HIGH,
                      0, nullptr, GL_TRUE);
```

Given our configuration, and assuming you have a context that supports debug output, every incorrect OpenGL command will now print a large bundle of useful data:

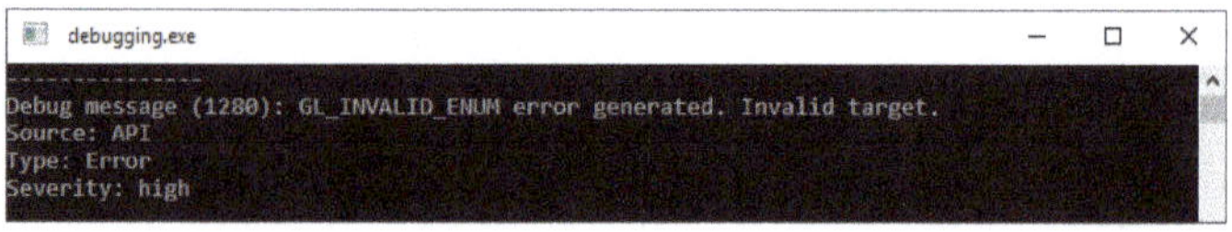

47.2.3 Backtracking the debug error source

Another great trick with debug output is that you can relatively easy figure out the exact line or call an error occurred. By setting a breakpoint in `DebugOutput` at a specific error type (or at the top of the function if you don't care), the debugger will catch the error thrown and you can move up the call stack to whatever function caused the message dispatch:

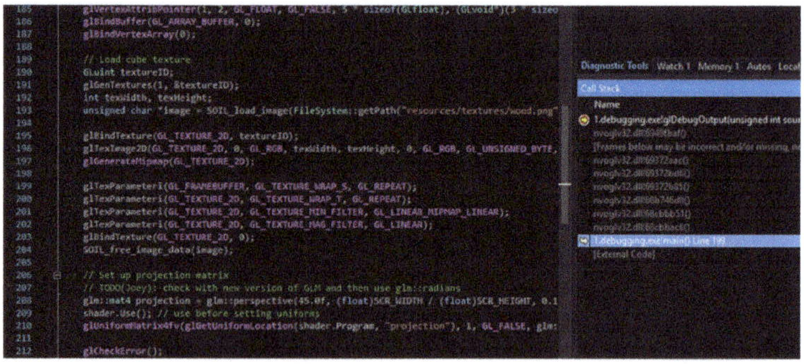

It requires some manual intervention, but if you roughly know what you're looking for it's incredibly useful to quickly determine which call causes an error.

47.2.4 Custom error output

Aside from reading messages, we can also push messages to the debug output system with `glDebugMessageInsert`:

```
glDebugMessageInsert(GL_DEBUG_SOURCE_APPLICATION, GL_DEBUG_TYPE_ERROR, 0,
                     GL_DEBUG_SEVERITY_MEDIUM, -1, "error message here");
```

This is especially useful if you're hooking into other application or OpenGL code that makes use of a debug output context. Other developers can quickly figure out any *reported* bug that occurs in your custom OpenGL code.

In summary, debug output (if you can use it) is incredibly useful for quickly catching errors and is well worth the effort in setting up as it saves considerable development time. You can find a source code example with both `glGetError` and debug output context configured at `/src/7.in_practice/1.debugging/`. See if you can fix all the errors.

47.3 Debugging shader output

When it comes to GLSL, we unfortunately don't have access to a function like `glGetError` nor the ability to step through the shader code. When you end up with a black screen or the completely wrong visuals, it's often difficult to figure out if something's wrong with the shader code. Yes, we have the compilation error reports that report syntax errors, but catching the semantic errors is another beast.

One frequently used trick to figure out what is wrong with a shader is to evaluate all the relevant variables in a shader program by sending them directly to the fragment shader's output channel. By outputting shader variables directly to the output color channels, we can convey interesting information by inspecting the visual results. For instance, let's say we want to check if a model has correct normal vectors. We can pass them (either transformed or untransformed) from the vertex shader to the fragment shader where we'd then output the normals as follows:

```glsl
#version 330 core
out vec4 FragColor;
in vec3 Normal;
[...]

void main()
{
    [...]
    FragColor.rgb = Normal;
    FragColor.a = 1.0f;
}
```

By outputting a (non-color) variable to the output color channel like this we can quickly inspect if the variable is, as far as you can tell, displaying correct values. If, for instance, the visual result is completely black it is clear the normal vectors aren't correctly passed to the shaders; and when they are displayed it's relatively easy to check if they're (sort of) correct or not:

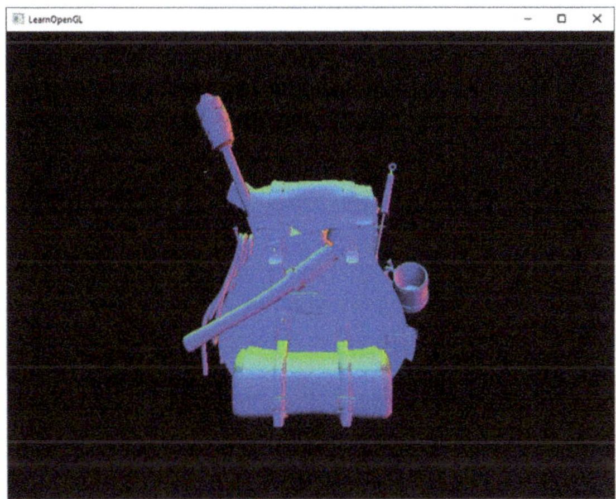

From the visual results we can see the world-space normal vectors appear to be correct as the right sides of the backpack model is mostly colored red (which would mean the normals roughly point (correctly) towards the positive x axis). Similarly, the front side of the backpack is mostly colored towards the positive z axis (blue).

This approach can easily extend to any type of variable you'd like to test. Whenever you get stuck and suspect there's something wrong with your shaders, try displaying multiple variables and/or intermediate results to see at which part of the algorithm something's missing or seemingly incorrect.

47.4 OpenGL GLSL reference compiler

Each driver has its own quirks and tidbits; for instance, NVIDIA drivers are more flexible and tend to overlook some restrictions on the specification, while ATI/AMD drivers tend to better enforce the OpenGL specification (which is the better approach in my opinion). The result of this is that shaders on one machine may not work on the other due to driver differences.

With years of experience you'll eventually get to learn the minor differences between GPU vendors, but if you want to be sure your shader code runs on all kinds of machines you can directly check your shader code against the official specification using OpenGL's GLSL reference compiler. You can download the so called GLSL lang validator binaries at `www.khronos.org/opengles/sdk/tools/Reference-Compiler/` or its complete source code at `github.com/KhronosGroup/glslang`.

Given the binary GLSL lang validator you can easily check your shader code by passing it as the binary's first argument. Keep in mind that the GLSL lang validator determines the type of shader by a list of fixed extensions:

- `.vert`: vertex shader.
- `.frag`: fragment shader.
- `.geom`: geometry shader.
- `.tesc`: tessellation control shader.
- `.tese`: tessellation evaluation shader.
- `.comp`: compute shader.

Running the GLSL reference compiler is as simple as:

```
glsllangvalidator shaderFile.vert
```

Note that if it detects no error, it returns no output. Testing the GLSL reference compiler on a broken vertex shader gives the following output:

```
C:\Users\Joey\Desktop>glslangValidator shader.vert
shader.vert
ERROR: 0:12: 'structure' : non-uniform struct contains a sampler or image: test
ERROR: 0:18: 'as' : undeclared identifier
ERROR: 0:18: 'assign' : cannot convert from 'temp float' to 'smooth out 2-component vector of float'
ERROR: 3 compilation errors.  No code generated.


C:\Users\Joey\Desktop>
```

It won't show you the subtle differences between AMD, NVidia, or Intel GLSL compilers, nor will it help you completely bug proof your shaders, but it does at least help you to check your shaders against the direct GLSL specification.

47.5 Framebuffer output

Another useful trick for your debugging toolkit is displaying a framebuffer's content(s) in some pre-defined region of your screen. You're likely to use framebuffers quite often and, as most of their magic happens behind the scenes, it's sometimes difficult to figure out what's going on. Displaying the content(s) of a framebuffer on your screen is a useful trick to quickly see if things look correct.

> Note that displaying the contents (attachments) of a framebuffer as explained here only works on texture attachments, not render buffer objects.

Using a simple shader that only displays a texture, we can easily write a small helper function to quickly display any texture at the top-right of the screen:

```glsl
// vertex shader
#version 330 core
layout (location = 0) in vec2 position;
layout (location = 1) in vec2 texCoords;

out vec2 TexCoords;

void main()
{
    gl_Position = vec4(position, 0.0f, 1.0f);
    TexCoords = texCoords;
}

// fragment shader
#version 330 core
out vec4 FragColor;
in vec2 TexCoords;

uniform sampler2D fboAttachment;

void main()
{
    FragColor = texture(fboAttachment, TexCoords);
}
```

```cpp
void DisplayFramebufferTexture(unsigned int textureID)
{
    if (!notInitialized)
    {
        // initialize shader and vao w/ NDC vertex coordinates
        // at top-right of the screen
        [...]
    }

    glActiveTexture(GL_TEXTURE0);
    glUseProgram(shaderDisplayFBOOutput);
        glBindTexture(GL_TEXTURE_2D, textureID);
        glBindVertexArray(vaoDebugTexturedRect);
            glDrawArrays(GL_TRIANGLES, 0, 6);
        glBindVertexArray(0);
    glUseProgram(0);
}

int main()
{
    [...]
    while (!glfwWindowShouldClose(window))
    {
        [...]
        DisplayFramebufferTexture(fboAttachment0);

        glfwSwapBuffers(window);
    }
}
```

This will give you a nice little window at the corner of your screen for debugging framebuffer output. Useful, for example, for determining if the normal vectors of the geometry pass in a deferred renderer look correct:

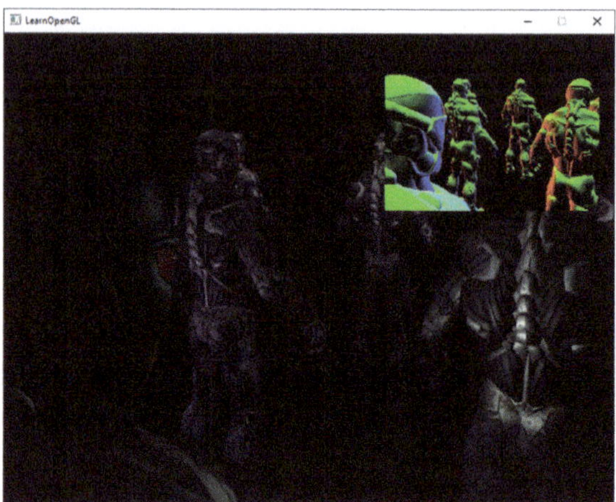

You can of course extend such a utility function to support rendering more than one texture. This is a quick and dirty way to get continuous feedback from whatever is in your framebuffer(s).

47.6 External debugging software

When all else fails there is still the option to use a 3rd party tool to help us in our debugging efforts. Third party applications often inject themselves in the OpenGL drivers and are able to intercept all kinds of OpenGL calls to give you a large array of interesting data. These tools can help you in all kinds of ways like: profiling OpenGL function usage, finding bottlenecks, inspecting buffer memory, and displaying textures and framebuffer attachments. When you're working on (large) production code, these kinds of tools can become invaluable in your development process.

I've listed some of the more popular debugging tools here; try out several of them to see which fits your needs the best.

47.6.1 RenderDoc

RenderDoc is a great standalone debugging tool with full source code available at `github.com/baldurk/renderdoc`. To start a capture, you specify the executable you'd like to capture and a working directory. The application then runs as usual, and whenever you want to inspect a particular frame, you let RenderDoc capture one or more frames at the executable's current state. Within the captured frame(s) you can view the pipeline state, all OpenGL commands, buffer storage, and textures in use.

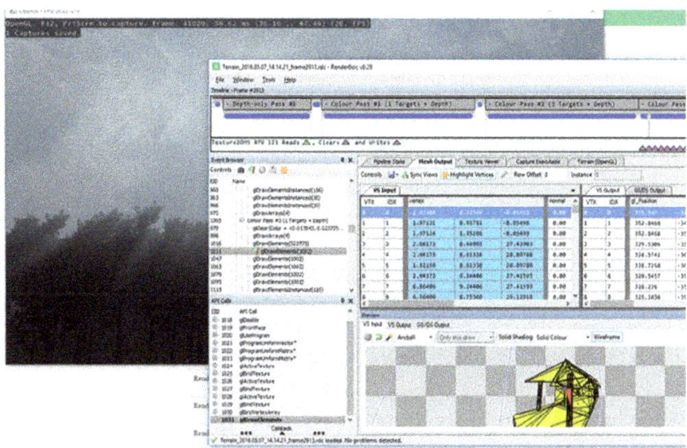

47.6.2 CodeXL

CodeXL[1] is GPU debugging tool released as both a standalone tool and a Visual Studio plugin. CodeXL gives a good set of information and is great for profiling graphics applications. CodeXL also works on NVidia or Intel cards, but without support for OpenCL debugging.

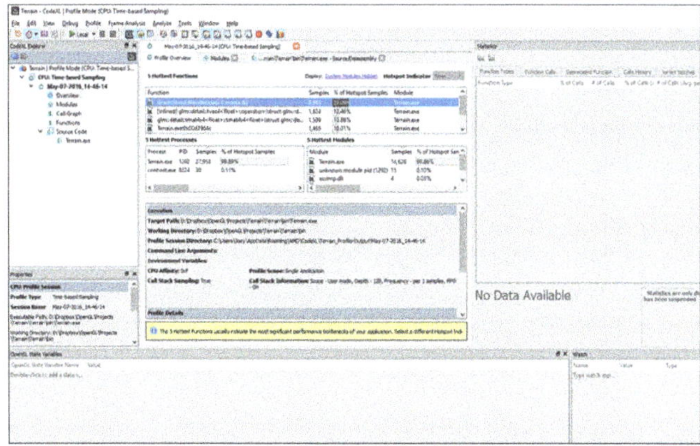

I personally don't have much experience with CodeXL since I found RenderDoc easier to use, but I've included it anyways as it looks to be a pretty solid tool and developed by one of the larger GPU manufacturers.

47.6.3 NVIDIA Nsight

NVIDIA's popular Nsight[2] GPU debugging tool is not a standalone tool, but a plugin to either the Visual Studio IDE or the Eclipse IDE (NVIDIA now has a standalone version[3] as well). The Nsight plugin is an incredibly useful tool for graphics developers as it gives a large host of run-time statistics regarding GPU usage and the frame-by-frame GPU state.

The moment you start your application from within Visual Studio (or Eclipse), using Nsight's debugging or profiling commands, Nsight will run within the application itself. The great thing about Nsight is that it renders an overlay GUI system from within your application that you can use

---

[1] gpuopen.com/compute-product/codexl/
[2] developer.nvidia.com/nvidia-nsight-visual-studio-edition
[3] developer.nvidia.com/nsight-graphics

to gather all kinds of interesting information about your application, both at run-time and during frame-by-frame analysis.

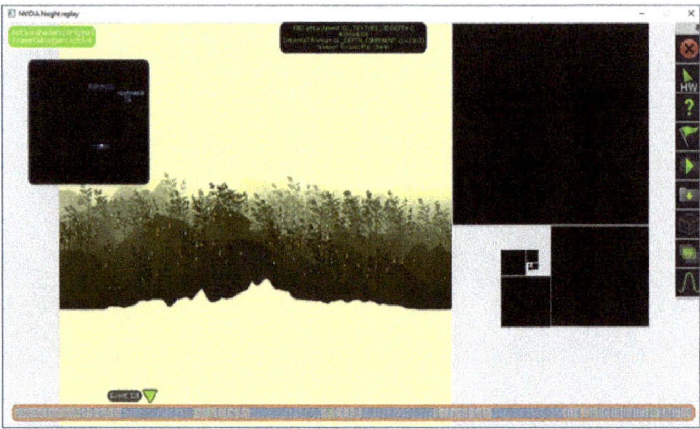

Nsight is an incredibly useful tool, but it does come with one major drawback in that it only works on NVIDIA cards. If you are working on NVIDIA cards (and use Visual Studio) it's definitely worth a shot.

I'm sure there's plenty of other debugging tools I've missed (some that come to mind are Valve's VOGL[1] and APItrace[2]), but this list should already get you plenty of tools to experiment with.

47.7 Additional resources

- `retokoradi.com/2014/04/21/opengl-why-is-your-code-producing-a-black-window/`: list of general causes by Reto Koradi of why your screen may not be producing any output.
- `vallentin.dev/2015/02/23/debugging-opengl`: an extensive debug output write-up by Vallentin with detailed information on setting up a debug context on multiple windowing systems.

---

[1] github.com/ValveSoftware/vogl
[2] apitrace.github.io/

48. Text Rendering

At some stage of your graphics adventures you will want to draw text in OpenGL. Contrary to what you may expect, getting a simple string to render on screen is all but easy with a low-level API like OpenGL. If you don't care about rendering more than 128 different same-sized characters, then it's probably not too difficult. Things are getting difficult as soon as each character has a different width, height, and margin. Based on where you live, you may also need more than 128 characters, and what if you want to express special symbols for like mathematical expressions or sheet music symbols, and what about rendering text from top to bottom? Once you think about all these complicated matters of text, it wouldn't surprise you that this probably doesn't belong in a low-level API like OpenGL.

Since there is no support for text capabilities within OpenGL, it is up to us to define a system for rendering text to the screen. There are no graphical primitives for text characters, we have to get creative. Some example techniques are: drawing letter shapes via `GL_LINES`, create 3D meshes of letters, or render character textures to 2D quads in a 3D environment.

Most developers choose to render character textures onto quads. Rendering textured quads by itself shouldn't be too difficult, but getting the relevant character(s) onto a texture could prove challenging. In this chapter we'll explore several methods and implement a more advanced, but flexible technique for rendering text using the FreeType library.

48.1 Classical text rendering: bitmap fonts

In the early days, rendering text involved selecting a font (or create one yourself) you'd like for your application and extracting all relevant characters out of this font to place them within a single large texture. Such a texture, that we call a bitmap font, contains all character symbols we want to use in predefined regions of the texture. These character symbols of the font are known as glyphs. Each glyph has a specific region of texture coordinates associated with them. Whenever you want to render a character, you select the corresponding glyph by rendering this section of the bitmap font to a 2D quad.

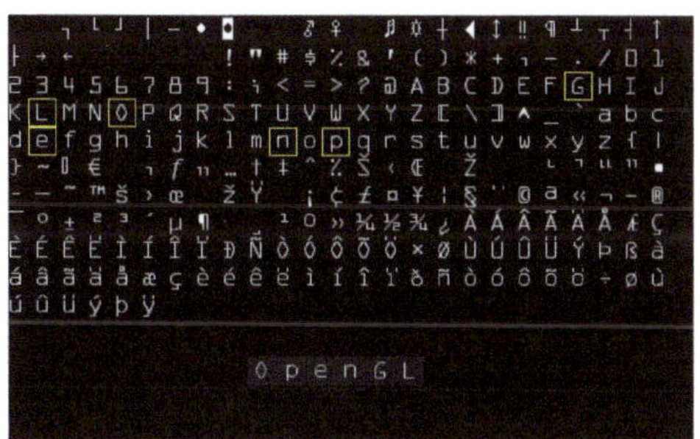

Here you can see how we would render the text 'OpenGL' by taking a bitmap font and sampling the corresponding glyphs from the texture (carefully choosing the texture coordinates) that we render on top of several quads. By enabling blending and keeping the background transparent, we will end up with just a string of characters rendered to the screen. This particular bitmap font was generated using Codehead's Bitmap Font Generator[1].

This approach has several advantages and disadvantages. It is relatively easy to implement and because bitmap fonts are pre-rasterized, they're quite efficient. However, it is not particularly flexible. When you want to use a different font, you need to recompile a complete new bitmap font and the system is limited to a single resolution; zooming will quickly show pixelated edges. Furthermore, it is limited to a small character set, so Extended or Unicode characters are often out

---

[1] www.codehead.co.uk/cbfg/

of the question.

This approach was quite popular back in the day (and still is) since it is fast and works on any platform, but as of today more flexible approaches exist. One of these approaches is loading TrueType fonts using the FreeType library.

48.2 Modern text rendering: FreeType

FreeType is a software development library that is able to load fonts, render them to bitmaps, and provide support for several font-related operations. It is a popular library used by Mac OS X, Java, PlayStation, Linux, and Android to name a few. What makes FreeType particularly attractive is that it is able to load TrueType fonts.

A TrueType font is a collection of character glyphs not defined by pixels or any other non-scalable solution, but by mathematical equations (combinations of splines). Similar to vector images, the rasterized font images can be procedurally generated based on the preferred font height you'd like to obtain them in. By using TrueType fonts you can easily render character glyphs of various sizes without any loss of quality.

FreeType can be downloaded from their website at `www.freetype.org/`. You can choose to compile the library yourself or use one of their precompiled libraries if your target platform is listed. Be sure to link to `freetype.lib` and make sure your compiler knows where to find the header files.

Then include the appropriate headers:

```
#include <ft2build.h>
#include FT_FREETYPE_H
```

> Due to how FreeType is developed (at least at the time of this writing), you cannot put their header files in a new directory; they should be located at the root of your include directories. Including FreeType like `#include <FreeType/ft2build.h>` will likely cause several header conflicts.

FreeType loads these TrueType fonts and, for each glyph, generates a bitmap image and calculates several metrics. We can extract these bitmap images for generating textures and position each character glyph appropriately using the loaded metrics.

To load a font, all we have to do is initialize the FreeType library and load the font as a face as FreeType likes to call it. Here we load the `arial.ttf` TrueType font file that was copied from the `Windows/Fonts` directory:

```cpp
FT_Library ft;
if (FT_Init_FreeType(&ft))
    std::cout << "ERROR::FREETYPE: Could not init FreeType Library" <<
    std::endl;

FT_Face face;
if (FT_New_Face(ft, "fonts/arial.ttf", 0, &face))
    std::cout << "ERROR::FREETYPE: Failed to load font" << std::endl;
```

Each of these FreeType functions returns a non-zero integer whenever an error occurred.

Once we've loaded the face, we should define the pixel font size we'd like to extract from this face:

```
FT_Set_Pixel_Sizes(face, 0, 48);
```

The function sets the font's width and height parameters. Setting the width to 0 lets the face dynamically calculate the width based on the given height.

A FreeType face hosts a collection of glyphs. We can set one of those glyphs as the active glyph by calling `FT_Load_Char`. Here we choose to load the character glyph 'X':

```
if (FT_Load_Char(face, 'X', FT_LOAD_RENDER))
    std::cout << "ERROR::FREETYTPE: Failed to load Glyph" << std::endl;
```

By setting `FT_LOAD_RENDER` as one of the loading flags, we tell FreeType to create an 8-bit grayscale bitmap image for us that we can access via `face->glyph->bitmap`.

Each of the glyphs we load with FreeType however, do not have the same size (as we had with bitmap fonts). The bitmap image generated by FreeType is just large enough to contain the visible part of a character. For example, the bitmap image of the dot character '.' is much smaller in dimensions than the bitmap image of the character 'X'. For this reason, FreeType also loads several metrics that specify how large each character should be and how to properly position them. Next is an image from FreeType that shows all of the metrics it calculates for each character glyph:

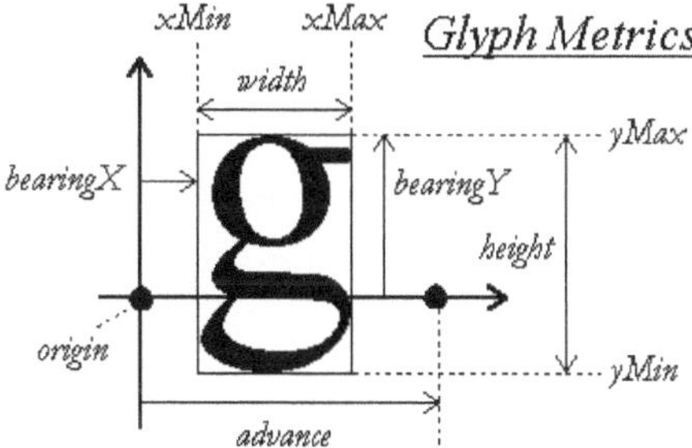

Each of the glyphs reside on a horizontal baseline (as depicted by the horizontal arrow) where some glyphs sit exactly on top of this baseline (like 'X') or some slightly below the baseline (like 'g' or 'p'). These metrics define the exact offsets to properly position each glyph on the baseline, how large each glyph should be, and how many pixels we need to advance to render the next glyph. Next is a small list of the properties we'll be needing:

- **width**: the width (in pixels) of the bitmap accessed via `face->glyph->bitmap.width`.
- **height**: the height (in pixels) of the bitmap accessed via `face->glyph->bitmap.rows`.
- **bearingX**: the horizontal bearing e.g. the horizontal position (in pixels) of the bitmap relative to the origin accessed via `face->glyph->bitmap_left`.
- **bearingY**: the vertical bearing e.g. the vertical position (in pixels) of the bitmap relative to the baseline accessed via `face->glyph->bitmap_top`.
- **advance**: the horizontal advance e.g. the horizontal distance (in 1/64th pixels) from the origin to the origin of the next glyph. Accessed via `face->glyph->advance.x`.

We could load a character glyph, retrieve its metrics, and generate a texture each time we want to render a character to the screen, but it would be inefficient to do this each frame. We'd rather store the generated data somewhere in the application and query it whenever we want to render a character. We'll define a convenient `struct` that we'll store in a `map`:

```cpp
struct Character {
    unsigned int TextureID;  // ID handle of the glyph texture
    glm::ivec2 Size;         // Size of glyph
    glm::ivec2 Bearing;      // Offset from baseline to left/top of glyph
    unsigned int Advance;    // Offset to advance to next glyph
};

std::map<char, Character> Characters;
```

For this chapter we'll keep things simple by restricting ourselves to the first 128 characters of the ASCII character set. For each character, we generate a texture and store its relevant data into a `Character` struct that we add to the `Characters` map. This way, all data required to render each character is stored for later use.

```cpp
glPixelStorei(GL_UNPACK_ALIGNMENT, 1); // no byte-alignment restriction

for (unsigned char c = 0; c < 128; c++)
{
    // load character glyph
    if (FT_Load_Char(face, c, FT_LOAD_RENDER))
    {
        std::cout << "ERROR::FREETYPE: Failed to load Glyph" << std::endl;
        continue;
    }
    // generate texture
    unsigned int texture;
    glGenTextures(1, &texture);
    glBindTexture(GL_TEXTURE_2D, texture);
    glTexImage2D(
        GL_TEXTURE_2D,
        0,
        GL_RED,
        face->glyph->bitmap.width,
        face->glyph->bitmap.rows,
        0,
        GL_RED,
        GL_UNSIGNED_BYTE,
        face->glyph->bitmap.buffer
    );
    // set texture options
    glTexParameteri(GL_TEXTURE_2D, GL_TEXTURE_WRAP_S, GL_CLAMP_TO_EDGE);
    glTexParameteri(GL_TEXTURE_2D, GL_TEXTURE_WRAP_T, GL_CLAMP_TO_EDGE);
    glTexParameteri(GL_TEXTURE_2D, GL_TEXTURE_MIN_FILTER, GL_LINEAR);
    glTexParameteri(GL_TEXTURE_2D, GL_TEXTURE_MAG_FILTER, GL_LINEAR);
    // now store character for later use
    Character character = {
        texture,
        glm::ivec2(face->glyph->bitmap.width, face->glyph->bitmap.rows),
        glm::ivec2(face->glyph->bitmap_left, face->glyph->bitmap_top),
        face->glyph->advance.x
    };
    Characters.insert(std::pair<char, Character>(c, character));
}
```

Within the for loop we list over all the 128 characters of the ASCII set and retrieve their corresponding character glyphs. For each character: we generate a texture, set its options, and store its metrics. What is interesting to note here is that we use `GL_RED` as the texture's `internalFormat` and `format` arguments. The bitmap generated from the glyph is a grayscale 8-bit image where each color is represented by a single byte. For this reason we'd like to store each byte of the bitmap buffer as the texture's single color value. We accomplish this by creating a texture where each byte corresponds to the texture color's red component (first byte of its color vector). If we use a single byte to represent the colors of a texture we do need to take care of a restriction of OpenGL:

```
glPixelStorei(GL_UNPACK_ALIGNMENT, 1);
```

OpenGL requires that textures all have a 4-byte alignment e.g. their size is always a multiple of 4 bytes. Normally this won't be a problem since most textures have a width that is a multiple of 4 and/or use 4 bytes per pixel, but since we now only use a single byte per pixel, the texture can have any possible width. By setting its unpack alignment to 1 we ensure there are no alignment issues (which could cause segmentation faults).

Be sure to clear FreeType's resources once you're finished processing the glyphs:

```
FT_Done_Face(face);
FT_Done_FreeType(ft);
```

48.2.1 Shaders

To render the glyphs we'll be using the following vertex shader:

```glsl
#version 330 core
layout (location = 0) in vec4 vertex; // <vec2 pos, vec2 tex>
out vec2 TexCoords;

uniform mat4 projection;

void main()
{
    gl_Position = projection * vec4(vertex.xy, 0.0, 1.0);
    TexCoords = vertex.zw;
}
```

We combine both the position and texture coordinate data into one `vec4`. The vertex shader multiplies the coordinates with a projection matrix and forwards the texture coordinates to the fragment shader:

```glsl
#version 330 core
in vec2 TexCoords;
out vec4 color;

uniform sampler2D text;
uniform vec3 textColor;

void main()
{
    vec4 sampled = vec4(1.0, 1.0, 1.0, texture(text, TexCoords).r);
    color = vec4(textColor, 1.0) * sampled;
}
```

The fragment shader takes two uniforms: one is the mono-colored bitmap image of the glyph, and the other is a color uniform for adjusting the text's final color. We first sample the color value of the bitmap texture. Because the texture's data is stored in just its red component, we sample the `r` component of the texture as the sampled alpha value. By varying the output color's alpha value, the resulting pixel will be transparent for all the glyph's background colors and non-transparent for the actual character pixels. We also multiply the **RGB** colors by the `textColor` uniform to vary the text color.

We do need to enable blending for this to work though:

```
glEnable(GL_BLEND);
glBlendFunc(GL_SRC_ALPHA, GL_ONE_MINUS_SRC_ALPHA);
```

For the projection matrix we'll be using an orthographic projection matrix. For rendering text we (usually) do not need perspective, and using an orthographic projection matrix also allows us to specify all vertex coordinates in screen coordinates if we set it up as follows:

```
glm::mat4 projection = glm::ortho(0.0f, 800.0f, 0.0f, 600.0f);
```

We set the projection matrix's bottom parameter to `0.0f` and its top parameter equal to the window's height. The result is that we specify coordinates with `y` values ranging from the bottom part of the screen (`0.0f`) to the top part of the screen (`600.0f`). This means that the point (`0.0`, `0.0`) now corresponds to the bottom-left corner.

Last up is creating a **VBO** and **VAO** for rendering the quads. For now we reserve enough memory when initiating the VBO so that we can later update the VBO's memory when rendering characters:

```
unsigned int VAO, VBO;
glGenVertexArrays(1, &VAO);
glGenBuffers(1, &VBO);
glBindVertexArray(VAO);
glBindBuffer(GL_ARRAY_BUFFER, VBO);
glBufferData(GL_ARRAY_BUFFER, sizeof(float) * 6*4, NULL, GL_DYNAMIC_DRAW);
glEnableVertexAttribArray(0);
glVertexAttribPointer(0, 4, GL_FLOAT, GL_FALSE, 4 * sizeof(float), 0);
glBindBuffer(GL_ARRAY_BUFFER, 0);
glBindVertexArray(0);
```

The 2D quad requires 6 vertices of 4 floats each, so we reserve 6 * 4 floats of memory. Because we'll be updating the content of the VBO's memory quite often we'll allocate the memory with `GL_DYNAMIC_DRAW`.

48.2.2 Render line of text

To render a character, we extract the corresponding `Character` struct of the `Characters` map and calculate the quad's dimensions using the character's metrics. With the quad's calculated dimensions we dynamically generate a set of 6 vertices that we use to update the content of the memory managed by the VBO using `glBufferSubData`.

We create a function called `RenderText` that renders a string of characters:

```cpp
void RenderText(Shader &s, std::string text, float x, float y, float scale,
                glm::vec3 color)
{
    // activate corresponding render state
    s.Use();
    glUniform3f(glGetUniformLocation(s.Program, "textColor"),
                color.x, color.y, color.z);
    glActiveTexture(GL_TEXTURE0);
    glBindVertexArray(VAO);

    // iterate through all characters
    std::string::const_iterator c;
    for (c = text.begin(); c != text.end(); c++)
    {
        Character ch = Characters[*c];

        float xpos = x + ch.Bearing.x * scale;
        float ypos = y - (ch.Size.y - ch.Bearing.y) * scale;

        float w = ch.Size.x * scale;
        float h = ch.Size.y * scale;
        // update VBO for each character
        float vertices[6][4] = {
            { xpos,     ypos + h, 0.0f, 0.0f },
            { xpos,     ypos,     0.0f, 1.0f },
            { xpos + w, ypos,     1.0f, 1.0f },

            { xpos,     ypos + h, 0.0f, 0.0f },
            { xpos + w, ypos,     1.0f, 1.0f },
            { xpos + w, ypos + h, 1.0f, 0.0f }
        };
        // render glyph texture over quad
        glBindTexture(GL_TEXTURE_2D, ch.textureID);
        // update content of VBO memory
        glBindBuffer(GL_ARRAY_BUFFER, VBO);
        glBufferSubData(GL_ARRAY_BUFFER, 0, sizeof(vertices), vertices);
        glBindBuffer(GL_ARRAY_BUFFER, 0);
        // render quad
        glDrawArrays(GL_TRIANGLES, 0, 6);
        // advance cursors for next glyph (advance is 1/64 pixels)
        x += (ch.Advance >> 6) * scale; // bitshift by 6 (2^6 = 64)
    }
    glBindVertexArray(0);
    glBindTexture(GL_TEXTURE_2D, 0);
}
```

Most of the content of the function should be relatively self-explanatory: we first calculate the origin position of the quad (as `xpos` and `ypos`) and the quad's size (as `w` and `h`) and generate a set of 6 vertices to form the 2D quad; note that we scale each metric by `scale`. We then update the content of the VBO and render the quad.

The following line of code requires some extra attention though:

```cpp
float ypos = y - (ch.Size.y - ch.Bearing.y);
```

Some characters (like 'p' or 'g') are rendered slightly below the baseline, so the quad should also be positioned slightly below `RenderText`'s `y` value. The exact amount we need to offset `ypos` below the baseline can be figured out from the glyph metrics:

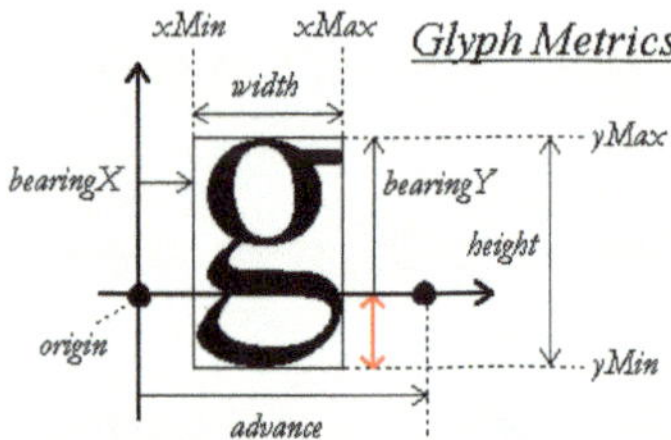

To calculate this distance e.g. offset we need to figure out the distance a glyph extends below the baseline; this distance is indicated by the red arrow. As you can see from the glyph metrics, we can calculate the length of this vector by subtracting `bearingY` from the glyph's (bitmap) height. This value is then `0.0` for characters that rest on the baseline (like 'X') and positive for characters that reside slightly below the baseline (like 'g' or 'j').

If you did everything correct you should now be able to successfully render strings of text with the following statements:

```
RenderText(shader, "This is sample text", 25.0f, 25.0f, 1.0f,
           glm::vec3(0.5, 0.8f, 0.2f));
RenderText(shader, "(C) LearnOpenGL.com", 540.0f, 570.0f, 0.5f,
           glm::vec3(0.3, 0.7f, 0.9f));
```

This should then look similar to the following image:

You can find the code of this example at `/src/7.in_practice/2.text_rendering/`.

To give you a feel for how we calculated the quad's vertices, we can disable blending to see what the actual rendered quads look like:

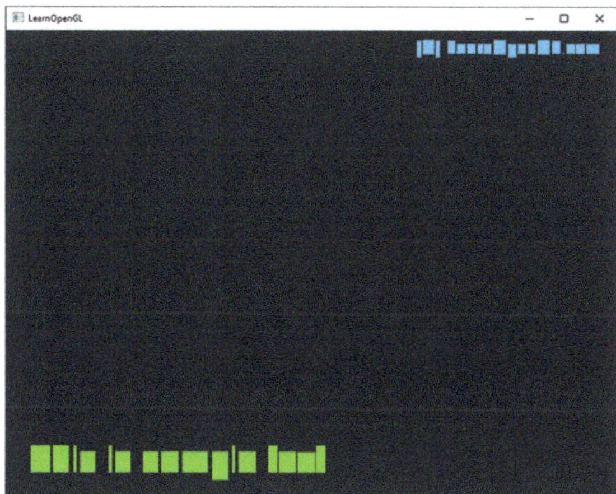

Here you can clearly see most quads resting on the (imaginary) baseline while the quads that corresponds to glyphs like 'p' or '(' are shifted downwards.

48.3 Going further

This chapter demonstrated a text rendering technique with TrueType fonts using the FreeType library. The approach is flexible, scalable, and works with many character encodings. However, this approach is likely going to be overkill for your application as we generate and render textures for each glyph. Performance-wise, bitmap fonts are preferable as we only need one texture for all our glyphs. The best approach would be to combine the two approaches by dynamically generating a bitmap font texture featuring all character glyphs as loaded with FreeType. This saves the renderer from a significant amount of texture switches and, based on how tight each glyph is packed, could save quite some performance.

Another issue with FreeType font bitmaps is that the glyph textures are stored with a fixed font size, so a significant amount of scaling may introduce jagged edges. Furthermore, rotations applied to the glyphs will cause them to appear blurry. This can be mitigated by, instead of storing the actual rasterized pixel colors, storing the distance to the closest glyph outline per pixel. This technique is called signed distance field fonts and Valve published a paper[1] a few years ago about their implementation of this technique which works surprisingly well for 3D rendering applications.

48.4 Further reading

- www.websiteplanet.com/blog/best-free-fonts/: summarized list of a large group of fonts to use in your project for personal or commercial use.

---

[1] steamcdn-a.akamaihd.net/apps/valve/2007/SIGGRAPH2007_AlphaTestedMagnification.pdf

VIII 2D Game

49. Breakout

Over these chapters we learned a fair share about OpenGL's inner workings and how we can use them to create fancy graphics. However, aside from a lot of tech demos, we haven't really created a practical application with OpenGL. This is the introduction of a larger series about creating a relatively simple 2D game using OpenGL. The next chapters will demonstrate how we can use OpenGL in a larger, more complicated, setting. Note that the series does not necessarily introduce new OpenGL concepts but more or less show how we can apply these concepts to a larger whole.

Because we rather keep things simple, we're going to base our 2D game on an already existing 2D arcade game. Introducing Breakout, a classic 2D game released in 1976 on the Atari 2600 console. Breakout requires the player, who controls a small horizontal paddle, to destroy all the bricks by bouncing a small ball against each brick without allowing the ball to reach the bottom edge. Once the player destroys all bricks, he completes the game.

Below we can see how Breakout originally looked on the Atari 2600:

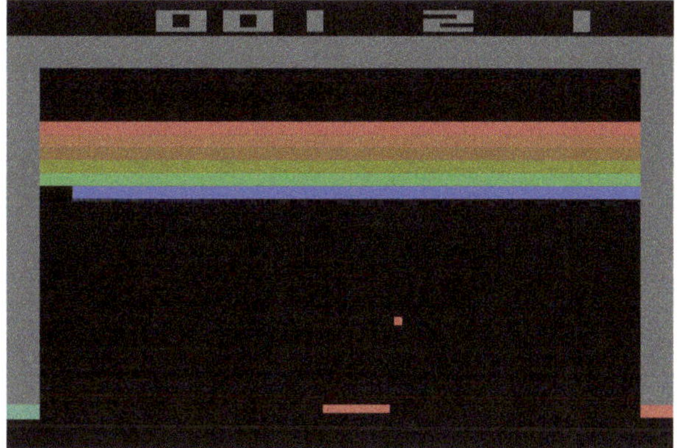

The game has the following mechanics:

- A small paddle is controlled by the player and can only move horizontally within the bounds of the screen.
- The ball travels across the screen and each collision results in the ball changing its direction based on where it hit; this applies to the screen bounds, the bricks, and the paddle.
- If the ball reaches the bottom edge of the screen, the player is either game over or loses a life.
- As soon as a brick touches the ball, the brick is destroyed.
- The player wins as soon as all bricks are destroyed.
- The direction of the ball can be manipulated by how far the ball bounces from the paddle's center.

Because from time to time the ball may find a small gap reaching the area above the brick wall, it will continue to bounce up and forth between the top edge of the level and the top edge of the brick layer. The ball keeps this up, until it eventually finds a gap again. This is logically where the game obtained its name from, since the ball has to *break out*.

49.1 OpenGL Breakout

We're going to take this classic arcade game as the basis of a 2D game that we'll completely implement with OpenGL. This version of Breakout will render its graphics on the GPU which gives us the ability to enhance the classical Breakout game with some nice extra features.

Other than the classic mechanics, our version of Breakout will feature:

- Amazing graphics!
- Particles
- Text rendering
- Power-ups
- Postprocessing effects
- Multiple (customizable) levels

To get you excited you can see what the game will look like after you've finished these chapters:

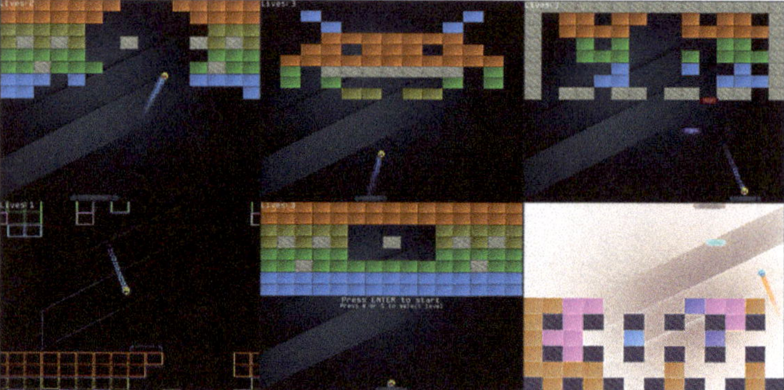

These chapters will combine a large number of concepts from previous chapters and demonstrate how they can work together as a whole. Therefore, it is important to have at least finished the *Getting Started* chapters before working your way through these series.

Also, several chapters will require concepts from other chapters (Framebuffers for example from the *Advanced OpenGL* section) so where necessary, the required chapters are listed.

50. Setting up

Before we get started with the game mechanics, we first need to set up a simple framework for the game to reside in. The game will use several third party libraries of which most have been introduced in earlier chapters. Wherever a new library is required, it will be properly introduced.

First, we define a so called uber game class that contains all relevant render and gameplay code. The idea of such a game class is that it (sort of) organizes your game code, while also decoupling all windowing code from the game. This way, you could use the same class in a completely different windowing library (like SDL or SFML for example) without much effort.

> There are thousands of ways of trying to abstract and generalize game/graphics code into classes and objects. What you will see in these chapters is just one (relatively simple) approach to solve this issue. If you feel there is a better approach, try to come up with your own improvement of the implementation.

The game class hosts an initialization function, an update function, a function to process input, and a render function:

```cpp
class Game
{
    public:
        // game state
        GameState       State;
        bool            Keys[1024];
        unsigned int Width, Height;
        // constructor/destructor
        Game(unsigned int width, unsigned int height);
        ~Game();
        // initialize game state (load all shaders/textures/levels)
        void Init();
        // game loop
        void ProcessInput(float dt);
        void Update(float dt);
        void Render();
};
```

The class hosts what you may expect from a game class. We initialize the game with a width and height (the resolution you want to play the game in) and use the `Init` function to load shaders, textures, and initialize all gameplay state. We can process input as stored within the `Keys` array by calling `ProcessInput`, and update all gameplay events (like player/ball movement) in the `Update` function. Last, we can render the game by calling `Render`. Note that we split the movement logic from the render logic.

The `Game` class also hosts a variable called `State` which is of type `GameState` as defined below:

```cpp
// Represents the current state of the game
enum GameState {
    GAME_ACTIVE,
    GAME_MENU,
    GAME_WIN
};
```

This allows us to keep track of what state the game is currently in. This way, we can decide to adjust rendering and/or processing based on the current state of the game (we probably render and process different items when we're in the game's menu for example).

As of now, the functions of the game class are completely empty since we have yet to write the actual game code. You can find the Game class's header at `/src/7.in_practice/3.2d_game/0.full_source/progress/2.game.h` and its cpp file at `/src/7.in_practice/3.2d_game/0.full_source/progress/2.game.cpp` file.

50.1 Utility

Since we're creating a large application we'll frequently have to re-use several OpenGL concepts, like textures and shaders. It thus makes sense to create a more easy-to-use interface for these two items as similarly done in one of the earlier chapters where we created a shader class.

We define a shader class that generates a compiled shader (or generates error messages if it fails) from two or three strings (if a geometry shader is present). The shader class also contains a lot of useful utility functions to quickly set uniform values. We also define a texture class that generates a 2D texture image (based on its properties) from a byte array and a given width and height. Again, the texture class also hosts utility functions.

We won't delve into the details of the classes since by now you should easily understand how they work. For this reason you can find the header and code files, fully commented at:

- **Shader**: `/src/7.in_practice/3.2d_game/0.full_source/shader.h`, `/src/7.in_practice/3.2d_game/0.full_source/shader.cpp`.
- **Texture**: `/src/7.in_practice/3.2d_game/0.full_source/texture.h`, `/src/7.in_practice/3.2d_game/0.full_source/texture.cpp`.

Note that the current texture class is solely designed for 2D textures only, but could easily be extended for alternative texture types.

50.2 Resource management

While the shader and texture classes function great by themselves, they do require either a byte array or a list of strings for initialization. We could easily embed file loading code within the classes themselves, but this slightly violates the single responsibility principle. We'd prefer these classes to only focus on either textures or shaders respectively, and not necessarily their file-loading mechanics.

For this reason it is often considered a more organized approach to create a single entity designed for loading game-related resources called a resource manager. There are several approaches to creating a resource manager; for this chapter we chose to use a singleton static resource manager that is (due to its static nature) always available throughout the project, hosting all loaded resources and their relevant loading functionality.

Using a singleton class with static functionality has several advantages and disadvantages, with its disadvantages mostly being the loss of several **OOP** properties and less control over construction/destruction. However, for relatively small projects like this it is easy to work with.

Like the other class files, the resource manager files are listed below:

- **Resource Manager**: `/src/7.in_practice/3.2d_game/0.full_source/resource_manager.h`, `/src/7.in_practice/3.2d_game/0.full_source/resource_manager.cpp`.

Using the resource manager, we can easily load shaders into the program like:

```
Shader shader = ResourceManager::LoadShader("vertex.vs", "fragment.vs",
                                    nullptr, "test");
// then use it
shader.Use();
// or
ResourceManager::GetShader("test").Use();
```

The defined Game class, together with the resource manager and the easily manageable Shader and Texture2D classes, form the basis for the next chapters as we'll be extensively using these classes to implement the Breakout game.

50.3 Program

We still need a window for the game and set some initial OpenGL state as we make use of OpenGL's blending functionality. We do not enable depth testing, since the game is entirely in 2D. All vertices are defined with the same z-values so enabling depth testing would be of no use and likely cause z-fighting.

The startup code of the Breakout game is relatively simple: we create a window with GLFW, register a few callback functions, create the Game object, and propagate all relevant functionality to the game class.

- **Program**: /src/7.in_practice/3.2d_game/0.full_source/progress/2.program.cpp.

Running the code should give you the following output:

By now we have a solid framework for the upcoming chapters; we'll be continuously extending the game class to host new functionality.

51. Rendering Sprites

To bring some life to the currently black abyss of our game world, we will render sprites to fill the void. A sprite has many definitions, but it's effectively not much more than a 2D image used together with some data to position it in a larger world (e.g. position, rotation, and size). Basically, sprites are the render-able image/texture objects we use in a 2D game.

We can, just like we did in previous chapters, create a 2D shape out of vertex data, pass all data to the GPU, and transform it all by hand. However, in a larger application like this we rather have some abstractions on rendering 2D shapes. If we were to manually define these shapes and transformations for each object, it'll quickly get messy.

In this chapter we'll define a rendering class that allows us to render a large amount of unique sprites with a minimal amount of code. This way, we're abstracting the gameplay code from the gritty OpenGL rendering code as is commonly done in larger projects. First, we have to set up a proper projection matrix though.

51.1 2D projection matrix

We know from the *Coordinate Systems* chapter that a projection matrix converts all view-space coordinates to clip-space (and then to normalized device) coordinates. By generating the appropriate projection matrix we can work with different coordinates that are easier to work with, compared to directly specifying all coordinates as normalized device coordinates.

We don't need any perspective applied to the coordinates, since the game is entirely in 2D, so an orthographic projection matrix would suit the rendering quite well. Because an orthographic projection matrix directly transforms all coordinates to normalized device coordinates, we can choose to specify the world coordinates as screen coordinates by defining the projection matrix as follows:

```cpp
glm::mat4 projection = glm::ortho(0.0f, 800.0f, 600.0f, 0.0f, -1.0f, 1.0f);
```

The first four arguments specify in order the left, right, bottom, and top part of the projection frustum. This projection matrix transforms all x coordinates between 0 and 800 to -1 and 1, and all y coordinates between 0 and 600 to -1 and 1. Here we specified that the top of the frustum has a y coordinate of 0, while the bottom has a y coordinate of 600. The result is that the top-left coordinate of the scene will be at (0, 0) and the bottom-right part of the screen is at coordinate (800, 600), just like screen coordinates; the world-space coordinates directly correspond to the resulting pixel coordinates.

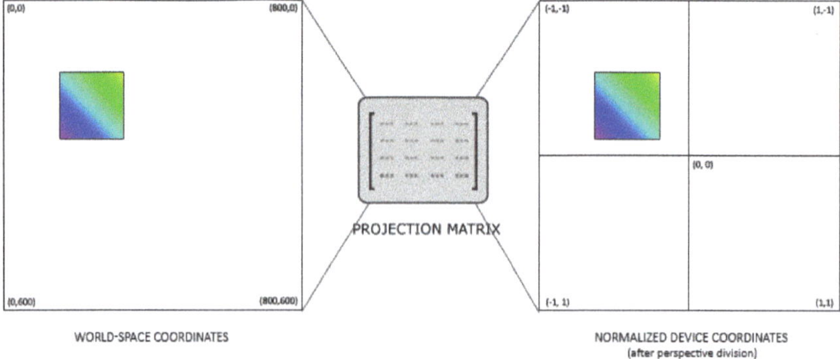

This allows us to specify all vertex coordinates equal to the pixel coordinates they end up in on the screen, which is rather intuitive for 2D games.

51.2 Rendering sprites

Rendering an actual sprite shouldn't be too complicated. We create a textured quad that we can transform with a model matrix, after which we project it using the previously defined orthographic projection matrix.

> Since Breakout is a single-scene game, there is no need for a view/camera matrix. Using the projection matrix we can directly transform the world-space coordinates to normalized device coordinates.

To transform a sprite, we use the following vertex shader:

```glsl
#version 330 core
layout (location = 0) in vec4 vertex; // <vec2 position, vec2 texCoords>

out vec2 TexCoords;

uniform mat4 model;
uniform mat4 projection;

void main()
{
    TexCoords = vertex.zw;
    gl_Position = projection * model * vec4(vertex.xy, 0.0, 1.0);
}
```

Note that we store both the position and texture-coordinate data in a single `vec4` variable. Because both the position and texture coordinates contain two floats, we can combine them in a single vertex attribute.

The fragment shader is relatively straightforward as well. We take a texture and a color vector that both affect the final color of the fragment. By having a uniform color vector, we can easily change the color of sprites from the game-code:

```glsl
#version 330 core
in vec2 TexCoords;
out vec4 color;

uniform sampler2D image;
uniform vec3 spriteColor;

void main()
{
    color = vec4(spriteColor, 1.0) * texture(image, TexCoords);
}
```

To make the rendering of sprites more organized, we define a `SpriteRenderer` class that is able to render a sprite with just a single function. Its definition is as follows:

```cpp
class SpriteRenderer
{
    public:
        SpriteRenderer(Shader &shader);
        ~SpriteRenderer();

        void DrawSprite(Texture2D &texture, glm::vec2 position,
            glm::vec2 size = glm::vec2(10.0f, 10.0f), float rotate = 0.0f,
            glm::vec3 color = glm::vec3(1.0f));
    private:
        Shader          shader;
        unsigned int quadVAO;

        void initRenderData();
};
```

The SpriteRenderer class hosts a shader object, a single vertex array object, and a render and
initialization function. Its constructor takes a shader object that it uses for all future rendering.

51.2.1 Initialization

First, let's delve into the `initRenderData` function that configures the `quadVAO`:

```cpp
void SpriteRenderer::initRenderData()
{
    // configure VAO/VBO
    unsigned int VBO;
    float vertices[] = {
        // pos      // tex
        0.0f, 1.0f, 0.0f, 1.0f,
        1.0f, 0.0f, 1.0f, 0.0f,
        0.0f, 0.0f, 0.0f, 0.0f,

        0.0f, 1.0f, 0.0f, 1.0f,
        1.0f, 1.0f, 1.0f, 1.0f,
        1.0f, 0.0f, 1.0f, 0.0f
    };

    glGenVertexArrays(1, &quadVAO);
    glGenBuffers(1, &VBO);

    glBindBuffer(GL_ARRAY_BUFFER, VBO);
    glBufferData(GL_ARRAY_BUFFER, sizeof(vertices), vertices,
    GL_STATIC_DRAW);

    glBindVertexArray(quadVAO);
    glEnableVertexAttribArray(0);
    glVertexAttribPointer(0, 4, GL_FLOAT, GL_FALSE, 4 * sizeof(float),
                          (void*)0);
    glBindBuffer(GL_ARRAY_BUFFER, 0);
    glBindVertexArray(0);
}
```

Here we first define a set of vertices with (0, 0) being the top-left corner of the quad. This
means that when we apply translation or scaling transformations on the quad, they're transformed
from the top-left position of the quad. This is commonly accepted in 2D graphics and/or GUI
systems where elements' positions correspond to the top-left corner of the elements.

Next we simply sent the vertices to the GPU and configure the vertex attributes, which in this case is a single vertex attribute. We only have to define a single VAO for the sprite renderer since all sprites share the same vertex data.

51.2.2 Rendering

Rendering sprites is not too difficult; we use the sprite renderer's shader, configure a model matrix, and set the relevant uniforms. What is important here is the order of transformations:

```cpp
void SpriteRenderer::DrawSprite(Texture2D &texture, glm::vec2 position,
    glm::vec2 size, float rotate, glm::vec3 color)
{
    // prepare transformations
    shader.Use();
    glm::mat4 model = glm::mat4(1.0f);
    model = glm::translate(model, glm::vec3(position, 0.0f));

    model = glm::translate(model, glm::vec3(0.5*size.x, 0.5*size.y, 0.0));
    model = glm::rotate(model, glm::radians(rotate),
                        glm::vec3(0.0, 0.0, 1.0));
    model = glm::translate(model, glm::vec3(-0.5*size.x, -0.5*size.y, 0.0));

    model = glm::scale(model, glm::vec3(size, 1.0f));

    shader.SetMatrix4("model", model);
    shader.SetVector3f("spriteColor", color);

    glActiveTexture(GL_TEXTURE0);
    texture.Bind();

    glBindVertexArray(quadVAO);
    glDrawArrays(GL_TRIANGLES, 0, 6);
    glBindVertexArray(0);
}
```

When trying to position objects somewhere in a scene with rotation and scaling transformations, it is advised to first scale, then rotate, and finally translate the object. Because multiplying matrices occurs from right to left, we transform the matrix in reverse order: translate, rotate, and then scale.

The rotation transformation may still seem a bit daunting. We know from the *Transformations* chapter that rotations always revolve around the origin $(0, 0)$. Because we specified the quad's vertices with $(0, 0)$ as the top-left coordinate, all rotations will rotate around this point of $(0, 0)$. The origin of rotation is at the top-left of the quad, which produces undesirable results. What we want to do is move the origin of rotation to the center of the quad so the quad neatly rotates around this origin, instead of rotating around the top-left of the quad. We solve this by translating the quad by half its size first, so its center is at coordinate $(0, 0)$ before rotating.

Since we first scale the quad, we have to take the size of the sprite into account when translating to the sprite's center, which is why we multiply with the sprite's `size` vector. Once the rotation transformation is applied, we reverse the previous translation.

Combining all these transformations, we can position, scale, and rotate each sprite in any way we like. Below you can find the complete source code of the sprite renderer:

- **SpriteRenderer**: `/src/7.in_practice/3.2d_game/0.full_source/sprite_renderer.h`, `/src/7.in_practice/3.2d_game/0.full_source/sprite_renderer.cpp`

51.3 Hello sprite

With the `SpriteRenderer` class we finally have the ability to render actual images to the screen! Let's initialize one within the game code and load our favorite texture[1] while we're at it:

```cpp
SpriteRenderer *Renderer;

void Game::Init()
{
    // load shaders
    ResourceManager::LoadShader("shaders/sprite.vs", "shaders/sprite.frag",
                                nullptr, "sprite");
    // configure shaders
    glm::mat4 proj = glm::ortho(0.0f, static_cast<float>(Width),
        static_cast<float>(Height), 0.0f, -1.0f, 1.0f);
    ResourceManager::GetShader("sprite").Use().SetInteger("image", 0);
    ResourceManager::GetShader("sprite").SetMatrix4("projection", proj);
    // set render-specific controls
    Renderer = new SpriteRenderer(ResourceManager::GetShader("sprite"));
    // load textures
    ResourceManager::LoadTexture("textures/awesomeface.png", true, "face");
}
```

Then within the render function we can render our beloved mascot to see if everything works as it should:

```cpp
void Game::Render()
{
    Renderer->DrawSprite(ResourceManager::GetTexture("face"),
        glm::vec2(200.0f, 200.0f), glm::vec2(300.0f, 400.0f),
        45.0f, glm::vec3(0.0f, 1.0f, 0.0f));
}
```

Here we position the sprite somewhat close to the center of the screen with its height being slightly larger than its width. We also rotate it by 45 degrees and give it a green color. Note that the position we give the sprite equals the top-left vertex of the sprite's quad.

---

[1] learnopengl.com/img/textures/awesomeface.png

If you did everything right you should get the following output:

You can find the updated game class's source code at `/src/7.in_practice/3.2d_game/0.full_source/progress/3.game.cpp`.

52. Levels

Breakout is unfortunately not just about a single happy green face, but contains complete levels with a lot of playfully colored bricks. We want these levels to be configurable such that they can support any number of rows and/or columns, we want the levels to have solid bricks (that cannot be destroyed), we want the levels to support multiple brick colors, and we want them to be stored externally in (text) files.

In this chapter we'll briefly walk through the code of a game level object that is used to manage a large amount of bricks. We first have to define what an actual brick is though.

We create a component called a game object that acts as the base representation of an object inside the game. Such a game object holds state data like its position, size, and velocity. It holds a color, a rotation component, whether it is solid and/or destroyed, and it also stores a `Texture2D` variable as its sprite.

Each object in the game is represented as a `GameObject` or a derivative of this class. You can find the code of the `GameObject` class below:

- **GameObject**: `/src/7.in_practice/3.2d_game/0.full_source/game_obj ect.h`, `/src/7.in_practice/3.2d_game/0.full_source/game_object. cpp`

A level in Breakout consists entirely of bricks so we can represent a level by exactly that: a collection of bricks. Because a brick requires the same state as a game object, we're going to represent each brick of the level as a `GameObject`. The declaration of the `GameLevel` class then looks as follows:

```cpp
class GameLevel
{
public:
    // level state
    std::vector<GameObject> Bricks;
    // constructor
    GameLevel() { }
    // loads level from file
    void Load(const char *file, unsigned int levelWidth,
            unsigned int levelHeight);
    // render level
    void Draw(SpriteRenderer &renderer);
    // check if the level is completed (all non-solid tiles are destroyed)
    bool IsCompleted();
private:
    // initialize level from tile data
    void init(std::vector<std::vector<unsigned int>> tileData,
            unsigned int levelWidth, unsigned int levelHeight);
};
```

Since a level is loaded from an external (text) file, we need to propose some kind of level structure. Here is an example of what a game level may look like in a text file:

```
1 1 1 1 1 1
2 2 0 0 2 2
3 3 4 4 3 3
```

A level is stored in a matrix-like structure where each number represents a type of brick, each one separated by a space. Within the level code we can then assign what each number represents. We have chosen the following representation:

- A number of 0: no brick, an empty space within the level.
- A number of 1: a solid brick, a brick that cannot be destroyed.
- A number higher than 1: a destroyable brick; each subsequent number only differs in color.

The example level listed above would, after being processed by `GameLevel`, look like this:

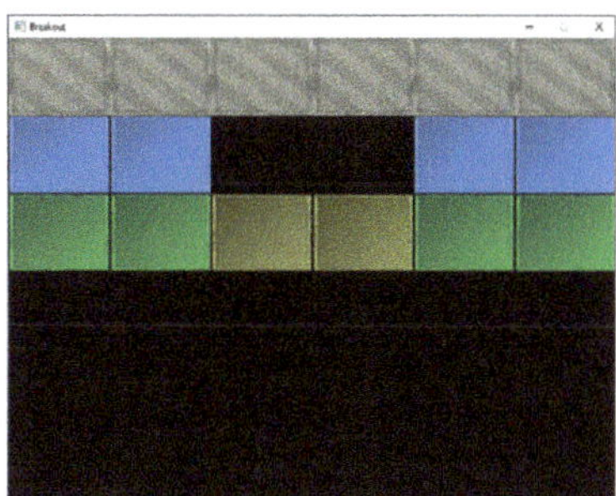

The `GameLevel` class uses two functions to generate a level from file. It first loads all the numbers in a two-dimensional vector within its `Load` function that then processes these numbers (to create all game objects) in its `init` function.

```cpp
void GameLevel::Load(const char *file, unsigned int levelWidth, unsigned
    int levelHeight)
{
    // clear old data
    Bricks.clear();
    // load from file
    unsigned int tileCode;
    GameLevel level;
    std::string line;
    std::ifstream fstream(file);
    std::vector<std::vector<unsigned int>> tileData;
    if (fstream)
    {
        while (std::getline(fstream, line)) // read each line from file
        {
            std::istringstream sstream(line);
            std::vector<unsigned int> row;
            while (sstream >> tileCode) // read each word
                row.push_back(tileCode);
            tileData.push_back(row);
        }
        if (tileData.size() > 0)
            init(tileData, levelWidth, levelHeight);
    }
}
```

The loaded `tileData` is then passed to the game level's `init` function:

```cpp
void GameLevel::init(std::vector<std::vector<unsigned int>> tileData,
                     unsigned int lvlWidth, unsigned int lvlHeight)
{
    // calculate dimensions
    unsigned int height = tileData.size();
    unsigned int width  = tileData[0].size();
    float unit_width     = lvlWidth / static_cast<float>(width);
    float unit_height    = lvlHeight / height;
    // initialize level tiles based on tileData
```

```cpp
    for (unsigned int y = 0; y < height; ++y)
    {
        for (unsigned int x = 0; x < width; ++x)
        {
            // check block type from level data (2D level array)
            if (tileData[y][x] == 1) // solid
            {
                glm::vec2 pos(unit_width * x, unit_height * y);
                glm::vec2 size(unit_width, unit_height);
                GameObject obj(pos, size,
                    ResourceManager::GetTexture("block_solid"),
                    glm::vec3(0.8f, 0.8f, 0.7f)
                );
                obj.IsSolid = true;
                Bricks.push_back(obj);
            }
            else if (tileData[y][x] > 1)
            {
                glm::vec3 color = glm::vec3(1.0f); // original: white
                if (tileData[y][x] == 2)
                    color = glm::vec3(0.2f, 0.6f, 1.0f);
                else if (tileData[y][x] == 3)
                    color = glm::vec3(0.0f, 0.7f, 0.0f);
                else if (tileData[y][x] == 4)
                    color = glm::vec3(0.8f, 0.8f, 0.4f);
                else if (tileData[y][x] == 5)
                    color = glm::vec3(1.0f, 0.5f, 0.0f);

                glm::vec2 pos(unit_width * x, unit_height * y);
                glm::vec2 size(unit_width, unit_height);
                Bricks.push_back(GameObject(pos, size,
                    ResourceManager::GetTexture("block"), color)
                );
            }
        }
    }
}
```

The `init` function iterates through each of the loaded numbers and adds a `GameObject` to the level's `Bricks` vector based on the processed number. The size of each brick is automatically calculated (`unit_width` and `unit_height`) based on the total number of bricks so that each brick perfectly fits within the screen bounds.

Here we load the game objects with two new textures, a block texture[1] and a solid block texture[2].

A nice little trick here is that these textures are completely in gray-scale. The effect is that we can neatly manipulate their colors within the game-code by multiplying their grayscale colors with a defined color vector; exactly as we did within the `SpriteRenderer`. This way, customizing the appearance of their colors doesn't look too weird or unbalanced.

---

[1]learnopengl.com/img/in-practice/breakout/textures/block.png
[2]learnopengl.com/img/in-practice/breakout/textures/block_solid.png

The `GameLevel` class also houses a few other functions, like rendering all non-destroyed bricks, or validating if all non-solid bricks are destroyed. You can find the source code of the `GameLevel` class below:

- **GameLevel**: `/src/7.in_practice/3.2d_game/0.full_source/game_level.h`, `/src/7.in_practice/3.2d_game/0.full_source/game_level.cpp`

The game level class gives us a lot of flexibility since any amount of rows and columns are supported and a user could easily create his/her own levels by modifying the level files.

52.1 Within the game

We would like to support multiple levels in the Breakout game so we'll have to extend the game class a little by adding a vector that holds variables of type `GameLevel`. We'll also store the currently active level while we're at it:

```cpp
class Game
{
    [...]
    std::vector<GameLevel> Levels;
    unsigned int           Level;
    [...]
};
```

This series' version of the Breakout game features a total of 4 levels:

- `/src/7.in_practice/3.2d_game/0.full_source/levels/one.lvl`
- `/src/7.in_practice/3.2d_game/0.full_source/levels/two.lvl`
- `/src/7.in_practice/3.2d_game/0.full_source/levels/three.lvl`
- `/src/7.in_practice/3.2d_game/0.full_source/levels/four.lvl`

Each of the textures and levels are then initialized within the game class's `Init` function:

```cpp
void Game::Init()
{
    [...]
    // load textures
    ResourceManager::LoadTexture("textures/background.jpg",
                                 false, "background");
    ResourceManager::LoadTexture("textures/awesomeface.png",
                                 true, "face");
    ResourceManager::LoadTexture("textures/block.png",
                                 false, "block");
    ResourceManager::LoadTexture("textures/block_solid.png",
                                 false, "block_solid");
    // load levels
    GameLevel one; one.Load("levels/one.lvl", Width, Height / 2);
    GameLevel two; two.Load("levels/two.lvl", Width, Height / 2);
    GameLevel three; three.Load("levels/three.lvl", Width, Height / 2);
    GameLevel four; four.Load("levels/four.lvl", Width, Height / 2);
    Levels.push_back(one);
    Levels.push_back(two);
    Levels.push_back(three);
    Levels.push_back(four);
    Level = 0;
}
```

Now all that is left to do, is actually render the level. We accomplish this by calling the currently active level's `Draw` function that in turn calls each `GameObject`'s `Draw` function using the given sprite renderer. Next to the level, we'll also render the scene with a nice background image[1] (courtesy of Tenha):

```cpp
void Game::Render()
{
    if(State == GAME_ACTIVE)
    {
        // draw background
        Renderer->DrawSprite(ResourceManager::GetTexture("background"),
            glm::vec2(0.0f, 0.0f), glm::vec2(Width, Height), 0.0f
        );
        // draw level
        Levels[Level].Draw(*Renderer);
    }
}
```

The result is then a nicely rendered level that really starts to make the game feel more alive:

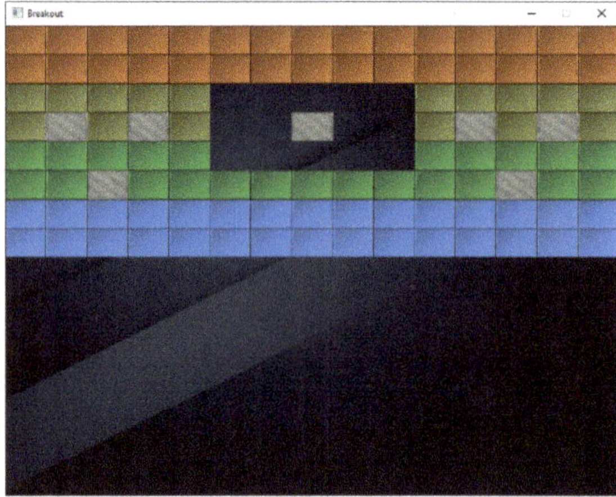

52.1.1 The player paddle

While we're at it, we may just as well introduce a paddle at the bottom of the scene that is controlled by the player. The paddle only allows for horizontal movement and whenever it touches any of the scene's edges, its movement should halt. For the player paddle we're going to use the following texture[2]:

A paddle object will have a position, a size, and a sprite texture, so it makes sense to define the paddle as a `GameObject` as well:

[1] learnopengl.com/img/in-practice/breakout/textures/background.jpg
[2] learnopengl.com/img/in-practice/breakout/textures/paddle.png

```cpp
// Initial size of the player paddle
const glm::vec2 PLAYER_SIZE(100.0f, 20.0f);
// Initial velocity of the player paddle
const float PLAYER_VELOCITY(500.0f);

GameObject     *Player;

void Game::Init()
{
    [...]
    ResourceManager::LoadTexture("textures/paddle.png", true, "paddle");
    [...]
    glm::vec2 playerPos = glm::vec2(Width / 2.0f - PLAYER_SIZE.x / 2.0f,
                                    Height - PLAYER_SIZE.y);
    Player = new GameObject(playerPos, PLAYER_SIZE,
                            ResourceManager::GetTexture("paddle"));
}
```

Here we defined several constant values that define the paddle's size and speed. Within the Game's `Init` function we calculate the starting position of the paddle within the scene. We make sure the player paddle's center is aligned with the horizontal center of the scene.

With the player paddle initialized, we also need to add a statement to the Game's `Render` function:

```cpp
Player->Draw(*Renderer);
```

If you'd start the game now, you would not only see the level, but also a fancy player paddle aligned to the bottom edge of the scene. As of now, it doesn't really do anything so we're going to delve into the Game's `ProcessInput` function to horizontally move the paddle whenever the user presses the A or D key:

```cpp
void Game::ProcessInput(float dt)
{
    if (State == GAME_ACTIVE)
    {
        float velocity = PLAYER_VELOCITY * dt;
        // move playerboard
        if (Keys[GLFW_KEY_A])
        {
            if (Player->Position.x >= 0.0f)
                Player->Position.x -= velocity;
        }
        if (Keys[GLFW_KEY_D])
        {
            if (Player->Position.x <= Width - Player->Size.x)
                Player->Position.x += velocity;
        }
    }
}
```

Here we move the player paddle either in the left or right direction based on which key the user pressed (note how we multiply the velocity with the deltatime variable). If the paddle's x value would be less than 0 it would've moved outside the left edge, so we only move the paddle to the left if the paddle's x value is higher than the left edge's x position (0.0). We do the same for when the paddle breaches the right edge, but we have to compare the right edge's position with the right edge of the paddle (subtract the paddle's width from the right edge's x position).

Now running the game gives us a player paddle that we can move all across the bottom edge:

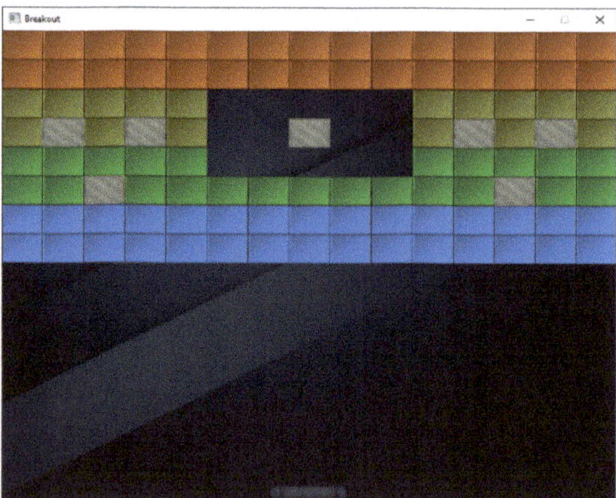

You can find the updated code of the Game class at:

- **Game**: `/src/7.in_practice/3.2d_game/0.full_source/progress/4.game.h`, `/src/7.in_practice/3.2d_game/0.full_source/progress/4.game.cpp`

53. Ball

At this point we have a level full of bricks and a movable player paddle. The only thing missing from the classic Breakout recipe is the ball. The objective is to let the ball collide with all the bricks until each of the destroyable bricks are destroyed, but this all within the condition that the ball is not allowed to reach the bottom edge of the screen.

In addition to the general game object components, a ball has a radius, and an extra boolean value indicating whether the ball is stuck on the player paddle or it's allowed free movement. When the game starts, the ball is initially stuck on the player paddle until the player starts the game by pressing some arbitrary key.

Because the ball is effectively a `GameObject` with a few extra properties it makes sense to create a `BallObject` class as a subclass of `GameObject`:

```cpp
class BallObject : public GameObject
{
    public:
        // ball state
        float Radius;
        bool  Stuck;


        BallObject();
        BallObject(glm::vec2 pos, float radius, glm::vec2 velocity,
                Texture2D sprite);

        glm::vec2 Move(float dt, unsigned int window_width);
        void      Reset(glm::vec2 position, glm::vec2 velocity);
};
```

The constructor of `BallObject` initializes its own values, but also initializes the underlying `GameObject`. The `BallObject` class hosts a `Move` function that moves the ball based on its velocity. It also checks if it reaches any of the scene's edges and if so, reverses the ball's velocity:

```cpp
glm::vec2 BallObject::Move(float dt, unsigned int window_width)
{
    if (!Stuck)
    {
        // move the ball
        Position += Velocity * dt;
        // check if outside window bounds; if so, reverse velocity
        // and restore at correct position
        if (Position.x <= 0.0f)
        {
            Velocity.x = -Velocity.x;
            Position.x = 0.0f;
        }
        else if (Position.x + Size.x >= window_width)
        {
            Velocity.x = -Velocity.x;
            Position.x = window_width - Size.x;
        }
        if (Position.y <= 0.0f)
        {
            Velocity.y = -Velocity.y;
            Position.y = 0.0f;
        }
    }
    return Position;
}
```

In addition to reversing the ball's velocity, we also want relocate the ball back along the edge; the ball is only able to move if it isn't stuck.

> Because the player is game over (or loses a life) if the ball reaches the bottom edge, there is no code to let the ball bounce of the bottom edge. We do need to later implement this logic somewhere in the game code though.

You can find the code for the ball object at:

- **BallObject**: /src/7.in_practice/3.2d_game/0.full_source/progress/ 5.1.ball_object_collisions.h, /src/7.in_practice/3.2d_game/0.f ull_source/progress/5.1.ball_object_collisions.cpp

First, let's add the ball to the game. Just like the player paddle, we create a `BallObject` and define two constants that we use to initialize the ball. As for the texture of the ball, we're going to use an image that makes perfect sense in a LearnOpenGL Breakout game: learnopengl.com/ img/textures/awesomeface.png.

```cpp
// Initial velocity of the Ball
const glm::vec2 INITIAL_BALL_VELOCITY(100.0f, -350.0f);
// Radius of the ball object
const float BALL_RADIUS = 12.5f;

BallObject *Ball;

void Game::Init()
{
    [...]
    glm::vec2 ballPos = playerPos + glm::vec2(PLAYER_SIZE.x / 2.0f -
                        BALL_RADIUS, -BALL_RADIUS * 2.0f);
    Ball = new BallObject(ballPos, BALL_RADIUS, INITIAL_BALL_VELOCITY,
                        ResourceManager::GetTexture("face"));
}
```

Then we have to update the position of the ball each frame by calling its `Move` function within the game code's `Update` function:

```cpp
void Game::Update(float dt)
{
    Ball->Move(dt, Width);
}
```

Furthermore, because the ball is initially stuck to the paddle, we have to give the player the ability to remove it from its stuck position. We select the space key for freeing the ball from the paddle. This means we have to change the `processInput` function a little:

```cpp
void Game::ProcessInput(float dt)
{
    if (State == GAME_ACTIVE)
    {
        float velocity = PLAYER_VELOCITY * dt;
        // move playerboard
        if (Keys[GLFW_KEY_A])
        {
            if (Player->Position.x >= 0.0f)
```

```cpp
        {
            Player->Position.x -= velocity;
            if (Ball->Stuck)
                Ball->Position.x -= velocity;
        }
    }
    if (Keys[GLFW_KEY_D])
    {
        if (Player->Position.x <= Width - Player->Size.x)
        {
            Player->Position.x += velocity;
            if (Ball->Stuck)
                Ball->Position.x += velocity;
        }
    }
    if (Keys[GLFW_KEY_SPACE])
        Ball->Stuck = false;
    }
}
```

Here, if the user presses the space bar, the ball's `Stuck` variable is set to `false`. Note that we also move the position of the ball alongside the paddle's position whenever the ball is stuck.

Last, we need to render the ball which by now should be fairly obvious:

```cpp
void Game::Render()
{
    if (State == GAME_ACTIVE)
    {
        [...]
        Ball->Draw(*Renderer);
    }
}
```

The result is a ball that follows the paddle and roams freely whenever we press the spacebar. The ball also properly bounces of the left, right, and top edge, but it doesn't yet seem to collide with any of the bricks as we can see:

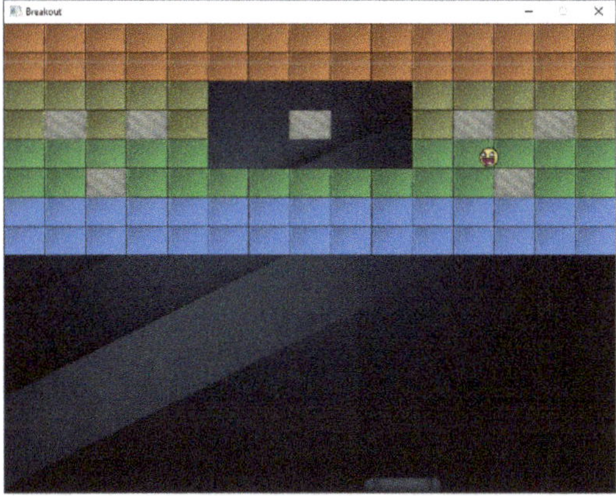

What we want is to create one or several function(s) that check if the ball object is colliding with any of the bricks in the level and if so, destroy the brick. These so called collision detection functions is what we'll focus on in the next chapter.

54. Collision detection

When trying to determine if a collision occurs between two objects, we generally do not use the vertex data of the objects themselves since these objects often have complicated shapes; this in turn makes the collision detection complicated. For this reason, it is a common practice to use more simple shapes (that usually have a nice mathematical definition) for collision detection that we *overlay* on top of the original object. We then check for collisions based on these simple shapes; this makes the code easier and saves a lot of performance. A few examples of such collision shapes are circles, spheres, rectangles, and boxes; these are a lot simpler to work with compared to arbitrary meshes with hundreds of triangles.

While the simple shapes do give us easier and more efficient collision detection algorithms, they share a common disadvantage in that these shapes usually do not fully surround the object. The effect is that a collision may be detected that didn't really collide with the actual object; one should always keep in mind that these shapes are just approximations of the real shapes.

54.1 AABB - AABB collisions

AABB stands for axis-aligned bounding box, a rectangular collision shape aligned to the base axes of the scene, which in 2D aligns to the x and y axis. Being axis-aligned means the rectangular box has no rotation and its edges are parallel to the base axes of the scene (e.g. left and right edge are parallel to the y axis). The fact that these boxes are always aligned to the axes of the scene makes calculations easier. Here we surround the ball object with an AABB:

Almost all the objects in Breakout are rectangular based objects, so it makes perfect sense to use axis aligned bounding boxes for detecting collisions. This is exactly what we're going to do.

Axis aligned bounding boxes can be defined in several ways. One of them is to define an AABB by a top-left and a bottom-right position. The `GameObject` class that we defined already contains a top-left position (its `Position` vector), and we can easily calculate its bottom-right position by adding its size to the top-left position vector (`Position + Size`). Effectively, each `GameObject` contains an AABB that we can use for collisions.

So how do we check for collisions? A collision occurs when two collision shapes enter each other's regions e.g. the shape that determines the first object is in some way inside the shape of the second object. For AABBs this is quite easy to determine due to the fact that they're aligned to the scene's axes: we check for each axis if the two object' edges on that axis overlap. So we check if the horizontal edges overlap, and if the vertical edges overlap of both objects. If both the horizontal **and** vertical edges overlap we have a collision.

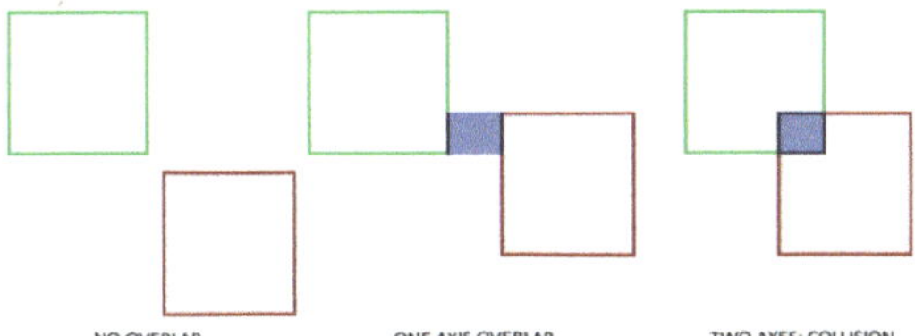

Translating this concept to code is relatively straightforward. We check for overlap on both axes and if so, return a collision:

```cpp
bool CheckCollision(GameObject &one, GameObject &two) // AABB - AABB
{
    // collision x-axis?
    bool collisionX = one.Position.x + one.Size.x >= two.Position.x &&
        two.Position.x + two.Size.x >= one.Position.x;
    // collision y-axis?
    bool collisionY = one.Position.y + one.Size.y >= two.Position.y &&
        two.Position.y + two.Size.y >= one.Position.y;
    // collision only if on both axes
    return collisionX && collisionY;
}
```

We check if the right side of the first object is greater than the left side of the second object **and** if the second object's right side is greater than the first object's left side; similarly for the vertical axis. If you have trouble visualizing this, try to draw the edges/rectangles on paper and determine this for yourself.

To keep the collision code a bit more organized we add an extra function to the Game class:

```cpp
class Game
{
    public:
        [...]
        void DoCollisions();
};
```

Within `DoCollisions`, we check for collisions between the ball object and each brick of the level. If we detect a collision, we set the brick's `Destroyed` property to `true`, which instantly stops the level from rendering this brick:

```cpp
void Game::DoCollisions()
{
    for (GameObject &box : Levels[Level].Bricks)
    {
        if (!box.Destroyed)
        {
            if (CheckCollision(*Ball, box))
            {
                if (!box.IsSolid)
                    box.Destroyed = true;
            }
        }
    }
}
```

Then we also need to update the game's `Update` function:

```cpp
void Game::Update(float dt)
{
    // update objects
    Ball->Move(dt, Width);
    // check for collisions
    DoCollisions();
}
```

If we run the code now, the ball should detect collisions with each of the bricks and if the brick is not solid, the brick is destroyed. If you run the game now it'll look something like this:

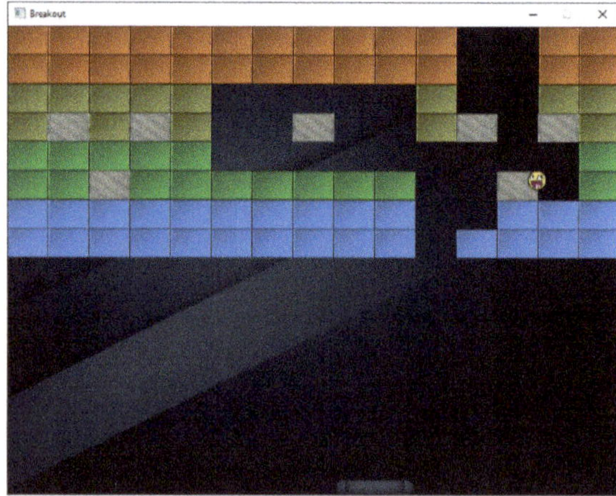

While the collision detection does work, it's not very precise since the ball's rectangular collision shape collides with most of the bricks without the ball directly touching them. Let's see if we can figure out a more precise collision detection technique.

54.2 AABB - Circle collision detection

Because the ball is a circle-like object, an AABB is probably not the best choice for the ball's collision shape. The collision code thinks the ball is a rectangular box, so the ball often collides with a brick even though the ball sprite itself isn't yet touching the brick.

It makes much more sense to represent the ball with a circle collision shape instead of an AABB. For this reason we included a `Radius` variable within the ball object. To define a circle collision shape, all we need is a position vector and a radius.

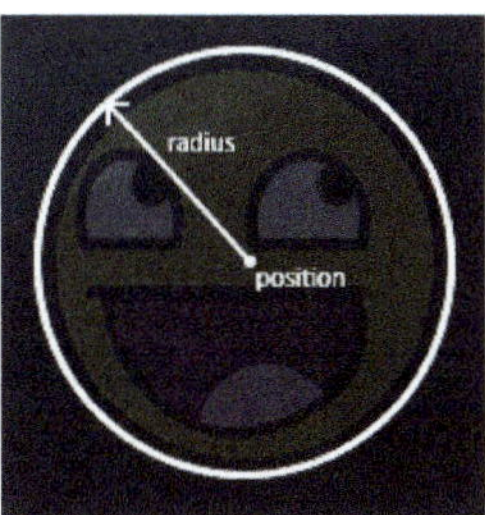

This does mean we have to update the detection algorithm since it currently only works between two AABBs. Detecting collisions between a circle and a rectangle is a bit more complicated, but the trick is as follows: we find the point on the AABB that is closest to the circle, and if the distance from the circle to this point is less than its radius, we have a collision.

The difficult part is getting this closest point $\bar{P}$ on the AABB. The following image shows how we can calculate this point for any arbitrary AABB and circle:

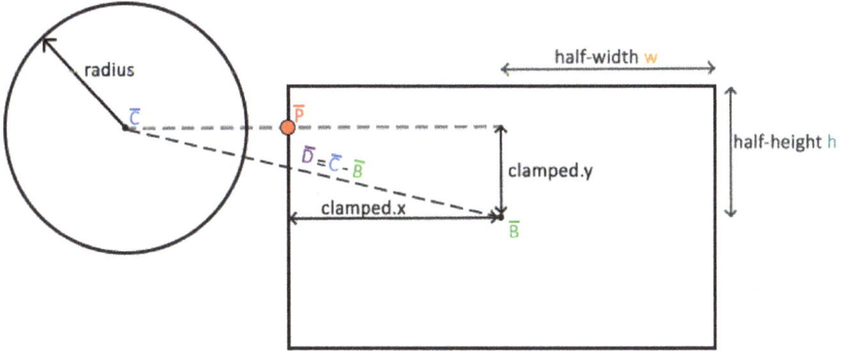

We first need to get the difference vector between the ball's center $\bar{C}$ and the AABB's center $\bar{B}$ to obtain $\bar{D}$. What we then need to do is clamp this vector $\bar{D}$ to the AABB's half-extents w and $\bar{h}$ and add it to $\bar{B}$. The half-extents of a rectangle are the distances between the rectangle's center and its edges: its size divided by two. This returns a position vector that is always located somewhere at the edge of the AABB (unless the circle's center is inside the AABB).

A clamp operation **clamps** a value to a value within a given range. This is often expressed as:

```cpp
float clamp(float value, float min, float max) {
    return std::max(min, std::min(max, value));
}
```

For example, a value of `42.0f` is clamped to `6.0f` with a range of `3.0f` to `6.0f`, and a value of `4.20f` would be clamped to `4.20f`. Clamping a 2D vector means we clamp both its x and its y component within the given range.

This clamped vector $\bar{P}$ is then the closest point from the AABB to the circle. What we then need to do is calculate a new difference vector $\bar{D}'$ that is the difference between the circle's center $\bar{C}$ and the vector $\bar{P}$.

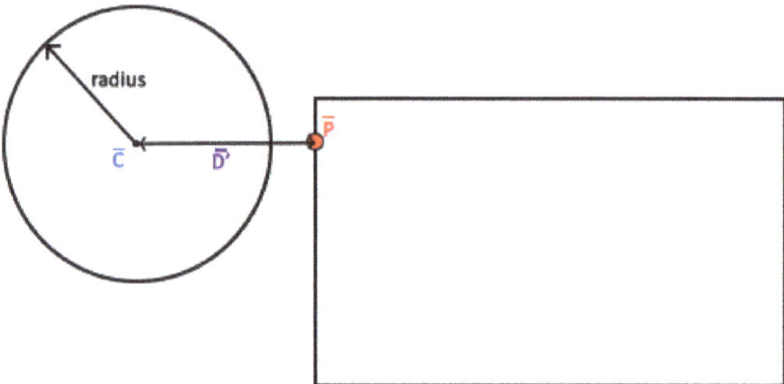

Now that we have the vector $\bar{D}'$, we can compare its length to the radius of the circle. If the length of $\bar{D}'$ is less than the circle's radius, we have a collision.

This is all expressed in code as follows:

```cpp
bool CheckCollision(BallObject &one, GameObject &two) // AABB - Circle
{
    // get center point circle first
    glm::vec2 center(one.Position + one.Radius);
    // calculate AABB info (center, half-extents)
    glm::vec2 aabb_half_extents(two.Size.x / 2.0f, two.Size.y / 2.0f);
    glm::vec2 aabb_center(two.Position.x + aabb_half_extents.x,
                          two.Position.y + aabb_half_extents.y);
    // get difference vector between both centers
    glm::vec2 difference = center - aabb_center;
    glm::vec2 clamped = glm::clamp(difference, -aabb_half_extents,
     aabb_half_extents);
    // add clamped value to AABB_center and get the value closest to circle
    glm::vec2 closest = aabb_center + clamped;
    // vector between center circle and closest point AABB
    difference = closest - center;
    return glm::length(difference) < one.Radius;
}
```

We create an overloaded function for `CheckCollision` that specifically deals with the case between a `BallObject` and a `GameObject`. Because we did not store the collision shape information in the objects themselves we have to calculate them: first the center of the ball is calculated, then the AABB's half-extents and its center.

Using these collision shape attributes we calculate vector $\bar{D}$ as `difference` that we clamp to `clamped` and add to the AABB's center to get point $\bar{P}$ as `closest`. Then we calculate the difference vector $\bar{D}'$ between `center` and `closest` and return whether the two shapes collided or not.

Since we previously called `CheckCollision` with the ball object as its first argument, we do not have to change any code since the overloaded version of `CheckCollision` now automatically applies. The result is now a much more precise collision detection algorithm:

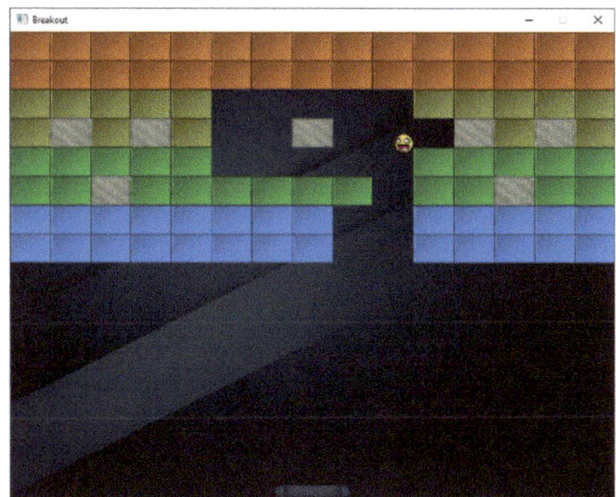

It seems to work, but still, something is off. We properly do all the collision detection, but the ball does not **react** in any way to the collisions. We need to update the ball's position and/or velocity whenever a collision occurs. This is the topic of the next chapter.

55. Collision resolution

At the end of the last chapter we had a working collision detection system. However, the ball does not react in any way to the detected collisions; it moves straight through all the bricks. We want the ball to *bounce* of the collided bricks. This chapter discusses how we can accomplish this so called collision resolution within the AABB - circle collision detection logic.

Whenever a collision occurs we want two things to happen: we want to reposition the ball so it is no longer inside the other object and second, we want to change the direction of the ball's velocity so it looks like it's bouncing of the object.

55.0.1 Collision repositioning

To position the ball object outside the collided AABB we have to figure out the distance the ball penetrated the bounding box. For this we'll revisit the diagram from the previous chapter:

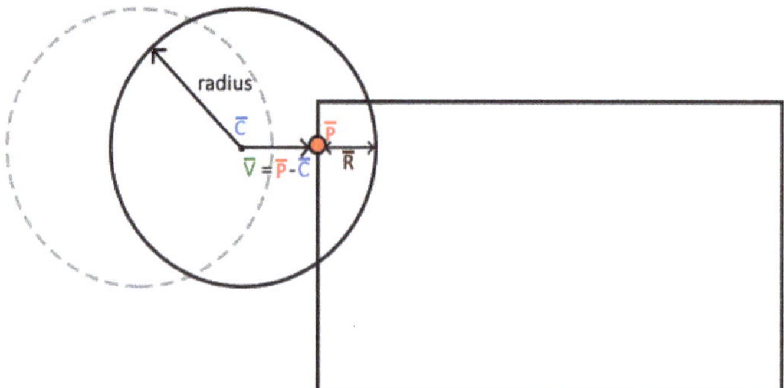

Here the ball moved slightly into the AABB and a collision was detected. We now want to move the ball out of the shape so that it merely touches the AABB as if no collision occurred. To figure out how much we need to move the ball out of the AABB we need to retrieve the vector $\bar{R}$, which is the level of penetration into the AABB. To get this vector $\bar{R}$, we subtract $\bar{V}$ from the ball's radius. Vector $\bar{V}$ is the difference between closest point $\bar{P}$ and the ball's center $\bar{C}$.

Knowing $\bar{R}$, we offset the ball's position by $\bar{R}$ positioning it directly against the AABB; the ball is now properly positioned.

55.0.2 Collision direction

Next we need to figure out how to update the ball's velocity after a collision. For Breakout we use the following rules to change the ball's velocity:

1. If the ball collides with the right or left side of an AABB, its horizontal velocity (x) is reversed.
2. If the ball collides with the bottom or top side of an AABB, its vertical velocity (y) is reversed.

But how do we figure out the direction the ball hit the AABB? There are several approaches to this problem. One of them is that, instead of 1 AABB, we use 4 AABBs for each brick that we each position at one of its edges. This way we can determine which AABB and thus which edge was hit. However, a simpler approach exists with the help of the dot product.

You probably still remember from the *Transformations* chapter that the dot product gives us the angle between two normalized vectors. What if we were to define four vectors pointing north, south, west, and east, and calculate the dot product between them and a given vector? The resulting dot product between these four direction vectors and the given vector that is highest (dot product's maximum value is `1.0f` which represents a `0` degree angle) is then the direction of the vector.

This procedure looks as follows in code:

```cpp
Direction VectorDirection(glm::vec2 target)
{
    glm::vec2 compass[] = {
        glm::vec2(0.0f,  1.0f), // up
        glm::vec2(1.0f,  0.0f), // right
        glm::vec2(0.0f, -1.0f), // down
        glm::vec2(-1.0f, 0.0f)  // left
    };
    float max = 0.0f;
    unsigned int best_match = -1;
    for (unsigned int i = 0; i < 4; i++)
    {
        float dot_product = glm::dot(glm::normalize(target), compass[i]);
        if (dot_product > max)
        {
            max = dot_product;
            best_match = i;
        }
    }
    return (Direction)best_match;
}
```

The function compares `target` to each of the direction vectors in the `compass` array. The compass vector `target` is closest to in angle, is the direction returned to the function caller. Here `Direction` is part of an enum defined in the game class's header file:

```cpp
enum Direction {
    UP,
    RIGHT,
    DOWN,
    LEFT
};
```

Now that we know how to get vector $\bar{R}$ and how to determine the direction the ball hit the AABB, we can start writing the collision resolution code.

55.0.3 AABB - Circle collision resolution

To calculate the required values for collision resolution we need a bit more information from the collision function(s) than just a `true` or `false`. We're now going to return a tuple of information that tells us if a collision occurred, what direction it occurred, and the difference vector $\bar{R}$. You can find the `tuple` container in the `<tuple>` header.

To keep the code slightly more organized we'll typedef the collision relevant data as `Collision`:

```cpp
typedef std::tuple<bool, Direction, glm::vec2> Collision;
```

Then we change the code of the `CheckCollision` function to not only return `true` or `false`, but also the direction and difference vector:

```cpp
Collision CheckCollision(BallObject &one, GameObject &two) // AABB - AABB
{
  [...]
  if (glm::length(difference) <= one.Radius)
      return std::make_tuple(true, VectorDirection(difference), difference);
  else
      return std::make_tuple(false, UP, glm::vec2(0.0f, 0.0f));
}
```

The game's `DoCollision` function now doesn't just check if a collision occurred, but also acts appropriately whenever a collision did occur. The function now calculates the level of penetration (as shown in the diagram at the start of this tutorial) and adds or subtracts it from the ball's position based on the direction of the collision.

```cpp
void Game::DoCollisions()
{
    for (GameObject &box : Levels[Level].Bricks)
    {
        if (!box.Destroyed)
        {
            Collision collision = CheckCollision(*Ball, box);
            if (std::get<0>(collision)) // if collision is true
            {
                // destroy block if not solid
                if (!box.IsSolid)
                    box.Destroyed = true;
                // collision resolution
                Direction dir = std::get<1>(collision);
                glm::vec2 diff_vector = std::get<2>(collision);
                if (dir == LEFT || dir == RIGHT) // horizontal collision
                {
                    Ball->Velocity.x = -Ball->Velocity.x; // reverse
                    // relocate
                    float penetration = Ball->Radius -
                                        std::abs(diff_vector.x);
                    if (dir == LEFT)
                        Ball->Position.x += penetration; // move right
                    else
                        Ball->Position.x -= penetration; // move left;
                }
                else // vertical collision
                {
                    Ball->Velocity.y = -Ball->Velocity.y; // reverse
                    // relocate
                    float penetration = Ball->Radius -
                                        std::abs(diff_vector.y);
                    if (dir == UP)
                        Ball->Position.y -= penetration; // move up
                    else
                        Ball->Position.y += penetration; // move down
                }
            }
        }
    }
}
```

Don't get too scared by the function's complexity since it is basically a direct translation of the concepts introduced so far. First we check for a collision and if so, we destroy the block if it is non-solid. Then we obtain the collision direction `dir` and the vector V as `diff_vector` from the tuple and finally do the collision resolution.

We first check if the collision direction is either horizontal or vertical and then reverse the velocity accordingly. If horizontal, we calculate the penetration value R from the `diff_vector`'s x component and either add or subtract this from the ball's position. The same applies to the vertical collisions, but this time we operate on the y component of all the vectors.

Running your application should now give you working collision resolution, but it's probably difficult to really see its effect since the ball will bounce towards the bottom edge as soon as you hit a single block and be lost forever. We can fix this by also handling player paddle collisions.

55.1 Player - ball collisions

Collisions between the ball and the player is handled slightly different from what we've previously discussed, since this time the ball's horizontal velocity should be updated based on how far it hit the paddle from its center. The further the ball hits the paddle from its center, the stronger its horizontal velocity change should be.

```cpp
void Game::DoCollisions()
{
    [...]
    Collision result = CheckCollision(*Ball, *Player);
    if (!Ball->Stuck && std::get<0>(result))
    {
        // check where it hit the board, and change velocity
        float centerBoard = Player->Position.x + Player->Size.x / 2.0f;
        float distance = (Ball->Position.x + Ball->Radius) - centerBoard;
        float percentage = distance / (Player->Size.x / 2.0f);
        // then move accordingly
        float strength = 2.0f;
        glm::vec2 oldVelocity = Ball->Velocity;
        Ball->Velocity.x = INITIAL_BALL_VELOCITY.x * percentage * strength;
        Ball->Velocity.y = -Ball->Velocity.y;
        Ball->Velocity = glm::normalize(Ball->Velocity) *
                    glm::length(oldVelocity);
    }
}
```

After we checked collisions between the ball and each brick, we'll check if the ball collided with the player paddle. If so (and the ball is not stuck to the paddle) we calculate the percentage of how far the ball's center is moved from the paddle's center compared to the half-extent of the paddle. The horizontal velocity of the ball is then updated based on the distance it hit the paddle from its center. In addition to updating the horizontal velocity, we also have to reverse the y velocity.

Note that the old velocity is stored as `oldVelocity`. The reason for storing the old velocity is that we update the horizontal velocity of the ball's velocity vector while keeping its y velocity constant. This would mean that the length of the vector constantly changes, which has the effect that the ball's velocity vector is much larger (and thus stronger) if the ball hit the edge of the paddle compared to if the ball would hit the center of the paddle. For this reason, the new velocity vector is normalized and multiplied by the length of the old velocity vector. This way, the velocity of the ball is always consistent, regardless of where it hits the paddle.

55.1.1 Sticky paddle

You may or may not have noticed it when you ran the code, but there is still a large issue with the player and ball collision resolution. The following shows what may happen:

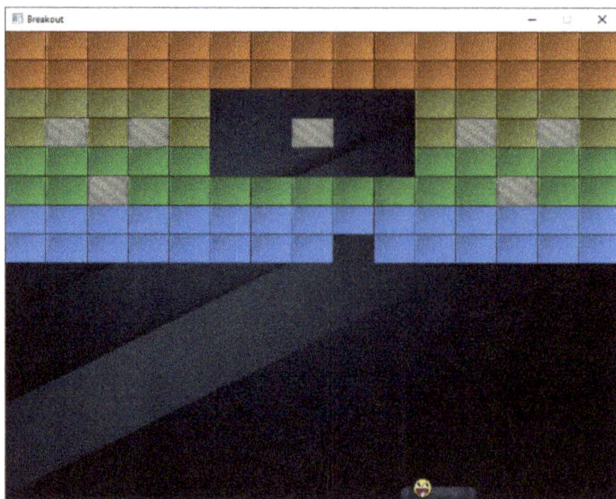

This issue is called the sticky paddle issue. This happens, because the player paddle moves with a high velocity towards the ball with the ball's center ending up inside the player paddle. Since we did not account for the case where the ball's center is inside an AABB, the game tries to continuously react to all the collisions. Once it finally breaks free, it will have reversed its y velocity so much that it's unsure whether to go up or down after breaking free.

We can easily fix this behavior by introducing a small hack made possible by the fact that the we can always assume we have a collision at the top of the paddle. Instead of reversing the y velocity, we simply always return a positive y direction so whenever it does get stuck, it will immediately break free.

```cpp
//Ball->Velocity.y = -Ball->Velocity.y;
Ball->Velocity.y = -1.0f * abs(Ball->Velocity.y);
```

If you try hard enough the effect is still noticeable, but I personally find it an acceptable trade-off.

55.1.2 The bottom edge

The only thing that is still missing from the classic Breakout recipe is some loss condition that resets the level and the player. Within the game class's `Update` function we want to check if the ball reached the bottom edge, and if so, reset the game.

```cpp
void Game::Update(float dt)
{
    [...]
    if (Ball->Position.y >= Height) // did ball reach bottom edge?
    {
        ResetLevel();
        ResetPlayer();
    }
}
```

The `ResetLevel` and `ResetPlayer` functions re-load the level and reset the objects' values to their original starting values.

And there you have it, we just finished creating a clone of the classical Breakout game with similar mechanics. You can find the game class' source code at: `/src/7.in_practice/3.2d_game/0.full_source/progress/5.game.h`, `/src/7.in_practice/3.2d_game/0.full_source/progress/5.game.cpp`.

55.2 **A few notes**

Collision detection is a difficult topic of video game development and possibly its most challenging. Most collision detection and resolution schemes are combined with physics engines as found in most modern-day games. The collision scheme we used for the Breakout game is a very simple scheme and one specialized specifically for this type of game.

It should be stressed that this type of collision detection and resolution is not perfect. It calculates possible collisions only per frame and only for the positions exactly as they are at that timestep; this means that if an object would have such a velocity that it would pass over another object within a single frame, it would look like it never collided with this object. So if there are framedrops, or you reach high enough velocities, this collision detection scheme will not hold.

Several of the issues that can still occur:

- If the ball goes too fast, it may skip over an object entirely within a single frame, not detecting any collisions.
- If the ball hits more than one object within a single frame, it will have detected two collisions and reversed its velocity twice; not affecting its original velocity.
- Hitting a corner of a brick could reverse the ball's velocity in the wrong direction since the distance it travels in a single frame could decide the difference between `VectorDirection` returning a vertical or horizontal direction.

These chapters are however aimed to teach the readers the basics of several aspects of graphics and game-development. For this reason, this collision scheme serves its purpose; its understandable and works quite well in normal scenarios. Just keep in mind that there exist better (more complicated) collision schemes that work well in almost all scenarios (including movable objects) like the separating axis theorem.

Thankfully, there exist large, practical, and often quite efficient physics engines (with timestep-independent collision schemes) for use in your own games. If you wish to delve further into such systems or need more advanced physics and have trouble figuring out the mathematics, Box2D[1] is a perfect 2D physics library for implementing physics and collision detection in your applications.

---

[1] box2d.org/

56. Particles

A particle, as seen from OpenGL's perspective, is a tiny 2D quad that is always facing the camera (billboarding) and (usually) contains a texture with large parts of the sprite being transparent. A particle by itself is effectively just a sprite as we've been using extensively so far. However, when you put together hundreds or even thousands of these particles together you can create amazing effects.

When working with particles, there is usually an object called a particle emitter or particle generator that, from its location, continuously spawns new particles that decay over time. If such a particle emitter would for example spawn tiny particles with a smoke-like texture, color them less bright the larger the distance from the emitter, and give them a glowy appearance, you'd get a fire-like effect:

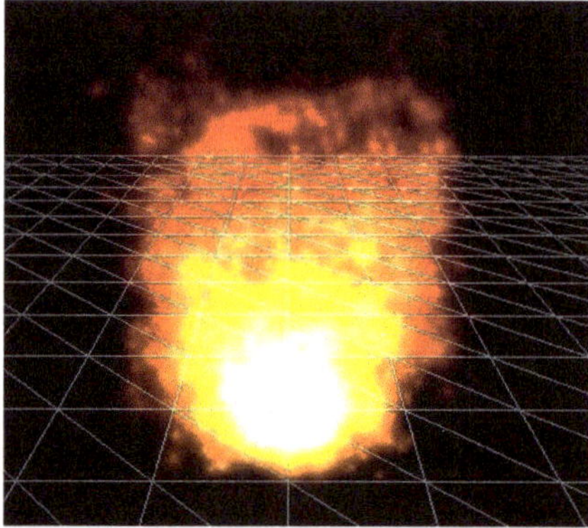

A single particle often has a life variable that slowly decays once it's spawned. Once its life is less than a certain threshold (usually 0), we kill the particle so it can be replaced with a new particle when the next particle spawns. A particle emitter controls all its spawned particles and changes their behavior based on their attributes. A particle generally has the following attributes:

```cpp
struct Particle {
    glm::vec2 Position, Velocity;
    glm::vec4 Color;
    float     Life;

    Particle()
      : Position(0.0f), Velocity(0.0f), Color(1.0f), Life(0.0f) { }
};
```

Looking at the fire example, the particle emitter probably spawns each particle with a position close to the emitter and with an upwards velocity. It seems to have 3 different regions, so it probably gives some particles a higher velocity than others. We can also see that the higher the y position of the particle, the less *yellow* or *bright* its color becomes. After the particles have reached a certain height, their life is depleted and the particles are killed; never reaching the stars.

You can imagine that with systems like these we can create interesting effects like fire, smoke, fog, magic effects, gunfire residue etc. In Breakout, we're going to add a simple particle generator that follows the ball to make it all look just a bit more interesting. It'll look something like this:

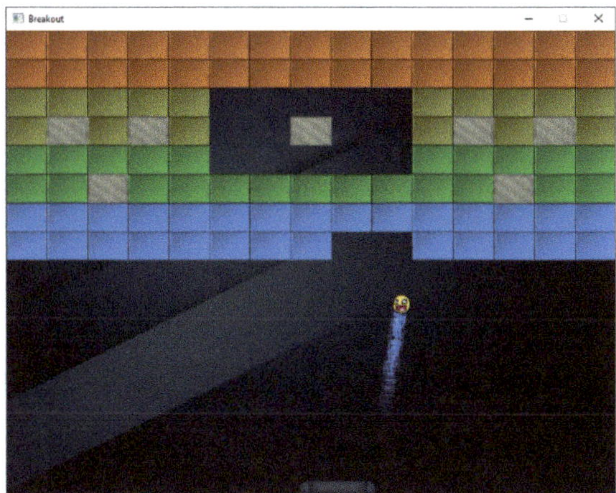

Here, the particle generator spawns each particle at the ball's position, gives it a velocity equal to a fraction of the ball's velocity, and changes the color of the particle based on how long it lived.

For rendering the particles we'll be using a different set of shaders:

```glsl
#version 330 core
layout (location = 0) in vec4 vertex; // <vec2 position, vec2 texCoords>

out vec2 TexCoords;
out vec4 ParticleColor;

uniform mat4 projection;
uniform vec2 offset;
uniform vec4 color;

void main()
{
    float scale = 10.0f;
    TexCoords = vertex.zw;
    ParticleColor = color;
    gl_Position = projection * vec4((vertex.xy * scale) + offset, 0.0, 1.0);
}
```

And the fragment shader:

```glsl
#version 330 core
in vec2 TexCoords;
in vec4 ParticleColor;
out vec4 color;

uniform sampler2D sprite;

void main()
{
    color = (texture(sprite, TexCoords) * ParticleColor);
}
```

We take the standard position and texture attributes per particle and also accept an `offset` and a `color` uniform for changing the outcome per particle. Note that in the vertex shader we scale the particle quad by `10.0f`; you can also set the scale as a uniform and control this individually per particle.

First, we need a list of particles that we instantiate with default `Particle` structs:

```cpp
unsigned int nr_particles = 500;
std::vector<Particle> particles;

for (unsigned int i = 0; i < nr_particles; ++i)
    particles.push_back(Particle());
```

Then in each frame, we spawn several new particles with starting values. For each particle that is (still) alive we also update their values:

```cpp
unsigned int nr_new_particles = 2;
// add new particles
for (unsigned int i = 0; i < nr_new_particles; ++i)
{
    int unusedParticle = FirstUnusedParticle();
    RespawnParticle(particles[unusedParticle], object, offset);
}
// update all particles
for (unsigned int i = 0; i < nr_particles; ++i)
{
    Particle &p = particles[i];
    p.Life -= dt; // reduce life
    if (p.Life > 0.0f)
    {   // particle is alive, thus update
        p.Position -= p.Velocity * dt;
        p.Color.a -= dt * 2.5f;
    }
}
```

The first loop may look a little daunting. As particles die over time we want to spawn `nr_new_particles` particles each frame, but since we don't want to infinitely keep spawning new particles (we'll quickly run out of memory this way) we only spawn up to a max of `nr_particles`. If were to push all new particles to the end of the list we'll quickly get a list filled with thousands of particles. This isn't really efficient considering only a small portion of that list has particles that are alive.

What we want is to find the first particle that is dead (life < `0.0f`) and update that particle as a new respawned particle.

The function `FirstUnusedParticle` tries to find the first particle that is dead and returns its index to the caller.

```cpp
unsigned int lastUsedParticle = 0;
unsigned int FirstUnusedParticle()
{
    // search from last used particle, often returns almost instantly
    for (unsigned int i = lastUsedParticle; i < nr_particles; ++i) {
        if (particles[i].Life <= 0.0f){
            lastUsedParticle = i;
            return i;
        }
    }
    // otherwise, do a linear search
    for (unsigned int i = 0; i < lastUsedParticle; ++i) {
        if (particles[i].Life <= 0.0f){
            lastUsedParticle = i;
            return i;
```

```
        }
    }
    // override first particle if all others are alive
    lastUsedParticle = 0;
    return 0;
}
```

The function stores the index of the last dead particle it found. Since the next dead particle will most likely be right after the last particle index, we first search from this stored index. If we found no dead particles this way, we simply do a slower linear search. If no particles are dead, it will return index 0 which results in the first particle being overwritten. Note that if it reaches this last case, it means your particles are alive for too long; you'd need to spawn less particles per frame and/or reserve a larger number of particles.

Then, once the first dead particle in the list is found, we update its values by calling `RespawnPa rticle` that takes the particle, a `GameObject`, and an offset vector:

```
void RespawnParticle(Particle &particle, GameObject &object,
                     glm::vec2 offset)
{
    float random = ((rand() \% 100) - 50) / 10.0f;
    float rColor = 0.5f + ((rand() \% 100) / 100.0f);
    particle.Position = object.Position + random + offset;
    particle.Color = glm::vec4(rColor, rColor, rColor, 1.0f);
    particle.Life = 1.0f;
    particle.Velocity = object.Velocity * 0.1f;
}
```

This function simply resets the particle's life to `1.0f`, randomly gives it a brightness (via the color vector) starting from `0.5`, and assigns a (slightly random) position and velocity based on the game object's data.

The second particle loop within the update function loops over all particles and for each particle reduces their life by the delta time variable; this way, each particle's life corresponds to exactly the second(s) it's allowed to live multiplied by some scalar. Then we check if the particle is alive and if so, update its position and color attributes. We also slowly reduce the alpha component of each particle so it looks like they're slowly disappearing over time.

Then what's left to do is render the particles:

```
glBlendFunc(GL_SRC_ALPHA, GL_ONE);
particleShader.Use();
for (Particle particle : particles)
{
    if (particle.Life > 0.0f)
    {
        particleShader.SetVector2f("offset", particle.Position);
        particleShader.SetVector4f("color", particle.Color);
        particleTexture.Bind();
        glBindVertexArray(particleVAO);
        glDrawArrays(GL_TRIANGLES, 0, 6);
        glBindVertexArray(0);
    }
}
glBlendFunc(GL_SRC_ALPHA, GL_ONE_MINUS_SRC_ALPHA);
```

Here, for each particle, we set their offset and color uniform values, bind the texture, and render the 2D quad. What's interesting to note here are the two calls to `glBlendFunc`. When rendering the particles, instead of the default destination blend mode of `GL_ONE_MINUS_SRC_ALPHA`, we use the `GL_ONE` (additive) blend mode that gives the particles a very neat glow effect when stacked onto each other. This is also likely the blend mode used when rendering the fire at the top of the chapter, since the fire is more 'glowy' at the center where most of the particles are.

Because we (like most other parts of the Breakout chapters) like to keep things organized, we create another class called `ParticleGenerator` that hosts all the functionality we just described. You can find the source code below:

* `/src/7.in_practice/3.2d_game/0.full_source/particle_generator.h`, `/src/7.in_practice/3.2d_game/0.full_source/particle_generato r.cpp`

Within the game code, we create a particle generator and initialize it with a particle texture[1].

```cpp
ParticleGenerator *Particles;

void Game::Init()
{
    [...]
    ResourceManager::LoadShader("shaders/particle.vs", "shaders/particle.
                                frag", nullptr, "particle");
    [...]
    ResourceManager::LoadTexture("textures/particle.png", true, "particle");
    [...]
    Particles = new ParticleGenerator(
        ResourceManager::GetShader("particle"),
        ResourceManager::GetTexture("particle"),
        500
    );
}
```

Then we change the game class's `Update` function by adding an update statement for the particle generator:

```cpp
void Game::Update(float dt)
{
    [...]
    // update particles
    Particles->Update(dt, *Ball, 2, glm::vec2(Ball->Radius / 2.0f));
    [...]
}
```

Each of the particles will use the game object properties from the ball object, spawn 2 particles each frame, and their positions will be offset towards the center of the ball. Last up is rendering the particles:

---

[1] learnopengl.com/img/in-practice/breakout/textures/particle.png

```cpp
void Game::Render()
{
    if (State == GAME_ACTIVE)
    {
        [...]
        // draw player
        Player->Draw(*Renderer);
        // draw particles
        Particles->Draw();
        // draw ball
        Ball->Draw(*Renderer);
    }
}
```

Note that we render the particles before we render the ball. This way, the particles end up rendered in front of all other objects, but behind the ball. You can find the updated game class code at `/src/7.in_practice/3.2d_game/0.full_source/progress/6.game.cpp`.

If you'd now compile and run your application you should see a trail of particles following the ball, just like at the beginning of the chapter, giving the game a more modern look. The system can also easily be extended to host more advanced effects, so feel free to experiment with the particle generation and see if you can come up with your own creative effects.

57. Postprocessing

Wouldn't it be fun if we could completely spice up the visuals of the Breakout game with just a few postprocessing effects? We could create a blurry shake effect, inverse all the colors of the scene, do crazy vertex movement, and/or make use of other interesting effects with relative ease thanks to OpenGL's framebuffers.

> This chapters makes extensive use of concepts from the *Framebuffers* and *Anti Aliasing* chapters.

In the framebuffers chapter we demonstrated how we could use postprocessing to achieve interesting effects using just a single texture. In Breakout we're going to do something similar: we're going to create a framebuffer object with a multisampled renderbuffer object attached as its color attachment. All the game's render code should render to this multisampled framebuffer that then blits its content to a different framebuffer with a texture attachment as its color buffer. This texture contains the rendered anti-aliased image of the game that we'll render to a full-screen 2D quad with zero or more postprocessing effects applied.

So to summarize, the rendering steps are:

1. Bind to multisampled framebuffer.
2. Render game as normal.
3. Blit multisampled framebuffer to normal framebuffer with texture attachment.
4. Unbind framebuffer (use default framebuffer).
5. Use color buffer texture from normal framebuffer in postprocessing shader.
6. Render quad of screen-size as output of postprocessing shader.

The postprocessing shader allows for three type of effects: shake, confuse, and chaos.

- **shake**: slightly shakes the scene with a small blur.
- **confuse**: inverses the colors of the scene, but also the x and y axis.
- **chaos**: makes use of an edge detection kernel to create interesting visuals and also moves the textured image in a circular fashion for an interesting *chaotic* effect.

Below is a glimpse of what these effects are going to look like:

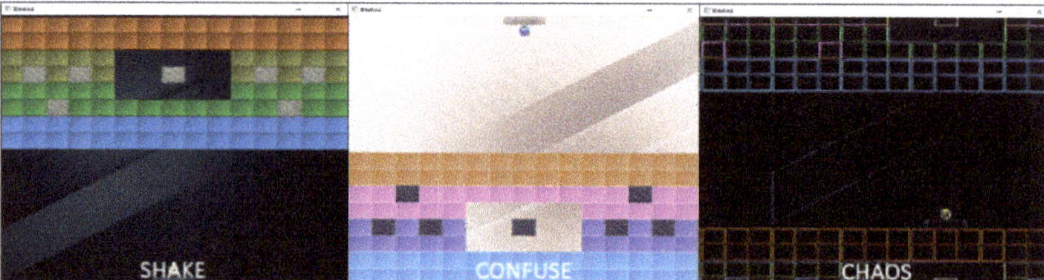

Operating on a 2D quad, the vertex shader looks as follows:

```glsl
#version 330 core
layout (location = 0) in vec4 vertex; // <vec2 position, vec2 texCoords>

out vec2 TexCoords;

uniform bool chaos;
uniform bool confuse;
uniform bool shake;
uniform float time;
```

```glsl
void main()
{
    gl_Position = vec4(vertex.xy, 0.0f, 1.0f);
    vec2 texture = vertex.zw;
    if (chaos)
    {
        float strength = 0.3;
        vec2 pos = vec2(texture.x + sin(time) * strength,
                        texture.y + cos(time) * strength);
        TexCoords = pos;
    }
    else if (confuse)
    {
        TexCoords = vec2(1.0 - texture.x, 1.0 - texture.y);
    }
    else
    {
        TexCoords = texture;
    }
    if (shake)
    {
        float strength = 0.01;
        gl_Position.x += cos(time * 10) * strength;
        gl_Position.y += cos(time * 15) * strength;
    }
}
```

Based on whatever uniform is set to `true`, the vertex shader takes different paths. If either `chaos` or `confuse` is set to `true`, the vertex shader will manipulate the texture coordinates to move the scene around (either translate texture coordinates in a circle-like fashion, or inverse them). Because we set the texture wrapping methods to `GL_REPEAT`, the chaos effect will cause the scene to repeat itself at various parts of the quad. Additionally if `shake` is set to `true`, it will move the vertex positions around by a small amount, as if the screen shakes. Note that `chaos` and `confuse` shouldn't be `true` at the same time while `shake` is able to work with any of the other effects on.

In addition to offsetting the vertex positions or texture coordinates, we'd also like to create some visual change as soon as any of the effects are active. We can accomplish this within the fragment shader:

```glsl
#version 330 core
in vec2 TexCoords;
out vec4 color;

uniform sampler2D scene;
uniform vec2      offsets[9];
uniform int       edge_kernel[9];
uniform float     blur_kernel[9];

uniform bool chaos;
uniform bool confuse;
uniform bool shake;

void main()
{
    color = vec4(0.0f);
    vec3 sample[9];
    // sample from texture offsets if using convolution matrix
    if(chaos || shake)
        for(int i = 0; i < 9; i++)
```

```glsl
            sample[i] = vec3(texture(scene, TexCoords.st + offsets[i]));

    // process effects
    if (chaos)
    {
        for(int i = 0; i < 9; i++)
            color += vec4(sample[i] * edge_kernel[i], 0.0f);
        color.a = 1.0f;
    }
    else if (confuse)
    {
        color = vec4(1.0 - texture(scene, TexCoords).rgb, 1.0);
    }
    else if (shake)
    {
        for(int i = 0; i < 9; i++)
            color += vec4(sample[i] * blur_kernel[i], 0.0f);
        color.a = 1.0f;
    }
    else
    {
        color = texture(scene, TexCoords);
    }
}
```

This long shader almost directly builds upon the fragment shader from the framebuffers chapter and processes several postprocessing effects based on the effect type activated. This time though, the offset matrix and convolution kernels are defined as a uniform that we set from the OpenGL code. The advantage is that we only have to set this once, instead of recalculating these matrices each fragment shader run. For example, the `offsets` matrix is configured as follows:

```cpp
float offset = 1.0f / 300.0f;
float offsets[9][2] = {
    { -offset,  offset }, // top-left
    {  0.0f,    offset }, // top-center
    {  offset,  offset }, // top-right
    { -offset,  0.0f   }, // center-left
    {  0.0f,    0.0f   }, // center-center
    {  offset,  0.0f   }, // center-right
    { -offset, -offset }, // bottom-left
    {  0.0f,   -offset }, // bottom-center
    {  offset, -offset }  // bottom-right
};
glUniform2fv(glGetUniformLocation(shader.ID, "offsets"), 9,
        (float*)offsets);
```

Since all of the concepts of managing (multisampled) framebuffers were already extensively discussed in earlier chapters, I won't delve into the details this time. Below you'll find the code of a `PostProcessor` class that manages initialization, writing/reading the framebuffers, and rendering a screen quad. You should be able to understand the code if you understood the framebuffers and anti aliasing chapter:

- **PostProcessor**: `/src/7.in_practice/3.2d_game/0.full_source/post_pro cessor.h`, `/src/7.in_practice/3.2d_game/0.full_source/post_proce ssor.cpp`.

What is interesting to note here are the `BeginRender` and `EndRender` functions. Since we have to render the entire game scene into the framebuffer we can conveniently call `BeginRender()`

and `EndRender()` before and after the scene's rendering code respectively. The class will then handle the behind-the-scenes framebuffer operations. For example, using the `PostProcessor` class will look like this within the game's `Render` function:

```cpp
PostProcessor *Effects;

void Game::Render()
{
    if (State == GAME_ACTIVE)
    {
        Effects->BeginRender();
            // draw background
            // draw level
            // draw player
            // draw particles
            // draw ball
        Effects->EndRender();
        Effects->Render(glfwGetTime());
    }
}
```

Wherever we want, we can now conveniently set the required effect property of the postprocessing class to `true` and its effect will be immediately active.

57.0.1 Shake it

As a (practical) demonstration of these effects we'll emulate the visual impact of the ball when it hits a solid concrete block. By enabling the shake effect for a short period of time wherever a solid collision occurs, it'll look like the collision had a stronger impact.

We want to enable the screen shake effect only over a small period of time. We can get this to work by creating a variable called `ShakeTime` that manages the duration the shake effect is supposed to be active. Wherever a solid collision occurs, we reset this variable to a specific duration:

```cpp
float ShakeTime = 0.0f;

void Game::DoCollisions()
{
    for (GameObject &box : Levels[Level].Bricks)
    {
        if (!box.Destroyed)
        {
            Collision collision = CheckCollision(*Ball, box);
            if (std::get<0>(collision)) // if collision is true
            {
                // destroy block if not solid
                if (!box.IsSolid)
                    box.Destroyed = true;
                else
                { // if block is solid, enable shake effect
                    ShakeTime = 0.05f;
                    Effects->Shake = true;
                }
                [...]
            }
        }
    }
    [...]
}
```

Then within the game's `Update` function, we decrease the `ShakeTime` variable until it's `0.0` after which we disable the shake effect:

```cpp
void Game::Update(float dt)
{
    [...]
    if (ShakeTime > 0.0f)
    {
        ShakeTime -= dt;
        if (ShakeTime <= 0.0f)
            Effects->Shake = false;
    }
}
```

Then each time we hit a solid block, the screen briefly starts to shake and blur, giving the player some visual feedback the ball collided with a solid object.

You can find the updated source code of the game class at `/src/7.in_practice/3.2d_game/0.full_source/progress/7.game.cpp`.

In the next chapter about powerups we'll bring the other two postprocessing effects to good use.

58. Powerups

Breakout is close to finished, but it would be cool to add at least one more gameplay mechanic so it's not your average standard Breakout clone; what about powerups?

The idea is that whenever a brick is destroyed, the brick has a small chance of spawning a powerup block. Such a block will slowly fall downwards and if it collides with the player paddle, an interesting effect occurs based on the type of powerup. For example, one powerup makes the paddle larger, and another powerup allows the ball to pass through objects. We also include several negative powerups that affect the player in a negative way.

We can model a powerup as a `GameObject` with a few extra properties. That's why we define a class `PowerUp` that inherits from `GameObject`:

```cpp
const glm::vec2 SIZE(60.0f, 20.0f);
const glm::vec2 VELOCITY(0.0f, 150.0f);

class PowerUp : public GameObject
{
public:
    // powerup state
    std::string Type;
    float       Duration;
    bool        Activated;
    // constructor
    PowerUp(std::string type, glm::vec3 color, float duration,
            glm::vec2 position, Texture2D texture)
        : GameObject(position, SIZE, texture, color, VELOCITY),
          Type(type), Duration(duration), Activated()
    { }
};
```

A `PowerUp` is just a `GameObject` with extra state, so we can simply define it in a single header file which you can find at `/src/7.in_practice/3.2d_game/0.full_source/power_up.h`.

Each powerup defines its type as a string, a duration for how long it is active, and whether it is currently activated. Within Breakout we're going to feature a total of 4 positive powerups and 2 negative powerups:

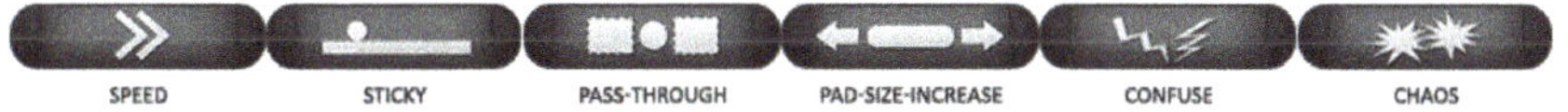

- **Speed**[1]: increases the velocity of the ball by 20%.
- **Sticky**[2]: when the ball collides with the paddle, the ball remains stuck to the paddle unless the spacebar is pressed again. This allows the player to better position the ball before releasing it.
- **Pass-Through**[3]: collision resolution is disabled for non-solid blocks, allowing the ball to pass through multiple blocks.
- **Pad-Size-Increase**[4]: increases the width of the paddle by 50 pixels.
- **Confuse**[5]: activates the confuse postprocessing effect for a short period of time, confusing the user.

---

[1]learnopengl.com/img/in-practice/breakout/textures/powerup_speed.png

[2]learnopengl.com/img/in-practice/breakout/textures/powerup_sticky.png

[3]learnopengl.com/img/in-practice/breakout/textures/powerup_passthrough.png

[4]learnopengl.com/img/in-practice/breakout/textures/powerup_increase.png

[5]learnopengl.com/img/in-practice/breakout/textures/powerup_confuse.png

- **Chaos**[1]: activates the chaos postprocessing effect for a short period of time, heavily disorienting the user.

Similar to the level block textures, each of the powerup textures is completely grayscale. This makes sure the color of the powerups remain balanced whenever we multiply them with a color vector.

Because powerups have state, a duration, and certain effects associated with them, we would like to keep track of all the powerups currently active in the game; we store them in a vector:

```cpp
class Game {
    public:
        [...]
        std::vector<PowerUp> PowerUps;
        [...]
        void SpawnPowerUps(GameObject &block);
        void UpdatePowerUps(float dt);
};
```

We've also defined two functions for managing powerups. `SpawnPowerUps` spawns a powerups at the location of a given block and `UpdatePowerUps` manages all powerups currently active within the game.

58.0.1 Spawning PowerUps

Each time a block is destroyed we would like to, given a small chance, spawn a powerup. This functionality is found inside the game's `SpawnPowerUps` function:

```cpp
bool ShouldSpawn(unsigned int chance)
{
    unsigned int random = rand() \% chance;
    return random == 0;
}
void Game::SpawnPowerUps(GameObject &block)
{
    if (ShouldSpawn(75)) // 1 in 75 chance
        PowerUps.push_back(PowerUp("speed", glm::vec3(0.5f, 0.5f, 1.0f),
                                   0.0f, block.Position, tex_speed));
    if (ShouldSpawn(75))
        PowerUps.push_back(PowerUp("sticky", glm::vec3(1.0f, 0.5f, 1.0f),
                                   20.0f, block.Position, tex_sticky));
    if (ShouldSpawn(75))
        PowerUps.push_back(PowerUp("pass-through", glm::vec3(0.5f, 1.0f,
                                   0.5f), 10.0f, block.Position,
                                   tex_pass));
    if (ShouldSpawn(75))
        PowerUps.push_back(PowerUp("pad-size-increase", glm::vec3(1.0f,
                                   0.6f, 0.4), 0.0f, block.Position,
                                   tex_size));
    if (ShouldSpawn(15)) // negative powerups should spawn more often
        PowerUps.push_back(PowerUp("confuse", glm::vec3(1.0f, 0.3f, 0.3f),
                                   15.0f, block.Position, tex_confuse));
    if (ShouldSpawn(15))
        PowerUps.push_back(PowerUp("chaos", glm::vec3(0.9f, 0.25f, 0.25f),
                                   15.0f, block.Position, tex_chaos));
}
```

---

[1] learnopengl.com/img/in-practice/breakout/textures/powerup_chaos.png

The `SpawnPowerUps` function creates a new `PowerUp` object based on a given chance (1 in 75 for normal powerups and 1 in 15 for negative powerups) and sets their properties. Each powerup is given a specific color to make them more recognizable for the user and a duration in seconds based on its type; here a duration of `0.0f` means its duration is infinite. Additionally, each powerup is given the position of the destroyed block and one of the textures from the beginning of this chapter.

58.0.2 Activating PowerUps

We then have to update the game's `DoCollisions` function to not only check for brick and paddle collisions, but also collisions between the paddle and each non-destroyed PowerUp. Note that we call `SpawnPowerUps` directly after a block is destroyed.

```cpp
void Game::DoCollisions()
{
    for (GameObject &box : Levels[Level].Bricks)
    {
        if (!box.Destroyed)
        {
            Collision collision = CheckCollision(*Ball, box);
            if (std::get<0>(collision)) // if collision is true
            {
                // destroy block if not solid
                if (!box.IsSolid)
                {
                    box.Destroyed = true;
                    SpawnPowerUps(box);
                }
                [...]
            }
        }
    }
    [...]
    for (PowerUp &powerUp : PowerUps)
    {
        if (!powerUp.Destroyed)
        {
            if (powerUp.Position.y >= Height)
                powerUp.Destroyed = true;
            if (CheckCollision(*Player, powerUp))
            {   // collided with player, now activate powerup
                ActivatePowerUp(powerUp);
                powerUp.Destroyed = true;
                powerUp.Activated = true;
            }
        }
    }
}
```

For all powerups not yet destroyed, we check if the powerup either reached the bottom edge of the screen or collided with the paddle. In both cases the powerup is destroyed, but when collided with the paddle, it is also activated.

Activating a powerup is accomplished by settings its `Activated` property to `true` and enabling the powerup's effect by giving it to the `ActivatePowerUp` function:

```cpp
void ActivatePowerUp(PowerUp &powerUp)
{
    if (powerUp.Type == "speed")
    {
        Ball->Velocity *= 1.2;
    }
    else if (powerUp.Type == "sticky")
    {
        Ball->Sticky = true;
        Player->Color = glm::vec3(1.0f, 0.5f, 1.0f);
    }
    else if (powerUp.Type == "pass-through")
    {
        Ball->PassThrough = true;
        Ball->Color = glm::vec3(1.0f, 0.5f, 0.5f);
    }
    else if (powerUp.Type == "pad-size-increase")
    {
        Player->Size.x += 50;
    }
    else if (powerUp.Type == "confuse")
    {
        if (!Effects->Chaos)
            Effects->Confuse = true; // only if chaos isn't already active
    }
    else if (powerUp.Type == "chaos")
    {
        if (!Effects->Confuse)
            Effects->Chaos = true;
    }
}
```

The purpose of `ActivatePowerUp` is exactly as it sounds: it activates the effect of a powerup
as we've described at the start of this chapter. We check the type of the powerup and change the
game state accordingly. For the `"sticky"` and `"pass-through"` effect, we also change the
color of the paddle and the ball respectively to give the user some feedback as to which effect is
currently active.

Because the sticky and pass-through effects somewhat change the game logic we store their
effect as a property of the ball object; this way we can change the game logic based on whatever
effect on the ball is currently active. The only thing we've changed in the `BallObject` header
is the addition of these two properties, but for completeness' sake its updated code can be found
below:

- **BallObject**: /src/7.in_practice/3.2d_game/0.full_source/ball_obje
  ct.h, /src/7.in_practice/3.2d_game/0.full_source/ball_object.c
  pp.

We can then easily implement the sticky effect by slightly updating the `DoCollisions`
function at the collision code between the ball and the paddle:

```cpp
if (!Ball->Stuck && std::get<0>(result))
{
    [...]
    Ball->Stuck = Ball->Sticky;
}
```

Here we set the ball's `Stuck` property equal to the ball's `Sticky` property. If the sticky effect is activated, the ball will end up stuck to the player paddle whenever it collides; the user then has to press the spacebar again to release the ball.

A similar small change is made for the pass-through effect within the same `DoCollisions` function. When the ball's `PassThrough` property is set to `true` we do not perform any collision resolution on the non-solid bricks.

```cpp
Direction dir = std::get<1>(collision);
glm::vec2 diff_vector = std::get<2>(collision);
if (!(Ball->PassThrough && !box.IsSolid))
{
    if (dir == LEFT || dir == RIGHT) // horizontal collision
    {
        [...]
    }
    else
    {
        [...]
    }
}
```

The other effects are activated by simply modifying the game's state like the ball's velocity, the paddle's size, or an effect of the `PostProcesser` object.

58.0.3 Updating PowerUps

Now all that is left to do is make sure that powerups are able to move once they've spawned and that they're deactivated as soon as their duration runs out; otherwise powerups will stay active forever.

Within the game's `UpdatePowerUps` function we move the powerups based on their velocity and decrease the active powerups their duration. Whenever a powerup's duration is decreased to `0.0f`, its effect is deactivated and the relevant variables are reset to their original state:

```cpp
void Game::UpdatePowerUps(float dt)
{
    for (PowerUp &powerUp : PowerUps)
    {
        powerUp.Position += powerUp.Velocity * dt;
        if (powerUp.Activated)
        {
            powerUp.Duration -= dt;

            if (powerUp.Duration <= 0.0f)
            {
                // remove powerup from list (will later be removed)
                powerUp.Activated = false;
                // deactivate effects
                if (powerUp.Type == "sticky")
                {
                    if (!isOtherPowerUpActive(PowerUps, "sticky"))
                    {   // reset if no other PowerUp of sticky is active
                        Ball->Sticky = false;
                        Player->Color = glm::vec3(1.0f);
                    }
                }
                else if (powerUp.Type == "pass-through")
                {
                    if (!isOtherPowerUpActive(PowerUps, "pass-through"))
                    {   // reset if no other PowerUp of pass-through is active
```

```cpp
                Ball->PassThrough = false;
                Ball->Color = glm::vec3(1.0f);
            }
        }
        else if (powerUp.Type == "confuse")
        {
            if (!isOtherPowerUpActive(PowerUps, "confuse"))
            {   // reset if no other PowerUp of confuse is active
                Effects->Confuse = false;
            }
        }
        else if (powerUp.Type == "chaos")
        {
            if (!isOtherPowerUpActive(PowerUps, "chaos"))
            {   // reset if no other PowerUp of chaos is active
                Effects->Chaos = false;
            }
        }
    }
}
this->PowerUps.erase(std::remove_if(this->PowerUps.begin(),
            this->PowerUps.end(), [](const PowerUp &powerUp) {
            return powerUp.Destroyed && !powerUp.Activated; }),
            this->PowerUps.end());
}
```

You can see that for each effect we disable it by resetting the relevant items to their original state.
We also set the powerup's `Activated` property to `false`. At the end of `UpdatePowerUps`
we then loop through the `PowerUps` vector and erase each powerup if they are destroyed **and**
deactivated. We use the `remove_if` function from the `algorithm` header to erase these items
given a lambda predicate.

> The `remove_if` function moves all elements for which the lambda predicate is true
> to the end of the container object and returns an iterator to the start of this *removed
> elements* range. The container's `erase` function then takes this iterator and the vector's
> end iterator to remove all the elements between these two iterators.

It may happen that while one of the powerup effects is active, another powerup of the same type
collides with the player paddle. In that case we have more than 1 powerup of that type currently
active within the game's `PowerUps` vector. Whenever one of these powerups gets deactivated,
we don't want to disable its effects yet since another powerup of the same type may still be active.
For this reason we use the `IsOtherPowerUpActive` function to check if there is still another
powerup active of the same type. Only if this function returns `false` we deactivate the powerup.
This way, the powerup's duration of a given type is extended to the duration of its last activated
powerup:

```cpp
bool IsOtherPowerUpActive(std::vector<PowerUp> &powerUps, std::string type)
{
    for (const PowerUp &powerUp : powerUps)
    {
        if (powerUp.Activated)
            if (powerUp.Type == type)
                return true;
    }
    return false;
}
```

The function checks for all activated powerups if there is still a powerup active of the same type and if so, returns `true`.

The last thing left to do is render the powerups:

```cpp
void Game::Render()
{
    if (State == GAME_ACTIVE)
    {
        [...]
        for (PowerUp &powerUp : PowerUps)
            if (!powerUp.Destroyed)
                powerUp.Draw(*Renderer);
        [...]
    }
}
```

Combine all this functionality and we have a working powerup system that not only makes the game more fun, but also a lot more challenging. It'll look a bit like this:

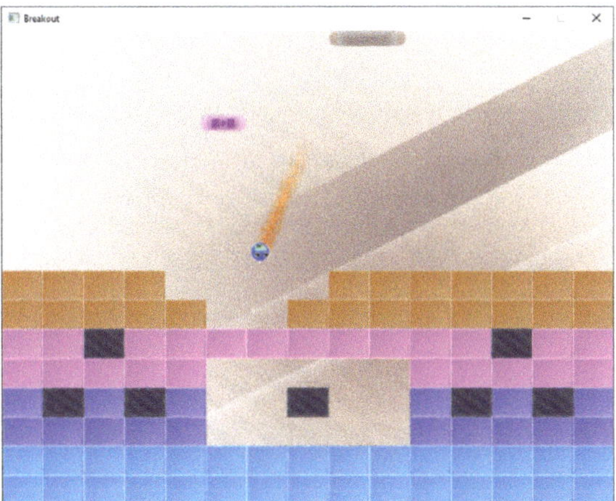

You can find the updated game code below (there we also reset all powerup effects whenever the level is reset):

- **Game**: `/src/7.in_practice/3.2d_game/0.full_source/progress/8.ga me.h`, `/src/7.in_practice/3.2d_game/0.full_source/progress/8.gam e.cpp`.

59. Audio

The game's making great progress, but it still feels a bit empty as there's no audio whatsoever. In this chapter we're going to fix that.

OpenGL doesn't offer us any support for audio capabilities (like many other aspects of game development). We have to manually load audio files into a collection of bytes, process and convert them to an audio stream, and manage multiple audio streams appropriately for use in our game. This can get complicated pretty quick and requires some low-level knowledge of audio engineering.

If it is your cup of tea then feel free to manually load audio streams from one or more audio file extensions. We are, however, going to make use of a library for audio management called **irrKlang**.

59.1 Irrklang

IrrKlang is a high level 2D and 3D cross platform (Windows, Mac OS X, Linux) sound engine and audio library that plays WAV, MP3, OGG, and FLAC files to name a few. It also features several audio effects like reverb, delay, and distortion that can be extensively tweaked.

> 3D audio means that an audio source can have a 3D position that will attenuate its volume based on the camera's distance to the audio source, making it feel natural in a 3D world (think of gunfire in a 3D world; most often you'll be able to hear where it came from just by the direction/location of the sound).

IrrKlang is an easy-to-use audio library that can play most audio files with just a few lines of code, making it a perfect candidate for our Breakout game. Note that irrKlang has a slightly restrictive license: you are allowed to use irrKlang as you see fit for non-commercial purposes, but you have to pay for their pro version whenever you want to use irrKlang commercially.

You can download irrKlang from their download page[1]; we're using version 1.5 for this chapter. Because irrKlang is closed-source, we cannot compile the library ourselves so we'll have to do with whatever irrKlang provided for us. Luckily they have plenty of precompiled library files.

Once you include the header files of irrKlang, add their (64-bit) library (`irrKlang.lib`) to the linker settings, and copy the dll file(s) to the appropriate locations (usually the same location where the `.exe` resides) we're set to go. Note that if you want to load MP3 files, you'll also have to include the `ikpMP3.dll` file.

59.1.1 Adding music

Specifically for this game I created a small little audio track[2] so the game feels a bit more alive. This background track is what we'll play whenever the game starts and that continuously loops until the player closes the game. Feel free to replace it with your own tracks or use it in any way you like.

Adding this to the Breakout game is extremely easy with the irrKlang library. We include the irrKlang header file, create an `irrKlang::ISoundEngine`, initialize it with `createIrrKlangDevice`, and then use the engine to load and play audio files:

---

[1] www.ambiera.com/irrklang/downloads.html
[2] learnopengl.com/audio/in-practice/breakout/breakout.mp3

```cpp
#include <irrklang/irrKlang.h>
using namespace irrklang;

ISoundEngine *SoundEngine = createIrrKlangDevice();

void Game::Init()
{
    [...]
    SoundEngine->play2D("audio/breakout.mp3", true);
}
```

Here we created a `SoundEngine` that we use for all audio-related code. Once we've initialized the sound engine, all we need to do to play audio is simply call its `play2D` function. Its first parameter is the filename, and the second parameter whether we want the file to loop (play again once it's finished).

And that is all there is to it! Running the game should now cause your speakers (or headset) to violently blast out sound waves.

59.1.2 Adding sounds

We're not there yet, since music by itself is not enough to make the game as great as it could be. We want to play sounds whenever something interesting happens in the game, as extra feedback to the player. Like when we hit a brick, or when we activate a powerup. Below you can find all the sounds we're going to use (courtesy of freesound.org):

- **bleep.mp3**[1]: the sound for when the ball hit a non-solid block.
- **solid.wav**[2]: the sound for when the ball hit a solid block.
- **powerup.wav**[3]: the sound for when we the player paddle collided with a powerup block.
- **bleep.wav**[4]: the sound for when we the ball bounces of the player paddle.

Wherever a collision occurs, we play the corresponding sound. I won't walk through each of the lines of code where this is supposed to happen, but simply list the updated game code at `/src/7.in_practice/3.2d_game/0.full_source/progress/8.game.cpp`. You should easily be able to add the sound effects at their appropriate locations.

Putting it all together gives us a game that feels a lot more complete. IrrKlang allows for much more fine-grained control of audio controls like advanced memory management, audio effects, or sound event callbacks. Check out their simple C++ tutorials[5] and try to experiment with its features.

---

[1] learnopengl.com/audio/in-practice/breakout/bleep.mp3

[2] learnopengl.com/audio/in-practice/breakout/solid.wav

[3] learnopengl.com/audio/in-practice/breakout/powerup.wav

[4] learnopengl.com/audio/in-practice/breakout/bleep.wav

[5] www.ambiera.com/irrklang/tutorials.html

60. Render text

In this chapter we'll be adding the final enhancements to the game by adding a life system, a win condition, and feedback in the form of rendered text. This chapter heavily builds upon the earlier introduced *Text Rendering* chapter so it is highly advised to first work your way through that chapter if you haven't already.

In Breakout all text rendering code is encapsulated within a class called `TextRenderer` that features the initialization of the FreeType library, render configuration, and the actual render code. You can find the code of the `TextRenderer` class here:

- **TextRenderer**: `/src/7.in_practice/3.2d_game/0.full_source/text_renderer.h`, `/src/7.in_practice/3.2d_game/0.full_source/text_renderer.cpp`.
- **Text shaders**: `/src/7.in_practice/3.2d_game/0.full_source/shaders/text.vs`, `/src/7.in_practice/3.2d_game/0.full_source/shaders/text.frag`.

The content of the text renderer's functions is almost exactly the same as the code from the text rendering chapter. However, the code for rendering glyphs onto the screen is slightly different:

```cpp
void TextRenderer::RenderText(std::string text, float x, float y,
                             float scale, glm::vec3 color)
{
    [...]
    for (c = text.begin(); c != text.end(); c++)
    {
        float xpos = x + ch.Bearing.x * scale;
        float ypos = y + (Characters['H'].Bearing.y - ch.Bearing.y) * scale;

        float w = ch.Size.x * scale;
        float h = ch.Size.y * scale;
        // update VBO for each character
        float vertices[6][4] = {
            { xpos,     ypos + h, 0.0f, 1.0f },
            { xpos + w, ypos,     1.0f, 0.0f },
            { xpos,     ypos,     0.0f, 0.0f },

            { xpos,     ypos + h, 0.0f, 1.0f },
            { xpos + w, ypos + h, 1.0f, 1.0f },
            { xpos + w, ypos,     1.0f, 0.0f }
        };
        [...]
    }
}
```

The reason for it being slightly different is that we use a different orthographic projection matrix from the one we've used in the text rendering chapter. In the text rendering chapter all y values ranged from bottom to top, while in the Breakout game all y values range from top to bottom with a y coordinate of `0.0` corresponding to the top edge of the screen. This means we have to slightly modify how we calculate the vertical offset.

Since we now render downwards from `RenderText`'s y parameter, we calculate the vertical offset as the distance a glyph is pushed downwards from the top of the glyph space. Looking back at the glyph metrics image from FreeType, this is indicated by the red arrow:

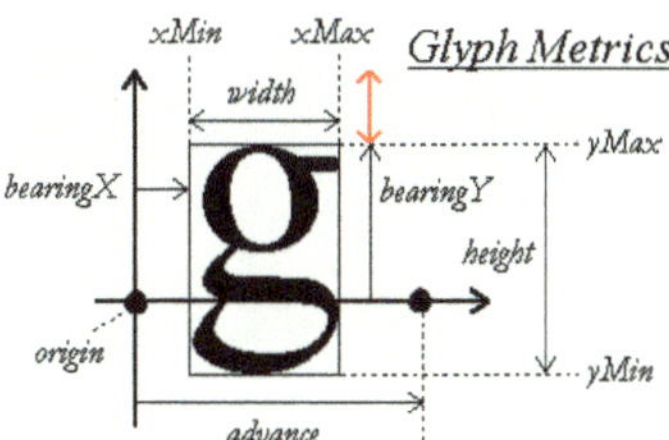

To calculate this vertical offset we need to get the top of the glyph space (the length of the black vertical arrow from the origin). Unfortunately, FreeType has no such metric for us. What we do know is that that some glyphs always touch this top edge; characters like 'H', 'T' or 'X'. So what if we calculate the length of this red vector by subtracting `bearingY` from any of these *top-reaching* glyphs by `bearingY` of the glyph in question. This way, we push the glyph down based on how far its top point differs from the top edge.

```
float ypos = y + (Characters['H'].Bearing.y - ch.Bearing.y) * scale;
```

In addition to updating the `ypos` calculation, we also switched the order of the vertices a bit to make sure all the vertices are still front facing when multiplied with the current orthographic projection matrix (as discussed in the *Face Culling* chapter).

Adding the `TextRenderer` to the game is easy:

```
TextRenderer *Text;

void Game::Init()
{
    [...]
    Text = new TextRenderer(Width, Height);
    Text->Load("fonts/ocraext.TTF", 24);
}
```

The text renderer is initialized with a font called **OCR A Extended**[1]. If the font is not to your liking, feel free to use a different font.

Now that we have a text renderer, let's finish the gameplay mechanics.

60.1 Player lives

Instead of immediately resetting the game as soon as the ball reaches the bottom edge, we'd like to give the player a few extra chances. We do this in the form of player lives, where the player begins with an initial number of lives (say 3) and each time the ball touches the bottom edge, the player's life total is decreased by 1. Only when the player's life total becomes 0 we reset the game. This makes it easier for the player to finish a level while also building tension.

We keep count of the lives of a player by adding it to the game class (initialized within the constructor to a value of 3):

---

[1] fontzone.net/font-details/ocr-a-extended

```cpp
class Game
{
    [...]
    public:
        unsigned int Lives;
}
```

We then modify the game's `Update` function to, instead of resetting the game, decrease the player's life total, and only reset the game once the life total reaches 0:

```cpp
void Game::Update(float dt)
{
    [...]
    if (Ball->Position.y >= Height) // did ball reach bottom edge?
    {
        --Lives;
        // did the player lose all his lives? : Game over
        if (Lives == 0)
        {
            ResetLevel();
            State = GAME_MENU;
        }
        ResetPlayer();
    }
}
```

As soon as the player is game over (`lives` equals 0), we reset the level and change the game state to `GAME_MENU` which we'll get to later.

Don't forget to reset the player's life total as soon as we reset the game/level:

```cpp
void Game::ResetLevel()
{
    [...]
    Lives = 3;
}
```

The player now has a working life total, but has no way of seeing how many lives he currently has while playing the game. That's where the text renderer comes in:

```cpp
void Game::Render()
{
    if (State == GAME_ACTIVE)
    {
        [...]
        std::stringstream ss; ss << Lives;
        Text->RenderText("Lives:" + ss.str(), 5.0f, 5.0f, 1.0f);
    }
}
```

Here we convert the number of lives to a string, and display it at the top-left of the screen. It'll now look a bit like this:

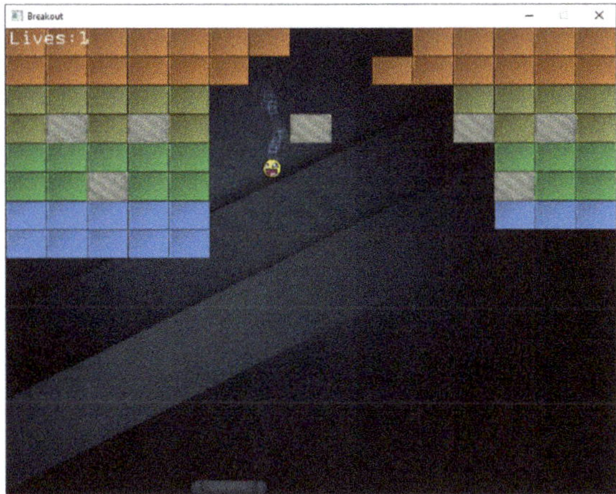

As soon as the ball touches the bottom edge, the player's life total is decreased which is instantly visible at the top-left of the screen.

60.2 Level selection

Whenever the user is in the game state GAME_MENU, we'd like to give the player the control to select the level he'd like to play in. With either the 'w' or 's' key the player should be able to scroll through any of the levels we loaded. Whenever the player feels like the chosen level is indeed the level he'd like to play in, he can press the enter key to switch from the game's GAME_MENU state to the GAME_ACTIVE state.

Allowing the player to choose a level is not too difficult. All we have to do is increase or decrease the game class's Level variable based on whether he pressed 'w' or 's' respectively:

```cpp
if (State == GAME_MENU)
{
    if (Keys[GLFW_KEY_ENTER])
        State = GAME_ACTIVE;
    if (Keys[GLFW_KEY_W])
        Level = (Level + 1) % 4;
    if (Keys[GLFW_KEY_S])
    {
        if (Level > 0)
            --Level;
        else
            Level = 3;
    }
}
```

We use the modulus operator (%) to make sure the Level variable remains within the acceptable level range (between 0 and 3).

We also want to define what we want to render when we're in the menu state. We'd like to give the player some instructions in the form of text and also display the selected level in the background.

```
void Game::Render()
{
    if (State == GAME_ACTIVE || State == GAME_MENU)
    {
        [...] // Game state's rendering code
    }
    if (State == GAME_MENU)
    {
        Text->RenderText("Press ENTER to start", 250.0f, Height / 2, 1.0f);
        Text->RenderText("Press W or S to select level", 245.0f,
                         Height / 2 + 20.0f, 0.75f);
    }
}
```

Here we render the game whenever we're in either the GAME_ACTIVE state or the GAME_MENU state, and whenever we're in the GAME_MENU state we also render two lines of text to inform the player to select a level and/or accept his choice. Note that for this to work when launching the game you do have to set the game's state as GAME_MENU by default.

It looks great, but once you try to run the code you'll probably notice that as soon as you press either the 'w' or the 's' key, the game rapidly scrolls through the levels making it difficult to select the level you want to play in. This happens because the game records the key press over frames until we release the key. This causes the ProcessInput function to process the pressed key more than once.

We can solve this issue with a little trick commonly found within GUI systems. The trick is to, not only record the keys currently pressed, but also store the keys that have been processed once, until released again. We then check (before processing) whether the key has not yet been processed, and if so, process this key after which we store this key as being processed. Once we want to process the same key again without the key having been released, we do not process the key. This probably sounds somewhat confusing, but as soon as you see it in practice it (probably) starts to make sense.

First we have to create another array of bool values to indicate which keys have been processed. We define this within the game class:

```cpp
class Game
{
    [...]
    public:
        bool KeysProcessed[1024];
}
```

We then set the relevant key(s) to true as soon as they're processed and make sure to only process the key if it wasn't processed before (until released):

```cpp
void Game::ProcessInput(float dt)
{
    if (State == GAME_MENU)
    {
        if (Keys[GLFW_KEY_ENTER] && !KeysProcessed[GLFW_KEY_ENTER])
        {
            State = GAME_ACTIVE;
            KeysProcessed[GLFW_KEY_ENTER] = true;
        }
        if (Keys[GLFW_KEY_W] && !KeysProcessed[GLFW_KEY_W])
        {
            Level = (Level + 1) % 4;
            KeysProcessed[GLFW_KEY_W] = true;
        }
        if (Keys[GLFW_KEY_S] && !KeysProcessed[GLFW_KEY_S])
        {
            if (Level > 0)
                --Level;
            else
                Level = 3;
            KeysProcessed[GLFW_KEY_S] = true;
        }
    }
    [...]
}
```

Now as soon as the key's value in the KeysProcessed array has not yet been set, we process the key and set its value to true. Next time we reach the if condition of the same key, it will have been processed so we'll pretend we never pressed the button until it's released again.

Within GLFW's key callback function we then need to reset the key's processed value as soon as it's released so we can process it again the next time it's pressed:

```cpp
void key_callback(GLFWwindow* window, int key, int scancode, int action,
                  int mode)
{
    [...]
    if (key >= 0 && key < 1024)
    {
        if (action == GLFW_PRESS)
            Breakout.Keys[key] = true;
        else if (action == GLFW_RELEASE)
        {
            Breakout.Keys[key] = false;
            Breakout.KeysProcessed[key] = false;
        }
    }
}
```

Launching the game gives us a neat level select screen that now precisely selects a single level per key press, no matter how long we press he key.

60.3 Winning

Currently the player is able to select levels, play the game, and fail in doing so to lose. It is kind of unfortunate if the player finds out after destroying all the bricks he cannot in any way win the game. So let's fix that.

The player wins when all of the non-solid blocks have been destroyed. We already created a function to check for this condition in the `GameLevel` class:

```cpp
bool GameLevel::IsCompleted()
{
    for (GameObject &tile : Bricks)
        if (!tile.IsSolid && !tile.Destroyed)
            return false;
    return true;
}
```

We check all bricks in the game level and if a single non-solid brick isn't yet destroyed we return `false`. All we have to do is check for this condition in the game's `Update` function and as soon as it returns `true` we change the game state to `GAME_WIN`:

```cpp
void Game::Update(float dt)
{
    [...]
    if (State == GAME_ACTIVE && Levels[Level].IsCompleted())
    {
        ResetLevel();
        ResetPlayer();
        Effects->Chaos = true;
        State = GAME_WIN;
    }
}
```

Whenever the level is completed while the game is active, we reset the game and display a small victory message in the `GAME_WIN` state. For fun we'll also enable the chaos effect while in the `GAME_WIN` screen. In the `Render` function we'll congratulate the player and ask him to either restart or quit the game:

```cpp
void Game::Render()
{
    [...]
    if (State == GAME_WIN)
    {
        Text->RenderText("You WON!!!", 320.0, Height / 2 - 20.0,
                         1.0, glm::vec3(0.0, 1.0, 0.0));
        Text->RenderText("Press ENTER to retry or ESC to quit", 130.0,
                         Height / 2, 1.0, glm::vec3(1.0, 1.0, 0.0));
    }
}
```

Then we of course have to actually catch the mentioned keys:

```cpp
void Game::ProcessInput(float dt)
{
    [...]
    if (State == GAME_WIN)
    {
        if (Keys[GLFW_KEY_ENTER])
        {
            KeysProcessed[GLFW_KEY_ENTER] = true;
            Effects->Chaos = false;
            State = GAME_MENU;
        }
    }
}
```

If you're then good enough to actually win the game, you'd get the following image:

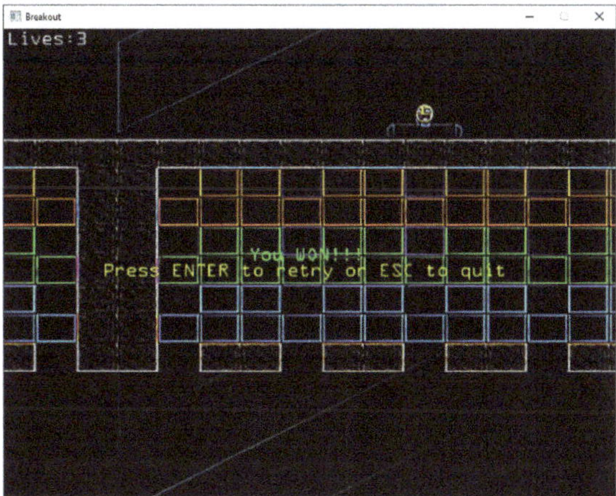

And that is it! The final piece of the puzzle of the Breakout game we've been actively working on. Try it out, customize it to your liking, and show it to all your family and friends!

You can find the final version of the game's code below:

- **Game**: `/src/7.in_practice/3.2d_game/0.full_source/game.h`, `/src/7.in_practice/3.2d_game/0.full_source/game.cpp`.

60.4 Further reading

- `www.websiteplanet.com/blog/best-free-fonts/`: summarized list of a large group of fonts to use in your project for personal or commercial use.

61. Final thoughts

These last chapter gave a glimpse of what it's like to create something more than just a tech demo in OpenGL. We created a complete 2D game from scratch and learned how to abstract from certain low-level graphics concepts, use basic collision detection techniques, create particles, and we've shown a practical scenario for an orthographic projection matrix. All this using concepts we've discussed in all previous chapters. We didn't really learn new and exciting graphics techniques using OpenGL, but more as to how to combine all the knowledge so far into a larger whole.

Creating a simple game like Breakout can be accomplished in thousands of different ways, of which this approach is just one of many. The larger a game becomes, the more you start applying abstractions and design patterns. For further reading you can find a lot more on these abstractions and design patterns in the wonderful `gameprogrammingpatterns.com` website.

Keep in mind that it is a difficult feat to create a game with extremely clean and well-thought out code (often close to impossible). Simply make your game in whatever way you think feels right at the time. The more you practice video-game development, the more you learn new and better approaches to solve problems. Don't let the struggle to want to create perfect code demotivate you; keep on coding!

61.1 Optimizations

The content of these chapters and the finished game code were all focused on explaining concepts as simple as possible, without delving too much in optimization details. Therefore, many performance considerations were left out of the chapters. We'll list some of the more common improvements you'll find in modern 2D OpenGL games to boost performance for when your framerate starts to drop:

- **Sprite sheet / Texture atlas**: instead of rendering a sprite with a single texture at a time, we combine all required textures into a single large texture (like bitmap fonts) and select the appropriate sprite texture with a targeted set of texture coordinates. Switching texture states can be expensive so a sprite sheet makes sure we rarely have to switch between textures; this also allows the GPU to more efficiently cache the texture in memory for faster lookups.
- **Instanced rendering**: instead of rendering a quad at a time, we could've also batched all the quads we want to render and then, with an instanced renderer, render all the batched sprites with just a single draw call. This is relatively easy to do since each sprite is composed of the same vertices, but differs in only a model matrix; something that we can easily include in an instanced array. This allows OpenGL to render a lot more sprites per frame. Instanced rendering can also be used to render particles and/or characters glyphs.
- **Triangle strips**: instead of rendering each quad as two triangles, we could've rendered them with OpenGL's `TRIANGLE_STRIP` render primitive that takes only 4 vertices instead of 6. This saves a third of the data sent to the GPU.
- **Space partitioning algorithms**: when checking for collisions, we compare the ball object to **each** of the bricks in the active level. This is a bit of a waste of CPU resources since we can easily tell that most of the bricks won't even come close to the ball within this frame. Using space partitioning algorithms like BSP, Octrees, or k-d trees, we partition the visible space into several smaller regions and first determine in which region(s) the ball is in. We then only check collisions between other bricks in whatever region(s) the ball is in, saving us a significant amount of collision checks. For a simple game like Breakout this will likely be overkill, but for more complicated games with more complicated collision detection algorithms this will significantly increase performance.
- **Minimize state changes**: state changes (like binding textures or switching shaders) are generally quite expensive in OpenGL, so you want to avoid doing a large amount of state changes. One approach to minimize state changes is to create your own state manager that stores the current value of an OpenGL state (like which texture is bound) and only switch if

this value needs to change; this prevents unnecessary state changes. Another approach is to sort all the renderable objects by state change: first render all the objects with shader one, then all objects with shader two, and so on; this can of course be extended to blend state changes, texture binds, framebuffer switches etc.

These should give you some hints as to what kind of advanced tricks we can apply to further boost the performance of a 2D game. This also gives you a glimpse of the power of OpenGL: by doing most rendering by hand we have full control over the entire process and thus also complete power over how to optimize the process. If you're not satisfied with Breakout's performance then feel free to take any of these as an exercise.

61.2 **Get creative**

Now that you've seen how to create a simple game in OpenGL it is up to you to create your own rendering/game applications. Many of the techniques that we've discussed so far can be used in most 2D (and even 3D) games like sprite rendering, collision detection, postprocessing, text rendering, and particles. It is now up to you to take these techniques and combine/modify them in whichever way you think is right and develop your own handcrafted game.